W9-CRI-890

## TABLE OF WEIGHTS AND MEASURES

### Length

12 inches = 1 foot
3 feet = 1 yard
5½ yards or 16½ feet = 1 rod
5280 feet or 1760 yards or 320 rods = 1 statute mile
6080 feet = 1 nautical mile
1 knot = 1 nautical mile per hour
6 feet = 1 fathom
660 feet = 1 furlong
7.92 inches = 1 link
100 links = 1 chain
80 chains = 1 statute mile
4 inches = 1 hand

### Area

144 square inches = 1 square foot
9 square feet = 1 square yard
160 square rods or 10 square chains = 1 acre
640 acres = 1 square mile
A square 208.71 ft. on each side = 1 acre or 43,560 sq. ft.

### Liquid Measure

16 fluid ounces or 4 gills = 1 pint
32 fluid ounces or 2 pints = 1 quart
4 quarts = 1 gallon (U.S.)
31½ gallons = 1 barrel
63 gallons = 1 hogshead

### Dry Measure

2 pints = 1 quart
8 quarts = 1 peck
4 pecks = 1 bushel

### Avoirdupois Weight

437.5 grains = 1 ounce
16 ounces (7000 grains) = 1 pound
1 ton = 2000 pounds
1 long ton = 2240 pounds

### Metric Conversions

1 millimeter = .03937 inch
1 centimeter = .3937 inch
1 meter = 39.37 inches or 3.2808 ft. or 1.0936 yards
1 kilometer = 3280.83 ft. or 1093.61 yards or .62137 mile
1 inch = 2.54 centimeters
1 foot = 30.48 centimeters
1 yard = .9144 meter
1 mile = 1.609 kilometers

1 liter = 1.0567 quarts
1 quart = .946 liter
1 gram = 15.432 grains
1 ounce = 28.35 grams
1 kilogram = 2.2046 pounds
1 pound = .4536 kilogram
1 degree Fahrenheit = .5556 degrees centigrade
1 degree centigrade = 1.8 degrees Fahrenheit

### Miscellaneous

12 = 1 dozen
12 dozen = 1 gross
20 = 1 score
24 sheets of paper = 1 quire
20 quires = 1 ream
1 league = 3 miles
1 horsepower = 33,000 foot-pounds per minute
1 cord = 128 cubic feet, usually piled up 8 ft. × 4 ft. × 4 ft.
1 board foot = 1 ft. × 1 ft. × 1 inch
1 imperial gallon = 1.20 U. S. gallon

## 50 YEARS OF DATES ON WHICH EASTER SUNDAY FALLS

| Year | Easter Sun. | Year | Easter Sun. |
|------|-------------|------|-------------|
| 1962 | April 22 | 1982 | April 11 |
| 1963 | April 14 | 1983 | April 3 |
| 1964 | Mar. 29 | 1984 | April 22 |
| 1965 | April 18 | 1985 | April 7 |
| 1966 | April 10 | 1986 | Mar. 30 |
| 1967 | Mar. 26 | 1987 | April 19 |
| 1968 | April 14 | 1988 | April 3 |
| 1969 | April 6 | 1989 | Mar. 26 |
| 1970 | Mar. 29 | 1990 | April 15 |
| 1971 | April 11 | 1991 | Mar. 31 |
| 1972 | April 2 | 1992 | April 19 |
| 1973 | April 22 | 1993 | April 11 |
| 1974 | April 14 | 1994 | April 3 |
| 1975 | Mar. 30 | 1995 | April 16 |
| 1976 | April 18 | 1996 | April 7 |
| 1977 | April 10 | 1997 | Mar. 30 |
| 1978 | Mar. 26 | 1998 | April 12 |
| 1979 | April 15 | 1999 | April 4 |
| 1980 | April 6 | 2000 | April 23 |
| 1981 | April 19 | 2001 | April 15 |

## CALENDAR FACTS

The astronomical or solar year is 365 days, 5 hours, 48 minutes and 46 seconds long.

Leap years are those whose date numbers are exactly divisible by four, except when they are also exactly divisible by 100. But the years that begin a century can be leap years when they are exactly divisible by 400. Thus 1900 was not a leap year, but the year 2000 will be.

SOLSTICE: literally "The sun stands." The summer and winter solstices, taking place about June 21 and December 21, occur when the sun reaches its greatest northern and southern declinations and appears for a day or two to stand still in its northern or southern advance.

EQUINOX: the spring and autumnal equinoxes, about March and September 21, occur when the sun crosses the equator, causing day and night to be of equal length throughout the world.

EASTER: the first Sunday after the Paschal full moon occurring on or after the vernal equinox (March 21). In the year 1818, Easter came at the earliest possible date —March 22. In the years 1886 and 1943 it came latest—April 25.

## WEDDING ANNIVERSARIES

1st—paper, plastics
2nd—cotton
3rd—leather or any leather-like article
4th—linen, silk, rayon or nylon or other synthetic silk
5th—wood
6th—iron
7th—wool, copper, or brass
8th—bronze or electrical appliances
9th—pottery or china
10th—tin or aluminum
11th—steel
12th—silk, nylon, linen
13th—lace
14th—ivory or agate
15th—crystal or glass
20th—china
25th—silver
30th—pearls
35th—coral or jade
40th—rubies or garnets
45th—sapphires or tourmalines
50th—gold
55th—emeralds or turquoise
60th—diamonds or gold
75th—diamonds or gold

# Good Housekeeping's

## GUIDE TO SUCCESSFUL HOMEMAKING

# Good Housekeeping's

## guide to

# SUCCESSFUL

# HOMEMAKING

### Revised Edition

compiled by the editors of

**GOOD HOUSEKEEPING**

HARPER & BROTHERS, PUBLISHERS, NEW YORK

GOOD HOUSEKEEPING'S GUIDE TO SUCCESSFUL HOMEMAKING
REVISED EDITION

Printed in the United States of America

# Contents

the oven, the broiler . . . taking care of your range . . . small appliances . . . the toaster . . . the electric mixer . . . the blender . . . the waffle baker . . . the electric roaster . . . infrared broilers . . . automatic fryers . . . electric coffeemakers . . . kitchen fans . . . garbage disposers.

hand iron . . . using the steam iron . . . ironing minute-savers
. . . special ironing problems . . . pressing equipment . . . pressing technique . . . sending clothes to the dry-cleaner . . . dry-
cleaning at home.

# Foreword

The philosophy of *Good Housekeeping* magazine always has centered upon the happiness of the home, not only the spirit but the mechanics. Without the mechanics, the spirit can falter. With all the poll-taking and statistics that we engage in at present, probably nobody ever has measured the value to the entire family of a well-run house. The woman who is able to manage the details of housekeeping—which continues to require time and effort even with all the marvelous modern equipment available—arms her husband against the pressures of twentieth-century business and secures her children with a happy environment.

From the very first issue of *Good Housekeeping* magazine many years ago, our predominant interest has been better, easier and happier homemaking. In fact, the now yellowed pages of that first issue, dated May 2, 1885, carry as the Editor's introductory preface an editorial titled "For the Homes of the World." The aims and purposes of the magazine are summed up in the editorial's final paragraph: "To produce and perpetuate perfection—or as near as may be attained in the Household—is the purpose and mission of *Good Housekeeping*."

In the years that have passed since then, the mechanics, indeed all the conceptions of housekeeping have changed as drastically as many of the products. In 1885 our readers were women whose sole occupation was homemaking. Living was more formal. Servants were more plentiful. Food preparation could (and did) consume many hours and much work. Keeping house was a manual procedure that was done on a strict time schedule—washing on Monday, ironing on Tuesday, upstairs-cleaning on Wednesday, and so on through a back-breaking week to baking on Saturday! Truly, in that day, woman's work was never done.

Today—how different it is! Homemaking may still be the woman's chief occupation, but it no longer demands all her time, nor so much manual labor. Modern appliances and methods help her keep her house cleaner with less effort than ever before. Her automatic washer and dryer stand ready to receive clothes as they are soiled, and have banished forever the old "blue Monday."

Her family is more nutritiously fed than it has ever been—and she does it with the help of precooked foods, frozen foods, prepared mixes, and all the other wonders of today's food industry.

No longer need she go to market every day as refrigerators and freezers with their long-term storage facilities put a grocery store right in her own home. Thanks to the freezer too, the old Saturday baking day can be changed to once-a-month baking—and this "baking day" has come to include practically all forms of cookery.

And so it goes with every phase of this big job of homemaking.

In keeping abreast, and sometimes ahead, of all these changes, *Good Housekeeping* has accumulated and published in the monthly pages of the magazine a vast share of information on all areas of housekeeping and homemaking. Between the covers of this book, much of that information has been condensed for you.

Whether you are a bride, just beginning your career of homemaking or a more experienced homemaker, you will find this book a modern, practical guide to taking care of today's house and apartment.

From our Studio and Building Forum come helpful pages on home furnishing—how to use color, how to buy furniture and floor coverings, how to arrange flowers, and what to do about your windows.

The Appliances and Home Care Department brings you the latest and best methods of keeping your house clean, best ways of washing clothes; plus how to buy, use and take care of appliances.

The Foods and Cookery staff tells you how to buy food, how to plan menus, how to set your table, and gives a variety of other valuable information.

From the Textile Laboratory comes the latest word on fabrics—from the old and familiar wools and silks to the newest synthetic. And there are points on buying clothing and taking the best care of it to get the most satisfactory wear.

The Sewing Center tells you all about sewing materials and sewing methods, including the fascinating story of today's sewing machines and attachments.

These are but the highlights of the material covered in these pages. A glance at the table of contents will show that the subjects range from the more fascinating topics we've mentioned to the less intriguing but equally necessary ones like repairing a leaky faucet and equipping a home medicine chest.

During *Good Housekeeping*'s long existence, in all the great changes that have come about, one thing has remained the same—*Good Housekeeping*'s firm conviction that no more important or challenging or rewarding occupation for women exists than that of homemaking. It is to that conviction, and to the women who are proving it in their daily lives, that this book is dedicated.

WILLIE MAE ROGERS
Director, *Good Housekeeping* Institute

# Good Housekeeping's

## GUIDE TO SUCCESSFUL HOMEMAKING

# How to Make Your Home More Attractive and Livable

### Basic Advice on Furnishing and Decorating

Whether you are planning the furnishings of your first home or just doing over one room you should begin with the budget.

You can have an attractive home on practically any budget if you plan intelligently and spend wisely. There's no hard-and-fast rule about exactly what you should spend for a particular piece, but there are some general rules for buying: Because major pieces of furniture are long-range investments that will undoubtedly move with you to other homes, they should always be of good quality. Be sure to buy well-designed, well-made sofas, upholstered chairs, dining tables, beds, etc. If you must economize, buy inexpensive rugs, curtains, draperies, because these may not fit the floor and window areas of future homes. And be sure to allocate a part of your budget to accessories—lamps, candlesticks, mirrors, etc. No room looks homelike without them.

**Decide What You Like and Need.** You'll waste lots of shopping time and possibly end up with some mistakes if you don't formulate a general picture of what *kind* of home you want. Should it be all-out modern, all-out traditional, or a contemporary combination of the two? Is yours a highly gregarious life with lots of entertaining, or do you prefer the books-records-television kind of evening? Entertaining means plenty of seating space, enough little tables, etc. Books and records call for shelves or cabinets. You'll want rooms that are easy to care for. If you can afford the time and the money, you may feel that more elaborate, more demanding furnishings are worth the effort. The important thing is to have a clear picture of your tastes before you buy.

**Consider the Possibilities of Color.** Color chosen wisely can work a minor miracle in any room. It can make a room look larger or change its apparent proportions. It can make a ceiling look higher or lower, dramatize a focal point, or minimize a defect. It can make a dark room seem sunnier, a bright room cooler. Perhaps most important, color has a definite psychological effect. Whatever you want it to accomplish, be sure you choose color you *like*. And unless you have a practiced decorating eye, it's a wise rule of thumb to use soft or clear shades lavishly on large areas, intense or highly dramatic colors only for smaller accents.

**Shop Before You Buy.** Even when your budget, your tastes, and your color scheme are all settled, it still isn't time to start charging and sending. But it *is* time to start collecting some tangible evidence. First buy yourself a loose-leaf notebook in which you can keep samples, swatches, measurements, and costs. Then start out on a "just looking" expedition. Collect all the samples of carpet, fabric, etc., that appeal to you. If you see a sofa you like, note size, price, and description, and, of course, which store you saw it in. Stop at a paint store and get color chips. But don't buy anything until you know definitely what every major purchase is going to be, have chosen a specific wall color, and have totaled up all the costs.

**Judge Quality by Firms' Reputations.** Since the marks of quality furniture are hard for anyone but an expert to detect, unless you take an expert along you will have to buy on faith. Even on a limited budget, it's good economy to buy major pieces by well-known manufacturers from a reliable store. Occasionally you may run across a bargain—a couch or chair that was a floor sample of a line that's being discontinued and happens to fit into your scheme.

**Don't Be Stampeded.** If your husband is very interested in furniture, decorating, and so on, he'll probably want to join you in your preliminary looking around. But if not, he's likely to become impatient with the whole business and want to start buying before the plan is complete. In this case it's a good idea to do most of the spadework yourself. However, before you actually buy, there are some items, such as chairs, couches, etc., that your husband should inspect and try out for comfort.

**Allow Time for Deliveries.** Most of the furniture you see on display in stores is sample furniture and is not from the floor. Some furniture may actually have

*Nothing could be lovelier in any bedroom than the use of matching fabric for the bedspread and draperies. Here, the bedspread is quilted.*

to be made up for you. You may find that it takes a month or two to get some of your purchases delivered.

**Choose Your Accessories Early.** Although it isn't necessary to select the last ash tray before you buy your furniture, it's wise to keep accessories in mind all along the way to be sure you don't run out of money before you get to them. Remember, much professional aid is free. If you are starting from scratch to furnish a home, the task may seem overwhelming to you. But don't forget there are independent decorators and decorators in furniture and department stores who will give you the benefit of professional know-how at no cost to you. If you do decide to take advantage of this service, here are two bits of advice: Consult the decorator in the beginning, not after you're halfway through. And tell him or her frankly just what your budget is. Most decorators welcome the opportunity to do a whole house or apartment, no matter how modestly. But they can't do the best job unless they know just how much you want to spend.

CHOOSING YOUR FABRICS

There's a choice of lovely fabrics for every purpose, but not every fabric fits every life. When you go shopping, carry along a clear picture of the kind of service you expect from the fabric you buy. If yours is an informal household peopled with youngsters or pets, or both, pale-pastel upholstery and frothy to-the-floor curtains are not for you. Buy sturdy, though no less attractive, materials in hardier colors and patterns. If you like to put everything in the washing machine, be sure the fabrics you choose are preshrunk. On the other hand, if you long for elegance and don't mind the extra attention it requires, as well as the extra cost of dry cleaning, by all means indulge yourself in the somewhat more demanding fabrics. Or use the latter in your own bedroom, and decorate the family rooms more practically.

**Begin with What You Have.** On a few occasions during a lifetime you may be able to start from the beginning in decorating a house or a room. But usually you do over a few pieces at a time. This means that the new fabrics you buy are going to have to live peaceably with furniture and, possibly, other fabrics that are not brand-new, which of course have color and character of their own. Start with these older pieces, and be sure that what you buy goes with them. If most of your furniture is covered with dark fabric, a single pale-pink chair or gossamer curtains may make the older pieces look somber and dingy. If the room runs to tweeds, satin is almost certain to

*Straight-lined furniture, which has a clean uncluttered look, is the choice of many of today's young homemakers. A softly tinted rug blends all of the components into a living room that is arresting and modern in character.*

be out of place. Try to keep all the fabrics in a room in about the same degree of formality.

**Design Calls for Discretion.** Every room needs pattern, and one of the prettiest and easiest ways to achieve it is through the use of patterned fabrics. But if you're not careful, it's easy to get too much design. If you have an Oriental rug with a prominent pattern, any other elaborate design is apt to clash with it. In such a room, use solids, stripes, or perhaps a small allover pattern in a not-too-large area. If you are combining two printed fabrics in one room, be sure there's a marked difference in scale, that one pattern is considerably larger than the other. Don't let a print dominate your room. If you have a large picture window, bold-print draperies drawn across the whole area will dwarf the rest of the room. Use more fabric design if you don't intend to hang pictures, less if you do.

**Careful Measurements Are Essential,** especially for curtains and draperies. Before you embark even on your exploratory shopping trip, you should measure your windows carefully. Measure windows from the top of the rod to the sill or floor (depending on whether curtains are to be sill or floor length), and from the outer edge of the window frame on one side to the outer edge on the other. Draw draperies should be one and a half to two times the width of the window, to allow for fullness. Sheer curtains should be two to three times as wide as the windows. Measure *each* window even though they all appear to be the same size.

**Follow Your Plan.** Take swatches of the materials now in the room that you do not intend to replace, including, if possible, a sample of your carpet. Bring home samples of all the fabrics you like. Compare them with colors and patterns now in the room in both daylight and artificial light. Don't buy a single piece of fabric until you have tried the samples all together in the room.

### Arranging Furniture

**Convenience:** Don't crowd any room, and this applies, especially to your living room, with big pieces that make moving around difficult. Place your furniture as people would use it when talking to one another. Many parties go flat because guests are too far apart and freeze up. Have small, low tables for ashtrays, etc., where each guest can reach one. Arrange lamps so no corner of the room glares or looks chilly and left out.

**Eye Satisfaction:** Weighting one wall with a heavy piece, with no similar weight opposite, makes a room seem to tilt. If you lack something as big, a smaller piece in darker color may do, because *dark colors seem to weigh more.* Never put rugs or large furniture "catty-corner" but always parallel to, or at right angles to, a wall. Place an upright piano against a wall, a grand with long side to the wall. And never put anything on top of a piano but music or a large vase of greens.

**How to Start Rearranging:** Get a tape measure, a big sheet of wrapping paper, some colored paper, and a sharp pencil. Measure room and furniture accurately. Draw room on big sheet, using an inch for a foot, so a 10-by-12 room is 10 inches by 12. Draw furniture on colored paper, so a 6-foot sofa is 6 inches. Move pieces about on plan till you get a good result.

**Call in the Family.** Too often, the woman of the house arranges the furniture mentally while her husband moves it physically. Husbands who have spent long Sunday afternoons pushing the piano from one wall to the other are apt to be cool on the subject of furniture arrangement. But if a change in plans involves nothing more than moving a piece of colored paper, a man can be surprisingly receptive. He may even be willing to contribute some very sound ideas.

Children are part of the family, too. Even a toddler likes to have his opinions considered, and teen-agers are genuinely interested in the appearance of their home.

# WALLPAPER

## Can Make Your Rooms Look Larger and Lovelier

It's astonishing the number of things wallpaper can do. A well-designed, carefully selected paper can alter the apparent size and shape of a room, make it seem larger or better proportioned. It can create a warm or cool atmosphere, generate excitement or serenity. Since today's good papers are designed by topflight artists, they often eliminate the need for pictures, accessories, etc. and some can be used on a single panel or a single wall almost as though they were paintings.

### Shopping for Wallpaper

**Style Advice.** Today your favorite store can give you more and more competent assistance. If not, write to well-known wallpaper manufacturers, stating your problem completely. You will be pleased by their interest and by the exciting ideas you can get from them. It is advisable to try a large sample, from your dealer's swatch book, against your wall before you make a final decision. Consider series of papers designed in harmony for adjoining rooms, so they will be keyed together.

**Look for the Label.** Choose a paper made by a well-known manufacturer. The brand name is his signature of responsibility, your assurance that he wants you to be satisfied. Save the directions for hanging and care of the paper—he has especially prepared them for you.

**Is It Washable?** There are several advantages in buying a washable paper. First, because the paper is washable, greater latitude in design is possible. You need not choose a small, nondescript pattern so that soil will be less noticeable; instead, imaginative designs on open backgrounds can be indulged in to your heart's content. Rain coming in through a window will not make colors run or streak. Fingermarks or other accidental soil can be removed with ease. If your paperhanger gets paste on the seams, it can be removed at once.

Not all wallpapers are washable, so if you want a paper that is, be sure to look for the manufacturer's label stating that the paper really is washable. Washability is accomplished without sacrifice of soft, water-color tones, so you can't tell by the appearance or texture whether or not papers are washable. However, you have every right to ask your dealer or paperhanger to test this in your presence before you buy.

**Will It Fade?** One of the most important economy and service qualities to look for in wallpaper is its ability to resist fading. Strangely, the use of the best pigments is not in itself adequate assurance. It is also essential that the colors be applied so that the paper is fully coated, or "grounded." This requires the utmost care and control in manufacturing, because no part of the raw-stock foundation may be left exposed to light, or "ungrounded."

**When It Comes to Cost,** a few cents more for a quality paper will be well spent. Buying a better paper represents real economy, as it will be a longer time before you need to replace it.

**Proper Wall Preparation.** Employ an expert paperhanger, and take his advice. He will know best how to deal with old or new plastered walls, old paper, calcimined or painted walls, etc.

If you prefer to do the work yourself, ask your dealer or write the manufacturer for full instructions, and follow them.

### Tips on Wallpapering

*1.* Always get an extra roll of wallpaper, so you can apply a whole new strip if your wall is seriously broken or soiled.

*2.* Consider the manifold uses of cutouts from patterned wallpaper—to decorate home-painted furniture, kitchen cupboards, nursery furniture, lampshades, wastebaskets, etc.

*3.* Think of wallpaper of any design you like, to line dresser drawers, cover screens, make mats for pictures, transform commercial hat or dress boxes into decorative accessories for your closet.

*4.* You may use a delicately patterned paper on the ceiling to dramatize a handsome overhead fixture such as a chandelier over a dining-room table.

*5.* You may frame a window with a wallpaper-covered valance. The result is pretty, practical, and economical.

*6.* If a television set is disturbing to your decor, cover it with the same paper used on the wall so it blends into the background. (If your television cabinet is wood, wash the surface with detergent, then attach wallpaper with wallpaper paste. If the cabinet has a plastic finish, sandpaper the surface, then apply wallpaper using vegetable glue.)

*7.* To brighten your bedroom, use a panel of patterned paper the same width as your bed to give the effect of a high headboard. Create a canopy with a plywood valance covered with the same paper at the top of the panel.

*8.* Cover the walls and doors of a small foyer with rich-looking, marbleized paper for a unified, unbroken look.

These four pictures show how wallpaper can add distinctive charm to any room. *Above left:* This Pillement wallpaper provides a more formal background for traditional elegance. *Above right:* An overall medallion pattern in wallpaper provides continuity in broken wall surface areas. *Below left:* Novelty wallpaper of heraldic shields can add a decorative note to a small dining area. *Below right:* This gaily patterned kitchen "paper" is not paper at all, but plastic-coated canvas which can be washed many times without any damage to its finish.

# GETTING THE MOST FOR YOUR FURNITURE DOLLAR

## Wood Furniture

### Living Room

The average living room needs the following wood pieces: (1) Four tables to hold lamps—a pair flanking the sofa, a pair flanking the fireplace. (2) Coffee table, the bigger the better, 12″ to 14″ high. (3) Two light pull-up armchairs. (4) Probably a desk or writing table, and a nest of small tables.

### Dining Room

You may decide to eat in your living room or dining alcove or breakfast nook; but if you have a real dining room, buy as follows: (1) Adjustable table to seat 8 or more. (2) Eight chairs, of which the two for head and foot of table might be armchairs covered to match living-room chairs, so they can be used as extras. (3) Serving table, sideboard, console, or chest for service.

### Hall

The average hall requires a console or chest with mirror over it and two chairs or a bench.

### Bedroom

(1) Twin beds or double bed. (2) Two night tables to hold lamps. (3) Two chests, best when of identical size. (4) Two side chairs. (5) Dressing table and bench, if you make up in your bedroom rather than in the bathroom. If you want a place to relax, choose (6) a comfortable chair with ottoman upholstered to match rather than the conventional chaise longue.

## Facts About Wood Furniture

### Solid versus Veneer

Good Modern furniture is generally solid throughout, as are Provincial and Colonial pieces. In some eighteenth-century styles, however, veneering adds to beauty. If you go to a reputable dealer, you needn't be afraid of today's veneers' cracking or splitting. With our dependable synthetic resin glues, even relatively inexpensive reproductions from a good dealer are often more practical than real antiques.

### Finishes

Most well-made furniture of any type is protected by shellac, lacquer, or varnish. Experts consider one of these finishes as good as another. All are rubbed down finally by hand. All make furniture more water and stain resistant than corresponding pieces of even a short time ago. But, especially in the case of coffee tables, it's wise to inquire just what the finish is planned to withstand.

### Woods

Approximately one hundred different kinds of wood can be used by furniture craftsmen. The most popular are mahogany and walnut (natural or bleached), beech, oak, ash, maple, and the fruit woods (apple, pear, and cherry, natural or bleached). All these are hardwoods, with the fruit woods in the extra-hard class. When pieces are to be painted, birch, maple, beech, pine, and occasionally cherry are used.

Most of the walnut is French, because American walnut turns black eventually. Fruit woods are imported, too. No mahogany is found in this country; our main sources are the Philippines, Santo Domingo, Cuba, and Africa.

### Construction

Side chairs, especially dining-room chairs, are strongest when back and back legs are in one piece. If the design prohibits this—as in some French chairs—back and back legs should be securely spliced and glued. Stretchers under chairs and tables add to strength, as does a lower shelf on a side table. Legs, braces, and corner blocks should be assembled with either dowel or mortise-and-tenon joints.

## Upholstered Furniture

### Style and Comfort

**1. Choose Simple Lines.** Avoid bulbous curves, curlicues on the ends of arms, conspicuous bumpy legs. If you don't plan to slipcover, it's wise to choose models upholstered to the floor, or with loose drops to give the same effect.

**2. Consider Size of Piece in Your Room.** Don't confuse comfort with size. A small, well-designed chair may fit the body better than a mammoth one that dwarfs everything else and is too heavy to move about. A round-backed chair is less bulky than the same model with a square back.

**3. Try Before You Buy.** Take your husband with you and sit on *each* chair and sofa. Decide whether these are comfortable: height from the floor, depth of the seat, position of the arms, way the back fits your back when you relax. Decide whether you prefer squashy down cushions or firmer ones.

## Construction

**1. A Good Upholstered Piece Is a Real Investment.** If you can't afford first-class construction in all pieces you need now, put your money into a sofa you plan to keep in the living room, and make do with cheaper chairs, which later can be retired to a bedroom.

**2. Go to a Dealer You Can Trust.** Since you can't cut open a chair or a sofa to see what's inside, you have to rely on what you're told. Ask questions about the following points and deal only with a store whose integrity you trust.

**What Is the Frame Made of?** The frame of an upholstered chair should be of ash, maple, or birch—not pine, cypress, or any of the several softer woods that will not hold the tacks and glue firmly. The angle-strengthening blocks should also be of a hard wood with wide shoulders and of ample thickness, and should be glued and screwed to the frame, not nailed. All joints should be doweled and glued.

**How Is the Seat Base Constructed?** Ask questions about the construction of upholstered furniture before you buy. The webbing is very important, for it is the foundation for the springs and filling; unless the webbing is well built, the structure will collapse. Webbing should be constructed of strong bands of hemp about 3½″ wide, interlaced and placed close together. Each band should be stretched and secured to the frame with four tacks at each end, the ends then folded and retacked.

**What About the Springing?** Often the seat of your prized easy chair gives way, and you wonder why. Usually the cause of this trouble is poor springing. The seat should be constructed of oiled, tempered-steel wire springs set close together. They should be firmly sewed to the webbing and harnessed or tied in four directions with smooth hemp cord. As each cord passes the springs, it should be tied twice, firmly, and anchored to the rails. Picture shows back and seat spring construction in a well-made chair.

**What Is Between Stuffing and Springs?** A heavy, closely woven burlap should be stretched over the springs and held in place by tacks and stitching. This done, the proper base exists for the stuffing—hair, in the case of flat upholstered seats; or down, in the case of deep cushioned seats. Essentials like this are concealed from view. If you want good furniture, ask what is inside. Two chairs may look identical on the outside, yet be totally different inside.

**How Should a Seat Cushion Be Made?** The casing of a seat cushion should be made of heavy downproof ticking. The better qualities cost little more and do not leak. There should be three dividers or walls

within the cushion, forming four crosswise compartments. The front pocket should be more firmly packed than the others, as there is more pressure there. The stuffing should be 70 per cent goose down and 30 per cent small feathers. Good white down is most desirable, but good quality gray down is better than poor white down.

**Foam Rubber Cushions.** More and more upholstered furniture today uses foam rubber padding and foam cushions instead of hair stuffing and down or spring cushions. Many people prefer the firm, resilient effect, and the necessity of "fluffing" cushions when housecleaning is eliminated. This type of cushion will probably outwear all other types, and does not require downproof ticking. A simple muslin covering plus slipcover or permanent upholstery does the trick. Foam also has the added advantage of being nonallergic.

*For lasting comfort and strength, the webbed foundation of a well-made easy chair is constructed of strong hemp, interlaced, and firmly secured to the frame.*

*Here an upholstered chair has been stripped of its fabric and stuffing, showing closely-set, tempered-steel, wire springs tied with smooth hemp cord.*

# REUPHOLSTERING

**What Is Involved in Reupholstering?** A good upholsterer strips the piece all the way down to its wood frame. He refinishes the frame if necessary; replaces webbing; reties springs; supplies new padding material for seats, arms, back, and cushions—all this before he even begins to put on the new covering fabric. A well-reupholstered piece is practically as good as new because most of it *is* new.

**What Kind of Fabric Should You Use?** A wide variety of upholstery fabrics is available today. Traditional wools and mohairs are durable and can be cleaned well. Heavy cottons come in several new textures, including a cotton velvet that doesn't shade or spot. Combinations of rayon and other synthetic fibers, and plastics, are also widely used. Your investment in reupholstering is a sizable one, so it is poor economy to buy inferior quality.

A sofa usually requires 9 to 14 yards of fabric; a fully upholstered chair, from 4 to 7 yards.

**Are There Advantages to Reupholstering?** Yes, if you have a good piece of furniture, reupholstering will probably cost less than buying an equally good piece at today's prices. Moreover, an upholsterer usually offers a much wider choice of fabrics than you can find on new stock furniture.

**Where Can You Get Reupholstering Done?** Three people can handle your reupholstering: an upholsterer; a decorator, who will advise you and then pass the job along to an upholsterer; or the upholstery section of a department or furniture store.

# TIPS ON FURNISHING YOUR ROOMS

### Where Will You Eat?

A dining room isn't a "must" today; but if you decide on one, don't necessarily buy a suite of furniture with pieces monotonously alike, some of which you don't need anyway. You can diversify your effect with, for example, a painted piece, one with a mirror top, or one of different period and wood. If you don't want a separate dining room, you can have a dining alcove with permanent setup—or choose a dining table to double as console between meals—or whisk out a card table when needed.

### Where Will You Put Accessories?

Occasional tables don't need to match the rest of your furniture. In fact, they make smarter accents when they contrast. Here are a few general rules for occasional tables: If in doubt between two, choose the larger. Never pick one that is fragile or likely to tip, if it must hold a lamp. If top of end table is higher than arm of chair or sofa by which it stands, cut legs to bring top level. Don't forget the usefulness of a nest of tables when you entertain. If top of any occasional table becomes too marred to use, have mirror or black glass cut to fit—it will be scarproof then, and smarter than ever.

### Where Will You Sleep?

A double bed takes less space, is more effective decoratively, calls for half as much linen, half the time to make. But if you're a twin-addict, you'll want twin beds. Remember that upholstered headboards—with the right material used the right way—go with any type of room. They can be re-covered later, to suit another room, a different mood. A single head-

*This handsome table-desk gives you that needed place for letter writing.*

*A double bed saves space for an armchair that is covered in the same fabric which bands the bedspread.*

*A built-in entertainment center is an asset in any family room.*

board for two beds is a smart note. The trick swing-out mechanism with which some single-headboard twins are equipped is an attractive spacesaver, and it helps considerably when the beds are being made.

### Where Will You Put Clothes?

In your bedroom you will need one or two chests of drawers for your clothes. Chests need not match other furniture. In choosing chests for a bedroom, don't get one high chest, one low. Get two alike; tops on a level have a more restful effect. Placed in oppo-site corners on one wall—or across from each other on facing walls—two chests balance, give symmetry to your room. Or if the form is simple, you can put them together and create one important piece of furniture, which looks much more expensive than it actually is and gives your room distinction.

### Where Will You Write?

Every home needs a good writing desk, in the living room or in your own bedroom. Choose the type that appeals to you, but check the following

*When you close these closet doors, you have a wall of checkered, bow-sprigged wallpaper.*

*Small writing table doubles as a lamp table for nearby easy chair.*

points: Is the writing surface of correct height? Is there enough drawer space? Is the chair truly comfortable?

### Where Will You Sit?

Chairs are both decorative and useful pieces of furniture. A small chair can often be used to fill an empty corner or to give unity to an arrangement.

Every room should have enough chairs to accommodate the number of people who might ordinarily use it. For special occasions, get additional chairs from other sources in advance. It is disturbing to both the hostess and her guests to have chairs moved with them from room to room.

As chairs are made to be sat in, comfort should be the first consideration. Stiff chairs at the dining table can spoil the best meal. Pull-up chairs in the living room that make relaxation impossible can ruin a party. Test each chair for comfort and suitability to purpose. Don't confuse comfort with bulk.

But good, clean line is equally important; chairs must please the eye as well as fit the body. Avoid much machine carving, extraneous ornament. "The simpler the smarter" is a good rule.

Check for reliable construction as explained before.

All these points are much more important than matching chairs in the same wood.

*Two chairs and an ottoman covered in an easy-to-clean vinyl provide comfort in any room.*

*A touch of elegance is added to this living room with a graceful Victorian chaise longue. The combination of antique and contemporary furniture is the choice of many homemakers.*

*The simplicity of Danish design is compatible with ideas of comfort. Left: Dining chairs with rush seats are harmonious with other furnishings.*

# DRESSING TABLES

On dressing tables, you can let your imagination run wild. This is one place where there is no standard pattern to which you could possibly be expected to adhere. Your dressing table is your inner sanctum where you can express yourself to your heart's content. There are only two things to remember here: have plenty of space for the things you will be using, and be sure the light is good. A word of caution: if the light is *too* bright you may end up looking as though you were made up for the stage.

*A dressing table need not be frilly to be fresh and feminine. The smooth lines of wood and wrought iron complete the graceful and certainly ladylike dressing area. Laminated plastic sheathes the closet doors and walls, and is even inlaid in the dressing-table top.*

*You will take the "lead" at this bath-and-dressing table with movie-star lighting. A room so delicate in its pastel color and accessories is surprisingly durable and easy to clean with a laminated plastic table top and vinyl-tiled walls and floors.*

## UNPAINTED FURNITURE

There are many types of inexpensive unpainted furniture on the market. You can get such things as bookcases, chests, high chairs, desks, vanity tables, wardrobes, etc. Make sure that whatever you get is strong enough for the use to which you expect to put it. For instance, see that drawers are all wood, not paperboard.

Sometimes unpainted furniture is sold already sanded. Even then it will require a final smooth sanding before you finish it. See page 81 for information on painting.

The tops of tables, chests, and dressers should have a good tough finish to withstand everyday wear. You may want to use one of the self-sticking plastic films that are available in solid colors as well as in attractive wood or marble grains. Or you can have a top made of plate glass and use a patterned paper or fabric or a print of your favorite painting under it.

Black glass also makes a very attractive top surface. A good grade of varnish applied over a painted or stained top surface offers some protection and an occasional waxing will keep it looking better longer.

The appearance of ready-made unpainted furniture can be greatly improved by putting on better looking drawer pulls, hinges, and other hardware, adding casters, and lining drawers and shelves with attractive and appropriate paper.

*A well-planned room can combine two important areas. Above: The living area with a rectangular arrangement of furniture gives a spacious and uncluttered air yet makes a definite division with the dining area.*

*Left: Style and décor are continued in the dining section of the above room, which is perfect for serving and eating as a foldaway door opens to the kitchen.*

## DINING AREAS

Many of today's homes are planned for dining areas instead of the standard dining rooms. It is often felt that this makes for easier living, as the dining area is used for other purposes when a meal is not in progress.

There are many ways of arranging a dining area. It can be an integral part of the living room, or it can be set off from the living room by a room divider. The room divider can be a wall with openings or it can be a low piece of furniture that doesn't obstruct the view into the living room. A breakfast bar (some people call it "snack bar") is often used between the kitchen and the dining area. This may be table height, so chairs may be used, or it may be regular bar height, in which case stools with or without backs are used.

# CHART OF HISTORIC FURNITURE STYLES

Furniture design isn't created in a vacuum. Nor does a wizard cabinetmaker pull it like a rabbit out of a hat. Every "new" design is an outgrowth and adaptation of older forms. It is also the result of the play of social, historic, and economic forces: the product of world-wide lending and borrowing of ideas, in which all countries participate. This is true whether we speak of modern or traditional design. Here are the high lights in the evolution of furniture design.

## Chests: Lowboys, Commodes, Dressing Tables

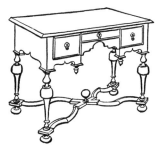

*William and Mary type lowboy of burl walnut. Bowl-turned legs, pear-drop brasses, and serpentine stretchers are typical. Late 17th century.*

*Early American lowboy, an elaboration of Queen Anne style; 1740. Carved fan motif, triple-arch skirt, acorn drops. Same design used today.*

*English mahogany chest, Thomas Chippendale type, with graduated drawers, early-type bracket feet; mid-18th century. Design is current today.*

*Dutch Colonial dower chest combines two drawers and chest; painted wood graining on pine. Simple country version. American, c. 1780.*

*English bow-front chest designed by George Hepplewhite; 1790. Veneered mahogany and holly wood, circular brasses. Design still used.*

*Late 18th-century French poudreuse; extremely refined curves typical of late Louis XV style. Cherry wood, hinged mirror. c. 1780.*

*French Empire fruit-wood commode; c. 1800. Simpler, bolder lines are emphasized. Note lion's-head handles. Style reached peak in 1820.*

*Mahogany dressing table by Duncan Phyfe; American, 1830. Curved supports, stretcher, feet. Lion's-head pulls — French adaptations.*

*Victorian black-walnut chest combines many earlier designs with little originality. Serpentine front, carved handles. American, c. 1850.*

*Queen Anne high chest on cabriole legs; bail handles, japanned design on drawers; fan ornament. Note straight top. English, c. 1710–35.*

*American mahogany double chest; typical block-front and shell design. Chippendale motifs; broken scroll pediment, flame finials. 1750–75.*

*American mahogany highboy; 1725–50. Broken pediment, fan motif, urn-and-flame finials. This basic design is still popular today.*

*Chippendale mahogany chest-on-chest, combining fretwork with gadroon edge around bottom, carved ogee feet. English, c. 1775.*

*Empire high chest of dark mahogany, gray marble top. Seven drawers. Classic heads top pilasters, ending in stylized human feet. French, c. 1810.*

*Sheraton tallboy. Veneered with figured mahogany. Simple chest-on-chest structure distinguished by architectural cornice. English, c. 1780.*

## Bookcases: Cabinets, Break Fronts

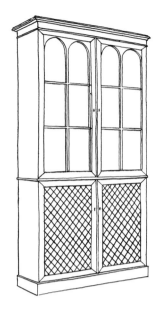

*Provincial wall cabinet in Louis XV style. Open shelves with scroll-cut framing. Graceful panels on lower portion. French, c. 1770.*

*Sheraton bookcase in cross-grain veneer. Purposely simple design to show off rare wood. Brass grille covers lower doors. English, c. 1800.*

*American break-front-case; design attributed to Thomas Shearer; c. 1790. Sheraton influence. Arched pediment, urn finials, squared legs.*

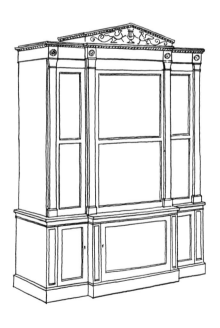

*English mahogany break front, Chippendale type. Center section emphasized by broken pediment, 2-door cabinet in base, flanked by drawers. Chinese fretted glazing is still duplicated today. c. 1750.*

*French Empire mahogany break front, c. 1810, has large-scale elegance. Outstanding elements are: leaf molding around top, ornamented pediment, plain pilasters topped by rosettes, gilded capitals. Base used today.*

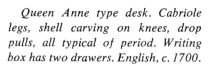

*Queen Anne type desk. Cabriole legs, shell carving on knees, drop pulls, all typical of period. Writing box has two drawers. English, c. 1700.*

*American adaptation of early 18th-century English slant-top desk. Top and base are one unit. Desk top has small drawers and pigeonholes within.*

*English Chippendale slant-top desk of mahogany. Serpentine front, bail handles, simple bracket feet, pull-out shelf. Middle of 18th century.*

*English mahogany pedestal desk of Chippendale period. First appearance of flat top. Cabinet doors in base. Popular design today. C. 1750.*

*George III pedestal desk of mahogany. Oval brasses; ogee bracket feet; chamfered, reeded corners. Leather top, drawers. C. 1750.*

*American slant-top mahogany desk. Lid carved with rope molding and shell. Same motif repeated on lower drawer. Claw-and-ball feet. 1750–70.*

*American block-front desk; 1765. Rhode Island type with reverse-shell carving on lid. Compare feet with those on pedestal desk above.*

*Small English curve-top desk. Satinwood with mahogany inlay and intricate marquetry. Rosettes, garlands on drawers, top, legs. Circa 1790.*

*Mahogany-inlaid tambour desk; English, c. 1790. Surmounted by box with tambour front, pigeon-holes within. Hinged top.*

*George Washington desk of mahogany. Fluted legs show fine detailing associated with the Sheraton period. Paper files on top, false drawers on ends. American.*

## Desks: Secretaries

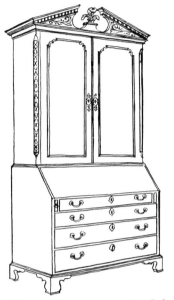

*Chippendale secretary; English, c. 1760. Detailed pediment with finial, canted corners atop early-type desk. Pull-outs hold desk lid.*

*American bookcase secretary; c. 1780. Chippendale-Hepplewhite period. Chinese lattice pattern on doors; high scroll pediment; five drawers.*

*American block-front secretary. Rhode Island type; credited to John Goddard; 1775. Note the elaborately carved shell-top pediment.*

*American mahogany secretary, modified Sheraton type. Classic pediment, finials. Gothic panels, tiny drawers. Hinged writing flap. c. 1795.*

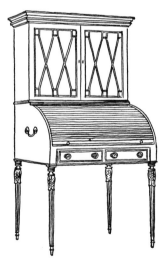

*Sheraton-type tambour desk-bookcase. Reeded legs with acanthus carving. Delicate, classic proportions indicate late Sheraton. English, c. 1800.*

*Duncan Phyfe secretary, with important elements of French Empire style. Half-round columns, paw feet. Massive, elegant. American, c. 1815.*

*American walnut table with plain H stretcher. Early Americans had neither the time nor craftsmanship to achieve fine carving, hence the simplicity shown here. Overhanging top prevalent in Colonial times. C. 1700.*

*English three-part table. Ends are separate, can be used against wall as consoles; center section becomes individual drop-leaf table. Compare concave curve of three pedestal legs with oval table below. Late 18th century.*

*Butterfly drop-leaf table; American. Name from shape of hinged brackets that support drop leaves. Type often made today. C. 1650.*

*American swing-leg maple table. Legs move to corners to support drop leaves. Table has cabriole legs, ball-and-claw feet. Circa 1760.*

*English oval table with single pedestal. Slight S curve in leg. Design of inlaid wood displaces carving. English, near end of 18th century.*

*Duncan Phyfe dining table. Note typically reeded pedestal, carved legs, and metal lion's feet. This table is expressive of French Empire style, which borrowed heavily from classic motifs. American, 1820.*

*Three-part American Sheraton table with characteristic reeded legs. Center section is a drop-leaf table. Ends can be used against wall as serving tables. Excellent example of early flexibility in furniture. Circa 1830.*

## Tables: Servers, Consoles

*An early American maple side table. Note legs resemble Dutch-type legs. Strong, sturdy stretchers. Made about 1720.*

*Early Georgian table. Marble top. Improved construction makes stretchers previously used unnecessary. Shell-carved knees. English, 1720.*

*French Provincial table of walnut or fruit wood. Light, curving contour is keynote of this period. Little ornamentation, tapered feet. C. 1780.*

*Hepplewhite semicircular side table in hardwood with marquetry of holly. Form, ornamentation resemble that of Louis XVI period. English, 1790.*

*American satinwood-and-mahogany side table in the Sheraton manner. Note serpentine top and reeded legs. Made about 1800.*

*Piecrust tilt-top table with tripod ornamented base, ball-and-claw feet. English, c. 1775. Contemporaneous with, though very unlike, Pembroke.*

## Tables: Tea, Game, Occasional

*Queen Anne Colonial-type tea table; American, 1725. Deep, shaped skirt, cabriole legs. This table is a fine interpretation of the English style.*

*Pembroke table, Chippendale style; American, 1775. Straight, square legs, crossed stretchers are features found in Chippendale's earlier designs.*

*Late Victorian console; American, 1860. Lyre-shaped support inspired by Duncan Phyfe. Serpentine top. Heavy footstool base, rope molding.*

*Sheraton - type Pembroke table. Curved drop leaves, reeded legs. Refer to delicate outlines of other late Sheraton pieces. American, c. 1790.*

*French Provincial game table with top removed, showing backgammon board. Country version of elegant French court tables. Louis XV, 1750.*

*Mahogany Hepplewhite card table; English, 1790. Special interest in quarter-round corners, holly-wood inlay. Movable legs support hinged top.*

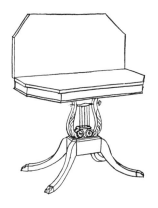

*Duncan Phyfe hinged - top card table. Lyre base and splayed feet of his design were both closely related to Empire styles. American, c. 1820.*

*Elaborately carved English mahogany tripod work table with spindle gallery for holding sewing or other small object. C. 1750.*

*Sheraton - type mahogany drum table; English, circa 1790. Deep apron with drawers; brass feet. This design is currently a great favorite.*

*French 18th - century worktable with tambour front; 1780. Made in walnut and fruit wood. An early version of present-day bedside tables.*

*American tilt-top side table. Cut-out, rounded corners; graceful stand; tapered legs. Used as candlestand. Still popular. C. 1790–1820.*

*English Regency sewing table corresponds to French Empire designs. Drawers for thread. Note ornate scroll supports on legs. Circa 1820.*

# Mirrors

*English walnut mirror; c. 1740. Scroll top and bottom, gilt crown. Often with Queen Anne lowboy.*

*Chippendale mirror. Ornately carved gilded frame, after the Louis XV manner. English, 1760.*

*American mirror, Chippendale type, but less elaborate. Scroll, pheasant ornament. C. 1750–1775.*

*American girandole gilded mirror. Candleholders on each side. Prototype of many used today. C. 1810.*

*Hepplewhite-style shaving mirror. Serpentine front. Shield form matches chair back. Made 1785–95.*

*American mirror. Transitional: Empire columns, classic beading. Our forefathers' favorite. 1800–20.*

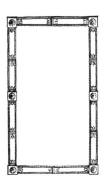

*American mirror; wood frame painted black and gold. Square medallions, carved rosettes. C. 1830.*

*Late Empire mirror with swirl columns, acanthus, lyre. Note high, narrow shape. American, 1820–50.*

## Sofas: Settees, Love Seats

*Queen Anne walnut settee upholstered in needlepoint. Scroll-curve arms, straight back, cabriole legs with club feet. Improved construction makes stretchers between legs unnecessary. English, circa 1710.*

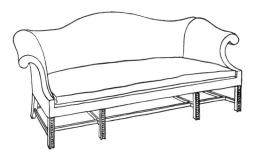

*English sofa, Chippendale type. Mahogany frame covered in damask. Straight, delicately carved legs. Plain, light stretchers. Observe flowing curve of back into arms. Often taken as a model for today's furniture. C. 1710.*

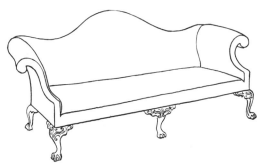

*American sofa in Chippendale style; c. 1775. Cabriole legs with intricate carving, naturalistic claw-and-ball feet. Note curve of back. Belonged to George Washington.*

*Louis XV sofa. Walnut frame covered in brocaded silk. Beautifully graceful lines. Back and arms joined in single continuous curve. French, late 18th century.*

*English Hepplewhite sofa with delicately curving back and arms, slightly serpentine front combines Louis XV and Louis XVI features. Late 18th century.*

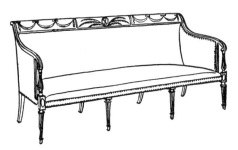

*American sofa, after Sheraton design, with reeded arms, turned and reeded legs. Brass nailheads outline frame. Top rail has bow, swag, wheat design. C. 1800.*

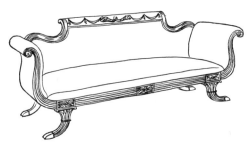

*Duncan Phyfe sofa with horizontally reeded base and scroll arms, outward-curving legs. Note similarity of motifs on top rail to Sheraton type. American, 1820.*

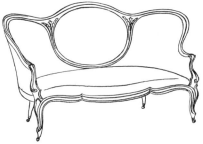

*American Victorian sofa of mahogany. Observe how curving lines resemble the more beautiful lines of Louis XV sofa. Back has carved, oval-panel inset. 1840–50.*

## Stools

*Early Georgian bench, shell-carved knee, ball-and-claw feet. Chippendale developed type. English, c. 1735.*

*Chippendale window seat of carved mahogany. Note scrolled arms, gadroon molding. English, 1760–75.*

*French banquette. Upholstered in velvet. Curved-X legs. Stool frequently copied today. Circa 1800.*

# Chairs: Side Chairs, Open Armchairs

*Early American slat-back armchair. Splint seat; simple, round stretchers. Late seventeenth century.*

*Queen Anne chair. Note typically curved lines of splat back, cabriole leg. English-made, c. 1720.*

*American comb-back Windsor chair; 1750. Originated in rural England. Note the back curve.*

*American bow-back Windsor chair; 1775–85 Bow often made of bent ash, hickory.*

*French Provincial armchair, Louis XV style; c. 1775. A country interpretation of court style.*

*Early Chippendale ladder-back chair. Straight legs, plain stretchers. English, mid-18th century.*

*Chippendale-type side chair. Decorated open splat, carved cabriole legs. English-made, circa 1770.*

*Shield-back, Hepplewhite-type chair. Tapered legs, spade feet, curved seat. American, c. 1795.*

*Sheraton-type armchair; American, c. 1800. Note continuous curve of back and leg, curved X in back.*

*Duncan Phyfe lyre-back chair; American, 1810. Note curve of back joining seat, outward flare of legs.*

*American Empire side chair, often called "Mme. Jumel"; 1810–30. Back curves into front legs.*

*English Regency open armchair; c. 1810. Upholstered seat, curved X in back. Still popular today.*

## Chairs: Wing and Open Armchairs

 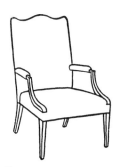  

*Queen Anne wing chair. Curved wings are protection from drafts. Cabriole legs. English, 1710–20.*

*Sheraton-type open armchair, often called "Martha Washington." American, c. 1790. Currently in favor.*

*American wing chair with wide flair. Square, straight legs; plain stretchers. Late 18th-century.*

*Hepplewhite wing chair; English, late 18th-century. Often copied today. Square, tapered legs.*

# GLOSSARY OF FURNITURE TERMS

**Acajou**  French word for mahogany

**Acanthus**  Conventionalized leaf

**Adam, Robert and James**  Scottish architects greatly influencing English decoration from c. 1750–1794

**Apron**  Structural part of a table, directly beneath the top, connecting the legs

**Bail Handle**  Handle hanging downward in a reversed arch

**Ball-and-Claw**  Chinese motif, symbolizing World Power; borrowed by English designers

**Baluster**  Spindle column supporting a railing or rail of chair

**Banquette**  Upholstered bench

**Baroque**  Style of art, architecture of curved and contorted forms; about 1550–1740

**Bergère**  French upholstered armchair with closed sides

**Bevel**  To cut to a slanted angle

**Block Front**  Front divided vertically into alternating concave and convex panels

**Bombé**  Bulging front and sides; common to Baroque design.

**Bonnet Top**  Rounded, bonnet-shaped top section of a highboy, secretary, etc.

**Boulle**  Marquetry of tortoise shell and metal; made in France by André Charles Boulle during the reign of Louis XIV.

**Bow Front**  Convex-shaped front

**Brasses**  Hardware, including handles and decorative metals

**Break Front**  Front formed on two or more planes, central portion being advanced or recessed, as in certain bookcases

**Bureau**  Chest of drawers; also French word for writing desk.

**Burl**  Growth on bole or root of tree; makes a beautifully marked or patterned veneer

**Cabriole**  Leg with double curve

**Cartouche**  Open scroll used as ornamental feature on furniture

**Cassone**  Italian decorated chest

**Chaise Longue**  French for "long chair." Usually with upholstered back; sometimes in two parts.

**Chamfer**  To bevel edge of a corner

**Chippendale, Thomas**  Most famous and influential of the English cabinetmakers. His early work was a refinement of Georgian. See "Georgian." Later, he borrowed and adapted from all periods and styles. 1718?–1779

**Classic Revival**  Styles influenced by Egyptian, Grecian, Roman, ancient architectural sources

**Console**  A table designed to be placed against a wall

**Cornice**  Horizontal top molding

**Credenza**  Elaborate sideboard, cupboard, or buffet

**Crewelwork**  Embroidery done with slackly twisted worsted yarn and a large-eyed needle

**Directoire**  Period of extreme simplicity of design; French; 1795–1799, and after

**Dresser**  Sideboard or buffet, chiefly for storage of clothing

**Dutch Foot**  Usually a thick, spoon-shaped foot

**Elizabethan**  Refers to reign of Queen Elizabeth in England; 1558–1603

**Empire**  Adaptation of the classic style of decoration endorsed by Napoleon when he became Emperor of France; 1804 to 1815. Vogue continued through 1830

**Farthingale Chair**  Chair made without arms to accommodate the voluminous Elizabethan skirts

**Fauteuil**  French open armchair

**Finial**  Terminating ornament on a post, pediment, or intersection

**Fretwork**  Interlaced ornamental work cut in low relief

**Frieze**  Running band of ornament

**Gadroon**  Carved, oval ornament repeated on a rounded molding

**Georgian**  Refers to reigns of Georges in England; 1714 to Regency. See "Regency"

**Girandole**  18th-century mirror, often convex, with candle sconces. Sometimes called bull's-eye mirror

**Goddard, John**  Cabinetmaker, designer of Newport, R. I.

**Grille**  Metal lattice work used in doors of cabinets, bookcases, etc.

**Hepplewhite, George**  Collaborated with Adam brothers, but his work was simpler; ?– to 1786.

**Jacobean** General term for merging of English Tudor design elements with those of Renaissance in England. Begins with reign of James I, through the Commonwealth period; ends with reign of James II. 1603–1701

**Japanned** Lacquered

**Knee** Upper convex curve of cabriole leg

**Lannuier, Charles Henri** French cabinetmaker and designer; worked in America. His furniture reflected Louis XVI classic tendencies and influenced Duncan Phyfe's work, ?–1820

**Lit de Repos** French for day bed

**Louis XIV** King of France, 1643 to 1715. Period of large-scale opulence in design. Ended with Regence. See "Regence"

**Louis XV** King of France, 1715–1774. Period during which design was characterized by flowing curves, rococo ornament, light colors

**Louis XVI** King of France, 1774–1792. Period of return to simpler forms, less ornate decoration, classic revival. See "Classic Revival"

**Lowboy** Table with drawers

**Marquetry** Elaborate-patterned inlay; usually, but not always, of wood

**Medallion** Design carved or painted within a circular or oval shape

**Melon Bulb** Thick turning, typical of Elizabethan and early Jacobean furniture (see "Elizabethan, Jacobean"); a motif retained from previous Gothic period

**Ogee** Line composed of a concave and convex curve; often used as a descriptive term for a type of table or chair foot

**Ormolu Mounts** Decorative gilded bronze on furniture

**Pediment** Broad, triangular piece with a long base; surmounts door, panel, bookcase, etc.

**Pembroke** Occasional table with drop leaves; said to be named after Pembroke family of England

**Phyfe, Duncan** Scottish cabinetmaker who worked in America. His designs were inspired by Empire. 1768–1854

**Pie-Crust Table** Round table with edge carved in scallops

**Pilaster** Upright column projecting from and attached to a wall or flat surface

**Poudreuse** French word for small powder table, often equipped with hinged mirror

**Provincial** Furniture imitating a definite style, but with its own rustic characteristics

**Pulls** Handles for drawers, cabinet doors

**Queen Anne** Queen of England, 1702–1714. Name applied to furniture made during or slightly after her reign

**Rails** Horizontal piece, part of a frame or paneling

**Reeding** Rows of beading or semicylindrical moldings used in close parallel lines

**Refectory** A dining table, generally long, narrow; often found in monasteries and nunneries

**Regence** Period following reign of Louis XIV in France. Furniture of this period is transitional in feeling. 1715–1723

**Regency** Period in England when Prince George, later George IV, was regent; 1811–1820

**Renaissance** Revival of interest in the arts; terminated Gothic design. Began in late 14th century, ended in early 17th century.

**Rococo or Rocaille** Flamboyant ornamental design with flowing curves. Height of popularity 1730–1765

**Rosette** Rose-shaped ornament of wood or metal

**Roundabout Chair** Chair with legs in front, back, and sides; slightly circular back supported by three legs

**Savery, William** Philadelphia cabinetmaker who worked in a highly ornamental Chippendale style; his highboys and lowboys considered the best in Colonial America

**Scritoire or Scrutoire** Desk with drop-down lid for writing

**Secretary** Fall-front desk, sometimes with drawers below and a bookcase or cabinet above

**Serpentine** Juxtaposition of a concave and convex form to create a sinuous line, as in the front of a chest of drawers.

**Shaker** Religious sect first introduced in America around 1780. Their furniture was free of what they called "wicked decoration"

**Shearer, Thomas** English designer and cabinetmaker; contemporary of Sheraton. Probably greatly influenced Hepplewhite. Published book of furniture designs in 1788. See "Hepplewhite," "Sheraton"

**Sheraton, Thomas** English cabinetmaker. Wrote *The Cabinetmaker and Upholsterer's Drawing Book.* 1751–1806

**Shield Back** Chair back in form of a shield. Often found in Hepplewhite's designs

**Slat Back** Chair back having horizontal rails or cross bars

**Spade Foot** Rectangular, tapered foot; common in Hepplewhite and Sheraton designs. See "Hepplewhite," "Sheraton"

**Spandrel** Triangular piece spanning the space between a vertical support and a horizontal piece or rail

**Spanish Foot** Grooved and flared foot often ending in a scroll

**Stile** Margin or space between panels or architectural elements

**Stretcher** Crosspiece connecting and strengthening legs

**Tester** Canopy on a fourposter or draped bed

**Toile de Jouy** Originally referred to fabric made and printed in Jouy, France

**Trumpet Turning** Turned leg with flaring profile resembling a trumpet

**Tudor** Reign of Tudor family in England from Henry VII to Elizabeth; 1485–1603

**Turkey Work** Oriental type of textile, or an imitation of it

**William and Mary** English monarchs, 1689–1702. Originally from Holland; brought Dutch influence to England

**Windsor Chair** So named because the withes and bowed shapes forming the spindles and back were cut and turned near Windsor, England

**Victorian** Pertaining to reign of England's Queen Victoria; 1837–1901

*Small portraits: "Mr. and Mrs. Wilson"*

*"Boat Races at Deauville," from a watercolor by Dufy*

SVENSKA VÄXTER

*Overscaled, contemporary Swedish botanical print*

*"Still Life; The Table," by Braque*

## PICTURES IN THE HOME

Carefully selected pictures, properly framed and hung, add immeasurably to the decorative interest of *any* room. You'll be able to find faithful reproductions of old masters, and colorful contemporary posters, for very little money. Even original water colors and oils are often available at budget prices.

You can choose one huge picture, or a number of smaller ones to group together. Related subjects such as the "Mr. and Mrs." prints at the top of the page make a natural grouping.

The framing of your prints is important. In most cases, a mat will enhance the picture as a part of your decoration. Keep the frames simple, and you will never tire of them. In any case, don't let either the mat or the frame compete with the picture for attention. The mat itself should be either a neutral tone or should be of a color taken from the picture; this is what the decorator means by "picking up a color." For instance, in the Swedish botanical print at the bottom of the page, the mat is the color of the leaves of the plants; this will in no way clash with the other colors or with the frame which is a light natural wood.

The usual rule on hanging pictures is to place them at eye level. In practice you will find that it quite often looks better to have them above eye level; when grouping pictures one above the other, keep the lower picture no lower than eye level. Experiment to find out what looks best in your room. In placing a picture behind furniture, make sure the top of the furniture comes below the frame of the picture; this is something that is quite often overlooked when a lamp is placed in front of a picture. Also be sure that the lampshade comes below the frame and if the lamp is supposed to light the picture, it should light the whole picture and not just part of it.

# BUYING A MATTRESS

One of the most important problems in selecting the furnishings for your home is deciding on your bedding. Because the right mattress is the basis for relaxing and restful sleep, it requires your careful attention. Confine your consideration to mattresses made by well-established manufacturers and handled by dealers who have built a reputation for giving good service.

Some stores have display rooms where you may try various mattresses and springs. A "rest test" will help you decide the type and degree of resilience you prefer.

The materials used and how they are put together determine the quality and comfort of the mattress. Most states and certain cities have bedding laws requiring that mattresses have labels describing the materials used in their making. So look for these labels, and read them before you buy. They tell what is inside the mattress and whether the material is new or renovated. Look for other tags or labels to identify special features. Read and understand any guaranty statements attached to the mattress.

## Innerspring Mattresses

There are two types of innerspring mattress. In one, each spring is held in an individual muslin pocket, permitting each to operate independently of the others. This contributes to the comfort of the mattress. In the second type, the springs are fastened securely to one another by metal ties or wires, forming an interlocked unit. For this type, a "prebuilt" border, which stiffens the edges and prevents sagging, is desirable.

The coils of innerspring mattresses are covered with a layer of sisal, quilted or stitched pads, or special, patented metal devices, which keep the mattress padding from sinking into the coils and so prevent that uncomfortable "coil feel." The mattress padding is made of layers of felted cotton, hair, or sponge rubber, held firmly in place.

## Solid Mattresses

The solid-core type of mattress has no innersprings; resilience is obtained from the filling materials, which may be formed from layers of felted cotton or hair. Usually, this type offers a firm sleeping foundation. If you suffer from back trouble or some other ailment that requires special consideration in selecting bedding, follow the advice of your physician. In time, some of these solid-core mattresses may tend to become lumpy and require renovation.

One increasingly popular type of solid-core mattress is the molded-latex or foam rubber unit. This has a core of spongelike rubber (over 80 per cent air). Such mattresses do not require padding. They have been in use for some years and have been found to retain a good degree of resilience. Because a latex mattress is usually not so thick as an innerspring or solid mattress, a special, extra-high box spring should be considered.

## Choosing a Bedspring

Every mattress should be supported by a suitable bedspring. Most mattress manufacturers furnish sets with box springs matched not only for ticking but also for resilience and comfort. The box spring is usually the most satisfactory type of support, and because it is enclosed in ticking, it is much easier to keep clean.

Coil and flat springs also are available. Coil springs, which are more resilient, are suited to the support of a solid-core type of mattress. But good coil bedsprings ought to be equipped with double-decker coils. Flat springs are usually less expensive but, in many cases, sag and do not provide proper support for the mattress.

*Springs held in individual pockets*

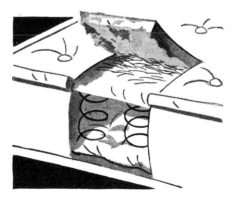

*Section of metal-tied innerspring type*

# FLOORS AND FLOOR COVERINGS

Your floor surface is really the cornerstone in building a decorating scheme. It can modify the size and shape of a room, be bold or retiring in pattern, bright-colored or neutral.

Within the framework of budget and structure, and with a practical eye on use and maintenance, you have a world of choice in deciding the finished "looks" of a floor. Here are a few general rules to remember, followed by a list of the basic types of flooring, exclusive of carpeting (which is discussed in a separate section).

In a small house, it is wise to choose one floor material throughout connected living areas, to make rooms seem larger and keep down cost. In a modern open plan, dining or conversation corners can be isolated visually with flood breaks: a switch in materials or cut-in patterns or borders. Extreme contrasts in texture and color are effective when there is a good reason. Color insets can direct traffic. A shaggy rug on a stone floor is an invitation to relax. A strip of clay tile under a picture window makes a safe base for indoor plants.

Before the final choice consider the long-range aspect of *keeping* a floor good-looking. Balance the factors of wear, budget and decoration against your own time, energy, and replacement dollars. First pick the right material for the hard or light use it will receive.

## The Eight Basic Types of Flooring

**Wood.** A favorite material because of its tradition and warm natural tones. Strip flooring goes with any decoration. Block or parquet creates an interesting effect and random plank has a Colonial or rustic feeling. Under carpeting, a plywood subfloor is economical.

**Linoleum.** Sheet form provides a smooth floor with few seams or joints; decorative borders, bands, or insets may be used. Also available in tiles that are easily installed by nonprofessionals. When color and material are the same throughout it is called "inlaid."

**Asphalt Tile.** A modestly priced, tile-shaped topping with a good history of wearability. Moisture-resistant and popular for all over the house. Easy to install oneself. Not impervious to certain household chemicals. Often marbleized or striated.

**Rubber and Cork.** Both offer the pleasure of warmth and resilience. Rubber has a color range, natural cork has woody brown tones. Not inexpensive, but durable, and lends air of quality.

**Plastics.** Newest addition to man-made floor coverings are the plastics (usually termed vinyl) in sheet or tile form and in rich colors. They are resilient, flexible, resistant to stains, easily maintained, but are not low in cost.

**Clay Tile.** Baked clay tile has proved its durability over the centuries. For kitchen, bath, or for any part of the house where ease in cleaning and impervious qualities count. Many sizes, colors, and types suit any decorating and wear requirement.

**Troweled.** Concrete, terrazzo, and other compounds that are poured into place. Some provide a self-finish, some need only sealing and paint, some serve as a subfloor for other finish materials. Long used in industry and public buildings, these materials

*Examples of two different types of vinyl floor covering used for a smooth, continuous decorative effect. Left: A terrazzo type in solid vinyl of mixed white and beige tones. Right: The popular vinyl asbestos in a confetti-like design. This is beautiful flooring that is easy to keep clean.*

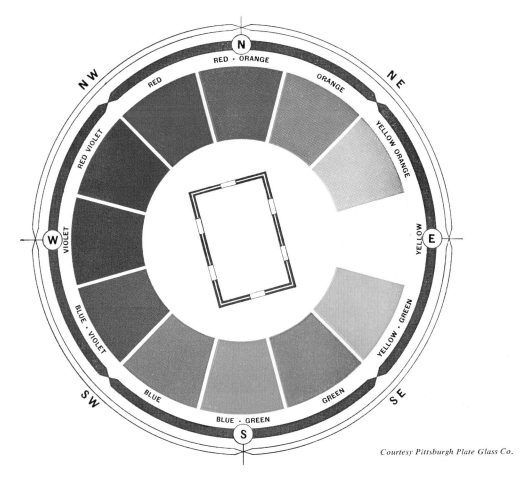

*Courtesy Pittsburgh Plate Glass Co.*

## HOW TO USE THE COLOR WHEEL

The color wheel is a simple and practical guide to the harmonious combination of colors.

It's made up of the three primary hues—red, yellow and blue—and a series of secondary and tertiary colors which are created by mixing these primary colors in varying proportions.

You can see that blues, greens and blue-greens are cool and restful. They are generally considered receding colors that "push" walls back, making rooms appear to be larger. Warm colors like red, red-orange, orange, yellow-orange and yellow are cheerful and warm. They are considered advancing colors that can make your walls seem closer and rooms appear smaller.

A simple way to determine the wall colors to use in a room is to make a rough sketch of the floor plan of your home and place it within the color wheel, with the north end of your house facing "N." This will serve as a guide to the type of color desirable for the rooms you wish to decorate.

To achieve a satisfactory color arrangement, all you have to do is to combine one or more colors that go well with your wall colors. For best results you will want to know these simple mechanical formulas that can be applied to the color wheel.

ANALOGOUS OR RELATED HARMONY— A series of neighboring colors on the color wheel are related by containing one color in common, may be used together.

COMPLEMENTARY OR OPPOSITE HARMONY—This color pattern makes use of hues and tints that are directly opposite each other on the color wheel.

SPLIT COMPLEMENTARY HARMONY— Offers a wider range of hues as it makes use of any color on the color wheel with the colors on both sides of its opposite on the circle.

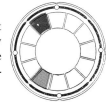

TRIAD HARMONY—Uses equidistant colors. One of the most frequently used harmonies and provides the basis of many beautiful and practical combinations.

have new importance in the home with slab construction.

**Brick and Stone.** The whole family of natural materials—slate, fieldstone, bluestone, marble, and brick—have a new role in the modern house. Formerly confined to terraces, patios, porches, or entrances, they are now used indoors for large floor areas. Range of soft colors, textures, patterns—bold or subdued.

### Wood Floors

There is a wide variation in the characteristics of wear, appearance, stability, cost, and maintenance of wood floors.

### Hardwood Floors

Oak and maple are the most commonly used hardwoods for finish flooring. These woods are manufactured, in several forms and grades, into excellent material that is generally available at mass-production prices.

There are also unusual woods that are not so well known, nor produced widely on a commercial basis for flooring, although they are entirely suitable for the purpose. In localities where such woods are native and can be milled economically near by, they often lend a distinctive charm to a house. Birch, beech, walnut, black and red gum, and many other hardwoods have qualities that make them satisfactory floorings in appearance and performance.

### Softwood Floors

Many white pine floors are still in use after hundreds of years. There are many softwoods such as redwood, southern yellow pine, larch, cedar, hemlock, Douglas fir, and cypress, that offer possible money savings, challenging design possibilities, and good service. Softwoods used for porch floors require paint or penetrating preservatives.

### Linoleum

One of the most versatile and best-known of floor coverings, linoleum usually comes in 6' sheets or in popular tile sizes. It is made of ground cork, wood flour, and linseed oil that is oxidized and pressed over a woven or felt backing. The choice of color and design is unlimited.

### Grades and Thicknesses

There is a wide difference in the quality of various linoleums. Only the "inlaid" type, in which the color and pattern go through to the base, can be considered an enduring floor covering. Standard thickness for use in homes is $\frac{3}{32}''$, for heavy traffic $\frac{1}{8}''$, for budget purposes $\frac{1}{16}''$. Ask a reliable supplier to help you with your choice.

*Because of its sound-quieting properties, wall-to-wall cork tile makes an excellent floor covering when no rug is used. In this room, the filtering of sound to other rooms is further diminished by the sound-absorbing quality of an acoustical ceiling and full-length draperies at the window.*

## Laying Linoleum

Because of its ease of cutting and workability, linoleum lends itself to custom patterns and rooms with difficult jogs. Decorative insets can be made to order, others are in stock. Sheets should be laid professionally, as a cutting mistake could ruin a whole roll. Dealers usually quote a price for material and labor together. Tile shapes can be set by the home workman. Per square foot, there is little more waste with sheet materials but not enough to make it much more expensive than tile. Both are economical.

### Asphalt Tile

Least expensive of durable manufactured floor coverings, asphalt tile has a new prominence in living areas. It is made of asbestos fibers and mineral color pigments in asphaltic and resinous binders, and comes in sheets, borders, and shapes, as well as the familiar squares.

### Sizes and Gauges

Most commonly used are the 9″ x 9″ tiles, although 6″ x 6″, 12″ x 12″, and others are available. Standard gauges are $\frac{1}{8}$″ and $\frac{3}{16}$″ thick. Although classed as a resilient material, asphalt tile is perhaps the least resilient in the group.

### Characteristics of Asphalt Tile

The shining merits of this material are its resistance to moisture and alkalies, and thus its ability to cover below-grade basement floors or on-grade concrete slabs. Do not expect it to do a waterproofing job, however. Its durability is proved by years of use in public buildings. It has sound-deadening qualities, is anti-slip and easy on the feet, and is termiteproof. The standard tile is not greaseproof, but there are special grease-resisting varieties for use in the kitchen.

Color range is wide but not quite so bright as in other materials, due to inherent ingredients. White, and light shades, are slightly more expensive because of necessary bleaching. Color and pattern go clear through. Usual pattern is "marbleized," either with high or gentle contrast—a practical design for disguising foot marks and dust. Room breaks, designs, and borders are simple to devise for individual rooms.

### Cork Tile

Cork tile is fabricated from a natural material: bark stripped from the cork oak is ground and baked under pressure, or it may be electronically processed. Natural gums provide the binder, trapping thousands of air cells within to give cork tile its distinctive characteristics of lightness, insulation, sound absorp-

tion, and resilience. Toasty colors range from light oak to dark walnut—no color is added.

### Decoration and Use

Cork tile most nearly resembles parquet wood but is like no other flooring material. About equal in cost to hardwood or carpet, it lends richness to a traditional interior and gives acoustic balance to a modern room with much glass. A subtle over-all pattern is achieved by the use of 6″ x 6″ tiles in random brown tones, while 6″ x 12″ shapes create an interesting diagonal design. Natural mottling disguises foot marks. Since cork tile is 50 per cent trapped air it is one of the best insulators. It is warm to the touch, and its resilience is kind to feet.

### Rubber Tile

Due to its flexibility, rubber tile resists indentations, chipping, and cracking. Its chief component is rubber—either synthetic, new, or reclaimed—and it is often reinforced by cotton fibers. It is a quality flooring noted for its resilience and bright coloring that goes clear through.

### Characteristics of Use

In a sense, a rubber tile floor is like having built-in rubber soles all over the house. The noise of footsteps is muffled, resilience underfoot reduces fatigue, and the surface discourages slipping. Its smooth, nonporous finish is highly resistant to abrasion and scuffing and maintains its good appearance for a long time. Rubber tile sheds dirt easily, so care is simple.

The flexibility of this product recommends it to locations where there may be structural movement, as in an old house or in climates with extremes of dampness and dryness. Rubber tile is not inexpensive, but its special qualities make it well worth while.

### Decorative Possibilities

A complete range of sizes, shapes, ornamental insets, borders, and molded coves allow a free hand in designing a custom floor to suit a room. Colors are clear and patterns include marbleized, textured, and jaspé (a muted stripe) for striking or subdued effects. Usual tile sizes are 6″ x 6″ and 9″ x 9″. Larger, smaller, and special sizes in stock or to order. Standard gauges: $\frac{1}{8}$″ and $\frac{3}{16}$″ thick.

### Plastic Flooring

Most of the large manufacturers are making this new floor material in tile or roll form. One product is made of coke, salt, and limestone; another is a combination of plastic binders and asbestos fiber.

Whatever the secret of the different formulas, the promise from all is a handsome and practical floor that is "everything-proof."

## Aspects of Plastic Floorings

Phenomenal claims have been made for the various plastics, loosely termed "vinyls." They earned their right to praise from their good performance under the most severe laboratory tests and accelerated wear tests that simulated years of use. Extremes of heat or cold, dampness, dryness, and the chemicals ordinarily used in most households do not seem to injure them.

Resilient, they have a good feel underfoot and accommodate to structural changes without cracking or buckling. This makes them ideal for covering an old floor that may be slightly uneven, or a wood floor with a normal play. Flexible, they may be curved to form stair nosings or coved bases for easy cleaning. Scuff-resistant and with color clear through, they will not show wear marks easily. Heavy furniture will not leave permanent indentations. Predictions are that plastics will outwear other floor-coverings. The relatively high first cost is balanced by the promise of long-range performance.

Impermeable to moisture, plastics will not rot and can be installed in situations where dampness might be injurious to other flooring materials. They can be installed directly over concrete, steel, or wood sub-floors, and are fire-resistant.

A complete palette of rich, true, fade-resistant colors makes plastic flooring a decorator's dream. It is usable for any room in the house, but particularly good in the kitchen because of its high resistance to grease, alkalies, solvents, and acids. Since the composition of the various products differs, it would be wise to check the individual resistance characteristics before making a final decision.

*Warm tans—found in this cork floor—keynote the color scheme of this attractive modern living room.*

*Quiet and easy to maintain, cork is a perfect choice where no rugs are used.*

### Clay Tile

Both glazed and unglazed tiles make extremely attractive and durable floors for bathroom, kitchens, plant rooms, halls, vestibules, and (recently) living areas where long and carefree service is required.

### Glazed and Unglazed Tile

A type of 4¼″ square matte or semimatte *glazed tile* known as "extra duty" is suitable for residence floors where there is no excessive abrasion or impact. (Often confused with this type because of similar appearance is a less durable kind called "glazed interior" which is made for wall surfaces but is *not suitable* for floors.)

A very durable *unglazed tile* termed "quarry" is resistant to moisture, stains, abrasion, freezing, and thawing. It is used for interior floors and outdoor terraces and walks.

### Ceramic Mosaics

In the tile trade the word "ceramics" refers only to small tiles about 1″ to 2″ in squares or hexagons —although properly all tiles are of baked clay and therefore ceramic. Glazed and unglazed tiles of this class make excellent floors.

### Troweled

Troweled materials are placed on the site while plastic and are leveled by troweling or "floating."

They make relative inexpensive, extremely durable colorful, and easily maintained floors. Unless seam are desired for design effect, troweled floors can b "all-in-one-piece." They may be used as a finished floor or serve as a base for rugs.

### Concrete or "Cement"

Sanitary, squeakless, strong, fireproof, permanent— concrete floors that are properly installed are also proof against moisture deterioration, termites, cracking, dusting, sagging, and impact. With buried radiant heating pipes in one-story basementless houses such floors are warm. Finished with a topping of colored cement, they never need renewing. Concrete of natural-colored cement can be painted after it is thoroughly dry.

### Terrazzo Has Texture

This flooring is composed of colored marble chips, called the "aggregate," and a binding cement known as the "matrix." Terrazzo is really a form of concrete and has the same characteristics. After the mixture is placed it is leveled as it hardens by troweling or floating at the proper time. After setting it is machine-ground to expose the aggregate which gives the surface its distinctive color and textured appearance. The color of the matrix, as well as the color of the chips, may be varied to result in a wide range of effects. Metal or colored plastic strips may be used to divide the field into interesting patterns and borders.

*A perennial favorite is the hardwood floor in random-width planks.*

*What could be prettier for a dining room than a vinyl-tiled floor in a high-style color?*

## Magnesium Oxychloride

The name suggests a patent medicine rather than the excellent flooring material it really is when used properly. It has many aliases including compo, sorel cement, magnesite, and numerous trade names. The product makes a resilient, low-cost floor which may vary in color from pure, brilliant hues to low-key grays. Unless of special type it should not be used where there is persistent dampness or where it might be exposed to acids or alkalies. This same material is used as a matrix with marble chips or cork granules for a type of terrazzo.

## Masonry

Brick and stone come very near to being everlasting and carefree flooring materials. They are fireproof and wearproof and may be handled in the spirit of either traditional or contemporary design. The floors of interior foyers, halls, and rooms with featured views can repeat the masonry paving of walks and terraces to create a feeling of oneness and unity with the area surrounding the house.

## Brick Is Versatile

Floor designs in infinite variety are possible because of the different colors, patterns, joint widths, and surfaces of bricks. Bricks are usually laid flat for minimum thickness and it is important that paving, face, or very hard-burned common brick be used for flooring because soft bricks will chip and dust. Pleasing effects can result from a combination of brick with troweled materials, with wood, or with clay tiles.

## Marble for Formal Luxury

Not all type of marble are suitable for floors—only those resistant to cracking from impact should be used. The material is sawed from quarry blocks to about an inch in thickness and the faces are polished. Relatively expensive, marble floors are most often found in luxurious homes or, where budget is a factor, used in small areas for emphasis.

## Flagging Has Natural Look

Flagstones can be of natural slate, sawed bluestone or limestone, cast concrete, or stratified fieldstone. Many patterns are possible, the character of the design depending on natural irregular shapes, hammer dressing, or machine sawed rectangular pieces. Since flagging is heavy it is usually laid over a concrete supporting slab. Sawed and cast types can be laid to accurate level. Since furniture will wobble on rough flag flooring, the tops of stones used to pave living areas should always be leveled.

*New red brick, waxed and polished, paves a hall and living room, gives a feeling of warmth and coziness.*

# RUGS AND CARPETS TO BEAUTIFY YOUR HOME

Although you select a rug or carpet chiefly for its decorative effect, there are some practical points to remember. For example, light shades will usually show soil more quickly than dark shades. In the dining room, food stains show up more readily on a solid-color, cut-nap rug than on a figured or a twist-type pile rug. Another vexing problem is shading (*described below*). This, too, is more noticeable in a solid-color, cut-nap rug than in a figured, patterned, twist- or pebbly-type rug.

### Use Proper-Sized Rugs

Rugs are available in sizes to fit any room, with a space between the wall and rug varying from 6″ to 15″. This space should be fairly equally divided on all four sides. If you are considering a wall-to-wall carpet, with its luxurious effect, keep in mind the problem of fitting it to another room if you move to another house. Wall-to-wall carpeting can easily be cleaned right up to the baseboards with a present-day vacuum cleaner.

### New Blends of Man-Made Fibers and Wool

There is a definite trend toward the use of man-made fibers in the manufacture of rugs and carpets. Most manufacturers are using such fibers in addition to the traditional wool. These are entirely satisfactory if made by well-established manufacturers, who use fibers specifically suited for rugs and carpets. Actually, this is not a new development; rugs blended of rayon and wool were offered years ago. Some were made of 50 per cent rayon and 50 per cent wool, and have stood up very well. Many rugs and carpets now have piles or naps made entirely of synthetic fibers

such as Acrilan, Creslan, nylon, etc., which resist soil and spotting. These should wear well, too.

### Rug Construction

In addition to Axminster and Wilton woven rugs, tufted and knitted rugs are now available. The type of construction is not an indication of the wear that may be expected. All other factors being equal (such as the yarns used in making the nap), the durability depends on the density of the tufts of yarn that make up the surface pile, and how well these are backed. The more closely the tufts are set, the more wear may be expected.

The term broadloom refers to carpet fabrics made on a wide loom, not to a type of carpet weave. Neither does it indicate that a rug or carpet is a solid color. It may be of any of the constructions and available in colorful patterns, plain colors, and in various embossed or sculptured designs.

### Life of Rugs and Carpets

While rugs and carpets made of synthetic fibers, or blends of synthetic fibers and wool, should wear as well as those made of all wool, it is impossible to predict how long any rug or carpet will last. This depends on how much traffic walks over it each day and the care it receives, as well as its own inherent wearing qualities.

### Fading

Fading of rugs and carpets is no problem, even if the nap is made of a blend of synthetic fibers and wool. While no dye is absolutely fadeproof, carpet and rug manufacturers use dyes highly resistant to the effects of sunlight.

*Look for the label on the back of the rug, and read it carefully. It gives useful information about the rug.*

*Open the face of the rug to examine pile. The closer the tufts, the greater the density and durability.*

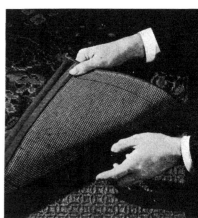

*Use cushions under rugs and carpets. They prolong their life and make them more comfortable to walk on.*

*An octagonal rug sets the scene and dramatizes it vividly in a dining corner. Strong patterns often add to the decorative impact of area rugs.*

*Here a burnt-orange rug is shown against a polished parquet floor. Accentuating color makes its strong point in the Danish-modern setting.*

## Shooting of Pile

The term "shooting" refers to yarn that extends above the surface of the pile. This does not indicate that the rug is in any way defective. Simply snip off these higher pieces of yarn to make them level with the rest of the surface.

## Fluffing, or Shedding

This is a perfectly natural occurrence in a rug or carpet, particularly a new one or one with a cut pile. When a rug is new, material that has been cut off in the manufacturing process to even the surface tends to shed. It is impossible to completely remove this in the manufacture. In fact, its removal may take months. Even after that you will find carpet fluff in the dust container of your vacuum cleaner. This does not mean your cleaner is hard on the rug. Some fluff may be cut off by walking on the rug. Fluffing occurs to a lesser degree in the twist-weave-type rug.

## Shading—Apparent Change in Color Tone

Shading, a normal condition in a rug or carpet, is due to the varying degrees in which light is reflected from different sections of the rug. It is caused by the nap's being brushed or laid in different directions. This effect is most noticeable in solid-color rugs and carpets. It can be corrected, at least temporarily, by steaming and repeated brushings in the opposite direction. Steaming can be done effectively only by a good professional rug cleaner.

## Prevent Bad Falls

Today, many manufacturers are applying to the backs of scatter rugs materials that lessen the danger of skidding or slipping. If your scatter rugs have not been so treated, place some good anti-skid material under them. Accident statistics show that many serious falls are caused by slipping on scatter rugs. Take a critical look at yours.

### Cotton Rugs and Carpets

Cotton rugs are of two types—nonwoven and woven. The nonwoven type is made by punching pile loops through a backing of cotton duck. The weight of the backing varies in rugs of different manufacture and style. The woven type doesn't have a separate backing. Its loops are actually a part of the weave, as in a Turkish or terry towel; they are very firm and resist pulling and snagging. Both types have cut pile or loops, depending on the design or texture. The looped rugs usually have a definite twist. The newest cotton rugs have a very fine, short, tightly twisted loop that wears well. Because of its hard twist, this pile can be cleaned with a vacuum cleaner more easily than rugs with longer, softer loops. Wear also is improved by the use of fine yarns, which increase the number of threads per square inch.

Cut-pile rugs have a soft, rippling texture. Both cut pile and loops sometimes are used in the same rug to obtain intricate designs and patterns. Interesting and pretty sculptured effects are obtained by having the pile of the rug at different heights.

### "Summer" Rugs

"Summer," or fiber, rugs are becoming more and more popular for indoor year-round use. They are made from a variety of materials. One kind is of twisted strips of paper, shellacked to resist friction. Durability depends on how tightly the strips are twisted. Dyes on such rugs are as sun-resistant as they can be made, but direct sunlight will gradually affect the brightness of the color. Sometimes these rugs have a stenciled pattern on one side and are solid color on the other, so you can turn them over for variety.

Another type of summer rug is the grass, or straw, rug. It's light yellow or greenish yellow. Since straw is too brittle to be woven, this kind of rug is sewed with cotton yarn.

Hemp rugs come in two versions: Manila hemp and sisal. Manila hemp is natural color or white. It is usually woven into squares, which reflect light and give the effect of a diamond pattern. The squares are bound together to any size or shape you want. Sisal may be dyed in any of several colors, and sisal rugs are sold in standard sizes.

### Pointers on Rug Colors

No matter what size, style, or kind of rug you choose, the most important thing to remember is to get a definite color—a really clear, light color, or a really bright, dark color. (Try not to get the dusty, dirty shades.) No matter how individual your taste, you should be able to find the color you are looking for in the stores today.

With a bold design on your floor, plan to have plain walls or striped wallpaper. With these use small-patterned or self-toned fabrics, stripes, or plain materials. For instance, if you have an Oriental or a floral rug that has a good deal of red and light blue in it, use the

light blue for the walls and the red for the furniture.

With a plain or tone-on-tone floor covering, plan to use brilliant, bold-patterned wallpaper. Use plain or striped fabric for slipcovers, upholstery, and curtains.

Always consider your rug as part of your decorating scheme, along with curtains, walls, and slipcovers. Buy carpets for color and design, rather than with the idea that they'll "wear forever." Styles change, new weaves and colors come on the market. Don't put so much into your first carpets that you feel you must keep them for life.

## SASH CURTAINS

The best curtains are the kind that are pretty and crisp to begin with and that stay that way. They don't attract dirt and don't yellow or gray with use. You can wash them easily, and they need little or no ironing. The only trouble with these curtains is that they don't exist—yet. There are many good curtains on the market today that have one or more of these desirable properties, but to date no one curtain fabric has them all. Textile manufacturers are working hard to produce the perfect curtain, but until they do you'll have to decide which feature means most to you.

### Are Cotton Curtains Still a Good Buy?

Cotton curtains in organdy, lace, or net are still popular. They wear well, wash out white, can be bleached in most cases, and can always be restored to crispness. They must, however, be starched and

*This carpet of a sturdy knitted construction and in a warm red shade adds texture interest to the room and complements the brick-fireplace wall.*

*Shaggy cotton is an attractive and sound choice for a bedroom, where carpets get light wear. Here, it is used luxuriously wall to wall.*

ironed after every washing. Some cotton curtains—organdies in particular—have a crisp finish, but the crispness decreases after several washings. The only troublesome feature of lace or net curtains is that you must put them on stretchers to restore them to their original shape and size—and this is not easy to do.

## Man-Made Fabrics

**Nylon Curtains** are beautiful when they are spanking white and crisp. They should be made of bright (never semidull) yarn, as this has greater resistance to the weakening and damaging effects of sunlight. And nylon curtains should be washed often, so they will not need hot water, bleach, and long washing to wash clean; such rigorous treatment often causes curtains to lose their finish, become limp, take on shadowy wrinkles—in short, never look really nice again. The newest nylon curtains are made of yarns that are sheerer, crisper, and can usually stay crisp longer than formerly.

**Fiberglas Curtains** are not attacked by sunlight, mildew, or insects. They need no drying or ironing. But keeping them white is a problem, and at their present stage of development they are better suited to use in the country or the suburbs than to city apartments where soot and grime are prevalent. Soaking badly grayed Fiberglas curtains in hot, sudsy water and chlorine bleach helps whiten them. The newest Fiberglas curtains are sheerer and crisper than ever before.

**Dacron and Orlon Curtains** are sheer and beautiful, although honors must go to Dacron for whiteness and for easy ironing. Orlon is strong, stands up well in sunny rooms, resists fumes.

Compared to cottons, these newer fibers need special care. It has always been easy to restore cotton curtains to whiteness and crispness with bleach and starch, so women have sometimes let them hang for months without a washing with no serious consequence. But curtains made of the newer fibers can be

difficult to whiten if they hang too long. Be sure to wash these curtains while a quick plunge into suds or washer will still do the job, so that no possibly damaging hot water or long soaking is necessary. Then give them a quick once-over with a steam iron to finish the job.

## Length and Width Are Important.

Curtains usually are one of three lengths: touching the sill, covering the trim below the sill, or reaching the floor. After you have decided the length, put up curtain rods; measure from top of rod to selected point. Add 1″ for heading above rod, and an allowance for expected shrinkage, so the curtains will be the right length after laundering.

For adequate fullness, each panel of straight-hanging or tied-back curtains should be the width of the rod. Each panel of crisscross curtains should be twice the width of the rod.

## Café Curtains

This curtain, borrowed from ubiquitous little restaurants in France (which have long employed this type of curtaining because it is cheerful, practical, and cheap), is a refinement of the familiar sash curtain. The café curtain is deservedly popular because it looks new, fresh, and charming; is easy to launder and hang; and is so flexible that it affords maximum control of light and air. Also, extending only to the sill, it requires less fabric, is inexpensive and easy to make. It works well in most contemporary interiors of informal nature, can be used with or without draperies. One of the charms of the café curtain is that it can be used without shades or blinds.

A wide range of fabric is suitable for café curtains, depending on the nature of the room where they are used. Plain or printed fabrics are equally successful and can be teamed together. Two tiers of café curtains on the same window can employ different colors. They can be made of lawn, dimity, chambray, Shantung, sheeting, gingham, muslin, challis, linen,

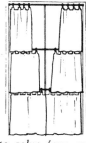

*Popular "café curtains" used to solve four common window problems: (1) two tiers of draw curtains which can be closed or opened for light and air without sacrificing privacy; (2) triple tiers to add eye appeal to a long, narrow window; (3) the French half-curtain, or "brise-* *bise," to solve the problem of privacy of picture and bay windows; (4) for patio doors, casement windows, and other problem treatments, hanging sill-length café curtains on big rings and making them wider than the opening enables you to pull them back easily.*

China silk, nylon, or any nonbulky material; for the kitchen, colorful toweling is effective. Most café curtains are unlined. Usually they are hung by rings on poles of brass, chromium, painted wood, or other ornamental metal. Café curtains should traverse (pull across) easily or their chief virtue is lost. They should be easy to hang and to take down. Flexibility is the basis of their usefulness.

### Points to Think Of in Buying

Measure the length from rod to sill. Then decide whether the curtains will just touch the sill or extend a few inches beyond. If the curtains are to hang to the floor, they should just miss it.

Measure the width of the window, and be sure you get plenty of fullness, so there will be no skimpiness. This is always very important, but especially so when you are covering a large window. Plain, very sheer curtains must be fuller than patterned. Of course, if you prefer, glass curtains need not cover the center of the window.

### Help Curtains Wear Longer

Be sure that rods and fixtures are smooth and free from rust so fabrics are not torn or hurt.

In children's rooms, drape curtains with tiebacks, so they will not be grasped and pulled out of shape.

Protect curtains by pinning them back out of the way when windows are washed.

A suitable radiator cover or deflector will save frequent washing of curtains that must hang above radiators and will help to protect the fabric from heat.

Curtains made ready-to-hang at either end, because of rod pockets at both top and bottom, will last longer, because you can turn them after each laundering and the bottoms will not wear out first. But don't forget to turn end for end every time you hang them.

Look for straight hems, full ruffles, square corners, and good construction.

Remember these cardinal rules:
1. Curtains must be the right length
2. Style and color must complement room
3. Hardware should be plain and unobtrusive
4. All curtains must be well tailored

## WINDOW TREATMENTS

The popular picture window and the tendency toward whole walls of glass have created new problems in window treatments, and new furniture designs are the result. There are no set rules for the treatment of windows. Every window or window group is a special case, and its handling requires advance *think-ing*. Several types of window and their treatments are shown in the illustrations in this section. Study them and adapt their ideas to the special problems offered by your windows. But before you make any decisions, ask yourself those questions: Are the curtains and draperies sufficiently flexible to permit control of light and air? Do they provide privacy? Do they regulate the view? Will they launder or clean? Do they present a pleasing *exterior* aspect? Do they suit the climate from the standpoint of fabric, lining, and interlining? Are they appropriate to the house's scale, quality, and uses? Do they look as well at night as in the daytime? Are they right for you?

## DRAPERIES

The draperies at the sides of your windows, framing the glass curtains or the blinds, are a vital part of your windows' charm, and one of the focal points of your over-all decorating scheme. Here are a few general pointers to help you in your selection of this important portion of your decorating scheme:

1. Old-fashioned draperies covered most of the glass. Today's draperies cover more wall, less glass. In an average room, the entire drapery is pushed softly together to form a band of color about 30" wide, all but 6" hanging over the wall.

2. Skimpy draperies are almost worse than none. Never split 50" material. Use one 36" width or more for each panel. Have plenty of fullness, even if that means that you must buy cheaper fabric.

3. There are two accepted lengths for draperies—to the sill or to the floor. In most cases, draperies look better if they hang to the floor. Lining improves their appearance, and, since it protects the drapery material from sunlight, helps to prevent fading. Therefore, lined draperies should wear better than unlined draperies.

4. Try to choose drapery material to suit your room. Good solid-color fabrics are: taffeta, heavy faille, satin or sateen, velvet or velveteen, rough-textured and diagonally woven fabric, plain or textured corduroys, self-patterned damask in silk, rayon, or cotton, etc. Among figured materials, best are florals (chintz and related fabrics), striped (satin to bedticking), modern or traditional geometric patterns (linen, rayon, etc.).

5. Most rooms look more intimate and friendly with the addition of sash curtains—not strictly necessary if you have Venetian or bamboo blinds. Many lovely rooms have no draperies at the windows, just full, crisp, ruffled, and tied-back organdy or fine muslin. For an informal room, sheeting can be used in the same way.

# AIDS TO SUCCESSFUL WINDOW TREATMENTS

Hardware and findings play an important part in professional-looking window treatments.

**1.** Silk cord for traverse curtain pulls; **2.** Tape for weighting curtain hems; **3.** 1-inch flexi-cord for welting; **4.** ⅜″ flexi-cord for welting; **5.** 1⅜″ wooden curtain pole; **6.** Crinoline for curtain headings; **7.** Extension curtain rod; **8.** Swing curtain rod; **9.** ⅜-inch curtain rods; **10.** Sim-pleat heading tape for pleated headings; **11.** Curtain holdback; **12.** Ceiling traverse rod; **13.** Wall traverse rod; **14.** Pin-on hooks; **15.** French-heading hooks; **16.** French-heading hooks; **17.** French-heading hooks; **18.** I-beam curtain carriers; **19.** Sew-on hooks; **20.** Rod rings; **21.** Pin-on hooks; **22.** I-beam pulley; **23.** Double-rod pulley; **24.** Single-rod pulley; **25.** I-beam curtain tracks; **26.** Silk drop for traverse cord; **27.** Lead weights for curtain hems; **28.** Varied brackets and sockets for curtain rods; **29.** Master carrier for I beam (traverse curtain); **30.** Master carrier for rod; **31.** Ceiling bracket for I beam; **32.** Wall bracket for I beam; **33.** Flat-rod bracket; **34.** Goose-neck bracket; **35.** Tassels for traverse cord; **36.** Wooden pole ends; **37.** Angle bracket; **38.** 1-inch brass tubing for curtain rods.

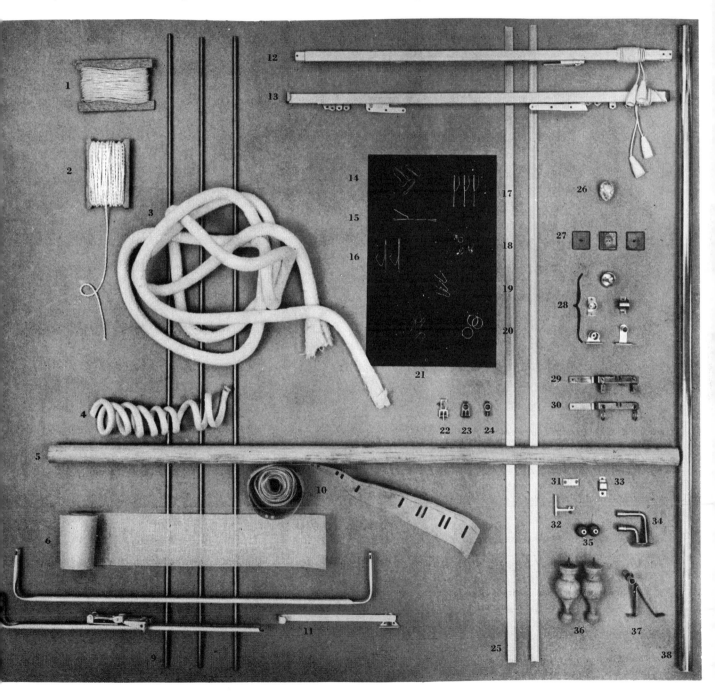

*Green café curtains on a brass rod give greater width to the window and complement the gay blue-green slip-cover on the armchair. A valance of matching material finishes the top of the window.*

*The ceiling-to-floor pattern which gives a room added dignity is now possible in the most sunproof of man-made materials—Fiberglas. This fabric responds fa-mously to hand washing and drips dry.*

*Here, a rich and colorful printed linen slipcovers the couch and chair in this living room. Floor to ceiling draperies done in a harmonious color make a handsome background.*

# SLIPCOVERS

Whether you are buying new furniture or re-covering old pieces, consider the practical advantages of using washable slipcovers instead of permanent upholstery on your sofas and chairs. If you want to change your color scheme or your fabrics for summer, you can buy two sets of slipcovers for each piece you intend changing, though more and more people are sticking to the same scheme throughout the year, removing their slipcovers only long enough to have them washed or dry-cleaned.

General rules for fabric, color schemes, and design combinations have already been covered in the sections on color, floor coverings, draperies, etc.

**1. Chintz,** in clear, fresh, gay colors, is our most attractive, charming, and versatile fabric for both slipcovers and curtains. Under this general term we include chintzlike printed materials, such as those with a satiny sheen; those a little heavier and with a slightly heavy weave and no sheen, known as printed cretonnes; printed twills; and printed and hand-blocked linens.

**2. Solid Colors or Stripes** are generally chosen for contrast. They often are used for seats of pull-up chairs or to slipcover a wing chair or a two-seated sofa. Smart materials in this class for slipcovers are: brocade, heavy faille or bengaline, velvet or velveteen, leather or imitation, corduroy, linen, sateen, cotton taffeta, damask, or twill, duck and denim, and felt.

If you prefer a solid color to a stripe for your contrast, pick one with an interesting weave: ridged, basket, slub, or rough-textured, herringbone or chevron; or one with lights and shadows, like velvet or velveteen; or one whose sheen is decorative, like satin.

**3. Avoid too many patterns** in one room, especially with a figured rug or wallpaper. Avoid dowdy fabrics like figured or plain plush, too-shiny rayon mixtures. Avoid buying a "set" covered in two or three different materials and colors. Unless you don't mind extra work, avoid fabrics containing wool (moth problem) and high-pile fabrics (dust problem).

**4. In Patterned Fabrics,** figures should be placed symmetrically on backs and seats. Back, cushions, and all other seams should be corded to match. If material is plain, heavier cords, welts, or fringe may be used in a contrasting color.

**5. The Skirt of Every Slipcover,** whether pleated, gathered, or plain with kick pleats at corners, should reach to or just clear the floor. No shorter length is smart.

**6. Unless a Washable Fabric Has Been Preshrunk,** slipcovers made of it should be roomy. In fact, an easy fit on any slipcover is better than a sausage-casing effect.

If you are making your slipcovers yourself, or having them custom made, don't economize on slipcover material. Buy a good grade of fabric—don't take chances with material that may shrink or stretch out of shape. It is cheaper in the long run to have your slipcovers fit properly after washing or cleaning than to have to go to the expense of making them all over again.

*When possible, buy upholstered pieces "in muslin," which may be any kind of inexpensive, sturdy cotton material, such as denim. Top photo shows what chair looks like when you get it, bottom photo shows same piece slipcovered in gay floral print.*

# LIGHTING

Choosing the proper lamps and other lighting fixtures for your home is not only a decorating problem but is important for the efficiency and health of your whole family. Today's wide range and selection in the lighting field is designed to help you solve both problems simultaneously.

Good lighting involves a choice of proper bulbs, (type, shape, size, etc.), appropriate lamps and fixtures (portable, built-in, wall-mounted, etc.), and location. Thanks to new designs and new concepts in the lighting industry, you now have a wider variety than ever before in each of these fields.

Your first decision will be between incandescent and fluorescent light, or a combination of both. Here are some of the advantages and uses for each. (*Information supplied by Westinghouse Electric Corporation.*)

### Incandescent Light Bulbs

1. Provide a point source of light that can be focused or directed over a limited area if desired.

2. Have the same size base in most household bulb wattages (25, 40, 50, 60, 75, and 100); thus lighting from fixtures or lamps can be increased or decreased within certain limits by a change to bulbs of a different wattage.

3. Can be operated on a dimmer switch for adjusting to various lighting levels in the room as the mood dictates.

4. Are less expensive to buy than fluorescent tubes. Incandescent lighting fixtures are also generally less expensive.

### Fluorescent Tubes

1. Provide a line of light; thus in work areas the light coming from several angles tends to wipe out the shadows. These "lines" of light can also be concealed behind window valances, cornices, or other architectural features of a home interior.

2. Provide three to four times as much light per watt as incandescent bulbs, with less heat. Warm light tubes are best for home use.

3. Will operate about 7 to 10 times longer than incandescent bulbs before replacement is required.

### Reading Lamps

A good lamp for reading must be designed for bulbs of sufficient wattage. For casual reading, a table lamp should have a minimum of 100 watts, a floor lamp 150 watts. For prolonged reading, a table lamp should have one or more bulbs totaling 150 watts, a floor lamp 300 watts. The lampshade lining should not absorb too much light, and the shade should be open at the top to throw light upward.

### General Lighting

Lighted valances, brackets, and cornices provide the newest and most glamorous general room lighting. Used alone, wall lighting creates a pleasant environment for conversation or music. Combined with upward lighting of portable lamps, it provides the soft, over-all general lighting needed for visual comfort and a feeling of increased space.

**Lighted Valances** are used at window areas to unify draperies, which should then be light in color. They provide both indirect lighting on the ceiling and dramatic down lighting on the wall.

**Lighted Wall Brackets** are the same in design as valances, but are used on unbroken wall spaces and may be mounted somewhat lower than valances. They may provide specific lighting for reading in bed, for range surfaces, for picture illumination, etc.

**Lighted Cornices** are mounted at the ceiling and

*New developments in incandescent bulbs include the decorator bulb, left, for use in unshaded fixtures designed for bare bulbs; the white indirect-light bulb for table and floor lamps without diffusing bowls; reflector bulbs, coated with an opaque silver finish to make them*

*useful as spotlights or floodlights; and tubular bulbs, some with standard screw type base, others (called "Lumiline") requiring special sockets, used mostly for decorating purposes in the home. Lumiline lamps are much softer and warmer than fluorescents.*

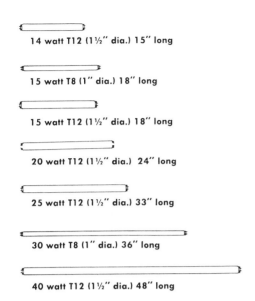

14 watt T12 (1½" dia.) 15" long

15 watt T8 (1" dia.) 18" long

15 watt T12 (1½" dia.) 18" long

20 watt T12 (1½" dia.) 24" long

25 watt T12 (1½" dia.) 33" long

30 watt T8 (1" dia.) 36" long

40 watt T12 (1½" dia.) 48" long

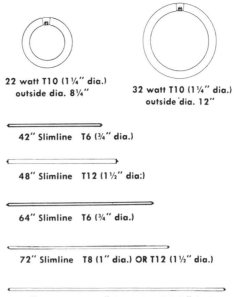

22 watt T10 (1¼" dia.) outside dia. 8¼"

32 watt T10 (1¼" dia.) outside dia. 12"

42" Slimline   T6 (¾" dia.)

48" Slimline   T12 (1½" dia.)

64" Slimline   T6 (¾" dia.)

72" Slimline   T8 (1" dia.) OR T12 (1½" dia.)

96" Slimline   T8 (1" dia.) OR T12 (1½" dia.)

direct all their light downward. They are best applied the full length of a wall or large window. They also give an illusion of height to low-ceilinged rooms. No single unit of any of these installations should be less than 4′ in length, and a total of 16′, singly or combined, is minimum in the average living room for the most charming and useful effect.

Shielding faceboards may be detailed to conform with the room's architecture and may be wallpapered, upholstered or painted to harmonize with the decorating scheme.

Warm or cool white deluxe fluorescent tubes, placed end to end, are generally used in 20, 25, or 40 watt sizes to fit space, although 40 or 60 watt incandescent Lumiline bulbs may be used. The warm white deluxe lamps create a warm atmosphere, blend with the light from incandescent bulbs, and compliment complexions, warm colors, and food. Cool white deluxe is often preferred when a cool atmosphere is desired or with color schemes predominant in blues and greens.

### Lighting Recipes

The following recipes for lighting specific areas have been developed by the Lighting Laboratories of General Electric Company Lamp Division to provide the proper amount of light (footcandles) for the average man and woman performing the everyday activities of family living. They are based on average eye heights and dimensions of commonly used furnishings and equipment. References to lamp diffusing bowls and harps should be checked with the diagram at the top of page 57.

*Here are some of the sizes of fluorescent tubes most commonly used in the home. "Slimline" and "Instant Start" tubes light instantly; the others, called "Preheat," do not. New equipment has been developed to provide either "rapid start" or "trigger-start" systems for the preheat type. Trigger-start is available for 14, 15 and 20 watt straight tubes, 22 and 32 watt circlines. Rapid start is designed for the 40 watt straight tube.*

*A nice way to add drama to a dining room without cluttering surface space is to use a striking overhead fixture. Here, a handsome crystal chandelier, hung relatively low, sheds a soft, flattering light.*

Well-planned lighting adds to decorative effect in any room. *Top left*, draperies become part of lighting scheme with lighted cornice supplemented by well-placed lamps. Draperies must be light in color so as not to absorb light. *Top right*, general lighting from valance encircling room is supplemented by a pair of table lamps and some spotlights strategically mounted on ceiling. *Center left*, soffit formed by lowered ceiling over sofa is lighted with two 33″ tubes to create attractive reading space. Same effect can be used over bed in many homes. *Center right*, recessed downspots provide even lighting over work area in kitchen. *Bottom left*, lighted bracket over bed provides good reading light, is wallpapered to blend with background.

*Decorator: Everett Brown. Photograph by Nowell Ward*

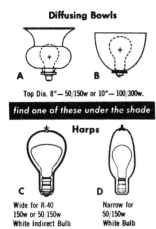

**Diffusing Bowls**

A      B

Top Dia. 8"— 50/150w or 10"— 100/300w.

*find one of these under the shade*

**Harps**

C      D

Wide for R-40
150w or 50/150w
White Indirect Bulb

Narrow for
50/150w
White Bulb

## Using a Floor Lamp for Reading or Sewing

**What to Use:** A senior or double swing-arm floor lamp with bowl A or B, 10". Height to lower edge of shade no more than 49" or less than 47" above floor; bottom of socket 1" below shade. Minimum shade dimensions: top 10½"; depth 10"; bottom 16" for *swing,* 18½" for *senior lamp.*

**Where to Place:** From center of reading material, measure 15" to right or left; from this point measure 26" at a right angle toward rear of chair; and place lamp so that the shade center is above this point.

## Using a Table Lamp for Reading or Sewing

**What to Use:** An end table lamp with bowl A or B, 8", or harps C or D. Lower edge of shade 15" to 17" above top of 25" table. Lamp socket in line with or slightly below shade. Min. shade dimensions: top 8½", depth 10", bottom 16". Table height plus lamp base should total 39"–42" (average eye level).

**Where to Place:** Measure 20" to right or left from center of reading material. From this point measure 16" at a right angle toward rear of chair. Place lamp so shade center is above this point—base about in line with shoulder.

## A Table or Floor Lamp for Desk Work

**What to Use:** Table lamp with bowl A or B, 8". Height to bottom edge of shade 15" above desk top. Bottom of socket 1" below shade. Minimum

shade dimensions: top 8½"; depth 10"; bottom 16". Shade should be light-toned but not highly translucent. When desk is used for short periods, table lamps of the same dimension as above may incorporate C or D.

**Where to Place:** Center of lamp should be above a point 15" to left of work center and 12" back from the front edge of the desk. If left-handed, place lamp to right.

## Television Viewing Using General Lighting

**What to Use:** Don't make the mistake of viewing television in a dark room. It's tiring to the eyes. The picture of a well-focused set is not decreased in visibility by a moderate level of lighting throughout the room.

Use your floor and table lamps, and turn to low level only if shades appear brighter than the screen. Opaque or dense fabric shades are preferable for lamps near screen.

**Where to Place:** Position portable lamps so that they do not form reflections in the screen and avoid bright spots of light on near-by walls.

## General Lighting for Dining

**What to Use:** A three-effect ceiling fixture, either close-to-ceiling or suspended. A central down light gives sparkling dramatic effect and uses an R-30, 75 watt spotlight or 100 watt standard bulb. Surrounding glassware (min. 18" across) contains four 50 watt or five 40 watt bulbs for general lighting. Ceramic-enameled or opal glass is preferred for its good diffusion and transmission qualities.

In addition, to supplement the down light, use a fluorescent wall bracket or a window valance. Minimum length is 33", 25 watt deluxe warm white tube.

## General Lighting for Kitchen

**What to Use:** A close-to-ceiling fixture centered in the area. Types for incandescent bulbs or fluorescent tubes suitable. Former require complete shielding in units at least 12" in diameter. Shielding of fluorescent tubes not essential but side-shielding

always desirable. Minimum lamp requirements: Incandescent—one 150 watt inside-frosted, three 60 watt inside-frosted, or one 200 watt silvered-bowl bulb; fluorescent (standard cool white)—three 24", 20 watt; two 33", 25 watt; or two circline, 8" and 12" diameter, 22 and 32 watts.

## Preparing Food at Counter

**What to Use:** A wall bracket for every work counter. Counters over 4' in length require a bracket for each 4'. Fluorescent types, min. one 24", 20 watt standard cool tube, do not require shielding if placed under cabinets not more than 58" above floor. Incandescent types require shielding and should use one 60 watt Lumiline or two 40 watt inside frosted bulbs.

**Where to Place:** Locate bracket on side wall just beneath the upper cabinets, 50"–58" above floor. An alternate position, essential if cabinet is less than 50" above floor, is on the underside of cabinet near front edge. Use similar units at range and sink.

## General Lighting for Bedroom

**What to Use:** A close-to-ceiling center fixture with shallow diffusing ceramic-enameled glass at least 17" in its widest dimension. There is a variety of glass shapes—circular, square, rectangular. Minimum of 4 sockets, 50 watts each; 5 sockets preferred (40 watts each).

## A Table Lamp for Reading in Bed

**What to Use:** A table lamp with bowl A or B, 8", or harps C or D. Height to lower edge of shade 15"–17" above 26"–28" high bedside table; bottom of socket in line with or 1" below shade. Min. shade dimensions: top 8½"; depth 10"; bottom 16". Table height plus lamp base height should locate lower edge about 20" above mattress—in line with eyes of reader, sitting up in bed.

**Where to Place:** Measure 22" from center of book out to table side. From this point measure 16" at a right angle toward wall. Place lamp so shade center is above this point.

## LAMPS AND LIGHTING FIXTURES

(Above left) *A hanging brass lamp on an arm floods any table or desk with strong, unshadowed light. The reflector eliminates glare of the bulb.*

(Right) *A nicely designed planter lamp like this provides a center of interest even when not lighted, and provides auxiliary light to the room at night.*

In addition to making sure that your lamps and lighting fixtures provide adequate light, it is important to remember their place in your decorating scheme. There is a tremendous variety from which to choose—and it is surprising how rarely you run into a duplication. A lamp or a lighting fixture is something you will have around for a long time, so be sure that you get one that you will not tire of.

# HOUSE PLANTS

House plants can be a decorative feature of your home. They are relatively inexpensive, and their cultivation can become a fascinating hobby. There are two different categories of house plants to be considered: plants grown for foliage, and plants grown for bloom. Consider the atmospheric conditions of your house before selecting plants. Generally speaking, plants prefer a cooler, more humid atmosphere than people do, and may require direct sunlight.

**Exposure.** If the window has southern or southwestern exposure, it will be possible to grow a wide variety of flowering plants as well as many of the spring bulbs which are available in endless variety and are most rewarding for the indoor gardener. Tulips, hyacinth, narcissus, amaryllis, and lily of the valley require very little care in return for their shown blossoms. Hyacinths will grow in water-filled glass vases, specially designed for the purpose; narcissus bulbs may be planted in pebbles with the water level kept just below the bulb. Lily of the valley pips will grow in soil or in bulb fiber. Small bulbs, such as crocus, may be grown in a dirt-filled dish. Amaryllis bulbs should be half-out of the soil. If, however, the window has northern or northwestern exposure, one's choice is necessarily more restricted, being limited to the ivies, the ferns, the dainty little African violets, and the group known as foliage plants. Several of the begonias, such as the Rex, will also do well in a north window. Philodendron, sansevieria, Chinese evergreen, and rubber plant are among the species that can grow in dim daylight or artificial light.

**Temperature** is almost as important as exposure. Most house plants thrive best in a temperature which ranges between 60° and 70°. If the temperature is consistently too high, the growth of the plants will tend to be weak and spindly. If the temperature drops too low at night, the growth may be temporarily or even permanently checked. Some plants are sensitive to temperature fluctuations, while others cheerfully withstand them. Practically all plants require an abundant supply of fresh air, but direct drafts should be avoided.

**Humidity.** Every effort should be made to increase humidity in rooms where plants grow. This can be done in a number of ways. Water pans may be attached to the radiators, or the pots may be placed on pebble-filled trays, in which the water is kept just below the bottom of the pot. Frequent syringing of the foliage is also a great help.

**Watering** should be done in the morning, and the water should be at room temperature. The pots should never be allowed to stand continuously in trays or saucers filled with water, as this makes the soil soggy and sour. A daily check-up is necessary, although daily watering may not always be advisable. Tap the pot with your knuckle. A dull, thick sound indicates that the soil is still moist; if it makes a hollow, ringing sound, the plant needs water. Plants vary greatly in their needs, and plants which are growing rapidly and forming flower buds will require more frequent watering than those in a less active stage. Most plants may be watered with a watering can that has a long, slender spout, from which the sprinkler has been removed. There are a few plants with thick, fuzzy leaves, such as African violets and gloxinias, which resent overhead watering. Such plants should be watered by placing the pots in a shallow pan of water and leaving them there until the soil on the surface becomes damp.

Foliage should be kept clean and dust-free. Plants with hairy leaves should never be washed; instead, clean the leaves gently with a soft brush. All others may be cleaned by spraying with water. Each plant is subject to its own variety of disease or blight and vulnerable to particular insects. A well-cared for plant is usually immune to such problems, but should they develop there are commercial preparations designed to combat them.

**Drainage.** House plants must have good drainage. This can be provided at the time of potting by placing pieces of broken crocks in the bottoms of the pots.

**Fertilizer.** Most house plants, particularly those that flower abundantly, are benefited by an application of fertilizer every four or five weeks while the plants are making active growth. There are a number of excellent fertilizers especially planned for house plants, but almost any type of complete fertilizer may be used when made into a solution—1 level teaspoonful to a quart of water.

**Danger Signs.** Healthy plants can be kept in good condition by following a few general rules. If the leaves and stem droop, the plant is not getting enough water; yellowing leaves usually indicate too much water, or improper drainage; undersized leaves mean the plant is not receiving proper nourishment.

# FLOWER ARRANGING

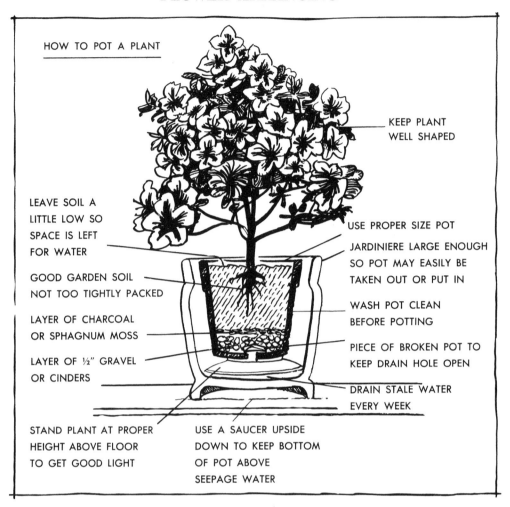

HOW TO POT A PLANT

KEEP PLANT WELL SHAPED

LEAVE SOIL A LITTLE LOW SO SPACE IS LEFT FOR WATER

GOOD GARDEN SOIL NOT TOO TIGHTLY PACKED

LAYER OF CHARCOAL OR SPHAGNUM MOSS

LAYER OF ½" GRAVEL OR CINDERS

USE PROPER SIZE POT

JARDINIERE LARGE ENOUGH SO POT MAY EASILY BE TAKEN OUT OR PUT IN

WASH POT CLEAN BEFORE POTTING

PIECE OF BROKEN POT TO KEEP DRAIN HOLE OPEN

DRAIN STALE WATER EVERY WEEK

STAND PLANT AT PROPER HEIGHT ABOVE FLOOR TO GET GOOD LIGHT

USE A SAUCER UPSIDE DOWN TO KEEP BOTTOM OF POT ABOVE SEEPAGE WATER

## FLOWER ARRANGING

Formal flower arrangement can trace its ancestry to the Orient, while the informal bouquet's genealogy is thought of as beginning in England. Probably the difference in the gardens in which the flowers were grown as well as the dissimilar temperaments of the gardeners had a great deal to do with it. While the formal arrangement is governed by as many rules as bridge, the informal is as ruleless as a game of tag. Colors are mixed with wild abandon; waxy roses mingle democratically with raggle-taggle cornflowers; pretty weeds pop up by the side of prize dahlias. All one needs is a watertight container, a scrap of chicken wire (or even half of a potato) to hold the arrangement in place, and imagination.

## BASIC PRINCIPLES

Some people are so gifted with a sense of form and color that they make fine flower arrangements without recourse to rules. The average person, however, profits by learning and following the basic principles and techniques.

**Design** is the basic pattern of the arrangement. It consists of a planned relationship among the component parts—flowers, foliage, and container. For the most satisfying flower picture, a design must have a definite relation to its location in the home. The most popular arrangement designs are variations of the triangle, the circle, and the Hogarth line (an open S curve).

**Scale** is achieved by selecting materials related in size to one another and to their container. An arrangement should be at least one and a half times a tall container's height, or about one and a half times a low container's width.

*The serene composition of iris is a flawless example of the Japanese naturalistic approach to arranging flowers. A needle-point holder secures the selected flowers and foliage in the same way they grow. Even the water level corresponds to the season of the flowers. Arranged by Mrs. Kenneth Leonard of Ikebana International.*

**Balance** is the grouping of materials within the design. It is usually achieved by working from light, delicate forms (buds and foliage tips) at the edges to darker, heavier materials in the center. Balance is of two types: *symmetric,* in which both sides of the arrangement are virtually the same; *asymmetric,* in which the two sides are distinctly different but have equal visual weight and therefore balance each other. A properly balanced arrangement looks good from any viewpoint and is therefore of the utmost importance in placing the arrangement in a room.

**Color** is ever present in flower arrangements. The ways of using it are numerous. Grouped color is more effective than spotty color. Dark, heavy flowers are best at the base or center of an arrangement, with buds and lighter, smaller, more delicate flowers placed near the outer edges.

**Focus** is the center of interest in an arrangement. Various elements should be placed so that the eye is led to a natural center of interest.

**Rhythm** is the feeling of motion in an arrangement, achieved by graceful lines leading to the center.

**Accent** is the emphasis obtained by contrast in color, size, form, or texture.

**Harmony** is created by blending the plant materials, container, accessories, and setting.

If your child makes you a gift of flowers he has picked—daisies, buttercups, field grasses, etc.—you can show your appreciation by arranging them in a low wicker basket. Of course, it will not be a formal arrangement, but it can make a refreshing spot wherever you place it, and he will know that you like his gift.

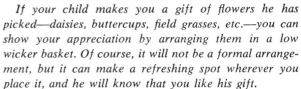

This permanent arrangement is made of cork tree and dried babies'-breath. Its vertical line with nice voids between the pieces gives it an Oriental feeling that would fit in well with both modern and traditional settings. The good thing about a permanent arrangement is that you can put it away for a while if you want to use something else, and then take it out and use it again.

# MAKING AN ARRANGEMENT

You will need some equipment to make your arrangement: something to hold the flowers in place in your container, and something to cut the stems to the length you want them. Flower holders are available either with holes in them or with pins; those with holes are not satisfactory for small stems or to hold flowers at an angle. Unless your holder is heavily weighted you will need something to hold it in the container. You can use floral clay, paraffin, or plaster of Paris. In any case, be sure that your container is completely dry before you try to get the material to stick. Don't have any air space between your material and container because water will get in, and your arrangement will topple over if it is in a shallow container.

After your holder is firmly fixed in the container, pour in some water to the depth of the holder so that your stems will stay wet while you are working.

Stick the tallest piece into the holder first. From there, add those pieces which will make the outline of your design and fill in with other flowers or leaves until your arrangement is complete.

If you are using a tall container, and it is awkward to anchor a holder in it, you can use crumpled chicken wire to hold your flowers. If the container is transparent, use broken twigs of short-needled evergreens; twigs of other types of trees muddy the water and make it smell bad.

Transparent containers are more difficult to use as they show the mechanics of your arrangement. In order to hide the works, you can use glass balls, marble chips, or leaves if you can anchor them so that they do not float. If you are going to keep the arrangement for only a short time, you can even add milk to the water.

There are many ingenious ways to hold flowers where you want them.

The main thing is not to have the mechanics show.

After your arrangement is made, your flowers may move around by themselves. Remember that many plants will automatically turn toward the light; others will open wide in heat or close in the cold. One of the most frustrating flowers to handle is a tulip; you make an arrangement for a lamp table with the tulips facing the room, and then you turn on the light—in a short time all your tulips are wide open and twisted around to look right at the light bulb. It is important, therefore, to consider the lighting of an arrangement.

Keep all your flower arranging tools in a handled basket. Then, when you have your flowers, decide on your container, where you are going to place the arrangement, and the type of arrangement you are going to make, you can work right on through without having to jump up to get a piece of wire, a holder, or whatever it might be that you have stored some place else.

## Garden Flowers

The best time to gather garden flowers is after sundown. If this is impossible, gather them very early in the morning. Cut the stems slantwise, and strip off all the lower leaves.

When cutting garden flowers, put them in a bucket containing several inches of water. Don't crowd your flowers in the bucket, or you will be unable to remove them without bruising the petals. When you return to the house, fill the bucket up to the necks of the flowers with cold water, and leave it in a cool, dark place overnight. Several hours of standing in deep water lengthens the flowers' lives and makes them easier to arrange.

Flowers should always be cut with a sharp tool. If the stems are roughly cut, squeezed, or pinched by a dull instrument, the tubelike cells that

take in water may become clogged. Cut off any leaves that will be under water in the arrangement as they would quickly decompose.

All flowers with woody or semi-woody stems—lilacs, chysanthemums, stock, and the like—live longer if the stem ends are scraped and split, to allow them to absorb additional moisture. Heavy stems may be split by making lengthwise cuts at the stem ends with sharp clippers.

Any flower stems that exude a milky substance—poppies, poinsettias, hollyhocks, dahlias, and the like—should have their stems sealed. This can be done either by steeping the ends for a few seconds in about 2" of boiling water (protect flowers and foliage from rising steam) before plunging them in deep, cool water, or by singeing the ends with a lighted candle as you pick the flowers. These processes seal the ends, but the stems can take in moisture through the pores above the sealed portion.

Always pick roses in the bud or partially opened stage. Keep them away from heat and strong sunlight.

## Florist Flowers

Flowers from the florist profit by having their stems recut and by being plunged in deep water for several hours. Don't let flowers from the florist lie in their box.

Among the most reliable cut flowers—usually available throughout the year—are gladioli, snapdragons, carnations, roses, and chrysanthemums.

Beware of cheap flowers; they sometimes look fresher than they are. Look at the foliage when you buy flowers. Leaves and stalks usually show signs of drooping before the blossoms.

Spring flowers are usually inexpensive but also short-lived, especially in steam-heated houses. However, a few jonquils, hyacinths, freesia, anemones, and tulips from the florist enable you to have arrangements during the tattered days of winter. If you use these flowers combined with distinctive foliage, you can get by with a small handful of them.

Florists provide greens that are long-lasting and can be used alone or with fresh or dried flowers. When buying greens or leaves, make sure the tip of each stalk looks alive.

The most durable leaves are Podocarpus and camellia foliage. They stay green from 4 to 6 months if you change the water weekly and do not allow scum to form. They should be sprayed or wiped off occasionally; the stems should be broken off (not cut), then split, about every 2 weeks. Rhododendron, huckleberry, and lemon leaves are three easily obtainable varieties that last many weeks. Treat them as you would Podocarpus and camellia foliage.

Chinese evergreens actually grow in water. They require lots of light and air. Eucalyptus leaves keep green in water for about a month.

Greens should be kept away from heat. A commercial spray can be used on smooth-surfaced leaves to make them shiny; or they can be wiped off with a piece of cotton dipped in milk. Both of these, however, shorten their lives.

*Pinch off a fairly small portion of waterproof clay; roll it in a cylinder around the holder.*

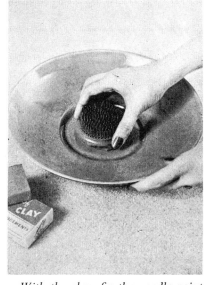

*With the clay, fix the needle-point holder firmly in position in the center of the container.*

*Form a main line with foliage, making the height about 1½ times the container's width.*

*The design shown here is basically a triangle. Establish an apex with a single carnation as shown.*

*Fill in the design with carnations, working first from the top down, then to the side as indicated.*

*Final step: Add several flowers, quite close together, as a visual focus for the entire arrangement.*

# The Care and Cleaning of Your Home and Its Equipment

### How It Is Done

There is just one way to have a clean house without seasonal upheavals. You must dispose of the dirt before so much accumulates that you've got to break your back to get rid of it. The better your cleaning equipment and supplies, the easier it is to keep your house shining and clean. The list below is a reminder of things you need.

### Cleaning Equipment and Supplies

Vacuum cleaner and attachments
Carpet sweeper
Wax applier
Cellulose-sponge mop
Dust mop
Corn broom or push broom
Dustpan
Brushes for radiators, bathtub, toilet bowl
Scrubbing brush
Sponges, cellulose or natural
Cheesecloth for cleaning and polishing furniture
Dustcloths, treated
Pail
Paper towels
Household gloves
Chamois
Cloths for washing up
Window cleaner
Basket for carrying cleaning supplies

Soap
Detergent
Chlorine bleach
Water softener
Silver polish and metal cleaner
Scouring powder
Furniture polish or wax
Disinfectant
Cleaning fluid and powder
Paint cleaner, liquid or powder
Floor wax, nonpolishing and polish types
Oven cleaner
Toilet-bowl cleaner or mop
Drain cleaner
Wallpaper cleaner
Upholstery and rug cleaner
Scratch-concealing polish
Rust remover

Most important is a good vacuum cleaner, because, more than anything else, it helps keep the house clean from top to bottom. With a good floor cleaner for removing dirt from rugs and carpets and attachments for all your dusting, you should be able to clean the modern way.

For quick, convenient brush-ups a carpet sweeper is indispensable.

Almost every housecleaning job can be done faster and better with a nonwoven cleaning cloth that looks and feels like paper. Dampen the cloth to make it soft and chamoislike, completely lint-free. Highly absorbent, it picks up dirt, grime, grease, and liquid. The fibers, protected by a special cellulose coating, will not hold soil or odor; the cloth can be washed out quickly and easily and made as good as new. You can use it to apply wax or furniture polish, then rinse out every trace.

Furniture care is made easier with chemically treated dusting cloths that clean and polish all types of furniture. Use one folded; as surface becomes dirty, fold it over. The cloth absorbs dust and dirt and can be used for months without harming fine finishes. When it is soiled, it can be washed in lukewarm water and suds.

For heavy-duty cleaning, use soft, knitted absorbent cleaning cloths. They're heavier and sturdier for washing and polishing furniture, woodwork, kitchen, and bathroom. Cheesecloth, too, is useful for cleaning and polishing jobs. Buy it in a roll, so you can cut off the length you need. Each time you cut a piece, shake out excess threads. Thereafter, the cloth is lint-free and highly absorbent.

The market offers an unlimited choice of furniture polishes, waxes, paint cleaners, wallpaper cleaners, metal polishes, rug and upholstery cleaners, etc., for practically any purpose you can name.

If you own a vacuum cleaner and a carpet sweeper you may not have much use for a broom. But for sweeping bare floors, porches, walks, and doorsteps, a broom is necessary. A soft-bristled push broom is useful for indoor use. Outdoors and for cement floors, a corn or palmetto-fiber broom does good work. Plastic bristles are colorful and easily washed. Wash brooms as soon as they show soil. Hang from hooks or stand them on their handles, so bristles don't rest on the floor. Brooms need a dustpan. One with a long handle saves having to bend over.

For washing floors in the kitchen, bathroom, and laundry, use a self-wringing yarn mop or one with a cellulose-sponge head. There is no need for putting your hands in mopping water.

### Brushes

Any housekeeper is more efficient for an intimate knowledge of brushes. Here are some descriptions to bring you up to date on a number of useful ones.

**Upholstery Brush.** A short-bristled, fairly stiff brush especially designed for cleaning curved surfaces of upholstered chair arms, backs etc. Also used on draperies and other fabric furnishings.

**Venetian-Blind Brush.** Two-, three-, or four-fingered soft-hair brushes for cleaning dust from the slats, especially around the tapes and the cords.

**Radiator Brush.** Fairly narrow, so spaces between the coils can be reached easily. Sturdy, stiff bristles fastened securely to a steel frame, long enough to reach the full depth of the household radiator.

**Lampshade Brush.** Soft hair or plastic bristles with curved, tufted end for reaching hard-to-get-at places.

**Scouring Brush.** Extra-stiff bristles for heavy-duty jobs. A handle that rests at an angle is convenient, because the full side of the brush can come in contact with the surface being cleaned.

**Vegetable Brush.** Available in stiff fiber or plastic bristles. Excellent for scrubbing potatoes, celery, carrots, etc. Have one or two extra ones on hand for washing dishes and cooking utensils.

**Bottle Brush.** Long-stemmed, with circular tuft for cleaning bottom rim of bottles. Use for all milk bottles, tumblers, pitchers, baby bottles, and other narrow-necked containers.

**Coffeemaker Brush.** Excellent for glass coffeemakers. Shaped in the form of a question mark to reach and clean inner surfaces.

**Toilet-Bowl Brush.** Shaped to clean all sections of the bowl. Plastic bristles are quick-drying.

**Comb Brush.** Choose a sturdy one that will slip between the teeth of your comb.

### Cellulose Sponges

Once you have used them in your housework, you'll never be without them. They wash dishes, walls, and woodwork, and are excellent for bathroom cleaning. The sponges fit the hand, don't drip, and rinse freely.

### Disinfectants

Sometimes you need a good household disinfectant to make cleaning doubly effective. The soapy type cleans as well as disinfects; the chlorine type, commonly used in laundering, bleaches as well as disinfects. Read the directions, and use the one that best fits the job.

### Liquid Cleaners

All-purpose liquid cleaners ease housecleaning in ways no single product ever did before. Only ¼ cup in a gallon of warm-to-hot water makes a hard-working solution for room-by-room cleaning of washable surfaces. Used full strength, these liquid cleaners will remove heel and scuff marks, and even wax build-ups from kitchen floors. They dissolve tar, grease, and oil; loosen adhesive and gum; take crayon marks off painted walls; clean white-wall tires. They can remove lipstick stains from table linen and clean old paintbrushes. Soak linens in the full-strength cleaner until stains disappear; soak paintbrushes overnight.

### Design Your Own Cleaning Center

Every home, even a small apartment, needs a place where cleaning things can be kept together. When supplies are scattered, even wiping up a few smudges can be an irritating job and a step-waster.

### Care of Cleaning Cloths and Brushes

**Cleaning Cloths and Sponges.** Wash in warm or very hot suds, depending on how soiled they are. If washing doesn't remove soil and stains, use a household bleach. Soak in a solution of 1 tablespoonful of bleach to 1 gallon of water for 10 or 15 minutes. Rinse well and dry. Cellulose sponges can be bleached or boiled, but natural sponges should be washed only.

**Dust Mops.** Instead of shaking your dust mop, use your vacuum cleaner to remove loose dirt. Treated and untreated dust mops can be washed. Dip the mop up and down in suds until clean. Rinse well, shake out thoroughly, and stand upside down on handle to dry. To re-treat a dust mop, use a product made for treating dustcloths. Soak the clean mop in the creamy mixture, wring out excess, and dry. Always hang a mop to store; never rest it on the floor.

**Wet Mops.** Wash yarn mops in hot suds after each use. Rinse, and then shake to separate the strands. Dry in the sun if possible. Never put away a damp or wet mop. Cellulose-sponge mop heads wash easily. After washing and rinsing, squeeze out water.

**Wax Appliers.** Lamb's-wool wax appliers can be kept soft and serviceable if you wash *immediately* after waxing. Otherwise, the wax hardens and the applier becomes stiff, sticky, and useless. Use hot suds, rinse in warm water until the water is clear, shake a few times, and let dry, resting on the handle. Wax appliers always should be hung when put away.

**Brushes.** Wash in suds, shake to remove excess water, and hang to dry. Shake several times during drying.

**Household Gloves.** Wash in warm suds, rinse well in clear water, and hang to dry. Gloves that are lined or have a satinized inside finish slip on very easily. Others sometimes need to be sprinkled with talcum before being put on.

### Carpet Sweeper Care

**Storing the Carpet Sweeper.** A carpet sweeper takes little storage space. It may be placed flat against the wall of the cleaning cupboard or hung on a hook suspended from the cupboard ceiling. When it is stored this way, be sure to empty it every time it is used; otherwise, fluff and dirt left in the sweeper may fall on the brush to be thrown on the floor again at the first stroke.

**Care of the Carpet Sweeper.** Empty the sweeper after each use. The brush must be free of hair ravelings, and fluff, because a tangled and matted brush cannot sweep well. With a sharp knife or shears, cut lengthwise through the brush between the rows of bristles. This will cut threads and ravelings into short lengths that are easier to remove. If the brush becomes sticky, rub it with a cloth saturated with dry-cleaning fluid, never water. To remove the brush for cleaning, follow the manufacturer's directions. Treat the sweeper to a thorough cleaning occasionally. Dust it and polish it with liquid wax or furniture polish.

**Service It Regularly.** If your sweeper does not clean as satisfactorily as it did when new, get in touch with your dealer or the manufacturer of the carpet sweeper, and let him put it in first-class condition.

Don't jerk the sweeper back and forth; run it smoothly with long, easy strokes. As you clean, occasionally turn the carpet sweeper around so sweepings will be taken up by both pans. Follow the manufacturer's directions for placing an occasional drop of oil in specific locations. The sweeper will run more easily and quietly, and last longer.

### Take Another Look at Your Vacuum Cleaner

If cleaning exhausts you, if your house has lost its bloom, take a look at your vacuum cleaner. Maybe you need a more up-to-date one.

**Does Emptying the Dirt Get in Your Hair?** Too often this is literally true, but now you can give up this job forever. New vacuum cleaners don't have messy bags to empty. Old vacuum cleaners that are still efficient can often be modernized merely by adding a new bag and disposable liner.

**Do the Attachments Come Apart?** There is nothing more maddening than having a dusting tool fall off just at the height of your cleaning. Up-to-date vacuum cleaners have featherweight attachments (called wands) with snug, airtight connections to make a positive lock.

**Do You Dread Getting Out Your Cleaner?** Store the cleaner and its parts without cluttering. Usually it is best to keep the cleaner set up for floor cleaning. This is no problem with an upright. The hose, wands, and floor tool of other types can be kept together, with hose looped over hooks, in closet.

**Does Vacuum-Cleaner "Whine" Get on Your Nerves?** Investigate antinoise developments in vacuum cleaners. Noise filters and interference eliminators have been added to muffle the sound of the motor and to prevent radio and television interference.

**Does Rounding Up Attachments Waste Your Time?** Studies made on time- and motion-saving methods show surprising wastes of time and energy in rounding up cleaner attachments. A cart on wheels, basket, or carrying caddy can simplify the job.

### Take Care of Your Vacuum Cleaner

A vacuum cleaner lags on the job when clogged with dirt. Empty the cleaner after each use. To clean a vacuum cleaner bag, brush it inside and out. *Never* wash it.

Handle your cleaner carefully. Don't bang it against stairs or drag the connecting cord against furniture. Keep the cord coiled on the handle when the cleaner is stored. When disconnecting, don't yank the cord; grasp the plug and pull.

Do not use your cleaner to pick up hairpins; pieces of glass, or any small or hard object. They can damage the mechanism.

### Use Your Vacuum Cleaner

The more frequently you use your vacuum cleaner on rugs and carpets, the longer they will last.

Don't hurry. Push the cleaner back and forth slowly in a straight line, lengthwise of the rug.

Unless your cleaner nozzle adjusts automatically, you cannot go from a thin rug to a heavy one, or vice versa, and get the best results with the same nozzle adjustment. With a motor-driven brush or agitator-type cleaner, the rug should vibrate slightly if the nozzle is adjusted right. With a straight-air type of cleaner, proper adjustment tends to lift the rug and hold it to the nozzle.

Get to know all your cleaner attachments and keep them handy. They will work for you in many ways.

### Clean As You Go

Work out a schedule for doing daily and weekly cleaning jobs in a systematic way. This will help keep your house looking good all the time and do away with those domestic upheavals called spring and fall housecleaning.

Making out your cleaning schedule is something you alone can accomplish. Every home is different—

city homes require constant dusting, houses where children live need more frequent washing of woodwork, and homes in industrial cities need weekly cleaning of windows and curtains. But whatever you plan, don't try to do everything in one day.

### Follow This Routine in Cleaning Each Room

1. First, bring order to the room. Pick up newspapers and magazines, carry out faded flowers, put away clothing, make beds, roll up scatter rugs.

2. Clean up grease spots or smudges on rugs under dining table, in front of fireplace and sofa, etc. A little cleaning fluid on a clean cloth usually will take care of them.

3. Now vacuum-clean rugs or carpets thoroughly. Some housekeepers like to do this after dusting; with modern cleaning equipment, one way is as good as the other.

4. Dust furniture, lamps, books, window sills. With flat upholstery tool, clean upholstery furniture. Use crevice tool behind and under pillows.

5. Change to wall or floor brush, and clean moldings, window and door frames, Venetian blinds, baseboards, bare floor, and areas under low furniture.

6. Change to upholstery attachment and thoroughly clean draperies from top to bottom, particularly around pleats and folds at top.

7. Put the furniture back in place, set the room in order, and put away your vacuum and other cleaning equipment.

### Use the Right Tool

**Round Dusting Tool** for cleaning: furniture, books, bookcases, fireplace screens, lamps, Venetian blinds.

**Floor Brush** for cleaning: polished wood floors, kitchen and bathroom floors, moldings, baseboards.

**Upholstery Tool** for cleaning: davenports, easy-chairs, draperies, chair and sofa cushions, mattresses, suits, overcoats, car upholstery.

**Spraying Attachments** for: quick convenient spraying of thin liquids (insecticides, garden sprays, etc.).

### Do You Need an Electric Floor Polisher?

For homes that have large areas of polished floors, an electric floor polisher is an invaluable aid. Not only does it save many hours of cleaning time, but its weight and buffing action take the hard work out of wax polishing.

Modern polishers are compact. Some brands are no larger than a vacuum cleaner, and you can buy an electric floor polisher that is light enough to be lifted up for polishing counters and table tops.

### Take Care of Your Hands

You want your hands to do tough jobs, yet feel soft. You plunge them into rough work and hope they will emerge smooth as cream.

**Avoid Deep-set Grime.** When dirt gets into knuckle creases and skin cracks, the effort to scrub it out reddens and roughens your hands. Don't give it a chance. Wear household gloves to guard your hands. Slip on a pair before you dust, sweep, scour, empty the vacuum-cleaner bag, hang up clothes, dispose of garbage, spade the garden, or turn your hands to any harsh or dirty job.

**Rub in Lotion** before you plunge your hands into water, as well as after. If your hands get very grimy, wash with lotion before you use soap and water. The grime will come out with much less scrubbing.

**Choose Soaps and Detergents With Care.** Women who take pride in the appearance of their skin and hands choose a dishwashing product as carefully as they choose toilet soap. This is the secret of avoiding garden-variety hands. Find the brand that is best for you.

# KEEPING YOUR KITCHEN SPARKLING

## Care for Cabinets

**Painted-Wood and Metal Cabinets.** Paint and enamel finishes are not impenetrable. Scrubbing with harsh abrasives will dull the gloss and make cleaning progressively harder. A cloth wrung out of sudsy water may whisk off grease and sticky finger marks, particularly if you make a habit of wiping the cabinet doors each day as you do the dishes. But stronger treatment is often needed. Kitchen wax (a creamy emulsion) takes off soil and leaves a film that makes the finish dirt-resistant. Avoid waxes and polishes that are dark in color, as they may discolor paint. A paste, powder, or liquid paint cleaner is good for neglected walls and woodwork. Use a mild solution made for this purpose. Be sure to follow label directions for using cleaner.

**Natural Wood Cabinets** barely show the usual kitchen smudges, but they need care. If you forget, natural wood will lose some of its luster and beauty, and may darken unpleasantly. Wax offers these cabinets the best protection, for it both cleans and preserves. Use regular liquid polishing wax, of the type you use on furniture, or kitchen wax for painted-wood cabinets. Wipe off sticky food smudges with a clean, damp cloth or sponge wrung out of warm sudsy water; then wipe the surface dry. Buff as you dry, to bring up the gloss.

## Kitchen Counter Tops

**Save That Surface!** A nick here, a mar there—soon the top of your range, drainboards, and other work surfaces look worn. Protective mats are the answer, and there is a wide choice of types. Particularly suited to use on the range are the asbestos mats with brightly colored or gleaming metallic finish. Household-utility mats, of heat-resistant rubber or rubber-like material, that withstand hot water, soap, or dishwashing cleansers can be used at range or next to sink.

**Stainless Steel, Monel Metal** counter tops need a little attention every day. They should be washed with hot suds, then wiped with a dry cloth. When the surface begins to look cloudy and dull, use any good metal polish (the label will tell you if it's for stainless steel). Or mix fine scouring powder with a few drops of ammonia. Work this into a paste with your cloth as you polish; then rinse and dry thoroughly. If scratches are a problem, buffing with very fine stainless-steel wool (0 or finer) will erase many of them.

**Linoleum, Plastic.** Wipe counter clean, using suds as necessary. When food sticks, lay damp cloth over spot to loosen; do not use abrasive cleanser or steel wool. Waxing plastic counters is not necessary, but may improve their gloss. Wax linoleum several times a year to give it water-resistance and lengthen its life.

To avoid spotting, don't let soapy water stand on a linoleum counter top for any length of time. If there are cracks and crevices in the counter top, water will get under the linoleum and eventually loosen it. Then it will have to be replaced. Watch out particularly for loose seams around the sink.

**Unfinished Wood.** Deep gouges make cleaning difficult, so use reasonable care. Deal with stains promptly. Meat-juice and grease stains can be removed with scouring cleanser. For other stains, use chlorine bleach (liquid or powdered) and apply it to the stain with a steel wool pad. If the entire board needs whitening, cover it with a bleach solution (about 1 tablespoonful to a cupful of water). Rinse well. Rub a new board with linseed oil to keep stains on the surface and make cleaning easier.

## Don't Neglect Your Range

### Two Ounces Plus of Prevention

Learn how to keep foods from boiling over and burning. Here are some how-to-cook suggestions that will help keep your pans gleaming and your range clean.

Boil foods gently. Then they won't splatter over the sides of the pan and give you two cleaning jobs —the stove and the utensil. Your foods will cook just as fast with low heat. You need high heat only to bring foods to a boil.

For top-stove pan-frying or sautéing with a small amount of fat, use medium heat in the initial browning. It will minimize spattering and brown foods more evenly than if the skillet is heated too fast. When you do a cooking job like this, move teakettle or salt and pepper shakers on range out of the way so they won't become spattered with fat.

When you cook foods that foam—applesauce, lima beans, rice, macaroni, etc.—a roomy utensil will help keep them from boiling up and overflowing. Stand at the stove until boiling begins, then lower heat. You will not waste so much time as you would if you had to clean the stove later.

When uncovered meats are roasted in the oven, keep the temperature low (325° to 350° F.). There's less spattering, and your oven stays cleaner. Meat shrinkage is minimized and the meat will be juicy and flavorful.

Do everything possible to avoid the syrup's boiling over when you bake juicy pies. Use a deep pie plate, and crimp the edges of the crust. Place a sheet of aluminum foil in the oven on a low rack where it will catch the drip.

**Exterior.** Cool range before cleaning to avoid crazing of porcelain enamel. Wipe with cloth wrung out of suds; dry. To remove stubborn spots, sprinkle on a little household cleanser; rub lightly with damp cloth. Rinse. To clean and wax, pour a little kitchen wax onto damp cloth; wipe cloth over surface of range. Let wax dry a few minutes; buff with dry cloth. This gives waxy, soil-repellent finish.

*Note:* Once porcelain enamel is stained by food acids, there is nothing you can do to remove the stains. Wipe up all spills promptly.

**Oven.** Wearing household gloves and using brush provided, spread special oven cleaner over all greasy or crusted surfaces. Close oven door. Allow cleaner to remain for 2 to 3 hours. Then rinse thoroughly with wet cloth or sponge. *Caution:* Spread newspaper in front of range to protect floor.

**Broiler.** Pour off fat while warm, then soak both pan and rack for 15 to 20 minutes in hot sudsy water in the sink. Dishwashing detergent has a penetrating and loosening effect on burnt-on grease. Finish up with a few whisks of a steel-wool soap pad, then rinse and let dry.

**Top of Stove.** Remove any parts that can be soaked in hot suds (drip trays, pans under electric elements, gas-range pan supports). While these soak, clean all surfaces of top of stove you can reach with damp cloth or steel-wool soap pad. If gas burners or electric elements are removable, clean with cloth wrung out of suds (do not immerse elements). Rinse or wipe clean all parts and replace.

### Cleaning the Refrigerator

**Exterior.** Wipe with cloth wrung out of suds; rinse, dry with soft, clean cloth. To remove stubborn stains, use damp cloth sprinkled with small amount of household cleanser; avoid harsh abrasives. Apply coat of kitchen wax; polish with soft cloth.

**Interior.** Wash walls of refrigerator with solution of warm water and baking soda (in proportion to 1 teaspoon of soda to 1 quart of water) or detergent and warm water followed by a baking-soda solution. Wash shelves and ice trays with warm water and detergent. If there is hardened food deposit on shelves, remove shelves to sink and soak in warm, sudsy water. Rinse with clear water; dry with clean cloth.

*Note:* Use *warm* water; hot water may damage protective coating on ice trays and thus cause difficulty in removing ice cubes. Also never put glass shelves into hot water immediately after removing them; sudden temperature changes may cause breakage.

**Gasket.** Wash the gasket (rubber or plastic seal on inside of refrigerator door) with warm suds; wipe with clean cloth wrung out of clear water; wipe dry.

### Cleaning the Freezer

**Exterior.** Wipe freezer with cloth wrung out of suds; rinse; dry with soft clean cloth. To remove stubborn stains, rub with cloth sprinkled with small amount of household cleanser; avoid harsh abrasives. Apply coat of wax; polish with soft cloth. (Waxing protects surface finish and helps maintain its gleaming luster.)

**Interior.** After defrosting freezer completely, wash the freezer shelves and walls with solution of warm water and baking soda (in proportion of 1 teaspoon of soda to 1 quart of water). Rinse with clear water; dry thoroughly before turning power on again.

**Gasket.** Wash gasket (rubber or plastic seal on the inside of freezer door) with cloth wrung out of suds; rinse with clear water; wipe dry.

### Removing Stains from Sink

To remove black marks and keep sink white, sprinkle household cleanser on damp cloth or sponge, or directly into sink or tub. (For best results, surface should be damp, not wet.) Rub with cloth until stains disappear; then rinse. (Most cleansers form suds when water is added; these help float away any greasy film.)

To remove stubborn food stains, fill sink with about ½″ of water; add 2 or 3 tablespoons of chlorine bleach. Swish solution around sides of sink with dishcloth. Let stand 5 minutes; drain; rinse.

To remove rust stains, wet surface; sprinkle on rust-removing cleanser; rub with damp dishcloth until stain disappears. Then rinse thoroughly. (Use rust-removing cleanser for stains only, not for daily cleaning.)

**Keep the Sink Drain Clean.** Even with the best of care, kitchen waste like sand, grease, and food particles may lodge in the sink drain and clog it. This trouble usually can be forestalled by weekly use of a drain-cleaning compound. If left in the drain overnight, such cleaners successfully remove even stubborn obstructions.

**When the Trouble Is Acute.** Most sinks have an extra strainer located well down in the pipe. Removing and cleaning this strainer at the first sign of sluggishness often is a simple and effective cure. Take out upper strainer; then remove lower strainer with screwdriver or piece of bent wire.

If this fails, see page 293 for directions on cleaning out a clogged drain.

**Electrical Disposal Units.** Electric waste-disposal units seldom cause drain trouble. In fact, they help prevent it, because the finely pulverized material they discharge into the drain acts as a scouring agent to remove and emulsify waste deposits. However, a few things like string, paper, and corn silk are not handled successfully by all makes of disposal units, so it is wise to dispose of these by other means.

### Cleaning and Disinfecting the Garbage Pail

Wash garbage pails or other containers at least once a week, using very hot suds. Long-handled brush makes job easy. Rinse well; dry thoroughly. Outside garbage containers can be dried in sun. In hot weather, disinfect every week or so. Use household disinfectant; follow directions on label.

### Cleaning Kitchen Ventilating Fans

Ventilating fans and ductwork accumulate grease on all surfaces. This grease is a fire hazard. An appliance serviceman should clean the entire system every year. Every month or so, wipe intake grill clean, first making sure fan is off, with damp cloth or sponge. Wipe every part you can reach. If fan is in an outside wall and has no ductwork, you may be able to clean the entire unit yourself by removing grill.

### Small Appliances

**Coffeemakers:** *Soaking method:* To remove stain, rancid oil, and sludge from any kind of coffeemaker, fill with water; add coffee-stain remover as directed on label. (Do not pour undissolved coffee-stain remover into polished aluminum pot; make solution in separate glass or enamel container, then pour into coffeemaker.) Proceed as in making coffee; drain; wash; rinse well.

*Scouring method:* Dip steel-wool soap pad into water; scour metal until all stains or film are removed. Use small percolator brush for cleaning hard-to-reach pump stem and spout. Rinse thoroughly. (This method is particularly good for aluminum coffeemakers.)

**The Waffle Baker.** Wipe outside of waffle baker with cloth wrung out of suds; polish with soft, dry cloth. To remove stubborn stains, use damp cloth sprinkled with household cleanser. Never immerse waffle baker in water, and avoid using harsh abrasives that will mar finish. Wipe grids with soft cloth or absorbent toweling. Use wire brush to remove any particles that stick to grids.

**The Portable Broiler.** Wipe the outside of broiler with damp cloth; polish with soft, dry cloth. To remove spattered fat or stubborn stains, use damp cloth sprinkled with household cleanser. Avoid using harsh abrasives that will scratch finish. Wash all removable parts, such as trays, racks, etc., in hot, sudsy water; rinse; dry thoroughly. Wipe inside with cloth wrung out of hot, sudsy water. To remove stubborn stains, use cloth sprinkled with household cleanser, or steel-wool soap pad. Never immerse broiler in water.

**The Electric Mixer.** Wipe motor housing and stand with cloth wrung out of suds. Rinse; dry with clean cloth. Never immerse motor in water. Wash bowls as you would any glassware. Use plastic hood to protect mixer against dust and moisture when it is not being used.

**The Electric Blender.** Wipe motor housing and stand with cloth wrung out of hot suds. Rinse with cloth wrung out of clear water; dry. Never immerse base in water. To clean blender jar, partially fill jar with water; add small amount of soap or detergent; turn on motor for few seconds. Then remove jar from base; drain; rinse in clear water; dry. If blades are detachable, wash all parts in hot suds; rinse in clear water; dry.

**Electric Skillets.** Wash with hot suds, rinse with clean hot water; dry. To remove food particles that cling to skillet, use steel-wool soap pads or cloth sprinkled with household cleanser. Never immerse the skillet in water unless the manufacturer recommends it.

**Deep-Fat Fryers.** After pouring off cooled fat, wipe out fryer with absorbent paper or cloth. Pour hot suds into fryer; wash thoroughly. Rinse with clear water; dry. To remove stubborn spots use steel-wool soap pad or cloth sprinkled with household cleanser. Wipe outside with damp cloth, then with dry cloth. Never immerse fryer in water.

**The Toaster.** Wipe outside of toaster with damp, not wet, cloth. Never immerse toaster in water. To remove stains use cloth sprinkled with household cleanser. If crumb tray is not removable, use small brush to remove crumbs; shaking toaster upside down may injure heating element.

### How to Clean the Floor

**To Wash a Linoleum Floor.** Never wash a linoleum floor with a streaming mop, for this floods the floor. Water never should be allowed to get under the floor covering; it will loosen seams and cause linoleum to buckle. With the mop wrung out lightly, go over only a small area at a time; wipe dry with a tightly wrung mop. Clean corners and baseboards by hand with a cloth wrung out of the washing solution. After washing the floor, allow it to dry thoroughly before applying wax.

**To Wax a Linoleum Floor.** Linoleum floors may be protected with polish or self-polishing wax. Self-polishing wax is more practical. It is easier to apply and requires no polishing. Use a wax applier made of yarn or lamb's wool, with a handle long enough to minimize stooping, or a mop of cellulose sponge.

The wax applier should be moistened evenly with water. Squeeze it out, so that it does not drip. Then pour a small pool of wax on the linoleum near the corner in which you are going to begin. Dip the applier into the wax until it is well coated. Remove excess by pressing the applier against the floor before waxing. Apply the wax in long, straight strokes, slightly overlapping each stroke as you go. Stroke in one direction. The wax applier, if moved back and forth, will leave a streaked finish. Let the wax dry for at least 20 minutes. Then buff with a clean, dry mop or polisher, if a higher gloss is desired. Before buffing, a second coat of wax can be applied when the first coat is thoroughly dry, if you want the greatest protection. *Wash your wax applier after every use.*

To remove an accumulation of old, soiled wax, use a prepared wax remover, or add a small quantity of a water-softening cleanser to the warm suds used for washing the floor. Use a scrubbing brush for complete removal.

Black marks can be removed from linoleum by rubbing them with a liquid polish wax (which contains a solvent), or a cleaning fluid, such as the kind used to remove spots from clothing. Some liquid cleansers designed for cleaning painted walls and woodwork do a good job. The floor can be rubbed lightly with steel wool.

### Paper for Protection

New shelf papers do a good job of protecting your shelves from dust and stains and also add cheerful color and gaiety to the kitchen. You have a choice of border designs—bright and modern, or conventional. Pure white, lacy patterns are particularly good for linen shelves. Such paper is of good quality with heavy, turn-down edges made of several thicknesses for durability. Frequently these edges are scalloped or cut out to add to their attractiveness, but plain paper is also available if you prefer it.

To line shelves, cut the paper to the correct length, place it on the shelf with the border turned down over the edge, and secure it with a few thumbtacks or some transparent tape. The paper can be kept clean by wiping it with a dry cloth. If it becomes stained, wring out a cloth in clear, hot water and wipe the spots gently. And, of course, badly stained shelving paper can easily be replaced, if necessary.

# EASIER DISHWASHING

It makes no difference whether you have hard or soft water—you can bring sparkle and gleam to your china, glass, and silverware if you use a dishwashing detergent. These new products, which come in powdered and liquid form, have special grease-cutting properties. You do not have to scrub dishes—dishwashing detergents actually penetrate greasy film and lift off food particles.

Dishes washed with one of these new products will drain dry without spotting, even in hard water, if they are rinsed well with hot water. A mechanical water softener or water-softening service solves the hard-water problem, not only in dishwashing but in many other ways.

Don't use so much detergent that you have mountains of suds. You waste time rinsing off the suds from your dishes and from the bottom of the sink after you've washed the dishes. Learn to use *light* suds. It's timesaving and economical.

The clean-up job always seems lighter if you take care of cooking utensils before serving dinner. Hot water and a few drops of detergent will soak most pots and pans clean. This method is especially good for greasy broilers and roasting pans. Drain off the grease while it is still liquid and wipe the pans with paper towels.

**Dishwashing Line-Up.** Convention says good dishwashing order calls for glasses and silverware first, then cups and saucers, then plates, with the cooking utensils last. Actually, so long as you change the dishwater often, dishes can be washed in any order. But it is not good practice to pile everything into the dishpan at one time. Dishwater should be as hot as your hands can comfortably stand it, unless you protect your hands with household gloves—then it can be even hotter.

If anyone in the family has a cold, dishes—especially glasses, cups, forks, and spoons—must *be* clean as well as *look* clean. Remove all greasy film in good suds, then rinse dishes in very hot water (preferably in a dish rack), for sanitary dishes.

Most women use a sponge or dishcloth instead of a dish mop because dish mops are harder to keep clean and sanitary. If you use a vegetable brush for pots and pans, try it for dishes, too. It keeps your hands out of water and quickly removes food that has to be rubbed off.

Rinsing dishes in hot water, the hotter the better, is important to get rid of suds and make dishes clean. If you are washing few dishes, rinse them under the faucet as you go. But after a complete meal, save time and water by putting the dishes in a dish rack and pouring or spraying hot, not boiling water over them. If you have a double-compartment sink, wash dishes in one side and rinse in the other. It's convenient to have a drainboard or counter on each side of the sink. When you buy a new sink, remember these conveniences.

**Take Care of Your Silverware.** Wash only a few pieces of silverware at a time, for if you try to wash too many, you may leave food between the fork tines. And though a few minutes in the dishpan does not harm silver, never soak it. Soaking can loosen knife handles and may affect the appearance of oxidized patterns.

**Drying Dishes.** Cut dishwashing time by letting dishes dry in a rack. To be practical, you should have a dish rack large enough to hold all the dishes from an average meal. But silverware and sometimes glasses need drying with a dish towel. Have a good supply of towels; keep them well laundered, so you'll always have fresh ones ready to use.

**After Storing China.** Even a tight cupboard doesn't keep out all dust and film, so look over stored china before using to see whether or not it needs washing. Last-minute washing of fine crystal brings out hidden sparkle. All it takes is a quick swish through very hot dishwashing-detergent suds in the dishpan. Wear lined household gloves, which enable you to put your hands in almost scalding water. Then rinse and polish with a lintless dish towel.

## How Much Work Does a Dishwasher Do?

**Do Dishwashers Save Time?** Just how *much* time depends on your definition of dishwashing. To most women, it means clearing the table, putting food in the refrigerator, wiping off the counter tops, etc. Obviously a dishwasher does not help with these jobs. But when you compare actually washing and drying the dishes by hand with loading the dishwasher, adding detergent, and setting it going, you find that a hand job that takes 45 minutes can be done in the dishwasher in 10, a saving of 35 minutes of clean-up time.

**Is It True That Dishes Must Practically Be Washed Before Putting Them into the Machine?** Dishes merely need to be scraped before they are put into the racks. Many women *do* rinse dishes quickly under the faucet, especially when the sink has a garbage disposer. But rinsing is really unnecessary unless the dishes are going to stand for some time before they're washed or are heavily coated with egg, chocolate, or mashed potatoes; then a rinse and a quick wipe with a nylon-bristled brush are all that's needed.

**Do Modern Dishwashers Ever Leave Glasses Filmy and Spotted?** Even the best dishwashing detergents cannot solve water problems caused by excessive hardness, high iron content, etc. In such cases the water condition complicates laundering, bathing, and even cooking. The only solution is the installation of water-conditioning equipment.

**Is Spotting a Problem under Normal Conditions?** Newer dishwashers dry the dishes with warm air from a heating element. But some of the older models depend upon unheated air for drying, and spotting can occur, especially on silverware and glassware. If spotting is a problem even with an up-to-date dishwasher and hot, hot water, try switching your detergent or varying the quantity you use.

**Do Dishwashers Break Dishes or Chip Glassware?** Dishes and glasses do not move while in a dishwasher; they rest securely in softly-cushioned racks while water swirls over, around, and inside them.

**Do Dishwashers Fade Colors on China?** China decorated with overglaze colors and patterns may eventually show loss of color. Gold, silver, and often platinum designs are particularly vulnerable. Of course such china is eventually affected by hand dishwashing too, but hot water and special dishwashing detergents used in a dishwasher accelerate the process. On the other hand, more and more china manufacturers are producing underglaze patterns and colors, which are not affected.

**Can Plastic Dishes Stand the Heat of the Dishwasher?** It's true that some types of plastic cannot stand the heat of a dishwasher during the drying period. These are the less expensive, lighter weight plastics of polystyrene and polyethylene, which are mainly used for picnicware, refrigerator storage dishes, etc. Most plastic dinnerware, made of one of the melamine plastics, are perfectly safe in the dishwasher.

**Are Dishes Cleaner and More Sanitary When Washed in a Dishwasher?** Dishes given one or more thorough washes with a cleanser and then rinsed and rinsed in *very* hot water, hotter than the hands could endure, are cleaner than those washed by even the best hand-washing methods. And bacteriological tests actually *prove* this.

**What Is the True Story on Washing Pots and Pans?** Pots and pans reasonably free from stuck-on or charred food can be washed in your dishwasher. In a small family, after a simple meal, they can be washed with the dishes. But often there is a full load of dinner things to wash and no room for bulky or odd-shaped cooking utensils and covers, so some women prefer to clean a few pots and pans by hand while the dishes are being washed automatically; others rerun the dishwasher.

**How Much Hot Water Does a Dishwasher Use?** The amount of water used is small—from 5 to 8 gallons—less than is needed to fill one of the new deep sinks.

**Is the Installation of the Dishwasher Costly or Difficult?** Nowadays installation does not pose the serious problem it did at one time. Before you buy a dishwasher, have the dealer or a plumber survey your home and see which model would be best for it, i.e., least costly to install. And get an estimate on cost of installation, including any plumbing and electrical work required.

**Which Is the Best Type of Dishwasher to Buy if You Live in an Apartment or a Home that You Do Not Own?** Portable dishwashers utilize detachable hoses, instead of pipes, for water supply and drain. They work automatically, have good capacity. Obviously they eliminate installation cost and inconvenience.

**If Your Family Is Small (Just Two of You), Is a Dishwasher Practical?** Any two people can collect a lot of dishes, even with simple meals. With a dishwasher, the sink never has messy-looking dishes in it; they're in the dishwasher.

### Faucet Dishwashing Device

This sturdy, beautifully tooled dishwashing device is designed to replace the faucets on your sink. It has

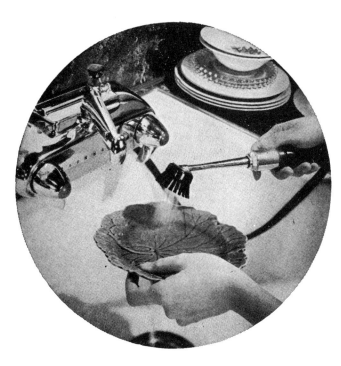

a tank for holding the detergent supply and a hose of convenient length and flexibility. A nylon brush for dishes or a wire brush for pots and pans is attached to the hose. Merely pressing a button produces suds for cleaning china and glassware; releasing it lets hot, clear water flow through the hose, for rinsing.

To save yourself as much work as possible, you must have a roomy dish drainer, so the clean, well-rinsed dishes can drain dry and be put away without toweling.

A dishwashing device like this makes fast work of all the hard dishwashing jobs—cleaning broiler pans and roasters, etc. It has several other advantages: There is no splashing, because of the aerated suds; there's no soaking of hands in dishwater; and you can run water from the faucets at any time.

This addition to the kitchen sink is more than a dishwasher. It does a fine job of flushing the sink, particularly when it contains leafy bits, sand, coffee grounds, or grease. You can direct the spray into any corner and use water as hot as you like.

The spray is an excellent vegetable washer, too, for with clear, cold water you can scrub and spray the vegetables until clean.

### Cooking-Utensil Care

Keeping your cooking utensils clean and shining is one of the best ways to make them last. Here are some things to remember:

1. Keep heat low enough to prevent burning and boiling over. This will save your pots and pans and a lot of your time, effort, and energy as well.

2. After using pots and pans, fill them with water and put them to soak on the range. Then with a good cleanser you can clean them quickly and easily and not have to resort to time-consuming scouring.

3. Hang your pots and pans where they are easy to get at. Don't keep them jumbled together in a cupboard, from which they'll come tumbling out and be dented and damaged.

4. If you use glass top-stove cooking utensils on an electric range with high-speed units you should use a rack or grid under them.

5. When cooking eggs and other foods that would darken and discolor aluminum, use enamelware, glass, or stainless steel. There's no use giving yourself an unnecessary cleaning job.

6. Be particularly careful in using skillets and griddles. They must not be left over heat too long before food is put into them. If they are, they may warp and buckle and become almost worthless. Habits like this are wasteful of fuel, too.

7. When utensils are piping hot from the range, it is better to let them cool a bit before filling them with water for soaking.

8. Don't put up with loose knobs and wobbly handles. Usually a screwdriver is all that is needed to tighten them. If knobs or handles break, have them replaced.

**Brightening Aluminum Pots and Pans.** Hard scouring is seldom necessary. If food has cooked on pan, first remove with dishwashing aid such as plastic or metal scouring pad. If scouring doesn't remove discoloration, fill pot with hot water; add cream of tartar, 1 or 2 tablespoons to 1 quart of water. Bring to boil; let simmer 5 or 10 minutes.

**Polishing Copper or Copper-Bottomed Pots and Pans.** Easiest way to use copper cleaner is to pour a little onto sponge; wipe sponge quickly over wet copper surface; rinse *promptly;* and dry thoroughly with dry towel. Most copper cleaners are slightly acid in action; it is wise to protect counter tops, clothes, and hands. Observe precautions on label.

**Cleaning Stainless-Steel Cooking Utensils.** High heat makes stainless-steel cooking utensils—particularly skillets—take on brownish or varicolored stains, called heat tints. To remove, scour with household cleanser; if they cannot be removed in this way, re-buffing of utensil by manufacturer may be necessary. To prevent stains from forming, use utensils over low or medium heat only.

**Cleaning Cast-Iron Cooking Utensils.** Always wash cast-iron utensil with *soap,* not detergent, which will remove all the seasoning years of use have given it.

To remove burned-on food, use steel-wool soap pads. Always rinse utensil with very hot water and completely dry over low heat, to prevent rust stains, before storing.

**To Season a Cast-Iron Pot or Skillet.** First scour utensil well with household cleanser; then wash, rinse, and dry thoroughly. With pastry brush, spread melted vegetable shortening or vegetable oil on inside of utensil and on inside of cover. Place in warm oven (250° to 300° F.) or on top of stove over low heat for several hours. Occasionally swab utensil; cover with more fat. Wipe off excess fat with paper towel. Repeat seasoning process, after which utensil will be ready for use. If rust appears after use, season utensil again. The more cast-iron utensils are used, the more seasoned they become and the easier they are to clean.

**Enameled Cooking Utensils.** Scour with household cleanser.

**Glass Cooking Utensils and Baking Dishes.** To remove burned-on food, soak utensil in solution of 1 tablespoon of baking soda to 2 quarts of water; wash with soap or detergent and hot water. To remove stubborn particles or stains, use a scourer, household cleanser, or steel-wool soap pad.

**Cleaning a Teakettle.** Fill kettle with water; add 2 or 3 tablespoons of water conditioner; let come to boil. Let simmer for 15 minutes; then empty kettle; rinse. This treatment should remove all but heaviest scale.

**Cleaning Vacuum Bottles.** Before cleansing bottle, rinse with cold water, especially if it has contained milk or cocoa. Then pour few drops of liquid dishwashing detergent into bottle; fill with very hot water. Let stand for a few minutes; then rinse thoroughly with clear hot water. Fill metal or plastic cover with sudsy water; swish cork around in water to remove odor.

### Stainless-Steel Flatware

**To most people, stainless steel** is a handsome material that will take the brunt of hard use—whether used for tableware, kitchen cutlery, or cooking utensils. But in some ways this is a misconception. For although so-called stainless ware is stainless for all practical purposes and is one of the easiest of materials to maintain, it is not completely stainproof.

**Because stainless steel** varies in composition and in the way it is finished (the higher the buffing, the greater the stain resistance), it is necessary to evaluate each stainless-steel product individually.

**After 16 hours of exposure** to food acids, stainless-steel cutlery and tableware should show little or no effect: Some stainless ware will come through completely unscathed. Some, upon close examination, will reveal faintly the areas where vinegar, mustard, or mayonnaise have been; these slight discolorations will usually fade and disappear without further washing or use. But it is not reasonable to expect even the finest stainless steel to retain its mirrorlike finish under all conditions of use. Often washing is not enough. Some foods leave a hazy white film that is unnoticeable until the utensil is dried; where this occurs, a sprinkling or two of household cleanser plus a little rubbing is the answer.

### Silver Care and Cleaning

**Save Hours of Silver Cleaning.** For your silver's and your own sake protect seldom-used silver from tarnish by methods like these.

**Make Your Own Silver Drawer.** Line and custom-fit a sideboard or other drawer for nontarnishing storage of flatware. You will need tarnish-preventive cloth, racks for separating the silver pieces, a base pad and tacks.

**Plastic Film.** The same crystal-clear plastic film that is so notable for food wrapping is the most convenient of all plastic films for storing silver. The film's characteristic of clinging by itself to the surfaces to which it is pressed is a big help in wrapping silver pieces tightly. Its quality of transparency is also helpful.

**Silver Cloth.** For long-time silver storage, years in fact, silver cloth is an outstanding shine protector.

**A Special Product** in a small glass jar effectively delays tarnishing if it is kept in your silver drawer. Use it according to directions.

The longer tarnishing is delayed, the less work you'll have.

### How to Polish Silver

Unless silver is used and washed every day or stored with special protection, tarnishing is inevitable. Polish it this way:

Rub silver polish, paste or cream, over silver until tarnish is removed. Then wash silver in hot sudsy water. Rinse in very hot water, and immediately polish dry, giving each piece a brisk rubbing with a clean dish towel. Change towels frequently. Silver-polishing cloths work on the same general principle; use with brisk rubbing.

**The Electrolytic Way.** Submerge magnesium-alloy leaf in hot detergent suds, then touch each piece of silver to leaf. Follow package directions exactly. Silver cleaned by this method often requires light polishing with silver-polishing cloth to give desired sheen.

# CLEANING DECORATIVE METALS

**Decorative Brass and Copper.** Decorative objects need cleaning and polishing to give them characteristic warm color and sheen. For smooth surfaces, apply metal polish with soft cloth or sponge; for embossed or carved designs, use brush. Rub until clean. Wash in hot, sudsy water; rinse in clear, hot water; dry with clean towel.

**Chromium.** Since chromium does not tarnish, it can usually be kept clean by washing with hot, sudsy water. Follow by polishing with soft, clean cloth to bring out gleam. When chromium fixtures, electrical appliances, etc., become dulled or covered with film, clean with any good metal polish, including silver polish.

**Pewter.** Wash with very hot, sudsy water to which ammonia has been added in proportion of 2 tablespoons to each quart of water. Rinse thoroughly in hot water; buff well with clean, soft cloth. When pewter becomes tarnished, clean with silver polish. Never use harsh abrasive.

**Wrought Iron.** Wrought iron seldom needs attention other than dusting. However, a thin coat of liquid polishing wax will give it gloss and resistance to rust. Apply just a little wax with a soft cloth; let dry 10 minutes or so; then rub with dry cloth. If spots of rust appear, wipe with dry-cleaning fluid; then rub with fine steel wool until rust disappears. If painted, first repaint rusty area.

**Aluminum.** Decorative aluminum, such as hammered, usually has a special finish that resists soil, stains, and discoloration. Wash in hot suds, just as you would an aluminum cooking utensil. Clean untreated aluminum with steel-wool soap pads. Tubular aluminum folding chairs may need scouring with steel-wool soap pads every year if chairs are used outdoors.

**Jewelry.** (Do not attempt to clean any costume jewelry unless you are sure water or cleaner will not loosen cement or dull finish. The following method is largely for gold and silver jewelry and for stones that have been set rather than cemented.) Dip jewelry in warm suds solution; brush gently with toothbrush, running tip of brush in behind stones if possible. When clean, rinse in warm water; dry with soft cloth. Clean tarnished silver jewelry with silver polish.

**Sterling and Plated Silver** can be cleaned with a good silver paste or polish. Use a soft brush on chased or embossed patterns. To protect display silver from tarnish, use a tarnish preventive. It's easy to apply and to remove and is effective for months.

**Wrap in Antitarnish Paper.** Silver showpieces such as those reserved for your state occasions—trays, candlesticks, tea-service pieces, etc.—will stay shining clean, ready for instant use, if they are wrapped in large (20″ x 30″) sheets of waxy coated paper. The paper is pliable but tough, and can be reused; the silver can be unwrapped, used, and then rewrapped in the same sheet.

**Good Metal Cleaners** include pastes, creams, liquids, treated cloths, and paper sheets, and special cotto fleece. All are suitable for cleanin tableware and decorative pieces. I most homes, the use of several differ ent types of metal cleaner is mos convenient.

**Use a Liquid Polish Protector.** Yo will save yourself many hours of un necessary cleaning and polishing o silver serving dishes, candelabra copper and brass chafing dishes i you protect them between uses with liquid polish protector. This is a trans parent liquid that can be used to coa metals which tarnish, chiefly silve copper and brass. Try to remembe these three important points whe you use this product: 1. The meta should be thoroughly clean, free from tarnish, and dry when the coating i applied. 2. The coating should b brushed lightly over the entire sur face. 3. If items are used for servin food or beverages, the coating mus first be removed. This is simple, how ever, merely break the film with you fingernail or a toothpick, and peel off.

**Lacquered Copper or Brass.** Man decorative copper or brass pieces— copper coffeemakers, toasters, bras fireplace accessories, etc.—are coate with lacquer in the manufacturin process, and the lacquer protect them against tarnishing for a lon time. However, when the lacque begins to wear off, and spots of tar nish appear, the best procedure is t have the old lacquer removed and new coat applied by an expert.

*Silver from Colonial days (about 1730). Cream pitcher and tray are easily recognized; the two other pieces are a trencher salt and a caster (spice shaker).*

*A chest with a treated lining helps to keep the silver bright and so saves a lot of unnecessary work repolishing.*

*Use a transparent liquid to protect clean ornamental copper from tarnish. Brush on a thin film, as if it were lacquer. But unlike lacquer this product can be removed easily.*

# KEEP YOUR BATHROOM SHINY

**Cleaning the Basin and the Bathtub.** Use water conditioner, household cleanser, or dry chlorine bleach, depending on the condition of the tub and hardness of the water supply. If a little water conditioner is sprinkled into the tub after every bath or shower and swished around with cloth or brush, the tub will seldom need scouring. But if soap scum has been allowed to accumulate, sprinkle household cleanser on cloth or sponge and go over entire surface; rinse until every grain of powder has been flushed away. About once a week, cleanse the tub with dry chlorine bleach, to whiten and disinfect at the same time. When using chlorine, apply with cloth instead of sponge, as chlorine causes some sponges to disintegrate.

**Cleaning and Disinfecting the Shower Floor.** Follow directions for cleaning the bathtub. About once each week disinfect shower floor, particularly if anyone in the family is afflicted with athlete's foot. Follow directions on the label of disinfectant for proper strength of solution and proper length of time solution should remain on surface.

**Cleaning the Walls.** *Ceramic.* If tile has a spattered, dull look, scrub with detergent suds and small, fairly stiff brush. Use toothbrush to remove dirt between tiles. Then rinse and dry tiles, rubbing to polish, with old Turkish towel.

*Plastic.* To give mastic (adhesive) a chance to set, do not wash new plastic wall tile for several days. To remove most soil, apply detergent suds with soft cloth. Then rinse wall; wipe dry with soft cloth. If tile attracts dust, wax with self-polishing wax. Do not use polishing wax.

**Cleansing the Bathroom Floor** (unglazed ceramic tile). Clean as for ceramic tile walls, using household cleanser to remove stains and black marks. (For other kinds of bathroom floorings, see "Floor Care," page 84–85.)

**The Toilet Bowl.** For quick daily cleaning, use mop with flush-away pad on plastic handle. Treated pad foams as it cleans. Swab bowl clean; open handle to release pad; then flush pad away like toilet tissue. For stubborn discolorations or lime deposit, shake ⅓ cup of toilet-bowl cleaner into toilet bowl; let stand for a few minutes. With long-handled brush, thoroughly swab solution all over inside of bowl. Then flush toilet.

**Rubber Shower and Bath Mats.** To remove scum and discoloration, scrub mat on both sides with brush dipped in suds or with cleaner; rinse well. Old, dingy mats should be discarded.

**Built-in Soap Dishes** (over a bathtub or basin) are hard to clean, because the soap scum is difficult to remove with either sponge or cloth. But one of the plastic scouring balls dipped in hot water does the job quickly. Or, to eliminate the soap-scum problem almost entirely, cut a thin cellulose sponge (the colored ones are pretty) to fit the bottom of the soap dish, and use it as a soap rest. When the sponge gets soapy, a squeeze in warm water will clean it.

**Chrome-Plated Towel Bars** and fixtures need very little care, but you can make them sparkle by using a good glass or metal cleaner. Use one of the cream or paste types recommended for chrome. Rub it on each surface, and then polish with a soft dry cloth.

**Mirrors.** An "antifog" cloth keeps them from steaming up for several days. Just rub this treated cloth over the slightly moistened mirror.

**Medicine Cabinets.** Too many of them are cluttered with old prescriptions and nearly empty jars and bottles that should be thrown out. After you have filed all the old containers in the wastepaper basket, thoroughly clean the cabinet inside and out. Then, to make the cleaning job easier next time, apply a coat of cream wax or one of the silicone or wax furniture polishes. The paint will then resist the inevitable finger marks and spills.

**Rust Stains** on porcelain-enamel fixtures that don't respond to a mild household cleanser can be given special treatment. A product made for rust stains makes short work of most of them. Rub it on with a damp cloth, and rinse off. This is not suitable for daily use, but can be used periodically to remove discoloration.

**Towels.** An extension rack that needs no special mounting slips over any conventional towel rack to provide temporary or permanent space for an extra supply of clean towels. It can also be used as a drying rack for stockings and gloves, without any fear of snagging.

**The Shower Curtain.** If shower curtains are used frequently, they get splashed with soap and water. If they are used seldom, they droop with dust. Fill the tub halfway with warm water, whip up lively suds with synthetic detergent, drop in curtain and hooks, and wash. Scum or film can be removed by gentle scrubbing with the bath brush.

**Washcloths.** Washcloths should be rinsed and wrung out after use. Soggy, wet washcloths quickly develop an unpleasant odor which is difficult to remove. A special clip-on rack can be attached to the sink to provide a place to hang damp washcloths.

# BEST WAYS TO CARE FOR WOOD FURNITURE

**Dust Before Polishing.** If dust and grit are not removed first, they may scratch the furniture when it is polished. Dusting should not be slapdash. Flicking an old cloth across a table or other surface doesn't remove dust; it merely displaces it temporarily. A good dustcloth (preferably chemically treated) is soft, lintless, absorbent, and clean. The soft, round brush attachment of a vacuum cleaner does the most thorough job of dusting flat surfaces, chair rungs, table legs, etc.

**Polishing Wood Furniture.** *The No-Rub Way.* Fold piece of clean, lint-free cloth into small square or pad. (Don't wad cloth; it will leave streaks.) Shake bottle of no-rub furniture polish well, wet pad with polish, wipe surface of wood with long strokes. Wait until polish has dried, leaving a whitish haze; then wipe off haze with clean dry cloth (you need not rub, just whisk off haze). Wood is left with bright, mirror-like finish.

*The Cream Way.* Put a little cream wax or polish on clean, dry cloth; rub cloth over wood with firm, even strokes. Remove any excess wax; then polish with another clean, dry cloth.

*The Liquid or Paste-Polishing Way.* Put a little liquid or paste wax on a clean, dry cloth, and rub on with grain of wood. Wipe off excess wax with another clean cloth—do not wait for wax to dry (this cuts down on the amount of rubbing or buffing needed). Use clean section of cloth for final buffing. For gleaming hard finish with much less effort, use an electric polisher with lamb's-wool buffing pad. This treatment for wood furniture gives long-lasting protection and a beautiful soft sheen or patina.

**Cleaning Wood Furniture.** *To remove greasy or sticky soil:* Make suds with warm water and just a little soap or detergent. Dip cloth or sponge into suds; wring out tightly; wipe off soil, rubbing if necessary. Rinse cloth; wipe wood again; dry thoroughly; polish.

*Note:* Waxing does remove most soil, but the suds method is necessary to remove sticky soil. It is also recommended before waxing when an oily polish has been used previously.

*To remove old polish and soil:* Dampen cloth, work a little paste cleaner (special cleaner for furniture or cars) into it. Rub small area of the wood at a time; as paste dries, use clean, dry cloth to remove it, along with old polish and soil. Polish as desired.

## Touch-ups for Wood Furniture

**To Remove Scratches.** Apply scratch-concealing polish or cream, or touch-up brush, as label says.

**To Remove Water Rings.** Rub on camphorated oil with grain of wood. Very bad rings may require several applications.

**To Remove Candle Wax.** First, with fingers, pick off all the wax you can. Then scrape *gently* with dull knife blade or plastic scraper. Remove last traces of wax by rubbing briskly with dry, soft cloth.

*Note:* To harden wax, making it easier to remove, hold an ice cube on it for a moment. Wipe up any melted ice promptly.

**To Remove Heat Marks.** To remove light damage, moisten clean, soft cloth with a little camphorated oil; rub cloth over mark with light strokes. Immediately rub vigorously with another clean cloth. To remove more severe damage, rub gently with dry steel-wool soap pad, a tiny area at a time, wiping up powdery substance before going on to next area. This method succeeds like a miracle, but you must work carefully.

**To Remove "Bloom" or "Fog."** Wash surface with cloth or sponge wrung out of warm suds. Rinse cloth; wipe again. Dry and polish as desired. Or wipe with cloth wrung out of solution of 1 tablespoon of vinegar in 1 quart of lukewarm water.

**To Remove Cigarette Burns.** To remove light burns or scorch on dark furniture, apply scratch-concealing polish or cream, rubbing with grain of wood. To remove more serious burns, mix a little rottenstone or powdered pumice with linseed oil to form a paste. Apply paste to stain, rubbing with grain of wood. (*Caution:* Do not get paste on unburned areas.) Wipe with dry, soft cloth. But note that even this kind of treatment will not restore badly charred wood.

**To Remove Perfume and Alcohol Stains.** Wipe up spilled alcohol or perfume immediately, since both these substances dissolve varnish and shellac. Apply scratch-concealing polish or cream as directed on the label. If this is not effective, try a combination of rottenstone or powdered pumice and linseed oil as suggested for removing cigarette burns.

### A Few Don'ts in Furniture Care

1. Don't place furniture too close to radiators or windows.

2. Don't put hot dishes on a table without protective pads.

3. Don't pull a vase across a table or place it directly on the surface.

4. Don't vie with the specialist in wood finishing.

5. Don't try to polish everything at one time.

## Fixing Furniture

**Loose Chair Rounds.** First remove old glue from rounds and inside hole so new glue will hold; then reglue. Or use a special wood-swelling fluid sold in hardware and dime stores. When wood is badly shrunken, metal fasteners often work well. Their barbs dig in, hold securely.

**Re-covering Side Chair Seat.** Fabric-covered seats on side chairs are fastened, from the underside, by a screw at each corner. Unscrew them, and lift out seat. Remove cambric covering and old fabric from underside. Tack new fabric along one side, then on opposite side, stretching it taut as you go. Miter corners, as in bedmaking. If seat is webbed, re-stretch webbing before re-covering.

**Gluing Large Pieces.** A "Spanish windlass" makes it easy to apply pressure to chairs and other large pieces until glue dries. Tie two turns of heavy cord around the piece; insert a stick between the strands, and twist until cord is rigidly taut. Tie or wedge stick, so it won't untwist.

**Loose Casters.** Fill hole solidly with plastic wood; when partially dry, replace caster. For a temporary repair, wrap Cellophane tape around shank of caster.

**How to Fix a Sticky Drawer.** Rub the runners of the drawer with paraffin or soap, and slide the drawer in and out a few times to lubricate the surface. Avoid using oil on sticky drawers; it soaks into the wood and will eventually stain or soil.

When a heavy drawer gives trouble, drive several large-headed thumbtacks into the runners. Then apply soap or paraffin. If this method doesn't work, you may have to resort to planing. First plane the side and bottom edges; then give them a coat of wax or paraffin. Plane the top edges only if necessary, as this spoils the drawer's appearance.

**Refinishing Old Furniture.** Remove the old varnish from the table top with a scraper, being sure the scraper is extremely sharp. If you use varnish remover, apply it with a full brush and let it remain undisturbed for 20 minutes. Then scrape with a broad

putty knife or a square-edged block of wood. Repeat if necessary, to remove all the old finish. Varnish remover is essential for curved or fluted table legs; use fine steel wool or stiff-bristled brush instead of a scraper.

Cover the floor with several thicknesses of newspaper and do only a small area of the table at a time. Be careful to scrape in the same direction as the grain of the wood.

Next wash the table with turpentine. Then apply an oil stain (or use a wood dye) and wipe it dry. Repeat this until you have the shade you want. Omit this step if the old stain is in perfect condition.

If you are working on open-grained woods, a new filler of the proper shade may be required. Apply it along the grain with a stiff brush or putty knife; in 10 or 15 minutes, when the gloss has dulled, rub off across the grain. After drying a day, the surface can be smoothed with No. 00 sandpaper wrapped around a block of soft wood. Then the table is ready to finish.

Using the best 2″ varnish brush you have, apply 3 coats of white shellac; allow each coat to dry overnight, smooth very lightly with fine sandpaper, and dust. Thin the shellac with 3 parts of painters' alcohol to 1 of shellac for the first coat; half and half for the next 2 coats, using a woolen cloth to rub the last coat with rottenstone and linseed oil for deep luster. Work in a dust-free place.

**Painting Unfinished Furniture.** Good results can be obtained in finishing new wood only if the surface is properly prepared. Dirt and grease must be removed before finish is applied. Use a nonsoapy cleaner, such as trisodium phosphate. Or clean by wiping with a cloth soaked in turpentine. *Caution:* Turpentine is highly flammable.

The next step is to smooth any rough spots with sandpaper (No. 0 usually is satisfactory). After sanding the surface should be brushed and wiped to remove dust.

*First Coat.* The first coat of paint will have to be thinned. Follow label directions for thinning according to the condition of the surface. Porous wood should be primed with a first coat thinned with linseed oil; resinous wood needs a primer thinned with turpentine. For the first coat, paint never should be applied as it comes in the can; it will not penetrate the pores of the wood properly to make a good bond between paint and wood.

*Puttying Cracks and Nail Holes.* When the first coat has dried, fill in cracks or holes with putty, and smooth off with a putty knife. This should be done only after the priming coat has been applied; otherwise, the oil in the putty will soak into the wood, causing the putty to dry out and crack. If necessary, smooth the putty by sandpapering it lightly after it has dried.

*Finishing Coats.* The second coat, which should be applied only after the putty has been allowed to dry for 24 hours, also should be thinned, but not so much as the first coat.

The third coat may be applied as it comes in the can, unless it has, at some time, been allowed to thicken. If the paint is so thick that it doesn't spread evenly, and leaves excessive brush marks, thin to the proper consistency. To thin the paint, use linseed oil for a glossy finish; turpentine for a flat or nonglossy finish.

*Using Enamel.* When a gloss enamel is used as the final finish, the first two coats should be flat. Enamel undercoat may be used, or a flat wall paint. Thin the first coat with turpentine. The second coat may be applied as it comes in the can. Then the enamel may be used directly from the can; apply in a thin, even coat. Allow 24 hours' drying between coats.

### Piano Care

Keeping a piano in tune is a job not only for the man with the tuning hammer, but also for the owner. A piano is more sensitive to environment than is generally realized. Wide changes in temperature or humidity are undesirable. The piano's location in a room affects its performance and the length of time it stays in tune. If it is close to a window or door that is habitually left open in warm weather, it will be exposed to maximum humidity and the wood will swell. If it is in a draft that blows hot one day and cold another, the alternating expansion and contraction of its metal parts invite trouble. It shouldn't be too near a radiator, hot pipes, or heat vents in floor or baseboard. If possible, place the piano near an inside wall or in a corner free from drafts and heat sources.

When the heat is on, the atmosphere is likely to become dry. Ordinarily, there is little you can do; it will help if you keep the temperature as even as possible and not too warm. With some heat dispensers you can use small vessels for water evaporation. Although you can modify temperature variations indoors, they cannot be entirely overcome, and tuning the piano becomes absolutely necessary.

Two *good* tunings a year, preferably soon after winter and summer, may suffice. For best results, it may need to be tuned 3 times a year. If it is used every day, it should be tuned 4 or more times a year. Four tunings the first year are not too many during "settling." *Good* tuning improves its condition and longevity.

If your home is near the sea or in a damp locale, the action will be affected by dampness. The parts will swell and cause sluggish key response. To remedy this condition, the action must be eased by a competent regulator. Also, dampness will cause rust on the strings. Rust should be removed.

Dust that accumulates inside a piano should be removed with a soft brush.

A piano need not be used every day.

Sometimes moths get at the felt inside a piano, and affect both action and tone. Frequent use may help keep moths away; but if a piano becomes infested, it will require professional care.

When the piano keys are soiled, they should be cleaned with a soft, damp cloth; rub the keys lengthwise.

Keep the outside of your piano free from dust, and protect its finish with polish. Not only will this protect the finish, but it also will help prevent the wood from drying out.

### Table Tops

**Leather.** Remove dust and dirt with soft brush or dusting attachment of vacuum cleaner. If leather is dingy, wash with saddle soap; apply light coat of paste wax or a special leather preservative, following label directions. Buff well.

**Hard Plastic** (Formica, Micarta, Nevamar, Textolite, etc.). First wash with warm suds and water. Wipe dry. Then if you want higher gloss, polish in any of the ways suggested under "Polishing Wood Furniture," page 80.

**Marble.** Wash with detergent suds and water. Do not use soap, which might leave a film. If marble is stained, wet with clear, hot water; spread with thick paste made by adding hot water to household cleanser to a depth of about ½ inch. Leave until paste is completely dry; this may take a day or two. When ready to remove dried paste, dampen slightly. Rinse marble; wipe dry.

## RESURFACING A TABLE TOP

*1. First remove the old finish from the table, using sandpaper wrapped around a block of wood. (Otherwise, the old finish may inhibit the bonding action of the cement.)*

*2. Using a fine-toothed saw, cut the laminated-plastic sheet to an over-all size a fraction of an inch (⅛" or less) longer and wider than the dimensions of the table top.*

*3. Using a grooved cement applicator, spread a thin coat of cement on the plastic sheet and another on the tabletop, then allow the coats to dry about 40 minutes.*

### Cleaning Painted Furniture

Use large cloth or sponge, well moistened, but not dripping with paint cleaner (liquid, powder, or paste). Clean small area with circular motion, then rinse before dirt resettles. Dry with clean cloth. Then move to next area, overlapping previously cleaned area by 2 or 3 inches. Follow with any furniture-polishing method recommended under "Polishing Wood Furniture," page 80.

### Porch Furniture

**Wood Furniture.** Wood furniture should be well scrubbed with soap and water and allowed to dry thoroughly. If the paint is in good condition, sand-papering the surface with fine sandpaper should be about all the preparation necessary.

Pay particular attention to smoothing rough and splintered edges that might catch clothing. Reset protruding nailheads. Loose nails should be withdrawn and replaced with others driven into new positions so they will hold securely. Fill the old nail holes with a filler made for this purpose, allow it to dry, and sand-paper smooth.

After all sandpapering is finished, remove the sandpaper dust clinging to the furniture, using a clean cloth or brush.

Now you're ready for painting. First apply a priming coat, allow it to dry, and then the finishing paint. Ask your dealer about priming when you buy the finishing paint. The priming paint should be of the same shade as the finishing. The finishing coat should be of a paint made especially for outdoor use.

If a second finishing coat is necessary, let first coat dry, and sandpaper it lightly before applying second coat.

If paint on wood furniture is blistered, badly cracked, or peeling, remove as much as possible by sandpapering with coarse sandpaper, or with scraper or putty knife. Smooth surface with fine sandpaper. Complete job with priming coat and two finishing coats, allowing each coat to dry thoroughly, and sand-papering lightly first finishing coat before applying second.

**Metal Furniture.** Metal furniture is prepared for painting in the same way as wood furniture. Special care should be used to remove rust spots. Emery paper usually does this efficiently.

**Canvas Chairs.** Canvas chairs that are faded but otherwise in good condition can be made to look almost new by painting with a paintlike dye made for this purpose.

The canvas is prepared simply by removing all loose dust and soil with a brush or vacuum cleaner. Awning paint is then applied with a brush according to the manufacturer's directions. On canvas chairs a special sealing coat should be applied to the canvas paint after it has dried, to prevent its rubbing off on skin or clothing. Your paint dealer can supply this.

**Wicker Furniture.** Examine the furniture carefully and mend any loose or broken ends. Be sure there are no protruding nailheads on which clothes could be torn, or rough spots that wreak havoc with stockings and fine fabrics. Smooth these with sandpaper.

Wash and dry the furniture thoroughly. If you wish color, apply several thinned coats of outdoor paint; otherwise, use spar varnish. Let each coat dry thoroughly before you apply the next one. The finish can be applied by using a spray gun or the spray attachment of a vacuum cleaner. Always do this work outdoors.

**Proper Care Pays Dividends.** Remember that all furniture used outdoors must stand up under sudden changes of temperature and weather. Rust, fading, peeling, and other signs of wear spread rapidly if not treated promptly. For longer wear, examine your outdoor furniture frequently and make repairs as soon as they are needed.

*4. Align one long edge of the sheet and table, then carefully lower the sheet into place. (Once the cemented surfaces have made contact, the sheet cannot be moved.)*

*5. Using an ordinary rolling pin and applying pressure, roll the entire surface. This squeezes out a small amount of cement that can simply be wiped off with your fingers.*

*6. Use a small plane to remove the fraction of an inch overhang of plastic around the edges. Then finish by filing the edges smooth and straight with a fine-toothed file.*

# CLEANING UPHOLSTERED FURNITURE

### The Dry-Clean Method

(For any fabric.) Pour about 2 cups of dry-cleaning fluid into a shallow pan. Dip special eraser into cleaning fluid, shake off excess. With long, even strokes, rub eraser over surface of fabric, overlapping each stroke.

### The Shampoo Method

(For fabrics not affected by water.) Mix foamy liquid cleaner with water as directed on label; use rotary beater to whip into thick, foamy suds. Test on back of furniture. Allow test patch to dry; examine to make sure color of fabric is unaffected before proceeding. Then, with a cellulose sponge or soft brush, using a circular motion, apply suds to fabric. (A stiff brush can be used on sturdy fabric.) Do a small area at a time, overlapping previously cleaned areas. When you have finished cleaning a few sections, wipe away suds with a piece of Turkish toweling wrung out of clear, warm water. (An electric fan blowing on furniture speeds drying.)

### The Powder Method

Sprinkle upholstery-cleaning powder over area 1 foot square; brush in thoroughly; leave for about an hour. When powder feels dry, remove it with vacuum-cleaner upholstery tool.

### The Vacuum-Cleaner Method

Vacuum sides, back, and cushions with upholstery nozzle, using brisk strokes. Then change to crevice tool to reach down into corners.

### Leather Upholstery

To clean leather upholstery, thoroughly wash with saddle soap, using enough soap on clean, wet cloth to make rich lather as you rub. While leather is still wet, wipe off with clean, dry cloth; then put on final light coat of saddle soap, and allow to dry. Buff with soft, dry cloth. For added protection, apply paste wax or special leather preservative. If leather upholstery is stiff from neglect or exposure, it can be softened by a light application of an oil such as neat's-foot oil. Put a little oil on clean, dry cloth; rub it into leather well. Do not use too much at one time; a little, at weekly intervals, is more effective.

### Plastic Upholstery

Wipe with warm light suds. For ground-in dirt, use a heavy concentration of laundering detergent and a medium-bristled brush; or a foam-type aerosol cleaner made especially for vinyl fabrics.

*For shoe polish or heel marks:* Sponge lightly with cleaning fluid. *Paint:* Sponge with turpentine. *Ballpoint ink:* Use rubbing alcohol. *Nail polish or polish remover:* Blot well, and sponge with cleaning fluid. *Brownish stain:* (This results from contact with products containing sulfur.) Place cloth saturated with 6% hydrogen peroxide on area for 30 minutes or more. Always rinse well after using a stain remover.

### Foam-Rubber Upholstery

Clean according to its fabric covering. Do not let cleaning fluid penetrate fabric because it may make the foam-rubber cushioning sticky.

# THE CARE OF FLOORS AND FLOOR COVERINGS

The 8 basic types of floorings (see p. 39) fall into 3 major categories: wood, composition, and ceramic or stone. Wood floors are still the most common, but as new materials are developed and old ones are improved, they are being put to use in almost every room in the house. With proper care, all floorings used today will give many years of service. Here is how to keep your floors clean and attractive so they add an extra note of beauty to your home.

### Cleaning and Polishing Wood Floors

**The Polishing-Wax Way.** If necessary, first remove old wax and soil, following directions carefully; apply polishing wax to clean floor only. If using paste wax, work well into large, folded cloth, and apply in light, even coat. Use another large cloth to wipe off excess wax. If using liquid wax, pour onto floor in pool; with long-handled lamb's-wool or chenille applicator, spread in thin film over floor, rubbing in well. To polish with electric polisher or polishing attachment on vacuum cleaner, let wax dry thoroughly before polishing. To polish with clean chenille pad or other cloth, let wax dry only 15 or 20 minutes.

**The Cleaning-Wax Way.** Follow label directions for use. This method is a timesaver in cleaning and polishing wood floors in traffic areas of house. Cleaning wax dissolves dirt and leaves a protective coating on floors; a little buffing brings up shine.

**Removing Heavy Soil, Old Wax.** Wear household gloves to protect hands; make sure the room is well ventilated to disperse fumes. Pour a little turpentine or dry-cleaning fluid on floor; rub with steel wool. With large cloth, wipe up soil and cleaner before going on to adjoining area. Continue until you have removed all old wax and soil. *Caution:* turpentine is flammable.

### Linoleum

**Cleaning and Care.** Use a mild soap, or detergent, and water; strong soaps contain an alkali that is damaging to linoleum oils. Be sure to follow the manufacturer's directions for the proper maintenance of their products. A coat of wax periodically will be protective and make for easier cleaning.

## Asphalt Tile

**Cleaning and Care.** Special cleaners are available for asphalt tile. It is not resistant to solvents in polishing type waxes; therefore, only a water-emulsion wax should be used, not a paste. A wax finish is recommended to keep down scuff marks and to maintain the original finish.

Standard tile is not greaseproof, but there are special grease-resisting varieties for kitchen use.

## Cork Tile

**Care and Cleaning.** Although the resins fuse to present a smooth surface, cork has natural minute pockets that can catch dirt unless the floor is kept well waxed. Twice a year use a heavy-duty wax, in between apply a lighter type. Do not use caustic or alkaline soaps or floor oils—instead use the manufacturer's own cleaning products—and avoid flooding floor. Because cork is susceptible to indentation and sharp edges protect it from damage by using furniture rests and cups under heavy furniture. A cigarette burn can be sandpapered out.

## Rubber Tile

**Care and Cleaning.** Rubber tile sheds dirt easily, so care is a simple matter: sweeping, an occasional washing with a mild cleanser, and waxing are all that is needed. A special cleaner is available for rubber-tile floors. Be sure to use a water-emulsion wax. Chemical solvents in a paste-type may damage some brands of rubber tile. Spilled ink and other usually stubborn stains may be wiped off easily.

## Plastic Flooring

**Care and Cleaning.** Dirt never seems to become ground in on a plastic floor, so it does not need hard scrubbing. It may be washed with any kind of packaged soap or detergent. Rubber-heel marks may be removed by rubbing them with a moistened steel-wool soap pad, then with a damp cloth. It is wise to keep a plastic floor waxed to enrich colors and luster and to act as a barrier against dirt. Make a special point of not overwaxing a plastic floor; the surface may become slippery, and scuff marks or actual discoloration from the wax may spoil the floor's appearance.

## Clay Tile

**Cleaning and Care.** Clay tile floors are seldom a problem, particularly when they're glazed. They are proof against almost any kind of wear and tear. Liquids can be mopped up with a paper towel. Tracked-in dirt can be removed by just a simple washing with soap, detergent, or cleanser (and a thorough drying). Even old stains and accumulated dirt don't call for hard scrubbing—they usually come off readily with a cleanser or fine steel wool.

## General Cleaning Instructions for Nonwood Floors

Wash floor, using warm water and soap or detergent. (For asphalt tile and rubber tile, use special cleaners.) When floor is clean and dry, pour pool of self-polishing wax onto floor; dip damp lamb's-wool applicator into wax, and spread over floor with straight, even strokes. Overlap strokes as you proceed, but do not retrace or scrub back and forth. Allow 20 to 30 minutes for wax to dry thoroughly.

**Removing Rubber-Heel Marks.** Moisten steel-wool soap pad; use to rub off marks.

**Removing Heavy Soil and Old Wax from Nonwood Floors.** Mix ¾ cup of concentrated floor cleaner with 1 gallon of water. Heat until steaming hot; keep hot over low heat. Pour about ½ cup at a time on the floor; spread around; let stand for a minute or so. Then scrub with stiff brush or fine steel wool. Wipe up loosened wax and dirt before cleaning next section of floor. When entire floor is clean, rinse well with warm water and let dry before rewaxing. (In small kitchens, half the quantity recommended here may be sufficient.)

## An Ounce of Prevention

Much of the work of keeping floors clean can be eliminated if you will protect the areas which receive the greatest wear or on which water or other liquids may be splashed.

Place mats at all entrances to prevent shoes from carrying in their accumulation of moisture, dust, and dirt from the street. Doormats may be of cork, metal links, rubber, plastic, wood, or other material. The important thing to remember is that they must be kept clean if they are to give your floors maximum protection. You may also use floor mats in front of the sink, washing machine, and tub, and alongside baby's bathinette. An extra piece of linoleum over a linoleum floor is inconspicuous, but serves the purpose.

If you have a sick child in the house, place a mat by the side of the bed to guard against accidents.

If food or other matter is spilled on your floor, wipe it up promptly and chances are all traces of it will be removed. Spots that have been allowed to harden often need to be scraped and may leave a discoloration. Crumbs may be tracked into another room and ground into a rug or carpet. A few seconds spent with a sponge or a broom and dustpan may save many minutes of scrubbing and vacuuming.

# CLEANING RUGS AND CARPETS

**Quick Cleaning.** Use carpet sweeper or junior-size vacuum cleaner to do speedy job of picking up surface dirt, lint, dog hairs, crumbs, etc., between weekly vacuumings. A carpet sweeper should be emptied frequently, and string and hair tangled around brush snipped with scissors and removed.

**Vacuuming.** To keep your carpets at peak of cleanliness, give them a going over every day. Two or 3 strokes of vacuum cleaner over each area will freshen and brighten them. However, once (or perhaps twice) a week does a good job. Ten or 15 minutes is not too much time to spend on a 9′ x 12′ rug.

If you have an upright cleaner, move it across carpet with slow, even strokes, giving revolving brush a chance to bounce out dirt down in pile. Finish by running vacuum with lay of pile, to prevent light and dark areas or ruffling of pile.

If your cleaner is a tank or canister type, use rug nozzle provided. This type of cleaner is particularly good for looped or shaggy rugs and carpeting, since it operates on a direct-suction principle.

A new rug should be vacuumed the same as any other. You may find a lot of fluff in your vacuum bag after cleaning a new rug. Loose fibers that cannot be removed during manufacture keep coming to the surface for several months; a vacuum cleaner is the best way to remove them.

Your vacuum cleaner should be emptied often; when it becomes too full, it slows cleaning.

**Cleaning Stair Carpeting.** A junior-size vacuum cleaner is good for cleaning stair carpeting. Using care to keep from pulling cleaner off steps, clean thoroughly with floor attachment at least once a week.

## Home Cleaning

**Wool and Wool Blends.** There are 3 methods for cleaning the surface of rugs and carpets at home—the suds or shampoo method, the powder method, and the dry-cleaning fluid method. Though valuable for freshening and touching up rugs between professional cleanings, when used to do a thorough job all 3 methods involve not only the cost of the supplies, but a great deal of time, inconvenience, and hard work. Moreover, such rug cleaning by home methods is a compromise at best.

**The Shampoo or Suds Method.** Vacuum rug or carpet thoroughly. Then, with brush or sponge, rub shampoo suds into area of about 1 square foot at a time. (One make of vacuum cleaner has attachment for shampooing rugs with a foam cleaner.) Finish by stroking nap to lay smooth; let dry undisturbed.

**The Rug-Cleaning Powder Method.** Vacuum rug or carpet thoroughly. Sprinkle rug-cleaning powder over a section of the rug about 4 feet square (laying newspaper under edges of rug first is a good idea). With long-handled brush, using a crisscross motion, scrub powder into nap of rug. Repeat process on adjoining area; continue until entire rug is covered. Let powder stand a few hours or overnight, then run vacuum cleaner over rug until all traces of powder have disappeared.

This treatment will revive the color of your rugs and the liveliness of the nap; however, don't expect it to remove heavy, neglected soil or eliminate the eventual need for professional cleaning.

**The Cleaning Fluid Method.** Vacuum rug or carpet thoroughly. Dip long-handled rug eraser into pan of cleaning fluid; shake to remove surplus. Then rub eraser over rug, one section at a time, following direction of weave. (If rug underlay is foam rubber, make sure cleaning fluid does not come in contact with it.)

**Home Cleaning of Cotton Rugs.** Small scatter rugs weighing not more than 5 pounds can be washed in a home washing machine. (In some machines it is necessary to balance one rug with a bathmat or bath towels.) Dry in tumble dryer (if rug is rubber backed, use low heat if possible) or on line (shake well to bring up nap). Send large rugs to commercial laundry or rug cleaner. *Note:* Special products for home cleaning of cotton and synthetic rugs help if rugs are not heavily soiled.

**Stains.** Whenever possible, stains should be removed promptly. Old or dried stains are often impossible to remove. See "Spot and Stain Removal," page 262, for information concerning specific stains.

## Professional Cleaning of Rugs and Carpets

Write to one of following sources for names of rug cleaners in your community who can give the kind of specialized care your floor coverings need:

National Institute of Rug Cleaning, Silver Spring, Maryland.

The Carpet Institute, Inc., 350 Fifth Avenue, New York, N. Y.

The Tufted Textile Manufacturers Assn., Dalton, Georgia.

## Treat Rugs and Carpets Promptly

If your rugs and carpets need a thorough cleaning, whether you plan to do it yourself or call in a professional cleaner, don't put it off. The longer dirt has to set, the harder it is to remove.

# RUG-CLEANING CHART

| TYPE OF RUG | CLEANING | SPOTTING |
|---|---|---|
| **COTTON** rugs come in all colors and sizes, in both tufted and woven pile. They often have rubber backing. Light colors soil readily and need frequent cleaning. | Tank or canister-type vacuum is best for looped or tufted cotton rugs. To keep colors clean, wash frequently. Wash small sizes in home washer. Send large rugs to commercial laundry or rug-cleaning establishment. Do not dry-clean rubber-backed rugs. | Don't try to spot-clean long-looped cotton-pile rugs. Short-pile or woven cotton rugs can often be spot-cleaned with detergent suds or a rug shampoo. |
| **ALL-WOOL** rugs and carpets of high quality are long-wearing, highly soil and crush-resistant. Colors are usually rather subdued. One make, Olson, is reversible. | Vacuum *thoroughly* from week to week, and clean with a rug powder or shampoo periodically. (See directions on previous page.) Send rug out for professional cleaning once a year. | All-wool rugs are easiest of all to spot-clean. Try detergent suds first. Let dry. If spot remains, sponge with grease-dissolving solvent. |
| **ALL-SYNTHETIC AND BLENDS** of synthetic-and-wool rugs have strong colors and generally cost less than wool of same weight. They wear well but tend to crush. | Clean same as wool rugs; however, all-synthetic rugs may need more frequent periodic cleaning. Because of special treatment, newer synthetic yarns have greatly increased soil resistance. | Spot-clean same as all-wool rugs. |
| **WALL-TO-WALL** carpets are cotton, all-wool, blends, or all-synthetic—woven or tufted 9′ to 18′ in width. The use of smooth-edge tackless installation simplifies care. | Clean same as all-wool rugs, but yearly cleaning will be more troublesome. Carpeting must either be cleaned on the floor by a reliable professional, or it must be taken up in order to be sent out. | Wall-to-wall carpets of cotton usually have a short pile, and if so can be spot-cleaned like all-wool rugs. |
| **FIBER RUGS** are woven in many designs, are frequently reversible, highly resistant to soiling, and can be used year round. They're a good value for little money. | Vacuum regularly, and shampoo periodically. | Spot-clean same as all-wool rugs, but the smooth, hard surface of fiber rugs is more difficult to spot-clean. |
| **ORIENTAL RUGS** are hand-woven, made in the Orient. They're rich in color and design. | Vacuum regularly, and send out for professional cleaning when necessary. Some Orientals have a high luster because of their finish. After washing, water-soluble finishes must be replaced with a sheen-producing resin. | Spot-clean same as for all-wool rugs, but spot-cleaned area may be dulled by treatment with suds if the rug has a high luster. |
| **RUG UNDERLAYS.** For longer rug life and more luxurious feel underfoot, use rug underlays beneath all except fiber and reversible rugs. | **HAIR** — Rug underlays made of hair are available in three weights—the difference being in thickness and price. When you take up a rug, clean the underlay by vacuuming it gently. | |
| | **RUBBER** — Underlays made of rubber, sometimes sponge rubber, are unusually soft. Rug cushions should measure about three inches less, both in length and width, than rug. | |

# DYEING FIBER RUGS

**When Does a Rug Need Dyeing?** Perhaps you have a fiber rug in your home that you have been unhappy with for a long time. Either the color has worn off, or it is not right for your decorating scheme. Why not consider dyeing it?

If you have been looking for a rug for your recreation room or for your children's play room, you may be able to find a discarded fiber rug in your attic or basement. Give it another life by dyeing it a bright new color. You will find that it fills your needs beautifully.

Dingy, faded fiber rugs can be dyed easily and successfully. Dyeing them is really more satisfactory than painting them as the dye penetrates the fibers, so the job lasts longer. If you paint them, the paint has a tendency to scuff off in a comparatively short time. Also, paint frequently rubs off on shoes and clothing—an important thing to remember if the rug is to be used where children may sit on the floor.

Fiber rugs are made of various materials, but most today are woven of Kraft fiber, with a smooth surface. This type of fiber rug dyes best.

The dye is available in ten shades: one shade of blue, various shades of gray, green, red, and brown. One quart of the dye is usually enough to do one 9' x 12' rug but you may wish to use more, particularly if the original color of the rug was much lighter than the color you are planning to dye it.

Before you start the actual dyeing operation, vacuum the rug well; then since dirt sifts through most fiber rugs, vacuum both sides, as well as the floor beneath. Remove all grease spots with a good spot remover because the dye cannot penetrate through grease.

Put several thicknesses of newspaper under the rug, and extending beyond its edges. Be sure to wear household gloves during the actual dyeing as it is difficult to remove the dye from your skin.

There are 2 methods of applying the dye. The brush-on method is described in the directions that come with the dye; it calls for mixing the dye with hot water and then brushing it onto the rug with broad, sweeping strokes. The spray-on method uses the sprayer jar of your vacuum cleaner. Mix the dye with the hot water the same as for the brush-on method, pay it into the sprayer jar, and spray the rug evenly. Shake the jar often to keep the dye well mixed. The spray-on method can be used with greater safety out-of-doors where there is less danger of your spraying something on which you don't want to get the dye color.

*Caution:* Be sure you know how to spray with your vacuum sprayer before you put the dye into the jar. Experiment with plain hot water first.

# CLEANING WALLS

**Painted Walls and Woodwork.** (Glossy, semiglossy, or washable flat paints.) Use paint cleaner—liquid, powder, or paste—best suited for the job. Prepared liquid cleaner, used straight from the bottle is most convenient for small jobs such as washing around light switches and doorknobs. If you are washing down an entire room, use a solution made from powder or paste.

If you plan to wash the ceiling, do it first so you won't smear walls. Wash walls *beginning at bottom and working up* to avoid streaks. Use a large cloth or sponge, well moistened but not too full of cleaning solution. Clean small area with circular motion, then rinse before dirt resettles. Dry with clean cloth (old bath towels are best). Then move to next area, overlapping previously cleaned area by a few inches.

*Note:* Flat paints vary in their resistance to washing. Some cannot be washed satisfactorily and must be repainted.

**Washable Wallpaper or Fabric Wall Covering.**
*Wallpaper Cleaner Method:* See "Nonwashable Wallpaper."

*Detergent Method:* Wring cloth or sponge out of detergent suds; wipe wallpaper gently. Rinse thoroughly with clear water. Fabric wall covering can take more moisture and harder scrubbing than paper, but rub no harder than necessary. To remove grease spots, apply a paste made of fuller's earth and cleaning fluid. Apply paste in thin coat (no more than ¼" thick), and let it dry. When paste is dry, remove by brushing with soft brush or cloth.

**Nonwashable Wallpaper.** Knead doughlike wallpaper cleaner into a large ball, and use it like a soft eraser. Wipe wallpaper from top to bottom, in one direction only. Use firm, sweeping strokes; as you work, fold soiled surface of pliable cleaner to inside, exposing clean surface.

*Reminder:* Wall cleaning is a hard job. If walls are dusted frequently, cleaning can be delayed for a long time. The dusting attachment of a vacuum cleaner is the best way to keep walls free from dust. However, a soft-bristled wall brush or a lamb's-wool duster will do an excellent job, too.

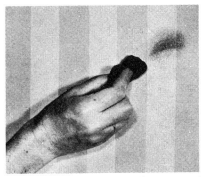

*Average dirt spots can be removed with a doughlike wallpaper cleaner. When the cleaner is rubbed lightly against the paper, dirt adheres to it. When it gets soiled, work it in your hand so that a clean part comes to the surface.*

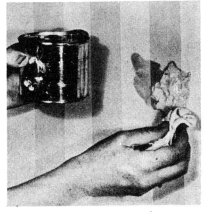

*Fuller's earth mixed with spot remover to make a stiff paste removes oil and grease spots. Apply a ¼"-thick coat over the spot and let it remain overnight.*

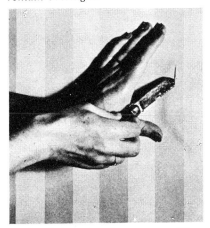

*Slit bulges in the paper with a razor or sharp knife and insert library paste. Press the paper flat with a soft, clean cloth. When paste is dry, wipe away excess with damp sponge.*

## Cleaning and Repairing Wallpaper

Wallpaper is so fresh-looking and attractive when it is new that it is worth while to do everything you can to retain its charm. The success of this depends to a large degree upon the quality of the paper you buy. But it also depends on the amount of care it receives. Proper cleaning and prompt repair will keep your wallpaper looking better longer.

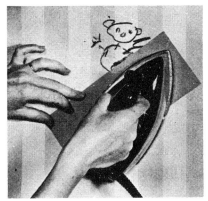

*Some crayon marks and grease spots can be removed simply by applying a clean blotter over the spot and pressing it with a warm iron. If the first blotter gets soiled, replace it with a clean one.*

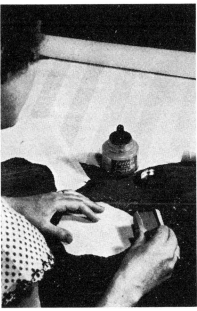

*Or you may find it easier to use one of the special wallpaper cleaning compounds, which are sold by most paint, hardware, and department stores. Follow directions on container.*

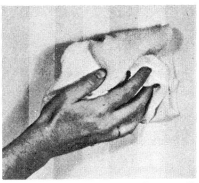

*Before cleaning or washing wallpaper, wipe off loose dirt and dust with a soft cloth or vacuum-cleaner dusting attachment. Washable papers can be cleaned with warm, sudsy water. Test all papers in an obscure part before washing.*

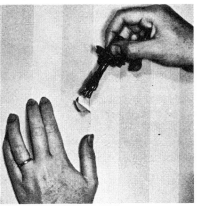

*When wallpaper becomes loose or torn at a seam, apply ordinary library paste or rubber cement to make it adhere again. Then press the spot lightly with a clean blotter until the paste is dry.*

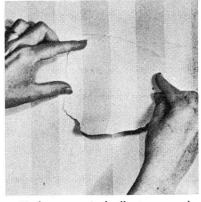

*If the paper is badly torn or defaced, tear a patch from matching paper, repeating the design of the worn area. Do not cut. Sharp edges are difficult to conceal.*

# CLEANING WINDOWS, MIRRORS, AND OTHER GLASS SURFACES

### Cleaning Methods for All Glass Surfaces

**The Spray Way.** Spray window cleaner in fairly uniform way over surface. Use large dry, lintless cloth to remove cleaner and polish glass.

**The Cream-Polish Way.** Use creamy window cleaner. Shake can; apply cream polish to slightly dampened sponge. Spread cleaner over glass; let it dry. When cleaner is dry, wipe off with soft, clean cloth.

**The Cleaning-Powder Way.** Use powdered or caked window cleaner. Apply thin film with moist cloth. When film is *almost* dry, polish it with a clean, dry cloth.

**The Cloth Way.** Wring out treated cloth or chamois in warm water, use it to wipe surface. If you are using chamois, add ammonia to water—1 tablespoon to each quarter of water.

### How to Make Your Windows Shine

**Wash Windows Often.** Window cleaning is not nearly so back-breaking a chore if you do it often, at regular intervals, before too much dust and grime settle on the panes and sills.

**Use a Sturdy Stepstool.** A good stepstool is an excellent help in reaching all parts of the windows when cleaning them.

**Do Window Frames First.** Before you wash your windows, clean the window frames. Dust them first; then wash them, using a liquid paint cleaner and a cellulose sponge. By this method you can get rid of soil without mixing the cleaner with water, as you would have to do with a powdered cleaner. Moisten the sponge with the cleaner, and rub it over the soiled

*It's quick and easy to spray windows with one hand, wipe dry with the other. Wash windows frequently.*

spots. Give the cleaner a little time to soften the dirt and dissolve grease, and you won't have to scrub or scour. Many of these cleaners do not need rinsing.

Treating window sills with wax is an excellent idea, because it prevents their becoming stained from rain spots. So when the window sills are completely dry, treat them with a liquid or paste wax of the polishing type or with a furniture polish with a wax base. Apply wax with a soft, clean cloth, in a light film. Let it dry; then buff until it has a bright, hard finish.

**What About the Outside?** Ground-floor windows offer no problem, but cleaning the outside panes of windows on higher elevations is not so simple, because only rarely can you reach far enough without taking chances. It is better to rely on a window-cleaning service than to risk falls or exposure to weather. To cut costs, get an estimate on cleaning only the outside of windows, and tackle the inside yourself.

**Cleaning Picture Windows.** There's more to cleaning picture windows than merely washing great expanses of glass. It's necessary to find a way of reaching the high sections safely. When working from the inside, use a kitchen stepstool that has wide, nonslip treads, to insure firm footing. But unless the window adjoins a terrace (on which you can use a stepstool), the outside work must be done from the ground. If the area in front of the window contains bushes and shrubs, it can be a real problem. The solution is a stepladder and two short planks. Place the planks on the ground to provide a level surface for the ladder and turn the ladder sideways beside the window (as you would to hang curtains). If a shrub or bush interferes, let the ladder straddle it. With the ladder set, climb up with your equipment. Clean the window; check the job from the inside; remove streaks missed the first time.

**Keep Your Window Screens Clean.** Window screens collect dirt and dust rapidly. When it rains, the dirt from the screens is splashed on your windows. For this reason, it is a good idea to clean your screens regularly. Use any stiff hand brush or the small brush attachment on your vacuum cleaner. Your windows will stay much cleaner longer.

### Cleaning Cloudy Glass Vases, Pitchers, Cruets

To remove cloudiness and mineral-deposit stains, fill vessel with hot detergent suds plus 2 or 3 tablespoonfuls of water conditioner. Let stand several hours; rinse. To loosen sediment, use stiff-bristled bottle brush.

# CLEANING BLINDS, SHADES, AND DRAPERIES

### Cleaning Venetian Blinds

**Dusting.** Frequent and thorough dusting of Venetian blinds is the best way to postpone the need for wet cleaning. The round-brush tool of a vacuum cleaner does the best dusting job, but a special flat Venetian-blind brush that dusts a slat or two at a time is the next best means. Lower the blind full length, and draw the slats tight. As you move the brush over the blinds, separate the slats, to clean overlapping areas. Then tilt the blinds in the opposite direction, and repeat.

**Washing.** Venetian blinds must be washed occasionally to remove the greasy film that settles on the slats. Use detergent-suds or paint-cleaning solution. Wipe off slats, one at a time, on both sides, with a small cellulose sponge tightly wrung out of the cleaning solution.

Venetian blinds should be treated with liquid wax and polished, to protect the surface.

*Metal blinds:* Metal blinds may be soaked to remove accumulated dirt. Remove the tacks that hold the tapes at the bottom of the blind to see how the cords are fastened. Often they're knotted, and untying the knot frees them. Or they may be fastened to metal clips that can be pried loose. When the cords are unfastened, pull them up and out of the slats, letting them dangle from the head of the blind. Then slip the slats out of the crosspieces of the blind tapes, on which they rest. To wash the slats, place them in a laundry tub, or if they are too long, use the bathtub, half filling it with hot water and adding a few sprinkles of dishwashing or laundering detergent. Let the slats soak a few minutes, and if necessary, give each one a quick rub with a sponge as you remove it from the tub.

Metal slats are so flexible that propping them up to dry is rather awkward. A plastic shell for drying stockings is perfect for handling the slats. Slip as many of them into the narrow slots as the shell will hold, and let them hang to drip for a few minutes. Then wipe them dry.

Replacing the slats in the blind is an exact reversal of removing them, except that the cords have to be threaded in a certain way. Begin by slipping each slat onto its two crosspieces on the tapes. When they are all in place, pull the cords down through the slats. The trick is to thread each cord so that it runs on one side of the first (or top) crosspiece, on the opposite side of the next crosspiece, and so forth. Start the right-hand cord on the right side of the top crosspiece, the left-hand cord on the left.

**Changing the Tapes.** You can use a liquid cleaner for sponging off the tapes, too. This will help remove light surface soil, but don't expect a miracle. If cotton Venetian-blind tapes are grimy, no amount of sponging is effective; but you can replace worn and soiled tapes with plastic tapes. The directions are simple, the colors lovely, and you'll find the cleaning future bright—merely wiping the tapes with a sudsy cloth will keep them spotless.

### Cleaning Window Shades

In cleaning very soiled window shades, success depends on whether or not they are washable. Unless you know they are washable, do not attempt to clean them with water. Washable shades should be removed from the window and unrolled on a flat surface such as a table top. Using a circular motion, clean the shade with a cloth or sponge wrung out of warm detergent suds. Wipe off the suds with a damp cloth wrung out of clean, cool water. Work on a small area at a time, overlapping each area. Wash shade on both sides. It must be hung to dry before rerolling.

The only way to improve the appearance of nonwashable shades is to lay them flat and erase the dirt with a dough-type cleaner or an art-gum eraser. Work with light strokes, and do not expect too much from the treatment. It will remove light soil only and cannot be expected to remove spots and stains. Window pulls can be washed or replaced.

### Window Draperies

Don't skip the draperies when you are in a hurry because they don't look as though they need dusting. A few minutes each week spent going over your draperies with the drapery tool of your vacuum cleaner will postpone an expensive dry-cleaning job and make the draperies last longer.

### Bamboo Draperies

Modern split bamboo draperies will keep their appearance a long time with just routine dusting. When they require further cleaning, merely wipe with a damp cloth. Do not attempt to submerge bamboo draperies in water—they may warp and be absolutely ruined.

Cotton cords that have become soiled from handling may be removed from bamboo draperies and washed. Make a diagram indicating exactly how they are attached in order to simplify replacement of the cords. Then put them back in just the same way.

## Taking Care of the Fireplace

**Cleaning Brass Andirons, Tools.** For brass andirons to be decorative and lend charm to a fireplace, constant effort is needed to preserve their shining luster. Scour blackened areas with a household cleanser until the soot is gone. If a heavy crust has formed, considerable rubbing and scouring are needed. When the brass is free and clean, pour a little metal polish on a soft, damp cloth; rub onto brass. Before polish dries completely, rub with a dry cloth.

**Cleaning the Hearth (Brick, Tile, Stone).** Brush off loose dust; scrub with stiff brush and solution of paint cleaner made according to label directions. No need to rinse. Wipe dry; then apply thin coating of any kind of floor wax (polish or self-polishing) to make hearth soil-resistant.

**Cleaning the Outdoor Grill.** Take removable wire grids to sink or laundry tub; quickly scour clean with steel-wool scouring pad moistened in water. Rinse grids; dry well with paper toweling. To clean permanent cast-iron grids and other parts of fireplace grills, scrub with stiff wire brush and plenty of hot suds. Rinse with pails of water, or hose off suds.

## Your Personal Objects of Art

**Valuable Crystal, Glassware, and Fine Ceramics,** such as porcelain dinnerware or a Meissen figurine, require unhurried, careful washing. To reduce the risk of chipping such pieces, use a rubber sink liner or a heavy bath towel to line the sink or dishpan. Wash one piece at a time in warm, sudsy water. Your regular dishwashing detergent will remove accumulated dust and banish the dull film from the inside of vases, making them sparkling and sweet-smelling again. Embossed and cut surfaces, filigree, and scrollwork can be cleaned best with a soft brush. Gently, but firmly, push the bristles into hard-to-clean corners. Don't use a cleanser on fine old pieces; the detergent will do the job and not endanger the glaze or painting. Rinse them well, and let them dry on the drainboard so there will be a minimum of handling.

**Ceramics** that are hand-painted or are crazed (covered with tiny cracks) should not be immersed in water. Clean them by wiping them gently with a damp cloth.

**Sculpture of Marble or of Other Nonporous Stone** can be scrubbed gently with a soft brush and warm suds. But the object should be rinsed and dried well. Cleaning solutions left on unpolished stone sometimes darken it.

**Paintings** can (and should) be dusted by a light brushing with absorbent cotton or a soft brush, but any other cleaning, brightening, or restoration work should be turned over to a professional painting restorer.

**Glass-Framed Pictures.** Clean the glass with a window cleaner that can be sprayed or wiped on and off. Keep the cleaner away from the wooden part of the frame, which should only be dusted.

## Lamps, Bulbs, and Bases

Rather than take the time to remove the shades and dust the lamp bulbs each time you clean, let them go a few weeks and then wash them. (The job should not be delayed too long, though, because a coating of dust on the bulbs reduces the amount of light in the room.) To wash a bulb, remove it from the lamp; hold it by the metal end; dip it into warm suds. Rinse and dry it carefully before replacing it in the socket. Lamp bases, too, need to be washed occasionally. Never immerse a lamp in water. Just wipe the base with a cloth that has been rinsed in sudsy water and then wrung tightly. To expedite the cleaning, carry a tray with the cloth and cleaning solution from room to room.

**Fabric Lampshades** are a problem to clean, because they don't take kindly to sponging and spots cannot be removed without leaving ugly rings. However, in most cases they respond to real shampooing. But before you start, make sure the lampshade is truly washable. *If you decide to take the risk:*

Examine the shade to see if seams are stitched and trimming is sewed on. If they are glued, soap and water will loosen them. A fabric shade with a paper-parchment lining should not be shampooed; it will buckle out of shape. Don't rule out all lampshades with glued bindings or trimmings. If you have patience, you can replace the trimmings after washing or buy new ones.

Work quickly. Fill a large container, preferably a laundry tub, with clear, lukewarm water. Add a generous amount of mild soap or detergent and whip up a rich suds. Hold shade by top of fixture, and plunge it up and down in the suds. Don't indulge in hard scrubbing. If spots show up, they can be rubbed very gently with a soft-bristle brush.

Rinse the shade thoroughly in at least two tubfuls of lukewarm water. Then pat it with a clean bath towel or cellulose sponge until it no longer drips.

Don't be discouraged if the lampshade looks somewhat bedraggled. As it dries, it usually comes back to shape. For quick drying, turn your electric fan straight on the shade, or hang it in a shady spot, where it can swing in the breeze.

**Parchment Lampshades.** Genuine-parchment and paper-parchment shades resist soil and can be sponged off with a damp cloth and rinsed with a cloth wrung out of clear water. General cleaners in liquid form that work on painted surfaces are fine, too, for cleaning paper, parchment, and paper-and-fabric shades. Don't get the shades completely wet.

### Exposed Radiators

If the radiator tool on your vacuum cleaner doesn't slip between the sections handily enough to draw the dust into the cleaner effectively, the blower end can be used to good advantage. Place newspapers beneath and behind the radiator; then use the radiator tool to blow the dust downward onto the papers. The suction end of the cleaner will pick up the dirt.

### Radio and Television Sets

Constant handling of all the knobs on radio and television sets leaves smeary fingerprints. A regular cleaning with a quick-polishing furniture cream makes short work of removing dust and smudges.

### How to Make a Bed

Turn the mattress (except foam rubber) at least once a week, and don't forget a well-fitting mattress pad for both protection and comfort. Smooth it out, and it will fill in the tuft hollows and make the sleeper more comfortable. You have now laid the foundation for a well-made bed.

Now put on the bottom sheet. Tuck it under the foot of the mattress, turning under a good 10 to 12 inches. Keep this tuck-under very even, so the sheet will be even at the top. Now pull the sheet smooth and as tight as you can at the top, and tuck snugly under the mattress. Do not be afraid to tug a bit—it will make the sheet taut and smooth, which is the secret of comfort. Now start on the mitered corners.

To make a mitered corner, first grasp the hanging-over portion of the sheet and fold it back over the top of the bed in a diagonal line. This leaves a section hanging at the side, which you must fold under the mattress. Then bring back the fold now lying on top of the bed, and tuck it tightly under the mattress. The result—a neat and tailored bed.

Top sheet is put on the bed in much the same way —that is, you must have the same amount of tuck-in at the foot. You will have a nice, generous turndown to cover the top of the blanket. This keeps the blanket clean, and it is easy on the sleeper's arms. The blanket should come almost to the top of the bed, so that it will cover the shoulders of the sleeper. Miter the corners at foot.

To tuck or not to tuck at sides is the next question to decide. Some like the tight, sleeping-bag effect, while others like the blankets hanging down loosely at the sides. And there are some who are annoyed if the top sheet is put on too tightly. So spoil your family and have their beds made as they like them.

To make a bed look inviting, fit the spread over the pillows. Make a crease through the center of the pillow with your arm out straight, and roll it over in half. Place it on the turned-down portion of the spread, and roll it back into its position on the bed, where it will cuddle into shape straight and smooth. Now you may put comforter or blanket at the foot of the bed if you wish.

It's up to you to decide what added protection and added warmth of a third sheet on top of the blanket are worth, considering the extra time and extra laundering it requires. When turning down the beds for the night, remove spread, plump up pillows and turn back the blankets and top sheet across the bed.

**Considering Fitted Sheets?** Contour sheets can now be purchased in sizes to fit any standard bed. They require less time for bedmaking, they are neat, and they need no ironing. In addition to standard long-wearing cotton, they come woven and knit in blends of quick-drying, man-made fibers like nylon and acetate. Be sure the fitted sheet you buy has been treated to control shrinkage; since the corners of fitted sheets receive the greatest strain, see that they are well seamed so they will not tear easily.

# SEASONAL HOUSEKEEPING

## Spring Cleaning

Spring cleaning is no longer the major overhaul it used to be, thanks to timesaving appliances and products. Nowadays, seasonal cleaning is supplementary cleaning—a sprucing up of furnishings, floors, and the house in general. If you know how to perform such jobs safely and effectively, you have a sound investment in your belongings.

Do your cleaning room by room, and before you know it the whole house will shine. But don't grab a pail, a mop, and a broom with the idea you are ready to plunge right in. Take stock of what you are going to do and what you are going to need. Is your vacuum cleaner in perfect shape? It should have a full set of attachments for high and low cleaning. Do you know about the latest in cleaning supplies? There are special cleaners for nearly every job. Take a trip to your hardware or housewares store. Make sure you have cleaners for windows, rugs, paint—and don't forget that you will need plenty of soft, absorbent cloths for washing, wiping, waxing, etc.

Then make up your mind about the plan you are going to follow, but don't let ambition run away with you. You can clean, and clean well, without driving yourself. Space your jobs over a period of time. Call on a handyman, if needed, or ask your husband to pitch in.

## Summer Housekeeping

The middle of the summer is no time for inspired housekeeping. Try to escape the hot, tiring jobs.

**Screens.** Be sure your screens are clean and in good condition before you put them up. Treat screens with an insecticide containing from 3 to 5 per cent DDT. It should be sprayed or brushed evenly on the screens. If this is done periodically, the DDT will kill insects that might otherwise creep in. If you want to replace your screens, consider not only copper and brass but plastic and aluminum. Plastic screening, like aluminum, can be left up the year round.

**The Garbage Problem.** The summer's heat, humidity, and insects make prompt garbage disposal necessary. Without doubt, a garbage-disposal unit is the ideal way to get rid of waste foods. But if you do not have one, use wax-treated, moisture-resistant bags to simplify handling garbage and help keep the inside garbage container clean and free from odor. Suburban families that have a large, outside garbage receptacle find the containers need an occasional scrubbing, even though the garbage is carefully wrapped. Use a household disinfectant, according to directions on the label, to clean and freshen the container.

**Fans for Greater Comfort.** During a heat wave the breeze set up by the familiar oscillating fan adds to comfort. Enclosed air circulators are quiet, portable, lightweight, and diffuse the air without gusty drafts. To cool the house at night, place a large ventilating fan in the attic. It discharges accumulated heat and lowers the temperature from 5 to 20 degrees. Fans that were stored during the winter may need cleaning and oiling. Take them to an electrical shop for servicing, if necessary.

**Cool the Air for More Comfort.** If you live where the weather is extremely hot and sultry, only air conditioning can do a thoroughly effective cooling job. The house temperature can be controlled by air-conditioning equipment located in the basement or utility room. Ducts distribute the air at suitable temperatures for summer cooling or winter comfort. If you want only one room—bedroom or living room, for

*The baby's plastic toys need cleansing. Give them all a good washing.*

*Frayed edges on your rugs and carpets? Cover with iron-on rug tape.*

*Fingerprints on your walls? Wipe them with liquid paint cleaner.*

*Difficult-to-dust areas are easy with a hand vacuum cleaner. Use one.*

*Nothing's gayer in closets than plastic shelving. And it can be wiped of*

example—cooled, consider a mechanical room cooler, which fits into a partly opened window and operates from a convenience outlet. Larger room-cooling units for greater cooling needs also are available, although special electrical and often extra plumbing facilities are required. With or without air cooling, heavy rugs and draperies make a room seem warmer. The beginning of the summer is a good time to send them to the cleaner's for cleaning and storage.

### Closing the House for the Summer

There always seem to be a number of small jobs to attend to when you are closing a house, even though you expect to be gone for only a short time. The following list may serve as a handy reminder of things to be done:

1. Before leaving, clean the house thoroughly.
2. Lock and bolt all windows and doors.
3. Lock up valuables.
4. Get rid of perishable food and turn off your refrigerator at outlet. Leave the door open.
5. Suspend delivery of milk, newspapers, etc.
6. Notify the post office to forward mail.
7. Make arrangements for the care of your pets.
8. If possible, ask a neighbor to come in occasionally to air the house and to give added protection against burglary. (Some people like to notify the police if they are going to be away. This is a wise precaution, particularly if your house is isolated.)

### Fall Housecleaning

Even though the old-time annual spring and fall housecleaning days are gone forever, it's nice to spruce up for winter, and there a few cleaning jobs that should be done a special way for best results. Instructions for cleaning rugs and carpets, floors, wood and upholstered furniture, wallpaper and paint,

windows, and other major jobs are given on the preceding pages. Plan what you will have to do, then find the best method to help you work your plan.

### Holiday Housekeeping

**Ready for the Christmas Rush.** There's not much time around Christmas to think about housecleaning. Get the children to pick out toys and books that will mean fun to other children. Have a quick rehearsal of your table settings. Plan your decorations, and don't forget holiday candles—with a bit of greenery, they dress up a table.

**Christmas Greens.** Here's a brief guide to some of the more attractive types of greens. *Fir:* Symmetrical, fragrant, and long-lasting. *Pine:* The long needles give a fuller, bushier appearance than firs or spruces. *Spruce:* Best for outdoor use because it sheds its needles after a few days indoors. *Cedar:* Short scale-like needles. Not very fragrant. Cedar aroma is released only when the wood is cut. *Hemlock:* Needles drop quickly, but makes a handsome outdoor wreath.

**Artificial Trees.** Sizes range from two to eight feet. *Vinyl* are the most realistic-looking. They are fire retardant, won't crush in handling, are easy to store. *Aluminum* trees cannot safely be strung with electric lights. *Metallic vinyl* trees can be strung with lights. Some manufacturers recommend small lights because heat from larger ones may wilt needles. *Viscose* trees are made of a fire-retardant rayon material. Somewhat easily crushed, but steam will restore some of their freshness. *Flocked* trees have needles coated with a white plastic or cotton material which resembles snow. *Brush* trees have limbs that look like bottle brushes.

*When you sweep up the cement basement floor, use a sturdy fiber broom.*  *Beat summer to the punch. Paint garden furniture in spring.*  *Clear off shelf space; bring down your magazines; store in order.*  *Take out harsh-glare bulbs; replace them all with new soft-glow lights.*  *Get some light on the subject. Use spray cleaner on grimy windows.*

# KEEP YOUR HOME FREE FROM INSECTS AND PESTS

This chart includes the most common insects that infest houses in the United States. They have been divided into groups according to the type of damage or annoyance they cause. Some of these pests are definite menaces to health and property; others are mainly annoying. All of them can be controlled if the recommendations are followed carefully.

The chart includes no mention of such wood-destroying insects as termites. We feel that their control can be adequately handled only by professionals. If you have any suspicion that your home is infested with termites, we urge you to seek professional counsel promptly. When professional help is needed for any type of insect control, excellent services are available in all parts of the United States.

Remember: Most effective insecticides are also poisonous to human beings and other warm-blooded animals. So use them and store them with care. Follow the detailed instructions on the label of the insecticide you buy. Take particular care that hands, food, and food-handling surfaces are well protected from any contamination by insecticides, no matter in what form these are used.

It has been possible to list here only the basic insecticides. Many insecticides available today are combinations of ingredients that, together, may do an even more effective job than one ingredient alone in higher concentration. To select the proper insecticide, study the label carefully to make sure the particular use to which you wish to put it is listed.

*DRAWINGS ARE FOR IDENTIFICATION, AND ARE NOT ALWAYS ACTUAL SIZE*

| FOOD-VISITING INSECTS | TYPE OF DAMAGE | METHOD OF CONTROL |
|---|---|---|
| **Housefly**  | Disease carrier (typhoid, dysentery, etc.); annoyance. | Eliminate breeding places when possible. Clean stables, barns, etc., thoroughly at regular intervals. Keep garbage and other refuse tightly covered, and dispose of it frequently. Provide adequate screening, tight-fitting door- and windowframes. Paint screens, window sills, doorsills, and other areas where flies alight or congregate with chlordane, lindane, DDT, terpene polychlorinates, dieldrin, or special formula including one of these. (Some fly strains have become "DDT resistant," so DDT may be ineffective.) Use 5% DDT or .1% lindane as space sprays to kill flies that do get in. |
| **Cockroach**  | Disease carrier; contaminates food; destroys book bindings, paper, and even starched clothing. | Use chlordane or dieldrin, the most effective insecticides for roach control: in liquid form along baseboards and around pipes, risers, and surfaces where roaches nest, run, or hide; chlordane in powder form in cracks and crevices. *Do not use chlordane as a space spray.* Insecticide-treated paper may be used in drawers and cabinets. |
| **Flour Beetle, Meal Moth, Cereal Weevil, etc.**    | Cause waste of otherwise edible foods. (None of these insects are disease carriers or are harmful in any way.) | Practice scrupulous cleanliness in kitchen and pantry. When infestation occurs:<br>1. Discard all packages of infested food.<br>2. Transfer contents of open uninfested packages to screw-top jars.<br>3. Scrub storage shelves thoroughly and spray with DDT, dieldrin or special formula containing one of them. |

| FOOD-VISITING INSECTS | TYPE OF DAMAGE | METHOD OF CONTROL |
|---|---|---|
| **Ant**<br> | Mainly annoyance and contaminator of food. Some species sting or bite. | *Outside the house:* Use chlordane dust directly on ant hills.<br>*Inside the house:* Where there is no danger of contaminating foodstuffs, use chlordane, dieldrin, lindane, DDT liquid or chlordane dust. In proximity to foods, use a pyrethrum or methoxychlor spray. "Ant traps," containing highly poisonous thallium salts, may be used if constructed so that children and pets cannot get at the contents. Insecticide-treated paper may be used in drawers and cabinets. |
| **Pomace Fly<br>(fruit fly)**<br> | Annoyance. | Discard bruised fruits promptly. Use a pyrethrum spray in infested areas. |

## BITING AND SUCKING INSECTS

| | TYPE OF DAMAGE | METHOD OF CONTROL |
|---|---|---|
| **Mosquito**<br> | Some species are disease carriers (malaria, yellow fever). Others are harmless, but cause great discomfort. | Provide adequate 16-mesh screening, tightly fitting door- and windowframes. Paint screens, window sills, doorsills with chlordane, lindane, DDT, terpene polychlorinates, or special formula containing one of these. DDT, dieldrin, or lindane (or special formula containing one of these) may be used as space spray to destroy mosquitoes that do get in. |
| **Bedbug**<br> | May be disease carrier; bite is highly annoying. | Spray mattresses and bedframes thoroughly with DDT or dieldrin. Treat wall cracks and baseboards in infested rooms with DDT or dieldrin in oil or DDT dust. Terpene polychlorinates may also be used. |
| **Flea**<br> | Disease carrier; in one stage of development, host of tapeworm. Bite is highly annoying. | Spray floors of infested houses with DDT, dieldrin, chlordane, or lindane. Treat infested dogs and their sleeping quarters with DDT dust, special lindane dust prepared for dogs, or special aerosol containing lindane. Treat cats and their sleeping quarters with rotenone or pyrethrum dust. |
| **Tick**<br> | Carrier of spotted fever; annoyance to pets, people. | Remove with forceps, being careful not to crush. (This is important! The fluid is dangerous.) Treat dogs with DDT dust, kennels with DDT dust or DDT in oil. |
| **Sand Fly,<br>Gnat**<br> | Annoying bite. | Paint screens, surfaces near light fixtures, with dieldrin, chlordane, lindane, or DDT in oil. |

## FABRIC-DAMAGING INSECTS

| | TYPE OF DAMAGE | METHOD OF CONTROL |
|---|---|---|
| **Clothes Moth,<br>Carpet Beetle**<br>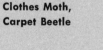 | Destroy clothing and upholstery materials of animal origin—wool, silk, fur, hair, etc. (Damage is caused by larvae, *not* by adult moth.) | Clean clothing, blankets, etc., thoroughly before storing.<br>Use paradichlorbenzene (1 lb. fine crystals per 100 cu. ft.) in storage containers. Keep containers tightly sealed; otherwise vapor will escape and moth-killing powers will be lost. Paradichlorbenzene may also be used in closets if periodically renewed. *NOTE:* Do not let paradichlorbenzene come in contact with vinyl plastics.<br>On clothes use mothproofing sprays containing DDT, methoxychlor, a fluosilicate, perthane, or terpene polychlorinates. Follow label instructions closely for method of application and amount to use. (Remember that laundering and/or dry cleaning may remove mothproofing.) Closets, etc., may also be sprayed with DDT, methoxychlor, perthane, or terpene polychlorinates. |

| FABRIC-DAMAGING INSECTS | TYPE OF DAMAGE | METHOD OF CONTROL |
|---|---|---|
| **Silverfish, Book Louse**  | Damage wallpaper, book bindings, and clothing. | Apply DDT in oil or DDT dust or terpene polychlorinates (or special formula containing one of these) to cracks and crevices. Repeat in 2 weeks if necessary. Insecticide-treated paper may be used in drawers and cabinets. |
| **Cricket**  | Damages any soiled fabric, also clean silk and rayon. | To infested places (usually warm and dark) apply chlordane in oil, DDT in oil, chlordane dust, or DDT dust. |
| **MISCELLANEOUS INSECTS** **Scorpion**  | Has extremely painful sting. | Search premises thoroughly, and destroy by mashing any scorpions found. Close all possible entrance holes from ground. Get rid of possible breeding places near house, such as rocks, decayed wood, etc. Use DDT spray directly on insect. |
| **Centipede**  | Bite may cause severe pain (rare). Otherwise, beneficial insect, since it destroys other insects. | If destruction is desired, mash with foot or use a pyrethrum dust or spray directly on insect, and areas where they have been seen. Keep house free of moist places. |
| **Millipede, Sow Bug**  | Mainly annoyance. Both may attack house plants; sow bugs may damage stored potatoes. | Use dieldrin, chlordane, lindane, or DDT in oil or chlordane or DDT dust in infested areas. (Do not use oil sprays where they may contact house plants.) |
| **Bee, Wasp, Hornet**    | Have painful sting. Some people have a violent allergic response to venom. | Screen ventilators leading to cellars and attic. Spray wasps' and hornets' nests with DDT in oil, or dust with DDT powder. Spray attic screens, windowframes, and walls with DDT in oil. |
| **Spider**  | Bite of black widow is poisonous. Other species only annoying. | Crush egg sacs as well as adult spider. Or use chlordane in oil. Brush away cobwebs. |
| **Cluster Fly, Elm Leaf Beetle**   | Annoyance. | Spray windowframes, doorsills, or other points of entrance with DDT in oil (being careful not to let it touch house plants). Spray congregations of insects on porches or sides of house with DDT. These insects are very difficult to control, particularly if trees are in close proximity to the house. If necessary, seek professional advice. |
| **ANIMALS INFESTING HOUSES** **Mouse, Rat**  | Disease carriers. Rat's bite dangerous and painful. | When possible, seek professional advice on rat-proofing buildings. Use bait containing warfarin. Follow label directions carefully. |
| **Bat**  | Makes annoying night noises, has very objectionable odor. | Block all entrance holes. Scatter flake naphthalene liberally in infested areas. Repeat as necessary. If this fails, secure the services of a professional exterminator. |

# Efficient Layout and Equipment Will Give You More Leisure

The job of meal getting really is three jobs—preparing food, cooking and arranging food for serving, and washing up. Storage cabinets, work counters, and equipment should therefore be placed so as to make three work centers, at which supplies, utensils, and appliances needed for each type of work can be kept together for convenience.

### The Food-Preparation and Mixing Center

The first need is an ample work surface or counter top at least 3′ long (but preferably longer). Cabinets above this work surface should be arranged for storing the things most frequently used in food preparation and mixing operations. In these cabinets one or two step-back shelves for small cans and packages in single rows add to visibility and convenience. Small equipment and gadgets should be stored within easy reach in drawers and compartments below or near the food-preparation counter. Flour and sugar in bulk may be stored at the food-preparation counter. A rack is preferable to drawers for storing knives, spoons, and spatulas. Some food preparation, of course, is most conveniently done at or in the sink, such as washing and preparing vegetables. Small equipment needed for this work should be kept near the sink.

The most satisfactory place for the sink is beneath a window where there is good light and a pleasant view. Two ample drainboards or counters are needed, one on each side of the sink. Needed, too, at the sink is a means of drying dish towels and cloths—a rack or an electrically heated drying compartment beneath a drainboard. The wastepaper basket and refuse can should be kept beneath the sink or drainboard. Near the sink is a good place for storage of vegetables and fruits not kept in the refrigerator. A 2-compartment sink is especially convenient. For example, dishes can be washed in one compartment and racked for draining in the other. A spray head attached to the sink is useful in rinsing dishes after washing and for cleaning vegetables. Most work-saving of all is the electric sink with dishwasher and refuse-disposal unit.

The refrigerator should be placed near the outside entry to the kitchen, at one end of the food-preparation counter, or as near to it as possible, so that perishable foods needed in meal preparation can be taken from the refrigerator without your moving more than a step or two. The refrigerator's door should open away from the counter, so it will not obstruct the counter.

### The Cooking and Serving Center

The principal piece of equipment at this center is the range. Near it should be grouped the pots and pans, small electric appliances, and other utensils and tools used in cooking and arranging food for serving.

Needed here is a work surface or counter at least 2' long—longer if possible—for "dishing up" and arranging food for serving.

Wall cabinets and base cabinets with counter tops provide storage and serving space at the cooking and serving center if placed next to the range, on one side or both sides.

A small cabinet or open shelves above the range, but not over the burners, is a good place to keep such supplies as tea, coffee, and cereals. Hooks below the shelves are convenient for hanging measuring cups and spoons and other small devices needed at the range.

### Dinette or Breakfast Nook

There's an informality about eating meals in the kitchen that many people like. A dinette also saves steps and simplifies the serving of children's meals and hurry-up breakfasts.

If you want an eating place in the kitchen, make room for it in your plans. Don't rob the kitchen of space needed to organize the kitchen work centers well. And don't make your eating place too small and cramped. If you can locate your snack bar strategically between kitchen and dining room you can also use this counter for arranging food for serving.

### Adequate Wiring Is Important

Below is a list of the electrical equipment that will be found in many modern kitchens. You may not have all of it now, but in planning the layout of your kitchen provide space for future purchases of the larger equipment such as a freezer or electric dishwasher. Provide for their wiring, too; alterations afterward are expensive.

An adequate wiring plan is as important as the arrangement of work centers. You will need *enough* outlets placed so you can use an appliance on a work counter wherever convenient—or several appliances at one time, if desired, with elbow room between and without an entangling clutter of connecting cords. In-

dividual outlets should be provided, too, for such equipment as the refrigerator, clock, and wall fan.

An equally important need is *enough wiring circuits*. No matter how many convenience outlets you have, if there are not enough circuits to supply them adequately with electricity, your appliances will not operate with maximum efficiency and economy. A good wiring plan will provide separate circuits for lights, for small appliances, and for larger equipment. Some equipment, such as an electric range, will require heavy-duty circuits or special wiring to meet operating requirements, or building-code or insurance regulations.

| | |
|---|---|
| Light fixtures | Fan |
| Roaster | Coffeemaker |
| Mixer | Refrigerator |
| Toaster | Freezer |
| Range | Clock |
| Disposer | Waffle Iron |
| Dishwasher | Deep Fryer |
| Blender | Broiler-Rotisserie |
| Radio | Electric Frying Pan |

### Suggested Layouts

#### One-Wall Layout

The one-wall arrangement of work centers shown below is basic. However, from a practical angle, this kitchen unit can be "broken" into 2 or 3 centers to fit the space available. In all the diagrams below the figure "1" refers to the food preparation area, "2" to the sink work center, "3" to the cooking and serving centers.

A continuous counter from one work center to another is the ideal arrangement, whether in a straight line, at a right angle (L-shape) or against 3 walls (U-shape). When this cannot be achieved, due to interruptions by doors or windows, work counters can be divided. However, due to dividing of work centers, additional work counter surface may be needed.

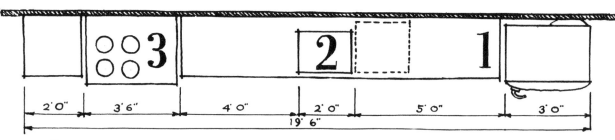

One-wall layout giving minimum work counter dimensions for each of the 3 centers. These dimensions would also apply to a 2-wall kitchen. Where work counters are separated, allow these minimums: 1' 6" each side of range, 2' 6" each side of sink, 5' 0" one side of refrigerator. Note that sink is always center of all layouts.

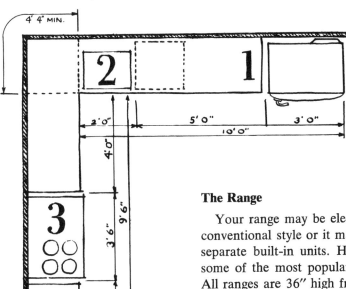

*In "bending" the kitchen into an L, as here, or into a U, additional wall space is required for corner base cabinets. Allow additional 4' 4" of wall space for each bend. Figures may vary with type and make of cabinets.*

## "U" and "L" Layouts

The arrangement of all kitchen appliances and cabinets in a straight line does not provide maximum convenience. In such an arrangement, appliances are too widely separated to form the desired "work triangle." Space limitations of kitchens and small apartments often dictate such a placement of appliances and cabinets. However, "U" or "L" shapes are preferred.

### Space Allowances for Appliances

In planning the kitchen, the space occupied by major electrical appliances is of first consideration. Sizes of most commonly used items of standard equipment follow:

## Refrigerators and Freezers

The capacity of refrigerators varies from approximately 6 to 12 cubic feet. Freezers (upright) vary from 8 to 25 cubic feet. Clearances needed for most capacities of refrigerators up to 12 cubic feet are as follows: width, 36"; depth, 30"; height, 72". An upright 18 cubic foot freezer requires a width of 39" to 44"; a depth of 31" and height of 74". If refrigerator and freezer are placed side by side, one should have a left-hand swing door, the other a right-hand swing door.

## The Range

Your range may be electric or gas. It may be the conventional style or it may be divided into the new separate built-in units. Here are the dimensions of some of the most popular sizes of standard ranges. All ranges are 36" high from floor to work top, and the oven door when open requires 45" clearance to back of range. A standard range is 38"–42" wide and 27" deep, and may have one or two ovens. A so-called "thirty-inch" range is 30" wide and 28" deep, with extra-width oven. An "apartment range" is 21"–24" wide and 26" deep, and has no extra work surface on top.

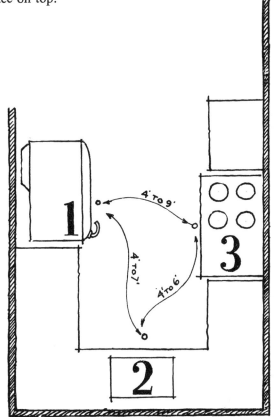

*To achieve maximum efficiency and convenience, "work triangle" should have the minimum and maximum distances shown here between appliances.*

## A Few Kitchen Tips

Try to include a meal-planning space in your kitchen. This might be a desk with drawers and space for cookbooks, recipe files, telephone and radio—or it might be only a shelf and bench.

A vertical file for serving trays is a great convenience, and requires only 9″ in width.

A maple cutting surface on or built into one small base cabinet at the preparation center saves your counter tops. Good for hot pots too.

A small table on wheels or casters helps in serving and removing dishes from the dining area, saves many steps between work centers in a large kitchen.

Keeping things in plain view when possible saves hunting in drawers and cupboards. Step-back shelves for spices, canned foods, even dishes and glassware illustrate this principle.

Pull-out shelves in base cabinets for large objects like mixing bowls, casseroles, roasters, cake tins, etc., facilitate finding utensils.

Revolving shelves in corner cabinets make best use of space, keep everything at your finger tips.

### Ventilating Fan

The ideal location for a ventilating fan is in the ceiling or in an outside wall directly over the range. If this is not possible, place fan on an outside wall as near the range as possible.

### Sink Bowls

Sinks are available in both single and double bowl types, and are generally made of porcelain enamel or stainless steel. Where a dishwasher is to be installed a single sink bowl is generally sufficient, otherwise a double bowl is recommended to make dishwashing easier—especially when there are many dishes.

Standard single sink bowls, to match standard sink cabinets and sink fronts, can be 21″, 24″ or 30″ wide. Double-bowl units range from 33″ to 42″.

### Dishwashers

Dishwasher and sink are available as a unit, or a dishwasher can be bought as a separate unit to be used in connection with any standard sink. The dishwasher may be top-loading, front-loading, or installed under a counter as a front-loading unit. A combination dishwasher-sink is 48″ wide and 24″ deep. A separate dishwasher is generally 24″ wide.

### Waste Disposer

An electric food waste disposer may be purchased as part of a combination sink-dishwasher unit, or it can be suspended from the bowl of any standard sink with 3½″ to 4″ sink opening. The drain line can be installed either under the floor or through the wall. Disposer and dishwasher can use either one drain line or separate lines.

*Three views of a kitchen (on this and the next page) show appliances built or fitted in. Above: combination washer-dryer, dishwasher, sink.*

*Across the aisle from the sink is a spacious refrigerator-freezer with a left-hand door which opens conveniently to the adjoining counter top.*

# EQUIPPING YOUR KITCHEN WITH UTENSILS

When you equip your kitchen, don't think you must buy every utensil we suggest here. Use our list as a guide. Buy enough good utensils to start with; then add others as you need them. Before long, you'll have a complete set that will give you years of good service. Many of these utensils have more than one purpose. The large, covered skillet has many uses. The loaf pan is good for both cake and meat loaf. When you're cooking, you often need boiling water, and it's easier and quicker to boil it in a teakettle than a saucepan. Besides, this reserves the saucepan for other use. A pie plate is useful even if you never make a pie—for baked apples, hot rolls, biscuits.

**Saucepans Come First.** A good saucepan balances well on your range, has a tight-fitting cover and well-shaped, heat-resistant handle. Before you buy saucepans, decide on the kind you want. They're available in several materials and styles. Perhaps you'll want a variety.

**Aluminum Saucepans** are stamped out of sheet aluminum; medium- or heavy-grade thickness gives best service. Cast-aluminum pans are heavier and thicker. Never soak aluminum in soap or other cleaning compounds; they darken the metal.

**Stainless-Steel Pans** heat less evenly—unless they have copper or aluminum bottoms or are of two layers of steel and an inner layer of metal that conducts heat evenly. The steel requires virtually no care except washing. Copper bottoms can be cleaned easily with one of the new cleaning products.

**Enameled Utensils** are well-known for their smooth and easily cleaned surface. But remember, enamel is a sort of glass fused onto metal; care is essential to prevent chipping. Don't let enameled pans boil dry. Never use steel wool to scour them; it may darken or scratch the surface.

**Glass Utensils** have an exceptional feature: You can watch the food as it cooks. They are easy to keep clean; but they cannot withstand rapid changes of temperature. If you have a modern electric range, put a grid over the element, so the glass won't crack. Glass made for baking cannot be used for top-stove cooking. Like enameled ware, glass utensils need care in handling and in use.

**A Pressure Saucepan** saves hours of cooking time. Pressure cooking is one of the best ways to make vegetables and the less tender cuts of meat taste good.

**Buying a Skillet.** These days, skillets are handsome and, with reasonable care, easy to keep clean. Skillets 2″ deep are best. Those with domelike covers are commonly called "chicken fryers," but they are by no means limited to frying chicken. They are good for all pan-frying, and are convenient for cooking asparagus, corn on the cob, other long foods. A covered skillet can go from stove to table when you use it for a one-dish meal. The 5″ or 7″ size is handy for frying eggs, browning onions and bread crumbs. Aluminum and stainless-steel skillets are hard to beat. But if you inherit one of cast iron, use it—it's especially good for slow, even browning. If you buy a cast-iron skillet, or if your old one is rusting, it must be seasoned. Scour it with household cleanser. Then coat it with unsalted fat or oil, and heat it for several hours in a warm oven (300° F.), occasionally swabbing it with a brush and adding more fat. Wipe off excess. Then repeat the seasoning process.

**Casseroles.** Casseroles are very popular, and rightly so. You can eliminate serving dishes—take the casseroles from oven to table. Place them on heat-resistant pads. The food stays hot all through the meal. Casseroles usually are made of oven glass, china, or glazed earthenware, may have matching covers. They range from small individual ones to large party sizes, covered or uncovered.

**Small Tools.** It is important to select food-preparation tools such as egg turners and kitchen spoons wisely. They must be strong enough to lift fairly heavy foods without bending or slipping; the spatulas

*The cooktop of the kitchen pictured on page 102 has storage above and below in space once used by just a range. Double ovens are directly opposite.*

must be flexible enough to be slipped under eggs and pan-fried foods. These tools should not rust, and the handles should be easy to grasp and heat-resistant. A stainless-steel set can hang on the wall, ready for use, near the range. Tongs are handy for turning steaks and chops and removing baked potatoes from the oven.

Cakes and cookies must be cooled on wire racks or coolers, to get a crunchy crust. A good egg beater is used for many cooking jobs. It should be easy to grasp and built to beat smoothly and evenly with a minimum of effort on your part. With a pastry blender you can cut fat into flour with professional ease. A rubber spatula has no equal for scraping down mixtures during beating and for getting that last bit of batter out of the bowl. A small sifter won't take much space, and it sifts cracker crumbs, flour, and sugar efficiently.

Brushes with long-wearing, quick-drying nylon bristles are the best buy for scrubbing vegetables and for special jobs like cleaning bottles, jars, coffee-makers, and strainers. You need strainers in food preparation and for washing fruits, vegetables, rice, etc. If you strain fruit juice, use a very coarse mesh, which will let the pulp through but hold back seeds and membrane.

A good can opener is a necessity. It opens round, square, and oval cans of all sizes easily and safely—no jagged edges on the can, no danger of cut fingers.

## A CHECK LIST FOR KITCHEN UTENSILS

### At or Near Kitchen Cabinet

1 standard glass measuring cup (for liquids)
1 standard metal measuring cup, or
  1 graduated set of measuring cups (for dry ingredients)
2 sets measuring spoons
1 set storage jars
1 nest of 5 mixing bowls
6 custard cups or ramekins
1 set of graters
1 fruit-juice extractor
1 coffee-making device
2 teaspoons for tasting
3 stirring spoons (1 wooden)
1 bottle opener
1 can opener (wall type)
1 jar opener
2 flour sifters (1-cup and 5-cup)
1 cake turner (if no broad spatula)
1 chopping bowl and knife
1 bread or cutting board
1 utility tray (on which to set measuring cups, spoons, etc., in use)
1 rolling pin with stockinet cover
2 sets muffin pans (6-8 in set)
1 square cake pan, 8" x 8" x 2"
1 loaf pan, 5" x 10"
2 layer-cake pans, 8" or 9"
1 cake tester
1 cookie sheet, 14" x 10"
1 open roasting pan, 10" x 15", and a trivet
2 wire cake coolers (racks)
2 casseroles
1 pastry blender
1 pastry brush
1 egg beater
1 pair kitchen shears

1 kitchen tongs
1 rubber spatula
1 knife sharpener
1 kitchen-cutlery set
1 cutlery rack
1 set biscuit cutters
1 bread box (if not part of cabinet)
1 cake box (if not part of cabinet)
2 pie plates, 9"
1 potato masher
1 electric mixer
1 set refrigerator dishes

### At or Near Range

1 pressure saucepan, 4 qts.
1 covered skillet, 10"
1 small skillet, 5" or 7"
1 tea kettle
2 lipped saucepans, 1 pt., 2 qts.
1 double-boiler, 1½-2 qts.
3 covered saucepans, 2-4 qts.

### At or Near Sink

Vegetable and bottle brushes (with nylon bristles)
1 colander
2 medium-size wire strainers, coarse and fine
1 dish-draining rack
1 wastebasket
1 garbage can
1 towel rack
Dishwashing supplies (soap, steel wool, kitchen cleansers, etc.)
Dishtowels and dishcloths
1 paper-towel holder and supply of paper towels
1 bottle of hand lotion to use after dishwashing
1 small fruit-juice strainer

### Storage Cabinet

1 Dutch oven
1 griddle, 10"
1 food chopper
1 covered kettle, 6-10 qts.
Waxed paper, foil, Saran
1 toaster

### Optional Equipment

Although these items are listed as optional you may consider some of them quite necessary.

Household scales
1 quart measure
1 or more molds
1 tube cake pan
1 doughnut cutter
1 ice-cream freezer
1 vegetable bin
1 deep-frying kettle with basket
1 deep-fat-frying thermometer
1 candy thermometer
1 roast-meat thermometer
1 electric skillet
1 funnel
1 pressure saucepan, 2 or 6 qts.
1 electric blender
1 electric broiler
1 ice crusher
1 waffle iron
1 egg poacher
Paper baking cups
Paper layer-cake pan liners
1 apple corer
1 board for rolling out dough (with cloth pastry cover)
1 dishpan, 12-quart capacity
Refrigerator bags and bowl covers

# MISCELLANEOUS KITCHEN EQUIPMENT

## Buy Good Utensils

Good top-stove pots and pans can save you time and work and turn out better food. They should have these qualities:

**Sturdiness.** Cooking utensils that are too light will warp, dent, and become wobbly.

**Proper Balance.** Pots and pans should be well balanced, so they will not tip over even when they are empty.

**Suitable Shape.** Top-stove cooking utensils cook with greatest efficiency when they cover heating units. Too-small utensils waste heat; too-large utensils with high heat may cause enamel on some range tops to craze.

**Tight-Fitting Covers.** To fit snugly; bring food to boiling point more quickly.

**Comfortable Handles.** Handles should be easy to grasp, securely attached, well proportioned.

## Thermometers

**Candy Thermometers.** Two major requirements for delicious homemade candy are a good recipe and a candy thermometer. Most candies must be cooked to a definite temperature, as stated in the recipe. The thermometer should be clipped to the edge of the pan before the mixture starts to cook. It must be completely covered with boiling syrup, but it shouldn't rest on the bottom of the pan.

**Deep-Fat-Frying Thermometers.** If your family's favorites are doughnuts, fried chicken, and French-fried potatoes, a deep-fat-frying thermometer is a wise investment. It will help you to maintain the temperature stated in the recipe for crisp, well-cooked, fried foods. No other method of determining the temperature is so accurate. Place the thermometer in the fryer before the fat is heated. Keep the thermometer in the fat while frying, so you can adjust the heat and keep the desired temperature. Be sure the bulb is immersed but does not touch bottom of utensil.

**Roast-Meat Thermometers.** For meat roasted just the way you like it, use a meat thermometer. Even with a good oven, set to the right temperature, and carefully determined time periods, the cooking time can be only an approximate guide to the degree of doneness. The size and shape of the cut, the amount of aging, the proportion of fat to lean—all affect the result. A good meat thermometer not only gives the desired temperature for different kinds of meat but also shows you when that temperature is reached. Before you insert the thermometer, make a hole for it with a metal skewer. Plunge the skewer through the outside fat into the center of the thickest, meaty part of the roast. Remove the skewer, and insert the thermometer. Be sure the bulb does not rest on bone, fat, or gristle. Here's a tip to help you determine the depth to which the meat thermometer should be inserted to reach the exact center of the meat. Place thermometer, with point at center of roast, against cut side of meat. Put your finger on the part of thermometer that is now just even with the top of the roast. This marks the depth to which the thermometer should be inserted in the roast.

Handle a glass thermometer carefully. Remember that glass fractures easily when quickly plunged from hot to cold water. Kitchen thermometers should be cooled before being washed.

## Kitchen Scales

Know how much per pound you pay for meat. And knowing the weight of roasts is almost essential; time and temperature charts call for cooking meat a specified number of minutes per pound. A standing rib beef roast, for example, weighing 5 pounds or less requires 21 to 26 minutes a pound for *rare* and 30 to 35 minutes for *well-done* roast in an oven of 325° F. So the weight is a guide to cooking the roast just the way you want it.

# KITCHEN CUTLERY

## Kitchen Scissors

A good kitchen shears is a tool of a hundred uses. Here are just a few:

1. To mince parsley and chives in practically no time at all.

2. To cut up candied fruits, such as cherries, citron, orange peel, etc.

3. To snip off the overlapping edge of pie crust after crust has been laid on the pie plate.

4. To cut off uniform pieces of yeast dough before shaping into balls for rolls.

5. To cut up pieces of cold, cooked chicken or meat for salad.

6. To cut up salad greens, green peppers, etc., for the salad bowl.

7. To remove the neck and wing tips from chicken, turkey, etc.

8. To cut large pieces of raw meat in smaller pieces.

9. To cut heavy skin from baked ham, before scoring and glazing.

10. To cut up giblets for gravy.

11. To cut the crusts from slices of bread.

12. To cut bread for fancy sandwiches.

13. To cut large fish fillets into small pieces before sautéing.

14. To cut up snap beans.

15. To cut pitted dates and prunes. Wet scissors to prevent sticking.

16. To cut taffy or other pulled candy into pieces. Wetting scissors helps here, too.

17. To snip cord used in trussing poultry, after roasting.

18. To open boiled lobsters. With scissors, cut a slit through the entire length of tail and body. Then it's simple to break away the flesh in one piece, starting from the tail.

**Other Cutlery.** Include in your cutlery a two-tined fork large enough to give you a good grip in lifting a roast out of the pan and to hold foods firmly while you are slicing. For carving, however—which is cutting *toward* you—always use a carving fork with a protecting finger guard.

## Kitchen Knives

**A Good Selection** includes a 10″ slicing knife, a knife for kitchen carving, a French or chopping knife (the blade is about 1½″ wide at the handle and tapers to a point), a spatula or two, a paring knife, and a utility knife with a 5″ blade.

**Special Knives.** Some very useful ones are the small knives with serrated edges for cutting such foods as tomatoes, cucumbers, and lemons in the thinnest of even slices; the very short-bladed knives designed just for paring, with handles a bit longer than the average to give a comfortable grip; and the large, sturdy, straight-edged butcher knives with points that stand up under pretty hard treatment —knives for getting through the hard shell of winter squash and pumpkin, or cutting larger vegetables like eggplant or turnips into slices or cubes before cooking.

Keep knives in a rack. Remember, nothing dulls and nicks knives more than cutting down on metal, glass, or enamel, so always cut down on a board. Use your knives properly. They'll serve you better and last

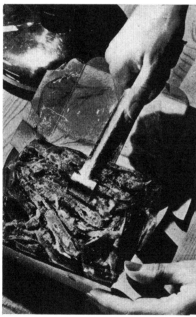

*Kitchen tongs used to lower a block of frozen vegetables into boiling water prevents splash. Use for deft handling of hot foods, putting green corn, stalk vegetables onto a platter, turn hamburgers, chops.*

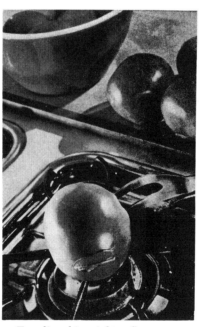

*To slip skin right off a tomato, hold it over a gas flame until it pops. Use fork to hold tomato. Owners of electric ranges can plunge tomatoes into boiling water, then into cold, for quick peeling.*

*Slice and peel onions without a tear. Slice them first with the heavy blade of a chef's knife—then just slip off the skin. Pivot knife on its tip for rapid and uniform slicing, dicing, and mincing.*

longer. If you have been using knives incorrectly, learn new habits.

**Safeguards.** Wash knives in fresh, warm suds as soon as possible after using them. Then rinse and dry immediately.

If your family raids the kitchen for a midnight snack, train them not to leave cutlery unwashed or soaking in water till morning. Soaking may ruin the handles.

**Keep Your Cutlery Sharp.** Sharpening knives is really a professional job, but we know it is not always possible or convenient to have this work done just at the time your knives need it. So we frequently turn to home knife sharpeners. There are several kinds available, but whichever you use, be sure to follow explicitly the manufacturer's directions for use, and take all the care you possibly can. And we can't overstress the fact that it's easier to keep knives sharp than to sharpen dull ones.

**Paring and Cutting.** For small, close jobs—peeling and eying potatoes, pitting cherries and grapes, hulling strawberries—where you need the tip of the blade, use the short paring knife. The closer you get your hand and the blade tip to the job, the faster the work goes. Hold the handle of the knife under the knuckle joints of four fingers, with the blade firmly guided by the index finger. Move the blade by using all the fingers, with the thumb as a pusher. You can slice radishes, small onions, and small fruit this way, too. Once you get used to using the paring knife like this, you'll never use it any other way. Use the longer utility knife for cutting up

cooked foods. You may prefer it for slicing string beans julienne style. This longer, thinner blade is a great help in cutting meat and fish off small bones, and it will be useful for countless small jobs every day.

**Preparing Vegetables.** The French or chopping knife is the tool for slicing and dicing raw vegetables. Angle the blade slightly away from you, hold the pared vegetable firmly on the cutting board, and slice with the wide part of the blade near the handle, without raising the tip of the knife from the board. The weight of the knife does the work. With practice you can regulate the thickness of the slices with professional ease. Lettuce or cabbage can be shredded for salad or cole slaw the same way.

To dice, slit the vegetables in thin strips lengthwise, pile the strips on the board, and slice them neatly, using the same knife the same way. To chop parsley, onions, and watercress evenly and finely, pick over, then slice as vegetables above. Place vegetables, as dry as possible, on the board, hold down the tip of the chopping knife with the fingers of your left hand, raise the handle, and chop in sharp, short strokes, working around in a half-circle.

In handling large vegetables, such as eggplant, turnips, and squash, remember to use a long-bladed, heavy knife. Cut the vegetable in half, so you can work with cut side down, to prevent slipping, then slice or dice.

**Cutting Fruit.** Use the long slicing knife instead of a paring knife to cut oranges, lemons, grapefruit, and apples. You can slice the fruit cleanly

with one long stroke, and there's less danger of the fruit's rolling. Use the shorter utility knife for cutting the rind off citrus fruit. Holding the fruit firmly in the left hand, with the thumb tucked well down out of harm's way, cut right through rind and skin at top of fruit. Now, slowly turning fruit in your hand, cut rind off with long, clean strokes all around fruit. By angling the knife blade, you can cut skin and rind off cleanly and neatly in a long strip, without wasting fruit or juice.

The long blade of the slicing knife is a must for sectioning peeled citrus fruit. Hold the fruit, and cut down close to the membrane on one side of a segment; then turn the knife in the fruit, and cut upward close to the membrane of the other side, using the knife as a lever to pull the fruit off the skin. Repeat all around the fruit, letting sections and juice drop into the fruit bowl.

**Carving and Slicing.** A good carving knife is a substantial, sturdy tool with a stiff blade and curved point that takes care of both raw and hot meats and gets in and under the joints of fowl. And you just can't get along without a good slicer, which is a bit longer and narrower than the carver, with a slightly flexible blade. Thin, even slices of cold meat, fruit cakes, and pound cakes fall away neatly from its efficient blade.

A good bread knife won't lie idle even though you may buy some breads sliced. Then there is bread to be cut very thin for sandwiches, and you will have to slice your homemade breads yourself.

## PAPER—THE HOUSEHOLD HELPER

### Paper Towels

Aside from their obvious uses for drying hands, wiping out greasy pans, draining fried foods, etc., paper towels have additional uses you may not have considered:

1. Wiping meats, fish, and poultry before they are cooked. It's a nuisance to keep a soft, clean cloth for this purpose, but a dampened paper towel is ideal.

2. Skimming stock is a tedious job when you use a spoon or ladle. Simply draw a piece of paper towel across the top to pick up fat without waste or fuss.

3. Handling hot foods, such as baked potatoes, toasted sandwiches, hot rolls, etc., is difficult. A paper towel usually supplies the necessary insulation. Place a paper towel over a pot holder when more thickness is needed.

4. Refreshing wilted greens with a dampened towel is an emergency measure. Wrap the greens in paper towels dampened with cold water, and store them in refrigerator until needed.

5. Draining berries or grapes sometimes leads to stained cloths or dish towels. Paper comes to the rescue again by doing the job neatly, leaving nothing to clean.

6. Tarnished silverware can be

treated as it's washed with a rub of silver polish on a dampened paper towel. This is particularly good for egg tarnish on forks.

7. Liquids spilled on the range should be wiped up immediately. A paper towel picks up grease or liquid without damaging hot enamel surfaces. Use dry towels; water should not be used until the surface has had time to cool.

8. Catchup and salad-dressing bottles are likely to get messy-looking after several uses. A quick wipe with a dampened paper towel keeps them clean.

9. Spills on kitchen floors may easily be tracked through the house. Keep the floor clean and avoid slippery spots by wiping up drops of water or grease as soon as you possibly can.

10. The kitchen sink will gleam if you clean it with a paper towel wrung out of suds after dishwashing. Save on sink cloths by using paper to apply scouring cleansers.

## Waxed Paper

Waxed paper is another old friend with many uses. You can use it when you're baking. You can sift dry ingredients onto waxed paper, use it to line the bottom of cake pans to prevent cakes' sticking, crush a small piece to help grease baking dishes. It's fine for wrapping and covering leftovers, of course, and when you pack lunches, it's indispensable. There are waxed-paper sandwich bags, too. They save time. A wall-mounted combination dispenser for both paper toweling and waxed paper keeps these kitchen stand-bys within easy reach.

## Garbage-Pail Bags

Everywhere in the kitchen paper products can save you messy clean-up jobs. Important are wax-treated bags to line the garbage pail. Folded newspaper and grocery bags are useful, of course, but they're not so neat and efficient. Because treated bags are moisture-resistant, they won't break open; the garbage pail stays dry and clean.

*Keep paper handy in the kitchen.*

*Dress up food in frills and flutes.*

**In Time of Illness.** Pin a garbage bag to the edge of the mattress to catch discarded tissue handkerchiefs.

**Traveling with a Baby.** On train and auto trips, used diapers often present a carrying problem. Take along a couple of garbage bags so damp diapers can be tucked away and kept separate from unused garments. If you use disposable diapers, the garbage bag serves as a container until you can throw them away.

**In the Laundry.** Keep a garbage bag in your clothes hamper to separate lingerie and hosiery from the regular laundry. Saves the trouble of sorting and prevents that calamitous accident—a colored sock in a load of white clothes.

When a few pieces, such as blouses, slips, and two or three shirts, already have been sprinkled, put them into a garbage bag until you are ready to iron them. You'll find the garments will be thoroughly and evenly dampened for easier ironing.

**Refrigerator Use.** Bulky foods—roast meat, chicken, boiled ham, corned beef—generally require endless yards of waxed paper for wrapping. Instead, fit them neatly into a garbage bag. This method of wrapping is convenient, too, for meats you plan to use for sandwiches: the meat can be easily slipped in and out of the bag for slicing.

**Extra Ice Cubes.** When you entertain, you can be sure of an adequate supply of ice if you empty trays of cubes into garbage bags and store them in the freezer.

**Wastebasket Lining.** Use garbage bags to protect the inside finish of wastebaskets. This is particularly important in the bathroom, where greasy cotton, paper towels, and facial tissues are tossed into the container.

## Other Efficiencies

**Paper.** Plates in a variety of sizes and shapes adaptable to almost any food on a menu, paper cups for hot or cold drinks, paper place mats, napkins, shelving, dusters, and many, many more.

**Aluminum foil,** well known and prized for its usefulness in the kitchen and for outdoor cooking, is now available in colors—red, blue, and gold—and in different widths. Besides the usual 15-inch width, look for the 7-inch (sandwich size), and 18-inch (extra-wide size). Regular foil has many household uses; heavy-duty foil is best for freezing foods.

**Plastic bags** for refrigerator and freezer storage come in many sizes up to those large enough to hold a turkey. These handy transparent pouches make convenient protectors for many items up to, and including, the packing of a still-damp bathing suit.

**Saran,** a strong, transparent plastic wrapping material (which clings to itself, as well as to anything it is wrapped around), is an excellent food protector. However, the very quality that makes Saran so distinctively useful—its ability to stick to itself—may make it a bit awkward to handle. Handling hint: If, in dealing with a large piece, you find that it sticks to itself, crumple the whole piece and then smooth it all out.

# PRESSURE COOKERS

You can find a pressure cooker to fit your needs. Capacities vary from the 2½- or 3-quart size to large cookers designed particularly for canning. Some of the smaller ones should not be used for canning, and the instructions that come with them give this warning. Aluminum or stainless steel is the usual metal for these utensils. The automatic pressure cooker has its own electric base; the timing, pressure control, and venting of the steam are completely automatic.

No matter what pressure cooker you use, follow the manufacturer's instructions carefully. Be sure you know exactly how to handle this equipment before you turn on the heat.

Don't overload your cooker. Foods should never come to more than two thirds of the depth of the pan. If any food rests against the cover, it may block the vent pipe or safety-release valve.

Check the steam vent before putting the cover on the pan. Make sure it is clean and free from food particles. Most manufacturers offer a cleaning wire that can be used to clean this tube.

Never use more nor less water than the amount called for. In cooking vegetables, start with hot water, to speed up pressure-reaching time. Brown meats in cooker first, to bring out richness of color and flavor; then use a rack under the meats for remaining cooking time. Be sure a steady flow of steam is issuing from the vent before you build up pressure. Turn the heat down as soon as cooking pressure is reached. Begin to count the time at this point.

Be sure all steam is out of the pan before removing the cover. Always remove the pressure weight or control *after pressure has been reduced* before even attempting to take off the cover. Never force cover off the pan if it seems to stick.

## Canning with a Pressure Cooker

Unless you use a pressure cooker in canning non-acid vegetables at home you cannot be sure you are not exposing your family to the death-dealing hazards of botulinus poisoning.

### Warning

**Botulism,** or botulinus food poisoning, is one of the deadliest of diseases. Statistics show that two out of three of its victims die. It is caused by bacteria, which live in the soil and cling invisibly to vegetables. Although more prevalent in some parts of the country than in others, botulinus bacteria are transported easily and probably are present in most soils in the United States.

If botulinus bacteria are not killed in the canning process, they create a poison that is certain death to almost all who swallow it. Because it usually does not change the food's appearance, odor, or taste, it cannot be detected.

Botulinus bacteria are extremely hard to kill except by high temperatures. They have been known to withstand continuous boiling for as long as 6 hours. This is why a steam-pressure canner is necessary when home canning nonacid vegetables. It is the only device by which canning temperatures can be raised high enough to destroy botulinus bacteria. The pressure cooker method of canning nonacid vegetables, as well as meats and fish, also results in less spoilage.

Home canning by other methods should be limited to acid foods (fruits and tomatoes). When foods are acid, all forms of bacteria are killed within a reasonable time at boiling water-bath temperature.

**All Home-Canned Foods Should Be Examined Carefully When Opened.** If there is any evidence of spoilage the food should not even be tasted.

## JARS FOR CANNING

Seal jars exactly as the manufacturer directs. Here are the three leading types of jars and caps and the way to use them.

**Lightning Type:** Dip rubber ring in hot water, place flat on the rim of the jar. Adjust lid on jar so upper wire clamp lies in center of groove on lid. Leave lower clamp up during canning. When jar is taken from canner, seal by pushing down the clamp.

**Combination Glass-and-Metal Cap.** Dip rubber ring in hot water. Fit it around projection on glass lid. Screw metal band tight; then unscrew slightly but not enough to make band loose. Turn screw band tight after jar is taken from canner. After 12 hours, remove screw band.

**Two-Piece Metal Cap:** Dip lid (the sealing composition is attached to lid) in hot water, or boil it—whichever the manufacturer directs. Place lid on jar, sealing side down. Screw band tight once and for all.

After you remove jars from canner, set them on a rack or cutting board, or on several thicknesses of toweling. After 12 hours, test them for seal. Turn over the lightning jars to see if they leak. Remove screw band on the combination cap and lift jar by lid. If the lid is sealed, it will hold the weight of the jar. You can test the two-piece metal cap by tapping the lid with a spoon. If the seal has been made, the sound will be clear and ringing; otherwise, it will be dull or low. If some of the jars did not seal properly don't try to reprocess them. Use the food immediately.

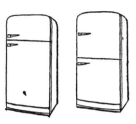

nette table with freez-
in base—suitable for
all kitchens and apart-
ent-house families.

Built-in flush-with-wall
refrigerator and freezer
units. They provide
14½ cu. ft. of storage.

Unique in its field, this
two-door refrigerator
freezer is just the thing
for large-family use.

Typical refrigerator-
freezer combinations.
The one at right is so-
called upside-down style.

Refrigerator and upright
freezer "twins" for a big
kitchen. They provide
about 24 cu. ft. of space.

## HOME FREEZERS

If there's a good buy to be found anywhere today, it's in a food freezer. It can cut your food costs; save you time, trouble, and transportation; provide delicious meals on short order; and add infinite variety to your menus. But in return for all this devoted service, you'll have to take time to get to know your freezer. And you'll probably discover that you have to change a few of your living habits to make fullest use of this new treasure.

You'll find that you have to plan shopping, and even cooking, weeks in advance. You'll need to keep a constant and knowing eye on price tags if you're looking for real savings. Just as you learned the facts about canning, you'll be obliged to learn the facts about packaging, freezing and storing, and thawing and cooking frozen foods. And unless you have the biggest freezer ever made, you'll have to decide how to use the space.

But the advantages more than outweigh the obligations. Freezing is fun, often for the whole family. And if there are men in the family who hunt or fish, they will welcome a freezer because it gives them a place to store their game or fish so they can be used over a period of many months. With a freezer in the house, you'll be an executive instead of a drudge, completely independent of the weather, crowded stores, the day's high prices, and the time of year. So here's what you'll want to know about choosing and using your freezer.

**Selecting the Right Freezer Is a Matter for Really Serious Consideration.** You'll have to choose from dozens of makes and sizes. If you have no previous experience to draw on, you may find it helpful to talk to friends and neighbors who own freezers. Read up on freezing, too, before you shop.

What make? Most freezer-manufacturing concerns are large and reputable, so there is little risk if you choose a well-known make. However, you'll have to

choose from three types of freezers: the upright type, with shelves like a refrigerator's; the chest type, sectioned off by dividers or baskets; and the recently introduced combination refrigerator-freezer with really larger low-temperature freezing and storing capacity. They are expensive, but if floor space is at a premium they are worth the price. The upright type occupies a smaller floor area and keeps packages readily accessible. Food freezes faster in uprights that have freezing coils in each shelf, because of the good contact. In chest freezers, you must place packages in a separate freezing compartment or against the walls. However, because the chest type is boxlike, you can store food in every nook and corner, but if you fill it too full you may have trouble getting at the packages on the very bottom.

**What Size?** This is a question that only you can answer. It depends entirely on what uses you hope to make of your freezer. Do you grow your own fruits and vegetables? Do you plan to market infrequently and to buy large quantities? Do you intend to cook and freeze whole meals? All these items are space-takers, so choose a size large enough to handle *all* your freezing projects.

**The Economy Story Is Not a Myth.** It is possible to save money with a freezer, but this saving doesn't come automatically. Making a year-round profit takes canny buying, a watchful eye for specials and quantity discounts, and a plan for freezing foods when they are in season.

If you live in a rural or suburban area, a garden is a perfect partner for a freezer; it can yield a winter's supply of fruits and vegetables for only a few cents a pound. In areas where there is a locker plant that helps slaughter and dress meat, some families are even raising their own livestock. Most locker plants offer other services, such as quantity discounts on frozen foods, a wide selection of packaging materials, and emergency storage in case of power failure.

**A Freezer Has Saving Ways for You Even if You Can't Grow Your Own Food.** You can take advantage of every special buy that comes along, whether it's a basket of peaches or a leg of lamb. Talk to the grocer, butcher, and near-by farmers about your needs. They can work with you to see that you get fresh food of the best grade or variety for freezing, and they may be able to give you special prices for quantity purchases or for their oversupplies. Some stores give quantity discounts on commercially frozen foods sold in dozen or half-dozen lots. Ice cream, too, costs less by the gallon or half gallon.

Don't underestimate the small economies of a freezer. You need never waste a scrap of food. You can cook at your leisure, and so spend time concocting those less expensive dishes that are complicated to make. There are fewer leftovers, because you can package in amounts to suit your family. Taken altogether, these small savings add up to a tidy sum.

**Buying Meat in Quantity** may or may not save you money. What many families with new freezers want to know first is whether to buy a side of beef or veal or a whole lamb. That can be a successful investment only if you ascertain, before buying, the quality of the meat and your saving. Be sure you know what cuts you'll get from the meat. Remember, every side of beef has its quota of stew meat as well as steaks.

The wholesale price of meat can be misleading if you don't know the percentage of waste fat and bone to expect. A 210-pound side of beef will give you 170 pounds or less of trimmed meat. Figure your cost per pound on this net weight, and add whatever you pay for aging, cutting, grinding, delivery, etc. Compare this with the retail cost of the same grade of meat.

Frozen-food locker plants are usually excellent sources of meat in quantity. For a minimum charge, they will age, cut, wrap, and freeze meat just as you want it.

**Managing a Freezer Is a Little Like Storekeeping.** You may want to specialize and stock certain foods, but more likely you'll keep a variety on hand. A running reorder tally just like the one that reminds you to restock canned goods will help you avoid emergency marketing trips or gaps in your menu.

An inventory of some kind is also good management. It can be complete or just a simple list of short-storage foods that will be used in a few weeks.

Make a few notes on how special foods were prepared for the freezer, so you can repeat your successes. Finally, to get the most in service and savings from your freezer, use it every day. A constant turnover of all but seasonal foods makes room for more good meals at a saving.

### Storing Food in a Freezer

The low temperatures in a freezer tend to draw moisture out of foods and make them lose flavor, volume, and texture. Special types of packaging material or containers must be used to guard against this loss of moisture; they should be moisture-vapor-proof. Commercially packed frozen foods need no additional wrappings, but foods frozen at home must have adequate protection.

Sheet wrappings are undoubtedly the best known and most versatile of all types of packaging. There is a wide variety of these—cellophane, Saran, aluminum foil, heavy paper (impregnated with wax or lined with cellophane), pliofilm and plastic films of other types. When you use these remember that casual wrapping is not enough. Edges must be folded over several times and sealed with freezer tape or heat.

**Freezer Jars.** Glass jars are handy for storing fruit juices, soups, and other high-moisture-content foods. They are made in pints and quarts, with wide mouths and screw caps. Ridges in sides make handling easier.

**Freezer Boxes.** Boxes of many different types are available for packing fresh fruits and vegetables, cooked foods, puddings, and the like. Those made of aluminum foil can be used for reheating foods. Others are clear plastic with flexible plastic lids that make the tight seal necessary. These can double for refrigerator storage, too. Heavily waxed cartons come in many sizes and shapes. Other paper containers are lined with moisture-vapor-proof material; frames and funnels make filling easier.

**Adequate Preparation.** Soon after you acquire a freezer, you'll find yourself preparing food in larger quantities than ever before. Perhaps you'll make enough stew for two or three meals, or cook vegetables by the peck and prepare fruit by the basket. Quantity cooking saves work in the long run; but it can be a confusing experience unless you have the proper equipment and facilities. Arrange a freezing center in your kitchen, where you can keep all the necessary tools and materials. Whenever possible, leave containers and rolls of sheet wrapping in their original packages, to protect them from dust, and place them on a separate shelf. Be sure to store Cellophane rolls and bags away from heat. Devote a kitchen drawer to the small freezing accessories—sealing tape, marking pencils, extra lids for containers, plastic ties for freezer bags, etc.

With a freezer, you need pots and pans larger than your everyday utensils to hold eight quarts or

*Packing meats*

*Packing planned leftovers*

more. Also, you must have a large-sized food mill for puréeing fruits and tomatoes that are to be frozen. Store these in a special place, outside the kitchen if necessary, where they'll stay clean and ready for action.

### Freezing Meats

Because meat is usually the most expensive food in a freezer, it requires special, careful attention. *Package* in amounts convenient for your family. *Wrap tightly* in freezer wrapping materials or containers; seal securely with freezer tape. *Label clearly*, noting date, kind of meat, cut, and weight or number of servings.

**Roasts.** Trim off excess fat. Pad sharp bone edges with fat, to avoid puncturing wrapping. Pack in bag or sheet wrapping; seal.

**Steaks and Chops.** Trim as desired. Package together, in bag or sheet wrapping, as many steaks or chops as you are likely to need for one meal. If there is more than a single layer of meat, separate layers with film or foil so they will come apart more quickly when thawing. Press wrapping flat against meat; seal edges securely with freezer tape.

**Chopped Meat or Cut-Up Meat for Stews.** Use only freshly cut or ground meat. Package chopped meat in bulk or in patties in any convenient freeze wrapping material or container, separating layers of meat with film or foil. Pack meat for stews in recipe amounts in any freezer material.

### Planned Leftovers

Keep your freezer well stocked without extra work by setting up a system of planned leftovers. When ordering meat, get an extra pound or so to cube after cooking. It will make wonderful skillet suppers.

**Leg of Lamb.** To get a larger proportion of meat to bone, buy a plump one. When the lamb is cooked, serve the smaller slices; save the perfect center slices for freezing. As you cut the meat from the cold roast, place it in freezer containers; one for perfect slices, one for chunks, and one for slivers. Heat the gravy just enough to liquefy it; pour it over the meat. Make soup stock from the bones, cool it, and freeze. You may use stock instead of gravy on the meat to be frozen.

**Rib Roast.** If you have the roast boned, ask for the bones for soup stock. Roast the meat the way your family likes it best. If rare, serve it cold after the first meal, as reheating will overcook and toughen it. Then freeze what is left the same way as freezing lamb.

**Pork Loin.** Buy a big, meaty piece, and have the backbone separated from the ribs. Cut and freeze several chops, leaving a piece large enough to roast. After roasting the loin, freeze leftover pieces.

**Veal Roast.** After roasting the veal, freeze the leftovers as you froze the lamb. Use in salads, sandwiches, hash, curries, and croquettes.

### Freezing Poultry

Poultry in parts or whole, cleaned and ready for cooking, can be frozen months ahead. Use wrapping materials recommended for freezing, and wrap them dripping wet; the coating of ice that forms helps protect them from "freezer burn."

**Broilers.** Clean as for cooking; then cut in half along breastbone, and wash. Package the halves together (place two pieces of waxed paper between the halves to make them easy to separate for faster thawing). In an emergency, you can broil without thawing. It takes about twice as long, and should be brushed often with melted butter.

**Fryers.** Disjoint and clean. Package in portions for one meal. Here's a special trick for packaging fryers. Get out your collection of loaf pans and oblong or square cake pans. As the cut-up chicken is washed, fit the pieces snugly into the pan, skin side down; top with a layer skin side up. Freeze right in the pan. Then release the chicken by running warm water over the bottom of the pan. This makes a solid block of chicken that is easy to wrap and takes little space.

The meaty pieces—breasts, legs, and thighs—can be wrapped together for an extra-special chicken dinner. Cook, then cut the meat from, the other pieces; cool the meat and the broth; package in plastic or glass containers. However, if the fryers are small, there may not be enough meat on the bony pieces to make handling them separately worth while. This is really a method to use with a larger fowl.

**Roasters.** Clean the bird as you would for cooking. Tie the legs and wings to the body to make packaging easier. The bird should not be stuffed before freezing. The seasonings often become too strong over a period of time and you run risk of spoilage. A better way is to make and freeze the stuffing a week or so ahead of use. When both are thawed, it's simple enough to stuff the bird just before roasting.

**Stewing Fowl** deserves better treatment than it gets in many kitchens. Instead of boiling or braising it all at once, try this: Simmer the wings, backs, and necks; freeze the stock and whatever meat is on these parts. Chicken stock in the freezer is like money in the bank. Of course, you can make soup from it. You can also use it in gravies, vichyssoise, and creamed dishes, and to moisten stuffing for roast chicken or turkey. Freeze the meaty uncooked pieces until you are ready to use them. Or cook them first, then freeze them; the cold slices and cubes can be used in summer salads and sandwiches. Package them in liquid-tight containers, with broth to cover. When you freeze chickens, be sure they are cleaned and ready to cook. Package in amounts for one meal, preferably in layers separated by waxed paper. Label according to use: "for soup," "for fricassee," "for creamed chicken," etc.

**Livers and Giblets.** A collection of livers and giblets can be used in many different ways. So freeze them in a separate container.

### Freezing Eggs

In containers, place convenient recipe amounts of yolks, whites, or whole eggs. To freeze whole eggs, break into measuring cup; add 1 tablespoon sugar or corn syrup, or 1 teaspoon salt, per cup, depending on future use (cake, omelet, or sauce, etc.). Stir to mix,

but do not beat. Freeze yolks as for whole eggs, using 2 tablespoons sugar or corn syrup, or 1 teaspoon salt, per cup. Freeze whites without adding salt or sugar. Be sure to label properly. Thaw completely and use promptly. Substitute for fresh eggs as follows: 1 tablespoon yolks for 1 egg yolk; 1½ tablespoons whites for 1 egg white; 2½ tablespoons mixed whole eggs for 1 egg.

### Freezing Dairy Products

**Butter** made from pasteurized cream may be frozen in original waxed carton. For storage longer than a month, overwrap with freezer material.

**Cheese**—Cheddar, Swiss, etc.—should be wrapped in convenient amounts up to 1 pound in freezer material. Creamed cottage cheese and cream cheese become grainy.

**Cream and Ice Cream** keep well in freezer for 2 or 3 months if repackaged in freezer containers. Both will keep up to a month in original containers. Buy economical gallon or half-gallon packages of ice cream; as they're used, keep cut surfaces covered with film or waxed paper. At end of churning period, homemade ice cream can be packaged and placed in freezer to harden.

### Freezing Fish and Shellfish

Clean and cut whole fish, fillets, or steaks as usual. Wrap individually in sheet material. Pack in flat carton (use liner for long storage). Wash oysters, clams, and scallops before and after shucking, to remove sand. Pack meat in containers and cover with salt solution, using 1 tablespoonful salt per 1 cup water; or cover with own juice. Leave 1″ head space for expansion. Shrimp may be frozen cooked or uncooked, with or without shells. For crabs and lobsters, cook, cool, and remove meat from shells. Pack tightly in containers, and freeze. They may also be frozen alive, without wrapping, for 1 or 2 weeks.

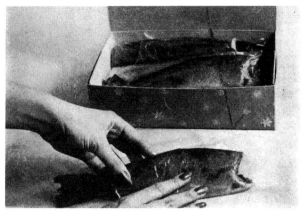

Frozen fish should be thawed just enough to separate pieces and cooked like fresh fish. If it is more convenient, cook frozen fish slowly, and allow extra cooking time.

### Freezing Fruits and Vegetables

Fruits and vegetables can be packed in several ways. You can use waxed cartons with a moisture-vapor-proof lining, plastic bags or boxes, glass jars, or aluminum foil boxes. As it is very important to pack fruits and vegetables as quickly as possible, cartons should be made ready before the foods are. Some cartons come flattened and have to be formed and the liners inserted.

## Vegetables

Freeze garden-fresh, tender vegetables. To heat: Boil 1 gallon or more water in large kettle; keep heat *high* at all times. Add vegetables (1 pound per 1 gallon water); cover; start timing. Give thick pieces or stalks longest time indicated. To chill: Plunge vegetables into iced water until cold. Drain before packing. Write your state agricultural extension service for varieties that are best for freezing.

**Asparagus.** Wash; break off tough ends; sort into narrow, medium, and thick stalks. Cut into 2″ pieces, or leave as spears. Heat 2 to 4 minutes. Chill; drain; pack.

**Broccoli.** Use compact dark-green heads. Wash; trim and peel stalks; cut lengthwise, leaving 1½″ heads. Heat 3 minutes. Chill; drain; pack.

**Brussels Sprouts.** Trim; remove coarse, outer leaves. Wash thoroughly; sort for size. Heat 3 to 5 minutes, according to size. Chill; drain; pack tightly.

**Corn on the Cob.** Use young, tender ears. Husk; wash; sort ears according to size. Heat small ears 7 minutes, medium 9 minutes, large 11 minutes. Chill; pack or wrap.

**Whole-Kernel Corn.** Use young, tender corn. Husk; wash. Heat 4 minutes. Chill thoroughly. Cut off kernels (avoid cutting into cob). Pack tightly.

**Green Beans.** Wash; remove ends. Cut into lengthwise strips or 1″ or 2″ pieces. Heat 3 minutes. Chill quickly, in iced water; drain well; pack.

**Mushrooms.** Sort for size; wash; trim ends. Slice mushrooms if larger than 1″. Place in 1 pint water with 1 teaspoon lemon juice, for 5 minutes. Drain. Heat whole ones 5 minutes, slices 3½ minutes. Chill.

**Peas.** Shell; discard immature or tough peas. Heat 1½ minute. Chill; drain; pack. Or freeze on tray; then put in container, for loose pack.

**Peppers.** Wash; remove stems and seeds. Cut as desired; freeze raw. Or heat halves 3 minutes, slices 2 minutes; chill; drain. Freeze raw if peppers are to be stuffed.

**Spinach.** Wash; remove tough stems and older leaves. Heat 1½ to 2 minutes. Chill; drain thoroughly. Chop if desired.

**Squash.** Summer: Wash; cut into ½″ slices. Heat 3 minutes. Chill. Winter: Wash; cut up; remove seeds. Boil or bake till soft; mash pulp. Set in cold water to chill.

**Lima Beans.** Shell; sort according to size; discard any overmature, white beans. Heat 2 to 4 minutes. Chill; drain; pack.

**Certain Vegetables Don't Freeze Well.** Potatoes may be frozen when they are French fried or baked, but they lose their texture if frozen after having been boiled. Cabbage, celery, and tomatoes can be used only for cooking after freezing. Beets, onions, and carrots are on the market practically all year and are better bought fresh or canned.

**Cooking Frozen Vegetables.** Only corn on the cob needs thawing before cooking. Leafy greens should be thawed at least partially. Put other vegetables in small amount of salted water, cover, and cook until tender. Frozen vegetables take less time to cook than fresh ones do.

### Freezing Fruits

Freeze only sound, fully ripe fruit. To make syrup: In 1 quart water, dissolve 2 cups sugar for light syrup, 3 cups for medium, 4¾ cups for heavy, 7 cups for extra heavy. Chill. To prevent darkening, add ½ teaspoon ascorbic acid per 1 quart syrup (or per 1 cup dry sugar); or use commercial preparation. Use liquid-tight containers; fill to within ½″ to 1″ of top.

**Apples.** Peel; core; slice. Add medium syrup if apples are to be used as is; ½ cup sugar per 1 quart apples if to be used in cooking. Add ascorbic acid.

**Apricots.** Wash; peel; pit; halve or slice. (To freeze unpeeled, heat ½ minute; then chill.) Sweeten as for apples. Add ascorbic acid.

**Blueberries.** Sort; wash. Add medium syrup. If berries are for pies, pack without syrup. To tenderize skins, steam berries 1 minute over boiling water; then chill.

**Cherries.** If you use sour cherries, add heavy syrup; if sweet, add medium syrup, ascorbic acid; if for pies, add ¾ cup sugar per 1 quart fruit.

**Cranberries.** Sort; wash. Pack without sugar; or cover with heavy syrup. Or make cranberry sauce or orange relish, adding sugar to taste.

**Grapefruit and Oranges.** Peel, seed, and section grapefruit and oranges. Drain; pack. Add medium syrup, made of juice plus water, and ascorbic acid.

**Grapes.** Wash; remove from stems. If to be used for jam or jelly, do not add sugar; or remove seeds and add medium syrup to cover.

**Melons.** Seed; cut into slices, cubes, or balls. Pack. Add light syrup. Several kinds of melon can be packed together, for fruit cups.

**Peaches.** Peel. Slice into medium syrup in container; or add ⅔ cup sugar per 1 quart peaches. Add ascorbic acid. Submerge fruit with waxed paper.

**Pineapple.** Pare; remove core and eyes. Slice, cube, or crush. Pack without sugar; or add light syrup made of water and juice.

**Rhubarb.** Wash; trim; cut. If to be used for pies, pack raw. Or heat 1 minute; then chill. Do not add sugar. Or cook; sweeten sauce to taste; then freeze.

**Strawberries.** Sort; wash; hull. Slice if large. Sweeten according to tartness (usually with ¾ cup sugar per 1 quart berries); or cover with heavy syrup.

### Thawing Frozen Fruits

If you have sometimes been disappointed in the quality of frozen fruits you have served, perhaps they have not been thawed properly. Speed in handling is the most important factor affecting quality of frozen fruits, and this applies as much to thawing as to freezing. Fruits must be thawed quickly, to prevent darkening, loss of fresh flavor, and mushiness. They should not stand at room temperature before they are served. They are at their best with the last few traces of ice clinging to them; then they look appetizing and taste delicious.

**To Speed Thawing.** There are several ways to speed the thawing process; but with any method, the fruit must be thawed in the original package. It takes 4 or 5 hours to thaw a pint package of frozen food at room temperature; the same package placed in front of an electric fan will thaw in about an hour. Let the fan blow directly on it; turn the package occasionally. If you don't have a fan and the package is watertight, place it in a bowl and let cold water run over it. Never use hot water. Immersed in cold water, pint packages thaw in about 45 minutes; quarts take a little longer.

### Salads and Sandwiches

**Salads as Such Don't Belong in the Freezer.** In fact, most of the "don'ts" in freezing are for this group of foods. Potato salad and coleslaw are unfreezable. After thawing, tomatoes, lettuce, celery, cucumbers, raw carrots, and other salad vegetables turn limp and soft; gelatine tends to weep; mayonnaise (except the small quantity in sandwich mixes) separates.

**Salad Ingredients** that *do* freeze well may be worth freezer space to you, particularly since they are often leftovers—for instance, cooked chicken; shrimp; lobster; vegetables; chunks of baked ham, pork, or veal; slivers of cold cuts; nut meats, pimento, and coconut; whipped cream. Wrap ingredients in freezer wrapping, or pack in freezer containers; don't mix several types in one package, or flavors will blend. If container is too large, cover top of food with freezer film or aluminum foil. Thaw in package, and mix into salad while still chilled. These ingredients can clutter a freezer; make a note to use them up.

**Sandwiches** made with sliced roast meats of all kinds, chicken, cold cuts, cheese, meat loaf, or turkey all freeze well. So do "salad" (tuna, ham, etc.) sandwiches when they're not too "wet"; use less mayonnaise than usual; omit lettuce, celery, tomatoes, and hard-cooked eggs. Spread bread with soft butter or margarine; add filling; wrap each sandwich in freezer wrapping and label. Stack sandwiches in any handy box; then freeze. Thaw, in wrapping, 3 to 4 hours at room temperature; *use promptly or refrigerate.*

**Sandwich Makings** freeze very well too. You can freeze bread, butter, prepackaged cheese and cold cuts—all in their original wrappings. Wrap sliced roast meat tightly. Before using, thaw 2 to 3 hours at room temperature.

**Buy One Loaf Each of Sliced Rye, Whole-Wheat, Raisin, Enriched, etc. Bread.** Remove a few slices from each, enough to last several days; then make up loaves of assorted breads, and freeze. This gives a choice of fresh bread. It thaws quickly at room temperature. If it's to be toasted, just pop bread from freezer into toaster.

### Freezing Casserole Dishes

**You can cook** almost any casserole dish, including macaroni and cheese, and freeze it; just postpone the final baking or browning until you are ready to serve. Fry chicken, chops, and cutlets as usual, but omit the "cook, covered," period (cook tender when you reheat them). Make dishes like chili con carne, meat loaf, corned beef, sauce for spaghetti, and pot roast as you would to serve them. In making stews, freeze the cubes of meat, browned and cooked tender; add the vegetables and finish cooking when you heat the meat for serving.

**You can freeze** a casserole mixture in its own dish. Cover the dish with freezer film or foil. To freeze other cooked foods, pack them in freezer containers, or wrap them. Before freezing cooked foods, chill them in the refrigerator.

**You can heat** small casseroles without thawing, but it is better to thaw large casseroles first. Heat fried chicken in 350° F. oven, without thawing, 30 to 40 minutes. Heat other cooked foods with or without thawing, to suit your convenience.

### Freezing Cakes, Pies, and Breads

Wrapping baked goods for the freezer presents no special problem. Bread, rolls, cakes, pies, cookies, etc., require moisture-vapor-proof wrappings—bags or sheets of aluminum foil, Cellophane, or plastic film. The wrappings must be sealed, and if the foods are to be stored more than a short time, protect the wrapping from moisture and tearing with an outer layer of stockinet or foil, or place in a cake box.

**Pies.** Most freeze well. But there is some difference in the way to prepare them. Two-crust pies (apple, cherry, etc.) and deep-dish pies will taste fresher if they are not baked until just before serving time. Prepare pie up to baking point; slip it into a freezer bag or wrap it in freezer wrapping; seal package with tape and freeze it. When time comes for serving, bake pie in 425° F. oven, without thawing, 40 to 60 minutes. If you are going to want pie shells to fill with fruit, ice cream, etc., bake them ahead and freeze them. The baked pie shell can be thawed at room temperature or heated in 375° F. oven, unthawed, 10 minutes. Chiffon pie should be allowed to set before it is wrapped for freezing. Thaw it 1 to 2 hours, in the refrigerator, before serving. *Note:* Never try to freeze a custard or cream pie or a meringue topping.

**Cakes** freeze wonderfully. Remember two things about freezing a frosted layer cake: Butter frostings freeze best, and it's wise to freeze your cake unwrapped until the frosting is set (this protects peaks and swirls). Any kind of cake—chiffon, angel food, spongecake, "butter" cake, poundcake, and fruitcake —freezes well; do not freeze batter. Wrap cake in freezer wrapping; seal with tape. Unwrap and thaw at room temperature—layers 1 hour, cakes 2 to 3 hours.

**Hot Breads.** Have on hand a variety of hot breads

— corn bread, blueberry muffins, coffeecake—home baked and ready to heat. You can make, bake, and wrap an assortment of rolls from one batch of yeast dough or prepared mix. It's smart, too, to have shortcake baked and ready for frozen strawberries or peaches. Wrap the breads in containers or plastic film or foil. To thaw, breads should be taken from the freezer and unwrapped. Then place frozen on a baking sheet in a 400° F. oven until heated through— about 15 to 20 minutes. Or thaw, wrapped at room temperature.

**A bakeshop coffeecake** is only a few minutes away from your table if you freeze it a week or two ahead. Thawing isn't necessary; it will be fresh and hot after 15 minutes in a 400° F. oven.

Besides helping you avoid crowds in stores, your freezer lets you buy a variety of baked goods—cakes, cookies, rolls, muffins, brownies, cupcakes—so you'll have whatever the family wants at a moment's notice.

**Most Baked Goods** should be served within 2 or 3 months after freezing. Unbaked rolls, muffins, and cookie dough should be used within 1 month. Breads to be served hot and pies do not need to be thawed before heating. Cakes and cookies should thaw several hours at room temperature.

**Store canapé ingredients in your freezer, especially if you often have unexpected guests or do lots of planned-ahead entertaining.** Cut assorted breads in variety of shapes (circular, oval, diamond, etc.), and pack enough in each package for a small party.

Adjacent to them in freezer, if possible, keep containers of several different spreads—chicken, ham, tongue, and fish seasoned and mixed with just enough salad dressing to hold them together. Pack in small amounts; then they'll thaw quickly and be used up at one time.

## Minor Miracles with Your Freezer

Here is a miscellany of minor miracles to perform with your freezer.

Freeze cream, whipped and sweetened, in small containers or as rosettes. Thaw an hour before serving.

Apple dumplings, steamed puddings, and fruitcakes take a long time to make. Bake and freeze them in advance.

Keep a stockpile of ice cubes in the freezer, in plastic or heavily waxed paper bags.

How about ham or chicken turnovers? Freeze them before baking; later, bake them, without thawing, at 400° F.—15 minutes if they're bite-size, 25 to 30 minutes if they're dinner-size.

Freeze French bread—sliced, garlic-buttered, and ready to pop into the oven.

Keep a bunch of parsley, chopped celery, onions, or peppers in the freezer, for use in soups, stews, etc. Mince parsley while it's still frozen and crisp.

Freeze rich soups in your ice-cube trays; then package cubes in bags, for quick single servings.

Nut meats of all kinds keep well in your freezer.

If you're busy during the jelly- and jam-making season, you can freeze fruits or fruit purée, and do your preserving in the fall.

Bake and slice meat loaf. Arrange layer of slices on heavy aluminum foil; cover layer with gravy or canned tomato sauce; fold foil tightly over meat; freeze. Reheat, without thawing, in 400° F. oven 40 minutes.

## Thawing and Cooking Frozen Foods

The more you use a freezer, the more your cooking habits will change. When you serve cooked foods from the freezer, getting dinner becomes a quick heating or baking process. But there are points you must know about the foods in your freezer.

Frozen food is more perishable after thawing than fresh food. Time thawing, so you will use food within a few hours. If food is thawed at room temperature, refrigerate until used.

Meat, poultry, and fish, like fruits, should not be overthawed, or they will lose flavor and juices. Learn to use a meat thermometer when you roast meat that has been frozen.

**Refreezing Frozen Foods.** As a general rule, avoid refreezing foods. The danger lies in the fact that refrozen foods may be partially spoiled, without your knowing it, from having been kept thawed too long. But, as with most rules, there are practical exceptions. If raw frozen food is cooked and then promptly refrozen, there is no danger. Food that has only partially thawed can be refrozen as long as it is still cold and contains a few ice crystals. Remember this if your freezer is accidentally disconnected or if power fails.

**Storage Time for Frozen Foods.** No one can tell you exactly how long you can keep foods in a freezer. Time limits depend on the temperature, kind of food, care taken in packaging, and the original quality of the food. These are general time limits at 0° F:

| | |
|---|---|
| Beef, lamb, veal | up to 1 year |
| Chopped beef | up to 2 or 3 months |
| Fruits and vegetables | up to 1 year |
| Pork (fresh), poultry, fish | 4 to 6 months |
| Ham | up to 1 month |
| Cooked and baked foods | 1 to 3 months |
| Franks | up to 1 month |
| Sandwiches | 2 weeks |
| Ice cream | up to 1 month |

Long storage causes loss of flavor. Use your freezer every day, so food is served fresh.

**Label and Date All Packages.** Labeling is important because it's very hard to identify food once it's frozen. The date will prompt you to use food before it loses quality.

**Freeze Packages Quickly.** Do not let packaged food stand; place in freezer promptly. Check your instruction booklet to see just where you should place packages in freezer.

## Facts on Freezer Care

**When You Freeze Food.** In any freezer, there is a limit to the amount of food you can freeze at one time. Check your instruction booklet. Overloading may not cause the motor to overheat, but it will increase running time. Besides, the food will freeze slowly and therefore be less appetizing when served. The size of your freezer determines how much food you can freeze at once—usually four to six pounds per cubic foot. Place each package in direct contact with a freezing surface.

**When You Defrost.** Just how often you'll have to scrape the frost off the walls of your freezer depends largely on the humidity and how often the freezer is opened. In most cases, defrosting is necessary only once or twice a year. The job is easy if you remove the frost while it is still "dry" and not too thick (half an inch or so), and if you scrape one section at a time. Remove food from one wall or shelf, and place a folded newspaper at the bottom of the freezer to catch the frost. Then, with a plastic scraper or a blunt metal or wood paddle, scrape off the frost. When the frost is thick and icy, you must disconnect the freezer. First remove all food packages and wrap them in newspapers and blankets to keep them frozen. If you direct a fan into the freezer or against the open lid, you'll hasten the melting. Use old towels or cloths to wipe up water. Finally, wipe out the interior with clear warm water; then wipe it dry. Connect the plug and return the food to the freezer.

**To Clean the Exterior.** Simply wipe off the outside of your freezer with a cloth wrung out of sudsy water. Then rinse and dry. Never use an abrasive cleaner on the finish. Use wax polish to protect the finish.

**To Clean the Condenser.** Your instruction booklet tells you when and how to clean the condenser. Do this with your vacuum-cleaner brush attachment, but disconnect freezer.

**When the Power Fails.** Keep the freezer tightly closed. Then it will keep all foods except ice cream frozen for about two days. If you are not sure power will be restored in a day's time, it's wise to use dry ice or to transfer the food to another freezer or to a locker plant. If power failure occurs frequently, get food insurance through a locker plant, bank, or insurance agent.

# REFRIGERATORS

## Buying a Refrigerator

Buying a refrigerator is a major investment for most families, so be sure your husband has a part in selecting one.

If you want your refrigerator to stay right through the years (at least 10), buy one large enough to allow for changes in entertaining and family life. Many young couples could get along nicely at the start with a 7-cubic-foot refrigerator. There is no excuse for considering anything smaller, because today's refrigerators are built for close quarters. However, there is much less chance of outgrowing a refrigerator with a capacity of 8, 9, or even 10 cubic feet, and the difference in cost is more than compensated by the roominess and convenience of the larger type.

## What Features Should It Have?

As you look over different makes of refrigerators, try to imagine each one filled with the foods you bring home from the markets. Notice the depth of the vegetable crispers. Will they take a large head of lettuce or cauliflower? If meat-storage drawers are provided, are they large enough for your needs?

Look at shelf arrangements, too, remembering the space you need not only for tall bottles but for the times when you have a turkey, a rib roast, or a watermelon. Some refrigerators feature high flexibility, with split shelves that can be arranged for your convenience. Some have special shelves on outer or inner doors—a feature that rates high in front-row storage. Other outstanding innovations are a foot pedal that opens the refrigerator door when you have both hands full; a compartment that keeps butter at spreading temperature; a swing-out rack with jars for leftovers; an ultraviolet lamp that retards the growth of mold; special racks for eggs, chilling trays, sandwich boxes; and even a built-in bottle opener. Some

have drawers or bins suitable for room-temperature storage of potatoes, onions, etc.; in others, the refrigerated area extends to the bottom of the cabinet. Choose the type that best fits your needs.

## What About the Freezer Section?

Some people mistakenly believe a large freezer section is unnecessary unless a lot of frozen foods are used. Besides keeping frozen foods, a freezing compartment safeguards your extra supplies of fresh meat, butter, bread, bacon, and cheese and gives you, on a small scale, the advantages of a home freezer. You can prepare casserole dishes, pies, cakes, rolls, and other cooked foods at your leisure and store them here for future use. All the people we know who own refrigerators with large freezer sections have remarked about the delight of having ice cream and ice cubes on hand at all times.

There are two types of freezer compartment: one keeps temperatures of 0° F. or below for long storage —6 months to a year; the other maintains temperatures from 10 to 15° F. or over for shorter storage— a few weeks to a month. Your habits of buying and using foods from day to day dictate the choice between the two. Discuss matters of temperature and cost with your dealer.

## Moist-Cold Storage

The most deluxe refrigerators are those having moist-cold compartments. In these refrigerators foods do not dry out, nor do odors intermingle. Foods stored in such refrigerators should not be covered, for the air, even though cold, is very moist (beads of moisture form on the walls). Eggs, bacon, cheese, meats of all kinds can be removed from their original wrappings and stored uncovered in the food compartment. Dairy products often have a special section or storage drawer of their own.

## The Defrosting Story

There is no need to worry about the defrosting job with today's refrigerators. Manufacturers have developed an ingenious mechanism that doesn't permit frost to accumulate on the freezer and yet keeps frozen foods at proper temperature. The food-storage compartment of refrigerators with a separate freezer does not require defrosting; the freezer needs only some scraping every few months. In the conventional type of refrigerator, where defrosting is necessary, improved design in controls and drip trays has made the job simple.

## Will a Home Freezer Affect Your Purchase?

Perhaps you hope someday to buy a home freezer, and you wonder how the freezer will affect your choice of refrigerator. In considering the size, keep in mind that you will need the same amount of refrigerator space for the storage of fresh meats, vegetables, fruits, etc., either with or without a freezer. So don't skimp on the size of your refrigerator. Whether or not you should buy a refrigerator with a large freezing section of its own will take a little thought. When a home freezer can be placed in or near the kitchen, the frozen foods it holds are conveniently at hand. But when the freezer has to be placed in a basement or other inconvenient spot, a freezing section in the refrigerator serves nicely as a supplementary storage place for several days' supply of frozen foods and saves you trips to and from the freezer.

## Storing Food in Your Refrigerator

The first thing that comes to mind in considering food storage is waxed paper, the old stand-by. It is on hand in every household and lends itself to all kinds of food storage. Somewhat more costly but high in convenience is aluminum foil or Saran. They can be shaped to fit a head of lettuce or cabbage as easily as they can be fitted over a bowl or dish. If kept clean and handled carefully, they can be used again.

## Fruits, Vegetables, Greens

Most of these need cold, moist air to keep them at their peak. Exceptions, of course, are potatoes, onions, etc., which are better left out of the refrigerator. If you don't have a vegetable crisper, get yourself a roomy enameled or plastic box, with cover, to keep salad greens, celery, radishes, parsley, etc., fresh and crisp. Supplement this crisper with plastic bags for bulky cabbage, cauliflower, melons. You can keep oranges, apples, and other fruits chilled in a crisper if there is room; if not, you can put them right on the shelf for a day or two.

## Keep Leftovers in Sight

There are many convenient types of container for leftovers. Best are those with clear-glass or plastic covers, as the contents are visible at a glance. Oven-glass dishes of different sizes and shapes can be used for baking, serving, and refrigerator storage. Plastic boxes are lightweight; sets of various sizes are available in holders that keep odds and ends in one place.

A set of bowl covers is a handy refrigerator accessory, too. The covers come in so many sizes that pitchers, jugs, glasses, and even your largest mixing bowl are quickly and neatly covered.

## Fruit Juice—Ice Cold

Frozen or canned juices, iced beverages, and ice water must be stored properly. A pitcher with a hinged cover holds a reasonable amount, yet takes up little of the precious space where tall bottles are stored.

## Butter, Eggs, and Cheese

Dairy products need careful storage. They should be kept covered and well chilled. For extra convenience there are specially designed containers for eggs, butter, and even for cheese. Butter dishes of different sizes are made for table use as well as storage.

## Storing Meat

When you are preparing a salad of chicken, seafood, meat, etc., for a home or community supper, take special pains to cook, cool, and refrigerate the meat or seafood just as quickly as possible. Because cut-up meat can spoil more quickly than uncut meat, delay preparing your salad mixture as long as possible. Once it is made, store immediately, carefully covered, in the refrigerator, and keep it there until served. (Reports of food poisoning at large gatherings often are traced to unclean preparation or to failure to refrigerate such foods.)

After you've simmered chicken, ham, or tongue until tender in boiling water, don't make the mistake of letting it cool on the back of the range. Spoilage or food poisoning can start too easily in this way. Instead, speed up the cooling by removing meat from boiling broth with 2 forks. Place on a clean plate; cover loosely with waxed paper; cool quickly to lukewarm; then refrigerate. Let kettle of broth stand in cold water until lukewarm; then refrigerate that, too. After cooling broth and meat, you may return the meat to the broth, and then store, covered, in the refrigerator.

## How Long Can Meats Be Kept?

Meat experts tell us that *unless a refrigerator is equipped with space for low-temperature storage of meat,* the best policy still is to cook and serve *fresh* meat as soon as possible after purchase. They recommend periodic marketing trips during the week, in preference to once-a-week shopping for meat. If you must buy 6 or 7 days' meat supply, choose longer-keeping, cured, or canned meats for the last few days.

Even smoked, cured pork cuts, such as hams and bacon, should be used soon. Their unmatched flavor and aroma are fleeting, so plan to hold them no longer than the list below indicates, for the full, superb flavor you purchased.

(Based on storage in a household refrigerator at 36° to 40° F.)

**Beef.** See page 147.
**Pork.** See page 150.
**Lamb.** See page 149.
**Veal.** See page 148.
**Cured Meats**

| | |
|---|---|
| Sliced Bacon | 7 days |
| Ham (halves) | 7 days |
| Picnic (whole) | 10 days |
| Sliced Dried Beef | 12 days |

**Table-Ready Meats**

| | |
|---|---|
| Franks | 4 to 6 days |
| Table-Ready Meats (bologna, baked loaves, luncheon meats) | 4 to 6 days |
| Dry and Semidry Sausage (uncut) | 2 to 3 weeks |
| Braunschweiger Liver Sausage (uncut) | 4 to 6 days |

**Poultry**

| | |
|---|---|
| Chicken (not frozen) | 2 days |

**Bread.** See page 142.
**Frozen Foods.** See pages 136 and 145.
**Meat Experts Recommend:**

1. Discard outer wrapper of meat.

2. If inner wrapper (or wrappers if more than one type of meat) is in good condition, refrigerate meat in this wrapper.

3. If inner wrapper is damaged or very moist, discard it; wrap meat *loosely* in waxed paper, aluminum foil, etc.

4. Store package of meat in the meat compartment of an automatic refrigerator, or as near cooling unit as possible.

### Storing Other Foods

**Vegetables, Especially Leafy and Green Ones,** begin to lose flavor, tenderness, and vitamins immediately after picking. The refrigerator slows the process, helps preserve their goodness. Clean all vegetables as soon as you get them from market or garden. Remove discolored, withered leaves. Then store at once in the refrigerator, in food bags, waxed paper, or a vegetable crisper. Vegetables like potatoes, onions, beets, and yellow turnips keep well in a vegetable bin, basket, or other receptacle, where cool air can circulate around them.

**Eggs.** See page 141.

**Letting the Morning Milk Wait on the Doorstep** after delivery, or stand around in the kitchen, not only robs it of vitamins, but steps up its bacterial content. So always take in the milk promptly, and keep it stored, covered, in the coldest part of the refrigerator. Before opening the bottle or putting it into refrigerator, wash it—particularly the top—under running cold water. Don't wipe. Never mix new and old milk except for immediate use. Adding some of yesterday's milk to today's hastens the spoiling process. This also applies to cream.

**If Quick-Frozen Foods Are Not Kept at a Very Low Temperature** they are liable to change in appearance and lose flavor and vitamins. Even though they can be kept frozen in the freezer compartment, you cannot long conserve all the vitamin content unless your refrigerator has a compartment especially designed for quick-frozen foods. Consider this in deciding what quantities to buy. Once quick-frozen foods are thawed, do not refreeze them. Use promptly.

### Storing Ice Cream and Desserts

**In a Refrigerator-Freezer** combination, the freezer temperature will be close to zero when the control is on the normal setting. Ice-cream desserts can be made and stored, right in serving dishes if you like, hours ahead. And in this type of refrigerator you can set the freezer control at a lower temperature for as long as you feel is necessary without affecting the lower food section.

**Keeping Ice Cream,** under any conditions, calls for care. Well-made ice cream, whether homemade or bought at a store, loses some of its velvety texture if it is handled too much. Remember, the richer the ice-cream mixture, the lower the freezing and storing temperature it needs; so keep the control turned as low as possible, especially for long storage.

**Ice-Cream Desserts** are even more sensitive to temperature than packages of ice cream. Keep them as cold as your refrigerator or freezer allows; unless the air is around zero, don't keep desserts more than a few hours. Wrap or cover them to protect flavor.

**All Gelatin Desserts** need the low temperatures in a good refrigerator to chill them for serving or unmolding. Desserts made with milk, eggs, or cream, like Spanish or Bavarian cream, are especially perishable and need continuous refrigeration. So after making such desserts, hasten their cooling by setting the container in cold water or in a cold place. Then store the cooled mixture, covered, in the refrigerator until serving time. Fruit gelatins keep better than those made with cream. But plan to serve even these within a day or two, to enjoy them to the fullest.

**Be Sure That the Cream-Filled Éclairs, Cream Puffs, Layer Cakes, and Pies** you make are refrigerated from the time of making. If you buy them, be sure, if you can, that the bakery refrigerates them, too. Cream and custard fillings call for extreme cleanliness in making. What's more, they easily may cause food poisoning if left standing at room temperature. So plan to serve cream puffs, cream pies, etc., soon after making or buying. Be sure, also, to store them in the refrigerator in the meantime, and to keep any left over there, too.

## Good Refrigerator Practice

Don't freeze more ice cubes than you need. It wastes electricity. Also, you can remove the unneeded ice trays and use this space for storing a few packages of frozen foods for a week or so.

**Canned food may be stored safely** in an open can if you put it in the refrigerator, covered, just as you would if the food were in a bowl.

Maybe it is your fault that you can't find space for that extra quart of milk, that package of choice cheese, or those luscious peaches you couldn't resist at the market. Could your refrigerator pass inspection? Or is it cluttered with bits of leftovers in small dishes, jars of food that should have been used long ago, bottles of relish the family would probably enjoy if you would give them a chance to? Declare a holiday on such practices, and your refrigerator will have better circulation of cold air, which is necessary with most makes, as well as more room to store perishables.

The advantages and disadvantages of putting hot foods into the refrigerator are debatable. This practice consumes more current, or ice, and requires more frequent defrosting of the unit; but people who are unusually vitamin conscious are willing to put up with these disadvantages for the sake of greater vitamin conservation, which rapid chilling of foods assures. Also the more rapidly you chill foods, the less liable they are to spoil. They can be partly cooled first by putting them in a suitable container and placing it in cold water.

## Where To Put Your Food

1. If your refrigerator has a freezer section, you will, of course, keep all frozen foods and ice cream in it. If it does not have a freezer section, keep frozen foods and ice cream in the ice-cube compartment.

*Caution:* If your refrigerator does not have a freezer section, do not buy more frozen foods than you can conveniently store in your ice-cube compartment. They will thaw out and will have to be used immediately or discarded.

2. Most refrigerators are equipped with covered hydrators for vegetables. If yours does not, you may purchase one. Keep it on the bottom shelf.

For crisper, fresher salad greens, wrap them in aluminum foil or in one of the clear plastic wrappings specially made for this purpose before you store them in your refrigerator.

3. Berries and ripe fruit are best kept in a shallow pan.

4. Meat and fish that are to be used promptly may be kept in the tray under the ice-cube compartment. Wrap fish to prevent odors.

5. Milk and cream should be kept next to the ice-cube compartment.

6. If your refrigerator does not have a special section for eggs, for safety's sake keep them in the egg box on the bottom shelf of your refrigerator.

7. Pickles and jellies need not be kept in your refrigerator. Don't let them take up valuable space. To chill pickles, place them in the refrigerator an hour or so before serving.

## Facts About Refrigerator Care

With a conventional refrigerator, the only care required is keeping the evaporator defrosted. If defrosting is a chore, you can attach an electric defroster merely by plugging it onto the refrigerator connection cord.

A high-humidity refrigerator needs no defrosting, but the very fact that high humidity exists in the food compartment makes it natural for moisture to collect on the walls of the box. Most refrigerators of this type have a moisture "collector" that should be taken out and cleaned once a week. At the same time, clear out your refrigerator in the usual way. Be sure to wipe the walls.

1. If the ice cubes have melted and the box starts to defrost, don't call for help until you've tried to find the trouble. If the light doesn't go on, it's a signal that there's no electricity at the outlet. First check whether the plug has been accidentally pulled out. Next, try the fuse. It may have blown from a temporary overload. If the light is on, check the cold con-

trol; maybe it was turned off and forgotten. If none of these is responsible, the refrigerator needs repair.

2. If the butter is too soft, milk bottles not cold, etc., examine your cold control. In some climates and under some conditions, the normal setting will not keep your refrigerator as cold as you want it. Turn control to a colder setting.

3. If foods freeze in the food compartment, again check the cold control. You may have used a very cold setting for too long a time. When you freeze foods, remember to use the cold setting only as long as necessary to freeze them; then return to normal setting.

4. If your refrigerator seems to be running too much of the time, it may or may not be a cause for concern. Normally, a refrigerator runs about one-third of the time.

5. If you're worried because the refrigerator drips with moisture, either inside or out, consider the weather. If it's hot and humid, dripping is normal, especially around the door. There's nothing to do but wipe it.

Keep your refrigerator spotlessly clean. Wipe up anything as soon as it is spilled. For a good clean-up, wash the inside with lukewarm water to which you've added some baking soda or borax. Keep a wary eye on the door gasket. Try not to touch it at all as you open and close the door, for grease from your hands is rubber's worst enemy. If you find black stains where the door gasket touches the refrigerator, it is usually a sign that the gasket is deteriorating. If you get grease on the gasket, wash it immediately with soap and water, and dry. The gasket must make a tight seal. Check the seal by closing the door on a dollar bill or piece of paper about the same thickness. Do this all around the door. If you feel a slight tug when you withdraw the bill, the gasket is making a proper seal. If not, it should be adjusted by a serviceman.

Don't let more than a quarter of an inch of frost collect on the freezer. If you don't have an automatic defroster, make defrosting time as definite as any other regular task. If your refrigerator has a fan-cooled, fin-type condenser, you should clean it at least once a year, as called for in the manufacturer's directions. *Before cleaning, disconnect the refrigerator cord from the electric outlet.*

Quickest, easiest way to defrost your refrigerator is: Turn off refrigerator; remove ice-cube trays, and replace with flat pans of warm (not boiling) water. The freezer trays can be used—unless manufacturer's instructions say not to. To catch ice that melts off bottom and sides of freezer, keep drip tray in place, spread clean paper on shelf below. When de-

---

### BEST TEMPERATURES FOR REFRIGERATING FRESH FOODS

| | |
|---|---|
| General Food Storage | 35° to 40° F. |
| Uncooked Meat (short storage) | 36° to 38° F. |
| Short-Storage Frozen Foods | 10° to 20° F. |
| Ice-Cream Storage | 10° F. |
| Long-Storage Frozen Foods | 0° F. |
| Fast Home Freezing | −20° F. |

---

frosting is completed, clean inside and outside of freezer. Then turn on the refrigerator.

### How Cold Should Your Refrigerator Be?

For general food storage, your refrigerator should be kept at a temperature of approximately 40 degrees F. But don't take it for granted that the average setting on the refrigerator dial will maintain this temperature under all conditions. If you have put hot food in the refrigerator, you may have to turn the control to a colder setting for a short period of time. If you have been opening and closing the refrigerator door constantly during preparation of a meal, or if you have neglected to close it tightly, the temperature inside the refrigerator may have gained a few degrees. Again, turn the control to a colder setting for a short period of time. However, don't forget about it or you will find ice in your milk and other foods partially frozen within several hours.

### When You Are Away

If you expect to be away from home for several days or more, you should follow this procedure:

1. Turn your refrigerator control to the lowest setting on the dial. (Sometimes marked "vacation.")

2. Remove all perishable food.

3. Make sure the refrigerator is clean. Wipe up any juice or sauces that may have spilled or splashed on the shelves or walls of the refrigerator.

4. Leave the door ajar.

(Of course, if you are planning to keep long-frozen foods in the freezer section of a refrigerator, you will have to maintain proper storage temperature even while you are away. However, it is most economical to plan to use up such foods before your departure date to save the cost of running the refrigerator.)

# KITCHEN RANGES

## Shopping for Your New Range

**Where to Begin.** If you have a choice of gas or electricity, determine which fuel is most suitable and economical. Public-utility companies in your town will give you their rates and perhaps approximate operating costs for both fuels.

**When Rates Don't Give the Answer.** If one rate is decidedly more to your advantage, you have the answer and there is no problem. But when the use of gas and electricity is fairly comparable, your decision becomes more difficult. In some cases, the proper fuel connection for the range is the deciding factor. Not all homes are wired for electric ranges or piped for gas, so use the available connection, to save expense.

When you consider the cost of installing suitable wiring for an electric range, find out whether your public-utility company can supply 230-volt 3-wire service in your home. Next, have an electrical contractor make a survey of your present wiring. Such a survey will reveal whether or not your utility company or dealer will share a part of the wiring costs, as they sometimes do.

Installing a gas range for manufactured or natural gas consists of running piping from the gas meter to your range. If bottled gas is to be used, determine the outside location for the tanks of fuel; then have the gas piped through suitable valves and regulators to your range.

**Special Features.** You will find many special features in both gas and electric ranges. Here are 9 for you to consider when you shop for a new kitchen range:

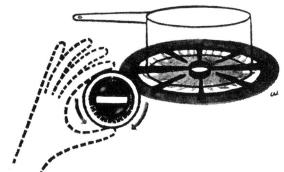

**1. Taming the Top Stove.** You can now have thermostatically controlled cooking on the top stove just as you do in the oven. Above, the gas burner has a dial marked in degrees; just set it to the prescribed temperature for sautéing, deep-fat frying, etc. Electric ranges have similar elements.

**2. For Short-Order Chefs.** A professional short-order chef is fussy about heat when making pancakes

because he knows that a few degrees can make the difference between light and fluffy or "sad" and tough pancakes. So the manufacturers of both gas and electric ranges have perfected the ever popular griddle and given it its own heat control. Without having to juggle the heat, you can make perfect hamburgers, grilled sandwiches, etc.

**3. Fine Engineering.** Broilers are easier to clean, smoke less, have generous broiler pans that glide in and out. And pan adjustment is easier with devices like those shown here—a lever (at left) and a crank (at right).

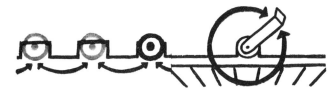

**4. Better Top-Stove Arrangements.** One range manufacturer has moved the burners to the back of the range, which gives 40 inches of front space. For busy cooks, ranges are available with 5 or 6 burners or elements.

**5. Robot Cooking on the Top Stove.** Here's an electric-range control that takes over completely and almost thinks for you. Suppose you've put a pan of potatoes on for dinner. Wouldn't you like to have it come to a fast boil, simmer gently, and then stop cooking when the potatoes are done? It will—with this control.

**6. Choice of Colors.** When you are buying a complete new kitchen, you'll want to consider all appliances in color. Today you can have a new range in one of a dozen colors. However, if a new range is all you are buying and you are uncertain about future color plans, you should choose white.

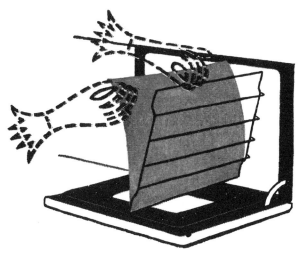

**7. Ranges Are Easier to Keep Clean.** The sketch above shows a brand-new idea for keeping the oven clean without work. Just fit special aluminum-foil sheets behind the removable rack glides, and replace them when they get spattered or crusty with grease. One new range has a disposable bowl under each top-stove unit, to catch spills. Another, a truly deluxe gas range, has a top, hinged at the back, that lifts up for a thorough cleaning underneath.

**8. Rotisseries.** Broilers equipped with motor-driven rotisseries do a wonderful job of roasting and barbecuing chicken, duck, turkey, pork, beef, etc. There's no storage problem, either; the rotisserie is part of your range. The spit on which you place the roast is suspended over the broiler pan, when you slide the pan into the broiler the spit engages the motor and starts turning.

**9. The Built-In Range.** A built-in range comes in two parts so the surface cooking unit can be installed in one place and the oven in another. Basically, the idea behind a built-in appliance of any kind is to make the appliance blend into the kitchen by becoming part of a wall or line of cabinets. This means expert and often costly installation.

A built-in range provides flexibility, for you can have a selection of heights at which to place the oven, and almost complete freedom about locating the surface unit. But a built-in must be planned for

carefully. You will have to answer such questions as where the surface unit will be put in relation to the oven, how you will place the ventilating fan so it will serve both parts of the range, where you will place two ovens if needed, what kind of counter material you will use adjacent to the surface unit, etc. In short, you will have to give built-ins some thorough study and get expert help in working one into your new kitchen.

### Know Your Range

#### The Top Stove

When you buy a new range, don't overlook the top stove, on which you'll probably do three-quarters of your cooking. In both gas and electric ranges, you'll find special features for closer control of heat.

**Just the Heat You Want.** Heats from "High" to "Keep Warm" are provided in different ways. On electric ranges, the switch or control can be turned to any one of several positions—usually 5 or 7, sometimes more. Modern gas burners are of 2 general types—dual or high-low. These burners are designed to give you a definite keep-cooking position as well as full heat. With the dual burner, the full flame quickly brings foods to the boiling point, and the small center flame keeps them cooking or keeps them hot. There's no uncertainty about setting this center flame, and there's no chance of its going out, as some burners do when turned low.

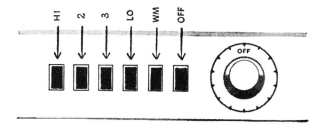

*On some electric ranges individual push buttons tune in, radio fashion, to just the heat you want. Each button has its own colored light to serve as a signal.*

*Two views of a gas burner that makes life easier for the cook. Foods simmer or stay hot on the tiny center flame, without worry about flame's going out.*

**Indicator Lights.** One of the good new features on top stoves are indicator lights (these remind you that heat has been left on), fluorescent lights illuminating the cooking top, and colored lights that signal cooking speed or heat to which each unit is turned.

**Cooking Charts.** Cooking charts, giving time and temperature information, are frequently incorporated on the top stove or on the oven door, so you can quickly verify the right times for cooking, baking, and roasting.

**Safety Guard.** A safety guard against the prying fingers of children also is provided on some ranges. A key arrangement makes it possible to lock the top-stove or oven controls so they cannot be turned on.

**Push-Button Control.** Instead of the usual round electric switch, some units have 6 small push buttons. They are marked for a particular cooking speed, and they glow with an indicating color—red for high, green for cooking speed, blue for keep-warm, yellow and purple for in-between heats.

**Well Cookers.** For many years, the well cooker was an established feature on electric ranges. It provided a convenient out-of-the-way cooking utensil large enough for cooking soups, stews, and bulky vegetables. Sacrificing the fourth unit was not wholly satisfactory to some housekeepers. Today, many ranges have a "three-way" unit, combining well cooker, pressure saucepan, or deep fryer and regular cooking unit. The heating unit is raised to surface level when desired.

## The Oven

**The Value of Two Ovens.** Two oven ranges offer greater convenience and flexibility. Simultaneously, one oven can be used for baking, the other for broiling. If one oven is busy with the main dish, use the other for baking the dessert.

**Oven Racks.** Good ranges are provided with sturdy, lock-stop, nontipping oven racks—a great improvement over the old-type racks.

**Heat Regulation.** Constant and accurate oven-heat regulation is another thing for which we can thank range manufacturers. Once the control is set, you can relax until baking or roasting time is over, thereby eliminating the watchfulness otherwise required.

**A Glass Door in the Oven.** For those who can't resist peeking, a range with a glass oven door becomes almost a necessity. Some ranges are equipped with switch-on lights, which operate without opening the door. On some ranges, the glass partition is removable and can be taken to the sink for cleaning.

**The Automatic-Timer Clock.** The automatic-timer clock is a deluxe feature on both electric and gas

*The trend to two-oven ranges delights women. They like being able to bake and broil at the same time, as well as the flexibility of so much oven space.*

ranges. This is not to be confused with the simple reminder clocks used for timing operations. It is a mechanism that turns heat on and off automatically. On many electric ranges, these clocks can be used to control not only the oven but also the well cooker and convenience outlet.

**Hours of Freedom.** Consider carefully whether or not such automatic cooking is important enough to you to warrant the added cost. There is no doubt that automatic cooking, if wisely used, can give hours of freedom from the kitchen.

**Let the Timer Clock Work for You.** Establish the habit of letting the timer clock work for you. To some women, the whole idea seems complicated—not just setting the clock, but planning menus and preparing foods considerably ahead of cooking time. Actually, the complete oven meal does not best illustrate the use of the timer. The automatic cooking of a roast while the family is at church makes you realize that having a range with a timer is like having an automatic cook.

## The Broiler

When you select a new range, make sure that the broiling facilities offer what you want.

In Electric Ranges, the direct unit of the baking oven's top element is used for broiling. Therefore, broiling is done at the same height as baking.

In Gas Ranges, the position of the broiling oven depends on the model. If the same burner is used for baking and broiling, the broiler is located below the baking oven. On these models, the broiler is quite low and close to the floor—objectionably so, in most cases.

Separate Broiler Compartments. The low broiler is eliminated in gas ranges having separate broiling compartments. This is a real convenience, because the broiler pan may be the pull-out type—it swings out when the door is opened—or a special, deep broiling section, designed particularly for broiling or "barbecuing" large cuts of meat.

The High Oven and Broiler. Some ranges have the oven placed well above the cooking top so baking and broiling can be done at a much higher and more convenient level. On such a range, the same burner can be used for baking and broiling, without any height disadvantages.

The Broiler Pan. Part and parcel of a good broiler on a modern range is a well-designed broiler pan, with its own rack or slotted grid. Most broiler pans are made of porcelain enamel or chrome for easy cleaning and have an adequate fat well.

*A "built-in" or "stack-on" range with a nonstoop oven and broiler. Individual units are installed so that the baking and broiling oven is at the right height for you.*

## Study Your New Range

When your range is installed and ready for use, familiarize yourself with its component parts and carefully study the instruction booklet. Then keep the book in a handy place. Remember that a well-designed, well-constructed range is about as perfect as engineering can make it; but its performance depends on its being used with forethought and care. If your range does not perform as you think it should, immediately call the public-utility company and ask them to send a home-service specialist. Undoubtedly she can put her finger on the trouble and save you waste of time and food.

## Take Care of Your Range

The Oven. Let the heat control help keep your oven clean: use the low-temperature method of roasting meat. When you bake casseroles, be sure to use a dish that won't have to be filled more than two-thirds full, so the food has room to expand. Apple and berry pies also are likely to create a cleaning problem. Don't take any chances of having the sugary juice boil out of the crust and onto the oven. On the bottom rack, under the pie, slide a cookie sheet or aluminum foil. Be sure it doesn't cover the entire bottom and shut off baking heat.

Oven doors on modern ranges are made to close easily and fit well. Slamming them shut isn't necessary and does them no good. Close-fitting doors conserve heat and fuel, help you do a better job of roasting and baking.

The Broiler. Getting rid of grease is the biggest problem in cleaning a range broiler. As soon as broiling is finished, remove the broiler pan and pour the hot fat into a drippings can. If the pan is left inside the range while the broiler section cools, the fat cools on the pan and cleaning is thus made more difficult, so be sure to take it out.

Top of the Range. If you cook carefully, you'll seldom have to do more than wipe off the top of your range with a damp cloth. A damp cloth should not be applied to the enamel top until the range has cooled, so have paper towels handy to wipe up spilled food, grease spatters, etc., before they dry and harden. Be especially prompt in wiping up acid-food spills, such as fruit juice and vinegar, which may discolor the surface. Although most modern range tops are food-acid-resistant, they are not acidproof.

To prevent spilling over, bring food or water quickly to a boil over high heat; then turn down the flame, and let the food boil gently or simmer. Also, cook in utensils large enough for the amount of food.

# SMALL APPLIANCES

**Is Your Home Properly Wired for Appliances?**
Successful use of today's appliances, both large and small, depends on the adequacy of your wiring system. Unless the wires are large enough, you may find yourself owning more appliances than you can use. If you plan to buy a new appliance, check your kitchen carefully to make certain your wiring will take the additional load. You may want to ask the help of a reliable electrical contractor or enlist the aid of your local power company in establishing just how much your kitchen wiring will take. It will make all your experiences with new appliances happier ones. Any serviceman will tell you that blown fuses account for more service calls than any other electrical difficulty. You may use several appliances on a circuit for months and never have any trouble. Then one day you turn them on simultaneously, and the fuse blows. The following list of typical wattage ratings show how easy it is to overload a circuit.

### Typical Appliance Wattages

| | |
|---|---:|
| Automatic Toaster | 1,100 |
| Coffeemaker | up to 1,000 |
| Waffle Baker or Sandwich Grill | up to 1,000 |
| Mixer | 100 |
| Radio | 100 |
| Television Set | 200 |
| Built-in Ventilating Fan | 100 |
| Electric Roaster | 1,650 |
| Refrigerator | 150 |

*Each time your refrigerator starts, it uses several times this wattage just for an instant.*

| | |
|---|---:|
| Automatic Hand Iron | 1,000 |
| Ironer | 1,650 |
| Floor Lamp | 150–300 |
| Table Lamp | 50–150 |
| Fluorescent Light (Each Tube) | 15–40 |
| Vacuum Cleaner | 125 |
| Portable Heater | 1,000 |
| Portable Electric Fan | 100 |
| Electric Bedcover | 200 |

**What Is This Thing Called a Warranty?** A warranty is a form of insurance on an appliance offered and guaranteed by the manufacturer. However, the manufacturer depends on his authorized dealers or distributors to carry out the guaranty's terms. These terms—the extent and duration of the warranty—are usually given on the last page of the instruction booklet. When you fulfill your obligation by returning this warranty as per instructions, you have an invaluable contract for service, replacement of defective parts, and general interest in the installation and smooth working of the appliance.

**Keep Your Instruction Booklets.** There's hardly an appliance sold today without specific directions for proper use. In spite of the fact that manufacturers strive to give new users understandable, easy-to-read instructions, women either throw the booklets away or put them in such a safe place that they can't find them. Losing yours may cost you a tidy sum, for directions are valueless after you have burned out a motor or thrown an automatic timer out of whack. The more expertly you use and understand modern appliances, the more money you'll save on service bills.

**What Appliances Will You Need?** There are a number of small appliances on the market today. Which ones you will want to have in your home depends on the kind of cooking and the amount of entertaining you are accustomed to. Certainly you need a good toaster, and a mixer is an invaluable aid to have in the kitchen. Described here is a number of other small appliances in popular use today. Which of them do you need to bring your home up to date?

*Don't buy blindly. Know what types of toasters are available.*

*Don't hide your toaster in a dark and inaccessible corner.*

*Do try to find a convenient, permanent place to keep it.*

## The Toaster

Of all electrical appliances, an automatic toaster that browns the toast just as you like it and pops it up, hot and crisp, can save you the most exasperation. It's a blue-ribbon performer in the household, whether it's working at breakfast, or making toast at the luncheon or dinner table.

The wide choice in types and styles of toaster may bewilder you. Before you make your decision, consider your budget. (1) Deluxe and most expensive toasters are completely automatic, pop up two slices, browned light or dark, and reheat toast. (2) Slightly less expensive is another type of pop-up toaster, which has a control for brownness, but is less reliable on cold toast or frozen bread. (3) Least in cost is the nonautomatic toaster—the bread must be turned and watched. Aim high—the more deluxe, the more convenient.

When you are looking over toasters, ask the salesman to point out differences. Most automatic toasters, because of their thermostats, must be used on alternating current. However, one or two automatics, and all nonautomatics, can be used on either alternating or direct current. Notice what provision is made for cleaning crumbs from the toaster. Many have easily removed crumb trays. Consider styling, too, so the toaster will grace your table when used in the dining room. Cords should be listed by Underwriters Laboratories.

All toasters, whether of the automatic's high wattage (1,000 or 1,100 watts) or the nonautomatic's somewhat lower wattage, must be plugged into an outlet *on which no other appliance is used while the toaster is in use.*

**Caring for Your Toaster** is simple. (1) Protect from dust with a plastic cover. (2) Don't wrap cord

around toaster or put on cover until toaster is cool. (3) Empty crumbs, and keep outside of toaster clean with soft cloth. If wiping doesn't suffice, use silver polish or cleaner.

## Your Electric Mixer

Mixers were made to be strong arms—to supply the continued power to make cakes, cookies, 7-minute frostings, mashed potatoes, candies, meringues, hard sauce, etc. The mixer does the work; you do the managing. Mixers take over the fruit-juicing job, too, for this attachment is often sold as part of the mechanism.

With a deluxe mixer like this in your kitchen, you have two bowls (one large and one small), a motor that is portable (so the beaters can be used with or without the stand), and lots of speeds clearly marked on the dial. You can take your choice, beginning with speed No. 1, which says, "for adding dry ingredients," going through No. 3—"beating prepared mixes, cakes, etc."—right up to No. 10—"icings, candy." You hardly have to think at all when a mixer takes over a job.

**The Simpler Mixers.** Portable mixers, with or without stands, smaller in size and with fewer speeds (just one speed in some cases), can be bought for something like half as much as the deluxe variety. These take the hard work out of mashing potatoes, making cakes, whipping cream, etc. However, it's not fair to expect them to work quite so fast as larger mixers, or with so little scraping of the sides of the bowl. Still, they *are* light, easy to handle, and simple to clean. Here's a big point for pocket-size kitchens: If you buy a small portable with its own wall bracket, you won't need to worry about giving up working space to the mixer. If you've already investigated mixers a bit on your own, you've seen the powerful model in which the bowl stands still and the beating device (this may be either a paddle or a whip) travels around inside the bowl. It's true that with this type of electric mixer you must use the mixer's own bowl, and you can't detach the mixer head, but you hardly ever have to scrape. And how it plows through heavy mixtures!

**Make Space for a Mixer.** Before trying to decide just which mixer you want, consider first where a mixer can be used in your kitchen. Reaching for and lifting a mixer any real distance will discourage your use of it; so be sure you can count on storing your mixer where it will be usable at all times. If your kitchen is small and working space is limited, give serious thought to fitting in a small, base cabinet or table, where the mixer can be kept conveniently on top, with the attachments readily available below. A mixer is a time- and labor-saving convenience *only* if it is on hand just when you need it.

**Look for These Features.** 1. Beater blades that slip in and out easily, so you won't have to handle them when they are sticky with batter. 2. A variety of speeds. Remember your mixer will have to take care of the slow blending of flour in cakes as well as the high-speed whipping of cooked icings and creaming of shortening and sugar, as in making cakes. Your direction booklet will be invaluable to you in learning to use your mixer. Study and use it until you're completely familiar with the mixer. 3. Ease of using the mixer while in operation. With the larger mixers, see how easily you can remove the beater stand and whether the handle feels comfortable. Ask the salesperson about the way you change from large to small bowl. In some mixers you move the platform; in one you have fingertip control of bowl position. Another mixer has a feature that keeps the beater speed uniform, and you don't have to turn the bowl by hand even with heavy mixtures. Notice the position of the speed control. Is it easy to reach and to read without peering closely at the individual speed markings? 4. Attachments that you want. A fruit juicer is usually a part of the beater, gives very fast, efficient extraction, and strains the seeds and pulp as you juice. Strainers differ in design. Some fit into your bowl; others hook on to it. One strainer joggles as you juice—a help in keeping it from becoming clogged. If you're interested in an attachment to make drinks, churn butter, shell peas, grind meat, or perform other special chores for which attachments are made, be sure to see whether they are available with the mixer that interests you. If you learn that such attachments are not available now, but will be, ask to see pictures of them and inquire about how they are used. (Direction booklets often display them.) If any strike you as complicated, look at those for other mixers.

**Mixer Care.** There are two very important points to remember: don't let water or juice splash or run into the motor, and be sure to follow directions for oiling the motor.

Unless you own the permanently lubricated type, occasionally apply a few drops of light household oil to the motor turntable. See your instruction book for when and how to oil.

After each use, go over the outside of the mixer with a damp cloth. Use a rubber spatula to scrape the bowl, but keep it away from those whirling mixer blades.

**A Blender at Work**

Distinctive with a blender are the whirlwind blades in a container. They have great power—with only a few seconds' whirling, the blades can blend, chop, grate, purée, or shred. Cream soups, sandwich spreads, salad dressings, frozen desserts are only a few of the almost countless things this amazing labor-saver can help prepare. What's more, with a blender most jobs take only seconds and are done right in the container, so there isn't an assortment of mixing bowls and tools to wash.

On the other hand, the business of making cakes in the blender is something we can't endorse wholeheartedly. With specific directions and recipes, an acceptable cake (or batter of any kind) can be turned out, but not as easily nor as well as in a mixer. At times, there are some spectacular uses to which blenders can be put. You can use it for grating bits of cheese and grinding bread crumbs. But be sure all these jobs will mean real timesaving to *you* before you buy.

Perhaps you have been considering the purchase of an electric blender only because it costs less than an electric mixer. Think it over carefully. An electric blender performs many useful services, but it cannot take the place of a mixer in the kitchen.

**Blender Care.** Disconnect the cord and wipe off the motor base after each use. If it has hard-to-clean ventilation slots, use a soft, dry brush, as water might seep into the motor. Wash the glass container along with your dishes. Blenders aren't cement mixers; the blades can break as well as the glass. So don't tempt fate by trying to crush large ice cubes. When you're making mixed drinks, crack the ice before putting it in the blender.

### Waffle Baker

An automatic waffle iron can be used without watching or guesswork. Satisfactory automatic waffle irons won't get too hot or too cool, so you needn't peek while a waffle is baking. As with toasters, set the dial for light, medium, or dark, and then bake. Automatic waffle irons should need little care. This is why it pays to determine the exact amount of batter needed for a perfect waffle from each iron. Use a suitable-size ladle.

Even an automatic waffle iron needs to be seasoned when new, unless the manufacturer advises to the contrary. To season, brush the cold grids thoroughly with unsalted, melted fat. Heat the iron to baking temperature; then let it cool. The first waffle baked after the iron is seasoned must be discarded, because it is likely to be greasy. After that, waffles shouldn't stick if you use a recipe containing shortening. Try the recipe on one of the packaged pancake, biscuit, or waffle mixes.

**Waffle Baker Care.** When the last waffle is baked, open the grids to let them cool. This helps prevent the seasoning from drying out. While the grids are still warm, wipe them with a dry cloth to remove excess grease and crumbs. Polish the outside just as you do the toaster. There's little you can do to brighten grids that have darkened; in fact, they brown waffles better than shiny ones do. Use the right amount of batter, and you'll save yourself a clean-up job. Everyone misjudges occasionally, but constantly overflowing batter causes burned-on grease that may never come off.

### Electric Roaster

**1. Set the Roaster in a Convenient Place.** The ideal arrangement is a table or cabinet on which the roaster can be kept and connected for use. Several roaster manufacturers make special cabinets (some of them

*The wonderful deep-fat fryer*

have casters, so the roaster can be rolled from one place to another). Shelves in the cabinet can be used as a storage place for baking and roasting utensils. A roaster requires between 1,320 and 1,650 watts, alternating (AC) current. It must have an appliance outlet that is not used for any other electrical device while the roaster is in use. If this rule is not followed, the roaster may heat improperly and the fuses may be blown.

**2. Follow the Manufacturer's Instructions.** Most cooking times and temperatures in a roaster are based on a preheated roaster and conform to usual recipe directions. Follow the manufacturer's booklet for temperatures and baking times when you bake cakes, pies, rolls, cookies, etc. Experience will prove them to be right.

**3. Don't Peek.** Every time you remove the lid, the roaster loses heat; the escape of heat slows cooking and retards browning. When you cook more than one dish, have the additional one ready the minute you open the roaster. The "peek-in" glass inserts in some roaster lids contribute to peace of mind, as you can check on the browning of cookies or a cheese soufflé without wasting heat.

**4. Let the Roaster Work for You.** Your roaster will do more than the usual baking, roasting, and broiling. Use it to heat canned soups, warm dinner rolls. Keep delayed meals warm without drying them out by setting the roaster's control dial at 150° F. Take the roaster to church suppers or on picnics (when the roaster can't be connected, cover it with a blanket; food can be kept hot several hours). Use the grid of the broiler unit for toasting; making griddle cakes; cooking bacon, ham, eggs, French toast, etc.

### "Infrared" Broilers

The portable electric broiler is far from a new appliance. As long ago as the twenties, closed-type table broilers with round or oval dome-shaped covers were available. And they're still popular today. But most asked about are open-front broilers that cook with so-called infrared rays. There is no magic about them. They simply cook with radiant heat, just as range broilers do. So these new broilers cannot possibly give you better results or broil faster than a good range broiler.

However, a well-designed, well-made portable broiler is a great convenience in a kitchen with an outmoded range or a broiler that is placed lower than you like. When meat is put directly under the electric element, you get a searing charcoal broil with a minimum of effort.

If you are considering buying a broiler, here are some facts you should know.

1. Many of these broilers are very easy to clean. The pan and grid are small enough to go into a dishpan, and the outer and inner broiler surfaces can be wiped clean easily.

2. Don't expect a broiler to be a smokeless miracle. When open-front broilers are used to broil meats that have a fair amount of fat, some smoking and spattering must be expected. The closer the meat is to the element, the more smoking and spattering there will be.

3. For safety's sake, the broiler should be listed by Underwriters' Laboratories.

4. If a broiler is going to be useful, you'll have to have a convenient place to keep it and plug it in.

5. Broilers are high-wattage appliances, and while they can usually be used safely on a household electric circuit, they should not be plugged into a line at the same time as other appliances. This may be a special problem in an old, poorly wired house or in apartments.

### Deep Frying—Automatically

The new automatic electric deep-fat fryers are reviving the fine art of frying. With one of these, it's easy to turn out hot, crisp, golden French fries, croquettes, batter-dipped sea food, chicken, etc.

In most fryers 3 to 6 pounds of shortening are required for deep frying. This fat can be reused a good many times if you strain it often and add some fresh fat every time or two. Smoking and a bitter, burned flavor are no problem with an automatic fryer, since the temperature control keeps the fat from overheating. Frying is safer, since you don't cook near an open flame.

Most fried foods cook in a comparatively few minutes, and even the smaller electric fryers can produce a meal for four in short order. And if you want menu variety, a fryer can add hundreds of new dishes to your collection.

### The Electric Frying Pan

The electric frying pan fries bacon and eggs beautifully, because the perfect temperature settings— bacon 340° F., fried eggs 300° F.—are given on the handle thermostat. At the handle-prescribed 380° F., pancakes turn out perfectly. At every temperature setting it offers the same kind of heat control for skillet cooking that you get with an oven.

### Automatic Coffeemakers

Automatic coffeemakers add a modern air and

*Electric frying pan with handle thermostat*

convenience to the old-fashioned art of making perfect coffee. Both percolator and vacuum-type turn out good coffee with identical ease and look handsome on the table. They handle the whole job of brewing coffee; then keep the coffee hot until you serve it. With any type of coffeemaker, stick to the rule of using level measurements and fresh coffee, because that is the only way we can be sure of good coffee every time. Most people like 2 level tablespoonfuls of drip-grind coffee to each 8-ounce cupful of water (one-half pint).

Automatic coffeemakers can be obtained in either percolator or vacuum types. There's a semiautomatic vacuum type, too. You must switch the heat from high to low to finish the brewing and keep the coffee hot. Keep your coffeemaker scrupulously clean. A special curved brush is excellent for cleaning glass bowls.

**Coffeemaker Care.** A few simple rules cover the care of electric coffeemakers. The heating element must never be put in water, so wash the pot carefully. You can save a trip to the service center if you don't allow the coffee to evaporate. If you do, the pot will overheat and the safety fuse will have to be replaced —a minor repair, but a needless bother.

### Fans

In hot, humid weather, electric fans give the air movement which provides a feeling of coolness and comfort even though the temperature is not actually lowered.

The kitchen and laundry are two rooms where fans are especially helpful. The kitchen fan removes warm air and cooking odors, and prevents their spread throughout the house. Fans installed in the laundry help remove moisture-laden air, which if not removed, may necessitate frequent repairs and redecorating.

The proper placement of a fan is of the utmost importance. Place it where it will have an unobstructed air path; never let it blow directly on a place where people usually sit or stand. The oscillating fan has advantages in this respect, as it circulates the air over a wide area but a short path. Large fans, if placed before an open window, effectively keep the air in circulation. Fans used on the floor should be of the circulator type or they should have special soft-rubber or ribbon-type blades to avoid injury from accidental contact. Children always should be kept away from exposed fan blades. Metal- or plastic-bladed fans usually are not well guarded at the rear and edges, where guards are needed. These fans should be placed out of reach.

**Care.** To keep a fan in repair, whether it is an air-circulating or exhaust fan, you only have to clean and oil it.

### Garbage Disposers

**What a Garbage Disposer Can Do.** Garbage disposers grind or shred rinds and peels, all vegetable and fruit trimmings, corncobs, eggshells, plate scrapings, coffee grounds, ash-tray contents, and small bones. The waste is pushed into the sink-drain opening, or into a hopper where it is ground to a pulp and washed away by a continuous flow of cold water.

**What a Garbage Disposer Cannot Do.** It will not get rid of large bones, seafood, nutshells (except soft ones), cans, jars, paper cartons, or string, including that on tea bags. Some instruction booklets advise against grinding any "fibrous matter": such things as artichoke leaves, sweet-corn silk, and husks.

**Types of Garbage Disposer.** Garbage disposers are sold as part of dishwashing or electric sinks, but one can be installed in your present sink if it is standard and has a sufficiently large drain opening. There are two general types of disposer. With one, the hopper is filled with waste, the cover put in place, and the disposer turned to "grind" position. Turning the cold-water faucet about halfway around starts the disposer. The other type, called the "continuous feed" type, grinds with the cover off, and the waste is gradually fed into the protected opening and ground as cold water flushes it away. Hot water never should be used for grinding, as it liquefies the grease and coats the interior of the drain line and clogs the drain. Cold water congeals the grease so it is easily carried away.

**Installation Facts.** 1. If you plan to buy a garbage disposer, check municipal regulations on its installation. Some cities and towns do not permit their use as yet.

2. Installing a disposer requires the services of a plumber and an electrician.

3. Garbage disposers can be used with septic tanks, but it provides an extra load (about 50 per cent) on the tank.

4. A garbage disposer is not a convenience-outlet device. It must have a permanent electrical connection, operating on AC current, protected by a 15-ampere fuse.

**The Best Way to Use a Disposer.** 1. Learn the difference in sound of grinding and of running the disposer with water alone.

2. Cut refuse into small pieces, so it drops easily into the hopper.

3. If bulky leaves are packed into the hopper, they won't feed into the unit.

4. The drain cover is an important protector of the disposer unit. When you are at the sink, and the disposer is uncovered, a paring knife, dishcloth, spoon, etc., may fall into the disposer.

5. Garbage disposers are self-cleaning, never have an odor, and are entirely sanitary.

**Will You Need a Garbage Pail?** Even with an automatic garbage disposer, you will need a container for cans, cartons, throw-away bottles, large bones, paper wrappings, berry baskets, twine, and bottle caps. These items cannot be put into the disposer.

For a tidier kitchen, get a covered step-on container. An enameled garbage can with a rust-resistant inner liner and a tight-fitting cover is most satisfactory. Moisture-resistant garbage bags greatly add to the neatness of handling.

**Change Your Ways.** Take full advantage of the convenience offered by an automatic garbage disposer. Instead of collecting parings and pits from fruits and vegetables on pieces of paper, work right over the sink, grinding the waste whenever enough is collected. And when you clear the table, rinse dishes for stacking while you scrape chicken bones, gravy, baked-potato shells, etc., into the garbage disposer. This scrape-rinse-stack procedure saves much of the time and energy of dishwashing.

### Other Small Appliances

The number of small electrical appliances on the market today is larger than it was ten years ago and it is growing every day. A visit to your small appliance store will turn up many new gadgets that save time and simplify the job of keeping house. There are deep-fat fryers, egg cookers, knife sharpeners, ice-cream freezers, casseroles, fruit juicers, and bottle warmers. Watch for other new developments that will lighten your chores and take over part of your daily work.

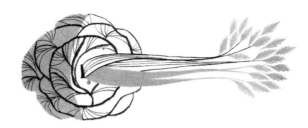

# Guide to Wise Eating

Read your local newspaper for the best food buys —you will find the market reports an excellent guide.

Don't wait until you get to market to plan your meals. Plan them at least a day ahead, taking into account foods on hand in refrigerator.

Prepare a businesslike marketing list. Avoid buying more than the family will eat by checking your recipes and amounts to buy. List alternate choices, in case foods are not available, or you find better buys.

It is best to go to market to buy perishables. Then you can check on quality, watch for bargains, and keep up to date on new foods.

Read descriptive labels on foods in cans, jars and packages for information on size, amount, variety, style, number of servings, kind of syrup, uses, etc. When you find a brand you like, remember the name.

Often you can save by purchasing a large rather than a small package of a product you use often and you know will keep well.

Get the full weight of a product for your money. Ask the price per pound, watch the scale while purchases are being weighed, and be sure to count your change. A customer's indifference is likely to encourage carelessness, if nothing worse.

## STOCKING YOUR SHELVES

Stock your pantry shelves not only with staples, but with foods in packages, cans, and jars, so you always have on hand the nucleus for a delectable meal. Replenish the stock regularly (keep a pad and pencil at hand to jog your memory) before the last of a much-needed staple or special favorite is used up.

When you make your purchases, buy the can, jar, and package sizes that suit the size of your family and your storage space.

Some canned meat products calls for storing them in the refrigerator.

See the label for this information.

Your first meals will be much easier if you start with well-stocked pantry shelves. Naturally you won't want to buy everything at once—just those items essential to the meals for a week or two. Stock up on other things as you need them.

The following list will guide you in stocking your shelves, not only with staples, but with foods in jars, cans and packages that fit your budget and the taste of your family. Scan your grocer's shelves for items not included in this list.

Baking powder
Baking soda
Bouillon cubes, meat-extract paste
Bread crumbs, dried
Canned foods or foods in jars:
    Baby pack: fruits, meats, vegetables, etc.
    Baked beans, chili beans, etc.
    Breads: brown, chocolate nut, date and nut, etc.
    Chicken: boned, fricasseed, whole, etc.
    Chinese foods: bean sprouts, chop suey, chow mein, chow-mein noodles, etc.

Cranberry sauce: jellied or whole
Cream for coffee: powdered
Fish: anchovies, crab meat, salmon, sardines, shrimp, tuna, etc.
Fruit juices: apple, cranberry, grape, grapefruit, lemon, orange, pineapple, prune, tangerine, whole-fruit nectar, etc.
Fruits: applesauce, cherries, fruit cocktail, grapefruit, peaches, pears, pineapple, purple plums, etc. Also dietetic packs
Gravy, beef
Meats: chopped ham, corned beef, corned-beef hash, deviled ham, ham, luncheon meat, meat *pâtés*, stews, tongue, etc.
Milk: evaporated, sweetened condensed, instant non-fat dried
Nuts
Pimentos
Popcorn
Preserved fruits and peels
Puddings: date, fig, plum, etc.
Rice: cooked or Spanish
Soups, chowders, etc.
Spaghetti and macaroni dishes
Tomato aspic, paste, purée, or sauce
Tomato juice or vegetable-juice cocktail
Turkey, boned
Vegetables: asparagus, beets, green beans; (Blue Lake, etc.), corn, limas, mixed vegetables, mushrooms, peas, potatoes, stewed tomatoes, etc.

Cereals: baby, hot, ready-to-eat
Cheeses
Chocolate: semisweet, unsweetened
Cocoa, instant-cocoa mix, etc.
Coconut
Coffee: regular, instant, decaffeinated, etc.
Cornstarch
Crackers and cookies
Dried apricots, figs, prunes, dates
Dried large California limas, split peas, etc.
Extracts
Flour: all-purpose, cake, etc.
Frosting mixes: "butter," fluffy, or fudge type
Frozen foods: fish, fruits, juices, lemonade, meats, poultry, prepared dishes, vegetables, waffles, etc.
Gelatin: fruit-flavored, unflavored
Herbs
Ice-cream and sherbet mixes
Ice creams
Jellies, jams, etc.
Macaroni, noodles, spaghetti
Macaroni, noodle, and spaghetti dinners
Marshmallow cream, marshmallows
Meat tenderizer, powdered
Mincemeat, prepared
Mixes: angel food, biscuit, cake, fudge or penuche, muffin, pancake, piecrust, popover, roll, salad-dressing bases, spaghetti sauce, brownie, frosting, cookie, etc.
Molasses
Monosodium glutamate

Mustard: dry, prepared, with horse-radish, etc.
Nuts: almonds, Brazil, pecans, walnuts, etc.
Olives: green, ripe, stuffed
Packaged puddings and pie fillings, instant puddings, tapioca pudding, etc.
Pectin, fruit: liquid or powdered
Pickles, relishes, etc.
Potato chips, corn chips, etc.
Raisins: light or dark
Rennet custard or Danish dessert
Rice: packaged precooked, regular
Salad dressings: cooked, French, mayonnaise, etc.
Salad oils: corn, cottonseed, olive, peanut, soybean, etc.
Salt: plain, seasoned, celery, onion, etc.
Sandwich spreads
Sauces: bottled sauce for gravy, bottled thick meat sauce, catchup, chili, cocktail, soy, Worcestershire, etc.
Shortenings
Soft drinks: sparkling water, etc.
Soup mixes, dehydrated; soups, frozen
Spices: cinnamon, nutmeg, cloves, curry, etc.
Stuffings, packaged
Sugars
Syrups: corn, maple-blended, maple
Tapioca, quick-cooking
Tea
Vinegars: cider, herb, wine, etc.

## VEGETABLES

**If fresh,** be fussy about the vegetables you buy. The longer they are held, the more vitamins they lose. Shop where vegetable turnover is quick and vegetables are kept on crushed ice or refrigerated.

Don't stock up more than a few days ahead (potatoes and onions excepted). They begin to lose flavor, vitamins, and tenderness as soon as they're picked.

Put fresh vegetables into refrigerator as soon as you get home, to reduce vitamin losses. (Of course, potatoes and onions belong in your vegetable bin.) Before storing vegetables, clean them with a dry cloth. If washing seems necessary, *dry well.*

**If frozen,** buy vegetables from a grocer who keeps them in a freezer cabinet that maintains a temperature near O° F. The package should be frozen solid, not beginning to soften. Keep frozen vegetables solidly frozen until ready to use. Once they thaw, do not attempt to refreeze them.

**If in cans or jars,** there is a great variety of vegetables from which to choose. Store in a cool, dry place until used.

Remember that canned vegetables labeled "substandard" are good, wholesome food—the difference lies in appearance and sometimes flavor. Just use ingenuity in preparing them.

**Compare prices** of fresh, frozen, and canned or glassed vegetables. They are all about equal in food value, so choose whichever fits your budget and your family's needs.

# FRESH VEGETABLES

**Artichokes, French or Italian,** should have compact heads.

**Artichokes, Jerusalem,** should be free from blemishes.

**Asparagus** is best with straight, green stalks with compact tips.

**Beets:** Buy smooth small or medium ones.

**Broccoli** should have tender firm stalks with tightly closed green flowerets without yellow color.

**Brussels Sprouts** should be without yellow spots or worm holes.

**Cabbage, all types,** should have fresh crisp leaves.

**Carrots** should be bright-colored and crisp. Remove tops at once.

**Cauliflower** should have a compact, crisp white head, few blemishes, and fresh green outer stalks.

**Celeriac** should be crisp.

**Celery** should have crisp stalks with fresh green leaves.

**Corn on the cob** should spurt milk when kernels are pressed. Refrigerate until ready to cook.

**Cucumbers** should be firm; not too plump or seedy.

**Eggplant** should be well shaped, purple, firm, shiny with no rust spots. Use soon after buying.

**Green Beans (Snap or Wax):** Pods should be crisp, slender, green or yellow, and snap easily.

**Green Limas** should have crisp green full pods.

**Green Peppers** should be thick-fleshed, crisp, and bright green. Use wide, chunky ones for stuffing.

**Greens (Beet Tops, Dandelions, Mustard, Spinach, Swiss Chard, Young Turnip Greens):** Avoid seedy or woody stems. Leaves should have good color, be crisp and clean.

**Kale or Collards** should have fresh, crisp leaves.

**Kohlrabi:** Buy small or medium ones with fresh tops and rind that can be easily pierced with the fingernail.

**Mushrooms** should be firm, plump, cream-colored, with short stems. For safety's sake, buy only cultivated ones.

**Okra** should have young, tender, crisp pods.

**Onions** should be clean, hard, well-shaped and with brittle skins. Avoid those with developed stems.

**Parsnips** should be smooth, firm, well-shaped, small to medium-sized. Soft or shriveled ones are apt to be pithy.

**Peas** should have well-filled, fresh, green pods.

**Sweet Potatoes or Yams:** Sweet potatoes have yellowish, fawn-colored skins and are mealy when cooked. Yams have white to reddish skins, are moist when cooked. Buy smooth-skinned potatoes with bright appearance. Buy in small quantity as they are perishable.

**White Potatoes** should be uniform and well-shaped.

**Pumpkin** should be bright-colored, firm, and free from blemishes.

**Salsify:** Buy firm, well-shaped medium roots.

**Squash, Acorn** should be acorn-shaped, ridged, green, firm, oval or round.

**Squash, Hubbard,** should have a hard, warted rind.

**Squash, Summer, Crookneck or Yellow,** should have curved neck and tender, warted rind, with a deep-yellow color. Rind becomes rough and less tender as it matures.

**Squash, Cymling, or Pattypan,** should be whitish, flat, scalloped, and disk-shaped.

**Tomatoes:** Buy large or small oval red and yellow ones. Sometimes they are purchased green. Regardless of type, look for firm, plump, smooth tomatoes with good color and no blemishes.

**Turnips, White,** should be firm and heavy with fresh green tops. Avoid those that are lightweight for their size; they may be woody, pithy, or strong in flavor.

**Turnips, Yellow, or Rutabaga,** should be heavy and firm. Avoid lightweight ones.

**Zucchini:** Buy small or medium-sized ones.

## FRUITS

**Apples.** Apples, on the market the year round, are at their peak from October to March. Listed below are some of the commercial leaders. About 3 or 4 apples equal 1 pound.

| Variety | Color | Season |
|---|---|---|
| *For Cooking* | | |
| Rhode Island Greening | Green | Oct. to Mar. |
| Rome Beauty | Red | Nov. to May |
| *For Eating* | | |
| Delicious | Striped | Oct. to May |
| *For Cooking and Eating* | | |
| Baldwin | Red | Nov. to Apr. |
| Gravenstein | Striped | July to Sept. |
| Grimes Golden | Yellow | Sept. to Jan. |
| Jonathan | Red | Sept. to Feb. |
| McIntosh | Red | Sept. to Mar. |
| Northern Spy | Striped | Oct. to Mar. |
| Winesap | Red | Jan. to Aug. |
| Yellow Newtown | Greenish-yellow | Jan. to June |

**Apricots.** Apricots, in season from May through August, are at their peak in June and July. Look for orange-yellow, plump, juicy apricots. About 8 to 16, depending on their size, equal 1 pound.

**To Store:** Keep in refrigerator.

**Avocados.** Available all year long, the peak season for California avocados is February through April; for Florida avocados, September through November.

When ripe it yields readily to gentle pressure from palms of hands. Always soften a firm avocado at room temperature before refrigerating it.

To prevent darkening, dip avocado slices into lemon juice. Wrap any leftover avocado in waxed paper or foil; store in refrigerator.

**Bananas.** Bananas are available the year round. Buy them by hand or cluster, at whatever stage of ripeness you find them in the store; they'll finish ripening at home. About 3 bananas equal 1 pound.

*For Baking, Broiling, or Frying:* Use firm bananas that are all-yellow or slightly green-tipped.

*For Eating out of Hand; Serving in Salads, Desserts, Milk Shakes; or Using as an Ingredient in Baking:* Use fully ripe bananas, flecked with brown, or all-yellow bananas.

**To Store:** Keep bananas in fruit bowl at comfortable room temperature, not in refrigerator. (Low temperatures prevent proper ripening, impair the delicate flavor.) They'll ripen as they stand.

To prevent darkening, dip banana slices into an acid fruit juice such as lemon or pineapple juice.

**Berries.** Fresh-berry time begins in April. The order of appearance is:

*Strawberries:* April through August; most plentiful in April, May, and June.

*Gooseberries:* April through August; most plentiful in June and July.

*Raspberries:* Mid-April through July; at peak July.

*Blackberries:* May through August; best in June, July, and August.

*Blueberries:* May to September; most plentiful in July.

*Loganberries:* June and July.

Choose berries that are ripe, well colored, and free from off-color spots.

**To Store:** Pick over berries, removing spoiled ones; spread out on tray; refrigerate, uncovered.

**Cherries.** Red, white, and black sweet cherries are available from May through August. They should be firm, shiny, plump, of fully ripe color, and free of spots.

**To Store:** Wash, examining any that float for worms. Drain; dry; refrigerate.

**Cranberries.** Fresh cranberries, available from September through March, are most plentiful from October through December. Choose berries that are firm, plump, fresh-appearing, and with high luster.

**To Store:** Refrigerate or freeze.

**Currants.** July is the month for currants. Look for bright, plump currants; make sure they are not so ripe they fall off stems. Refrigerate on shallow tray.

Use white or red currants for eating, or in salads, fruit cups, or desserts; black currants for jelly or jam.

**Figs.** Fresh figs, in season from June through November, are most plentiful in September and October. They should be soft. Kadota figs should be greenish yellow; Black Mission, purplish. Buy them slightly underripe; refrigerate until fully ripe.

**Grapefruit.** Grapefruit are especially delicious January through May. They should be firm, well shaped, heavy with juice, and thin-skinned. The color varies from pale yellow to reddish brown. Rust spots and green tinges do not affect the inner quality.

Very often small grapefruit are sweeter and juicier than the large sizes. Small grapefruit can be easily reamed for fresh juice too.

Grapefruit meat is white or pink, with or without seeds. Under U. S. Department of Agriculture rulings, any grapefruit containing fewer than 17 seeds is considered seedless.

**To Store:** Store grapefruit in a cool place, preferably in refrigerator.

**Grapes.** June to April is the grape season. Choose firm, fresh-looking bunches, in which plump grapes cling to stems when gently shaken.

**To Store:** Refrigerate.

**Kumquats.** Kumquats are in season November through February. Choose firm fruit, heavy for its size.

**To Store:** Refrigerate.

**Lemons.** Big juicy fresh lemons are in season all year.

**To Store:** Refrigerate.

**Limes.** Florida limes are most available between June and September; California limes, between October and December. Look for limes that are green, not yellowish, and heavy for their size.

**To Store:** Refrigerate.

**Mangoes.** Mangoes, in season from May to September, vary in size from a few ounces to 3 or 4 pounds.

**To Store:** Wrap in waxed paper; refrigerate.

**Melons.** Most ripe melons yield to pressure at the blossom end, and have a typical melon fragrance and yellowish tinge.

*Cantaloupes* are in season from May to November; imported ones may come in earlier. When ripe, they have a yellow ground color, distinct aroma, and smooth scar on the stem end. Blossom end yields to pressure.

*Casabas* are in season from July to December. When fully ripe, their rind is golden yellow; the white flesh is very juicy and sweet. Melon weighs 4 to 10 pounds.

*Cranshaws* are in season from July to November. Melon weighs 4 to 8 pounds.

*Honeyballs* are in season from May to October.

*Honeydews* are in season from January to November. When vine-ripened, they are creamy or yellowish in color, show softening at the blossom end, have smooth, well-rounded ridges next to stem, and are definitely fragrant.

*Papayas,* in season from December through February, are ready to eat when the rind is yellow and the fruit feels soft.

*Persians* are in season from July to November. When ripe, rind has yellowish cast; flesh is pink. Melon may weigh as much as 10 pounds.

*Santa Claus, or Christmas,* melons are winter melons. Signs of ripeness are light yellowing of rind, softness at blossom end.

**To Store:** Wash melon; dry; place in paper bag or waxed paper; refrigerate.

**Nectarines.** Nectarines are available in June, July, and August. Choose firm fruit, free from cuts and decayed spots.

**To Store:** Refrigerate.

**Oranges.** Oranges are available all year round. All oranges must pass state maturity requirements before they can be shipped. To enhance the eye appeal of certain varieties, Florida oranges are sometimes colored with harmless color; such fruit is stamped "Color Added."

Look for oranges that are firm and heavy for their size. If space is available, and there are several persons in the family, it is economical to buy oranges by the box or bag.

**To Store:** Keep oranges in a cool place, refrigerating those to be used for juice or salad next day.

**Peaches.** Peaches, in season from late May to mid-October, at their best in July and August. They are white- or yellow-fleshed, either clingstone or freestone. Cling peaches are used for canning; freestones are fine for all uses.

Ripe peaches should be firm but yield to gentle pressure, and should be free from brown spots or other signs of decay. The flesh should be either yellow or white, not green. About 4 peaches will weigh 1 pound.

**To Store:** Refrigerate.

**Pears.** For cooking, slightly underripe pears are best. Varieties of pears include:

*Bartlett:* In season from July through October.

*Bosc:* In season September through February.

*Comice:* In season October through February.

*Anjou:* October through May.

*Nelis:* February through June.

Check ripeness by pressing slightly near stem end. If pears are not quite ripe, let ripen at room temperature in paper bag or fruit bowl.

**To Store:** When ripe, refrigerate.

**Persimmons.** Persimmons are in season October, November, and December.

**To Store:** Refrigerate.

**Pineapple (fresh).** In season all year, pineapple is at its peak from March through June. Quality fruit is heavy for its size and has no signs of decay or mold at bottom or around eyes.

When ripe, fruit has sweet fragrance, golden-yellow flesh; center leaves loosen easily when pulled.

**To Store:** Keep, wrapped, in refrigerator.

**Plums and Fresh Prunes.** Plums are in season May through September; fresh prunes are available July to November. Choose those that are plump and yield slightly to pressure.

**To Store:** Refrigerate.

**Pomegranates.** Pomegranates are in season September through December.

**To Store:** Refrigerate.

**Rhubarb.** Rhubarb is in largest supply from March through July, and is at its peak May and June. Early rhubarb has light-pink stalks; late rhubarb stalks are dark reddish green. Buy fresh crisp stalks.

**To Store:** Refrigerate.

**Tangerines.** Tangerines are in season from November to late February. December and January are best months.

**Watermelons.** Watermelon is available the year round except for a short period, usually in December. When ripe, underside is turning yellow, not light green; flesh is crisp, juicy, red. Your best bet in judging ripeness is to have watermelon "plugged," i.e., have a piece cut out so you can examine the flesh.

The small icebox watermelon, sometimes called New Hampshire midget, is available April to September.

**To Store:** Refrigerate.

### Fruits in Cans or Jars

Your grocer has a wonderful assortment of fruits in cans or jars. Look for pineapple, peaches, orange slices, plums, fruit cocktail, pears, grapefruit, cherries, etc.

# CANNED FOOD BUYING GUIDE
## Giving Common Container Sizes with Their Approximate Net Weight and Cup Content

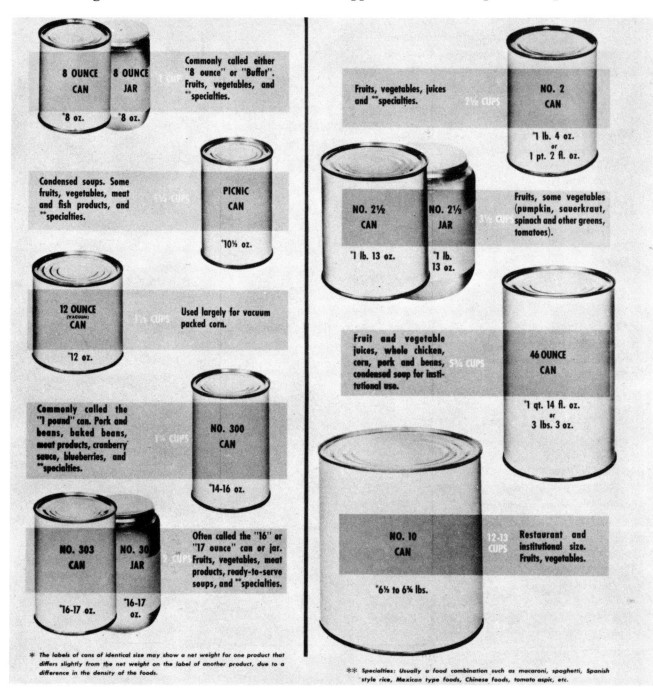

**8 OUNCE CAN** • **8 OUNCE JAR** — *8 oz. • *8 oz.
Commonly called either "8 ounce" or "Buffet". Fruits, vegetables, and **specialties.

Condensed soups. Some fruits, vegetables, meat and fish products, and **specialties.
**PICNIC CAN** — *10½ oz.

**12 OUNCE (VACUUM) CAN** — *12 oz.
Used largely for vacuum packed corn.

Commonly called the "1 pound" can. Pork and beans, baked beans, meat products, cranberry sauce, blueberries, and **specialties.
**NO. 300 CAN** — *14-16 oz.

**NO. 303 CAN** • **NO. 303 JAR** — *16-17 oz. • *16-17 oz.
Often called the "16" or "17 ounce" can or jar. Fruits, vegetables, meat products, ready-to-serve soups, and **specialties.

Fruits, vegetables, juices and **specialties. 2½ CUPS
**NO. 2 CAN** — *1 lb. 4 oz. or 1 pt. 2 fl. oz.

**NO. 2½ CAN** • **NO. 2½ JAR** — *1 lb. 13 oz. • *1 lb. 13 oz.
Fruits, some vegetables (pumpkin, sauerkraut, spinach and other greens, tomatoes).

Fruit and vegetable juices, whole chicken, corn, pork and beans, condensed soup for institutional use. 5¾ CUPS
**46 OUNCE CAN** — *1 qt. 14 fl. oz. or 3 lbs. 3 oz.

**NO. 10 CAN** — *6½ to 6¾ lbs.
12-13 CUPS
Restaurant and institutional size. Fruits, vegetables.

\* *The labels of cans of identical size may show a net weight for one product that differs slightly from the net weight on the label of another product, due to a difference in the density of the foods.*

\*\* *Specialties: Usually a food combination such as macaroni, spaghetti, Spanish style rice, Mexican type foods, Chinese foods, tomato aspic, etc.*

## CAN SIZES

**Don't Hesitate to Store Leftovers in Opened Cans.** Canned foods may be safely left in the opened can if they're covered and kept in the refrigerator like any leftover cooked food.

**Strained and Homogenized foods for infants, and** chopped junior foods, come in small jars and cans suitable for the smaller servings used. The weight is given on the label.

Meats, poultry, fish and seafood are almost entirely advertised and sold under weight terminology.

# EGGS

High-quality eggs will retain their original quality for some time if they are properly handled in shipment and storage. Proper handling of eggs means keeping them under constant refrigeration——in transit, in the wholesaler's warehouse, in the retail stores —until they are purchased. That is why we urge you to buy eggs only from sources that follow this important practice. Eggs that are not properly refrigerated lose quality rapidly.

You can tell a good deal about an egg's quality in your own kitchen through a very simple test—one, incidentally, that is a part of official grading procedures. Just break an egg into a saucer. If the egg covers a small area (does not spread unduly), has a high, firm yolk surrounded by thick white, the chances are excellent that it is a high-grade egg. A lower-grade egg will have a yolk with a flat curve and a thinner, spreading white.

Even though it may be the fashion in your community to prefer eggs of one color or the other, pay no attention to this in your buying. There is no difference between white and brown eggs. Weight for weight they are equal in flavor and nutritive qualities.

Buy only graded, cartoned, refrigerated eggs, labeled with a well-known brand name or trade-mark, or the letters "U.S." Such eggs have been carefully graded for quality and size. Graded cartoned eggs come in 4 quality grades, all referring to the freshness of the eggs. Grade AA or Grade A are top quality. They have a large amount of firm white and a well-rounded, upstanding yolk. While good for all uses, their high quality and freshness are most appreciated for poaching, frying, or cooking in the shell. Grade B and C have thinner whites and somewhat flatter yolks, which may break easily. But many families buy these lower-graded, less expensive eggs for scrambling, thickening sauces, baking, making omelets and salad dressings, and combining with such other foods as tomatoes, cheese, onions, etc.

**Egg Size.** Graded cartoned eggs are sorted for size, based on their weight per dozen. These sizes fall into the 6 weight classes below, although Jumbos and Peewees are not too often available.

|  | One Dozen Eggs Must Weigh at Least |
|---|---|
| Jumbo | 30 oz., or 1 lb. 14 oz. |
| Extra large | 27 oz., or 1 lb. 11 oz. |
| Large | 24 oz., or 1 lb. 8 oz. |
| Medium | 21 oz., or 1 lb. 5 oz. |
| Small | 18 oz., or 1 lb. 2 oz. |
| Peewees | 15 oz. |

In the summer and early fall, when medium and small eggs are in surplus, they are likely to be an especially good buy.

*To separate eggs, break shell with sharp tap at its center with knife blade or on bowl edge. Press thumb tips into crack; pull shell apart, retaining yolk in one half, letting white pour out of other. Rock yolk from one half of shell to other, so rest of white pours off.*

*If any yolk gets into white, whites will not beat up to full volume. Remove every trace of yolk with a piece of egg shell or paper towel, working carefully.*

*For leftover yolks or whites, store yolks, covered with cold water, in refrigerator; use within 2 or 3 days. Refrigerate egg whites in a covered dish; use within 10 days.*

# COFFEE

**Ground Coffee** comes in 3 grinds: regular, drip, and fine. The best all-purpose grind has been found to be the drip grind; however, if the manufacturer of your coffeemaker specifies some other grind, try it and compare the results you get with the drip grind. You can stock coffee if you buy it in a vacuum-sealed can. Once you open the can, try to use it up within a week. If you buy coffee that is not vacuum-packed, make sure it was roasted and ground within the last few days. If a little coffee is left over at the end of the week, don't mix it with a fresh supply.

Coffee is grown in tropical climates in various parts of the world, so you may find that you prefer the blend in one brand to that in another.

**Instant Coffee** is obtained by removing the water from a strong coffee brew. Practically all brands consist of just the dehydrated coffee brew, with nothing added. Whatever brand you buy, follow the directions on the label.

**Decaffeinated Coffee** has practically all the caffein removed. It comes in ground and dehydrated forms.

**Cereal Beverages** contain no coffee but are made from cereal grains. There are two kinds: one is prepared like regular coffee, the other is an instant type.

## CHOCOLATE AND COCOA

**Unsweetened Chocolate** is made from cocoa beans from which no cocoa butter has been removed.

**Semisweet Chocolate** has sweetening added to give a half-sweet taste. Some of the cocoa butter has been removed.

**Cocoa** is prepared from the bean by removing varying amounts of cocoa butter.

**Breakfast Cocoa** contains at least 22 per cent cocoa butter.

**Dutch Process Cocoa** is made from cocoa beans that have been alkalized to give the cocoa more color and flavor.

**Instant Cocoa Mix and Ready-to-Serve Cocoas** have sweetening and dry milk solids added. They require only the addition of hot or cold water or milk to be served as a beverage. See label directions for making frosting, sauce, etc.

## TEA

Tea leaves are sold by the pound, in a package, or in tea bags.

**Black Tea,** grown in India, Ceylon, and Indonesia, owes its flavor to the fermenting process the leaves go through before they are heated and dried. Flavored and spiced teas are frequently made from black teas.

**Green Tea,** from China and Japan, is not fermented.

**Oolong Tea,** from Formosa, is fermented only a short time.

**Orange Pekoe and Pekoe** indicate the size and type of leaf. These names have nothing to do with the kind or quality of the tea.

**Instant Tea** is the dried extract of freshly brewed tea. Some brands contain equal parts of the dried extracts and carbohydrates. (The latter protect the flavor.)

**To Store:** Be sure to store tea in a tightly sealed container or jar away from cooking odors and spices. After 6 months it tends to lose flavor.

### Bread

There are many kinds of bread on the market, such as white, whole wheat, rye, gluten, protein, etc. Most white bread is now made with enriched flour. Whether you buy the fluffy or the firm type of white bread is a matter of personal taste.

**To Store:** The first choice is the freezer where the temperature is 10° F. or lower. Properly cooled bread, in an airtight, moistureproof wrapping will retain its moisture, remain free of mold, and keep its freshness up to 3 months. If left in its original wrapper, limit bread storage to 2 weeks.

The second choice is a ventilated breadbox. Properly wrapped, bread will stay acceptably fresh for several days, but it is subject to mold.

The third choice is the refrigerator. Here wrapped bread retains its moisture and is less subject to mold than in a breadbox, but it stales more rapidly.

## THE MACARONI FAMILY

Macaroni products include macaroni, spaghetti, and egg noodles in a great variety of shapes and sizes.

**Macaroni** is tubular and hollow.

**Spaghetti** is solid.

**Egg Noodles** are ribbonlike and must contain at least 5.5 per cent egg solids by law. Only egg yolks are used because the whites tend to make noodles tough.

The better macaroni products are a mixture of semolina (made from durum wheat) and water. Some are enriched with vitamins $B_1$, $B_2$, niacin, and iron. The label will indicate whether the product is enriched.

Macaroni products are no mere "starchy fillers." They contribute fine supplementary proteins and,

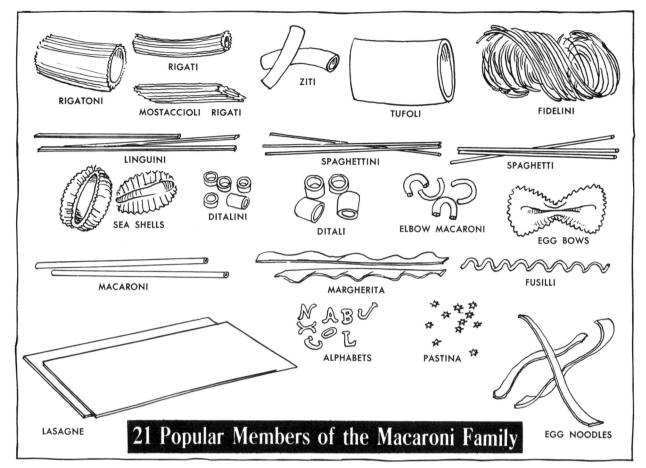

**21 Popular Members of the Macaroni Family**

RIGATONI • RIGATI • MOSTACCIOLI RIGATI • ZITI • TUFOLI • FIDELINI • LINGUINI • SPAGHETTINI • SPAGHETTI • SEA SHELLS • DITALINI • DITALI • ELBOW MACARONI • EGG BOWS • MACARONI • MARGHERITA • FUSILLI • LASAGNE • ALPHABETS • PASTINA • EGG NOODLES

when enriched (many brands are), B vitamins and iron too. One-half cup cooked spaghetti or macaroni supplies only a little over 100 calories, noodles even less.

Endless in variety, spaghetti, macaroni, and noodle dishes delight the eye, please the palate, are a fine prop for a shaky budget. Even small additions of meat, fish, cheese, eggs, or milk to these dishes give a big "lift" to their cereal proteins.

Never overcook macaroni, spaghetti, or noodles. The actual number of cooking minutes depends upon how well cooked you like your macaroni—"al dente," which is just tender, or well done. Test degree of doneness by biting a piece while cooking. If it's firm all the way through and not hard in the center, it's

ready. Drain off all water and prepare for serving.

Do not rinse macaroni products unless they are to be chilled and used in a salad. Then use cold water.

### How to Eat Spaghetti

There are two schools of thought on the question of just how spaghetti should be transferred from plate to mouth. Take your choice of these two methods.

With fork in right hand, spear 3 or 4 strands. Hold tines against plate. Twist spaghetti into ball. Lift to mouth.

Pick up strands with fork. Twist against spoon held on plate with left hand. Lift with fork. Support with spoon part way.

# CHEESE

*Varieties so marked are made in U.S.A. and are normally available*

## Natural Cheeses

### *American Cheddar

*Surface:* Waxed yellow brown
*Interior:* Light cream to orange. Close texture.
*Flavor:* Mild to pronounced
*Uses:* Sandwiches
With pies and cobblers
In salad dressings
In dishes such as casseroles, etc.

### *Bel Paese

*Surface:* Slate gray
*Interior:* Light yellow. Soft to solid
*Flavor:* Mild
*Uses:* Dessert—with fruit or crackers

### *Blue

Blue mold cheese from cows' milk
*Flavor:* Piquant
*Uses:* Dessert—with crackers or fruit
Salads and salad dressings
Appetizers—as a spread

### *Brick

*Surface:* Yellowish brown
*Interior:* White to light cream
*Flavor:* Mild to pronounced
*Uses:* Sandwiches and with cold cuts

### *Caciocavallo

Odd shapes, often in pairs
*Surface:* Light brown and paraffined
*Interior:* Rather hard, dry
*Flavor:* Somewhat salty, smoky
*Uses:* As table cheese when fresh
Cured for grating and cooking

### *Camembert

*Surface:* Thin, whitish crust
*Interior:* Soft, creamy, yellowish
*Flavor:* Luscious flavor all its own
*Uses:* Dessert or salad

### *Chantelle (Trade-mark name)

*Surface:* Red-coated
*Interior:* Cream to light orange. Semi-hard
*Flavor:* Mild to pronounced
*Uses:* With cold meats
As dessert or party refreshment

### *Cottage

Made from skim milk. Some has cream added. White
*Flavor:* Pleasing, slightly acid
*Uses:* Salads. Season with chives, pickle relish, diced tomatoes, also with fruits

### *Cream

Made from a mixture of cream and milk with minimum fat content of 33 per cent. Comes with chives, relish, pimento, and pineapple added.
*Flavor:* Delicate, slightly acid
*Uses:* Sandwiches
Salads and salad dressings
Dessert—with crackers and jelly

### *Edam

*Surface:* Red-coated ball
*Interior:* Body and texture usually grainy
*Flavor:* Mild. Slightly salty when fresh, pronounced when cured
*Uses:* Dessert—with fruit or salad
Appetizer or nibbler

### *Gorgonzola

Blue-mold cheese from cows' milk
*Surface:* Clay color
*Interior:* Blue streaks
*Flavor:* Rich, piquant, when cured
*Uses:* Salads and salad dressings
Dessert

### *Gouda

*Surface:* Usually red
*Interior:* If imported, solid; if domestic, softer
*Flavor:* Often slightly acid
*Uses:* Same as Edam

### *Liederkranz (Trade-mark name)

*Surface:* Russet
*Interior:* Creamy yellow, soft
*Flavor and odor:* Robust
*Uses:* Appetizer—on crackers, toast
With salad, crackers
Dessert—with crackers, fruit

### *Limburger

*Surface:* Grayish brown
*Interior and flavor:* When fresh, white, odorless, and tasteless. As curing progresses, odor, flavor, and color develop
*Uses:* Sandwiches—on dark breads, or on crackers

### *Mozzarella

Irregularly spherical in shape
Semisoft. Light cream-colored
*Flavor:* Mild
*Uses:* In main dishes such as eggplant or veal *parmigiano*, pizza, etc.

### *Munster

*Surface:* Yellowish tan
*Interior:* White when fresh. Turns light cream when fully cured
*Flavor:* Mild to pronounced
*Uses:* Sandwiches—with dark bread
Appetizers or nibblers

### *Mysost (Gjetost or primost)

Made from whey. White to brown
*Flavor:* Sweet with distinct odor
*Uses:* Thin slices on bread or crackers

### *Neufchâtel

2- or 3-pound loaves
A cream cheese with 20 per cent minimum fat content. White. Soft
*Flavor:* Mild
*Uses:* Sandwiches and salads
Nibblers or light refreshments

### Oka (Port du Salut)

Circular cakes, 1 and 5 pound
*Surface:* Russet
*Interior:* Creamy yellow. Semisoft
*Flavor:* Robust
*Uses:* Dessert, with port wine

### *Parmesan (Reggiano)

*Surface:* Black or very dark green
*Interior:* Light yellow. Very hard. Has to be grated
*Flavor:* Mild unless cheese is old
*Uses:* Grated, serve with Italian spaghetti or soups

**\*Provolone**

Pear, ball, or sausage shape

Includes such styles as Provolette, Provolone, Provoloni, Salami

*Uses:* Dessert or with crackers

**\*Ricotta**

Made from whey, with milk added

*Flavor:* Mild

*Uses:* In ravioli, lasagna, etc.

**Roquefort**

Made from sheeps' milk

*Surface:* Yellowish-brown rind

*Interior:* White, with blue-green mold

*Flavor:* Spicy

*Uses:* Dessert—with fruit, crackers

Salad dressings

Appetizers, nibblers—blend with cream or cream cheese

**\*Swiss—Domestic**

*Surface:* Grayish brown

*Interior:* White or cream color. Round, shiny holes throughout

*Flavor:* Mild, sweetish to sharp

*Uses:* Sandwiches

Sliced—with cold meats

Salads, etc.

*Note:* Natural cheeses such as Cheddar, Swiss, brick—usually pasteurized—come in factory-wrapped packages in a variety of sizes.

The flavor of all natural cheeses, except cream and cottage cheeses, is enhanced if the cheese stands at room temperature a while before serving.

### Process Cheeses

**\*Packaged Process Cheese**

(¼- to 5-pound packages)

Made by mixing 2 or more "wheels" of same variety of cheese, or 2 or more varieties (except cream or Neufchâtel cheese), with aid of heat and with (or without) water, salt, harmless coloring, and emulsifier. Pasteurized in manufacturing; labeled "process cheese"

*Flavors:* American, white American, pimento, swiss, brick, sharp, etc.

*Uses:* Cookery, sandwiches

**\*Packaged Process-Cheese Slices**

(8-ounce packages)

*Flavors:* American, Swiss, etc.

*Uses:* Sandwiches

**\*Process-Cheese Spreads**

Jars and packages

*Flavors:* Pineapple, pimento, olive-pimento, Swiss, American, sharp, Limburger, etc.

*Uses:* Sandwiches

Salads

Nibblers, etc.

**\*Process-Cheese Foods**

Packages

*Flavor:* Mild to sharp. Pimento may be added.

*Uses:* Sauces

Sandwich spreads

**\*Process Grated Cheese**

In canisters or glass jars

Two types: American and Italian

*Uses:* American—for au gratin dishes, soups, etc.

Italian—for sprinkling on dishes

**\*Process Smoked Cheese**

Hickory-smoked or with smoke-flavored solids added

*Uses:* Appetizer or nibbler

**\*Triple-Use Cheese Spread or Sauce**

In jars or glasses

Can be spread, spooned, or heated

*Uses:* Sauce—on vegetables, meats, etc.

Spread—on bread, crackers, etc.

## JUICES

**Canned juices come in:**

5½- to 6-oz. can (5½ to 6 fl. oz.)—about ¾ cup

No. 211 (12 fl. oz.)—about 1½ cups

No. 300 can (13½ fl. oz.)—about 1¾ cups

No. 2 can (1 pt., 2 fl. oz.)—about 2½ cups

46-oz. can (No. 3 cylinder)—about 5¾ cups

**Unopened Canned Juices:** Will keep for months in cool, dry spot. Never store near heat, or damp walls.

**Leftovers:** It's safe to store canned juices in opened cans. Cover tightly; store in coldest part of refrigerator; use next day or so. For best flavor, if can is large-sized, store juice in refrigerator container.

**Frozen juices come in:**

6-oz. cans

Some in 4-oz. and 12-oz. cans

**Unopened Frozen Juices:** Put in freezer or refrigerator-freezer at once. They'll keep many months at 0° F; several weeks in ice-cube compartment of refrigerator. Unopened cans stored at room temperature may burst after 2 or more days.

**Frozen Concentrate:** Reconstitute as label directs, *making sure to shake or stir briskly and thoroughly.* Use within 24 hours for best flavor.

## NUTS

Unshelled nuts are convenient and thrifty. Shell the whole bagful at once, immediately storing any not used.

A good nutcracker works well on all kinds of nuts with little effort. If your nutcracker is the family hammer, hold each nut by the seam and give the pointed end a sharp, bouncing blow.

As for Brazil nuts, they'll be easier to shell if you cover them with cold water, bring water to boil, boil 3 minutes, and drain. Then cover them with cold water, let stand 1 minute, drain, and crack.

*In an Unshelled Pound*

1 lb. walnuts . . . . . . . . . About 2 cups nut meats

1 lb. pecans . . . . . . . . . . About 2¼ cups nut meats

1 lb. Brazil nuts . . . . . . . . About 1⅔ cups nut meats

1 lb. almonds . . . . . . . . . About 1¾ cups nut meats

1 lb. peanuts . . . . . . . . . About 2 cups nut meats

1 lb. filberts . . . . . . . . . . About 1½ cups nut meats

*Storage*

Nuts (unless vacuum-packed) keep fresh for weeks in the refrigerator or tightly covered in a home freezer or freezing compartment.

*Chopping Nuts*

Nut choppers do a good job. So does the electric blender, especially when you have a quantity to do.

# MEAT

**The Inspection Stamp.** All meat packers who slaughter or manufacture meat food products shipped in interstate commerce (that is, shipped outside the state in which they are located) must operate under Federal inspection. The inspection includes meats sold within the state as well, so long as any shipments are made outside the state. In addition, some states and cities operate their own inspection services. However, if the packer sells only within his own state, Federal inspection is not required.

The Federal inspection stamp is a guarantee that the meat comes from a healthy animal, was slaughtered and processed under sanitary conditions, was entirely suitable for consumption when it left the processing plant, and carried no misleading statements on any label attached to it. The number on the stamp refers to the official number of the processing plant. The ink used to make the stamp is a vegetable color and is harmless, so it does not have to be trimmed from the meat.

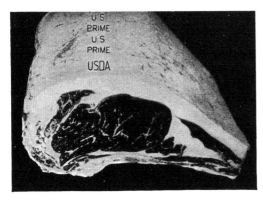

**The Grade Stamp or Brand Stamp.** This stamp refers to the quality of the meat. Grade and brand names are affixed to a carcass for its full length by a roller which uses the same type of marking fluid used for the inspection stamp.

These are the U.S. official grades for meats graded in Federally inspected plants. Meat that is only locally inspected carries the same grading without the "U.S." before the name. All grading is on a

voluntary basis. Many packers use brand names that closely parallel the official grade designations. Pork is not graded like the other meats, but is graded by quality and weight by the packer. Cured and smoked pork products are easily identified by the packer's brand. Your meatman will tell you which is the top quality in his stock.

| | Beef | Veal | Lamb | Mutton |
|---|---|---|---|---|
| 1. | Prime | Prime | Prime | |
| 2. | Choice | Choice | Choice | Choice |
| 3. | Good | Good | Good | Good |
| 4. | Commercial | Commercial | | |
| 5. | Utility | Utility | Utility | Utility |

The top grade—prime—is sold at retail only in the most expensive meat markets. It is usually reserved for higher-priced hotels and restaurants.

## Aging of Meat

Only high-quality beef, mutton, and lamb have fat coverings thick enough to permit aging without excessive evaporation. Aging is the storage of the meat for from 3 to 6 weeks at temperatures of from 34° F. to 38° F. The purpose of aging is to develop tenderness and flavor.

## Storing Meat

**To Store Fresh Meat,** see that it lies flat, not curled, and then wrap it loosely to allow circulation of air. Refrigerate in coldest part of refrigerator. If your refrigerator has a special meat compartment, you may store the meat unwrapped. You can store freezer-wrapped veal, lamb, and beef (with the exception of chopped meat) up to one year in your freezer. In the frozen-food compartment of the refrigerator, you can keep freezer-wrapped meat for 1 to 2 weeks.

**To Store Cured or Smoked Meats,** refrigerate at once in their original wrapper.

**To Store Cooked Meats,** refrigerate within 2 hours of cooking to avoid danger of food poisoning. Do not keep cooked meat for more than 4 days.

## Can You Identify Meat?

Identification is an important factor in the buying and utilization of meat. In learning to recognize the different cuts, remember that in beef, lamb, pork, and veal there is a difference in color and size, but the muscle and bone structure of all four meats are alike. Know your beef and you will be able to identify the others.

# BEEF

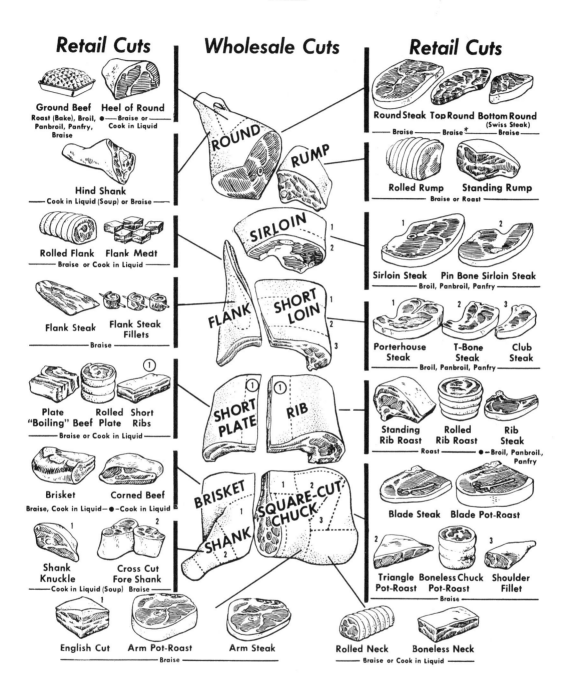

## Retail Cuts

**Ground Beef** — Roast (Bake), Broil, ●—Panbroil, Panfry, Braise

**Heel of Round** — Braise or Cook in Liquid

**Hind Shank** — Cook in Liquid (Soup) or Braise

**Rolled Flank** **Flank Meat** — Braise or Cook in Liquid

**Flank Steak** **Flank Steak Fillets** — Braise

**Plate** **Rolled Plate** **Short Ribs** — "Boiling" Beef — Braise or Cook in Liquid

**Brisket** **Corned Beef** — Braise, Cook in Liquid — ●—Cook in Liquid

**Shank Knuckle** **Cross Cut Fore Shank** — Cook in Liquid (Soup) Braise

**English Cut** **Arm Pot-Roast** **Arm Steak** — Braise

## Wholesale Cuts

ROUND

RUMP

SIRLOIN

FLANK

SHORT LOIN

SHORT PLATE

RIB

BRISKET

SQUARE-CUT CHUCK

SHANK

## Retail Cuts

**Round Steak** **Top Round** **Bottom Round** (Swiss Steak) — Braise — Braise* — Braise

**Rolled Rump** **Standing Rump** — Braise or Roast

**Sirloin Steak** **Pin Bone Sirloin Steak** — Broil, Panbroil, Panfry

**Porterhouse Steak** **T-Bone Steak** **Club Steak** — Broil, Panbroil, Panfry

**Standing Rib Roast** **Rolled Rib Roast** **Rib Steak** — Roast — ●—Broil, Panbroil, Panfry

**Blade Steak** **Blade Pot-Roast**

**Triangle Pot-Roast** **Boneless Chuck Pot-Roast** **Shoulder Fillet** — Braise

**Rolled Neck** **Boneless Neck** — Braise or Cook in Liquid

## BUYING AND STORAGE GUIDE FOR BEEF

|  | Approx. Amt. per Serving | Storage Limit at 36° to 40° F. |
|---|---|---|
| Corned beef | ¼ lb. | 7 days |
| Hamburger | ¼ lb. | 2 days |
| Pot roast | ⅓ lb. bone in or ¼ lb. boned | 5 to 6 days |
| Rib roast | ⅓ lb. bone in or ¼ lb. boned | 5 to 8 days |
| Steak | ½ lb. bone in or ⅓ lb. boned | 3 to 5 days |
| Stew meat | ⅓ to ¼ lb. | 2 days |

# VEAL

## Retail Cuts

## Wholesale Cuts

## Retail Cuts

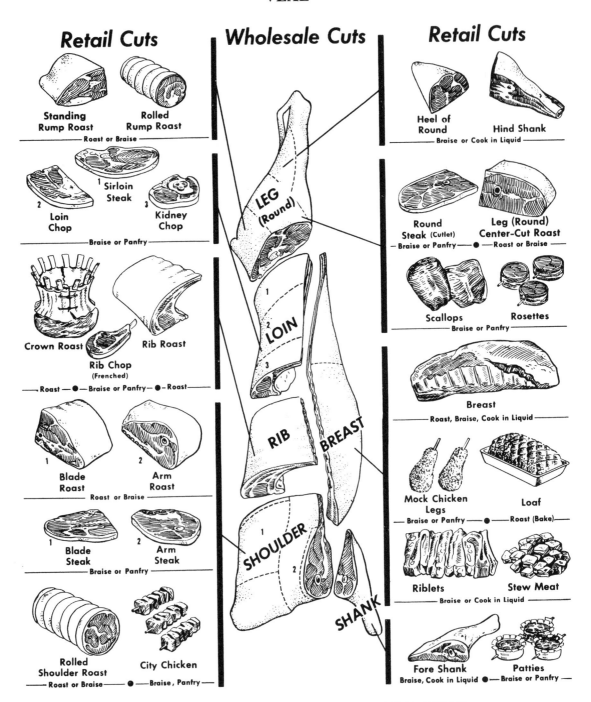

**Standing Rump Roast** — **Rolled Rump Roast**
— Roast or Braise —

**Sirloin Steak** (1) — **Loin Chop** (2) — **Kidney Chop** (3)
— Braise or Panfry —

**Crown Roast** — **Rib Chop (Frenched)** — **Rib Roast**
— Roast — ● — Braise or Panfry — ● — Roast —

**Blade Roast** (1) — **Arm Roast** (2)
— Roast or Braise —

**Blade Steak** (1) — **Arm Steak** (2)
— Braise or Panfry —

**Rolled Shoulder Roast** — **City Chicken**
— Roast or Braise — ● — Braise, Panfry —

LEG (Round)

LOIN

RIB

BREAST

SHOULDER

SHANK

**Heel of Round** — **Hind Shank**
— Braise or Cook in Liquid —

**Round Steak (Cutlet)** — **Leg (Round) Center-Cut Roast**
— Braise or Panfry — ● — Roast or Braise —

**Scallops** — **Rosettes**
— Braise or Panfry —

**Breast**
— Roast, Braise, Cook in Liquid —

**Mock Chicken Legs** — **Loaf**
— Braise or Panfry — ● — Roast (Bake) —

**Riblets** — **Stew Meat**
— Braise or Cook in Liquid —

**Fore Shank** — **Patties**
Braise, Cook in Liquid ● — Braise or Panfry —

## BUYING AND STORAGE GUIDE FOR VEAL

|  | Approx. Amt. per Serving | Storage Limit at 36° to 40° F. |
|---|---|---|
| Chops and steak | ⅓ to ½ lb. | 4 days |
| Roast |  |  |
| Bone in | ⅓ to ½ lb. | 5 to 6 days |
| Boned | ⅓ to ¼ lb. |  |
| Stew meat | ¼ to ⅓ lb. | 2 days |

**148    FOOD AND DIET**

# LAMB

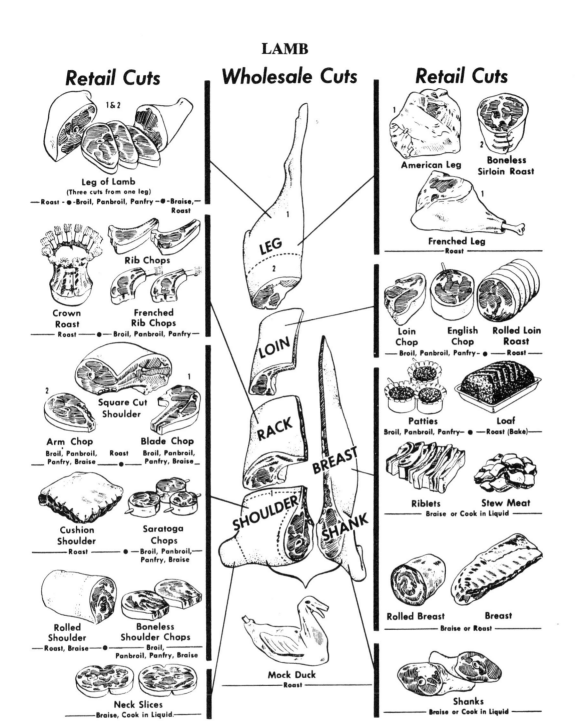

## Retail Cuts

**Leg of Lamb**
(Three cuts from one leg)
—Roast - ●-Broil, Panbroil, Panfry -●-Braise,—
Roast

**Rib Chops**

**Crown Roast**
— Roast —

**Frenched Rib Chops**
● — Broil, Panbroil, Panfry—

**Square Cut Shoulder**

**Arm Chop**
Broil, Panbroil, Panfry, Braise

Roast
●

**Blade Chop**
Broil, Panbroil, Panfry, Braise

**Cushion Shoulder**
— Roast —

**Saratoga Chops**
● —Broil, Panbroil, Panfry, Braise

**Rolled Shoulder**
—Roast, Braise—●

**Boneless Shoulder Chops**
Broil, Panbroil, Panfry, Braise

**Neck Slices**
—Braise, Cook in Liquid.—

## Wholesale Cuts

LEG

LOIN

RACK

SHOULDER

BREAST

SHANK

**Mock Duck**
— Roast —

## Retail Cuts

**American Leg**

**Boneless Sirloin Roast**

**Frenched Leg**
— Roast —

**Loin Chop**

**English Chop**

**Rolled Loin Roast**
— Broil, Panbroil, Panfry- ● — Roast —

**Patties**
Broil, Panbroil, Panfry- ● —Roast (Bake)—

**Loaf**

**Riblets**

**Stew Meat**
— Braise or Cook in Liquid —

**Rolled Breast**

**Breast**
— Braise or Roast —

**Shanks**
— Braise or Cook in Liquid —

## BUYING AND STORAGE GUIDE FOR LAMB

|  | Approx. Amt. per Serving | Storage Limit at 36° to 40° F. |
|---|---|---|
| Chops | ⅓ to ½ lb. | 3 days |
| Roast |  |  |
|   Bone in | ¼ to ½ lb. | 5 days |
|   Boned | ¼ to ⅓ lb. |  |
| Shank | ¼ to ½ lb. | 2 days |
| Stew meat | ⅓ to ¼ lb. | 2 days |

# PORK

## Retail Cuts | Wholesale Cuts | Retail Cuts

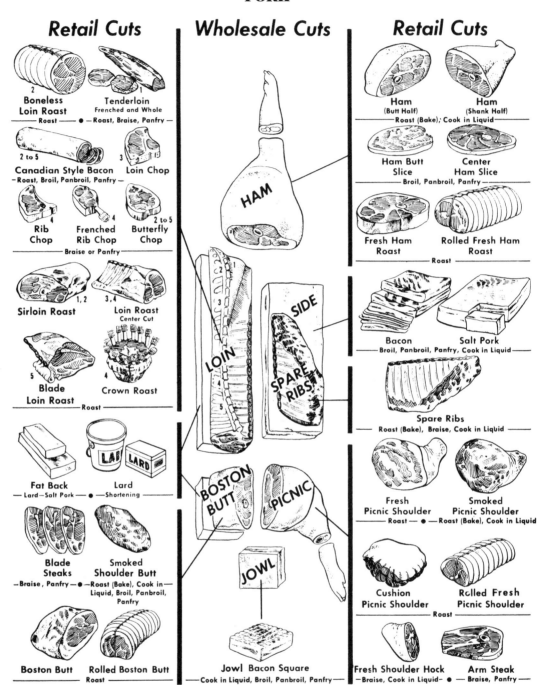

**Retail Cuts (left)**

2 Boneless Loin Roast — Roast —
1 Tenderloin Frenched and Whole — ● — Roast, Braise, Panfry —

2 to 5 Canadian Style Bacon — Roast, Broil, Panbroil, Panfry —
3 Loin Chop

4 Rib Chop
4 Frenched Rib Chop
2 to 5 Butterfly Chop
— Braise or Panfry —

1, 2 Sirloin Roast
3, 4 Loin Roast Center Cut

5 Blade Loin Roast
4 Crown Roast
— Roast —

Fat Back — Lard—Salt Pork — ● —
Lard — Shortening —

Blade Steaks — Braise, Panfry — ● —
Smoked Shoulder Butt — Roast (Bake), Cook in Liquid, Broil, Panbroil, Panfry —

Boston Butt
Rolled Boston Butt
— Roast —

**Wholesale Cuts (center)**

HAM
LOIN
SIDE
SPARE RIBS
BOSTON BUTT
PICNIC
JOWL
Jowl Bacon Square — Cook in Liquid, Broil, Panbroil, Panfry —

**Retail Cuts (right)**

Ham (Butt Half)
Ham (Shank Half)
— Roast (Bake); Cook in Liquid —

Ham Butt Slice
Center Ham Slice
— Broil, Panbroil, Panfry —

Fresh Ham Roast
Rolled Fresh Ham Roast
— Roast —

Bacon
Salt Pork
— Broil, Panbroil, Panfry, Cook in Liquid —

Spare Ribs — Roast (Bake), Braise, Cook in Liquid —

Fresh Picnic Shoulder
Smoked Picnic Shoulder
— Roast — ● — Roast (Bake), Cook in Liquid —

Cushion Picnic Shoulder
Rolled Fresh Picnic Shoulder
— Roast —

Fresh Shoulder Hock — Braise, Cook in Liquid — ● —
Arm Steak — Braise, Panfry —

## BUYING AND STORAGE GUIDE FOR PORK

| | Approx. Amt. per Serving | Storage Limit at 36° to 40° F. |
|---|---|---|
| Chops | ½ to ¾ lb. | 3 days |
| Sausage | ¼ lb. | 2 to 3 days |
| Roast | ⅓ to ½ bone in or ¼ to ¼ boned | 5 to 6 days |
| Spareribs | ¾ to 1 lb. | 3 days |
| Bacon | 2 slices | 6 to 7 days |
| Half ham | ½ to ¾ bone in or ⅓ lb. boned | 7 days (whole ham 2 wks.) |

# VARIETY MEATS

Variety meats are known in some sections of the country as fancy meats, meat specialties, extra edible parts, meat sundries, or unusual meats. You can usually figure on a quarter-pound per serving in buying, except on tongue, where there is considerable waste due to the skin and the heavily fatted section; on tongue and oxtails, figure about a half-pound per serving. Keep variety meats loosely wrapped in coldest part of refrigerator. Plan to use within 24 hours. If bought frozen, keep frozen until time to use.

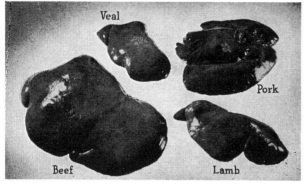

**Liver** is an excellent source of iron, vitamin A, copper and B vitamins. Pork liver generally contains even more iron than calf or beef liver.

**Heart:** Beef makes 10 to 12 servings; lamb 1 serving; pork or veal 2 servings.

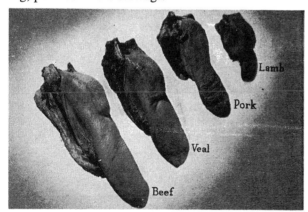

**Tongue** can be bought fresh, smoked, corned, or pickled. There are also ready-to-eat whole tongues, as well as canned whole or sliced.

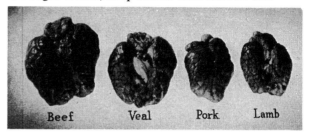

**Brains:** Veal brains are the most popular. Frozen brains are available, too.

**Kidneys:** Veal kidneys weigh 8 to 12 ounces each; lamb, 2 ounces each; and beef about 1¼ pounds.

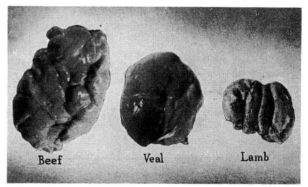

**Sweetbreads** are the thymus glands of beef, calf, or lamb. Each animal has two kinds: heart sweetbreads, which are rounded; throat, or neck sweetbreads, which are elongated.

**Tripe** is the inner lining of the stomach of beef. There are three kinds: honeycomb, which is considered a great delicacy; pocket; and plain or smooth. All three come fresh, pickled, and canned.

**Oxtails** are sold fresh or frozen.

# POULTRY

Ninety per cent of all poultry of every class—chicken, turkey, duck, and goose—now offered for retail sale, is in ready-to-cook form—that is, fully drawn, pin-feathered, and cleaned inside and out. It may be fresh or frozen. Dressed poultry has been plucked, but head and feet are still on, viscera still in. Usually the meatman will draw (remove viscera from) a dressed bird, but you still have considerable cleaning to do at home.

**Appearance.** Poultry should be clean with no bruises or discolorations. A meaty bird has a short body and a broad breast. A frozen bird has a slightly darker skin.

**To Store:** Buy fresh poultry *only* from retailer who refrigerates them. Once they're home, quickly remove film or other wrapper; then wrap loosely, with ends open, in waxed paper or foil. Store just below freezing unit. Use in 1 or 2 days. Keep frozen poultry frozen until used.

After mealtime, get leftover poultry into refrigerator at once. For safety's sake, remove stuffing from roasted bird; refrigerate it with gravy.

If you stew a bird for later use, cool it quickly by lifting from broth to wire rack. Cool kettle of broth in cold water in sink, changing water, stirring often. Refrigerate cooled bird, broth, at once.

**To Avoid Food Poisoning,** *never* stuff poultry day ahead. Prepare stuffing ingredients ahead, then refrigerate; combine just before you stuff and roast.

## Chickens

Chicken is available ready-to-cook whole, cut-up (may be trayed and wrapped), or parts (by the piece, or trayed and wrapped).

**Broil-Fryer Chickens** weigh from 1¼ to 3 pounds.
**Roasters** weigh over 3 pounds.
**Stewing Chickens** are usually hens in which the tip of the breast bone has hardened.
**Capons** are unsexed chickens weighing 4 pounds or more. They are exceptionally tender and have a large proportion of white meat.

## How Much to Buy per Serving

This means per serving, *not* per person. Some people take more than one serving.

*Ready to Cook*

| | |
|---|---|
| For Broiling | ¼ to ½ bird |
| For Frying | ⅔ to ¾ lb. |
| For Roasting | ⅔ to ¾ lb. |
| For Stewing | *¼ to ⅔ lb. |

*Dressed*

| | |
|---|---|
| For Broiling | ¼ to ½ bird |
| For Frying | ¾ to 1 lb. |
| For Roasting | ¾ to 1 lb. |
| For Stewing | *⅓ to ¾ lb. |

* Smaller amount is suggested if you serve with rice, macaroni, or biscuits, etc.

## Turkeys

Small turkeys are specially bred for less weight at maturity. Large turkeys have a greater proportion of edible meat per pound than small turkeys. Turkey parts, available in some markets, come by the piece and include breasts, drumsticks, wings, thighs, etc.

Allow about ½ pound ready-to-cook turkey per serving.

## Ducklings

Ducklings—tender meaty ones—either fresh or frozen, come ready-to-cook throughout the year.

Allow at least ¾ to 1 pound ready-to-cook per serving.

## Geese

Geese come frozen ready-to-cook, or they come dressed. There are smaller birds now.

# SEAFOOD
## Fish

*Selection*

Fresh fish will have:
   Eyes—bright, clear, full
   Flesh—firm, elastic
   Gills—bright, fresh color; not gray
   Scales—clinging to the skin and with characteristic sheen
   Odor—clean, fresh; not tainted, stale

*Amounts to Buy*

   3 lb. whole fish makes 3 servings
   2 lb. dressed fish makes 4 servings
   1 lb. fillets or steaks makes 3 servings

*Fish to Broil*

FILLETS

| | | |
|---|---|---|
| Sea bass | Haddock | Pike |
| Bluefish | Hake | Pollack |
| Carp | Mackerel | Porgy |

| Cod | Mullet | Sole |
|-----|--------|------|
| Flounder | Ocean perch | Weakfish |

STEAKS

| Striped bass | Muskellunge | Tuna (fresh) |
|-----|-----|-----|
| Cod | Salmon | |
| Halibut | Swordfish | |

DRESSED WHOLE

| Sea bass | Flounder | Shad |
|-----|-----|-----|
| Bluefish | Mackerel | Smelts |
| Butterfish | Mullet | Weakfish |
| Carp (up to | Pike | Whitefish |
| 3 lb.) | Porgy | Whiting |

SPLIT

| Sea bass | Hake | Porgy |
|-----|-----|-----|
| Bluefish | Mackerel | Weakfish |
| Bonito mackerel | Mullet | Whitefish |
| Carp | Pike | Whiting |

*Fish to Fry*

DRESSED WHOLE

| Bass | Mackerel | Smelts |
|-----|-----|-----|
| Butterfish | Perch | Trout |
| Flounder | Pike | Whitefish |
| Lake herring | Pompano | Whiting |

FILLETS OR STEAKS

| Cod | Red snapper |
|-----|-----|
| Flounder | Rockfish |
| Haddock | Shad (and/or |
| Halibut | shad roe) |
| Ocean perch | Sole |
| Pickerel | Swordfish |
| Pollack | |

*Fish to Bake*

FILLETS

| Cod | Hake | Sole |
|-----|-----|-----|
| Flounder | Mackerel | Whitefish |
| Haddock | Ocean perch | |

STEAKS

| Cod | Pollack | Tuna (fresh) |
|-----|-----|-----|
| Haddock | Salmon | |
| Halibut | Swordfish | |

*Fish to Boil, Poach, or Steam*

Any of the fish listed except the very oily ones like mackerel and bluefish.

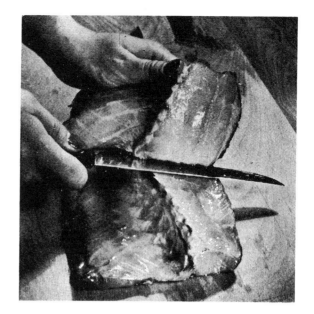

**How to Bone and Fillet a Fish**

Some fish have a very tender skin, which can be left on. In this case, if there are scales, scale the fish, as follows: Place it on a cutting board with the tail toward you, and scrape with a knife from tail to head. If skin is to be removed, do not scale.

To clean the fish, cut off the fins with shears. Clean out the entrails. In flat fish, such as flounder, and in small fish, the entrails are near the head and are removed easily when the head is cut off. In large fish, it is necessary to slit the fish along the underside of the body, from the fin nearest the tail to the mouth. Then remove the entrails.

Next, cut off the head just back of the gills. Then, holding the knife at an angle, scrape the lining surrounding the entrails. Wash the fish well, and dry with paper toweling.

To bone the fish, place it on the board, with the slit or underneath part of the body toward you. Keep the fish flat on the board during the boning and skinning process.

Insert the knife at the head end of the fish between the top surface of the backbone and the flesh. Keep the cutting edge of the knife close to bone and cut flesh free from bone all the way to the tail, using a clean cutting motion and cutting completely across fish. Use the left wrist to hold down the lower part of the fish and the left hand to lift the flesh gently from the bone as you cut.

With the fish still in the same position—with the exposed bone uppermost—again insert the knife at the head end, this time just under the backbone. With the cutting edge of the knife close to the bone, cut the bone free from the flesh all the way to the tail.

As you cut, press down on the lower part of the fish with the left wrist, and with the left hand pull up gently on the end of the bone, using a clean cutting motion with the knife.

As you cut, press down on the lower part of the fish with the left wrist, and with the left hand pull up gently on the end of the bone, using a clean cutting motion with the knife.

After removing the backbone, you probably will find some bones that surrounded the entrails. To remove these, cut them out with shears or pull them out with tweezers. In some fish you may find it necessary to cut away these bones with a sharp knife. To do this, cut a slit in back of the bones, where they formerly joined the backbone; then cut to the outer edge of the fish, removing the bones.

You now have two fillets of fish, free from most bones and ready to skin. To skin, place fillet on cutting board, flesh side up, with the tail end toward you. One inch in from the end of the tail, make a cut through the flesh just to the skin. Hold the end of the fish taut with the left hand and cut the flesh free from the skin the entire length of the fish, pushing downward on the knife and using a clean cutting motion.

## Shellfish

### Lobsters

East Coast lobsters are more plentiful in the summer, although they are on the market all year. The shell of a live lobster is bluish-green with touches of red. Cooking turns the lobster red. Uncooked lobsters should always be bought alive. A cooked lobster should have a tail that springs back in place after it is straightened. The female can be recognized by the softness of the two uppermost finlike appendages.

**Amount to Buy:** If you serve lobster in the shell, allow 1 small or ½ large lobster per person (they generally weigh 1 to 2 pounds). If you use lobster meat, allow about 1 pound lobster in shell for each ⅔ cup diced, cooked meat. One 6-ounce can of lobster yields about 1 cup.

**To Store:** Refrigerate lobster or lobster meat, and use as soon as possible.

### Frozen Rock-Lobster Tails

The meat of rock lobsters lies in the tail section. Because they are usually sold frozen, wrapped individually, or 2 to a carton, you can keep a few in your freezer. Each weighs ¼ to 1 pound; ½-pound size makes 1 generous serving.

### Crabs

Crabs should be alive when purchased. Hard-shelled crabs, greenish-blue in color, are available throughout the year. Soft-shelled crabs, dark-greenish brown in color, are available from June through September. Ready-cooked crab meat is sold in pry-open cans and regular cans.

**Amount to Buy:** Allow 2 live crabs per person. Crab meat comes in 1-pound, pry-open cans (about 3 cups); the 6½-ounce regular can holds about 1¼ cups.

**To Store:** Refrigerate crabs or crab meat; use as quickly as possible.

### Shrimp

Frozen or fresh raw shrimp (some come deveined) are widely distributed. Their shell ranges from a grayish-green to a soft pink in color. Sold by size, they vary from 15 to 42 shrimp per pound.

You may also buy frozen cooked, deveined shrimp, as well as frozen, ready-to-fry, breaded fantail shrimp, and canned shrimp.

**Amount to Buy:** One pound frozen or fresh raw shrimp yields 1⅓ to 1⅔ cups (or ½ pound) after cooking and shelling, and makes 2 or 3 servings. One 5-ounce can yields about 1 cup.

**To Store:** Wrap raw or cooked shrimp well; refrigerate; use as soon as possible. Keep frozen shrimp frozen until used.

### Oysters

East Coast and Gulf of Mexico shucked oysters are sold by the dozen, or in ½-pint, 1-pint, and 1-quart containers. Pacific Coast oysters are smaller.

Oysters in the shell are sold by the dozen. If serving oysters on the half-shell, allow 6 to 8 per serving. Oysters are also sold canned or frozen.

**To Open Oysters in the Shell:** Scrub shells well; rinse in cold water. Insert point of sharp, thin knife into hinged end of oyster; push blade between shells until muscle at center is cut and valves begin to separate. Run knife around shell; separate valves; loosen oyster from shell.

### Clams

**Hard-Shell:** Large size (quahogs) used for broth and Manhattan-style clam chowder. Smaller sizes (littlenecks and cherrystones) served raw on shell, or in clam cocktails.

**Soft-Shell:** Usually small and popular for broth, steaming, New England clam chowders, frying, etc.

**Pacific Coast:** Range from little butter clams to 1½ pound-Pismo clams to giant 6-pound geoducks. Nice for stews, bisques, etc.

**In Shell:** Sold by peck, dozen, or quart. Shells of live clams are tightly closed, or close quickly when touched. Reject clams with opened or broken shells.

**Shucked:** Sold by quart, for chowders, frying, etc.

**Canned Minced:** Fine for quick clam chowders.

**To Open Clams in the Shell:** See "Oysters" above.

### Scallops

These are the muscles which open and shut scallop shells:

**Bay:** Tiny, pinkish white cubes, about ¾" in size. Especially delicate.

**Sea:** Larger cubes, of 2" or more. May be split across grain before using.

Frozen plain or breaded scallops are also available.

**Amount to Buy:** Allow 1 pound for 3 or 4 servings.

### Mussels

Mussels have black, oblong shells about 3" long. They are delicious and at their best from October to May.

### Abalone

An extra-large, one-shelled sea snail found chiefly along shores of Pacific. As sold in market, it has been pounded, neatly sliced, and is ready for cooking.

## MILK AND CREAM

### Fluid Milk

Be sure that the milk you buy comes from a reputable dealer, and that it is pasteurized. In some communities, several grades of milk are sold. Ask your local health department to explain the differences; then buy the best grade you can afford. Insist that milk be pasteurized. Undulant fever and many streptococcal infections are traceable to raw milk.

**Homogenized Milk** is pasteurized fluid whole milk in which the fat globules have been reduced in size so that all portions of the milk have the same butter-fat content.

**Skim Milk** is milk from which butter fat has been removed.

**Heavy, or Whipping, Cream** contains not less than 30 per cent butter fat.

**Light, Coffee, or Table Cream** contains not less than 18 per cent butter fat.

**Half-and-Half Cream** is a mixture of half milk and half cream containing 11.5 per cent butter fat.

**Commercial Sour Cream** is light pasteurized cream of custardlike consistency with characteristic tangy flavor produced by the addition of a culture or starter.

### The Care of Milk and Cream

1. Take delivered milk in promptly and store at once in the coldest part of the refrigerator. Refrigerate continuously until used.

2. Wash top of container and cap before opening or putting milk away.

3. Always keep milk covered.

4. Never mix new and old milk or cream except for immediate use. Adding yesterday's milk or cream to today's hastens the souring process.

### Evaporated Milk

Canned unsweetened evaporated milk is pasteurized and homogenized, fresh, whole cow's milk from which half of the water content has been removed. Vitamin D is added, and the milk is sterilized after the can is sealed.

**To Store After Opening:** Keep evaporated milk in the can. Cover and refrigerate.

### Instant Nonfat Dry Milk

Instant nonfat dry milk is pasteurized milk with only the fat and water removed. It's a wonderfully thrifty type of milk.

**To Store:** Keep it in its protective package on a cool, dry pantry shelf; close the package carefully after each use. Once it's liquefied, refrigerate.

### Condensed Milk

Canned sweetened condensed milk is a mixture of pure, whole cow's milk and sugar, from which about 60 per cent of the water is removed before the mixture is sealed in cans.

**To Store:** After opening, cover and refrigerate.

# FLOUR

**All-purpose flour** is sometimes referred to as general-purpose, or family flour. It comes in bags, and gives good results for home baking.

It may be a blend of hard wheats, soft wheats, or of both. Enriched flour contains thiamine, niacin, riboflavin, and iron, in addition to excellent, energy-yielding carbohydrates and supplementary protein.

Sift all-purpose flour just before measuring.

**Bread flour,** which also comes in bags, is excellent for yeast breads but is not so satisfactory for general use. It is made from hard wheats and has a higher, stronger gluten than all-purpose flour.

**Cake flour** comes in packages. It is made from selected soft wheats and is especially milled to be very fine.

Always sift cake flour just before measuring.

**Self-rising flour** is all-purpose flour to which leavening and salt have been added in proper amounts for most home baking except yeast breads. Use as label directs.

**Self-rising cake flour** comes in packages and is cake flour to which salt and leavening have been added in proper amounts for home baking. Use as label directs.

**Whole-Wheat, Entire-Wheat, and Graham Flour** are synonymous terms. Such flour contains, in natural proportions, all the constituents of the entire cleaned wheat grain.

Do not sift before measuring.

## LEAVENING AGENTS

**Baking powders** are classified according to the acid ingredients they contain. There are 3 types. Nationally known brands clearly indicate the type on the label.

**Double-Acting Baking Powder** reacts very slowly, releasing about one-fifth to one-third of its leavening in the cold mixture; the rest in the heat of baking.

**Phosphate Baking Powder** reacts slowly and requires heat to liberate about one-third of its leavening.

**Tartrate Baking Powder** reacts rapidly and begins its action at room temperature when liquid is added.

**Baking soda** is used alone or with baking powder to leaven baked goods made with buttermilk, sour milk, chocolate, molasses, fruit juices, etc. Acid from these ingredients reacts with soda to release leavening. When using soda, don't delay mixing or baking.

**Yeast: Active Dry Yeast** stays fresh for several months on a cool shelf and gives uniformly fine results until expiration date on package. If refrigerated, it is good well beyond expiration date on label. When dissolved, one package of dry yeast equals one cake of compressed yeast.

**Compressed Yeast** must be kept in the refrigerator, no longer than a week or two. It can be frozen, but must be thawed at room temperature and used immediately. If it crumbles easily between your fingers, it is still good, even though the edges are slightly brown from drying.

## SHORTENING

**Butter** is churned from sour or sweet cream. It may be marked with a grade: AA, A, etc. It is available salted, lightly salted, or without salt (sweet). It comes in prints, rolls, or whipped.

**Margarine** is usually made entirely from vegetable oils processed to give them desirable spreading and cooking properties. A culture of skim milk used in the manufacturing process is largely responsible for its appetizing flavor. Margarine has the same energy value as butter, and since it is fortified with a minimum of 15,000 units of vitamin A per pound, it is nutritionally comparable to butter and is uniform in food value throughout the year. Buy margarine only from a store that keeps it refrigerated. Store, covered, in refrigerator.

**Emulsifier-Type Shortenings.** Whether these shortenings are all-vegetable or a combination of meat fat and vegetable oils, they are specially adapted for quick-method cakes. They are also used for other forms of baking, sautéing, frying, etc. Creamy white in color, bland in odor and flavor, they are light, workable, easy to blend with other ingredients. They require no refrigeration.

**New Type Lard** is processed to make it creamy and smooth, slightly hardened to produce a higher melting point. A little antioxidant is added so it may be kept without refrigeration.

**Regular Lard.** The quick-blending properties of regular lard make it excellent for pastry. It is also used for sautéing, shallow and deep frying, baking breads, etc. Keep it covered, in the refrigerator.

## SALAD AND OLIVE OILS

**Salad Oils** are made of corn, cottonseed, or peanut oils, or a blend of two or more oils. They are excellent for sautéing, deep or shallow frying, making salad dressings, preparing dishes that call for melted fat, a wide selection of cakes, etc.

**Olive Oil** is popular for salad dressings, Italian-style dishes, etc.

**To Store:** After pouring what you need, wipe off neck of bottle or can, and inside of cap. Only olive oil requires refrigeration.

## VINEGARS

**Cider Vinegar** is a stand-by for salads and salad dressings.

**Distilled White Vinegar** is ideal for pickling and preserving.

**Malt Vinegar** is for salad dressings, meat and fish sauces, seafoods.

**Wine Vinegar** is made from select table wines.

**Tarragon Vinegar** is malt, cider, distilled, or a blend of vinegars with tarragon added.

**Basil, Herb or Spice, or Mixed Herb Vinegar** is a vinegar to which spices and/or herbs have been added.

**Garlic Wine Vinegar** has been flavored with garlic.

## SALTS AND SEASONINGS

**Table Salt** comes plain or iodized, and in several shaker sizes.

**Seasoned or Seasoning Salt** is a flavorful blend of spices with salt.

**Celery Salt** is a mixture of ground celery seeds with salt.

**Garlic Salt** is a mixture of garlic powder with salt. Use with, or instead of, salt.

**Onion Salt** is a blend of dehydrated onion and salt.

**Monosodium Glutamate** is a white crystalline seasoning that enhances the natural flavors of many foods.

## HERBS

**Amount to Buy:** Small quantity at a time. **To Store:** Keep tightly covered in cool place.

**Basil** has a spicy taste, somewhat resembling pepper.

**Bay Leaves** come from a laurel tree grown in eastern Mediterranean countries.

**Chervil** resembles parsley and is slightly peppery.

**Dill** has an herb flavor that is delightful in pickles.

**Marjoram,** one of the mint family, is slightly bitter and aromatic.

**Orégano** is used frequently in Italian cookery.

**Poultry Seasoning** is a combination of fragrant herbs with sage.

**Rosemary** is both sweet and sharp. It is strong, so use lightly.

**Sage** is the most familiar herb next to parsley. It is the most powerful in flavor. Use it lightly.

**Savory** has a flavor similar to, but milder than, sage and mint.

**Tarragon,** with an anise flavor, is sharp, clean, and tangy. It is so decided in flavor that it is often used alone.

**Thyme** is a versatile herb of many uses.

## SPICES

**Allspice** resembles blend of cinnamon, nutmeg, and cloves.

**Aniseed** has a licorice-like flavor.

**Caraway Seeds** have a pleasant spicy flavor, and when bruised, an agreeable odor.

**Cardamom Seeds** have a strong spicy odor and taste like anise.

**Celery Seeds** taste like celery.

**Chili Powder** is a blend of chili peppers and spices.

**Cinnamon** is the spicy bark of an Oriental tree.

**Cloves,** the nail-shaped flower bud of the clove tree, is a heavy, aromatic spice.

**Curry Powder** is a blend of hot spices.

**Dill Seeds** resemble caraway seeds in flavor.

**Ginger,** the root of an Oriental plant, is pungent and aromatic, with a bitey flavor.

**Mace,** the dried pulp around the nutmeg kernel, has a flavor similar to nutmeg.

**Nutmeg,** the kernel of nutmeg fruit, has a flavor somewhat resembling mace.

**Paprika,** a mild member of the pepper family, adds color and flavor.

**Pepper,** the world's most popular spice, comes from the East Indies.

**Poppy Seeds** are fragrant seeds from Holland.

**Saffron,** the world's most expensive spice, adds a golden color to food. A little goes a long way.

## SUGARS

**Brown Sugar** gets its color from its molasses content. There are two kinds:

*Light brown sugar* has a delicate cane flavor.

*Old-fashioned brown sugar* contains more molasses and is, therefore, darker, with more flavor.

Brown-sugar packages are designed to retain the sugar's moisture longer and keep the contents soft and fresh. After each use, fold down the inner paper liner carefully, and tuck in the flap.

**Granulated Sugar** is made from sugar cane or from sugar beets. Use either kind in all cookery.

**Confectioners' Sugar** is a very fine pulverized white sugar with a soft, smooth, fluffy texture. Cornstarch is added to prevent caking. It is often known as 10X sugar.

**Fine Sugar** for fruits, cereals, drinks, etc. is finer than granulated sugar and dissolves quickly.

**Cube and Tablet Sugar** are convenient sweetings for hot drinks. Use cubes for demitasse, tea, etc.; tablets for any hot drink.

## MOLASSES

**Dark Molasses** has a full, tangy flavor and deep color, and is excellent for all cooking in which many spices are present.

**Light Molasses** has a more delicate flavor than dark, a lower iron content, and a golden color, and is excellent for general cooking purposes.

## SYRUPS

**Corn Syrup,** used widely in cooking and as a table syrup, comes in 3 styles:

*Dark:* deep-amber in color.

*White or light:* colorless.

*Maple-flavored:* golden.

**Maple-Blended Syrup** is a blend of maple and cane syrups. It is delightful on pancakes, in candies, etc.

**Maple Syrup** is the pure boiled-down sap from the maple tree. A favorite on pancakes, in candies, on ice cream, etc.

## EXTRACTS

Buy well-known quality brands to insure full, uniform flavor. Keep tightly closed. Try new flavors or plan to combine flavors.

## CEREALS

Whole-grain or enriched, in ready-to-eat and hot styles, are ready to serve or cook quickly. Latest comer to the field is the presweetened kind.

**To Store:** Store all cereals in a cool, dry, convenient spot. Packages and inner wrappings should be carefully opened so that they may be resealed after each use. This is particularly important with ready-to-eat cereals, which are only at their best when crisp.

Keep cereals that require cooking in original packages, so label directions may be followed.

## COCONUT

**Packaged Shredded:** Sweetened packed in moisture-retaining cartons.

**Canned Shredded:** Coconut shreds that are more moist come in vacuum-packed cans. One style has short shreds, another mixed shred lengths.

**Fresh:** It's easy to open a fresh coconut with a long nail, by puncturing the 3 indentations at end of the coconut. Drain milk out; then bake whole coconut at 350° F. 15 minutes to crack shell. Complete cracking with hammer; pry out white meat in large pieces. With knife, cut brown skin from white meat. Grate meat, rubbing each piece full length of grater.

# PYRAMID FOR SOUND HEALTH

## The Basic Pattern for Good Diets — Normal and Special

### What foods you should select, how much, how often, and why

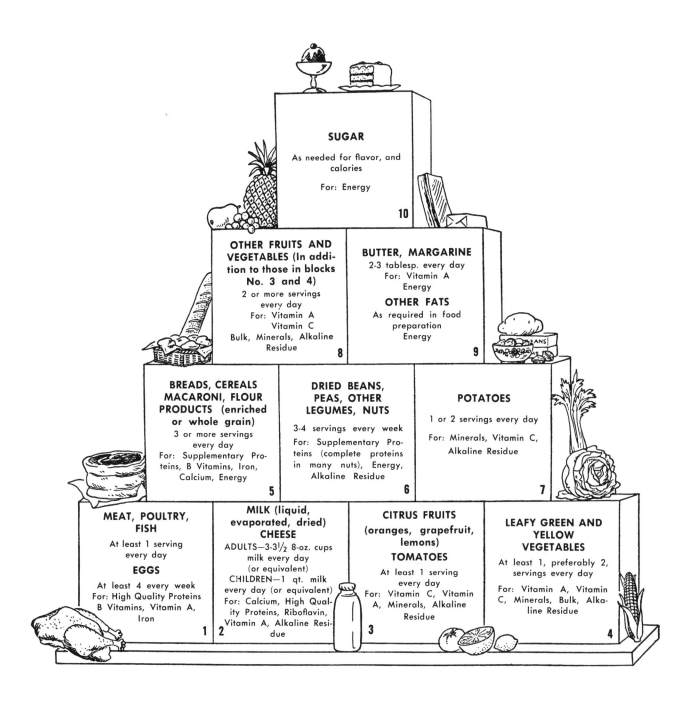

**SUGAR**

As needed for flavor, and calories

For: Energy

**10**

**OTHER FRUITS AND VEGETABLES** (In addition to those in blocks No. 3 and 4)

2 or more servings every day

For: Vitamin A
Vitamin C
Bulk, Minerals, Alkaline Residue

**8**

**BUTTER, MARGARINE**

2-3 tablesp. every day
For: Vitamin A
Energy

**OTHER FATS**

As required in food preparation
Energy

**9**

**BREADS, CEREALS MACARONI, FLOUR PRODUCTS** (enriched or whole grain)

3 or more servings every day

For: Supplementary Proteins, B Vitamins, Iron, Calcium, Energy

**5**

**DRIED BEANS, PEAS, OTHER LEGUMES, NUTS**

3-4 servings every week

For: Supplementary Proteins (complete proteins in many nuts), Energy, Alkaline Residue

**6**

**POTATOES**

1 or 2 servings every day

For: Minerals, Vitamin C, Alkaline Residue

**7**

**MEAT, POULTRY, FISH**

At least 1 serving every day

**EGGS**

At least 4 every week
For: High Quality Proteins B Vitamins, Vitamin A, Iron

**1**

**MILK (liquid, evaporated, dried)
CHEESE**

ADULTS—3-3½ 8-oz. cups milk every day (or equivalent)
CHILDREN—1 qt. milk every day (or equivalent)
For: Calcium, High Quality Proteins, Riboflavin, Vitamin A, Alkaline Residue

**2**

**CITRUS FRUITS (oranges, grapefruit, lemons)
TOMATOES**

At least 1 serving every day

For: Vitamin C, Vitamin A, Minerals, Alkaline Residue

**3**

**LEAFY GREEN AND YELLOW VEGETABLES**

At least 1, preferably 2, servings every day

For: Vitamin A, Vitamin C, Minerals, Bulk, Alkaline Residue

**4**

# HOW TO EAT TO CONTROL YOUR WEIGHT

People often forget that calories are by no means the whole story on food values. It is possible to eat 1,500 calories a day and feel marvelous and yet "starve" on 2,000.

Women who plan meals should know about calories. But they must also know the rest of the story on food values—which foods provide proper proteins, minerals, vitamins, and other diet necessities. Here is the information. Read it carefully, and you can always serve healthful meals.

We Americans have little excuse for not eating well and wisely. And a need to be budget-conscious is no hindrance either to eating enjoyment or to a sound diet. A well-seasoned meat loaf with a tasty sauce provides as high-quality protein as prime ribs of beef. Pie fillings, puddings, and sauces made with evaporated milk or nonfat dry milk need make no apology for either flavor or food value. The preparation of delicious and nutritious low-cost meals challenges the skill and ingenuity of the homemaker.

You will find our "Pyramid" a guide to wise food selection. The pyramid is divided into the following ten blocks:

1. Meat, poultry, fish, eggs
2. Milk (liquid, evaporated, dried) and cheese
3. Citrus fruits and tomatoes
4. Leafy green and yellow vegetables
5. Breads, cereals, macaroni, flour products (enriched or whole grain)
6. Dried beans, peas, other legumes, and nuts
7. Potatoes
8. Fruits and vegetables (in addition to those in 3 and 4)
9. Butter, margarine, and other fats
10. Sugar

Here are the important reasons for choosing each class of food. Isn't it really easy to assure your family of all the essentials of a sound diet and at the same time serve them mouth-watering meals? Some foods, such as pure fat and pure sugar, supply principally calories, or energy units. Others contribute, in addition, vitamins, minerals, proteins and other values vital to our health and well-being. The latter are what we call protective foods; they are the four blocks which form the base of the pyramids.

Whether you are planning normal family meals, trying to reduce, or attempting to collect a few extra pounds, you will be vitally concerned with calories. A calorie is a unit of energy—the energy needed to stoke the engines of our bodily processes and provide the fuel for our physical activities. Everyone has a calorie requirement: the number of energy units he needs daily for his physical activities. If the food you eat supplies this number, you neither gain nor lose.

## Reducing Diet

The only practical way to attain a weight and stay there is to control your diet and form a habit of daily moderate exercise. A few more sets of tennis or 50 bends a day won't take off fat. Exercise is wonderful to change your figure, but it's difficult to exercise enough to decrease your weight. To take off one pound, you must walk about 36 miles or wash on a washboard for 24 hours. It's easier to eat with regard for your figure.

If you need to lose weight, reduce the number of calories you are now taking daily—but not too drastically and never at the expense of the necessary protective foods. Fortunately, many of these essential foods are not too high in energy units (for example, fruits, vegetables, skim milk, and lean meat). **Don't reduce your calories below 1,200 to 1,300 or try to lose more than 2 pounds a week. Consult your doctor before going on a reducing diet.**

1. Cut down but don't omit breads, cereals, fats and sugar. Use enriched or whole grain bread, flour.
2. Eat fruit fresh without sugar, or use canned dietetic packs.
3. Eat plenty of salad, but go easy on dressing, or use a low-calorie dressing.
4. Substitute skim milk or buttermilk for whole milk.
5. Don't skip meals, but eat less at mealtime.

Individual food preferences are legion. We think it is *particularly* important for you to have foods you like to eat when you are taking off weight.

Now, how much do you need to lose? The best way to find out is to have your doctor tell you. It's *always* a good idea to have a medical check-up and go-ahead before starting a reducing plan.

Based on 2,000 calories daily as an average requirement for maintaining your normal weight:

To lose 5 lb. in approximately 3 weeks you must omit a total of 17,500 calories.

To lose 10 lb. in approximately 6 weeks you must omit a total of 35,000 calories.

To lose 15 lb. in approximately 9 to 10 weeks you must omit a total of 52,500 calories.

If you have a particularly heavy frame, or do an unusual amount of physical work, you may need more than 2,000 calories to maintain your normal weight (your doctor can help you on this point). In such cases, your diet can be a little more liberal (1,500 to 1,600 calories daily) and still allow you to lose about 2 pounds weekly.

## To Gain Weight

The problem of gaining weight often seems more difficult than taking it off. The underlying cause of an underweight condition may be found in some physical disturbance; therefore, the first step in trying to put on pounds should be a complete physical examination.

Sometimes loss of weight is due to lack of proper food which results in poor appetite. A poor appetite can be caused by poor tone of the digestive tract induced by an inadequate supply of certain vitamins in the diet. Excessive smoking also affects the appetite. Try to confine smoking to the end of the meal if you are trying to gain weight. Here are some other suggestions that may help you:

1. Use cream generously on fruits, cereals, etc.
2. Between-meal snacks are fine—midmorning, midafternoon, and before bed.
3. Use mayonnaise generously on salad.
4. Allow time for a hearty breakfast.
5. Try to increase the size of portions of all dishes.
6. Plenty of sleep is a must.
7. Immediately after arising in the morning, drink a glass of cold, unsweetened fruit juice. It washes mouth surfaces and stimulates the appetite.

8. Eat dessert at lunch and dinner.
9. Eat gravies, sauces, and extra cream.

Remember, you will not accomplish wonders overnight; don't watch the scales too closely. And don't worry. Just map out a campaign, form good eating and sleeping habits, and see if each month doesn't register a steady gain.

## Facts About Age and Weight

How Much Should You Weigh? During the years of childhood and early youth, it is considered desirable to weigh a few pounds more than the average for your height and age group.

By middle age, most doctors agree, it is better to maintain the ideal weight for a twenty-five year old of your height and sex. The reasoning behind this advice is based on studies that show that people over twenty-five tend to slow down their activities, particularly their participation in sports, yet retain a hearty appetite. As a result, they eat more than they should. Unless they are among those few who stay thin no matter what, they gain weight. For this reason, the statistical average weight after twenty-five is not likely to be the ideal weight.

As you grow older, you should not exceed this ideal weight. The table shown below will give you the ideal weight, as charted by experts, for persons of your build, weight, and sex.

Weight problems in teen-agers are treated just like weight problems at any other age level. If your child is too thin or too fat, enlist his aid.

## DESIRABLE WEIGHTS

### Women, Ages 25 and Over*

| Height (with shoes) | | Weight in Pounds (as ordinarily dressed) | | |
|---|---|---|---|---|
| Feet | Inches | Small Frame | Medium Frame | Large Frame |
| 4 | 10 | 92– 98 | 96–107 | 104–119 |
| 4 | 11 | 94–101 | 98–110 | 106–122 |
| 5 | 0 | 96–104 | 101–113 | 109–125 |
| 5 | 1 | 99–107 | 104–116 | 112–128 |
| 5 | 2 | 102–110 | 107–119 | 115–131 |
| 5 | 3 | 105–113 | 110–122 | 118–134 |
| 5 | 4 | 108–116 | 113–126 | 121–138 |
| 5 | 5 | 111–119 | 116–130 | 125–142 |
| 5 | 6 | 114–123 | 120–135 | 129–146 |
| 5 | 7 | 118–127 | 124–139 | 133–150 |
| 5 | 8 | 122–131 | 128–143 | 137–154 |
| 5 | 9 | 126–135 | 132–151 | 141–158 |
| 5 | 10 | 130–140 | 140–155 | 145–163 |
| 5 | 11 | 134–144 | 144–159 | 149–168 |

### Men, Ages 25 and Over*

| Height (with shoes) | | Weight in Pounds (as ordinarily dressed) | | |
|---|---|---|---|---|
| Feet | Inches | Small Frame | Medium Frame | Large Frame |
| 5 | 2 | 112–120 | 118–129 | 126–141 |
| 5 | 3 | 115–123 | 121–133 | 129–144 |
| 5 | 4 | 118–126 | 124–136 | 132–148 |
| 5 | 5 | 121–129 | 127–139 | 135–152 |
| 5 | 6 | 124–133 | 130–143 | 138–156 |
| 5 | 7 | 128–137 | 134–147 | 142–161 |
| 5 | 8 | 132–141 | 138–152 | 147–166 |
| 5 | 9 | 136–145 | 142–156 | 151–170 |
| 5 | 10 | 140–150 | 146–160 | 155–174 |
| 5 | 11 | 144–154 | 150–165 | 159–179 |
| 6 | 0 | 148–158 | 154–170 | 164–184 |
| 6 | 1 | 152–162 | 158–175 | 168–189 |
| 6 | 2 | 156–167 | 162–180 | 173–194 |
| 6 | 3 | 160–171 | 167–185 | 178–199 |

*From Tables Metropolitan Life Insurance Co.

# VITAMINS AND MINERALS—HOW TO GET THEM AND WHY

| WHY YOU NEED THEM | THEIR RICHEST NATURAL SOURCES | |
|---|---|---|
| **Vitamin A**<br>Helps resist nose and throat infections (colds)<br>Helps prevent night blindness and other eye diseases<br>Promotes children's growth | Liver<br>Fish-liver oils<br>Yellow vegetables (carrots, sweet potatoes)<br>Butter or margarine | Cream<br>Milk (whole, evaporated)<br>Whole-milk cheese<br>Egg yolk<br>Dried apricots |
| **Vitamin B₁ (Thiamine)**<br>Necessary for functioning of nerve tissues<br>Affects body's utilization of carbohydrates, fats<br>Promotes children's growth<br>Stimulates appetite and good muscle tone | Lean pork<br>Whole-grain or enriched breads, cereals, and flours<br>Peanuts<br>Dried peas<br>Dried beans<br>Variety meats (liver, kidneys, sweetbreads) | Lentils<br>Lean meats<br>Fish<br>Chicken<br>Milk (whole, skim, evaporated, non-fat dry)<br>Brewer's yeast<br>Wheat germ |
| **Vitamin B₂ (Riboflavin)**<br>Necessary for healthy skin and hair, good digestion, sound nerves<br>Increases resistance to infection, general weakness, and poor eye conditions | Liver<br>Kidney<br>Lean meats<br>Fish<br>Chicken<br>Milk (whole, skim, evaporated, non-fat dry) | Eggs<br>Green and leafy vegetables (turnip greens, beet greens, kale, green limas, collards, mustard greens, etc.)<br>Dried peas<br>Brewer's yeast<br>Wheat germ |
| **Vitamin C (Ascorbic Acid)**<br>Prevents and cures scurvy<br>Increases strength of capillary walls, lessening the possibility of hemorrhages<br>Increases resistance to infection<br>Necessary for sound teeth and gums | Citrus fruits (oranges, grapefruit, lemons, tangerines)<br>Strawberries<br>Cantaloupe<br>Pineapple | Tomatoes<br>Raw cabbage<br>Potatoes<br>Green and leafy vegetables (green peppers, mustard greens, Brussels sprouts, kale, parsley, etc.) |
| **Vitamin D**<br>Aids in utilizing calcium and phosphorus in building bones, teeth<br>Prevents rickets in children | Sunshine<br>Fish-liver oils<br>Vitamin-D enriched milk and evaporated milk | Liver<br>Vitamin-D enriched cereals<br>Fresh and canned oily fish<br>Egg yolk |
| **Niacin**<br>Is chief factor in cure and prevention of pellagra<br>Helps maintain a healthy skin condition | Liver<br>Kidney<br>Heart<br>Lean meat<br>Fish<br>Green and leafy vegetables (green beans, broccoli, kale, cabbage, etc.) | Brewer's yeast<br>Wheat germ<br>Green peas<br>Milk (whole, skim, evaporated, non-fat dry)<br>Whole-grain or enriched breads, cereals, and flours |
| ***Calcium**<br>Builds strong bones and teeth<br>Necessary for lactation; coagulation of blood; heart, nerve, and muscle functions<br>Helps maintain alkalinity of the blood | Milk (whole, skim, evaporated, non-fat dry)<br>Cream<br>Cheese | Sardines<br>Green and leafy vegetables (green beans, broccoli, kale, cabbage, etc.) |
| ***Phosphorus**<br>Builds bones and teeth<br>Necessary for utilization of fats and carbohydrates by the body | Green and leafy vegetables (green beans, broccoli, kale, cabbage, etc.)<br>Milk (whole, skim, evaporated, non-fat dry)<br>Cheese<br>Cereals<br>Wheat germ | Eggs<br>Fish<br>Shellfish<br>Liver<br>Meats<br>Brewer's yeast |
| **Iron**<br>Helps form red blood corpuscles<br>Helps carry oxygen in blood<br>Aids in tissue respiration<br>Prevents nutritional anemia | Liver<br>Oysters<br>Molasses<br>Green and leafy vegetables (green beans, broccoli, kale, cabbage, etc.) | Dried apricots<br>Egg yolk<br>Potatoes<br>Whole-grain or enriched breads, cereals, and flours |

* *The correct functioning of calcium, phosphorus, and vitamin D depends on sufficient amounts of each.*

# APPROXIMATE DAILY CALORIE REQUIREMENTS

(Normally Active People)

| MEN (143 lbs.) | CALORIES | | CHILDREN UP TO 10 YEARS | CALORIES |
|---|---|---|---|---|
| 25 yrs. | 3,200 | | Under 1 year | 50 per lb. |
| 45 yrs. | 2,900 | | 1 to 3 (27 lbs.) | 1,200 |
| 65 yrs. | 2,600 | | 4 to 6 (40 lbs.) | 1,600 |
| | | | 7 to 10 (59 lbs.) | 2,000 |

| WOMEN (121 lbs.) | CALORIES | CHILDREN OVER 10 YEARS | | CALORIES |
|---|---|---|---|---|
| 25 yrs. | 2,300 | GIRLS: | 10 to 12 (79 lbs.) | 2,300 |
| 45 yrs. | 2,100 | | 13 to 15 (108 lbs.) | 2,500 |
| 65 yrs. | 1,800 | | 16 to 20 (120 lbs.) | 2,400 |
| | | BOYS: | 10 to 12 (78 lbs.) | 2,500 |
| | | | 13 to 15 (108 lbs.) | 3,200 |
| | | | 16 to 20 (139 lbs.) | 3,800 |

These tables should make your calculations simple. People's daily calorie needs vary, because of differences in build, activities, etc. These figures, compiled by the Food and Nutrition Board of the National Research Council, will help you determine the number of calories you should have each day.

# COMPLETE CALORIE GUIDE

(These calorie values are based on Composition of Foods—Handbook #8, U.S.D.A.)

## Breads and Cereals
### (Grain Products)

| | AMOUNT | APPROX. CALORIES |
|---|---|---|
| Baking-Powder Biscuits | 2 small | 95 |
| Bread: Boston brown | 1 slice | 100 |
| Cornbread | 1 piece, 2" x 2" x 1" | 100 |
| French | 1 slice | 80 |
| Melba toast | 1 slice | 20 |
| Rye | 1 slice | 60 |
| White, enriched | 1 slice | 60 |
| White, raisin | 1 slice | 100 |
| Whole wheat | 1 slice | 75 |
| Buns: Cinnamon with raisins | 1 | 155 |
| Hot Cross | 1 | 105 |
| Cereals, Cooked: | | |
| Corn meal, yellow or white | ¾ cup, cooked | 100 |
| Farina or granular wheat | ¾ cup, cooked | 100 |
| Rolled Oats | ¾ cup, cooked | 100 |
| Cereals, Ready to Eat: | | |
| Corn, wheat, rice flakes | 1 cup (approx. 1 oz.) | 105 |
| Puffed wheat, rice, corn | 1 cup (approx. ½ oz.) | 50 |
| Shredded Wheat | 1 biscuit | 100 |

| | AMOUNT | APPROX. CALORIES |
|---|---|---|
| Wheat bran | 1 cup | 100 |
| Wheat germ | 1 tablesp. | 30 |
| Coffee cake, iced with nuts | 1, 4½" wedge | 250 |
| Cornstarch | 1 tablesp. | 35 |
| Crackers: Graham | 1, 2¾" square | 40 |
| Ritz type | 1 | 15 |
| Saltine | 1, 2" square | 15 |
| Soda | 1, 2¾" square | 25 |
| Thin wheat | 1 | 10 |
| Danish Pastry | 1, small | 130 |
| Doughnuts: Cake type | 1 | 135 |
| Jelly | 1 | 175 |
| Flour: All purpose | 1 cup, sifted | 400 |
| Cake | 1 cup, sifted | 370 |
| Whole-wheat | 1 cup, sifted | 450 |
| French Toast | 1 slice | 105 |
| Griddlecake | 1, 4" diameter | 60 |
| Macaroni, Noodles, and Spaghetti | ¾ cup, cooked | 150 |
| Muffins: Blueberry | 1, 2¾" diameter | 150 |
| Bran | 1, 2¾" diameter | 100 |
| Corn meal | 1, 2¾" diameter | 140 |
| English | 1, 3½" diameter | 130 |
| Plain | 1, 2¾" diameter | 130 |
| Popover | 1 medium | 100 |

| | AMOUNT | APPROX. CALORIES |
|---|---|---|
| Pretzels | 1 small, 1″ x 2″ or 5, 2″ sticks | 10 |
| Rice: Brown, processed, white | ¾ cup, cooked | 125 |
| Rolls: Plain | 1 | 100 |
| Sweet | 1 | 150 |
| Waffle | 1, 6″ diameter | 220 |

## Dairy Products and Eggs

| | AMOUNT | APPROX. CALORIES |
|---|---|---|
| Butter (see Fats, Oils and Shortenings) | | |
| Buttermilk, cultured | 1 glass (8 oz.) | 85 |
| Cheese: American, Cheddar, Swiss (processed or natural) | 1 slice (1 oz.) | 110 |
| Camembert | 1, 1¾″ wedge | 100 |
| Cheese Food | 1 ounce | 105 |
| Cottage, creamed | ⅓ cup | 85 |
| Cottage, plain | ⅓ cup | 75 |
| Cream | 1 ounce | 105 |
| Parmesan, grated | 2 tablesp. | 35 |
| Roquefort | 1 piece, 1½″ x 1″ x 1″ | 100 |
| Spread | 2 tablesp. | 100 |
| Chocolate-Milk Drink | 1 glass (8 oz.) | 180 |
| Cream: Heavy | 1 tablesp. | 50 |
| Light | 1 tablesp. | 30 |
| Sour, light | 1 tablesp. | 30 |
| Egg: Fried | 1 medium | 105 |
| Omelet | 2, with butter | 215 |
| Scrambled | 2, with 2 tablesp. milk, butter | 245 |
| Whole fresh, cooked or poached | 1 medium | 75 |
| Eggnog | 1 glass (8 oz.) | 230 |
| Ice Cream Soda, vanilla | 1 regular | 270 |
| Milk: | | |
| Condensed | 1 tablesp. | 60 |
| Dried (nonfat milk solids) | 4 tablesp. (1 oz.) | 85 |
| Dried (whole milk solids) | 4 tablesp. (1 oz.) | 160 |
| Evaporated | ½ cup (undiluted) | 170 |
| Liquid (skim) | 1 glass (8 oz.) | 85 |
| Liquid (whole) | 1 glass (8 oz.) | 165 |
| Malted (dry powder) | 3 tablesp. (1 oz.) | 110 |
| Yogurt (made from skim milk) | 1 cup (8 oz.) | 80 |
| Yogurt (made from whole milk) | 1 cup (8 oz.) | 160 |
| Milk Shake | 1 glass (8 oz.) | 400 |

## Fresh Fruits

| | AMOUNT | APPROX. CALORIES |
|---|---|---|
| Apple | 1 medium, 2½″ diameter | 75 |
| Apricots: Dried | 4–6 halves | 80 |
| Fresh | 2–3 medium | 60 |
| Avocado | ½ medium | 250 |
| | ½ cup, ½″ cubes | 165 |
| Banana | 1 medium, 6″ long | 100 |
| Blackberries | ½ cup | 40 |
| Blueberries | ½ cup | 45 |
| Cantaloupe | ½″, 5″ diameter | 40 |
| Cherries, sweet | 20, ⅞″ diameter | 100 |
| Dates, dried | 4 dates | 100 |
| Figs, dried | 2 medium | 100 |
| Grapefruit | ½ medium | 75 |
| Grapes: Concord | 15 | 45 |
| Malaga | 15 | 75 |
| White | 15 | 45 |
| Honeydew Melon | 2″ x 7″ wedge from 6½″ x 7″ melon | 50 |
| Loganberries | ½ cup | 50 |
| Orange | 1 medium, 3″ diameter | 70 |
| Peach | 1 medium | 50 |
| Pear | 1 medium | 45 |
| Pineapple | 1 slice, ¾″ thick | 50 |
| Plum | 1, 2″ diameter | 30 |
| Prunes, dried | 4 medium | 75 |
| Raisins | ¼ cup, seeded and seedless | 100 |
| Raspberries | ½ cup | 50 |
| Strawberries | ½ cup, or 10 large | 40 |
| Tangerine | 1, 2½″ diameter | 35 |
| Watermelon | 1 slice, 10″ diameter x ¾″ thick | 50 |

## Cooked and Canned Fruits

| | AMOUNT | APPROX. CALORIES |
|---|---|---|
| Applesauce: Sweetened | ½ cup | 85 |
| Unsweetened | ½ cup | 45 |
| Apricots: Canned in syrup | 4 medium halves, 2 tablesp. syrup | 100 |
| Stewed and sweetened | ½ cup | 200 |
| Cherries, canned in syrup | ½ cup, 3 tablesp. syrup | 100 |
| Cranberry Sauce, sweetened, canned or cooked | 1 tablesp. | 35 |
| Fruit Cocktail | ½ cup fruit and syrup | 90 |
| Grapefruit Sections | ½ cup, 1 tablesp. syrup | 90 |
| Peaches | 2 large halves, 3 tablesp. syrup | 100 |
| Pears | 2 halves, 2 tablesp. syrup | 80 |
| Pineapple, sweetened | 1 slice, ¾″ thick, 1 tablesp. syrup | 85 |

| | AMOUNT | APPROX. CALORIES |
|---|---|---|
| Prunes, stewed and sweetened | 4 with 4 tablesp. syrup | 120 |
| Rhubarb, stewed and sweetened | ½ cup | 175 |

### Frozen Fruits (with Syrup)

| | AMOUNT | APPROX. CALORIES |
|---|---|---|
| Apricots | ½ cup | 90 |
| Blueberries | ½ cup | 120 |
| Melon Balls | ½ cup | 80 |
| Peaches | ½ cup | 90 |
| Pineapple chunks | ½ cup | 105 |
| Raspberries | ½ cup | 110 |
| Rhubarb | ½ cup | 120 |
| Strawberries | ½ cup | 95 |

### Fresh, Frozen and Canned Juices

| | AMOUNT | APPROX. CALORIES |
|---|---|---|
| Apple | ½ cup (4 oz.) | 60 |
| Cider, sweet | 1 glass (8 oz.) | 120 |
| Cranberry | ½ cup (4 oz.) | 40 |
| Grape | ½ cup (4 oz.) | 90 |
| Grapefruit: | | |
| Sweetened, canned | ½ cup (4 oz.) | 65 |
| Unsweetened, canned, or fresh | ½ cup (4 oz.) | 50 |
| Lemon, fresh, canned or frozen | ¼ cup (4 tablesp.) | 15 |
| Orange, fresh, frozen, canned | ½ cup (4 oz.) | 50 |
| Pineapple, unsweetened | ½ cup (4 oz.) | 60 |
| Prune | ½ cup (4 oz.) | 85 |
| Tomato, canned | ½ cup (4 oz.) | 25 |
| Vegetable Cocktail | ½ cup (4 oz.) | 25 |
| Whole-Fruit Nectars: | | |
| Apricot, peach, pear, plum | ½ cup (4 oz.) | 55 |

### Meats, Fish, Poultry

#### (All values on cooked basis)

| | AMOUNT | APPROX. CALORIES |
|---|---|---|
| Bacon, lean | thin strip, 5" long (crisp) ⅕ oz. | 30 |
| Beef: | | |
| Corned, canned | 2 slices, 3" x 2" x ¼" (2 oz.) | 100 |
| Dried or chipped | ½ cup (2 oz.) | 115 |
| Hamburger | 1 patty, 2¾" diameter, 1" thick (1½ oz.) | 150 |
| Roast or steak | 1 serving, 4½" x 3" x ½" (3 oz. without bone) | 275 |
| Bologna | 2, ⅛" slices, 2¾" diameter (3½ oz.) | 250 |

| | AMOUNT | APPROX. CALORIES |
|---|---|---|
| Fish and Sea Food: | | |
| Bass | 1 piece, 3" x 2¼" x 1" (3½ oz.) | 100 |
| Bluefish | 1 piece, 3½" x 3" x ½" (4 oz.) | 190 |
| Clams, raw | 6 (4 oz., meat only) | 100 |
| Cod fish cake | 1, 2½" diameter | 125 |
| Cod Steak | 1 steak, 3¾" x 2½" x ¾" (4 oz.) | 85 |
| Crab, deviled | 1 medium | 200 |
| Crab meat, canned or fresh | ½ cup (2½ oz.) | 70 |
| Halibut | 1 steak, 4" x 3" x ½" (4 oz.) | 225 |
| Lobster, canned or fresh | ½ cup (3 oz.) | 80 |
| Mackerel | 1 piece, 3" x 3" x 1" (3 oz.) | 160 |
| Oysters, raw | 5 medium (2¼ oz., meat only) | 60 |
| Salmon, baked | 1 steak, 4" x 3" x ½" (4 oz.) | 200 |
| Salmon, canned | ½ cup (2½ oz.) | 100 |
| Sardines, canned in oil | 4, 3" long (1¼ oz.) | 75 |
| Scallops | 6 medium | 225 |
| Shrimp | 10–12 medium (2¾ oz.) | 75 |
| Swordfish | 1 steak, 3" x 3" x ½" (4 oz.) | 225 |
| Tuna, canned in oil | ½ cup, drained (2¾ oz.) | 155 |
| Tuna, canned dietetic pack | ½ cup (2¾ oz.) | 125 |
| Whitefish | 1 piece, 3¾" x 2¼" x ¾" (2½ oz.) | 100 |
| Lamb: | | |
| Chop | 1 rib, 2" x 1½" x ¾" lean (3 oz.) | 100 |
| Roast | 1 slice, 3½" x 4½" x ⅛" (1¼ oz.) | 100 |
| Liver: | | |
| Beef, Calf, Pork | 1 slice, 2¾" x 2" x ¼" (2 oz.) | 85 |
| Liverwurst | 1 slice, 3¼" diameter, ¼" thick (1 oz.) | 70 |
| Luncheon Meat, canned | 1 slice (1 oz.) | 80 |
| Pork: | | |
| Ham, fresh or smoked | 1 slice, 4½" x 4½" x ¼" (3 oz.) | 330 |
| Loin | 1 chop, ¾" thick (4 oz.) | 350 |

| | AMOUNT | CALORIES | | AMOUNT | CALORIES |
|---|---|---|---|---|---|
| Sausage | 1 link, 3″ long, ½″ diameter (¾ oz.) | 95 | Mustard Greens | ½ cup | 15 |
| | | | Okra | 5 pods | 20 |
| Poultry: | | | Onion, raw | 1 medium | 50 |
| Chicken | 1 average serving (3½ oz.) | 200 | Parsley, raw | 2 tablesp. chopped | 5 |
| | | | Parsnips | ½ cup | 50 |
| Duck | 1 average serving (3 oz.) | 315 | Peas, green | ½ cup | 55 |
| | | | Peppers, raw green | 1, 3½″ long | 20 |
| Turkey | 1 average serving (4 oz.) | 300 | Potatoes: Baked or | | |
| | | | boiled | 1 medium | 95 |
| Sweetbread | ¾ cup (3¼ oz.) | 175 | French fried | 8 pieces, 2″ x ½″ x ½″ | 160 |
| Tongue | 4 slices, 3″ x 2″ x ⅛″ (1¾ oz.) | 100 | Sweet, baked | 1 medium, 5″ x 2″ | 185 |
| Veal: | | | Sweet, candied | 1 small, 3½″ x 2¼″ | 315 |
| Cutlet, breaded | 1 chop, 4″ x 2¼″ x ½″ (3 oz.) | 280 | White, mashed, with milk and butter added | ½ cup | 120 |
| Roast | 1 slice, 4″ x 2½″ x ½″ (3 oz.) | 190 | Pumpkin | ½ cup | 35 |
| | | | Radishes, raw | 5 medium | 10 |
| | | | Rutabaga | ½ cup | 25 |
| | | | Sauerkraut, canned | ½ cup | 15 |
| | | | Spinach | ½ cup | 20 |

## Vegetables (Fresh, Frozen, Canned)

*(Cooked unless otherwise specified. No butter or margarine used)*

| | AMOUNT | CALORIES | | AMOUNT | CALORIES |
|---|---|---|---|---|---|
| Asparagus, fresh | 12 medium stalks, 5″ long | 25 | Squash: | | |
| | | | Summer | ½ cup | 20 |
| Beans: | | | Winter | ½ cup | 50 |
| Baked, canned, with pork and tomato sauce | 1 cup | 295 | Succotash | ½ cup | 130 |
| Green | ½ cup, 1″ pieces | 30 | Tomatoes: | | |
| Limas, dried or fresh | ½ cup | 100 | Canned | ½ cup | 25 |
| Beet Greens | ½ cup | 20 | Fresh | 1 medium | 30 |
| Beets | 2, or ½ cup, diced | 35 | Turnip, white | ½ cup | 25 |
| Broccoli | ½ cup | 20 | Water Cress, raw | 1 bunch, 3″ long, 3″ diameter | 20 |
| Brussels Sprouts | 7 | 60 | | | |
| Cabbage | ½ cup | 20 | | | |
| Carrots: Cooked | ½ cup, diced | 25 | | | |
| Raw | 1, or ½ cup grated | 20 | | | |
| Cauliflower | ¼ small head, 4½″ diameter | 25 | | | |

## Salads

*(Each salad includes 2 leaves of lettuce and 1 tablespoon of dressing)*

| | AMOUNT | CALORIES |
|---|---|---|
| Celery, raw | ½ cup, or 4, 7″ long pieces | 10 |

| | AMOUNT | CALORIES |
|---|---|---|
| Chard | ½ cup | 30 |
| Coleslaw | ½ cup | 50 |
| Collards | ½ cup | 40 |
| Corn, sweet fresh | 1 ear, 5″ long, 1¾″ diameter | 85 |
| Cucumbers, raw | 6 slices, ⅛″ thick | 5 |
| Dandelion Greens | ½ cup | 40 |
| Eggplant, fried | 1 slice, 4″ diameter, ⅜″ thick | 135 |
| Endive, raw | 2 stalks, 5¾″ long | 25 |
| Escarole, raw | 4 leaves | 20 |
| Kale | ½ cup | 25 |
| Kohlrabi | ½ cup | 25 |
| Lentils, dried, split peas | ½ cup (2½ tablesp. raw) | 120 |
| Lettuce, raw | 3 large leaves | 10 |
| Mushrooms | 4 large | 10 |

| | AMOUNT | CALORIES |
|---|---|---|
| Apple and Carrot with Mayonnaise | ½ cup | 100 |
| Avocado with Tomato, Cottage Cheese, and French Dressing | ¼ avocado, ½ tomato, 2 tablesp. cheese | 245 |
| Banana and Nut with Mayonnaise | ½ banana, 1 tablesp. walnuts | 260 |
| Cabbage Salad with French Dressing | ½ cup, shredded | 65 |
| Chicken and Celery with Mayonnaise | ½ cup | 250 |
| Crab and Celery with Mayonnaise | 3 heaping tablesp. | 160 |
| Cream Cheese and Pineapple with French Dressing | 1 slice pineapple, 2 tablesp. cheese | 200 |

| | AMOUNT | APPROX. CALORIES | | AMOUNT | APPROX. CALORIES |
|---|---|---|---|---|---|
| Fruit (fresh orange, grapefruit, and grapes; canned peach and pineapple; mayonnaise and whipped cream) | 3 heaping tablesp. | 160 | **Cakes:** | | |
| Mixed Greens with French Dressing | ½ cup | 50 | Angel | 1, 2″ wedge | 115 |
| Perfection Salad (jellied veg., no dressing) | ½ cup | 40 | Cheesecake | 1 piece, 2½″ wedge | 275 |
| Potato with Mayonnaise | ½ cup | 200 | Chocolate layer cake with icing | 2-layer piece, 2″ wedge | 400 |
| Salmon and Celery with Mayonnaise | ½ cup | 195 | Cupcake with icing | 1, 2¾″ diameter | 200 |
| Shrimp and Celery with Mayonnaise | ½ cup | 170 | Fruitcake | 1 piece, 1⅞″ x 1⅞″ x ⅜″ | 100 |
| Salad Dressings: French | 1 tablesp. | 50 | Poundcake | 1 slice, 2¾″ x 3″ x ⅝″ | 125 |
| Mayonnaise | 1 tablesp. | 100 | Spongecake (6 eggs) | 2″ wedge (1/12 of 8″ cake) | 115 |
| Russian | 1 tablesp. | 80 | White layer cake, iced | 2-layer piece, 2″ wedge | 325 |
| Salad | 1 tablesp. | 85 | **Cookies:** | | |

### Sandwiches and Soups

| | AMOUNT | APPROX. CALORIES | | AMOUNT | APPROX. CALORIES |
|---|---|---|---|---|---|
| **Sandwiches** (with 2 slices lightly buttered bread) | | | Fig Bar | 1 small | 100 |
| Bacon, Lettuce, and Tomato (4 slices crisp bacon, 2 slices tomato) | | 300 | Gingersnap | 1 small, 1¾″ diameter | 20 |
| Chicken Salad with Lettuce (2 tablesp. chicken, 2 teasp. mayonnaise) | | 245 | Iced Sandwich | 1 small | 70 |
| Cream Cheese and Jelly (2 tablesp. cream cheese, 1 tablesp. jelly) | | 340 | Macaroon | 1 large | 110 |
| Egg Salad with Lettuce (½ egg, 1 tablesp. mayonnaise) | | 290 | Oatmeal | 1 large, 3½″ diameter | 120 |
| Frankfurter on Roll (1 frankfurter) | | 180 | Plain | 1, 3″ diameter | 110 |
| Ham, with Lettuce (1 slice ham) | | 270 | Sugar | 1 medium, 2½″ diameter | 50 |
| Hamburger on Roll (1 hamburger patty) | | 250 | Vanilla Wafer | 1, 2½″ diameter | 20 |
| Peanut Butter (1½ tablesp. peanut butter) | | 300 | Cornstarch Pudding | ½ cup | 140 |
| Swiss Cheese (1 slice cheese) | | 270 | Custard, baked or boiled | ½ cup | 140 |
| **Soups:** | | | Eclair, iced, custard filling | 1 | 200 |
| Asparagus, Pea, Cream of | ¾ cup (6 oz.) | 150 | Gelatin Dessert | ½ cup | 75 |
| Bean | ¾ cup | 145 | Gingerbread | 2″ square | 100 |
| Bouillon | ¾ cup | 10 | Ice, Orange | ½ cup | 150 |
| Chicken Noodle | ¾ cup | 95 | Ice Cream, vanilla | ½ cup, or ⅙ of quart | 200 |
| Clam Chowder | ¾ cup | 75 | Junket | ½ cup | 115 |
| Consommé | ¾ cup | 10 | **Pies:** | | |
| Mushroom, Cream of | ¾ cup | 150 | Apple | 3½″ wedge (⅛ of 9″ pie) | 230 |
| Pea | ¾ cup | 115 | Blueberry | 3½″ wedge | 255 |
| Tomato | | | Cherry | 3½″ wedge | 300 |
| Clear | ¾ cup | 80 | Chocolate meringue | 3½″ wedge | 255 |
| Cream of | ¾ cup | 160 | Custard | 3½″ wedge | 230 |
| Vegetable | ¾ cup | 65 | Lemon meringue | 3½″ wedge | 275 |

### Desserts

| | AMOUNT | APPROX. CALORIES | | AMOUNT | APPROX. CALORIES |
|---|---|---|---|---|---|
| | | | Mince | 3½″ wedge | 300 |
| | | | Pumpkin | 3½″ wedge | 240 |
| | | | Strawberry | 3½″ wedge | 225 |
| | | | **Puddings:** | | |
| Apple, baked | 1 medium | 160 | Bread with raisins | ½ cup | 250 |
| Apple Brown Betty | ½ cup | 170 | Chocolate | ½ cup | 200 |
| Apple Dumpling | 1 medium | 360 | Tapioca | ½ cup | 125 |
| Brownie | 1 piece, 2″ x 2″ x ¾″ | 145 | Strawberry Shortcake | 1 tablesp. whipped cream, 1, 2½″ biscuit | 300 |

| | AMOUNT | APPROX. CALORIES |
|---|---|---|
| **Sugars, Candy, Sweets, and Syrups** | | |
| Candy: | | |
| Bar | 1 | 295 |
| Caramel nut candy | 1 oz. square | 140 |
| Caramel, plain | 1 small piece | 45 |
| Chocolate cream | 1 medium piece | 50 |
| Chocolate mint | 1 patty, 1″ diam. | 45 |
| Fudge, plain | 1 piece, 1″ square | 100 |
| Chocolate, semi-sweet | 1 oz. | 150 |
| Chocolate, sweetened | 1 oz. | 135 |
| Corn Syrup | 1 tablesp. | 60 |
| Honey | 1 tablesp. | 65 |
| Maple Syrup | 1 tablesp. | 55 |
| Marmalade, Jam, Jelly | 1 tablesp. | 60 |
| Marshmallow, plain | 1 average | 25 |
| Sauces: | | |
| Butterscotch | 2 tablesp. | 210 |
| Chocolate | 2 tablesp. | 130 |
| Hard | 2 tablesp. | 120 |
| Sugar: | | |
| Brown | 1 tablesp. | 50 |
| Granulated | 1 tablesp. | 50 |
| Powdered | 1 tablesp. | 45 |
| Sundaes: | | |
| Chocolate ice cream with chocolate sauce and chopped pecans | ½ cup ice cream, 2 tablesp. sauce and 2 pecans | 425 |
| Vanilla ice cream with butterscotch sauce | ½ cup ice cream, 2 tablesp. sauce | 410 |
| **Beverages** | | |
| Ale | 1 glass (8 oz.) | 100 |
| Beer | 1 bottle (12 oz.) | 170 |
| Champagne | 1 glass (3½ oz.) | 90 |
| Cocktails: | | |
| Dry Martini | 1 | 90 |
| Manhattan | 1 | 110 |
| Old-Fashioned (rye) | 1 | 100 |
| Tom Collins | 1 | 125 |
| Whiskey Sour | 1 | 110 |
| Cocoa, with milk | 1 cup | 180 |
| Coffee without sugar and cream | 1 cup | — |
| Cola Drinks | 6 oz. | 75 |
| Distilled Liquors: | | |
| Brandy | 1 brandy glass (1 oz.) | 75 |
| Gin | 1 jigger (1½ oz.) | 120 |
| Rum | 1 jigger | 150 |
| Ginger Ale | 1 glass (8 oz.) | 80 |

| | AMOUNT | APPROX. CALORIES |
|---|---|---|
| Soft Drinks (carbonated beverages) | 1 glass (8 oz.) | 90 |
| Tea without sugar or cream | 1 cup | — |
| Whiskies: | | |
| Bourbon | 1 jigger | 120 |
| Rye | 1 jigger | 120 |
| Scotch | 1 jigger | 110 |
| Wine: | | |
| Dry | 1 wineglass (2 oz.) | 90 |
| Sweet | 1 wineglass (2 oz.) | 160 |
| **Miscellaneous** | | |
| Catsup, Chili Sauce | 1 tablesp. | 15 |
| Chocolate, unsweetened | 1 square (1 oz.) | 160 |
| Cocoa | 1 tablesp. | 20 |
| Coconut, dried | 2 tablesp. | 80 |
| Gravy | 2 tablesp. | 50 |
| Hollandaise Sauce | 2 tablesp. | 100 |
| Molasses | 1 tablesp. | 50 |
| Olives: | | |
| Green, stuffed | 3 medium | 35 |
| Green, unstoned | 3 medium | 25 |
| Ripe, unstoned | 3 medium | 25 |
| Peanut Butter | 1 tablesp. | 100 |
| Pickles: | | |
| Dill | 1 large | 15 |
| Sour | 1 large | 15 |
| Sweet | 1 | 20 |
| Popcorn, popped | 1 cup | 55 |
| Potato Chips | 10 medium, 2″ diameter | 110 |
| Yeast: | | |
| Dried brewers' | 1 tablesp. | 25 |
| Regular | 1 package dry, or 1 cake compressed | 15 |
| **Nuts** | | |
| Almonds | 12 | 90 |
| Brazil nuts | 2 | 95 |
| Chestnuts, roasted | 8 | 100 |
| Hazelnuts, roasted | 8 | 110 |
| Peanuts, roasted | 8 | 45 |
| Pecans | 12 | 105 |
| Pistachios | ¼ cup | 130 |
| Walnuts | 12 | 95 |
| **Fats, Oils, and Shortenings** | | |
| Butter | 1 tablesp. | 100 |
| Cod-Liver Oil | 1 tablesp. | 125 |
| Lard | 1 tablesp. | 125 |
| Margarine | 1 tablesp. | 100 |
| Oils: | | |
| Corn, cottonseed, olive, peanut, soybean | 1 tablesp. | 125 |
| Vegetable shortenings | 1 tablesp. | 110 |

*Fine china, silver, and linen lend an air of elegance. Miniature lighted candles denote an evening meal.*

*This informal setting using place mats has a festive note for a Christmas party.*

*The polished Colonial table is left bare, and the food is served in bright pottery for a late snack.*

*A formal setting with wine for one course can also use place mats. The coffee service waits on the buffet.*

# Setting and
# Serving

## DINNERWARE

*Fine china is translucent.*

The word "china" covers a variety of wares. There is true china, which is translucent when it is held up to the light—costliest, loveliest. Then there is the heavier earthenware, often beautiful as a picture, especially when it is a reproduction of old designs.

**China:** Sometimes called porcelain, it is made of fine clays and is fired at high temperatures. It is nonporous, and resistant to chipping and cracking. *Bone china* contains animal bone ash to give it its characteristic whiteness. *Vitrified china* is thicker than fine china and is not translucent; this is used in restaurants and institutions.

**Earthenware:** Sometimes called semiporcelain or semivitreous ware, it is made of coarser clays than china and is fired at lower temperatures. It has a somewhat porous texture and is less resistant to chipping and cracking than china. This ware varies in thickness and is opaque.

**Pottery:** Generally thicker than earthenware and usually decorated with bolder designs.

### Decoration and Glaze

The kind of decoration affects both the cost and wear of dinnerware, due to an important step in the manufacturing process. Dishes are dipped or sprayed with a glasslike coating called a glaze, which is fired or baked on. Decorations are applied either over or under the glaze, and there is considerable difference between the two in wearing qualities. Underglaze decorations last as long as the dishes. Overglaze decorations usually are less resistant to wear. On good-quality dishes, overglaze decorations are well fired into the glaze, and will last a long time if reasonable care is taken in washing. However, overglaze decorations on low-priced dishes are often fired at low temperatures and may soon wear off. Gold decorations are always applied over the glaze, and here again, the resistance to wear depends mostly on the quality. Dishes in the low-priced range may be decorated with bright, shining gold when new, but the gold is often thin and wears off quickly. On more expensive pieces, the decorations are usually thicker and much more resistant to wear. Dinnerware with gold or overglaze decorations is not a good choice if you use a dishwasher. The high water temperatures, dishwashing detergents, and the forceful washing action in efficient dishwashers wear off gold and overglazes much more rapidly than hand dishwashing does.

**Open-Stock Patterns.** If you choose an open-stock pattern, it will be available for years to come. Then you can buy only the pieces you need now and add more later. You can also replace broken pieces.

Look at all the pieces in the pattern you prefer, to see if you like their shape and size, even if you do not want them now. At some future time you may want some of these pieces—another size in a platter or vegetable dish, a chop plate, or a sugar bowl.

Ask your store how long the pattern you prefer has been selling and what its chances for survival are. The well-known potteries here and in England have made certain patterns available for many years, some for generations. So look for the name and the trademark or back stamp of the pottery on the underside of the dishes.

**Essential Dinnerware.** The quantity of each piece of dinnerware you need depends upon the type of entertaining you do and the size of your family. You may prefer some items in silver (tea service, vegetable dishes, salts and peppers, gravy boat, etc.) and others in glass (salad or dessert plates). A service for twelve is customary.

**Plastic dinnerware** is made of melamine, a smooth, hard material which is also used for counter tops, knife handles, and other hard-wear items. (Most picnicware is styrene, which may crack and break more easily than melamine.) Melamine dinnerware is extremely resistant to breakage.

Melamine dinnerware can be washed in a dishwasher. Hot water and detergents won't affect it, nor will the heat of drying. If you wash it by hand, be sure the water is hot enough to dispose of streaks or greasy film. To prolong its good looks, avoid using scourers or harsh abrasives or scoring it with sharp knives. Keep all plastic dinnerware away from the oven or direct heat.

The biggest complaint from users is the way cups become stained by tea and coffee. To prevent this, rinse cups promptly after use. After washing, wipe them dry. If cups do stain, use one of the stain removers sold for the purpose.

## APPROXIMATE SIZES OF DINNERWARE

| | Size in Inches | Uses |
|---|---|---|
| Service plate | 11½–12 | On table between courses |
| Dinner plate | 10½–11 | Main course |
| Luncheon plate | 9½–10 | Also for buffet |
| Salad plate | 8½–9 | Salads, fish, dessert, with sherbet glass, or under lug soup |
| Pie plate | 7½–8 | Dessert or salad |
| Bread and butter plate | 5½–6 | Also for relishes |
| Coaster | 3½–4 | For glass, butter pat or as ash tray |
| Fruit dish | 5½–6 | At breakfast for fruit, for individual vegetable servings |
| Cereal dish | 6–7 | Cereal, green salad, soup, dessert (baked apple, etc.). Place on salad plate to serve |
| Soup plate, coupe | 8–9 | Often used for cold cereals too |
| Rim soup plate | 8–9 | Serve on service plate |
| Cream soup | | Two-handled cup (more formal) is served with own saucer |
| Lug soup | 6–7 | Soup, cereal, tossed salad, or dessert |
| Covered soup plate | 6–7 | Onion soup or marmite |
| Vegetable nappie (round) | Varies to 10 | Vegetables, fruit desserts |
| Baker (oval) | | Vegetables only |
| Covered nappie | Varies to 12 | For keeping vegetables warm |
| Covered casserole | | Usually oven proof, otherwise used like covered nappie |
| Platter, oval, small | 10–11 | Breakfast platter. Also for asparagus or corn |
| Platter, oval, medium | 12–15 | Luncheon size |
| Platter, oval, large | 14–17 | Roasts, large steaks, turkey |
| Platter, chop | Varies to 15 | Meats, sandwiches, iced layer cake, hors d'oeuvres |

# GLASSWARE

Your glassware should complement your dishes and silver. A few shapes of glasses that can do double duty will prove to be a better investment than a wide assortment of special glasses for each particular use. Open stock in glasses has the same advantage it has in china: you can replace broken pieces or add to your supply.

A great deal of fine glass is made in this country, and even the least expensive American glass stands up well under constant use. Don't be fooled into buying a foreign glassware because of a low price tag. Only the best (and relatively expensive) European glass can compete in service with American glass.

You will probably get most use out of colorless glass, but you may want a few pieces in color to add variety to your table setting.

**Glass Is Made in 3 General Grades.** The finest is lead or flint glass, commonly known as "crystal." In this, lead oxide has been added to potash and silica to give a brilliant, clear quality to the product. It is distinguished by the long-ringing tone it produces when you tap it. This glass lends itself beautifully to cutting and engraving.

Medium-grade glass, which accounts for most glassware, is made of silica and soda ash. It is a good serviceable grade, but it does not have the sparkle of lead crystal.

Glass in the lowest price bracket of tableware is the type that is also used for bottles and jars. It lacks brilliance and tends to have a somewhat murky appearance.

Glasses for wines and liquors are shown on the next page. Average table glass requirements:

- 12 stemmed water glasses
- 12 water tumblers
- 12 fruit juice glasses
- 12 stemmed sherbets
- 12 tall iced-tea glasses

*Shown above are five types of glasses which make up the average table glass requirements. Reading from left to right, they are: juice glass, water tumbler, iced-tea or iced-coffee glass, stemmed sherbert, and water goblet. These shapes are typical; however, a wide variety of styles and designs is available.*

PONY BRANDY     BALLOON BRANDY     SHERRY     SPARKLING BURGUNDY     HOLLOW STEM CHAMPAGNE

# GLASSES FOR
# WINE AND LIQUOR

CLARET     SAUCER CHAMPAGNE     PARFAIT OR STEM
WHISKEY SOUR     COCKTAIL

MARTINI     DELMONICO     OLD FASHIONED     HIGH-BALL     PILSENER

# WINE

Wine is the pure, naturally fermented juice of fresh, ripe grapes. It is a product of Nature, and in winemaking, man's role is simply that of guiding the development and constantly watching to see that Nature does her work to perfection. If we crush a handful of grapes and leave the juice in a cup, it will turn into wine. The refinements of wine growing are in the choice, planting, cultivating, and harvesting of the grapes; the control of fermentation; care, watchfulness, and sanitation in the winery; proper aging, and expert blending.

The alcohol in wine is simply Nature's means of preserving the juice of the grape. The grape is the only fruit that will naturally preserve itself, without anything being added to it or taken away.

## When You Buy Wines

If you are not too well acquainted with different wines or what you should pay for them, talk to a reliable wine dealer. Let him suggest good wines, notable vintage years for imported wines, etc., in keeping with your tastes and budget.

## Only 5 Classes of Wine

There are only 5 classes of wine, and anybody can tell them apart. They are Appetizer Wines, White Table Wines, Red Table Wines, Sweet Dessert Wines, and Sparkling Wines.

But there are hundreds of different names. This need not be confusing as long as we remember that virtually all wines fit into the 5 classes.

## 12 Well-Known Wine Types

In the 5 classes of wine, and among the hundreds of wine type names, there are 12 distinct wine types well known in the United States. These are Sherry and Vermouth (Appetizer); Claret and Burgundy (Red Table); Sauterne and Rhine Wine (White Table); Port, Muscatel, Tokay and White Port (Dessert); and Champagne and Sparkling Burgundy (Sparkling). All other wines are similar to these, but because of minor differences in the grapes used, or in the vintner's blending methods, or even his whims of nomenclature, are given different names.

If you can recognize by sight, taste, and smell the 12 well-known types—Sherry, Vermouth, Claret, Burgundy, Sauterne, Rhine Wine, Port, Muscatel, Tokay, White Port, Champagne and Sparkling Burgundy—you know your wines as well as the average well-informed wine merchant does. Don't expect to be able to recognize all the minor differences of the wines bearing other names than these 12. A professional wine taster can't recognize them all, either!

## The Care of Wine

Because of their low alcoholic content, table wines are perishable after opening of their containers brings them into contact with air. Table wine left in a partly empty container will spoil even though corked. That is why many retail stores advise customers against buying table wine by the gallon unless they intend to use it up or rebottle it into smaller containers within a few days after opening—sooner if the weather is warm. Actual spoilage begins between a few days and a few weeks, varying according to the weather and the individual wine. Storage in a refrigerator slows but does not prevent spoilage.

## When Wine Is Left Over

**Appetizer and Dessert Wines:** Once opened, these wines keep well for weeks unless they are exposed to air for very long periods.

**Table Wines:** Contact with air and heat makes them "go off" (spoil). Care for them as follows:

1. If it's a fifth bottle of wine, cork it tightly; refrigerate; use the next day. If it must be held longer than a day, pour into clean smaller bottles; close with conical cork from drugstore; refrigerate. Plan to use within a week.

2. If it's a gallon jug of wine, pour what is left into clean smaller bottles; cork tightly; refrigerate. Plan to use within a week.

3. If you intend to use leftover wine for cooking, it need not be refrigerated. Just add enough olive oil to form a thin film on wine; then close bottle with conical cork. Such wines are best used in meat and fish cookery, not in desserts or with fruit.

Wine stored for long periods should be kept in a moderately cool place (ideal is about 55°), away from furnaces, steam pipes, radiators, preferably where the temperature does not change.

Wherever possible, bottles of corked table wines and sparkling wines should be kept lying on their sides. This keeps the corks moist and therefore airtight. When bottles of corked table and sparkling wines must be kept upright for display and sales purposes, old stocks should be moved to the front of shelves every time new stocks are added. Bottles with screw caps, whether table or dessert wine, should be stored standing upright.

## Storage in Refrigerators

It does not ordinarily injure wine to store it in refrigerators. Many people regularly keep a few bottles or half-bottles in their home refrigerators, ready to serve. Even a week's or two weeks' supply may be kept safely on ice, but some wines may lose quality if refrigerated for much more extended periods.

White table wines and sparkling wines are those regularly kept iced ready to serve, but Sherries, white dessert wines and even red wines are also often preferred when chilled. The best wine-chilling temperature is 40° to 50° F. Wine should not be chilled below 26° F., because excessive chilling may cause extra sediment to deposit. It may occasionally be found that some one delicate wine will cloud or deposit when chilled, in which case that particular wine should be kept out of the refrigerator thereafter.

## How Wine Is Served

The serving of wine is as easy and simple as the serving of any other beverage. There are certain formal wine customs, some of them quite practical, but these are considered "in order" only on very special occasions, and even these are not rigid.

Normally only one or two wines are served with a meal—an appetizer like Sherry at the start, and a table wine with the main course. Serving only one table wine with the main courses is customary at luncheons and informal dinners, and in that case the table wine is poured as soon as the first course is begun. On the other hand, when it is the desire to be very formal, as at a banquet, any number of wines can be served; three, four, or as many as eight or ten.

## Serve Wine with Style

At the simple one-wine dinner, bring on the wine with the main course. Pour it just before, or at the same time as, the main dish is served. Then everyone can enjoy a sip after his first taste of the food.

**Here's How:** Before meal begins, have wine bottle on small tray on table. (It's good practice for host to sample the wine beforehand, to be sure of its quality.) Host pours a bit of wine into his glass, to make certain no pieces of cork remain in bottle. The hostess is served next, then the person to her right and so on around the table to the right. The wine is poured from the guest's right and the glass is not lifted from the table. The way to avoid dripping wine on the tablecloth is to give the bottle a slight twist before raising it from the pouring position, thus catching the last few drops on the lip of the bottle. Or let bottle pass from hand to hand, in the European manner.

**Here's Why:** Guests enjoy knowing the wine they are drinking. So they can examine the label, pass the bottle as is or, if it's chilled, with a cloth wrapped around the lower part only. Wrapping the bottle completely makes guests feel they are expected to guess what the wine is or to believe it is better than it is.

## The Glasses

Unless you go in for elaborate entertaining, 3 standard glass sizes are all you need.

**For Appetizer and Dessert Wines:** Use 2- to 3-oz. cocktail glass.

**For Red and White Table Wines:** Use 4- to 6-oz. wineglass.

**For Sparkling Wines:** If available, flute glasses are often preferred. Or use saucer or hollow-stemmed champagne, water goblet, or high sherbet glass.

Wine will taste best if you fill glasses only one-half to two-thirds full. Space left in glass permits you to enjoy wine's aroma.

## What Wine with What Food

Exaggerated in its importance by popular belief, the question of "which wine goes best with which course" nevertheless deserves to be understood clearly by those with wine knowledge.

| Foods | Wines that Harmonize Best |
|---|---|
| Appetizers . . . . . . . . . | Sherry, Champagne |
| Seafoods . . . . . . . . . . | Any white table wine, like Rhine Wine or Sauterne |
| Fowl with white meat | Same wines as with seafoods |
| Fowl with dark meat . | Any white table wine, like Rhine Wine or Sauterne, or any red table wine, like Claret or Burgundy |
| Steaks, roasts, chops, game, pastes . . . . . | Any red table wine, like Claret or Burgundy |
| Desserts . . . . . . . . . . | Any sweet dessert wine, like Port, Muscatel, White Port, Tokay, or Sweet Sauterne, Sweet Champagne or Sparkling Burgundy |
| Cheeses . . . . . . . . . . | Port or Burgundy |
| Nuts . . . . . . . . . . . . | Port |

The exaggerated idea of "which wine with which food" was originally popularized in the lore of connoisseurs who make wine a lifetime hobby. Millions who use wine daily throughout their lives enjoy dry red table wine with all kinds of food and are amused at any suggestion that this could be wrong. Personal taste and trial are better guides than any rules, because the academic authorities on the subject differ among themselves, and the many consumers who actually enjoy the "wrong" wines with various foods are pleasing their individual tastes.

Table setting illustrating the placement of wine glasses. Even though the dinner is elaborate no more than two wine glasses are on the table at any one time. The glasses may be arranged in either of two ways. One, as shown here, the glasses are set slightly to right of place and towards center of table—the water goblet on line with knife, one wine glass above and one to the right, forming a triangle. Glasses may also be set in a straight line in front of and to the right of place—the water goblet and the wine glasses in that order. When additional wines are served, the glasses are exchanged as each course is finished and the next course is served.

## BOTTLE SIZES

| | | | | | |
|---|---|---|---|---|---|
| Split or nip | (Wine) | 6 ozs. | Rehoboam | (6 quarts) | 156 ozs.–1.22 gals. |
| Half-pint | (Whisky) | 8 ozs. | Methuselah | (8 quarts) | 208 ozs.–1.65 gals. |
| Half-bottle | (Wine) | 12½ ozs. | Salmanasar | (12 quarts) | 312 ozs.–2.44 gals. |
| Tenth (four-fifths of a pint) half-bottle | | 12.8 ozs. | Balthasar | (16 quarts) | 416 ozs.–3.3 gals. |
| Pint | (Champagne) | 13 ozs. | Nebuchadnezzar | (20 quarts) | 520 ozs.–4.07 gals. |
| Pint | (Whisky) | 16 ozs. | Demijohns | | 4.9, 3 and 2 gals. |
| Bottle (three-fourths of a quart) | (Wine) | 24 ozs. | Half-gallon jug or bottle | | 64 fluid ozs. |
| | | | Vermouth bottle | | 30 fluid ozs. |
| Fifth | (All Spirits) | 25.6 ozs. | Chianti bottle | | 30 fluid ozs. |
| Quart | | 32 ozs. | Champagne bottle | | 24 to 26 fluid ozs. |
| Quart | (Champagne) | 26 ozs. | Champagne half-bottle | | 12 to 13 fluid ozs. |
| Magnum | (2 quarts) | 52 ozs. | Table wine splits | | 6 and 6.4 fluid ozs. |
| Dbl. mag. or jeroboam | (4 quarts) | 104 ozs. | Chianti split | | 8 fluid ozs. |
| Tappit-hen | (1 gallon) | 128 ozs. | Champagne splits | | 6.2 and 8 fluid ozs. |

# SILVERWARE

There are two general types of silverware: sterling and silverplate.

**Sterling** is 82.5 per cent pure silver; copper is added for strength and hardness. Differences in cost depend on the weight of the silver and to some extent on intricacy of pattern. So in making your choice, note the weight of individual pieces. Each piece is marked "sterling" and carries the manufacturer's trade-mark.

**Silverplate** is less expensive than sterling silver. It is made by coating a special base metal with pure silver. "Silver plated" means that at least 2 ounces of silver per gross of teaspoons has been used. Double, triple, or quadruple silver plating contains two, three, or four times as much silver as a single plating. Because the basic things that affect wearing quality are not apparent, it is important to buy silverplate from a reputable manufacturer. With good care, it will give lasting satisfaction. In general, differences in quality depend on the base metal used, the thickness of the silver plating, the care with which plating is applied, and the reinforcing of the plating at points of greatest wear. Reinforcing is very important and may be done in several ways:

*Inlaid* silver has an extra coating on backs of spoons and forks under the over-all plating. Some brands have special blocks of sterling silver inlaid at points of greatest wear.

*Overlaid* silver has extra silver added over the plating where each piece receives the greatest wear.

Note carefully each manufacturer's description of his reinforcement method. Other guides to quality are fine design, smooth edges, feel of good balance.

Low-cost silverplate usually carries no manufacturer's name or mark and is "flash," or very thin plate with no reinforcements. It cannot be expected to give long service.

*Sheffield* plate is silver-coated copper. It was made by fusing sheet silver to a copper base, whereas modern pieces are electroplated.

### Flatware

Flatware consists of the pieces you eat *with:* knives, forks, spoons, and serving pieces. Hollow ware consists of the pieces you eat *from:* dishes, platters, etc., plus such accessories as vases and candlesticks.

### Place Pieces

**Dinner Knife,** the largest table knife, is used for formal or informal dinner as well as for breakfast or luncheon.

**Luncheon Knife,** sometimes called breakfast or dessert knife, can be used for informal dinners. In a formal setting, it can be used for the fish course; and if the salad requires cutting, it is used for the salad course.

**Fish Knife** is for the fish course only.

**Fruit Knife** is for fresh fruit at any meal.

**Butter Spreader** is for any spreading use. It can be used as a serving piece in place of the butter knife.

**Dinner Fork,** the largest table fork, is used with the dinner knife, for formal or informal dinner. Can also be used for breakfast or lunch. May be used with table spoon for serving.

**Luncheon Fork** is sometimes known as the breakfast or dessert fork. May be used for the fish course in formal dinners and with luncheon knife, for informal dinners.

**Fish Fork,** for the fish course.

**Salad Fork** can double as a fish fork. It is also suitable for dessert, pastries, and sandwiches that require a fork.

**Oyster Fork** is also used for seafood cocktails. As a serving piece it is used for olives, lemon, or pickles.

**Ice Cream Fork,** for ice cream only.

**Iced Tea Spoon** is used for tall drinks.

**Dessert Spoon,** or oval soup spoon, can be used for soup served in plates, and for cereal, as well as dessert. Can also double as a small serving spoon.

**Soup Spoon** can be used for dessert served on a plate as well as for soup.

**Cream Soup Spoon,** smaller than the regular soup spoon, is for soup served in a soup cup or bowl. It is also correct for cereal and dessert.

**Bouillon Spoon,** smaller than the cream soup spoon, is for consommé in a bowl or bouillon cup.

**Orange Spoon,** for orange or grapefruit.

**Teaspoon** is used with hot beverage when served in a large cup, and for fruit cocktail, cereal, liquid vegetables, frozen desserts and almost everything served in a small dish.

**Coffee Spoon,** for after-dinner demitasse. Also for tiny bowls of relishes.

**Individual Salt Spoon** is used with open salt-cellar.

### Serving Pieces

**Pie and Cake Servers** (or pastry servers) can also be used to serve waffles and hot cakes, frozen desserts, fish or cutlets.

**Cheese Server** is especially for cheese.

**Butter Knife** can also be used for cream cheese.

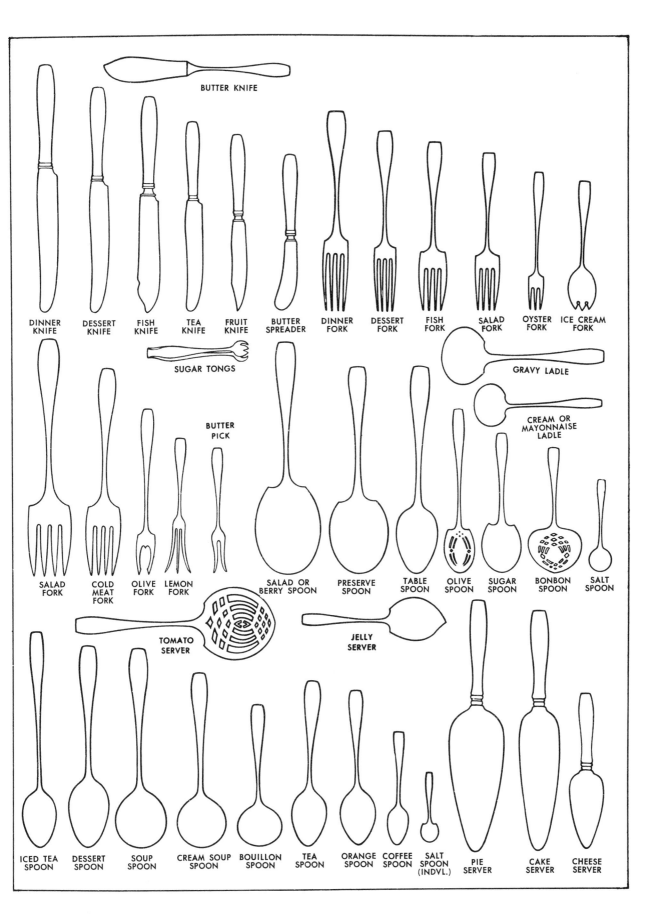

BUTTER KNIFE

DINNER KNIFE — DESSERT KNIFE — FISH KNIFE — TEA KNIFE — FRUIT KNIFE — BUTTER SPREADER — DINNER FORK — DESSERT FORK — FISH FORK — SALAD FORK — OYSTER FORK — ICE CREAM FORK

SUGAR TONGS

GRAVY LADLE

CREAM OR MAYONNAISE LADLE

BUTTER PICK

SALAD FORK — COLD MEAT FORK — OLIVE FORK — LEMON FORK — SALAD OR BERRY SPOON — PRESERVE SPOON — TABLE SPOON — OLIVE SPOON — SUGAR SPOON — BONBON SPOON — SALT SPOON

TOMATO SERVER

JELLY SERVER

ICED TEA SPOON — DESSERT SPOON — SOUP SPOON — CREAM SOUP SPOON — BOUILLON SPOON — TEA SPOON — ORANGE SPOON — COFFEE SPOON — SALT SPOON (INDVL.) — PIE SERVER — CAKE SERVER — CHEESE SERVER

**Salad Fork** is most useful of serving forks. Can also be used for cold meats, meat loaf, and fish.

**Cold Meat Fork** has same use as salad fork.

**Olive, Lemon, and Butter Forks** can be used interchangeably.

**Sugar Tongs** is needed for lump sugar.

**Salad or Berry Spoon** can also be used for vegetables, puddings, and casserole dishes.

**Preserve Spoon** can be used for the same purpose as the salad and berry spoon.

**Tablespoon** is the most useful serving piece. It can be used for almost every type of serving.

**Olive Spoon** may be used in place of the olive fork.

**Sugar Spoon** can double as jelly server.

**Bonbon Spoon** is for candy and nuts.

**Salt Serving Spoon** is used with open salt.

**Gravy Ladle** is also for stews, soups, creamy dishes, dessert sauces, and whipped cream.

**Cream or Mayonnaise Ladle** can also be used for dessert sauces.

**Tomato Server** is used for many vegetables, for fish, eggs, croquettes, casserole dishes, and chopped meats.

**Jelly Server** can also be used for cut cheese or relishes.

### Essential Pieces

Adequate silver service for 12 would consist of the following pieces, to which you can add as your requirements demand:

| | |
|---|---|
| 12 dinner knives | 12 luncheon forks |
| 12 dinner forks | 12 coffee spoons |
| 12 salad forks | 3 tablespoons |
| 24 teaspoons | gravy ladle |
| 12 butter spreaders | cold meat fork |
| 12 dessert spoons | sugar tongs |

### Discontinued Patterns

If you own sterling silver flatware of a discontinued pattern, you can order new pieces from your silverware dealer during January and February. If enough orders for the same pattern and pieces are received, the manufacturer then considers it feasible to make them up, and you will get delivery by autumn of that year. Each manufacturer has a list of inactive patterns, from which he will make up an order. Unless your silver dates back many generations, you should be able to obtain any pieces you may need.

### Hollow Ware

Hollow ware pieces are available in sterling or plated silver in practically all the types in which china and glassware are made. You can have a complete silver dinner set or just a few of the serving dishes to vary the appointments of your table.

### Stainless Steel

Flatware of stainless steel is available in a wide range of grades from inexpensive utensils you would not want to use outside your kitchen to beautifully made pieces that cost as much as sterling silver.

Although stainless steel is one of the easiest of materials to maintain, not all of it is entirely stainproof. In most instances slight discolorations will fade and disappear in time. As a general rule, the pieces finished with the highest buffing show the greatest stain resistance.

Stainless ware is not affected by climatic conditions, never oxidizes, and never has to be polished.

Stainless tableware is made in such a variety of patterns that it can be fitted into most table settings. Like sterling silver, it is the same metal all the way through so it will give a lifetime of service if it is of a weight that will not bend or otherwise become distorted.

### Monogramming Your Silverware

Beautiful silverware is always a joy to own and an asset to any table decoration, but personalized silver is the pride of the discriminating hostess. It is a family heirloom to be handed down from generation to generation with stories of the mothers and grandmothers who have used it.

If you have recently purchased silverware, or if you have been fortunate enough to have received it as a gift, consider the advantages of having it monogrammed.

There is little that dictates correctness in personalizing silverware. One, two, or three initials may be used. The script should harmonize with the silver's decoration, but it may be sharply contrasting, as in the case of simple lettering on a handle decorated with elaborate scrollwork.

Follow these rules when having silver monogrammed:

*If you want only one initial:*
1. Use the last initial of the wife's maiden name.
2. Use the last initial of the husband's name.

*If you want two initials:*
1. Use the wife's maiden initials, first and last.
2. Use the wife's last initial plus the husband's last initial.

*If you want three initials:*
1. Use the first and last initials of the wife's maiden name plus the last initial of the husband's name.
2. Use the wife's three maiden name initials.

# TABLE LINENS

**Tablecloths** should be of a sturdy fabric because .hey must be able to withstand repeated laundering. Before buying a cloth, know the size of your table. The cloth should be large enough to hang well over the edge of the table (15″ to 18″ for a formal table setting).

Linen, whether plain weave or damask, usually gives the best service. There are two kinds of damask —single and double. Double damask has approximately twice as many filling, or crosswise, threads, making a more distinct pattern. Single damask with a high thread count and high-quality thread is a better value than double damask with a low thread count and inferior thread. Rayon-and-cotton and all-cotton damasks wear well and are less expensive than linen. When buying all-cotton damask, be sure the label says it has been treated with a durable finish. This finish helps keep the surface of the material smooth.

Solid-color or printed tablecloths should be dyed with fast colors to withstand repeated washing.

Lace cloths are long-wearing and are easy to spot-clean and launder.

Whatever the size of your tablecloth, limit the creasing to one sharp fold lengthwise down the center of the cloth; fold your cloth from selvage to selvage right side out, so the crease will look right on your table.

To preserve the finish of your table, use a table pad under your cloth, or use individual pads under hot dishes. Damask hangs better over a table pad than over bare wood. Pads can be made to order to fit your table. They usually have a felt surface underneath, with a waterproof plastic top. They are never used under lace cloths or table mats.

**Place Mats** are available in endless variety. In addition to the materials used in tablecloths, they are also made in raffia, plastic, glass, and paper. They are available in many shapes and colors, and some of them are intended to hang over the edge of the table.

**Napkins** may match, blend, or contrast with your tablecloth or mats. Dinner napkins are ordinarily made in 18″ x 18″ or 22″ x 22″ sizes. Napkins for informal use, or for breakfast and luncheon, come in many sizes.

Fold dinner napkins in thirds, with the hems toward each other, then in thirds as shown. Folds may be smoothed in by hand. The open edge is usually placed toward the right whether at the left of the setting or on the service plate. Informal napkins may be folded the same as dinner napkins, or they may be folded in quarters, into a triangle, or rolled into a tube. There is no definite rule regarding informal napkins, except that the hem or (if folded into a point) the point is usually placed toward the setting. Some place mats have a pocket to hold a napkin.

*Have one lengthwise fold in your tablecloth.*

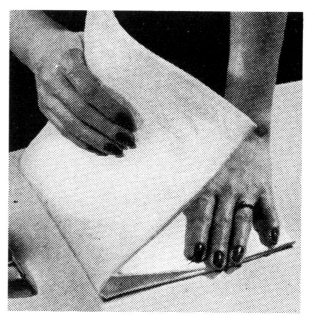

*This is the way to fold a dinner napkin.*

# SETTING THE TABLE

Here are some general rules to guide you in setting the table. The settings may be varied to fit your menu and equipment.

**Table Mats:** Mats are usually placed 1″ from the edge of the table unless they are to hang over the edge.

**Dinnerware:** The luncheon, dinner, or service place is placed in the center of the place setting. The bread-and-butter plate goes to the left, above the forks.

**Silverware:** Set 1″ in from the edge of the table or mat. Forks are placed to the left of the plate, except the oyster fork which goes to the right of the spoons. Knives and spoons are set to the right of the plate, with the knives nearest the plate. The butter spreader is placed on the bread-and-butter plate. Knife blades are turned toward the plate. All pieces are placed in the order of their use, from the outer edge of the setting toward the plate. Dessert silver is usually brought in with the dessert. The spoon for coffee or tea is customarily placed on the saucer, not the table.

**Glassware:** The water glass is set to the right of the plate, above the knives. Fill ¾ full just before announcing the meal. Wineglasses go to the right of the water glass.

**Napkin:** The napkin is placed to the left of the forks; or on the service plate at a formal meal.

**Accessories:** The ash-tray is usually placed above the service plate, or to the right of the spoons. Salts and peppers are set in pairs at both ends of the table; individual sets go between each two places.

**Centerpiece:** For a meal at which people are seated around the table, the centerpiece should be low enough so guests can see over it easily. For buffet serving, or a meal at which only one side, or two adjoining sides, of the table are used for seating, there is no rule as to height of the decoration.

**Candles:** White or cream should be used for formal dinners; for informal meals, any color may be used. Candles are usually not lighted for any meal except dinner, unless the room is dark. They should not be on the table unless they are to be lighted. It takes at least 4 candles to light the average-sized dining room. Keep the flame above eye level by using 18″ to 24″ candles in holders under 7″ in height; 10″ to 16″ candles in holders from 7″ to 10″; and 10″ to 12″ candles in holders more than 12″ tall.

**Dessert and Coffee Service** is usually placed on the buffet or serving table, with the water pitcher. Coffee may be served in the living room.

**Chair:** If a tablecloth is used, the front edge of the chair should be just under the cloth.

## Place Settings

The diagrams that follow are given as an aid to your table setting. They are not to be taken as hard-and-fast rules. The modern trend is away from rigid rules.

*Breakfast setting shows luncheon plate, knife and fork, bread-and-butter plate with spreader, in place. Dessert spoon or teaspoon is used for cereal. Remove the bowl and serve the main course on the plate. Juice glass can go to right of the water glass. Coffee cup and saucer are shown with spoon on saucer.*

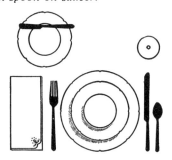

*Luncheon setting uses luncheon plate, knife, fork, teaspoon, bread-and-butter plate with butter spreader. The teaspoon is used for the fruitcup which is then removed, and the luncheon plate is ready for the main course. A dessert fork or spoon is brought in with the dessert.*

*Three-course dinner setting shows wine glass to right of the water glass. Use dinner plate, bread-and-butter plate with butter spreader, dinner knife and fork, salad fork, and cream soup spoon. Salad is served with the main course which is served on the dinner plate. Dessert service follows.*

In these diagrams, wherever the circle indicating a glass has a smaller circle inside it, it denotes a stemmed glass. The butter spreader on the bread-and-butter plate does not have to be at right angles to the rest of the silver. It can be placed on the plate parallel to the other silver.

*Family dinner service shows a juice glass beside the water glass. Dinner knife and fork are to be used. The salad plate at the left is for the salad course which will be served with the main course. The dessert spoon has been placed with the initial setting to save time. The spoon for the coffee will be on the saucer when the coffee is brought in.*

*Formal dinner setting shows the oyster fork at the right for a seafood cocktail which will be placed on the service plate. Then the soup spoon will be used for the soup that will replace the seafood cocktail. The service plate will be removed when the main course is served. Two wines are planned. Bread-and-butter plates are generally omitted for the more formal dinner.*

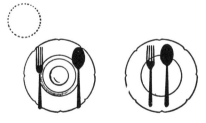

*Dessert service is shown with and without a finger bowl. At the left, the finger bowl is centered on a doily on the dessert plate, flanked by dessert spoon and fork. The guest removes bowl to the left, the spoon and fork to right and left of plate. At the right a dessert service minus finger bowl is shown.*

## Setting the Buffet Table

Napkins are placed so a guest can pick one up as soon as he approaches the table. Then comes a stack of dinner or luncheon plates to which he helps himself. The food is placed on the table with serving silver beside it. The hot food will stay hot if served in a chafing dish or one of the many types of serving dishes available for that purpose. The knives and forks are placed at the end of the line. The spoons are placed on the saucer of the coffee or tea service.

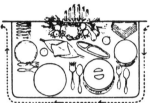

*When the buffet table is placed against a wall, the guests will move as shown by the arrows. Note that the table decoration is placed at the back of the table. It does not have to be in the center of the back, but could be placed to either side. If rolls are served already buttered, it not only saves space on the buffet table, but also makes it easier for the guests to handle their plates of food. A water pitcher and glasses could be set up on a side table, if the buffet does not have enough room.*

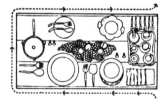

*With the buffet table in the center of the room, traffic would be as indicated by the arrows. The table decoration could be placed in the middle of the table as shown here, or it could be placed at the open end if the number of guests was not too large and the table of sufficient size. Round or oval tables would be set the same as rectangular ones.*

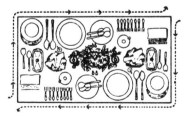

*If the crowd is large, it is well to set up duplicate service as shown so that two lines can serve themselves at the same time. For a setting like this, it is best to keep the decoration in the center, although it could be placed at the beginning or end of each serving line if the table is large enough.*

*This breakfast table setting has a fruit and vegetable centerpiece of artichokes, lemons, and ivy in a square shallow basket. The ivy repeats the ivy in the dishes. This same setting could be used for any informal meal.*

*A family breakfast setting lined up along one side of the table makes serving easier. The mats and simple china would look just as well for a Sunday supper; for a larger crowd simply use both sides of the table.*

*This informal luncheon setting shows how to place silver on oval mats. Note that the pieces are not set in a straight line with the edge of the table, but 1" in from edge of mat. Water glass may be set on bare table.*

*The coarse texture of the tablecloth with a metallic thread running through it co-ordinates with the rough texture of the carnations in the centerpiece. Other flowers are snapdragons and asters with eucalyptus leaves.*

*For luncheon, a runner may be used down the center of the table, with only the place settings at each end on the cloth. Here a centerpiece of fruit and variegated leaves contrasts with the plain china.*

*This informal dinner setting uses a centerpiece of flowers to carry out design of china and silver. Large salt and pepper shakers are placed at each end of table. The fruit cup is served on a glass plate on the dinner plate.*

This setting could be used for an informal dinner or luncheon. To be strictly formal the bread-and-butter plates would be omitted, and the napkins would be on the service plates when the guests sit down.

On this buffet table, the silverware is rolled up inside the napkin. The two copper chafing dishes keep the food piping hot. The candles will be lighted as a signal that the guests should start to serve themselves.

# HOW TO CARVE

To get the full co-operation of your carving set you must give it good care. Keep it separated from other cutlery so the knife will not be dulled or nicked. A good blade needs only occasional sharpening. Well-kept tools add confidence.

Carving is a pleasure when you know how to do it with ease. Start by placing the roast on a large platter, and go easy on the garnishes so the carver will have plenty of room. Place carving fork at left of platter, carving knife (with razor-keen edge) at right, blade in.

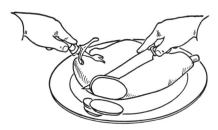

## How To Carve a Leg of Lamb

1. One side of a leg of lamb is a thick, meaty section; the other is a thinner, less meaty section. Place leg with shank to right and thinner, less meaty section near. Insert fork firmly, with guard up, in large end of leg and carve 2 or 3 slices from thin side, as above.

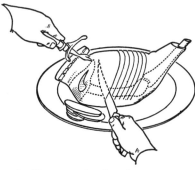

2. Now turn lamb so it rests on cut surface. This brings thick, meaty section to upright position, shank end pointing upward. Then, with fork in large end, start slicing from right end of roast, close to shank end. Cut straight down to bone, as shown.

3. Continue to cut parallel slices down to bone, as many as are needed for serving, keeping slices about ¼″

thick, as illustrated. Then, with fork still in place, run knife under slices, parallel to and along leg bone. This releases all the slices at one time.

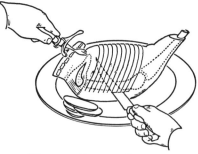

## How to Carve a Standing Rib Roast

1. It will be much easier to carve a standing rib roast if you have meat-man cut backbone from ribs when you buy it. Place roast on platter with broader cut surface down. Place it on table with rib side to left and ends of ribs pointing toward carver.

Insert the carving fork securely, with the guard up, between the two top ribs of the roast to left. Then, starting at right outside edge, at broadest part, slice across face of roast towards rib side, as above, making slices about ¼″ thick.

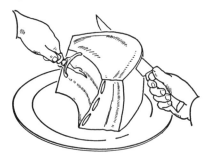

2. When knife blade meets the rib bone, loosen slice by cutting along rib bone with knife, as shown.
3. As each slice is cut, steady it with the fork and lift it, on knife blade, to the platter as illustrated.

## How to Carve Tongue

Place trimmed, skinned tongue on

table with tip to right. With fork inserted at top, near small end, slice from thin part straight down, at such an angle as will produce largest slices. Keep slices parallel.

## Rolled Rib Roast

Place rolled rib roast on the platter with the larger cut surface down. With the guard up, push the carving fork firmly into the roast on the left side an inch or two from the top. Slice across the grain toward the fork from the far right side. Uniform slices of ⅛″ to ⅜″ thick make desirable servings.

As each slice is carved, lift it to the side of the platter or to another hot serving platter. Remove each cord only as it is approached in making slices. Sever it with the tip of the blade, loosen it with the fork and allow it to drop to platter.

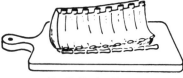

## Pork Loin Roast

It is easier to carve a pork loin roast if the backbone is separated from the ribs at the market. The backbone becomes loosened during roasting; note in the illustration that it has fallen away from the ribs.

Before the roast is brought to the table remove the backbone by cutting between it and the rib ends. Now place roast on platter so the rib side faces you. This makes it easy to follow the rib bones, which are the guides for slicing. Make sure of the slant of the ribs before carving, as all ribs are not perpendicular to platter.

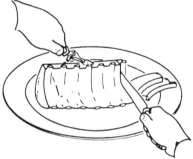

Insert the fork firmly in the top of the roast. Starting at right end of loin, carve vertical slices, progressing toward left end as you slice. Cut close against both sides of each rib. In a small loin each slice may contain a rib; if the loin is large it is possible to cut two boneless slices between ribs. Two slices for each person is the usual serving.

### Porterhouse Steak

Contrary to most carving rules a steak is carved with the grain because the meat fibers are tender and already relatively short.

Use the steak set, a blade of 6″ or 7″. Place steak on table with tapered

end at left. Holding the steak with the fork inserted at the left, cut close around the bone. Then lift the bone to the side of the platter where it will not interfere with carving.

Next, with fork in position, cut across full width of steak into thick or thin slices are preferred.

### How to Carve a Whole Ham

Place whole ham on table with scored side up and shank end to right. The thin side of ham, from which first slices are made, will be facing carver if the ham is a left leg; on far side if ham is a right leg.

1. The ham shown here is a left leg. After securing fork in heavy part cut 2 or 3 thin oval slices, parallel to length of ham, from nearer side.

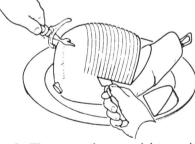

2. Then turn ham upright, so it rests on cut surface. Next, about 6″ in from shank end, make a straight cut to leg bone, as for slicing. Make another cut at an angle to this, close to shank end, and remove this wedge of meat. Then ham is easy to slice.

3. With carving fork steadying ham, cut thin slices down to leg bone —as many as will be needed for serving. Then run knife along bone, at right angles to the slices, releasing them all at one time, as illustrated.

### How to Carve a Chicken or Turkey

1. Place roast bird on table, with legs to right. Starting on side facing you, cut leg from body while bending it back with left hand.

2. Next, lift leg to a side plate near by. While holding leg with left hand, sever thighbone from drumstick, just over the round bone.

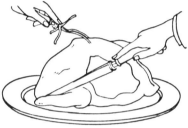

3. Slice all meat from leg. Then, with fork astride breastbone, cut down sharply where wing joins body, severing wing completely.

4. Now start, just above joint where wing was removed, to cut thin slices of white meat, working upward, always cutting parallel to breastbone.

5. After breast has been sliced, it's easy to reach stuffing. For second servings, turn platter and carve other side of bird.

# SERVING

## Seating the Guests

As a general rule, the host sits at the end of the table near the service entrance. The hostess sits at the opposite end of the table. It is the duty of the hostess to indicate the seating arrangement. The lady guest of honor sits to the immediate right of the host; the gentleman guest of honor sits to the immediate right of the hostess. The hostess distributes the rest of the guests so that a lady and a gentleman alternate around the table if possible. At a large party, place cards will avoid confusion.

## Order of Service

The hostess is served first, when there is a host, or if the meal is served by a maid. When the hostess serves the meal, she serves herself last.

## If the Maid Serves

**Before the Guests Are Seated:** she fills the water glasses three-quarters full; if bread-and-butter plates are used, she puts a pat of butter on each plate. She sees that all chairs are in place. If fruit cup or seafood cocktail is to be the first course, she puts it in place; soup is served after the guests are seated. Then she appears at the door of the living room, waits to catch the hostess' eye and announces that dinner is served.

**After the Guests Are Seated:** 1. She makes sure that everything for a course is ready before she starts to serve it.

2. She serves the hostess first, then continues around the table except when there are only four at the table: in that case, she serves the host last. Each succeeding course is served in the opposite direction to avoid having the same person always served last.

3. She stands to the left of the person being served, to place, remove, and offer dishes, except for those things which are used on the right, such as beverages. She always avoids reaching in front of anyone.

4. In offering food, she holds the platter flat on the palm of her left hand over a napkin folded into a square; if the dish is heavy, she steadies it with her right hand. She holds the dish low and close enough to make it easy for the guest to serve himself. The handles of the serving pieces are pointed toward the guest. For serving small dishes, she uses a small tray with the napkin under it.

5. To exchange plates, the maid removes the plate with her right hand, placing the new one with her left. Until the dessert course, she never leaves a place setting empty, but always replaces the dish she removes with one for the next course.

6. She keeps the water glasses three-quarters full, without lifting the glass from the table. A napkin is used to catch any stray drops from the pitcher.

7. She always serves hot food on hot plates; cold food on chilled plates.

8. She moves about quietly, without touching any of the guests as she serves.

9. She waits until everyone has finished with a course, before she starts removing it from the table.

10. She clears the table for dessert by removing all food, unused silver, salts and peppers. Then, if necessary, she removes crumbs from the table with a small napkin, by brushing them onto a plate.

11. For the dessert course, she puts each dessert service in place before bringing in the dessert; or for a simple dessert, the service may be placed on the dessert plate.

12. She may serve coffee already poured in the kitchen, or she may set coffee service at the hostess' place for her to serve. Or the hostess may prefer to serve coffee in the living room.

## Serving Without a Maid

Up to the time the guests are seated, the procedure is the same, except that the hostess does the chores. The actual serving of the meal is much simplified after that by having the host serve the main course and passing it to the hostess in exchange for her plate, which he fills and passes on to the person to the right of the hostess and so on, around the table, serving himself last. Bread is passed around the table. If the meat is carved before it is brought to the table, it will save time. If the host carves at the table, have someone else serve the rest of the meal. If the hostess is within easy reaching distance, she can take care of it; otherwise, a guest (or member of the family) sitting next to the host can take over.

No one—least of all the hostess—enjoys a meal during which the hostess is constantly jumping up from the table to replenish this dish or bring on that. Here are a few simple rules that will cut steps, dishes, and time when you must be cook and hostess, too.

1. Choose the right menu. Plan meals with not more than two or three easy-to-serve courses. Casseroles are ideal for this.

2. Eliminate last-minute chores. If you cannot complete your cooking in advance, prepare as much as possible early in the day and keep it in the refrigerator.

3. Choose dishes that can wait without spoiling if the serving may be delayed.

# Buying and Caring for Linens, Bedding, Towels, and Clothing

For thousands of years, cloth has been woven from fibers that come from plants and animals. But fabrics woven from natural fibers now have new uses and vary in texture and appearance because of scientific developments.

Science has also developed many man-made fibers. At first, man-made fibers were judged according to how nearly they conformed to fabrics we already knew, rather than on their own merit. Now a new era in textiles is here—an era of better appreciation of man-made fibers and of the discovery that they can be blended successfully with natural ones. Blending is the scientific combining of two or more fibers to produce certain desired results. Weight, texture, color, drapability, etc., are the factors that determine what fibers will be blended and how.

For example, rayon is often blended with wool in dress fabrics to lighten weight and to add luster. Acetate and rayon are used together to give striking color effects and interesting textures. Cotton is blended with synthetic fibers to increase absorbency and to widen range of colors. It may also be mixed with nylon to make a cooler, more comfortable fabric.

Man-made fibers have also been built to specification, as well as blended, with a considerable amount of success. The proof: Orlon, Dacron, Dynel, Acrilan, Nylon, etc. Each is a man-made fiber, planned from the test tube to do a specific job. They may be mixed with other fibers or used by themselves. Manufac-

turers are continually working to give the consumer new and better fabrics that are easy to care for, long-wearing, and inexpensive.

Since these new fabrics are built to specification and others are blended with a particular purpose in mind, it is obviously important that you know what you are buying, and that you choose fabrics according to the way in which they are to be used.

**Labels Pay Dividends.** Many terms found on labels designate qualities in fabrics that are important not only in use but in care. Looking for labels pays dividends in the form of better service and satisfaction from your purchases of clothing, sheets, blankets, curtains, hosiery, and other textile products. Good labels can help you choose garments and other articles that will keep their color, finish, and fit throughout their normal lifetime.

But do you sometimes find words relating to textiles whose meanings aren't clear to you? It's not surprising, for every year brings additions to the vocabulary of textiles; new weaves, fibers, and finishes are constantly being introduced. Here is an up-to-date glossary of the terms that refer to the fibers, processes, or special finishes you may encounter in your textile shopping. Learn what they stand for and remember to watch for them: they will save you time and money. Read about new developments in current periodicals and newspapers to keep your textile vocabulary up to date.

# A GLOSSARY OF TEXTILE TERMS

## Fibers and Yarns

Acetate, Acrilan, Cotton, Dacron, Dynel, Nylon, Orlon, Rayon, Silk, Vicara, Fiberglas, Linen, Wool, Arnel. Fibers spun into yarns used in manufacturing cloth.

**Blend.** Two or more fibers mixed together to make one yarn.

**Slubs.** Thick, uneven places in yarns. Some slubs are natural to the fiber, as are those in linen; others are artificially produced in spinning, as are those in certain kinds of cotton.

**Nubs.** Small knots or balls of fibers, often brightly colored, added to yarn for interest.

**Carded Cotton Yarn, Woolen Yarn.** Made from mixture of long and short staple cotton or wool fibers cleaned of most impurities. Yarn twisted from these fibers may be fibrous and uneven, with many fiber ends protruding from surface, as in denims and tweeds.

**Combed Cotton Yarn, Worsted Yarn.** Made from long cotton fibers or long staple wool both carded and combed, which gives a smooth, even yarn. Used in such fabrics as gabardine, cheviot, broadcloth, organdy, etc.

## Dyeing Processes

**Stock-Dyed Fabrics.** Made from fibers dyed before they are spun into yarns. Can produce mottled effect seen in some flannels.

**Yarn-Dyed Fabrics.** Made from yarns dyed before weaving.

**Piece-Dyed Fabric.** Dyed after it is woven or knitted.

**Chromspun, Celaperm, Color-Sealed, Coloray.** Trade names of acetate yarns—pigment is part of fiber.

**Cross-dyed Fabrics.** 2 or more dyeing processes produce multicolored effect on fabrics made of 2 or more fibers which take dye differently.

## Fabric Constructions

**Knitted Fabrics.** Composed of interlocking loops that can expand or contract; hence usually fairly elastic.

**Woven Fabrics.** Made on loom from number of warp (lengthwise or straight) yarns that are alternately raised and lowered while filling (crosswise) yarn is interlaced across them.

## Weaves

Plain, twill, and satin weaves, with their variations, are considered the 3 standard weaves in the construction of textile fabrics.

**A Plain Weave** is the simplest form of weaving and is used more than any other. Each filling yarn passes alternately under and over each warp yarn, making a very firm construction. About 80 per cent of all woven fabrics are made with plain weave. Examples are chambray, percale, taffeta, and crepe.

**The Rib Variation** of the plain weave uses heavier filling than warp threads or heavier warp than filling. Examples of the former method are rep, faille, and cotton broadcloth; the latter, crossbar dimity and fancy gingham. This variation tends to be less firm than the ordinary plain weave because of the unbalanced thread count.

**A Basket Variation** of the plain weave is constructed from two or more filling yarns passed alternately over and under two or more warp yarns. It can be a balanced or unbalanced yarn construction. This is a decorative weave, but usually a loose one, and thus may cause yarn slippage, fraying, stretching, or shrinking. Examples are Oxford cloths and monk's cloth. Monk's cloth is used frequently in draperies and bedspreads. This variation is also found in women's dress and suit fabrics.

**The Twill Weave** is one of the most durable of all weaves. The filling yarns are interlaced with the warp in such a way as to form diagonal ridges across the fabric. This is also called the serge, or diagonal weave and can be varied for ornamentation. The herringbone, in which the diagonal runs in one direction for a few rows, reverses, and runs in the opposite direction, is an excellent example of the twill weave. Others are the broken twill and the zigzag twill. The twill weave is used mainly in wools, cottons, and lining fabrics.

**The Satin Weave,** in which warp yarns are floated over several filling yarns, has a smooth, lustrous sheen. It is usually made with acetate, rayon, silk, or Orlon fibers. **The Sateen Weave** is made by floating filling yarns over several warp yarns. Cotton drapery linings are often made of sateen weave. The floating yarns, loosely twisted, interlace infrequently and hence are susceptible to distortion. These constructions give reasonably good service if not subjected to excessive hard wear.

**The Crepe Weave,** which may be plain or combined with the satin weave, gives the fabric a pebbly, creped surface.

**Fancy weaves are pile, gauze, Jacquard, and dobby. Ornamental effects are created by swivel and lappet types.**

**A Pile Weave** uses the plain or twill base with a pile made from clipped yarns on the right side of the material. A fabric with tight interlacing and close pile usually wears better than a loosely constructed one. Examples of some pile fabrics are velvet, corduroy, terry cloth, and plush.

**Gauze Weave** is a term applied to sheer, loosely woven fabrics made either in plain or leno weave. In the leno weave, the warp yarns are arranged in pairs that twist like a figure 8 around filling yarns and thus help prevent slippage or distortion. This weave produces a slight lacy effect—for example, as in marquisette, which is used for curtains, evening wear, dresses, and children's wear. This weave is also combined with other weaves to produce fabrics of unusual surface, texture, and appearance. It is found in cotton, synthetics, silk, and wool.

**The Jacquard Weave** produces complicated woven designs or patterns and requires a special loom to accomplish this. It is a combination weave—satin with sateen, satin with twill, or perhaps pile with plain. Damask and brocade are examples of Jacquard weaves. Jacquard cloths are found in draperies, upholstery fabrics, and tablecloths. Matelassé, a double-woven Jacquard fabric, is used for dresses and bedspreads.

**The Dobby Weave** creates a small design such as found in bird's-eye, used for diapers, and huck toweling, used for face towels. The closer the weave, the more stable the fabric.

**The Swivel Weave** resembles embroidery and usually is woven into cotton fabrics. The design appearing on both sides is done with extra filling yarns that are cut on both sides. The figures are not knotted to the groundwork of the cloth and therefore will not wear well if subjected to friction. This weave is used in men's shirts and pajamas.

**A Lappet Weave,** similar to the swivel, is produced by using extra warp yarns. Its pattern often has a zigzag effect produced with one continuous thread on only one side. It is not interwoven in the basic cloth, but, if fastened securely, it will not pull out with friction. An illustration of this is domestic dotted swiss used in dress fabrics and curtains.

**Double-Woven Fabrics** are usually two cloths united with extra fillings and warps. This construction is primarily used for heavier fabrics such as chinchilla cloth, for women's coats and hats, and mackinaw cloth, for heavy jackets. Many yarn and color combinations are possible. Usually, heavier yarns are used, but sometimes this construction is varied by using lightweight yarns on the surface, giving the illusion of lightweight fabric. Double-woven gloves are an example of this variation.

### Descriptive Terms

**Textured Surface.** Has pebbly, mossy, nubbly, or embossed surface, to give depth effect.

**Plaid.** Pattern made of colored stripes crossing at right angles to form squares of various sizes.

**Bouclé.** Woven or knitted fabric identified by knotted or looped surface.

### Fabrics

**Alpaca.** Fiber from South American llamas, extensively used to make pile fabric for lining cold weather clothing or lightweight, soft, plain-woven dress fabrics.

**Barathea.** Closely woven fabric with pebbly weave, usually made of silk or rayon.

**Broadcloth (Woolen).** Woolen cloth with smooth, untextured surface. No weave can be detected on face of fabric, and nap is brushed to lie in one direction.

**Butcher Rayon.** Plain-weave fabric made from slub yarns. Also made in crease-resistant finish.

**Cashmere.** Fabric with very soft "hand," made from extremely fine wool of Indian Kashmir goats for outerwear. These fabrics are generally expensive and luxurious.

**Gabardine.** Firmly woven steep twill weave fabric made of worsted, cotton, rayon staple, and in blends. Characterized by distinct, closely set, diagonal lines on face.

**Helanca.** Nylon yarn which has the ability to stretch as much as 5 times its length. Used in hosiery and underwear.

**Jersey.** Plain or knitted tricot fabric available in most fibers.

**Velvet.** Lustrous fabric with short thick soft pile in lengthwise direction. Ordinarily silk or rayon with cotton backing.

**Velveteen.** Cotton, looks like velvet. Pile in crosswise direction.

**Zibeline.** Thick woolen coating fabric with long hairy nap.

## GOOD WEAR STARTS WITH THE FINISH

All fabrics, except some industrial fabrics and unbleached muslin, are "finished" in various ways before they reach you. Some finishes are as old as the art of weaving. Others are very new. All are intended to make fabrics more attractive, more serviceable, and enhance their value and their usefulness to you. Some important finishes are:

**Ease-of-Care Finishes.** Today's cottons as well as a number of blends are finished by the use of resins or chemical treatments to provide a fabric which may be washed by machine and hand- or machine-dried to require a minimum of ironing for a pleasing appearance. These are also called "Wash-and-Wear Finishes." Garments from fabrics with such finishes must be washed or cleaned according to the instructions on the individual hang tag for optimum results. Pay careful attention to manufacturer's bleaching instructions.

**Crease-Resistant Finishes.** Certain fabrics—especially some of the spun rayons—crease and wrinkle easily because of their construction, but are desirable because of their beauty. Their general appearance is greatly improved by crease-resistant finishes, which make them crisper and firmer, and minimize distortion in wear. Fewer pressings are needed. These finishes improve fabrics, especially rayons, in other ways, too. Shrinkage may be lessened considerably and the wet strength increased. Crease-resistant finishes are found most often on spun rayons, cottons and some velvets. Besides being used on suits and dresses, they are used on neckties and shirts. Crease-resistant finishes are also resistant to dry-cleaning and usually are not affected seriously by repeated launderings. Don't use chlorine bleach.

**Flame-Resistant Finishes.** Although nearly all fabrics will burn, some fabrics, such as chenille, knit brushed rayon, high-pile and napped fabrics, are especially hazardous because of the rapid rate at which their surface fibers burn. Many serious and often fatal accidents have occurred when such fabrics came in contact with a flame from a match or a kitchen range. These fabrics, however, have become far less dangerous to wear because of flameproofing finishes that retard burning.

**Glazed Finishes.** In the past, glazed finishes were not satisfactory, because they were removed easily in laundering. The modern glazed finishes are usually found on plain-weave cotton fabrics of various weights in printed designs or solid colors. No starch is needed in laundering. On draperies, upholstery, and bedroom ensembles, glazed finishes have the advantage of dust-resistance and better draping qualities. When you buy glazed fabrics, look for tags telling that the finish is resistant to laundering or dry-cleaning. Also look for special directions on other care. Glazed fabrics look best when ironed while damp on the *right* side.

**Moth-Resistant Finishes.** Each year, moths and carpet beetles cause millions of dollars' damage to fabrics containing wool. In recent years, some knitting yarns, blankets, rugs, and other fabrics have been treated to resist moth damage. These finishes now have been applied to many more types of fabric, including the ones used in men's suits and topcoats. Some of these finishes withstand repeated dry-cleaning and laundering; others do not. Look for tags or labels stating durability of moth-resistant finish. Even if a garment has a moth-resistant finish, be sure it is clean before storing. Moths will be attracted to stains.

**Shrink-Resistant Finishes.** To get the kind of service you want from your clothing, shrinkage after repeated washings or dry-cleanings should be held to a minimum. A good finish can reduce the shrinkage to such a small percentage that it does not noticeably affect the fit of a dress, blouse, or skirt after it has been laundered or dry-cleaned. Cottons can be finished by a mechanical process that reduces residual shrinkage to not more than 1 per cent, assuring maximum freedom from shrinkage problems. Shrinkage of linen, wool, and rayons can be controlled by chemical processes. However, these methods are not applied to all preshrunk fabrics so it is important to read the tags on labels telling the amount of residual shrinkage you can expect (not to exceed 3 per cent for garments).

**Spot-Resistant Finishes.** Easier-to-care-for, more serviceable garments are possible with spot-resistant treated fabrics. They fend off water-soluble stains, such as coffee, fruit juices, and ink. They are not impermeable to oily stains. One qualification about such finishes is this: you must wipe off the stain immediately or it will spot. You'll find that spot-resistant fabrics aren't penetrated by rain as quickly as others. Suits are made in this fabric for both men and women, and they carry an identifying label.

**Starchless Finishes.** Starchless finishes, used mostly on cottons, impart desirable crispness to fabrics, es-

pecially sheers. These finishes, obtained by resin or chemical treatment of fibers, withstand repeated launderings without great loss of stiffness. Curtains with starchless finish do not shrink so much, absorb soil so easily, become so wrinkled and mussed during humid weather as untreated ones.

**Waterproof Finishes.** Many fabrics are coated with a continuous film of a substance that seals the fabrics' pores to water and to free passage of air. The most familiar coatings are rubber and plastic. Some are more durable than others and may have special properties, such as high resistance to acids and oils. Good plastic finishes have high resistance to heat, light, and freezing temperatures and lend themselves to many interesting uses besides making garments waterproof. These coatings are used in shower curtains, raincoats, crib sheets, mattress covers, baby pants, beach bags, outdoor furniture covers, etc. They are highly resistant to spots and stains and can be washed safely with soap and water. This also is true of rubber-coated fabrics. Be sure you get "waterproof," not "water-repellent," if that's what you need. Completely waterproof garments are warm to wear. They will be more comfortable if they contain perforations to allow air to enter.

**Water-Repellent Fabrics** have been so treated that they shed water readily. However, they retain all the outward appearance and texture of untreated fabrics. There are two types of water-repellent treatment: durable and nondurable. Durable water-repellency withstands repeated laundering or dry-cleaning without any major loss of water-repellency. The nondurable finishes should be replaced after laundering or dry-cleaning. Many laundries and dry-cleaning establishments can replace these finishes. An important feature of water-repellent fabrics is their ability to "breathe," because spaces between the yarns are not sealed. They are therefore more comfortable to wear than waterproof garments.

**Other Special Finishes.** The finishes produced with resins and heat change the appearance of a fabric. Sculptured cottons have a raised, shiny design with background remaining unglazed. Embossed cottons give interesting patterned effects to a material. The same method is used to give a durable moiré (watered appearance) finish on cotton and acetate fabrics, and a polished appearance on cottons (chintzes and chambrays). It is also used on durably pleated cottons.

### Natural Fibers

A fiber is just an inconsequential-looking little wisp. It must be made into yarn, then fabric, then clothes before you can wear it. But if you know the fiber's properties, you will have some idea of what to expect of the garment.

## Cotton

Cotton, one of the first fabrics woven by man, still heads the list in popularity—for several good reasons.

It is comfortably absorbent and easy to launder. It is also inexpensive. Cotton is strong and can be woven into a wide variety of fabrics, from lightweight batistes to heavy sailcloth. It can be dyed in many fast colors and finished to give the fabric wrinkle-resistance, water-repellency, shrinkage control, or an embossed surface.

# DICTIONARY OF COTTON TERMS

When you shop for cotton clothes, you'll probably see the following terms on tags or labels. Be a wise shopper—learn to identify them.

## Yarns

**Carded Cotton Yarn** is made from short uneven cotton fibers that have been cleaned of most impurities. Carded yarns generally are used in all except the finest cotton fabrics.

**Combed Cotton Yarns** are made from long, choice fibers that have been combed to remove short fibers and all impurities. Combed yarn is made into fine, high-grade fabrics.

**Sea Island Cotton.** Longest and finest of all cotton fibers. This is used in the finest woven goods and laces.

**Pima Cotton.** Intermediate in fiber length, it allows greater strength or finer yarns than regular cotton.

**Egyptian Cotton.** High-grade, fine, long fiber, used to manufacture fine fabrics, threads, and laces.

**Mercerized Cotton.** An alkali-treated yarn or fabric which shows increased strength, luster, and absorbency.

## Dyeing Processes

**Vat Dyes.** Class of dyes with an excellent degree of colorfastness.

**Yarn-Dyed** fabrics are made of yarns dyed *before* they are woven or knitted into cloth.

**Piece-Dyed** fabrics are dyed *after* they are woven.

**Iridescent Cottons.** These fabrics are made by weaving two contrasting colors.

## Fabrics

**Batiste.** Soft, lightweight, sheer, plain-woven fabric made of mercerized yarns. It is used in infants' wear and lingerie. A heavy fabric, used to make foundation garments, is also called batiste.

**Broadcloth.** Tightly woven, lustrous cotton fabric with a fine crosswise rib. The best quality is made of combed yarns and usually is mercerized. Broadcloth is used extensively for men's shirts, pajamas, women's sport clothes.

**Calico.** Plain-woven, printed cotton fabric. The name is derived from Calcutta, where it was first made.

**Chambray.** This popular fabric is made in several weights for various purposes. It is a plain weave made with a colored warp (lengthwise) yarn and white filling (crosswise) yarn. Blue chambray is widely used for work shirts. Lighter-weight chambray, woven from finer yarns, is popular for women's and children's dresses. **End-on-End Chambray** is woven with a colored yarn and a white yarn, or two colors, alternating in the warp direction.

**Cretonne.** Plain-woven fabric, printed in bright colors on a white or colored ground. Used for draperies and upholstering. Resembles chintz but does not have a glazed finish.

**Denim.** Durable twill-weave cotton fabric, usually an indigo-blue warp and gray or white filling, used for work clothes. A lighter-weight denim with a soft finish, in a variety of colors and patterns, is used for sport clothes.

**Dimity.** Sheer cotton fabric characterized by corded stripe or checked effects, with a starched finish. Used for women's and children's dresses and lingerie.

**Dotted Swiss.** Sheer, plain-weave, crisp fabric, with woven or applied dots.

**Lawn.** Lightweight, plain-weave, sheer cotton fabric, solid color or printed, with a crisp, starched finish.

**Madras.** Fine shirting fabric with a woven design. These shirtings are made in colors, with checks or fancy patterns. Usually mercerized.

**Mull.** Plain-woven, soft, sheer.

**Nainsook.** Fine, soft, lightweight cotton similar to lawn, but with a soft, lustrous finish.

**Organdy.** Thin, transparent, crisp cotton fabric. Some specially treated organdies retain their crisp, transparent finish after laundering.

**Percale.** Printed plain-weave cotton fabric with a smooth finish. Used for women's and children's clothes.

**Piqué.** True piqué is characterized by raised cords or welts running crosswise in the fabric. Usually the fabric sold is piqué with lengthwise cords is really a lightweight Bedford cord and is also known as warp piqué. **Bird's-Eye Piqué** has a raised-diamond effect on the surface. **Waffle Piqué** is characterized by a honeycomb weave; it is not a true piqué.

**Poplin.** Fine, durable, plain-woven fabric characterized by crosswise ribs.

**Plisse.** Thin cotton fabric with a puckered or blistered effect in stripes or designs, made by treating sections of the fabric with a caustic-soda solution. This shrinks parts of the cloth and gives it a characteristic crinkle.

**Seersucker.** Lightweight cotton fabric characterized by woven-in crinkled stripes, made by weaving some warp threads tight and others loose.

**Gingham.** Yarn-dyed, plain-weave fabric woven with check patterns. Qualities vary from coarse carded yarns to fine combed yarns, and may be mercerized or Sanforized. **Tissue Gingham** is a very lightweight, sheer, combed-yarn fabric that may be trimmed with cord stripes or checks. **Zephyr Gingham** is a lightweight, soft-finish fabric.

# LINEN AND WOOL

**Linen** continues to be popular for resort and summer wear. It absorbs perspiration freely and quickly, making it a cool fabric for warm-weather apparel. It is readily washable and doesn't require special handling during laundering. The characteristic thick-and-thin look of uneven yarns gives it a distinctive beauty. In the past, linen had one disadvantage—it wrinkled easily. Today, many linens have a crease-resistant finish. There are 3 main fabrics used in linen clothing. All come in a variety of colors—dark, bright, and pastel shades.

**Dress Linen.** A plain-woven, durable, and serviceable fabric. Quality varies considerably, depending on the yarn and thread count.

**Cambric** (also called handkerchief linen). A plain-woven fabric that may be sheer or coarse. It is used for handkerchiefs and dress goods.

**Butcher's Linen.** A strong, substantial, plain-weave fabric used for suits and dresses. Often confused with butcher linen—a rayon fabric, not linen at all.

Look for the "all linen" label. If there is no label, do not assume the article is linen. The consumer is protected by Federal Trade Commission rulings, which govern fair-trade practices in the industry and stipulate that the word "linen" can be used only when the fiber content is exclusively linen.

**Wool.** For some purposes, there isn't anything like wool. It has great warmth; it is soft and resilient. But wools vary, so you should know something about them.

If you want a wool that will give long, hard wear, choose a worsted, such as gabardine or covert. Because of their construction, worsteds have a relatively smooth, hard surface, which resists wear. The weave pattern is clearly visible. Worsteds hold a press well and do not wrinkle easily, but they tend to develop a shine. The long-wearing worsteds are probably best used for tailored classic garments, such as suits. Some lightweight worsteds drape well and are suitable for dresses. These cannot, of course, take the hard wear that wiry worsteds can.

On the other hand, if you want a less tailored, more casual garment, choose a woolen such as flannel or broadcloth. These are made from softer yarns than worsteds and frequently have a nap, which obscures the weave. The nap may rub off in areas of great wear. However, some woolens, such as tweeds, have exceptional wearing qualities. Good woolens feel soft but are also firm and springy.

## Know Your Wools

**Worsteds** are made from yarns of long wool fibers with a high or hard twist. Compared with woolens, worsteds have a hard, smooth, unnapped surface. Typical worsteds are serge, gabardine, sharkskin, and covert.

**Wool Gabardine** is made from very firmly woven worsted yarns. It has distinct, raised diagonal lines (twill) on the face, but not back, of the fabric.

**Wool Serge,** made from worsted yarns, is characterized by prominent diagonal lines on both sides of fabric; usually has hard, smooth finish.

**Wool Sharkskin,** a hard-finished worsted characterized by small dots of white on a colored ground, has a white and a colored thread alternating in the fabric's length and width.

**Covert** is made of woolen or worsted yarns. Each thread contains two shades of a color (light and dark). Fine twill construction is popular for topcoats and men's suits.

**Homespun,** plain- and loose-weave fabric, includes hand-woven tweeds, generally with twill construction.

**Scotch Tweed** has a very rough appearance, because the yarns are irregular and the fibers are of varying lengths. Scotch tweeds usually have white warp and heather-toned or vividly colored filling threads.

**Irish Tweed** is made of white warp yarns and black or dark shades of gray, blue, brown in the filling.

**Cheviot Tweed.** Warp and filling yarns are dyed the same color. A distinctive, loosely woven, shaggy material.

**Donegal Tweed** is a firm fabric hand-woven in Ireland. Generally it is plainly woven with coarse yarns. Colored nubs on the yarn distribute tufts of different colors throughout.

**Harris Tweed,** a hand-woven woolen twill, is produced only on the Outer Hebrides islands off the coast of Scotland. It is used for suits, topcoats, overcoats, and sportswear.

**Melton Cloth** is a thick, heavyweight cloth resembling felt. It has a short nap, a dull surface, and usually is dyed in solid dark colors. Used for overcoats and jackets.

**Virgin Wool.** New wool, used for no other purpose than the yarn or fabric in which it first appears.

**Wool.** The fibers from fleece of sheep or hair of angora or cashmere goat, camel or vicuna that have not been reclaimed from woven or felted products.

**Reprocessed Wool.** Wool that has been woven, knit, or felted, then reduced to fibers and manufactured again without having been used by consumers. Reprocessed wool may be obtained from mill ends and clothing manufacturers' clipping of unused- or virgin-wool fabrics. Reprocessed-wool fibers retain most of their original resiliency and, when blended with the longer fibers of wool or virgin wool, make excellent fabrics.

**Reused Wool.** Wool reclaimed from products used by consumers and remade into new products. Used garments and fabrics are garneted (shredded) into fibers, which are made into yarns and cloth. Reused wool is sanitary; the reclaiming process cleans and disinfects it.

# TYPES OF SILK FABRIC AND FIBER

**Shantung** has a rough, nubby surface. This slub effect, as it is sometimes called, is produced by using doupion—a special type of silk. For added interest, some Shantungs have small designs woven in self colors.

**Crepe** is recognized by its crinkly surface. Although there are many varieties, the best known are Canton crepe, flat crepe, and crepe de Chine. Flat crepe is the smoothest. Because crepes contain yarns with a high twist, they shrink in washing. So when you buy crepe, look for a tag giving care information. Or ask the clerk whether it can be laundered successfully, or must be dry cleaned. No dress or blouse, to keep its fit, should shrink more than 3 per cent.

**Faille** is characterized by soft, flat, horizontal ribs or cords.

**Bengaline,** like faille, has pronounced cords running across the fabric, but it is heavier than faille. Bengalines also are made from rayon, worsted, cotton, or combinations.

Both bengaline and faille are durable and especially suitable for suits and dresses. Bengaline, because it is heavier, also is used for coats.

**Surah** is a soft, lightweight fabric characterized by its fine, diagonal twill. Used for blouses, dresses, and ties.

**Taffeta** is a closely woven, smooth fabric characterized by its crisp finish. "Changeable" taffetas are woven from yarns of two colors. **Faille Taffeta** is woven with a fine cross rib. **Paper Taffeta** is lightweight, specially treated to give it a crisp finish. **Pigment Taffeta** has the normally lustrous finish dulled by white pigment.

**Satin** is characterized by its smooth, lustrous face and comparatively dull underside. There are variations of the fabric's weave, quality, and weight. Satins drape beautifully and are used for all types of apparel.

**Brocade** is an elegant fabric woven with an all-over design of flowers, scrolls, or other figures. The figures are often of a contrasting color or metallic threads on a rich satin or twill background. It is used wherever decorative fabrics are needed.

**Foulard** is a lightweight, soft fabric (usually printed) with a twill weave. This wears well and is used extensively for ties and dresses.

**Tie Silk** used in dresses is similar to foulard and usually is of good quality. It is suitable for men's ties because it is resilient, pliable, and holds a firm knot. However, the term "tie silk" also applies to any silk fabric used for neckties, some of which are not quality fabrics.

## Fibers

**Silk Fibers** are obtained by unreeling silkworm cocoons. The cultivated worms produce smooth creamy-white or yellow fibers used in most silks.

**Tussah Silk** comes from the cocoons of wild silkworms. It is coarse, irregular in size, and brownish-tan in color. It cannot be bleached satisfactorily. Tussah silk is used to make such fabrics as pongee.

**Doupion Silk** is reeled from two or more entangled cocoons. It makes an uneven yarn particularly useful for such fabrics as Shantung.

**Spun Silk** is made from short fibers of silk from various sources—such as pierced cocoons, reeling waste, and double or triple cocoons.

## Weighted Silks

When silks are immersed in a tin-salt solution they absorb some of the salts, which add body and weight to the fabric. Small amounts of weighting (up to 20 per cent) are not injurious. Higher amounts cause eventual deterioration of the fabric.

## Characteristics of Silk

Silk fabric has a smooth, lustrous appearance and drapes beautifully. Although the silk fiber is very fine, it is quite strong and elastic. Silk, though absorbent, does not conduct heat away from the body and is, therefore, a warmer fabric than cotton or linen of the same construction. Resistance to sunlight and perspiration is not especially good, particularly if the fabric has been weighted. Thus silk is more appropriate for dressy occasions than for sportswear. Depending on the fabric's construction and the particular garment, a silk garment may or may not be washable. Check the label for instructions on care and cleaning.

# FUR AND SPECIALTY FABRICS

Luxurious fabrics are being made by blending fur fibers with fibers of cotton, wool, acetate, and viscose rayon, or combinations. These blends are used with equal success for soft fabrics that drape easily and crisp fabrics for fine tailoring. The fabrics, which have fur's delightful softness, are used for dresses, slacks, sports shirts, jackets, lounging robes. Fur fibers also are blended in knit fabrics. Usually fur fabrics cost more than ordinary fabrics.

Mink, muskrat, raccoon, squirrel, wolf, opossum, and silver fox can be blended successfully. Seldom is one fur fiber used alone. Usually similar furs, such as mink and muskrat, or fox and wolf, are blended. The percentage of fur varies from 10 to 25 per cent.

The fur fibers do not add or detract from the serviceability of a particular weave, although sometimes there may be a slight shedding, especially from knit fabrics, because of their loosely twisted yarns. The fur fibers impart desirable properties, such as crease-resistance and light weight warmth. Some fur fabrics are washable, most should be dry-cleaned.

**Specialty Fibers** such as camel or cashmere may be added to wool for greater softness and sheen. Fabrics are dry-cleanable.

# MAN-MADE OR SYNTHETIC FIBERS

The basic materials from which man-made fibers are made are coal, water, petroleum, natural gases, and various chemicals, as well as wood and corn. In the following list the most important of these synthetic fibers especially created by man to meet man's textile needs are described.

**Arnel** is one of the newer man-made fibers. It has characteristics similar to other synthetics—quick drying, shrink-resistance, wrinkle-resistance, durable crease retention and pleatability, and moth-and-mildew-resistance. It is unlike some other man-made fibers in that it can be washed and ironed at high temperature settings. Since sensitivity to heat has been one of the faults of synthetic fibers, this property makes Arnel an important new development.

**Rayon,** first of man-made fibers, is one of the most versatile. Fine yarn made from this fiber can be woven into crepes. Rayon behaves much as cotton does. It's absorbent and slow to dry. Some rayon fabrics are vat-dyed and highly resistant to fading. Very sheer rayon nets and highly napped rayon fabrics should have a fire-retarding finish. Rayon can be made wrinkle-resistant, water-repellent and shrink-resistant, degree of washability depends on dye and finish. Recently, rayon fiber has proved serviceable for tufted carpets.

**Acetate** is soft to the touch and lustrous in appearance. Acetate fabrics drape easily; acetate colors have good resistance to sunfading and washing. Acetate, like rayon, is cool and easy to care for. It does not dry as quickly as the newer man-made fabrics and requires ironing at a low temperature. Normally acetate resists wrinkling; but don't wring too vigorously or you may find wrinkles that are hard to iron out.

Be sure any blue shade of acetate is treated to resist fume fading. Solution-dyed acetates (the color is part of the fiber) have the best colorfastness.

**Nylon** is one of the strongest of all fibers. Its long-wearing qualities and easy launderability are outstanding. Knit tricots and woven sheers require little if any ironing; shrinkage is held to a minimum. Nylon has good elasticity and is therefore popularly used for hosiery. Because of the nature of the fiber, fabrics can be durably pleated. Nylon is not very absorbent and therefore not particularly cool. The coolest versions are tricot fabrics.

Fabrics that can be made from nylon yarn are as many and varied as those made from rayon yarn: beautiful satins, taffetas, crush-resistant velvets, sheer marquisettes and nets, and fabrics made from mixtures of nylon and rayon or other fibers; heavy damask drapery fabrics and other sturdy drapery fabrics; rugs and heavy frieze used for upholstery.

Crimped nylon is particularly elastic. It is used with great success in "stretch" socks and stockings.

**Orlon** has good shape retention and will not shrink or sag when laundered. It can be made into lightweight sheers or heavier napped fabrics. It is especially noted for warmth without weight or bulkiness and its soft and lovely feel. It holds pleats during washing, has good wrinkle recovery, sheds dirt, dries quickly, and needs little ironing. It has very good resistance to sunlight. Orlon is popular for use in making sweaters and other knit fabrics. Sweaters made from Orlon fibers often look and feel much like cashmere.

**Acrilan** is like Orlon in many properties. It can be bought in a wide color range, and can be used alone or blended with other fibers to make useful and attractive apparel and household items.

**Dynel** has such properties as shape retention, natural wrinkle-resistance, warmth without weight and easy care. While Dynel will not burn readily, it will fuse and harden if too hot an iron is used. Thus, though little ironing is needed, one must be cautioned to use a low iron setting. It is mildewproof, and mothproof; shrinkage and stretching are so slight that they're not worth mentioning. Dynel is used mainly as a blend with other fibers.

Recently Dynel has been blended with Orlon to make a synthetic fur that is beautiful and inexpensive and at the same time maintains many desirable properties of a synthetic fabric.

**Dacron** requires little care because of its unusual wrinkle-resisting property even in humid heat. Another outstanding feature of Dacron is its ability to retain pleats or creasing set under heat and pressure. Dacron ranks second to nylon in fiber strength and, like nylon, it has good strength and abrasion resistance and, therefore, will give exceptionally long wear. Probably the best news of all about Dacron is that it has the ability to transfer many of its wrinkle-resistant, shape-retaining qualities to the fabrics in which it is blended.

**Polyesters.** A number of new fibers such as Fortrel, Kodel, and Vycron are now available. These are related chemically to Dacron and have somewhat similar properties.

## Blends

A variety of fabrics has been successfully developed by (1) combining synthetic fibers with each other and also by (2) using man-made fibers blended with natural fibers.

Synthetics are used with each other because, though all have remarkable properties, degrees vary. When used in correct proportions, the most desirable features of each fiber can be incorporated in a fabric.

Synthetics are often used with natural fibers. No new fiber is comparable to wool in springiness, or to silk in soft drapability, or to cotton in absorbency. But by blending synthetic with natural fibers, it is possible to produce a fabric with the good features of both.

**Dacron and Cotton** (65%–35%) is an excellent example of proper blending to achieve the best characteristics of each fiber. This fabric, used extensively in blouses, shirts and lingerie, has minimum shrinkage, is wrinkle-resistant, and requires little if any ironing. All these properties are contributed by the Dacron content. Cotton contributes absorbency and makes the fabric comfortably cool for summer clothes.

### Plastic Fabrics

For beauty, durability, ease of care, and all-round versatility plastics rival many of the textile fabrics and, in some cases, offer advantages textile fabrics cannot. Among the things being made from plastic fabrics are draperies, window and shower curtains, belts, wall coverings, aprons, raincoats, umbrellas, upholstery fabrics, slipcovers, baby pants, washable stuffed toys, bowl covers, food bags, dress shields, beach bags, card-table covers, tablecloths, pillow covers, garment-storage bags, hats, shoes, luggage, and golf bags.

Plastic fabrics are of 3 types: plastic-film, "supported-film" fabric, and fabric woven from plastic thread.

Plastic-film fabric is made entirely from plastic and is familiar in the form of raincoats, baby pants, shower curtains, and bowl covers. Plastic-film fabrics may vary from very clear to opaque.

Plastic-coated or "supported-film" fabric is made by coating various textile fabrics with a plastic film. Most of the base fabric's original appearance is retained, but it is endowed with new characteristics that often improve good looks and durability and make for easier care.

Woven plastic fabric is used mainly for rugs and upholstery. It resembles other upholstery fabrics. Woven plastic fabric is fairly expensive, but it is long-wearing and serviceable.

All are highly stain-resistant, waterproof, mothproof, and mildew–resistant—a quality that is especially welcome in shower curtains and food covers. When waterproofness of an entire plastic garment is essential, examine the seams to make sure they have been heat-sealed.

Many types of plastic are impervious to most acids and can be used safely where acid-resistance is necessary—as for work gloves and aprons.

Luggage made from the proper plastic fabrics stands up well under the rigors of traveling, as it is very resistant to abrasion, scuffing, and staining.

Plastic fabrics for draperies, window curtains, and upholstered furniture are very durable and lend themselves to almost any treatment. The plastic upholstery fabrics compare closely with textile fabrics in general comfort. They do not become sticky or tacky on humid days.

As plastic fabrics are both waterproof and stain-resistant, cleaning is simply a matter of sponging with soap and warm water and wiping dry with a clean cloth. It is advisable, however, to remove stains as soon as possible.

Plastic fabrics should not be pressed or ironed, because they will melt at ironing temperature. If wrinkles occur, hang up the article, and the wrinkles usually will come out.

*Highly decorative, easily cleaned*

*Wispy light, but waterproof*

*Mildew is no problem*

# HOUSEHOLD LINENS

## How to Buy Sheets and Pillowcases, Towels, Bedspreads

| | HOW MANY PER PERSON? | WHAT ARE STOCK SIZES? | WHAT ABOUT SHRINKAGE? | TYPES TO CHOOSE FROM |
|---|---|---|---|---|
| **SHEETS AND PILLOWCASES** | Each bed needs at least 6 sheets—2 for current use, 2 at the laundry, 2 in reserve—and 3 cases per pillow. Keep your reserve replenished, so as to avoid large cash outlay at any one time. Some use a third sheet over the blanket, to protect the blanket and to add warmth. | For a double bed, the sheet should be 81″ or (better still) 90″ wide and 108″ long; for a single bed, 72″ x 108″; for a twin bed, 63″ x 108″. The 108″ length provides ample tuck-in to keep the lower sheet smooth and allows a generous fold-over at top of upper sheet, to protect blankets. Pillowcase sizes are: 42″ x 36″; 42″ x 38½″; and 45″ x 38½″. Measure the width of your pillow, double the measurement and add 2″ or 3″. | Cotton sheets do not shrink noticeably in width. In length, they shrink about 5 per cent, which amounts to a little over 5″ for 108″ length. This shrinkage is enough to spoil tuck-in allowance unless you buy the 108″ length in the first place. Remember, too, that 5″ of the 108″ are used in hems. Man-made fiber sheets have minimum shrinkage. | The types are percale muslin and nylon and blends of nylon-and-acetate. Percale is made of finer threads, more highly twisted, more threads to the inch, and is smoother and lighter in weight than muslin. Both have varying numbers of threads to the inch. Man-made fiber sheets are woven or tricot knit (which are cooler than woven). |
| **TOWELS** | 6 terry bath towels and 6 terry hand towels are a minimum supply per person. If your laundering is not done often, you will need more. Keep another half-dozen in each size ready for guests. Twelve of the very small, "one-wipe" terry towels will be handy for occasional use. | Average bath-towel size is about 24″ x 46″; but you can get a man-size towel as large as 38″ x 72″. If you do your own washing, you may prefer medium-size bath towels, about 20″ x 40″, as they are easier to handle when wet. An even smaller size, the "hand towel," is about 18″ x 30″. Smallest size, "one-wipe" terry towel, is 11″ x 18″. | The shrinkage of terry towels is practically nothing in width, and not over 5 per cent in length. All-over shrinkage is not an important factor in towel performance. Sometimes too tightly woven borders pull in at the sides after washing, unless eased gently to shape when hanging to dry. | Terry-towel looped surfaces are either plain all over or have patterns raised as if sculptured. Both types come in a variety of colors and with a feel varying from soft and caressing to rough enough for a glowing massage. Some are reversible, with white predominating on one side and color predominating on the other. |
| **BEDSPREADS** | Each bed should have at least 2 spreads for everyday use. Thus one can replace the other during laundering. A third spread on hand for special dress-up occasions is usually a good idea. | Woven spreads come 74″ x 108″ for single or twin beds; 88″ x 108″ for double beds. Chenille spreads come marked "Single," "Double," or "Super Size." The Super Size is about 99″ x 114″ and is right for a very large double bed or to cover two twin beds pushed together. | Good-quality woven spreads do not shrink excessively, because the last operation in manufacture is a thorough wetting on both sides, so that practically all the shrinkage takes place before you buy the spread. Chenille bedspreads usually do not shrink excessively because they are made of material that has been washed before tufting is put on. | Chenille tufting runs in uninterrupted rows of soft, short pile. Candlewick type has a skip stitch separating the tufts. Woven spreads come in a variety of patterns and colors, to suit every taste. |

# HOUSEHOLD LINENS

## How to Buy Sheets and Pillowcases, Towels, Bedspreads

| IMPORTANT POINTS TO CHECK | OTHER INTERESTING DETAILS | WHAT SHOULD THE LABEL TELL? |
|---|---|---|

Sheets should be "Torn," not "Cut." "Torn" means the cloth was torn along one thread and thus will not later develop a bias appearance. Remember that the "Torn Size" is the size before hemming, and therefore turning the hems makes the sheet about 5″ shorter. Hems should be well fastened at the ends. Cotton sheets and pillowcases need a very small amount of finishing material called sizing. Low-grade ones have an excess of sizing. Rub a piece of sheet between your fingers. Excess sizing will come out in fine powder.

Bed linens in pastel colors, stripes, and patterns are on the market; hang in the shade to dry, to help preserve their hue. The fitted sheet is specially processed to reduce shrinkage; it is easy to slip on, less bulky. "Combed" percale for sheets and pillowcases is a smoother firmer cloth, but higher in price than "carded" muslin. Man-made fiber sheets take up less closet room. Fewer sheets are needed as they wash and dry quickly.

Many sheet labels give you valuable shopping information, which will help you understand where the quality lies. Some manufacturers enclose booklets with each sheet. These booklets take the form of a guide explaining the construction, service values, etc. Other manufacturers will send helpful data if you request it. Remember that a well-known brand name is your assurance that the sheet has been carefully made to give you satisfaction.

Hold to the light to see if underweave is close and firm. White towels are more absorbent than solid-color towels. Some towels are treated to make them thirstier, and, if so, the label may tell you this. Buy towels large enough, as hard tugging in use may break the edges. The selvage should be firm and closely woven. Consult the members of your family as to their preferences in texture, size, and color.

A good towel is downy, spongy, and resilient when crushed in your hand. Deep-toned colors may bleed onto other clothes during the first washings, so must be washed alone until danger from this is past. Do not iron terry towels or put them through a tight wringer. Shake terry towels well before you hang them up to dry.

The label will state the size in inches. Look for information about color resistance to washing and light. Some towels have been treated to increase the absorbency, and this may be stated on the label. Some of these treatments do not withstand repeated launderings; others do. If you send your towels to the laundry, washing directions on some labels tell you to instruct your laundry to "tumble-dry" or "fluff-dry" your terry towels. Otherwise instruct your laundry to do this, as it may put them through the flat-work ironer, which flattens loops, makes them harsh, lessens absorbency. All laundries can do this, and it does not cost extra.

To be sure you get a spread wide enough to hang almost to the floor, without touching, measure the bed. The spread must be long enough completely to cover the pillows and tuck under them in a soft fold before continuing on down the bed. The background material of a chenille spread must be closely woven and strong, with tufts well anchored. A woven spread must also be firm and close in weave. Colors should resist light and laundering.

Suit the spread to its purpose. Woven spreads, for instance, are excellent for children's and young people's use, since they will stand hard wear. They will not wrinkle or shed lint; they launder easily and need no ironing. Chenille spreads are best for the stylized bedroom, where beauty is the prime consideration. The tufts should be uniform in height, not jagged.

The size of the spread, either in inches or designated by "Single" or "Double," should be on the label. Look for information as to whether a chenille spread is "Vat Dyed," "Piece Dyed," or "Dip Dyed." "Vat Dyed" on the label means that the colors will last longer and withstand repeated launderings. The label may state also that the spread has been treated for shrinkage. Washing instructions should be clear and full.

# BLANKETS

*Labels tell you the inside story.*

*Tuck blankets in gently.*

*For comfort, choose a generous size.*

**Blankets for Warmth.** The warmth of a blanket does not depend on its weight, but largely on the nap —its thickness and resilient qualities. A good blanket is relatively light in weight. It retards the escape of body heat because of the countless insulating air cells held in the nap, which should remain resilient through years of wear and repeated washings. So when you buy a blanket, examine the nap. It should be of good depth, fine, even, and springy, and should not shed when brushed with your hand.

**Blanket Fabrics.** There are blankets of wool, cotton, and Acrilan, many blends of wool with man-made fibers, and blends of man-made fibers with each other.

**All-Wool Blankets** are usually highest in price. Their warmth-retaining qualities and the resilience of their nap will remain high through years of use if the blankets are properly laundered.

**Acrylic Fiber Blankets** have a dry hand. Though they are soft, they are not so springy as wool. They're as warm as wool blankets of comparable construction. Representatives of these fibers are Acrilan, Creslan, and Orlon. To minimize pilling (fuzzing) and wrinkling, follow the manufacturer's washing instructions. Shrinkage is negligible.

**Blended Blankets,** especially those containing rayon, are lower-priced. They have good warmth retention. Launder carefully to keep their good appearance.

**Cotton Blankets** are popular for lightweight summer coverings.

**Blanket Bindings** are usually made of satin or twill weave of acetate, rayon, or nylon. The latter is the longest-wearing.

**Sizes of Blankets.** Choose a blanket long enough— 90″ rather than 84″—for a good tuck-in at the foot of the bed. There are two standard widths, 72″ and 80″, the latter for double beds. There are, of course, smaller sizes for cribs and cots.

**Look at the Labels.** Most blankets carry labels that give much useful information, including the fiber content, size, weight, and washing directions. The brand name of the manufacturer is important, if well known, because it gives you added assurance of good quality.

**Care of Blankets.** When you make a bed, fold the top sheet well down over the blanket, for comfort and as a protection against soil. The blankets should come well up over the shoulders and should be tucked snugly under the mattress at the foot. Some people prefer to have the blanket hang down at the sides; others, to have it tucked in. In the latter case, it should be handled gently when you make the bed, as vigorous tugging may injure it.

## Electric Blankets

**How an Electric Blanket Keeps You Warm.** This single covering can keep you warm and comfortable all night, even though the north wind howls outside. The extra blankets you pile on your bed in cold weather restrict the loss of heat from your body. An electric blanket does this and more. By means of an automatic control, it provides the warmth needed to make up for temperature changes in your bedroom. You merely turn on the switch when you go to bed and turn it off in the morning.

**Its Advantages.** The advantages of an electric blanket can be listed quickly; but until you've actually used one, you'll not realize how wonderful it can be.

1. It gives you warmth without weight. For example, an electric blanket weighs just about as much as an ordinary blanket—but you use only one instead of two or three.

2. If you turn it on before you get into bed, it will take the icy chill off the sheets.

3. It takes care of you all night. You don't have to lie and shiver or get up in the cold to get another blanket.

4. It simplifies making the bed. You have to take care of only one blanket instead of several.

**Safety Features.** If you buy an electric blanket, make sure it is listed by Underwriters' Laboratories, Inc. Such listing means that the blanket has the safeguards deemed necessary for your protection.

**Cost of Using an Electric Blanket.** It is impossible to give the exact cost of operating an electric blanket, because the temperature in different localities and rooms varies so much. But in one study it was found that the cost of an electric blanket used every night from December to May in a room where the average temperature was about 55° F. and in a locality where electricity cost four cents per kilowatt hour was about fifty cents a month.

**Care of an Electric Blanket.** Most electric blankets are all or part wool, so you keep them clean much as you do ordinary wool blankets. The best advice, however, about washing or dry-cleaning them comes from the manufacturers of the blankets. In most cases washing is suggested. But be sure to follow carefully the manufacturer's directions given on the label. You need not look forward with dread to a seasonal cleaning job, for an electric blanket will stay clean a surprisingly long time if you protect it. Always remember to turn down a generous section of the sheet over the upper part of the blanket. And if the blanket user is ill, cover the entire blanket with a clean sheet. Don't sit or lie on an electric blanket—you may pull the interior wires loose.

### Quilts and Comforters

Quilts and comforters are made in a variety of fabrics. Quilts are washable if their covering is washable; many comforters are not, though the newer ones made of Acrilan or Dacron are washable.

Comforters stored during the summer present the problem of moth protection if wool filling is used. Cotton-filled quilts usually aren't stored, because they may be used all summer.

Quilts, customarily filled with cotton batt, do not compare in warmth with down-, or wool-filled and man-made fiber-filled comforters. Decide how much warmth you require—whether you need a lightweight, extra covering or maximum warmth in a single covering.

**Know Facts about Fillings.** Read the label to find out about the filling. Wool and down usually are used as comforter fillings; though Acrilan and Dacron are becoming more popular because they're washable, lightweight, yet warm, and not affected by moths; sometimes cotton is used for lightweight, summer comforters; also, combinations of wool and fur or wool and down are used.

Better-quality cottons and wools are free from foreign matter and are composed of longer fibers, which mean in cotton a smoother batt, and in wool greater warmth and resiliency. The presence of foreign matter, such as burrs, may be detected by feeling the quilt or comforter carefully.

Down is more expensive than wool, but may be preferred because of its lightness. White goose down, finest and most expensive, is softer and more resilient than the down of gray geese and other waterfowl. Acrilan and Dacron have excellent resiliency.

### Features to Look for:

**1.** A well-made quilt or comforter is quilted in a *regular* pattern with *small, even* stitching. The design has a purpose—it keeps the filling from shifting.

**2.** Side seams should be neatly turned under and stitched down close to the edge.

**3.** Fabrics should be closely woven, so the filling won't come through.

**4.** Washable coverings should be resistant to fading from light and laundering.

**5.** Many comforters are covered with acetate satin or taffeta. As acetate, especially in blues and greens, is susceptible to fume fading, you should have some assurance that the colors will not fume-fade readily. Look for label giving this information.

**Making a Quilt.** Whether you use materials from your scrapbag or buy them, be sure they have good resistance to laundering. Buy approximately "eighty-square" material—80 threads per inch in warp and woof. You know it as percale. Fabrics below eighty square may let bits of the filling through; those much above make quilting more difficult.

### Mattress Protectors

Mattress protectors, besides keeping the ticking clean, help prevent perspiration and other moisture from penetrating the mattress, corroding built-in springs, and making the filling unsanitary. Mattress protectors are of two types—the mattress cover and the mattress pad—both of which vary in construction and material.

**Mattress Covers.** One type of cover is a boxlike envelope that fits over the entire mattress. Usually one end is closed. The open end is fastened with snaps, buttons, ties, or slide fastener. Another type, with an elastic binding, fits over the top and sides and extends a few inches under the mattress, like an ironing-board cover.

Muslin and plastic-film mattress covers come in sizes to fit all beds, cribs, and cots. Covers made with two rows of stitching along the binding will withstand long, hard wear without bursting at the seams.

**Mattress Pads.** The quilted mattress pad is made of muslin and filled with cotton. A newer-type pad consists of foam rubber covered with muslin. (It's machine-washable, but it should never be put in an automatic dryer.) Placed on top of the mattress, a mattress pad covers tufts or buttons and adds to sleeping comfort.

Muslin pads are excellent moisture absorbers. Some are plastic-covered. Both protect the mattress from getting soiled and absorbing moisture and odors, thus prolonging the life of a mattress.

When you buy a mattress pad, examine the stitching. The common zigzag stitch is used in lower-priced pads. Better pads have closer stitches, often made in little squares. This stitch makes a more firmly quilted pad that can withstand frequent washing—a point for mothers of young children to remember.

The binding and how it is applied also affect the mattress pad's length of wear. Again, pads with two rows of stitching along the binding are firmer and longer-lasting.

**Sizes.** Mattress pads are made to fit cots and beds of all sizes. For children, pads range from carriage and lap sizes to bassinet, crib, and full-crib sizes. Also, you can buy padding by the yard and cut it to any size. It is wise to select a pad larger than the bed, to allow for shrinkage in laundering. Buy two pads for each bed, so one can be on the bed while the other is being laundered.

### Pillows

Since we spend a third of our lives in bed, sleeping comfort demands the same care in choosing pillows as in a bed or a mattress. Much depends on what was used to stuff a pillow. You can get this inside information easily by reading the labels attached to pillows which describe their contents. Many states have sanitation and health laws requiring such labels. Better manufacturers usually use them anyway.

**Feather Pillows.** Feathers and down from geese and ducks make the most durable, resilient feather pillows. Down (a relatively expensive filling) makes a very soft pillow; feathers make a firmer one. A mixture of goose feathers and down is the most popular choice, the percentage of each determining the cost and degree of resilience; naturally, the higher the per-

centage of feathers, the firmer the pillow will be.

Chicken feathers are a cheaper but less durable pillow filling than goose or duck feathers. The feather quill lacks the natural curl, of goose and duck feathers. Chicken feathers are often chopped or artificially curled to make the pillows resilient when new, but this does not last very long.

**Other Fillings.** Acrilan or Dacron filling in the form of batting offers many advantages—nonallergenic, vermin- and mothproof, highly resilient and washable. Hand laundering is recommended. Machine laundering tends to disturb the batting, causing lumpiness in the washed pillow, but most can be dried in an automatic dryer to fluff up the filling.

Foam latex, a natural rubber filled with air spaces first used for allergics, is now popular for general use. It is durable and it springs back to its original shape without plumping. Pillows of foam latex are made in two thicknesses—"regular" and "extra-plump."

Curled-hair filling is satisfactory for those who like a very hard pillow.

**Ticking Is Important.** A closely woven 8-ounce twill ticking makes a good pillow cover for feathers. Down pillows require a closer weave to make the covering strictly downproof. An extra pillow cover of ticking, with a zipper closing, can easily be removed for laundering and helps keep the pillow clean. Extra covers in a plastic film, with a zipper closing, are also available. They are especially good for allergics.

**Buying Pillows.** The standard size is 21″ x 27″, but smaller pillows are available. Read the label for information about the filling and the weight. A full-sized goose-down pillow may weigh only 1½ pounds. A mixture of goose down and goose feathers weighs more, depending on the percentage of feathers. Chicken feathers may weigh up to 3½ pounds. A comparatively light pillow is a good choice.

Feel a feather pillow to see if there are any large feather quills; these should not be present. Test a pillow's springiness or resilience to find out if it suits you.

**Care of Pillows.** You can wash feather pillows at home, but commercial laundries offer a pillow-washing service which gives a thorough renovation, including additional filling if needed. If chicken-feather or turkey-feather-filled pillows are washed, the curl may be removed with subsequent loss of resiliency. It is best to protect pillows against soil by plumping and airing them frequently.

Wash Acrilan- and Dacron-filled pillows by hand and dry in an automatic dryer. Latex foam rubber pillows are also hand-washable, but they must be dried in the open air, never in an automatic dryer.

## Table Linen

For a discussion of table linens, see page 179.

## Kitchen Linen

### What You Will Need

- 6 oven cloths or pot holders
- 6 dishcloths
- 6 cloths for washing-up work in kitchen
- 12 dish towels and glass towels
- 2 or 3 floor cloths for floors and baseboards
- 4 to 6 dusters (outing flannel, cheesecloth, or dustless dusters)
- 1 chamois or window washer

### A Good Dish Towel

The handsome patterns and bright colors of today's dish towels will bring cheery atmosphere to your kitchen. However, certain qualities add to their serviceability and the satisfaction you can get from them.

To judge a dish towel's worth, consider its fiber content, degree of linting, general construction, and colorfastness to laundering, particularly since dish towels are often laundered with a household bleach. Many dish-towel manufacturers indicate fiber content and colorfastness on labels; look for these labels on the towels when you shop.

**Fiber Content.** Linen has several properties that make it desirable for toweling. Flax fibers, from which linen is made, are hollow and quickly absorb moisture. As the fibers are long and have few ends at the surface, linen has little tendency to lint. Also, linen is very strong and durable. Its strength increases when wet.

Linen toweling fabrics include:

**Bird's-Eye Linen.** This is a novelty twill with a small-diamond, over-all pattern. The loosely twisted filling yarns increase absorbency.

**Fisheye Linen** has a diamond effect similar to bird's-eye, but the pattern is larger.

**Glass Toweling.** A plain-woven, absorbent fabric made in solid colors, stripes, checks, or prints. It is comparatively free from lint.

**Huck.** The foundation of this durable fabric is a plain weave; its face has a rough, pebbly texture with long surface floats, giving the fabric good absorbent properties.

However, linen no longer has a monopoly as the only fiber used in dish towels. Latest manufacturing methods successfully use many other fibers in towels —cotton and linen; all cotton; cotton, rayon, and linen; and cotton and rayon. These fabrics are woven and finished in such a way as to minimize linting and

increase absorbency. Choose a firm, rough-textured fabric that is not too thin for drying dishes.

Don't wipe a soiled pot or pan with a towel. Crumpled paper, a paper towel, or a brush should be used instead, to protect dishcloths and towels from stains.

While the heavier towel is good for general wiping, the thinner type is needed for glasses and cups. So choose both weights when you stock up on towels.

**Color Harmony.** Gay and attractive colored dish towels can add much charm to a kitchen if they are selected with color harmony in mind. Towels are available to fit into any decorating scheme. There are plaids, checks, stripes, floral and scenic prints. For you who are handy at sewing, and enjoy making your own kitchen accessories, toweling also can be bought by the yard up to 54″ wide, to make matching or contrasting curtains, tablecloths, napkins, aprons, chair pads, and many other items. You may even buy ready-made ensembles of matching dish towels, tablecloths, napkins, and curtains.

Most of the well-known brands of towels being sold today are dyed or printed with fast colors to withstand frequent washing and bleaching.

# WOMEN'S CLOTHING

### How to Shop

A few women are accomplished shoppers, and fewer still stretch their money as far as possible. Shopping requires common sense, self-restraint, and an imagination keen enough to visualize oneself in whatever is to be purchased. Those are not common attributes. They must be cultivated. Here are 8 shopping hints:

**1. Make a List at Home.** Know what you want before you shop. Consider the type of life you lead, the money you have to spend, the articles you need as against those you merely want.

**2. Buy Twice a Year for the Main Items of Your Wardrobe.** Make a list in March and in September for the next months.

**3. Don't Go Shopping with a Group of Friends** or even with your best friend, unless you consider her taste so much better than your own that you are willing to follow her advice.

**4. If Your Budget Is Limited, Buy Things You Can Wear for Several Years.** A well-made tailored suit or coat, bought with common sense and restraint, can be worn, with minor alterations, for five years. Good material will last that long. The cut, if not exaggerated, can be modified with the times, and tailored clothes are always best in conservative colors.

**5. Never Lose Sight of Yourself.** Be the complete egoist. Visualize yourself in the clothes you are buying. If you can't wear suits, don't buy them. Buy dresses and coats, instead. You must use restraint and imagination to see only what is attractive for *you*.

**6. Never Buy Anything Just Because It Is Cheap.** Look for fabric labels, good workmanship. Always it is better, when buying tailored clothes, to buy the very best you can afford.

**7. Think Before You Buy Novelty Gadgets.** When something comes into fashion publicity that is fantastic, be wary of it. No matter how stylish a fashion or trend may be, wear it only if it suits you.

**8. When You Buy Dresses, Coats, or Suits, Take Time to Have Them Fitted Carefully and Altered If Necessary.** It is a rare figure that does not need some slight alteration in a ready-made.

### Choosing Colors

Color is the most subtle element in good taste. You can cheapen the most beautifully cut dress with the wrong color, and you can kill your good looks with the same mistake.

Skin, hair, and eyes are important in your choice of colors—in the order mentioned. White skin calls for pure tones of medium strength. Skin with a pink undertone looks florid in purples, mauves, orchids, and most blues. Olive skin can take striking colors; but purples and blues will make it seem yellow. Sallow skin is difficult and requires careful make-up. Cream skin is the easiest, as almost any color goes with it—provided the figure is fairly good.

Hair is important. The main thing is not to kill it with monotony. Don't wear a color to match your hair. Use contrast. Rich browns with gray hair, also warm greens or blues or red. Dull greens and grays and blues with bright-auburn hair. Fairly strong, pure colors with mousy hair. No yellows or orange with blonde hair; no tan with light-brown hair. Black and white hair are, of course, exceptions to the rule of contrast. With them you can wear any color if the weight and skin are suitable.

Certain colors bring out the eyes. Hazel eyes, for instance, have more character with greens, browns, grays, or yellows. The woman who has very blue eyes should go in for true, rich blues, always a shade lighter or darker than her eyes. With definitely brown eyes avoid blues, and when brown is worn, choose it dull and deep, not bright.

**Blue** is a difficult color. It will make sallow or olive skin look yellow. Gray blues and deep, dull blues are best. Midnight is easier to wear than navy, because navy in any but the finest material is likely to be purplish.

**Red** is an easy color to wear. Even a sallow skin looks well in dull, garnet red. Black- and white-haired women look lovely in crimson or strawberry red. Mousy types can be stepped up with a judicious choice of lipstick red if the figure permits it. But beware of the common wine reds and fuchsia shades—wines are uninteresting, and fuchsias are too purple. Deep-garnet, dark-strawberry, and raspberry reds are best.

**Yellow** is excellent for summer or evening wear; but it should be in off-shades, never bright butter yellow. Dull, pale canary, old gold, or mustard are all smart, both for sports and in heavy evening crepes.

**Green** is much more adaptable than is generally supposed. Yellow greens, such as moss, grass, leaf, and evergreen, go with most skins, all colors of hair. They are excellent with hazel, gray, or brown eyes. Blue greens—those special tones of turquoise and peacock—are not usually becoming.

One woman in a thousand looks good in **mauves and purples.** That woman should have deep-blue eyes, black or white hair, creamy skin. And even she should stick to the bluish purples such as periwinkle or madonna purple. No orchids or reddish purples.

**Orange,** like yellow, should never be worn pure. It should be toned down almost to the point of being no longer orange.

### Choosing Fabrics

Half your success in being well dressed lies in the effectiveness of the fabric you wear—whether you buy your clothes ready-made or make your own wardrobe. Take great care that the fabric is right for *you*—in drapability, in texture, and in appropriateness for the style in which it is made.

In the main, here are some rules which should be remembered when you shop for fabrics—either by the yard, or in ready-made dresses:

1. Choose patterns that are in scale with your figure. As an example of what we mean, little people should wear little figures.

2. Shiny surfaces make things appear bigger. Dull surfaces make for slimness.

3. Deep-piled or deep-textured materials add pounds in appearance.

4. The draping quality of the fabric partially determines how it should be used.

5. The mating of fabric with dress design should be done with a sensitive eye to appropriateness.

---

### Basic Ready-to-Wear Sizes

**Junior Sizes:** 7–9–11–13–15

For the woman who has a small, high bust, a small waist and a short one, round hips, slight shoulders, a young figure.

**Misses Sizes:** 8–10–12–14–16–18–20

For the woman who is fairly evenly proportioned, whose waist is exactly in the middle of the torso, and who is slightly above average height.

**Petite Sizes:** 8–10–12–14–16–18–20

For the woman who is 5'5" or less and is evenly but diminutively proportioned.

**Half-Sizes:** 12½–14½–16½–18½–20½–22½–24½–26½

For the woman who is short and a little plump. The shoulders are narrow, waist is high, and bust full.

**Women's Sizes:** 34–36–38–40–42–44–46–48–50–52

For the woman, whose shoulders are wide, hips and stomach substantial, and waist long.

---

### How to Care for Your Clothes

The good-grooming habit should be practiced daily. Here are some tips to help keep your clothing trim and spotless.

**Keep your drawers and closets in order.** Sort out seldom-worn accessories and clothes. Arrange them neatly on shelves and in the back of your closet to allow more convenient room for your current wardrobe. Carefully examine garments you seldom wear. You may wish to dye or alter some of them to more fashionable colors and styles; others should be stored elsewhere or given away.

**Buy a good clothesbrush.** Then hang it in the most convenient place—the inside of your closet door, for example.

**Provide yourself with a well-equipped mending basket.** Include thread in a variety of colors, needles, tape measure, hooks and eyes, snap fasteners, scissors, thimble, single-edge razor blade, mending tape, buttons. Besides the usual mending care given to loose buttons, broken slip straps, etc., be particularly careful to keep coat and jacket linings and shoulder pads tacked firmly in place to avoid an untidy appearance.

### Daily Care of Clothing

**For that spic-and-span look, wear a blouse only one day.** Nylon, Dacron, Orlon, and acetate blouses launder readily. Weight for weight, however, rayon, cotton, and linen will be cooler and more absorptive.

**Protect your clothes from perspiration.** Use a deodorant, an antiperspirant, or dress shields.

**Wear an apron or smock when you work. Don't overload suit and coat pockets.** Overloaded pockets look untidy and usually stretch out of shape.

**Brush each garment after wearing it to remove loose surface dirt.** This will help each garment stay clean longer and will cut down on cleaning bills.

**Hang each garment straight on a hanger.** Soft knit garments should *not* be hung but folded neatly in a drawer. Use hangers the same width as the shoulders of the garment. Wide hangers are better than narrow ones. Garment bags give additional protection from dust.

### Airing, Pressing, Cleaning

**Air clothes frequently to keep them fresh.** Sunning and airing woolen garments help protect them against moth damage.

**Press clothes often.** The fabric, construction, and amount of wear given a winter suit or dress will determine how frequently it needs pressing. When garments start to get out of shape or become badly wrinkled, they should be pressed. Many cotton and rayon dresses and suits require frequent pressing in order to maintain their neat appearance. Cottons, rayons, and linens with crease-resistant finishes and synthetic fabrics such as Orlon, Dacron, Acrilan, and blends of these man-made fibers, require less frequent pressing.

**Remove all stains before pressing.** The heat and pressure of the iron may set stains almost indelibly. Simple stains may be removed at home by the prompt use of water or dry-cleaning fluid. Use nonflammable cleaning fluids and be sure to work in a well-ventilated room.

Periodically sponge dress collars with dry-cleaning fluid to keep them free from powder.

Send clothes to be dry-cleaned before they become badly soiled and as soon as possible after a hard-to-remove stain appears. If you know what the stain is, tell the dry cleaner.

**Clean all clothes before storage.** Long storage of soiled clothes ages many stains, making them very difficult or even impossible to remove. Cleaning before storage is also a good protection against damage from insects.

**Before sending each garment to the dry-cleaner,** examine it for the following:

Check the shoulder pads. If they are covered with a plastic material, or if they contain sponge rubber, they should be removed. Plastic-covered pads usually become stiff and shrink excessively, while sponge-rubber shoulder pads are seldom dry-cleaned satisfactorily.

Remove all ornamental buttons, as they may be damaged during dry-cleaning.

Clean out all pockets. Certain types of matches left in pockets are particularly hazardous. They may ignite during the deodorizing process, which follows the dry-cleaning, and start a serious fire.

Be careful not to leave lipstick in pockets. It can cause great damage to clothes during dry-cleaning.

### How to Care for Furs

Your furs will look lovely longer if you follow these simple rules:

**1. Fit.** Make sure you buy a good fit. Skimpiness strains seams and skins, helps cause rips.

**2. Hanging.** Never let your furs lie on a flat surface for long periods; this flattens or crushes the fur. Hang your coat on a hanger, your scarf on one of the large rings made for this purpose. Before hanging, shake gently.

**3. Brushing.** Vigorous brushing or rubbing should be avoided. Use a soft brush and be gentle. Brushing seldom is needed if furs are shaken often.

**4. Damp Furs.** Shake thoroughly; hang to dry in a cool flow of air, if possible. When dry, again shake gently. Wet or dry, furs never should be near heat.

**5. Wearing.** Keeping your coat buttoned when you are standing helps prevent its being pulled and ripped. When you're sitting, unbutton and ease the coat. This relieves strain on seams, skins, and buttons. Carry purse and parcels carefully, not tucked under the arm, to avoid rubbing fur. Don't overload pockets. A narrow ruching sewed at the back of the neck helps prevent fur's being soiled. When carrying a coat, hold it fur side in.

**6. Packing.** When packing, fold with fur side out; place crumpled tissue between folds where fur touches fur. After unpacking, shake gently and hang for 24 hours, to let the fur fluff.

**7. Cleaning and Repairing.** Fur should be cleaned thoroughly by a furrier at least once a year, more frequently if there is much soot in the air. Glazing to restore luster should be done whenever necessary. Have small rips repaired. Entrust cleaning and repairing to a furrier or cleaner who has a good reputation for handling furs.

**8. Storing.** Furs should be placed in cold storage during warm weather to prevent drying and protect against moths. Choose a reliable storage company, and get a receipt.

### Garment Shields

**Underarm Shields.** These shields come in several different sizes and shapes. The regular shape is recommended for normal perspiration; this shape also comes in large sizes, for heavy perspiration. If perspiration is light and protection is needed only directly under the armpit, the crescent shape may be used.

The shield designed so that one side is shorter than the other is recommended for short-sleeved dresses and blouses. Also, special shields are available for dresses with cap sleeves and those with deep armholes.

The shields mentioned above must be pinned or sewed directly to the dress or blouse. In many cases, the pins are bar-tacked to the shield to prevent possible damage to the shield.

**Back Shields.** If you have experienced the annoyance of staining the back of a dress with perspiration, you may find back shields the answer to your problem. These are made of lightweight, cotton nainsook, and are shaped like the back of a dress. Tiny pins fasten the shield at the shoulders, sides, and waistline.

**Skirt Shields.** This is an apron-shaped shield that ties at the waistline and helps keep skirts from wrinkling and creasing.

# BELTS, BUTTONS, AND TRIMMINGS

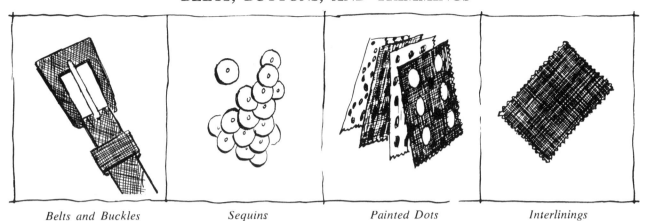

*Belts and Buckles*  *Sequins*  *Painted Dots*  *Interlinings*

Pay attention to belts, buckles, ornamental buttons, shoulder pads, and other trimmings and accessories when you shop for a dress. If trimmings and accessories do not stand up well in use and in laundering or dry-cleaning, your new dress may soon become unwearable.

### Belts and Buckles

Many belts are made with a cardboard or paper backing coated with lacquer or linseed oil. Such belts will not withstand laundering or dry-cleaning. To identify this construction, bend the belt sharply, to see if the backing cracks at the crease.

On fabric-covered belts, the fabric should be stitched to the back of the belt. It should not be fastened with an adhesive, which invariably loosens and comes off in laundering or dry-cleaning. The fabric should be sewn around the buckle frame, too.

### Buttons

Some highly transparent plastic buttons dissolve in dry-cleaning. These buttons look like glass, but can be distinguished from glass by scratching their surface with a pencil or fingernail. Glass buttons do not show scratch marks. Transparent-plastic, ornamental, and fragile buttons should be removed before the garment is dry-cleaned.

Plastic buttons sometimes soften and are distorted from the iron's heat. To avoid this, test the button by touching it with the tip of the iron.

### Sequins

Sequins may be made of glue, plastic, metal, or mica. The last three are the most durable. Sequins made of glue will dissolve in water. Both glue and plastic sequins may melt or distort if touched by a hot iron. To prevent or minimize this, press on the wrong side the parts of dresses trimmed with sequins.

Use a moderately hot iron, and work quickly. Avoid buying dresses trimmed with sequins—or beads—that are attached by an adhesive instead of by thread. They may drop off in dry-cleaning.

### Interlinings

Interlining of hair canvas, linen, or cotton is used for shaping tailored coats. The newer nonwoven fabrics seldom give trouble in dry-cleaning, but may in wet-cleaning or laundering, if dark-colored interlinings are used under light-colored fabrics. The dyes may bleed and stain the outer fabric. The fault is the coat manufacturer's. Report such an experience to your store.

### Painted Dots

Fabrics decorated with polka dots or other designs applied with paint or lacquer may prove unserviceable in dry-cleaning. The dots or designs peel off or distort and pucker the fabric. A dress may withstand one dry-cleaning, but not a second or a third.

### Trimmings

Pay particular attention to dress trims, as their attractiveness may be outweighed by the difficulty and bother of keeping them clean. White cotton-piqué trim on a dry-cleanable dress is an example. This trim becomes soiled readily. Washing it is the best way to make it fresh again; but removing collar, cuffs, or other trim after a brief wearing is tedious.

Unless they are washable, colored trimmings on light-colored dresses may bleed and stain the dress. When trimmings are washable, don't invite trouble by leaving a dampened dress rolled up for more than a short time before ironing. Even properly dyed trimmings may "print off" when damp, if left too long in contact with other damp fabric, and the resulting stains may make the dress unwearable.

# CHECK LIST FOR BUYING DRESSES, BLOUSES, SWEATERS

## Dresses

**Does It Really Fit?** When you try on a dress, pay particular attention to the shoulder line and armholes—among the chief factors in a good fit. If the shoulders are too wide, the armhole seam falls below the level of the shoulders; if too small, the seam is in from the edge of the shoulders, causing too much snugness and giving the illusion of narrow shoulders. Make sure, too, that the armhole and the sleeves are large enough for free, easy movement with no strain on the armhole seam. Raise the arms and bring them forward to note this strain. For good fit, the dress should come to your normal waistline. If the dress seems too short or too long at the waistline, a different size range may solve the difficulty. Finally, look at the dress length. It should be sufficiently long for your height and in keeping with the style trend. The depth of the hem may be 1½", but 2½" is better. The hemline should be relatively straight and even.

**Is It Well Made?** Examine the dress carefully for the following details: buttons, buttonholes, belts, seams, shoulder pads, trim. A well-made dress is carefully finished at each of these points.

**Seams.** They should be finished neatly, have a generous allowance so they will not pull out. Pinking is used on the seams of many woven dresses; the machine overcast stitch, on most knit dresses. Some more expensive dresses have French seams, with all seam edges turned under. All types of seam should be free of raw edges, which may ravel in use.

Tape reinforcement at the shoulder and waist seams is a good point to look for—especially on knit garments. Tape keeps the seams neat and firm, prevents stretching and sagging.

**Shoulder Pads** have a dual purpose —to portray the shoulder-line silhouette of the season whether it be built up or sloping, and to hold the shoulder line in place. Most pads on better dresses are covered with the self dress material. Some pads in dry-cleanable

winter dresses have snaps or other fasteners, so they may be removed.

**What Does the Label Say?** An informative label is your best means of identifying hidden qualities that mean good wear. If you are buying a cotton dress, for example, look for a shrink-resistant label. This means that the dress will not shrink out of fit. With assurance of low shrinkage, you can buy the size that fits you best. The label should also tell you if the dress is colorfast to sunlight, washing.

## Blouses

**Does It Really Fit?** Try on the blouse. Are the shoulders wide enough? Is the blouse full enough across the back and under the arms to permit free-and-easy action? Is it long enough to allow you to tuck a substantial portion under your skirt? If you can't answer yes to all these questions, try another size or style. Blouses are sized according to bust measurements. If, for example, your bust measures 34, buy size 34 blouses.

**Is It Well Made?** Full, firmly stitched, pinked or taped seams, and trim that is fastened securely with straight and even stitches, are tailoring details that add to a blouse's style and durability. These features are especially important on washable blouses, particularly nylon and rayon, to prevent fraying. At dart points and trim ends, the stitching should be held securely by backstitches or tied threads. Fagoting, lace inserts, and hand embroidery should also be firmly stitched to the blouse. Buttonholes should have close stitching to avoid fraying.

**What Does the Label Say?** Look for a tag or label to find out what the blouse is made of and what care it should be given. If it is washable, it should not shrink out of fit or fade in washing. If the blouse is acetate, it should have been treated to resist fume fading. If it is organdy, it should retain its crispness through many washings.

When special instructions are given on care, such as proper washing technique and ironing temperature, be

sure to keep the label or tag on file for future reference.

## Sweaters

**Does It Really Fit?** In well-made sweaters, the number of stitches varies according to the size. Some manufacturers, however, have been known to make several sizes from one run of sweaters by shrinking some and stretching others. Obviously, such sweaters do not keep their original fit after washing.

As you can't tell whether or not a sweater has been knit—not stretched or shrunk—to size, it is best to buy from a reliable store and look for tags or labels that assure washability.

As sweaters aren't pretty when they cling, it's wise to buy a size larger than your regular blouse size.

**Is It Well Made?** Look for straight, firmly sewed side seams. Some manufacturers sew tape on the shoulder seams. This holds the shoulders in place and keeps them from sagging or stretching after repeated wearings.

Also, carefully note the sweater's neckline. Merrowed and looped necks are the kinds used. A merrowed neck can be recognized easily by an inside seam at the neck. This seam joins the separately made ribbing to the body of the sweater. A looped neck doesn't have a seam, because it is a continuation of the body of the sweater. It is smooth, firm, and appears hand-finished.

Looped necks, which are more expensive, give excellent wear, will not sag and stretch out of shape.

Buttons, ribbon, and trim should withstand laundering. Buttonholes should be firmly stitched, to help prevent raveling. If the outside of the center front is bound with ribbon, be sure the ribbon is color fast to washing and to light. Some manufacturers place the ribbon on the inside. Then any difference between sweater and ribbon shades isn't so noticeable.

**What Does the Label Say?** Be sure to check labels for the fiber content— 100 per cent wool, nylon, Orlon, Acrilan, Vicara, or blends of these fibers, and note washing instructions.

# SPORTSWEAR

## Slacks and Shorts

Good fabric, good fit, good lines, and the right color determine how you will look in slacks. Here are some rules to keep in mind when buying and wearing them. In general, the same principles apply to all tailored sportswear: shorts, pedal pushers, etc.

**1. Don't buy slacks that have too deep a crotch, wide flapping legs, long, dragging cuffs.** Slacks are a tailored fashion and must look smooth.

**2. Follow masculine preference in fabrics and colors.** Decide what becomes you—fly front or side closing. Be sure slacks have well-pressed creases.

**3. Regard slacks as part of an ensemble**—not as a pair of trousers. Complement them with the right accessories—low-heeled shoes, simple, tailored blouses, right-length jackets, informal hair-dos, appropriate headgear.

**4. Consider the occasion.** Wear utility slacks for utility jobs; dark faille or jersey slacks for evening comfort.

## Buying a Bathing Suit

If you counted them, you'd discover that a surprising number of your summer hours are spent in a bathing suit. So we think it deserves careful buying.

Choose the right fabric for your needs. Bathing suits are available in a variety of woven, knit, and lace fabrics. Much of the performance of a suit depends upon the fibers from which it is made.

**Acetate** is a popular fabric for bathing suits because it resists shrinking and dries quickly. But when you select a suit made of acetate, make certain that the color resists fume fading. Fabrics made of solution-dyed acetate have excellent colorfastness.

**Cottons**—lace, broadcloth, denim, gingham, satin, seersucker, piqué, poplin, and twill—are used chiefly for dressmaker suits, which are flattering to most figures. These fabrics are very absorbent and dry slowly, but are cool when dry. To assure good fit, buy only those cottons that are treated to resist shrinking and fading caused by perspiration, sunlight, and chlorinated or salt water. Cotton is subject to mildew, but you can forestall such damage by washing and drying your suit between wearings.

**Nylon** is very desirable for bathing suits because it is strong, dries quickly, and can be dyed in beautiful bright colors.

**Orlon** is also excellent; it dries quickly and resists shrinkage. Bathing suits of Orlon or nylon should be washed in warm water, dried away from heat, and ironed with a warm, never hot, iron.

**Wool** is preferred by many professional swimmers because it has natural elasticity and clings to the body. Because it's very absorbent, it dries slowly; on the other hand, it does not feel clammy when wet. Wool suits must be thoroughly washed and dried between wearings to prevent mildew; when in storage, they should be protected against moth damage.

To prolong its life, protect your suit against cosmetics, antiperspirants, deodorants, and tanning lotions and oils—any of these can damage color or fabric. And after each wearing, rinse the suit and dry it thoroughly, away from heat.

## HOW TO MAKE SURE YOUR BATHING SUIT FITS

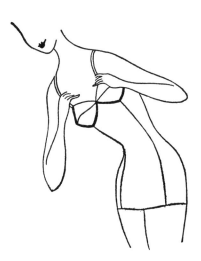

Open zipper. Turn top half of suit down and fold it over 3″ below waistline. Step into suit; grasp fold firmly and work suit over hips to waist. Do not use fingernails. Gradually roll top of suit over body. Adjust. Fasten hook and eye before closing zipper to prevent undue strain on suit and to avoid catching flesh in zipper. Bend over, allow bust to fall into bra cups.

Straps should allow movement without falling, but should not cut shoulders or lift bust out of place.

To check bra for fit and comfort, make this action test: Raise your arms; note whether bra provides ample coverage in this position.

Now check hipline, or lower part of suit, for fit and comfort.

*Fasten straps and check their length. Do they bind or cut your shoulders?*

*Sit on chair or floor. Is suit long enough for comfort and coverage?*

# TYPES OF SUITS AND THEIR ACCESSORIES

### The Dress Suit

**Material:** Wool crepe, worsted-silk blends, fine gabardine, twill or suitable synthetic fabric

**Accessories:** *Hat:* Straw, felt, or ribbon, with flowers, feathers, veil or other trim

*Bag:* Dressy, of suede, faille, or patent leather

*Shoes:* Pumps, sandals, or ties, of kidskin, patent leather, or suede

*Gloves:* Kidskin, fabric, suede

**Blouse:** Feminine, ruffled, or lace trimmed; with jabot, bow, or pleated and tucked collar

### The Street Suit

**Material:** Cheviot, twill, gabardine, fine worsteds, covert, flannel or suitable synthetic fabric

**Accessories:** *Hat:* Breton, sailor, beret, bonnet cloche

*Bag:* Envelope, pouch, of calf, alligator, felt, gabardine, or patent leather

*Shoes:* Pumps and ties, of calf, suede, gabardine

*Gloves:* Doeskin, capeskin, fabric, suede

**Blouse:** Tailored, simple lingerie blouse, shirtwaist, gilet, or dickey

### The Sports Suit

**Material:** Tweed, flannel, wool, gabardine, covert or suitable synthetic fabric

**Accessories:** *Hat:* Classic sports with brim, cloche, beret, calot

*Bag:* Classic and big, of calf, alligator, pigskin, felt

*Shoes:* Low-heeled moccasins, ghillies, monks, brogues, or oxfords, of calf or alligator

*Gloves:* String, capeskin, pigskin, chamois

**Blouse:** Casual—sweater, jersey shirtmaker blouse, gilet, dickey

## How Your Suit Should Fit

Most women should not step into a ready-made suit without having it altered. The price of alterations is economy in the long run. The value of perfect fit is unlimited. A suit is more expensive than a dress. You wear it longer, so it should be right. Take time to have it fitted, and choose your suit to flatter your particular figure.

The tall, slim woman should choose a much longer jacket than the short, plump woman. It should also close higher and have wider revers. Low closing point, near waist, and long, narrow revers are necessary to lengthen and slenderize the large-all-over woman or the woman with a big bust. This kind of suit, however, is definitely mature. Double-breasted jackets are also unbecoming to heavy women. Patch pockets, other horizontal trimmings are not becoming to short women. Set-in pockets, long lines are more becoming.

Hips must fit smoothly, be neither too loose nor too tight. Sleeves should follow arm lines closely and not pull from around armhole. Inner sleeve seam often needs raising. Have your sleeves short enough to avoid wrinkles at the wrist.

The plain, classic, rather narrow skirt, so often shown with tailored suits, is only for the tall and slim. The woman of medium height and weight should wear a skirt with an easy flare. Bias cutting, six or eight gores, a group of pleats front and back—all these are good. But there should be the same amount of fullness in the back of the skirt as in the front, to achieve a slight and even ripple around the legs. A straight back is likely to cut in below the seat.

The collar must stick close to the neck when seen from the side. It must not rise in back too high for the length of your neck, nor cause the upper part of your jacket in back to pull and wrinkle below it.

Jackets often need lifting under the collar in back.

If your waist is normal, be sure waist pinch on jacket comes in the right place. If your waist is short, choose a jacket that is only slightly fitted in back, so your real waistline does not show. A short waist cannot be disguised in a tight jacket. But a good tailor can put the waist pinch where he pleases in a semi-fitted suit.

### There's More Than Style to Your Coat

Style and attractiveness are important, but there is much more to consider when you buy a winter coat. The fabric, fastenings, trim, fit, and workmanship need careful examination.

**Linings.** Many coats, particularly sport and box models, have removable linings held in place with buttons or slide fasteners. These coats provide warmth when you need it, and with the lining out, their usefulness is extended well into the spring.

**Lining Fabrics.** A lining should be woven closely and firmly. An acetate lining should be dyed or treated to resist fume fading; otherwise, it may change color after a short period of wear. Look for the label giving this information. Solution-dyed acetate linings offer excellent resistance to fume and sun fading.

Linings made of nylon or Orlon should always be used in garments made of man-made fabrics to avoid uneven shrinkage between the outer fabric and the lining.

For extra warmth, coats may be interlined with wool or glass fiber, or lined with leather, alpaca, or fur. Alpaca pile, sheepskin, and fur linings are especially desirable where low temperatures prevail.

**Check the Fit.** Remember you'll be wearing suits and woolen dresses under your coat, so check its fit for both looks and comfort. Raise your arms to detect any binding or straining at the armhole, indicating you may need a size larger. Some coats have elastic panels set in at the armholes to increase freedom of action. If you shop for a coat with a removable lining, with the intention of wearing it in the warmer months, try it without the lining to make sure it will not be too large and full.

**Woolens and Worsteds.** Worsted fabrics are made from tightly twisted wool yarns and have a smooth, unnapped surface and a firm texture. Individual threads in the weave are very distinct. Woolens, on the other hand, are made from yarns with a loose twist, and are soft in texture. The short, protruding fibers of the fabric can be easily napped. Examine heavily napped woolens to see if the underweave is firm and close. Weak, sleazy fabrics sometimes are heavily napped to disguise their shortcomings. Although woolens offer somewhat more warmth than worsteds, they are less durable.

**Coat Fastenings.** Fastenings should close securely and be adapted to the coat fabric. Loops are better than buttonholes on loosely woven fabrics. Smooth buttons of simple design last longer than irregular-shaped buttons, particularly cloth-covered ones. Novelty or ornamental buttons should be removed before coat is sent to the dry-cleaner. Buttons should not be sewn close to the fabric but attached by a stem of thread. Closely sewn buttons may strain the fabric and cause it to tear.

**Fur Trim.** If you plan to buy a fur-trimmed coat, pay careful attention to where the fur is placed on the coat. Certain sections—the cuffs and sleeve trim, for example—receive considerable rubbing and wear. While it is expected that fur cuffs will wear in time and need repair, see that other trim, such as that on the sleeves, is so placed to be spared rubbing against the coat as much as possible.

### On Buying Fur Coats

First, decide your price range. If price is no object, you can look at chinchilla, ermine, fisher, marten, mink, and Russian sable. Expensive but not astronomical are beaver, blue fox, kolinsky, leopard, Alaska seal, weasel, and most types of lamb, such as broadtail, caracul, and Persian. The moderate range includes badger, fitch, many types of fox, skunk, mole, muskrat, ocelot, otter, raccoon, and squirrel. In the low-priced group are hare, guanaco, mouton-processed lamb, marmot, Persian paw, and rabbit or lapin or coney.

Next, determine the purpose of your purchase. Is the coat to be for only sports wear, or must it serve for daytime and evening, or is it to be an elegant extra coat? Although wearing qualities depend greatly on the particular pelts and the care they receive, experts generally advise that, when durability is a prime consideration, you steer clear of leopard, cat, fox, hare, kidskin, marmot, and some types of lamb.

Fair durability is credited to broadtail, ermine, fox, kola, krimmer, muskrat, mink, nutria, opossum, pony, sable, squirrel, weasel, and some types of marten. Muskrat, which authorities consider one of the best buys, has a service expectancy of 5 years for the northern type, 3 for the southern.

Greatest wearing qualities are attributed to badger, beaver, bear, fitch, fisher, American mink, marten, plasticized lamb, otter, raccoon, Alaskan seal, skunk, and Persian lamb with high luster and well-developed curl. This last fur demonstrates how little price may have to do with durability—pelts with tight, large curls outwear those with tight, small curls, although the small-curled furs are costlier. Good beaver, a favorite of the experts, will last 8 years or more and is exceptionally warm. Alaska seal may wear many years, although it is so light and pliable an entire pelt can be passed through a napkin ring. Otter often is called the most durable of furs. Plasticized lamb, or mouton—sheepskin treated with resinous material that straightens the hairs—is rugged stuff when properly processed.

Fit has a great deal to do with the wearing qualities as well as the comfort of a fur coat. Your coat should be one size larger than your dress, and it is best to try it on over a suit. Walk toward a mirror in it—it should open and close with your steps, not remain open, and if the closing is an overlap, it should remain closed except when you are sitting. Remember, a fur coat is heavy. Unless it's fitted so that the shoulders rather than the neck bear the weight, you're unlikely to get much pleasure from it.

### On Buying Raincoats

When you shop for a raincoat, you'll surely run across the terms waterproof and water-repellent. And although they sound much alike, there are some important differences between them. See page 192 for a discussion of the two terms.

Make your choice between these two kinds of rainwear by considering who's going to wear the coat where. For children or adults who must spend a lot of time outdoors, regardless of weather, plastic waterproof coats are undoubtedly the best bet. But for the men and women who, when it's raining, simply hurry from train to office, or from house to car, a water-repellent garment is more satisfactory.

## Some Dos and Don'ts about Hats

**Dos**

If you wear glasses, your hat should show most of your forehead. With that one exception, there are no hard-and-fast rules. Pick any hat that becomes you, watching these other points.

Avoid gauzy, flowery, or multicolored hats if your skin is coarse or blotchy. Rich, solid materials are best.

Wear soft lines and fabrics to offset angular features.

Avoid center trimming if your nose is no asset. The eye travels down the feature you prefer to minimize.

Be sure that your hat is as wide as the widest part of your face.

Avoid a strictly symmetric hat if your features are irregular.

Choose an eye veil instead of a full one if you want to look younger.

Reject any hat that must be clamped on with elastic or a great many hatpins. The right hat clings to your head even on windy days with no apparent help —or, at the most, with one hatpin.

**Don'ts**

If you have a large face and an ample figure, don't choose a tiny or a very big hat. Pick a fairly bulky hat with upward lines.

Don't match the fabric of your hat with that of your suit. A tweed suit is enough tweed, and another color or texture may be more flattering to your face and hair.

Don't repeat a bad line. For example, don't let the brim of a hat follow the line of a too-large nose.

Don't wear a cartwheel if you are under 5'2". It will dwarf you. Pick a hat scaled to your dimensions.

Don't wear elaborate earrings when your hat is elaborate or flower-bedecked.

Don't wear the same type of hat year in and year out.

Don't wear hats with high crowns or vertical lines if you are tall. Hats with horizontal lines cut your height.

Don't choose a wide-brimmed or drooping hat if your neck is short and thick.

Don't wear a hat with tired band, veil, or flowers. Replacing them will revive your hat.

### Care of Your Hats and Veils

Hats need frequent brushing. Felt and velvet hats look better if they are steamed as they are brushed. Hold the hat over the spout of a steaming tea kettle, and turn the hat as you brush. Too often hats are jammed together in a crowded hatbox. To preserve their shape, hats should be put on individual hat stands or stuffed with paper and set on their crowns.

Keep veils perky by placing a piece of waxed paper over them when you press them. This restores crispness and makes the veils last longer. Even rain-soaked veils look better after this treatment.

### Shoes and Their Care

**How Should a Shoe Fit?** A shoe should be roomy enough at the tip so that, while standing, you can at least wiggle your big toe; behind the base of the big toe, it should be snug enough to grip your instep and your heel firmly.

When you stand up in your new shoes, see if you *can* wiggle your big toe. Then, as you walk around, see if the shoe is slipping at your heel or bulging under your ankle. If you can't move the big toe, try the next length or width; if your heel slips, try a narrower width. If the shoes still don't fit, try a different style.

**How to Get the Right Size.** While sitting, draw a pencil outline of your foot. Then stand up and draw another. Now pick up a heavy weight, or press down as hard as you can, and draw a third outline. As you can see, your foot is more than one size. The weight you put on it as you stand spreads it lengthwise and crosswise. Your foot can "grow" a full size longer in the course of an active day, the extra length being added by the constant weight you've had on your foot.

If your foot has lengthened slightly, or if the particular last demands a shoe that is half a size larger, the clerk will be correct if he brings you a narrower width. Size 7½A, for example, is approximately the same width as size 7B; to get the same width in a 6½ would require a C.

**Repairs:** Important in the care of shoes is keeping the heels straight. Run-over heels misshape the entire shoe and throw the body out of line.

**Cleaning and Polishing:** Clean, well-polished shoes give the longest service. Polish "nourishes" the leather, restoring the oils, and protects against water and scuffing.

Before applying polish, clean the shoes. Smooth leather should be wiped with a clean cloth. Colored smooth leathers such as calf, kid, elk, alligator, and lizard need a paste polish in neutral or matching color. As it is very hard to remove stains from light-colored shoes, a light bootmaker's stain may be used on the entire shoe, to mottle the leather and make stains less noticeable.

Suede, buck, and similar leathers should be brushed with a bristle or wire brush or with a firm rubber sponge designed for suede. When there are grease spots or the nap has become flattened or shiny, buff with an emery board, then apply liquid suede cleaner the color of the shoe. Stuff shoes with tissue paper before applying liquid, and leave tissue in place until dry; it will keep the inside clean. Colorless liquid suede cleaners may be used for brightly colored suede shoes; but they should be used sparingly, because they often remove color as well as dirt. Brush white napped leather shoes thoroughly. Then use a white shoe cleaner, following the manufacturer's directions for best results.

Fine walking shoes are best cleaned with saddle soap or a saddle-soap-type cleaner, with a small amount of water. Follow with paste polish for a high shine.

The best cleaners for patent-leather are a liquid wax and a special thin paste cleaner. If neither is available, petroleum jelly may be used. Plastic patent leathers can be wiped with a damp cloth.

Scuffs on grain leather can be treated by applying shoe dye to the scuffed portions, then polishing the shoes when they have dried.

### The 11 Key Leathers

**Karung Snakeskin** takes high colors very well and makes wonderful stripping sandals.

**Cobra Snakeskin** dyes well, too. It is used for sandals, pumps.

**Calfskin,** the best-known leather, polishes easily, wears well.

**Calcutta Lizard** is a serviceable, sturdy, and hard-wearing leather.

**Chameleon Lizard** is a hard-surface novelty leather used mostly as a trim.

**Suede** is a perennial favorite for almost all shoe styles.

**Alligator** wears well, is used for formal and informal shoes.

**Buckskin** is good for white summer shoes because it is a comfortably porous, light, and attractive material.

**Kidskin** is a soft leather recognizable by the tiny pores that appear on the surface.

**Textured Leather** is a favorite for sports.

**Patent** is side leather with a shiny varnish applied. Always fashionable, it is most popular in the spring.

### You May Be Judged by Your Handbag

For the sake of your bag as well as your costume, switch handbags often, and when you empty the contents, take time to clean the inside of the bag. Brush the dust from the folds of linings and pockets of both fabric and leather-lined bags. To clean and protect the outside of your smooth-leather bags, like calf or alligator, use saddle soap and a neutral cream or special leather preserver. Rub a thin coating of the neutral cream or leather preserver over the bag, wipe off the excess and polish with a clean, dry cloth. *Special note*: A wax treatment is ideal for colored bags that tend to rub off on gloves and clothing. Apply liquid wax sparingly (the same type of wax you use on your furniture). Then polish well. It may take a little time, but when a good film of wax has been built up it will go a long way in correcting the trouble.

### Gloves

**Your Size and Fit.** If you are not certain of your glove size, try on gloves before buying. Turn ring settings toward palm, and put the glove on whichever hand is larger. The right hand usually is one-quarter size larger than the left, except for a left-handed person. You can determine your glove size with a tape measure. Pull it taut across the palm and over the knuckles of your hand. The number of inches measured is your glove size. Leather gloves come in quarter sizes (6, 6¼, 6½, 6¾, 7, etc.). Fabric gloves come only in half sizes (6, 6½, 7, 7½, etc.).

**Care of Gloves.** The way you don and remove your gloves greatly affects their fit and life. If your hands are hot and moist, dust a little powder on them. Insert four fingers into the glove, and gently smooth the glove fingers downward, keeping seams straight. When the four fingers are fitted, gently ease your thumb into the glove.

To remove gloves, work them off finger by finger, instead of pulling them off by the cuff. You will prolong the life of your gloves if, after wearing, you blow into them; then smooth, reshape, and fold them. Damp gloves should be air-dried before they are put away, to prevent mildewing and spotting. Mend rips with strong thread that is not too coarse and as fine a needle as possible, to avoid tearing the leather.

# CHOOSING THE RIGHT FOUNDATION GARMENT

**What is a foundation garment?** A foundation garment is any garment that supports or controls the figure. For some reason many people associate this term with corsets or corselets only. Actually it covers many other types of underclothing. Girdles, panty girdles, and even garter belts are foundation garments. So are brassières and bandeaux, maternity and surgical garments.

**How should you buy a foundation garment?** There is only one completely satisfactory way of selecting a foundation garment, and that is to try it on before you buy it. Have a trained fitter recommend a girdle, bra, or corselet for you. Try on several models, and let a *corsetière* check the fit at the appropriate points. Then move around in the garment. Sit down. Bend over. Walk around. If you're buying a girdle or corset, ask yourself whether or not the garment you have on gives the abdominal support you want. Is it long enough to make a smooth thighline? If it's intended to, does it control your diaphragm? Does it fit snugly at the waistline without pinching or bulging? Are the bones placed so they don't gouge?

**How do foundation garments correct specific figure faults?** Good foundation garments are "engineered" in the same way that shoes are. It's no longer necessary to compress flesh into heavy, uncomfortable garments. The principle of modern girdles, bras, etc., is control through gentle molding and support. A girdle with a reinforced front panel flattens a protruding abdomen. A one-piece corselet or a waist-length bra controls the diaphragm. A waistlet or a high-waisted girdle reduces waist measurements. A corselet or corset disciplines heavy thighs. So analyze your figure and its flaws thoroughly and decide just what you want foundation garments to do for your figure.

**What should you expect of a bra?** If you're buying a bra, check these points. Are the bust cups the correct size? Do they shape and lift without any bulging flesh around the edges? Are the shoulder straps comfortable and easily adjustable? Does the back band fit snugly without pinching, and is it high enough in back to avoid your having a spare tire above it? Is it anchored below the shoulder blades? Is the band beneath the cups wide enough to help support the bosom and control the diaphragm? There is a bra for every figure type, so find one that fits you perfectly.

**Care and Wear Suggestions.** Avoid any unnecessary pull on elastic panels when putting on garments. Folding over the waistline edge to double thickness before grasping it eases the strain.

Permanently close the bottom hook of a girdle placket to eliminate strain there. Squeeze closed with pliers or tap gently with a hammer.

Mend worn spots immediately. Just before laundering is a good time to examine and repair.

Launder frequently for ease in getting garments clean and for longer wear.

## Good Fit and Wear in Slips

**Fabrics.** The most popular types of fabric are nylon tricot, woven nylon, multifilament acetate, and cotton. Woven Dacron is used to some extent. Silk is used in expensive slips. Nylon and Dacron are long-wearing, quick-drying, and need no ironing;

## What To Ask For

**Brassière.** A garment that lifts and molds the bustline.

**Bandeau.** A brassière that extends less than 3″ below the breasts.

**Padded Brassière.** A bra that has a padding of fabric or foam rubber stitched into it. There are also bras with pockets, into which pads may be inserted to round out the bustline.

**Strapless Brassière.** A bra that has no shoulder straps, but supports the bust with wiring or boning.

**Bra-lette.** A bra, usually strapless, that extends to the hipline and has garters that are usually detachable.

**Girdle.** A hip-confining garment that may be made of alternating panels of rigid fabric and elasticized material. It may have a front, side, or back opening, or no opening at all. If rigid material is used, it is relatively lightweight.

**Roll-on.** A knitted, elastic girdle without opening or boning.

**Panty Girdle.** A girdle with leg sections. It may or may not have a detachable crotch.

**Waistline Girdle.** Any girdle whose upper edge is at the natural waistline.

**High-Waisted Girdle.** A girdle whose upper edge extends 1″ or more above the natural waistline. This is also called a high-top girdle.

**Waistlet.** A waist band, from 3″ to 6″ wide, usually boned and fastened with hooks and/or lacing, to decrease the waist measurement. This is also called a waist nipper or cinch.

**Corset.** A hip-confining garment made principally of rigid fabric. It varies in length and is more disciplinary than a girdle. It has a full-length opening.

**Corselet.** A one-piece foundation garment that combines girdle and bra.

**Garter Belt.** A band from 3″ to 8″ wide with garter attachments. Its upper edge may extend to the natural waistline or above it.

multifilament-acetate slips are quick-drying, but they require ironing.

**Fitting Your Figure.** The type of slip you wear depends on the proportions of your figure. For example, if you usually buy misses-size dresses, 8 to 20, but have a 4″ difference between your bust and hip measurements, a bias-straight slip is recommended. This type has a bias top and a straight skirt. Its construction allows for comfortable, easy movements and it will not ride up on figures of these proportions.

Stocky women (dress sizes 12½ to 26½) and the full-figure women (dress sizes 38 to 52) who have more than a 4″ difference between bust and hip measurements should choose an all-bias slip—a 4-gored slip, for example. Besides allowing ample hip room, many of these 4-gored slips are without a midriff section. This gives a smooth contour and better fit to women of these proportions.

Either the bias-straight or the all-bias slip is satisfactory for the slender woman (junior dresses 7 to 15) who has a small bust and small hips, with little difference in measurement between the two.

**Try on for Size.** Try on the slip at the store. Most slips are sized by bust measurement, a few by dress measurement. One make of slip requires that the bust, waist, hip, and height measurements be taken before the correct size and type can be determined. Slip sizes usually range from 7 to 15 (junior sizes), 12½–26½ (half sizes), 32 to 40 or 8 to 20 (misses sizes), 38 to 44 (women's sizes), and 46 to 52 (extra sizes). Every woman should be able to get a slip fitted to the proportions of her figure.

**The Length Problem.** A solution to the length problem is the proportioned slip. This takes into consideration both figure type and height. Proportioned slips come in three height ranges: 5′ 6″ and over, 5′ 4″ to 5′ 6″, and 5′ 4″ and under. Designs for youthful, average, and heavier types are found in each range.

### Panties

**Fabrics.** The most popular knits of rayon, acetate, and nylon are two-bar tricot and run-resistant circular. Two-bar tricot (mainly of acetate of nylon) is knitted in a way that makes it run-proof. The run-resistant circular knit (mostly of rayon) is constructed to minimize runs and give elasticity. Acetate is quick drying, fairly absorbent; rayon has good absorbency and stretch; nylon is quick drying and retains its shape.

Wool, part-wool, cotton, and Dynel-cotton panties also are available in several knit constructions, most common of which are rib and flat knit. Wool and part-wool panties are warm; Dynel-cotton are warm yet lightweight; cotton panties are absorbent.

**Construction.** Look for good construction when you buy panties. There should be sturdy, neatly finished, lock-stitch seams, bar tacking at points of strain, reinforced or double-fabric crotch, and neat stitching at the waistband and leg openings.

The elastic waistband varies with the style. Panties with a yoke front and elastic back are good for a woman who has large hips but does not take an extra size.

**Sizes.** There are no set standards of sizing. Once you have decided on a particular brand, check with a salesperson for sizing method. Here are some symbols used in sizing: *small*: sizes 4–5, hip measurement 34–36; *medium*: sizes 6–7, hip measurement 38–40; *large*: sizes 8–9, hip measurement 42–44; extra-large: over 44.

### Hosiery Wardrobe

**For Longer Wear.** Follow the old rule: buy three pairs of the same shade and weight at one time. Then, when a run or snag ruins one stocking, you can use its mate with any of the other two matching pairs.

Both denier and gauge are important in selecting hose for your wardrobe. The higher the denier, the thicker the yarn. Therefore, 15 and 12 denier stockings are gossamerlike and cannot be expected to withstand hard wear. For your walking or sports shoes, choose 30 denier.

The higher the gauge, the more threads per inch. Those with more threads promise longer wear. The most popular gauges are 51, 60, and 66.

**Size:** The chart below is a guide for buying stockings according to shoe size if the proportions of your legs are more or less average. Note that it isn't only the length of your foot that matters but the width as well.

| Shoe Size | Below 4½B | 4½B–5½AA | 5½A–6D | 6E–7C | 7D–8B | Above 8B |
|---|---|---|---|---|---|---|
| Hose Size | 8½ | 9 | 9½ | 10 | 10½ | 11 |

**A Word on Care.** You can't expect to get long wear from your stockings unless you give them proper care. Of course, keep them away from rough surfaces, which cause snags.

When you put on your stockings, gather the entire leg portion in both hands, slip your foot into the toe, and draw the stocking over your leg, keeping the seam straight. Reverse the procedure when you take off your stockings.

# SHOPPING FOR MEN'S CLOTHING

## Shopping Points

1. Buy only what he needs and will use at present. Don't overstock.

2. Buy only what he likes and wants. Consider his tastes and preferences.

3. Know in detail all sizes and measurements.

4. Always look on the label for information about shrinkage, color-resistance to washing, size, etc.

5. Be conservative in choosing patterns and colors. Remember he is the one to be pleased. When in doubt, buy solid color or white.

## Men's Underwear

Many fiber combinations are used in men's underwear. You can buy knitted underwear in all-wool, cotton, wool and cotton, or either of these two natural fibers mixed with man-made fibers such as nylon, Orlon, or Dynel. The warmest and heaviest garments are all-wool. Garments which contain a high percentage of synthetic fiber are usually lighter in weight, but have good warmth properties. Knitted underwear containing any of the newer man-made fibers resists shrinking and distorting in laundering and dries quickly. Arm and neck openings in knitted shirts must be roomy to avoid chafing. Nylon-reinforced neck openings keep their shape through many washings. Knitted shorts need no ironing, fit comfortably. Look for heat-resistant elastics.

## A Wife's Guide to Neckties

When buying a man's ties, select colors or combinations of colors that point up the color of his suits and shirts. Prominently striped ties clash with boldly striped shirts or suits; choose solid colors or subdued pattern. Striped and figured ties go best with white and solid-colored shirts.

Clear, bright colors tend to brighten a dark complexion. Soft colors and patterns are best for a man with high coloring. Color of the eyes is a good guide for a man of average coloring. Much white in a tie points up blue eyes; green, bright browns, and yellows flatter brown eyes.

For sportswear, men prefer sport or casual ties. Satins and Jacquard fabrics are best for dress occasions.

It was once considered improper to wear a sport shirt without a tie. But the trend toward more leisurely living has popularized the wearing of sport shirts without ties for most occasions.

Bow ties are entirely suitable for casual and sports wear, and provide a change from the conventional four-in-hand. The best-looking bow ties are tied by the wearer, although the convenience of snap-on bow ties has made them very popular.

The accompanying diagrams show your husband how to achieve a well-tied knot. All pictures show him as he appears to himself in reflection—the right is his right in the mirror.

## Pajamas

Well-cut pajamas give comfort at the shoulders and have no annoying, tentlike bulk at waist. Some pajama coats button down the front; others slip over the head, with the opening large enough for ease in putting on. When you buy pajamas, be sure that waistbands are large enough and that sleeves and legs are long enough. Ill-fitting pajamas can cause loss of sleep.

## MEN'S HAT STYLES

Homburg

Snap Brim

Lightweight

Derby

Tyrolean

Roll Brim

### Windsor Knot

*1. Pull wide end 12" below narrow, around narrow, up through center. 2. Bring behind narrow end. 3. Turn wide end up. 4. Pull down through center; turn across narrow end. 5. Pull up through center. 6. Pull down through knot. Tighten.*

### Four-in-Hand Knot

*1. Cross wide end over narrow. 2. Bring it around and behind narrow end. 3. Turn it around and over front. 4. Continue back, then up through the center. 5. Then pull down carefully through knot. 6. Now tighten and adjust so knot is centered.*

### Bow Knot

*1. Hold left end 1½" below right. 2. Pull left end up through center. 3. Form one section of bow. 4. Holding this section, drape long end over it. 5. Form second section of bow; slide it through loop behind knot. 6. Make the ends look even.*

### Handkerchiefs

Narrow, closely machine-stitched edges have taken the place of hand-rolled hems and make a firm, masculine finish. Colors are available, but better be sure and buy white. Hemstitching may break; plain hems wear longer.

### Men's Socks

All socks are stamped with data about the material used in making them. Socks are made of silk, rayon, nylon, cotton, wool, and various blends of these fibers. Nylon yarn is strongest and longest-wearing, but not so absorbent as rayon and silk. Rayon compares favorably with silk in wearing qualities, but is less expensive. Cotton and wool are soft and absorbent. Nylon blended with wool reduces shrinkage and gives added strength. Look for shrink-resistant finishes in all-wool socks. They withstand repeated launderings without noticeable change in fit. Cotton sweat socks with wool inner soles provide a foot cushion. They are good for active sportswear. Mercerized cotton socks are made of yarns chemically treated to increase the luster and strength of the fiber.

Socks made of Durene, a mercerized, combed-cotton yarn, have especially good service qualities.

English rib hosiery, formerly imported from England, is knit with a 6 x 3 rib. These socks are now being made by domestic firms under license on English machines. They fit well and are comfortable and durable.

Men's hose are available in sizes 9½ to 13; outsizes are carried in some styles. Hosiery and shoe sizes are related. Use the following table to determine what size you should buy.

| Shoe Size | Hosiery |
|-----------|---------|
| 6½–7 | 10 |
| 7½–8 | 10½ |
| 8½–9 | 11 |
| 9½–10 | 11½ |
| 10½–11 | 12 |
| 11½–12 | 13 |

Sizes correspond to the length of the sock measured from toe to heel. If the shoe width is "D" or wider, it is wise to buy socks a size larger than those indicated in the table.

**Stretchable Socks,** made from stretch nylon, stretch to fit all parts of the foot, then spring back to their original size when taken off. They do not bind, bag, nor slide under the heel. Although the initial cost of stretchable socks is more than that of ordinary socks, they usually wear longer than most other types.

Choose socks to fit the wearer's activities and to go with his suits and ties. Stretchable nylon socks are sized in small, medium, and large for comfortable fit.

### Buying Washable Workclothes

Men need work clothes that fit well, allow easy movement, and are durable and washable. Tightness of weave and weight of fabric are helpful guides in determining durability. Labels state whether or not garments are shrink- and color-resistant to washing. Collar size and sleeve length are clearly marked on all shirts; leg length and waist measurement on labels attached to pants. Loose, baggy clothes are uncomfortable and unsightly. If clothes are tight, seams and fabric wear out faster. Choose clothes that are cut full enough to allow for comfortable fit and free movement.

**Shirts.** Sleeves should be full, particularly at the elbow. Seams should be felled and double-stitched, collars well tailored for proper fit and good appearance. Neckbands, like those on dress shirts, should button at the center of the throat. Cuffs should have a double thickness of material and a double row of stitching, with buttons at the wrists. Two patch pockets, with button flaps, are usual. The yoke at the back shoulder should be double and deep. The hem should be narrow and cleanly finished. Colors can match or contrast with pants or breeches. Even the brightest colored and plaid shirts are available in special finishes which allow machine washing and drying. They can usually be worn without having to be ironed.

**Work Pants.** Seams, like those on dress trousers, should be pressed flat, with overcast edges and generous seam allowance. There should be an adjustable outlet at the center back, in case waistband measurement changes. Most pants have a slide-fastener fly closure. If not, buttons should be sewed on firmly and securely, and the buttonholes neatly finished. All pockets and other points of strain should be bartacked at ends or reinforced with metal rivets. For long wear, look for sturdy duck or sailcloth pockets on work pants.

Newer fabrics and finishes are used to produce work pants which can be machine washed and dried and be worn after a minimum of ironing.

**Waist Overalls or Dungarees** are used as trousers or over trousers. They have large patch pockets and loops for tools.

**Bib Overalls** give more protection than waist overalls. Special pockets with pencil and tool compartments usually are sewn on bibs. All have suspenders over the shoulders.

**Overall Coats or Jackets,** designed to be worn with overalls, usually have big patch pockets for carrying tools. Some are lined with cotton or wool-and-cotton flannel, for extra warmth. Look for a label that states the lining is washable. Otherwise, the coat may have to be dry-cleaned.

**Coveralls** are one-piece garments, designed to be worn over other clothing. Many have pockets slit through, so items in pants' pockets can be reached easily.

Denim, standard fabric for overalls, provides long wear and good washability at low cost. Pin stripes, hickory stripes, white drill, and brown duck are more color-resistant than most blue denim.

Shoulder straps on overalls should be adjustable and buckles washable. Points of strain should be reinforced with bar-tacking or metal rivets. Buttons should be rust-resistant.

**Aprons.** Shop aprons, cut in uniform size to fit any figure, usually are made of blue denim or white twill. Average length is 38″. These aprons may have a double pocket at the top and a waist patch pocket. Tape ties at the waist should be reinforced with a double row of stitching.

### Men's Shirts

**The Conventional Business Shirt** is designed to be worn with a tie. Its collar top is stitched to the collarband, and it has one left-side pocket.

Most popular of the cotton-weave shirting materials is broadcloth. Oxford cloth has a softer weave. Madras and chambray, made with colored and white yarns, have stripes, patterns, or other color effects woven into the fabric.

Shirts of nylon or Orlon fibers are easy and inexpensive to care for, wear well, and maintain a neat appearance even after a long day. Open-weave constructions now used enable the fabric to "breathe," eliminating the sealed-in feeling of the first nylon shirts. Acrylic-and-cotton or rayon-and-polyester blends with cotton or rayon are used in dress shirts that exhibit wash-and-wear characteristics when the laundry instructions on the label are followed.

Details vary with the price of the shirt. Buttonholes should be closely stitched and buttons, sewed securely to the shirt in parallel lines of stitching, should slip through easily. Ocean pearl or carefully-selected plastic buttons will last the life of a shirt. If the label is marked "two-ply yarn," two yarns have been twisted together in each thread, thus giving a stronger fabric. Chemical or resin treatment of cotton produces fabrics which are used in shirts requiring minimum care—so-called wash and wear.

**Collars** are manufactured in three general types: one designed to be worn either soft or stiffened with starch; one that depends on mechanical devices to hold it in place; and one, called the fused collar, that is held stiff by its construction. (A fused collar should never be starched.) Individual styles vary in length of point, spread, and height of collarband, depending on the manufacturer.

**Cuffs** may be straight, button style; French cuff, which folds back and fastens with cuff links; or a variation cut like the straight cuff, but fastened with cuff links instead of buttons. Most men prefer either the conventional button cuff or the French cuff.

White shirts are most popular, but colored and striped shirts are acceptable for all but very special occasions.

**Shirt Sizes** are standardized. Labels carry two designations: collar size and sleeve length. Other dimensions are proportionate.

**When Buying Sports Shirts:** There must be plenty of fullness across the shoulders, in the form of gathers or an inverted pleat.

Buy a collar that can be worn open or buttoned up and with a tie.

Sleeves come both full length and above the elbow.

As to chest measurement, buy a shirt loose enough to be comfortable. The best way to get the right size is to try the shirt on. A tight shirt is ugly.

Some manufacturers skimp on length; so buy on the long side.

The shirt that can be worn either tucked in or hanging out is practical.

Some shirts have four pockets. All are usable when the shirt is worn out, only two when it's tucked in.

### When Buying Slacks

Be sure of waist measure. Know whether wearer is "short" or "long" type. Insist on full cut, especially at the top, so there will be room in the seat. Sizes are indefinite, so trying on is the best bet. Fullness is assured by tailored pleats.

Buy on the short side. Slacks dragging about heels are unsightly. They should just touch the instep. Since leg bottoms come unfinished, know the in-seam measurements (from crotch to bottom of cuff), so the store can do the finishing. Seam finishes should be inspected. Many slacks have matching belts and non-skid buckles. Some have two sets of belt loops—one for active sports, one for spectator.

## SOME COLLAR STYLES

*Button-Down Collar*

*Wide-Spread Collar*

*Short-Point Collar*

*Round Collar*

*Conventional Collar*

# CHILDREN'S CLOTHES

Since children's clothing sizes are designed to fit the child's body, not his age, getting the right size is simple. You need only to measure your child and know his weight. You don't have to take him along when you shop.

Underwear sized according to the height-weight system will have labels giving size number and weight or height, or both. Other clothes labels may give additional measurements.

The following charts show "height-weight" sizes, with corresponding measurements for children of normal proportions.

### Infants

| Measure-ments | Size Numbers (Not Age) | | | | | |
|---|---|---|---|---|---|---|
| | 3 mo. | 6 mo. | 12 mo. | 18 mo. | 24 mo. | 36 mo. |
| Height | 24 | 26½ | 29 | 31½ | 34 | 36½ |
| Weight | 13 | 18 | 22 | 25 | 28½ | 32 |

*Note:*

Infants, particularly very young ones, outgrow their clothes rapidly; therefore most people prefer to buy clothes for babies a size or two larger than necessary.

However, in order to serve their purpose, waterproof pants *must* fit.

### Boys and Girls

| Measure-ments | Size Numbers (Not Age) | | | | | |
|---|---|---|---|---|---|---|
| | 2 | 3 | 4 | 5 | 6 | 6x |
| Height | 34 | 37 | 40 | 43 | 46 | 48 |
| Weight | 28½ | 32½ | 37 | 42 | 48 | 52 |
| Chest | 21 | 22 | 23 | 24 | 25 | 25½ |
| Waist | 20½ | 21 | 21½ | 22 | 22½ | 23 |

### Girls Only

| Measure-ments | Size Numbers (Not Age) | | | | | |
|---|---|---|---|---|---|---|
| | 7 | 8 | 9 | 10 | 12 | 14 |
| Height | 50 | 52 | 54 | 56 | 58½ | 61 |
| Weight | 58 | 64 | 72 | 80 | 92 | 104 |
| Chest | 26 | 27 | 28 | 29 | 30½ | 32 |
| Waist | 23 | 23½ | 24 | 24½ | 25½ | 26½ |

### Infants' Wear

What you buy depends on several factors: whether your baby is born in summer or winter; the heating of your house; and, of course, your budget. Buy only a few garments for the first 6 months.

Have at least three sets of clothing: one on the baby, one in the wash, and one in reserve. It is wise to purchase only basic items for the layette. Relatives and friends usually give such things as dainty dresses, sacks, and bootees.

If you want to make some of the baby's clothes, we suggest that you concentrate on dresses and bootees instead of layette essentials. Because of the hand sewing on the former, prices are relatively high; but you will save little by making diapers, shirts, and gowns.

Sleeping bags that bind the neck or tie to the baby's crib are not recommended.

### Boys Only

| Measure-ments | Size Numbers (Not Age) | | | | | |
|---|---|---|---|---|---|---|
| | 7 | 8 | 9 | 10 | 11 | 12 | 13 |
| Height | 48 | 50 | 52 | 54 | 56 | 58 | 59½ |
| Weight | 53 | 58 | 64 | 71 | 78 | 85 | 91 |
| Chest | 25¾ | 26½ | 27¼ | 28 | 28¾ | 29½ | 30½ |
| Waist | 23 | 23½ | 24 | 24½ | 25 | 25½ | 26 |

| Measure-ments | Size Numbers (Not Age) | | | | | |
|---|---|---|---|---|---|---|
| | 14 | 15 | 16 | 17 | 18 | 19 | 20 |
| Height | 61 | 62½ | 64 | 65 | 66 | 67 | 68 |
| Weight | 98 | 105 | 113 | 119 | 124 | 130 | 136 |
| Chest | 31½ | 32¼ | 33 | 33¾ | 34½ | 35¼ | 36 |
| Waist | 26½ | 27 | 27½ | 28 | 28½ | 29 | 29½ |

### Undershirts

| Age | Weight | Length |
|---|---|---|
| 3 mos. | 13 lb. | 10 in. |
| 6 " | 18 " | 11 " |
| 12 " | 22 " | 12 " |
| 18 " | 26 " | 14 " |
| 24 " | 29 " | 16 " |
| 36 " | 32 " | 17 " |

### Underpants

| Size | Weight |
|---|---|
| 1 | Up to 22 lb. |
| 2 | 22-27 lb. |
| 3 | 28-32 lb. |
| 4 | 33-38 lb. |

### Diapers

Diapers are made in attractive designs and pastel shades as well as the usual white. There's a large choice of fabrics and types, too.

Absorbent bird's-eye diapers are available in cotton and cotton-and-rayon combinations. They tend to soften with repeated launderings. Gauze diapers, which are very soft, dry quickly because of their porous construction. Fitted diapers need not be folded and are less bulky under baby's clothes. Highly absorbent cotton-flannel diapers are also available.

Disposable paper diapers and diaper liners are especially useful when baby goes visiting or traveling. The completely disposable diapers are made of a soft fibrous material, an absorbent filler, and a firm backing. Disposable diaper liners are constructed of durable paper and may be used in regular diapers or in plastic or plastic-coated diaper holders. They are fastened to the holder with tabs and snaps.

There are even some diapers that do not require pins. They are fastened by means of cotton tapes that snugly tie together in front and back of the diaper.

## Baby Pants

**Fabrics.** Baby pants are made of a variety of plastics, plastic-coated fabrics, rubber, rubber-coated fabrics, and plastic-and-fabric combinations.

Pants of good-quality plastic will remain soft and pliable through numerous launderings. Plastic pants are stain-resistant and washable. Some are boilable.

Coated-fabric baby pants usually are made of rayon, silk, acetate, or nylon impregnated with plastic or rubber. These are usually strong and durable. Plain rubber and latex are used in baby pants, too; usually perforations allow sufficient ventilation.

Colorful fabric pants made with plastic linings keep baby not only dry but smartly dressed. Rayon and nylon tricot are widely used as outer fabrics on these pants. Some have an outer fabric of seersucker.

**Construction Details.** Most baby pants are finished at the leg and waist openings with narrow rubber or plastic binding, or narrow elastic about a half inch from the edge, which forms a ruffle. Seams are heat-sealed or machine-stitched. Pants may be of the pull-on type, or they may have snaps on each side. A tab above the snaps makes opening easier.

**Sizes.** Care should be taken to buy pants that will be large enough for the child. Baby pants are sized small, medium, large, and extra-large, depending on the size of leg and waist openings and distance from waist to crotch.

### Suggestions for a Basic Layette

#### For Dressing the Baby

2 or 3 wrapping blankets
4 or 5 shirts
3 or 4 nightgowns
4 dozen diapers
2 sweaters (if necessary for warmth)
1 bunting (if necessary for warmth)
Bands are not necessary, as most hospitals furnish them.

#### For Bathing the Baby

Oval tub or bathinette
2 to 4 large, soft bath towels
2 or 3 face towels
3 or 4 washcloths
Do not buy such items as soap, talcum, baby lotion, and oil until your doctor has advised you.

#### For the Baby's Bed

1 bassinet or crib, with mattress to fit
1 water-resistant mattress cover
4 to 6 diaper pads
2 pieces of rubber sheeting
4 cotton sheets
2 lightweight, 1 heavier blankets

### Togs for Toddlers

Clothes for young children should be chosen for good looks, good wear, and ease of care.

**Self-Help Features.** Construction features that help a child dress himself are desirable. Plackets are managed more easily at the front of a dress or suit than at the back or side. Look for those that automatically release caught fabric and therefore won't jam. Buttons should be flat, medium size, and preferably with grooves, to keep little fingers from slipping. Buttonholes should be large enough to insert buttons with ease; snaps, medium size and firmly attached.

**Washables Are a Must.** Choose fabrics that can be washed by machine and don't require extra work.

**Proper Fit Is Important.** Select clothes that fit well and will not hamper the child's activities. Drooping shoulder seams, too-long sleeves, and big necklines can be as uncomfortable and restricting as a garment that is too tight. For longer wear, look for wide hems, fullness at chest and back, and long blouse tails.

### Underwear for Small Fry

When you buy undershirts and underpants for your youngster under 3, be sure the garments have enough stretch to allow for active play and are absorbent enough to keep your child comfortable. Look for garments that will wear well and will hold their shape after many launderings. Cotton knit is a good choice.

**Construction.** There are two popular kinds of cotton knit—flat knit and rib knit. Flat knit is lighter in weight and less expensive than rib knit, which is usually more elastic and durable.

A garment's seams as well as fabric should have give. Look for seams sewed with an overlock stitch, which is elastic enough to stretch with the garment and still keeps threads from breaking.

**Care.** All children's underwear should be processed so that it won't shrink out of fit. Buy garments with brand names known for reliability; read the labels.

### Knit Shirts

Knit shirts are becoming the basis of a young child's wardrobe. Their service qualities should be examined carefully.

**Construction.** Are the seams and buttonholes overcast, to prevent fraying in laundering? Are the fastenings sewed securely? Are there tape reinforcements at the shoulder seams, to prevent sagging? Is the shirt long enough to allow for shrinkage? Do the stripes match at the side, shoulder, and sleeve seams?

**Launderability.** Knit shirts do not require ironing to restore original size and fit. Just shape them while damp, and let them dry on a flat surface.

**Light-Fading.** Because knit shirts are worn in the bright sunlight, they must meet definite requirements for colorfastness to light. Frequently you will notice a tag with a "Durene" trademark. This identifies mercerized-cotton yarns that have been produced under the quality-control requirements of the Durene Association of America. Compared with ordinary cotton knits, Durene fabrics offer uniform quality embodying extra comfort, strength, and service.

### Knit Suits

Knit suits are a must in any child's wardrobe. They are timesavers for busy mothers, because they don't need ironing, and they always look smart. Use the following suggestions as buying guides:

**1.** Examine the fabric closely to be sure of a firm, even knit. A ribbed knit has greater elasticity than a plain knit and provides a smooth fit. Stripes should be matched at side, shoulder, and sleeve seams. Note the elasticity of the garment by carefully easing it between your hands. If the fabric feels tight, it will shrink excessively and lose its shape in washing.

**2.** Inspect the garment thoroughly, and look for construction details that will assure better wear and better fit. Seams and buttonholes should be overcast with close, even stitching, and seams should be wide enough to prevent raveling. Buttonholes reinforced with tape are most satisfactory. Buttons large enough to be handled easily by small fingers are desirable. Buttons sewed to a double thickness of knit fabric or a single thickness backed with tape remain secure under strain. Snap fasteners are managed easily and launder well. Shoulder seams reinforced with tape do not sag and stretch out of shape. Gently stretch cuffs and neckbands, to make sure they will return to their original size during wear. Elastic, which makes a neat, snug-fitting waistband, should be well secured and wide enough to eliminate curling. Watch for extra length at suspender ends, so buttons can be lowered as the child grows. Shirts should be long enough to tuck in and stay down when the child twists and turns. If pants and skirts have deep hems, which can be let down, you are assured of an extra season's wear.

**3.** Read labels carefully, and note all information given by the manufacturer. Washing directions should be followed closely, to prolong the life of the garment. If a suit contains wool, this will be stated on the label or tag. A garment containing combed cotton is soft and wears well. Look for fabric that is color-resistant to repeated washings and wearings.

**4.** Check the size of the garment with the body measurements of your child. These should include chest, arm, neck to waist, and waist to crotch. Allow for shrinkage in selecting the size. However, do not buy a suit that is too large, because it would be too bulky and would hamper the child's activities. Try the suit on the child to be sure it fits properly.

### How to Buy a Snow Suit

In many sections of the country, the snow suit has become a wardrobe necessity for children. Today, you'll find various weights and styles to choose from.

**Fabrics.** Among the most popular choices are cotton suits made of firmly woven gabardine, Byrd Cloth, poplin, and corduroy. Most of them are wind-resistant and water-repellent. Rayons and acetates are used chiefly in the one-piece, or pram-type, suits. Because of the high price of new wool, its use is greatly restricted; however, reprocessed wool makes very satisfactory snow suits.

Part- or all-nylon suits are very serviceable because they are highly resistant to wear. The all-nylon ones (with nylon linings and interlinings) can be washed quickly and easily.

Lightweight shell fabrics usually are lined with wool, alpaca pile, or cotton flannel quilted to wool batting. Battings made of acetate, Dacron, and Fiberglas fibers have excellent insulating properties.

Suits treated with durable water-repellents, which withstand repeated washings and dry cleanings, usually cost slightly more than those with nondurable finishes; however, the former eliminate the bother and expense of reprocessing after each cleaning.

**Styles.** One-piece suits are rarely made in sizes larger than 3 years. They have conveniently placed zippers, so that the task of dressing a toddler is made easier for Mother and less annoying for Baby. These zippers may run from neck to ankle, from ankle to hip, or across the shoulders and down the sides to the ankle cuffs.

Two-piece suits, generally preferred for older children, come with trouser-type or knit-cuff pants. The former may have elastic bands or knit cuffs fastened inside the legs near the ankles. These help keep out wind and snow and allow the trousers to hang straight and free at the bottom. Some trousers have bib tops front and back for added protection, and reinforced knees for longer wear. Most two-piece suits have zipper openings at the ankles, so that the pants can be put on over shoes or rubbers. Boys' suits are available with zipper fly fronts.

Most jackets have elasticized waistbands, which fit snugly. Sleeves may have knit cuffs, elastic inserted in the sleeve linings, or knit cuffs sewed to the linings.

You'll find separate or detachable hoods on most outfits, though some boys' suits come with peaked caps. Mouton collars provide extra warmth around the neck.

**Fit.** Most suits are sized by number according to age, though some manufacturers use the United States Government standards for height and weight.

A suit should fit loosely enough to accommodate sweaters and bulky winter clothing, yet it shouldn't be droopy. An improperly fitted suit is uncomfortable and restricts the child's action.

**Care.** To keep a snow suit looking good, brush and air it frequently. Hang it up between wearings. Remember that spots and stains are easier to remove when fresh. Follow the manufacturer's directions for cleaning. All clothing should be clean when stored. If the suit contains wool, be sure to protect it from moths.

### Choosing Your Children's Socks

Important things to consider when buying socks for your children:

**Size.** Remember, a child's foot grows quickly. Don't automatically buy the size sock you bought last time, for a sock, like a shoe, affects the healthy growth of a young foot. Whenever there has been a change in shoe size, there should be an equivalent change in sock size.

**Fabric.** Cotton socks should be closely knitted and made of combed mercerized cotton.

Stretch nylon socks should be sized small, medium, or large.

**Heel, Toe, and Sole.** These parts should be of heavier fabric than the rest. Check the sock by holding it up to a strong light; reinforcement should extend above the counter (back) of a low shoe. There should be no loose ends of yarn to catch on the foot. You'll get added wear from four- or six-ply yarn or nylon reinforcement.

**Color.** If the label or tag says "colorfast" or "vat-dyed," the sock will probably cost a little more; but it will look better longer, with no excessive fading or bleeding.

**Top.** If the top of the sock is elasticized or ribbed, it should have plenty of give. Always make certain the top of the sock is not skimpy; otherwise it will be uncomfortable and will wear out sooner.

### Shoes for Young People

**A Child's Shoe Must Fit.** A young child's feet grow so rapidly that his shoes rarely wear out. But the exact way in which his shoes are wearing provides a clue as to whether or not they're still the right size. If the soles are curled at the tip, the chances are the shoes are getting too short. If the edges of the soles look as though they're taking a special beating, the shoes are probably too narrow. Excessive wear on the instep-side edge of the heel suggests an ankle weakness. And worn linings are an indication that the shoes are too small. When any of these signs are found on a pair of shoes, the shoes must, for the child's foot health, be discarded. Never let a child continue to wear shoes he's outgrown, and never hand shoes down from one child to another.

**When New Shoes Are Required,** don't shop without your child if you can possibly help it. (If the youngster cannot accompany you, take along a tracing of his feet. Have foot measurements taken properly. The Brannock device measures the length of the arch from ball of foot to heel. If a measuring stick is used, be sure the child stands up on it to apply proper pressure. The shoe should extend about half an inch beyond the big toe. To test roominess of vamp, lift leather between thumb and forefinger; there should be enough to form a small wrinkle. To make sure the heel fits snugly and clears the ankle-bone, run your finger around the top back of the heel line.

**Don't Try to Save Your Pennies on Children's Shoes.** Avoid extra-heavy shoes, for they can hurt delicate young feet. And don't buy orthopedic shoes or shoes with built-in corrective devices, except on medical advice. Keep a careful check on your child's socks, too, making sure they're large enough. Strict attention to these details will promote the lifelong health of your child's feet.

#### What Size Is a Child's Shoe?

| Age | Sock Size | Shoe Size | Check |
|---|---|---|---|
| 1 year and under | 5 to 5½ | 0 to 5 | Every 4–8 weeks |
| 1 to 3 | 6 to 6½ | 5½ to 8 | Every 4–8 weeks |
| 4 to 5 | 7 to 7½ | 8½ to 11 | Every 4–8 weeks |
| 5 to 7 | 8 to 8½ | 11½ to 13½ 1 to 2 | Every 8–12 weeks |
| 7 to 14 | 9 to 10½ | 2½ to 9 | Every 12 to 16 weeks |

# LUGGAGE AND PACKING

Luggage is an important long-term investment, and should be considered carefully. Buy from a good dealer who carries well-known brands. So-called "bargain luggage"—the kind sold at a half or a third off—can be a dubious risk. Buy enough luggage to fill your needs. Nothing ruins a suitcase faster than overpacking. It is an unnecessary strain on the seams. Your suitcase should close easily. If you have to sit on the lid in order to close the catches, it is too full.

There are many different kinds of luggage materials. Those described below are most commonly used today.

**Leather:** Most leather luggage comes from cowhide, which, because of its thickness, is split or layered. The top layer is called "top grain," and from this we get our finest luggage. It takes a finer finish, wears better, and keeps its smooth appearance longer than "split cowhide," which comes from the second or third layer. Don't feel that smooth leather is not fine leather just because the finish is not uniform. The lives that animals lead leave markings on their hides that are characteristics, not defects.

Leather is not a good choice for use in the tropics, not only because of moisture there, but also because ants will eat it. In dry climates, leather loses its natural oil and dries out unless the oil is replaced. So, to get good wear and long life from leather luggage, you must preserve its richness and beauty by frequent saddle soapings and the use of a leather preserver or neutral wax.

Rawhide is not tanned, but natural oils and hairs are removed. It is a popular material for luggage. This long-wearing hide is used most frequently in its natural white or ivory shade. Because of its light color, rawhide soils quickly but is easily cleaned with a damp sponge. Imbedded stains respond to treatment that sounds drastic but isn't: Use a household cleanser or fine steel wool to erase the stains.

**Canvas:** It's our guess that few people recognize canvas-covered luggage when they buy it. There is something about the term "canvas" that sounds unglamorous. Actually, clear-coated canvas is the most popular luggage today. It comes in all price ranges; it is smart in appearance, strong, lightweight, washable, gay-looking. Unlike leather, which suffers in dry or damp climates, canvas-covered luggage is suitable for world-wide use.

**Plastic:** The plastics used in covering luggage today are resistant to scuffs and mars and stand a lot of roughing. The cases travel well in any climate. Cleaning is simple—wiping with a damp cloth is all that's necessary.

**Aluminum:** Aluminum is very lightweight, distinctive-looking, and simple to keep clean. It should not be banged, however, because dents disfigure it and may affect proper closing.

**Nylon:** For weight and durability, nylon-covered luggage compares well with canvas-covered pieces. Nylon coverings are colorful and easy to clean. A damp cloth and a little suds refreshen the fabric.

**Be Conscious of Details.** No matter what type of luggage you buy, look for marks of good workmanship and quality. Expect such things as metal studs to protect the bottom of the case, well-sewn linings with at least 3 pockets. The hardware should be well aligned, easy to open and close. Obviously, the frame should be substantial. A wood-veneer box or metal frame is a mark of quality, but cardboard is often used in low-priced luggage.

Set your sights on matching or co-ordinated luggage, even though you buy a piece or two at a time. Luggage is sold in open-stock patterns, so you can start with a color scheme and add more pieces from time to time. Basic pieces fill various travel needs:

1. **Hatbox.**

2. **The Smaller 21″ Week-End Case** for women holds a reasonable, small wardrobe for the average 4-day trip. The roomier 26″ Pullman case for longer trips makes a good companion piece in matching color.

3. **Lady's Wardrobe Case** contains large hanger section, as well as roomy section for flat packing.

4. **Hat-and-Shoe Case,** designed to carry 4 or 5 pairs of shoes and a few extra hats.

5. **Train Case**—all you need for overnight trips. This small, deep, easy-to-carry case holds cosmetics, slippers, fresh lingerie, etc.

6. **Man's Two-Suiter,** with hanger section to keep suits from wrinkling, plus space for other clothing essentials.

7. **Attaché Case,** excellent for men's overnight business trips, has an expandable file for papers and room for clothing essentials.

8. **Traveling Garment Bag,** useful for either men or women. Clothes do not need to be folded; they are just hung in the bag.

## Keep Leather in Good Condition

*Don't* store it in a damp basement. Leather absorbs moisture, may mildew.

*Don't* store it in a very warm attic. Leather dries out and cracks in hot air.

*Don't* overpack. Luggage will not retain its shape unless you respect the capacity of each piece.

*Do* nourish the leather regularly with saddle soap, or with a leather cleaner and conditioner. As a general rule, saddle soap is best for black and tan hides, rawhide, and pigskin, and a leather conditioner is best for crocodile, lizard, patent leather, and moroccos.

*Do* wash off, with soap and warm water, the first signs of mildew, or simply wipe it off with a moist cloth. Dry well.

*Do* watch out for small gouges and tears. If the damage is not too deep, the torn leather can be pasted down and polished.

*Do* keep your luggage in repair by turning it over to a reliable luggage shop when bindings and linings become torn.

### Packing Tricks

Packing for a trip, whether long or short, has always been an onerous task. Here are a few hints to make the chore easier and the results better.

**The Irreducible Minimum.** Keep your luggage to the irreducible minimum. Resist the temptation to take your entire wardrobe. Choose clothes that will fit the occasion (don't forget matching belts!), and group them for travel, sports, dress, etc. Lingerie comes next; then accessories.

**Two Bags Are Better Than One.** If you can take a medium-size and a small bag rather than one large one, by all means do. All the heavy, hard-to-pack articles like shoes, jewelry boxes, tennis balls, and hangers can go into the small bag, leaving the other for clothes, so they lie flat and smooth. If one bag has

to do, pack the flat articles first, and cover them with a piece of cardboard the size of the suitcase. Arrange other articles on top. Whatever you do, try not to overcrowd.

**Tissue Combats Wrinkles.** Whether you are packing a dress, suit, or blouse, the fundamentals of using tissue in folding clothes are the same. In folding a dress, for example, place it front down on the bed and spread tissue over the back of the skirt and the upper part of the dress. Then fold sleeves and skirt lengthwise over the tissue, smoothing out wrinkles. Finally, fold the dress in halves or thirds to fit your bag. Use tissue, also, to wrap shoes (if you don't have shoe mittens), bottles, and cosmetic jars and to stuff hats to keep their shape.

**Essential Extras.** The wise traveler keeps a list of the little things that are so easy to forget: clothes hangers, shoe polish, pins, manicure essentials, stationery, stamps, pen, and pencil. Be prepared for broken shoulder straps and snags in stockings. You'll also be glad to have a small container of soapflakes or a bar of soap and a bit of cleaning fluid, in case you smear lipstick or get a grease spot; and for play shoes that soon become dingy, a small bottle of general household cleaner—the kind you use at home for walls and woodwork.

**Press As You Unpack.** Even with careful packing, the sooner you get your clothes out of the bags and onto hangers, the better they will look. While crease-resistant fabrics take a trip very well, others need pressing. If you own a traveling iron, take it with you; also, a treated pressing cloth. As each garment is pressed, place it on a hanger, centering shoulders so that it hangs straight. Button as many buttons as may be necessary to keep it from sagging, and close the slide fastener.

## HOW TO PACK A SUIT JACKET

*Men who travel fold their suit jackets in a deft way that women might borrow. No tissue is needed. Start by slipping hands into suit shoulder, to support jacket, as shown.*

*Grasp end of shoulder pads, pull toward you, turning suit shoulders inside out. Support shoulders in hands and bring them together. Hold both in right hand as you turn up collar.*

*Hold suit shoulders with right hand; lay jacket on flat surface. Straighten side seams; make parallel. Jacket is now inside out. Line up lapels, smooth sleeves. Put in suitcase.*

# CLOTHES STORAGE

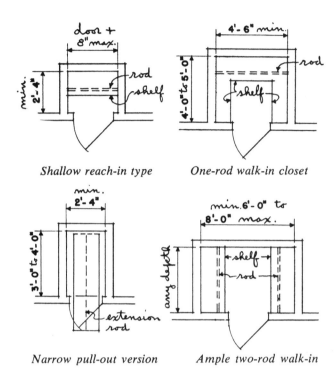

*Shallow reach-in type*          *One-rod walk-in closet*

*Narrow pull-out version*          *Ample two-rod walk-in*

The first step in reorganizing a closet is to find out just how much cubic space you have to work with. Measure the height of your existing shelves, the width, depth, and height of the closet, the width and height of your door. Use these measurements in fitting equipment. "Dead" unreachable spots should be avoided by proper arrangement of hanging rods, hooks, and shelves. Wide, shallow, narrow, or deep: convenience depends on how space is adapted to contents.

A closet hang rod that is too high will be difficult to reach and wasteful of space. If too low, hems drag on the floor. If you want your closets to have a neat and convenient arrangement, place the rods to conform to these simple rules: For evening dresses, men's overcoats, and garment bags, the rod should be 6' above the floor. Dresses and short coats require a 5' 3" rod. Skirts, men's suits, and children's clothes can hang from a 3' 9" rod. Toddlers will learn to store their own clothes if the rod is 2' 6" above the closet floor. For more storage space, combine two or more hang rods of different heights in each closet. Use upper space for shelving or bin-type storage.

Crowding damages clothes. Pushing and pulling to extricate one garment from a hard-to-reach spot means strain and wrinkles for all the others. Plan space in order to use every bit of it, but let clothes hang free and accessible, with air around them. If the closet isn't big enough, provide auxiliary storage.

Closet accessories are so ingeniously and attractively designed today that your closets can look as delightful as the rest of your home, and harmonize perfectly with the rooms they adjoin.

Garment bags—particularly transparent plastic ones—are the answer to a multitude of problems. Clothes are kept dust- and wrinkle-free, and you can always reach them. Transparent-plastic hatboxes come in several sizes. Boxes that fold when not in use are important spacesavers. When putting hats away, pack tissue in the crown and around the edges to prevent crushing or sliding. Drawer-like boxes are convenient for stockings, gloves, odds and ends.

Skirt-and-blouse or shirt hangers that hold several garments on one hook also save closet space. Three-row metal shoe racks keep shoes off the floor in orderly rows. A trouser valet holds several pairs of slacks or trousers flat against the wall or door. A specially designed hanger holds a fur scarf securely.

Most closets are poorly lighted, if at all. If there's no illumination whatsoever, have your electrician give you an estimate on installing fixtures. Where you install a fixture makes a great difference. The best place is on the inside door trim, near the center of the door. A ceiling light is bad, because it casts dark shadows under the shelves and in corners. Make sure you use an adequate bulb—60 to 100 watts, or, for a large closet, 150 watts. Light-color walls reflect light, make the closet bright as well as efficient.

*Mr. & Mrs. Closet. Strict segregation maintains neatness and harmony and prevents closet quarrels.*

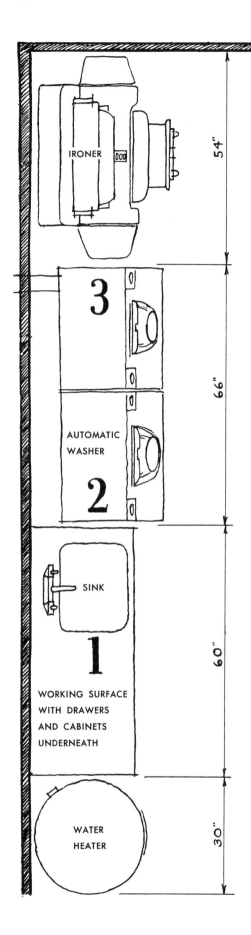

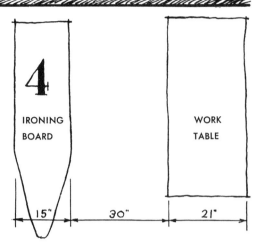

## A SIMPLE AND EFFICIENT LAYOUT PLAN FOR YOUR LAUNDRY

Even though it may be some years before you expect to be able to purchase all the equipment needed for a completely mechanized, modern laundry, you should arrange what you now have in a space large enough to allow for additions.

The four basic work areas that make up an efficient laundry are:

1. The preparation center
2. The washing center
3. The drying center
4. The finishing center

Their separate functions are described on the next page.

This may seem like a lot of space to devote to the job of washing and ironing the family clothes, but an efficient laundry may actually take up very little room. If you are really cramped for space, consider combining your laundry with one or more other house operations. For instance, the preparation center may double as a breakfast bar, or it may be your food preparation center during meal time if your laundry is located in your kitchen. Or put your home freezer in your laundry room and keep wrappings, labels, and other freezer supplies there, too.

If possible, have your sewing center near your laundry so clothes may be repaired promptly. (You are most likely to notice small tears, missing buttons, etc., when you are looking for stains or sorting clothes to go into the washer.)

The four basic areas of the laundry should be arranged in such a manner as to assure a smooth flow of work. In a long narrow room, the centers may be located in logical sequence along one wall. In a smaller but wider room, try an L- or U-shaped arrangement.

# A Guide to Home Laundering and Dry-Cleaning

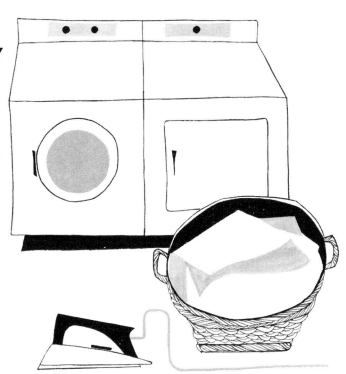

Not too many years ago, the job of washing, drying, and ironing the family laundry was a dreaded chore. Automatic laundries have replaced the washboard, and the concept of "washday" is now practically obsolete, but better planning and new developments can improve your laundry routine and cut down the number of hours devoted to what used to be a chore.

### Locating the Laundry

No longer is it accepted practice to place the laundry in the basement: in homes without a first-floor utility room, it may be near the kitchen, if not an actual part of the kitchen. A small space—about 9' x 9'—is sufficient. (Of course, a de luxe laundry with elaborate facilities will take more space.) Try to arrange essential equipment as conveniently and compactly as is practical. The ironing board may be used for folding sheets and towels, the top of the dryer for dampening, and a folding basket on wheels may serve as a temporary hamper for soiled clothes.

Home economists have divided work in the laundry into four major tasks—preparation, washing, drying, and finishing—and operations follow in the sequence given. For maximum efficiency and convenience, place equipment in order.

**1. Preparation Center:** Sorting and mending is done; stains are removed. Ample counter or table space with a deep-bowl sink or tub is desirable. Storage space for soaps, starches, bluings, etc.

**2. Washing Center:** Clothes washer.

**3. Drying Center:** Automatic clothes dryer. (In homes without a dryer, line space in the basement or outdoors is necessary.)

**4. Finishing Center:** Clothes are sprinkled and ironed here. Equipment includes ironing board, a hand iron and possibly an automatic ironer.

The laundry must be located near a water supply line. If the hot water supply is insufficient, a separate water heater may be needed. Electric washers and dryers should be connected to individual outlets served by individual circuits. The dryer may require installation of a vent pipe to the outside of the house.

### Equipping the Laundry

**What Kind of Washer?** The field of modern washers now offers a wide choice both of brands and types of machine. The range is from the well-known portable washers with spinner or wringer to the fully automatic, plumbed-in machine that fills, washes, rinses, and empties without attention. In between these types are washers that vary in their degree of automatic operation, like the washer with a spin-rinse, or the washers which work automatically for the most part but which do not have to be plumbed in. Most of these, automatic or not, wash by means of an agita-

*Combination washer-dryer.*

tor in the center of the tub. But there are automatic washers in which the clothes are tumbled in a revolving cylinder. Either type of washer permits you to wash clothes clean without concern about their wearing out. Very hot water, a good soap or detergent, and a willingness to follow the manufacturer's directions are the simple, basic requirements for getting the everyday family wash clean in any good washer. However, with a tumbler washer, you must use a soap or detergent suited to the tumbling principle. It cannot be one that quickly develops very heavy suds, because the washer will oversuds before you have added enough cleanser to do a good washing job. In the agitator-type washer (or a modified agitator type, as some of them are called), there is more leeway in types of soap or detergent. A tumbler washer is undoubtedly gentler and causes less strain on fragile things than other types. However, if you have lots of sturdy cottons to wash (usually families with children do), or work clothes or other articles in which soil is likely to be heavy or ground in, the agitator-type washer might be the wiser choice. A study of your own washbasket will tell you.

There is quite a difference in the amount of water various washers require. Some use as much as fifty gallons or more, but even those most sparing of water require at least twenty-eight or thirty gallons each time you wash eight or nine pounds of clothes and use the full rinsing cycle. This need not be all hot water by any means. Even when you wash cottons, for which all-hot water is desirable, rinses on automatic washers usually mix both hot and cold to give warm water. Special water-saving features on certain washers are of value. One type supplies just the right amount for small or medium loads when you do not have enough pieces to fill the washer. In another, wash water is reserved for a second use.

Some automatic washers have two completely automatic cycles, one for washing the regular family wash, and the second cycle for "delicate fabrics" or a small, lightly soiled load. This cycle shortens wash, rinse, and spin periods; saves water, detergent and time.

**Apartment-Size Washing Machines.** Small kitchens in modern apartments do not allow much space for a washing machine. To solve this problem, manufacturers have designed a semiautomatic washer which occupies less space and is lighter than conventional machines. Casters permit it to be rolled into a corner when not in use.

A conventional machine may be used in an apartment if sufficient space is available. It need not be installed; a temporary connection which attaches to a standard faucet is available.

If you are buying your first washer, go around to your dealers and see what they have to offer. You are the only one who can measure cost against need and convenience.

### When You Use the Washer:

1. If your clothes don't come out clean, don't jump to the conclusion that the washer isn't working right and frantically call the dealer; first explore a number of other possibilities.

Are you using a suitable soap or detergent? Some of the new washday detergents make such heavy suds that you can't add enough detergent to do a good washing job (especially true of the tumbling-cylinder washers, but true also of some of the agitator automatics). A low-sudsing detergent, or a washday soap plus water softener, does a fine job.

Do you stuff too many clothes in the washer at one time? Overloading a washer is hard on the motor and doesn't give the wash water a chance to flush thoroughly through the clothes.

Is the water hot enough? Soiled cottons won't come clean with lukewarm water. Use water of at least 140° F.

*Automatic washer with spinner basket.*

2. If you've accidentally dumped in too much soap or detergent and your washer won't spin when it should, you have oversudsed it. Stop the washer and throw in cold water to quench the foam. Repeat the cold-water treatment until you can spin the water out.

3. If the washer thumps around while it is spinning out water, the load is unbalanced, with more weight in some places than in others. Many washers shut themselves off when this happens. If yours doesn't, stop it and redistribute the clothes.

### The Dryer

A clothes dryer looks much like an automatic washer. Inside the cabinet is an electric-motor-driven metal drum. Clothes inside this drum are tumbled around in heated air until they become dry. The air is heated either by gas or electricity. Electric dryers operate on heavy-duty, 230-volt wiring, as an electric range does. If you do not already have this type of wiring, you may find installation expensive. Similarly, a gas dryer requires gas piping. If you do not have it, investigate the installation costs and compare them with wiring costs.

There are 110-volt dryers on the market, but don't buy one blindly. It may require the installation of a 110-volt branch circuit. And you cannot expect it to dry clothes as quickly as a gas dryer or an electric dryer operating on 230 volts.

An electric dryer uses about 2½ to 4 kilowatt-hours per load of clothes. A gas dryer requires from 15 to 25 cubic feet of manufactured gas, or half that amount of natural gas. The figures vary according to the amount of moisture in the clothes.

Most dryers have a method of venting moisture to the outdoors. In some models, venting facilities are built into the dryer; in others, attachments must be purchased as accessories.

Usually a screen is used to catch the lint as air leaves the dryer. Lint screens must be cleaned frequently. Otherwise, lint may cause trouble.

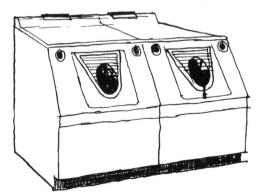

*Laundry Twins: Tumbler washer and matching dryer.*

*Agitator washer and matching dryer.*

**When You Use the Dryer:** If your dryer throws off so much moisture that walls and windows in the rooms are constantly steamed up, you should improve the room's air circulation.

A new dryer owner is always startled by the amount of lint that collects in the lint trap with every load. This is a normal result of drying clothes by any method; but in outdoor drying, the lint blows away and you don't see it. The only thing you need be concerned about is emptying the trap *after each use*. Occasionally, you'll have to brush out the air-intake passage and the floor of the cabinet. Caution: If lint is allowed to accumulate in any part of the dryer, it can cause overheating.

**The Combination Washer-Dryer** is the newest development in automatic home laundering equipment. This appliance is particularly suited to homes where floor space is limited and both appliances are desired. The washer-dryer may be used as a combination—clothes come out automatically washed and dried, ready for ironing or storing—or separately as either a washer or a dryer.

When using this appliance, it is necessary to sort clothing and linens according to drying time as well as washability. Since the washer-dryer is completely automatic, it is easier to wash smaller loads more frequently than to allow laundry to accumulate.

There's danger in overdrying clothes. Letting them tumble around in hot air after they are dry adds hard-to-remove wrinkles and can cause serious shrinkage. But if you use the right technique, you'll have no reason to overdry and shrink clothes; and you can eliminate at least a third of your ironing, because sheets, work clothes, pajamas, shorts, etc., will dry soft and almost wrinkle-free.

You use the same washer and dry the same clothes week after week, so experiment until you find out how long it takes to dry clothes the way you want them. For example, 20 minutes may damp-dry your sheets just right for pressing; but if you don't intend to iron the sheets, the drying time will be closer to 30 minutes. There's a drying-time chart in your dryer's instruction book; use it as a guide to start you off.

It's easy to use your dryer efficiently. When you wash several loads of clothes on one day, sort your items into loads that can be dried together. Your first load should be the one that takes the least drying time, so your dryer will be free when the next batch is ready to be dried. Keep heavy Turkish towels until last, for they take longest to dry. If you wash clothes every day or so, your problem will be one of drying a mixed load. In such a load you will have some items that you will want to remove while they're slightly damp for ironing, some pieces that will dry quickly, and some heavy terry towels or bath mats that will take longer to dry. Set your time dial for the lightest-weight fabrics, and remove these first. Then continue to reset the time dial as needed until the load is completed. You'll find it handy to put small items like socks, gloves, etc., in a small mesh bag; you save time by keeping them all together.

A good way to guard against shrinkage of T shirts and knit underwear is to dry them in the same load as Turkish towels, which keep knit things from getting too dry. After about 20 minutes, the knit pieces can be removed, folded, and placed on top of the dryer; there they can finish drying while the towels continue to tumble.

### Other Laundry Equipment

A washer, a dryer, and an electric ironer represent the three major investments in furnishing a home laundry. Here is a list of other equipment and supplies, some essential, some optional. Don't skimp. A well-equipped laundry will save time and make the job of washing and ironing clothes much easier.

Combination steam-dry iron
Adjustable ironing board
Comfortable chair
Sleeve board
Ironing-board pad and covers
Clothes hamper
Laundry cart
Pressing cloth (treated)
Sprinkling device
Cord control for iron
Curtain stretcher
Drying rack
Sweater drying forms and wool-sock drying forms
Clothes hangers
Sponge for moistening fabric
Mixing bowls; measuring cups and spoons
Mending tape for quick repairs
Soaps, detergents, water softener, bluing, starch, bleach
Clothespins, clothesline

### Soap or Soapless Detergent?

Washing clothes is a complicated job because so many things enter into the picture. Fabrics require different treatment in washing; there are many different types of soil; water varies in the amount of hardness it contains—and all these things must be taken into account when you choose laundry supplies.

The chart shown below classifies laundry soaps and other detergents by types and uses for the express purpose of helping you choose the right product for your laundry, whatever you may be washing. Con-

## SOAPS AND OTHER DETERGENTS

**Mild Soaps:** Suitable for washing, by hand, nylon hosiery, lingerie of all kinds, baby clothes, wool, silk, Dacron, or Orlon in soft water or water that is only slightly hard. Can also be used in washers for fabrics that need special care. For best results in hard water, add water conditioner or softener to basin or washer before adding soap.

**Regular Soaps:** Unexcelled for heavy-duty washing of clothes with ground-in dirt in soft or conditioned water. Excellent for all fabrics with the exception of silk or wool, whose color they may affect. These soaps dissolve less readily than mild soaps, so they are better suited to use in washer than in basin or tub.

**Mild Synthetics:** Like mild soaps, these mild synthetics are excellent for washing fine fabrics, particularly by hand. (Most of them produce too many suds to be effective in washers.) Their outstanding advantage is that they work as well in hard as in soft water without the addition of any other product. They are particularly good for colored fabrics.

**Regular Synthetics:** These newer detergents were developed to meet the need for a heavy-duty product that could be used alone in hard water, in basin, tub, or washer. Like regular soaps, they can be used for all kinds of fabrics, but they are a little more likely to fade delicate colors than the mild detergents. Some produce fewer suds and so are better for certain types of washers.

**Water Conditioners:** These products work quickly and leave the water clear, thus preventing the formation of curds and soap scum on clothes.

**Water Softeners** aid in water softening, but are less effective than water conditioners. They can be used very satisfactorily where the water is only slightly hard, but for very hard water, a water conditioner is well worth the added cost.

fusion sometimes arises from misuse of the word detergent, which actually means a cleansing agent and of course includes soap.

While soaps and synthetics can be used for the same general purposes, there is one outstanding difference in the way they are used. A synthetic is unaffected by hard water (or salt or cold water, for that matter), whereas soap, because of its chemical nature, is most effective in warm or hot, soft water.

### How to Bleach

In laundering normally soiled family wash, you can't get by for long without bleaching. When clothes are new, they stay white and fresh through quite a number of *good* launderings. Eventually, however, soil and yellowing does build up. Then bleaching is necessary.

Chlorine bleach, long the routine product for stain removal and whitening, comes not only as a liquid but also as a powder. Powdered bleaches that do not contain chlorine come under the heading of fine-fabric bleaches; the bleaching power is perborate.

When you shop for bleaches, know what you are buying. Read the label—it will give you the clue to whether you are buying chlorine or perborate, and it will tell you when and where to use the bleach and in what quantity.

The chlorine bleach you buy at the grocer's is effective in whitening soiled clothes and linens and removing stains, but it can be damaging to fabrics when it is improperly used. To determine the right quantity of liquid bleach, use it in proportion to the amount of water your washer holds. Your washer's instruction booklet should tell you how much water is used during the wash period, but if it doesn't follow this guide: Top-opening automatic washers average 12 to 16 gallons of water; front-opening ones, about 8 gallons of water; wringer or spinner washers, 18 to 20 gallons.

One tablespoonful of liquid chlorine bleach to a gallon of water is a good proportion for occasional bleaching; for weekly bleaching, use half that amount.

With powdered chlorine bleach, the directions on the label usually suggest ¼ to ½ cup of bleach for top-opening automatic washers, ⅛ cup for front-opening washers. With wringer or spinner washers, use ½ cup of bleach.

When using a powdered chlorine bleach, mix it with the water and suds before adding the clothes. If you use a spinner or a wringer washer, do a *thorough* job of rinsing.

Labels on some garments may warn you not to use a chlorine bleach, even though the fabric is cot-ton. The fabric has probably been treated with a chemical that holds chlorine. If you ignore the warning, the fabric may become badly discolored and, in some cases, permanently affected. If you do make a mistake and use chlorine, here's the remedy: Soak the garment in a solution of sodium sulfite and warm water (1 teaspoonful of sulfite to each gallon of water). Rinse well.

### Bluing the Wash

Using bluing in the wash makes clean white clothes appear whiter by giving them a slight bluish cast. It can be used on all white clothes, but it is particularly helpful in keeping silk and wool white, for these cannot be bleached.

There are two methods of bluing in a nonautomatic washer. One is to use a soapflake-bluing combination or a soapless cleaner containing bluing. Both are used with some extra soap in the wash water. The other is to add a few drops of liquid bluing to the last rinse water. Follow the manufacturer's directions carefully for the amount to use. To avoid streaking, be sure to mix the bluing and water thoroughly before adding the clothes. If you use a prepared starch containing bluing, you can blue the pieces you are starching individually.

In an automatic washer, use a soapflake or soapless-cleaner type of bluing. Follow the manufacturer's directions for amount.

### How to Starch

Many articles of clothing look better when they have been given a finish of starch. Do this right in the washing machine. For a full load of clothing, use 6 tablespoonfuls starch to 4 cupfuls water, make according to the directions on the package. Add the starch solution to the final rinse water, and run the washer for 3 or 4 minutes. Remove water by wringer or spinner basket.

Starching in an automatic washer is not usually recommended. However, follow the directions provided by the manufacturer of your machine.

When starched garments do not take on the proper crispness, it may be that they were not wrung sufficiently before starching and the water diluted the starch mixture. Also, the clothes may have been dried in a strong wind or in a damp atmosphere. In very humid or freezing weather, hang starched garments indoors.

White starch often shows on dark-colored garments. Use bluing to tint the starch for dark blue or black and strong, clear tea to tint starch for brown. Commercial tints also may be used.

Men's shirts are starched more frequently than any other garment in the home laundry. Here is a simple way to handle them. For all-over starching, use the "starch rinse" described above, or dip in a light starching solution. Then starch the colors, cuffs, and buttonhole bands in a thicker, hot-starch solution— or in a cold-starch solution, if desired. The trick is to gather together the buttonhole band, the collar, and the button band as if you were pleating them. Hold tightly and dip in the starch. Squeeze in the starch, squeeze out the excess, and dip again. Repeat several times before finally squeezing out the starch and slapping the material between your palms. Hang up and dry completely; then sprinkle the shirts well, and let them season about an hour before ironing.

If starch sticks to your iron, you may have the fabric too wet or you may not have worked the starch into the fabric properly. You can buy a special ironing aid to add to a starch solution—a form of wax that prevents starch from sticking to the iron.

Slightly different in nature from ordinary starch is a new type of liquid-plastic starch. Unlike the "permanent" plastic kind, it comes out with each washing. It can be used on silks, rayons, and nylons where ordinary starch isn't always effective. On table linens, it gives body without harshness and washes out almost all stains, including lipstick and grease.

### For Easier Laundering

**Wash Often.** Whether or not you have a washing machine, wash several times a week. It lightens the work; there is more likely to be enough hot water to last to the end of the job and less hurry in the general handling of the clothes. Divide your wash logically— bath towels and bedclothes one day; dish towels, table linen, and clothing another; fussier things a day to themselves. Such management will prevent frazzled nerves and a completely upset household.

Freedom isn't the only gain derived from washing often. There are other advantages: (1) You can really save, especially in children's clothes, when buying. Junior may need only two pairs of size 2 pajamas if they can be back on the shelf clean the same day they're washed. (2) Perspiration stains and other types of soil oxidize and become more difficult to remove the longer they remain on garments. So clothes come clean more easily when they are washed the day after they are worn. (3) There need never be a crisis in which there are no clean bedclothes for a sick child, no dry diapers for an infant.

**Start by Sorting.** Sort clothes according to soil. Divide into piles the clothes that are slightly soiled, and those that have heavy soil. Distribute sheets, etc., so that no one pile is made up of all large flat pieces. Each pile should hold about 6 or 8 pounds. Two sheets, 2 pillowcases, 2 bath towels, 2 shirts, and a few guest towels will usually weigh about 6 pounds. Sorting is examining, too, and emptying trouser cuffs and pockets of sand, grass, and other collections.

**What About Soaking?** Long, overnight soaking, which used to be routine, is no part of automatic washing. But a short soak, or prewash, of soiled work clothes, curtains, etc. is still a good idea. Some machines provide this automatically; for the others, fill the washer on "Rinse," add a detergent, and let the machine wash and spin until the water is out. Use a chlorine bleach in the prewash when clothes are very dirty.

**Avoid Clothes-Tangle in the Washer.** Instead of tossing clothes hit or miss into the washer, take time to separate them. Place bundles of clothes on all four sides of the agitator, instead of stringing them around it. When you remove the clothes, shake them to loosen them.

### Don't Believe These

**Soaking colored clothes in salt water sets colors.** If dyes in colored fabrics are not fast to laundering, there is nothing you can do to prevent bleeding.

**A little soap in the last rinse makes woolens softer.** Good Housekeeping Institute has tried this many, many times and never once found it to be an improvement over thorough rinsing.

**Shrunken woolens can be restored to shape.** When woolens have become shrunken and felted from improper washing, there is no way to restore their size and fluffiness completely.

**Washable dresses that have been dry-cleaned cannot be laundered successfully.** Any really washable garment can be laundered satisfactorily even though it has been dry-cleaned several times. Exception: washable leather gloves that have been dry-cleaned.

**Chlorine bleaches "eat" clothes.** Not if they are properly used and the directions on the label closely followed. Damage to clothing from chlorine bleaches comes from:

1. Failure to mix the bleach and water thoroughly before adding clothes.
2. Using too much bleach.
3. Failure to rinse out bleach properly.
4. Carelessness in using a bleach—splattering it on clothes or spilling it on tabletops where wet clothes are placed.

**Milk takes out ink stains.** Best known of the old remedies, it not only is unreliable but adds to the complications.

# SIX BEST WAYS TO WASH YOUR CLOTHES

Sometimes it seems that washing machines have *oversimplified* the job of doing the family laundry. Frequently, women give it little, if any, thought at all. Actually the job of washing your clothes can be done more easily and more efficiently if it is done right.

Just because your washing machine takes care of the filling, washing, and rinsing without any effort on your part after you have pushed the button does not mean that you should toss your clothes in, push the button, and go on to something else. There is more to sorting the family wash than merely separating the clothes into two piles, one to go in the washer, the other to be done by hand.

There are *five* different methods of machine washing, depending on the kind of wash that you are planning to do. Read through the following list of Wash Ways so you will be familiar with them. Know the method that applies to your own type of washing machine. Refer to these pages again whenever you are in doubt. (Wash Way 6 is hand washing.)

---

**Wash Way 1** (Washable Whites). For the white cottons and linens that make up the bulk of the family laundry; they can be washed in any type washer. To maintain whiteness, a heavy-duty bleach (chlorine) is included. (*Important:* Watch for labels that warn against use of a bleach.) Typical items: sheets, pillowcases, dish towels, bath towels, facecloths, men's shirts (including striped and light colors), T shirts, shorts, aprons, gloves, handkerchiefs, children's cotton underwear, etc.

*Automatic method:* When using an automatic washer, set the temperature dial on "Hot." We recommend 160° F. as a good all-round temperature, but water as hot as 180° F. can be used. The hotter the water, the cleaner the wash. Set the time dial for 10 minutes. Follow washer instructions for putting in clothes and laundry supplies. Let the washer go through the complete cycle.

*Laundry supplies:* Soap with water conditioner, or detergent; liquid or powdered chlorine bleach.

*Wringer or spinner method:* Use water only as hot as your hands can stand—not hotter than 120° F. Fill washer to water line; add enough soap and water conditioner, or detergent, to make 2"- to 3"-deep suds; add bleach; mix. Then add clothes for 10-minute wash. With wringer washer, rinse twice in laundry tub, or once in washer (for 5 minutes); put clothes through wringer. With spinner washer, put clothes in spinner basket; rinse and spin them as washer manufacturer directs.

---

**Wash Way 2** (Washable Colors). For colorfast cottons, linens, rayons, and special acetates (Celaperm and Chromspun); also suitable for the following fabrics in white: nylons, acetates, Orlons, and Dacrons. These fabrics should not be put into colored loads. If bleach is needed to remove stains, use a fine-fabric (perborate) bleach. Typical items: colorfast dresses, blouses, sport shirts, tablecloths, napkins, pajamas, pastel sheets and bath towels, children's clothes, aprons, bedspreads.

*Automatic method:* The temperature of the water should not exceed 160° F.; wash for 8 to 10 minutes. This will protect colorfast dyes. As an extra precaution, wash any item with a very deep color by itself the first time, to be sure it doesn't bleed onto other pieces. *Note:* Check colored napkins and tablecloths for grease and lipstick stains. Soak these in cleaning fluid before laundering.

*Laundry supplies:* Use a fine-fabric (perborate) bleach instead of a chlorine bleach.

*Wringer or spinner method:* Same as wringer or spinner method in "Wash Way 1" except for one important difference: No chlorine bleach is used. (If you use wash water for more than one load of clothes, be sure you don't put colored clothes in water that contains bleach, previously used for white clothes.) Good practice in using a wringer: Straighten each item as you take it from washer; fold buttons to inside to avoid breakage; then put item carefully through wringer.

---

**Wash Way 3** (Dual-suds, or Heavy-duty, Wash). The dual-suds method calls for a warm, short wash followed by a hot, longer wash. It is useful for items that have heavy soil, ground-in soil, dust, stains, or other complicating factors. Typical items: work and garden clothes, sweat shirts, denims, children's clothes, curtains, diapers, and crib pads. *Note:* Dusty curtains, denims with colors that bleed, diapers, and pads must be washed alone.

*Automatic method:* Use special "Soak" setting for the first suds. With washers having no "Soak" setting, turn the temperature dial to "Warm"; set the time dial for 5 minutes. Stand by so you can turn time dial at proper moment to skip the rinses. For second suds, use "Hot" setting and give 8- to 10-minute wash. Let washer complete the cycle.

*Laundry supplies:* As for "Wash Way 2," use a fine-fabric bleach, not a chlorine bleach.

*Wringer or spinner method:* Use washer for first wash, washing clothes for 5 minutes in water of 105° F. temperature. Or, to save time and work, use laundry tub to soak clothes, soaking them 15 to 20 minutes in warm sudsy water; then put clothes through wringer, or spin them in spinner basket (you don't need to rinse them); after that give them regular 10-minute wash in washer. *Note:* Sheer or old curtains should be washed only 5 minutes in washer.

**Wash Way 4** (Short, Gentle Wash). The method that protects color, finish, or delicate construction. Also use it for all silks, Dynels, colored acetates (except Celaperm, Chromspun and other solution-dyed acetates), and for colored Orlons, Dacrons, nylons, and blends of Vicara. When washing blends, use the method for the most delicate fiber in the blend. (For washing woolens, see "Wash Way 5.")

Fabrics that are too delicately constructed and those that contain colors that may run or bleed should not go in your washer. See Wash Way 6.

**Wash Way 5** (Washing Wool or Wool Blends). Developed specifically to minimize shrinkage of washable woolens. Typical items: blankets of all-wool or wool blends, bathrobes, slacks and skirts that have been treated for shrinkage protection, scarves and stoles, infants' wear. This method must always be carefully controlled.

Wool or wool blends that cannot be washed by this method should be hand washed. See Wash Way 6.

*Laundry supplies:* Mild soap with water conditioner; or mild detergent, unless washer directions call for low-sudsing products.

**Wash Way 6** (Hand Washing). Obviously suited to articles that cannot, for one reason or another, stand washer action. They may be too fragile in fabric or construction, or they may contain colors that run or bleed and must therefore be washed alone to keep them from discoloring other articles. Typical items: nylon stockings; sweaters of all kinds; fragile blouses or lingerie; silk scarves; Fiberglas curtains; blouses or dresses trimmed with rhinestones or sequins.

**Don't Overwork Your Washing Machine.** It's unfair to washer and clothes. For a load of lightly soiled cottons, 5 minutes are enough; for average or heavily soiled pieces, 7 to 10 minutes of washing are plenty. Acetates shed soil easily. Allow 3 minutes for washing.

*Automatic method:* Some washers automatically provide short washing time and less rinsing and spinning. With others, set temperature dial to "Warm" and time dial for 3 minutes. Reduce rinsing and spinning by adjusting the dial yourself. Automatic washing of articles made of manmade fibers may leave them more wrinkled than hand washing and drip drying. A quick pressing will remedy this.

*Laundry supplies:* Mild soap with water conditioner; mild detergent; unless directions call for a low-sudsing product.

*Automatic method with agitator-type washer:* Fill washer with warm water (about 105° F.). Add laundry supplies. Run washer 1 to 2 minutes to make suds. Stop; immerse woolens; close cover. Allow to soak for 10 minutes; run washer a few seconds and spin water out. Fill for rinse, agitate 1 minute, spin water out again. Repeat rinse if necessary.

*Automatic method with tumbler-type washer:* Place woolens in washer. Fill with warm water (105° F.); add ½ cup low-sudsing detergent. Stop washer. Soak 5 minutes; tumble 1 minute. Fill deep rinse; run 1 minute; spin until draining stops.

*Wringer or spinner method:* Use clean, fresh water at 105° F. for each load and a 3-minute washing period. Whether or not you find it practical to wash delicate garments or fabrics in washer depends largely on number of pieces to be washed and whether washer would save work, as, for example, in easier handling of voluminous housecoats or billowy petticoats. With wringer-type washer, avoid setting creases by taking out articles and letting them drip dry. Most wringers are too harsh on delicate fabrics anyway.

*Wringer or spinner method:* Fill washer with warm water (105° F.); add laundry supplies, and run washer long enough to build up billowy layer of suds. Stop washer; immerse blanket or other woolens, and let soak without agitation for 10 minutes. Then put through wringer (with wringer rolls loosened); or spin in spinner basket 2 to 3 minutes or until drain stops ejecting. Rinse woolens in washer or in laundry tub until water is clear, Since woolens, particularly heavy items such as blankets and bathrobes, tend to hold water, wring or spin them between rinses.

*Hand-washing method:* Use warm water with enough soap or detergent for suds. Squeeze suds through article until clean. Difficult part is getting water out after rinsing. Press between clean bath towels, or hang article to drip dry. Latter method is primarily used for articles of manmade fibers—Orlon, Dacron, etc.—which need little or no ironing. Always use it for permanently pleated skirts. Lay sweaters flat.

*Laundry supplies:* Mild soap or mild detergent.

**Another Watchword: Fix Rips and Tears in Clothes Before Washing.** Mending tape, which needs no sewing, comes in handy. It's simple to press the tape on with a hot iron. Match the tape with the color of the article.

### The Blessing of Colorfastness

**What Are "Fast Colors"?** The term "colorfastness" refers to the degree of a color's resistance to sun and cleaning. Vat dyes are the fastest dyes developed. They are ideal for articles that require frequent washing, or that are exposed to the sun. They are also highly resistant to perspiration stains.

**Look for Informative Labels.** Many textile manufacturers now emphasize colorfastness in their fabrics. Most fabric makers specify on their labels the *degree* of color-resistance to washing and to light. The label gives you information about the resistance of the color to both sun and cleaning and tells you whether the article should be washed or dry-cleaned. Some labels give washing directions. In many cases soap manufacturers have co-operated with fabric makers in working out these directions. If the article should be washed separately, this should be specified.

Colors having a high degree of resistance to fading or running are not affected by washing, if reasonable care is taken. They can be washed in the machine with other clothes, the great advantage in being sure of your colors.

*However, brightly colored fabrics should never be hung in the sun to dry, as this may cause fading.*

### What Does Shrinkage Mean to You?

Shrinkage may present no serious problems to you, if you watch for labels giving the percentage of residual or expected shrinkage when shopping. "Residual shrinkage" means the shrinkage you can expect from repeated washings or dry-cleanings, predetermined by laboratory tests. It is so important that the Federal Trade Commission issued rules for its mention on woven cotton goods. These rules say that no words like "Shrunk" or "Preshrunk" may appear on a label without giving the percentage of residual shrinkage.

Shrinkage of 1 per cent or less is hardly noticeable. Residual shrinkage up to 2 or 3 per cent is satisfactory. Higher shrinkage may or may not be satisfactory depending on the use of the article. For example, bed sheets and blankets that were the correct length will be too short after washing if shrinkage exceeds 5 per cent.

Remember: if shrinkage is mentioned in any way on the label of woven cotton yard goods, you may expect the residual shrinkage declared.

### Know What You Are Washing

When you read the word "washable" on the label of a dress or pair of curtains, you know it means certain plus values: you're going to have fewer dry-

# WASHING TEMPERATURE AND TIME CHART

Many women allow their clothes to remain in the washing machine longer than necessary or wash them in water that is considerably hotter than the fabrics or the colors can stand because they erroneously believe that this harsh treatment will make their clothes cleaner. Actually, it will only make clothes wear out sooner. Find the proper Wash Way for each load you wash (see pp. 235–236); then consult the following table for washing time and water temperature.

#### Wash Way 1

| Method | Water Temperature | Washing Time |
|---|---|---|
| Automatic | 160° F. | 10 Minutes |
| Wringer or Spinner | 120° F. | 10 Minutes |

#### Wash Way 2

| Method | Water Temperature | Washing Time |
|---|---|---|
| Automatic | Not to Exceed 160° F. | 8–10 Minutes |
| Wringer or Spinner | Not to Exceed 120° F. | 8–10 Minutes |

#### Wash Way 3

| Method | First Wash | Second Wash | First Wash | Second Wash |
|---|---|---|---|---|
| Automatic | 105° F. | 160° F. | 5 Minutes | 8–10 Minutes |
| Wringer or Spinner | 105° F. | 120° F. | See Below | 10 Minutes |

#### Wash Way 4

| Method | Water Temperature | Washing Time |
|---|---|---|
| Automatic | 105° F. | 3 Minutes |
| Wringer or Spinner | 105° F. | 3 Minutes |

#### Wash Way 5

| Method | Water Temperature | Washing Time |
|---|---|---|
| Automatic | 105° F. | (See Text, p. 236.) |
| Wringer or Spinner | 105° F. | (See Text, p. 236.) |

#### Wash Way 6

Since this is a hand-washing method for delicate fabrics and dyes, obviously the water temperature should be kept fairly low. Water that feels comfortably warm to the hands is best suited to this kind of washing. Rinse water should be cool.

## WHAT SHRINKAGE COSTS YOU IN INCHES

| RESIDUAL SHRINKAGE | SLACKS | SHIRT SLEEVE | DRESS | | | CURTAINS |
| | | | BUST | WAIST BAND | LENGTH, NECK TO HEM | |
| | 44" long before washing | 33" long before washing | 35" before washing | 28¼" before washing | 41" before washing | Length 72" before washing |
|---|---|---|---|---|---|---|
| 1% residual shrinkage | .44" (Less than half an inch) | .33" (One-third of an inch) | .35" (About a third of an inch) | .28" (Approximately a quarter of inch) | .41" (Less than half an inch) | .72" (Less than three-quarters of inch) |
| 2% residual shrinkage | .88" (Almost an inch) | .66" (Two-thirds of an inch) | .70" (Nearly three-quarters of an inch) | .56" (Approximately half an inch) | .82" (Almost an inch) | 1.44" (Almost an inch and a half) |
| 3% residual shrinkage | 1.32" (One and one-third inches) | .99" (Just about an inch) | 1.05" (Just over an inch) | .85" (Almost an inch) | 1.23" (Almost an inch and a quarter) | 2.16" (Well over two inches) |

cleaning bills. After each laundering, the material will have the freshness that washing produces. But before you buy, there's something else you need to find out. The label says it's "washable," but does it tell you *how* to wash it?

**Cottons.** Most new cottons can breeze through automatic washing and drying. It's only the deep colors—reds and blues—that need special care. Cottons with these colors should be washed separately the first time or two, to get rid of excess dye.

**Corduroy.** Clothes made of washable corduroy (look for labels that say "vat dyed" and "Sanforized") are easy and simple to wash. Because colors are fast, corduroy of this kind can go into the wash water with white cottons, but avoid linting of dark colors—greens, browns, and maroons—by washing with other dark colors.

Vat-dyed corduroys can be washed with water as hot as you would use with other cottons. For machine washing, use your usual laundry soap or other cleanser, and try a 5-minute wash period—it's usually enough. Avoid crushing or wrinkling by loosening wringer rolls. If you use a spinner, don't let it run longer than necessary. After corduroy has been washed and rinsed and is ready to hang up, give it a good shaking just as you would bath towels or bathmats. Shape it by smoothing and straightening, then hang to dry. Children's playthings need little attention, but tailored sports clothes will dry best on hangers.

**Wools.** Although antishrink treatments minimize shrinkage, you should not expect woolens to launder like cottons. Wool is affected adversely by high temperatures, and wool colors seldom are so resistant to washing as cotton colors.

**Silk.** If a silk fabric or garment is not labeled washable, have it dry-cleaned. Washable silks should be washed in lukewarm suds from soap or a synthetic detergent. Then rinse thoroughly, and iron with the heat control at "Silk" setting. To prevent white silk's yellowing after wear and repeated launderings, use the cake-type bleaching agent made by home-dye manufacturers according to directions before the fabric has become seriously discolored. *Do not use chlorine bleaches.* They discolor the silk and damage the fabric.

**Acetates.** When the tag says "washable," you should be able to wash the garment by hand with a good laundry soap; or if the seams are well finished and well tailored, there is no reason why it should not be put into a washing machine. Almost invariably cool or lukewarm water has been recommended for acetates, but if necessary, use water no hotter than you use in your dishpan.

In machine washing, some precautions must be kept in mind. The washing time for acetates should be short, because they are weaker when wet. Wash acetates for 3 or 4 minutes and allow about 2 minutes for each rinse.

**Nylon** may be washed by hand or machine. As in all other fabrics, the tendency toward bleeding or running of dyes during washing depends on how well the fabric was dyed. Wash white and colored goods separately. This is especially true of white nylon fabrics, which have a tendency to absorb dyes that bleed from other fabrics.

The easy washing of nylon fabrics has been over-emphasized. Wash garments thoroughly. Although nylon washes readily, it needs more than a light dipping in soap and water.

**New Man-Made Fabrics.** Dynel, Dacron, and Orlon are machine-washable if blended with washable fibers. Consult the label before washing. Follow the manufacturer's directions.

**Plastic Film.** When plastic-film products are apron size or less, they can easily be washed by hand or wiped clean. But washing by hand (or wiping) larger articles like kitchen curtains, draperies, and shower curtains is difficult and impractical. Although soil doesn't penetrate plastic film as it does fabric, it doesn't come off easily.

Fill the washer with warm water, add a water conditioner and some detergent, and run the washer 5 minutes. Before the washer begins to spin, stop the action and transfer the curtain to the laundry tub, rinse it, and hang it to dry.

The longer soil is allowed to remain, the more firmly it adheres. For easier washing, launder your plastic-film pieces frequently.

### Laundering Treasured Pieces

The lovely things you treasure—appliquéd guest towels, monogrammed bridge sets, embroidered doilies, and other rather elaborate pieces—deserve extra care in laundering.

If you have a clothes washer, the washing part of the job is quite simple. Usually, fancy pieces of rayon, cotton, and linen are soiled only slightly; warm water, a good soap or synthetic detergent, and a short washing period (about 5 minutes) will get them clean. Rinse in clear, warm water. If you haven't a washer, a short soaking period (10 to 15 minutes, or so) in warm, sudsy water, with just enough dip-squeezing to get them clean, makes hand washing less tiresome. Be sure to rinse each piece thoroughly. After each washing and rinsing, squeeze out as much water as possible.

Before washing your bridge sets (both cloths and napkins), examine them for stains from cream, salad dressing, and other greasy foods. Washing does not always remove such stains, even though they may seem to disappear. Rather than take the chance of setting the stains (as ironing sometimes does), give any suspicious spots a preliminary treatment. Use a cleaning fluid. Gather the sections surrounding the stains, and place them in the cleaning fluid to soak for at least 10 minutes. Then wash and rinse.

For detailed instructions for treating specific stains, consult the next chapter.

### Lingerie Laundry

Gather all your slips, blouses, bras, rayon or nylon gowns and pajamas, petticoats, and underthings. (If your lingerie is especially filmy and delicate, do not put in washer. See page 236, "Wash Way 6," for laundering instructions.) If you don't have a full load for the washer, you can add light cotton dresses that aren't too soiled, or you can wash half a load. White nylon is particularly susceptible to picking up other colors, so if anything in the load will bleed even slightly, save the white nylon for another batch. Hook bras and close all zippers before washing. Bows on blouses are less likely to be pulled and possibly torn if you tie them loosely.

Wash lingerie in water that's just comfortably warm, using a mild soap or detergent. The actual washing time should be very short. A minute or two is ample. Use a mesh bag for fragile articles. In this, even nylon hose will go through the wash without damage.

### Washing Gloves

**Dark-Colored Fabric Gloves** may bleed and cause streaks. Wash them off the hands by squeezing in warm suds, and then rinse thoroughly. Before hanging them to dry, squeeze out as much water as you can and continue to press out moisture with old cloths or paper towels until gloves are dry enough to prevent settling of dye. Shake out, and straighten cuff and finger seams. Hang straight with clip clothespins, or slip a glove over each end of a wooden clothes hanger. Dry in a warm place.

**Wool Gloves.** Draw an outline of the gloves on paper before washing them. Squeeze rich, warm suds through and through, avoiding hard rubbing. Rinse well, and with an old Turkish towel press out as much moisture as you can. If colors from embroidery or trimming tend to run, stuff towel inside gloves. Shape them to drawn outline, and allow to dry away from excessive heat. To restore the fluffiness to heavily napped gloves and mittens, brush them well with a medium-stiff brush when they're dry.

**Leather Gloves** can be washed successfully if they are of the washable type and have not been dry-cleaned. Wash leather gloves on the hands. Work in a little extra soap on soiled fingertips and cuffs. Roll gloves off the hands, turning them inside out. Wash inside. Rinse thoroughly; turn right side out. Pat out excess water, as described for fabric gloves; shape, and puff out fingers by blowing in them. Lay flat to dry and when they're almost dry, soften by working them gently with the fingers.

### Washing Wool Socks

Wool socks that haven't been treated to resist shrinkage need laundering care. Follow these rules:

1. Wash wool socks *after each wearing*. This helps counteract the felting that results from wear and perspiration.

2. Use a detergent suitable for fine fabrics or wool only. It preserves the color, keeps wool soft. If there is color loss, it will be considerably less than if you hadn't used a detergent.

3. Wash by hand. Use slightly warm water for the job; after the last rinse, press out as much water as you can, to hasten drying. Dry on frames.

4. To remove socks from frame, pull top down over ankle and instep until cuff reaches toe. Then slip entire sock off frame. Stored like this, folded inside-out-in-half, socks lie flat and cuffs are stretched less than if socks are rolled.

### How to Wash Sweaters

**Trace on Paper.** Before washing a sweater, or any knitted garment, place it on a piece of clean, heavy wrapping paper, and draw its outline. If you have several sweaters, make an outline of each, label, and save for future washings.

**Wash Gently.** Make a rich suds in tepid water, just barely warm to the back of your hand. Use one of the mild soaps or synthetic detergents. If you prefer to use soap but the water is hard, add a water conditioner. If the sweater is heavily soiled, soak it for 2 or 3 minutes, but not longer. Then wash it very gently. When necessary, give the sweater a second washing in fresh suds. Don't try to rub out heavy soil, for hard rubbing may make wool sweaters shrink or mat. Squeeze the suds lightly through the garment, being especially careful if you are washing a beaded sweater. Do not hold the sweater by the sleeves or shoulders. Instead, support the whole garment with both hands to prevent its stretching.

**Rinse Thoroughly.** To give a good rinsing, use water the same temperature as the suds. Squeeze out as much water as possible, still supporting the sweater with both hands. Then roll the garment in a bath towel to absorb moisture. If the sweater is heavy or if it has more than one color, insert a towel between the front and back. Unroll towel. Repeat procedure, using dry towels.

**Dry on Outline.** Remove the towel (or towels), and place sweater on the wrapping paper. Ease the sweater into the prepared outline. Pay particular at-

tention to the ribbing at the neck, cuffs, and waist, for these must be dried to exact size in order to fit snugly. If the sweater has shrunk in washing, stretch it gently and pin it to the paper outline, using rustproof pins. Dry it flat, away from heat. A sweater can be blocked by pressing it with a warm iron over a damp cloth, or a steam iron does an excellent job.

### Washing Delicate Blouses

Whether it is a man-tailored, shirtmaker style or a dainty, lace-and-gauze creation, a blouse lends charm to a suit or skirt only when it is fresh and clean. Most tailored blouses can go right into the washing machine with your regular laundering; some can be treated like machine-washable lingerie. But almost everyone has a blouse or two that must be washed by hand, without rubbing or wringing. The instructions on the label usually tell you that the garment should be washed in lukewarm water. It may also specify the use of mild soap flakes; fine-fabric detergent will work just as well.

Sprinkling silk blouses after drying may result in a spotty effect. Iron while there's still enough moisture in the fabric.

### How to Wash a Quilted Robe

As a general rule, quilted robes in pastel colors are color-resistant to laundering and, with care, can be washed satisfactorily. Robes of deeper hues and robes trimmed with dark colors are somewhat of a risk, and it is better to have them dry-cleaned. For washable robes, use lukewarm water, and make a rich suds with quick-dissolving soap. Squeeze the robe gently through the suds until it is clean. Avoid wringing, twisting, and hard rubbing. Rinse thoroughly in lukewarm water until the last rinse water is clear. Get rid of as much water as you can by squeezing. Press out excess moisture in clean bath towels.

Quilted robes and bed jackets are dried best on wooden or plastic hangers. Straighten the shoulders and smooth out the robe. Then loop over the tie on a wraparound robe or close the slide-fastener. A bath towel placed over the hanger under the shoulders will help quicken the drying. Quick drying is important, because it lessens the danger of the colors' bleeding.

### Stocking News

Have you stockings that are unattractive because of too-intense color? Tone the color down by washing the hose and adding bluing to the last rinse. On silk, rayon, and nylon hosiery, it changes the hue ever so slightly, but enough to make it more pleasing.

### Washing Baby Clothes

**Diapers.** If you have a washer and dryer, and from 4 to 5 dozen diapers, washing every other day will keep the supply going. To care for diapers after use, you'll need a large covered pail. (A 2-gallon enameled one is usually adequate.) After you remove diapers or soiled sleeping togs, flush away any soil. Then half-fill the pail with cold water, deodorize it with 2 tablespoonfuls of borax, and put the diapers in to soak.

When you're ready to wash the diapers, wring them out and put them in your clothes washer. Use very hot water and enough soap or synthetic detergent to make lively suds. Wash about 10 minutes, and rinse thoroughly. Rinsing is important. Babies have sensitive skin, and a rash can develop easily.

Discuss the matter of boiling diapers with your pediatrician. Some doctors say boiling isn't necessary if diapers are washed properly; others recommend boiling daily or at least several times a week.

If you have a tumbler dryer, diapers will dry quickly in any kind of weather. But if you must use a line, hang each diaper by two corners, in the sun whenever possible. When they are dry, smooth, fold, and put away. Do not iron. Ironing wastes time and makes the diapers less absorbent.

**Other Baby Clothes.** Such articles as bibs, shirts, wrappers, nighties, and crib sheets collect so fast that you'll have to wash every day or so. Use hot suds for 3 or 4 minutes, and rinse thoroughly. If the clothes are stained from spinach, carrots, fruit and meat juices, etc., first let them soak in cool or lukewarm water. If stains from these foods are set, you must use a chlorine-bleach treatment.

Cod-liver-oil stains are particularly troublesome. Soak the spots in a grease-dissolving spot remover. Then, after the bib or dress has been thoroughly washed in very hot suds, the stains should disappear.

### How to Wash a Stuffed Toy

Many stuffed animals and dolls are made with foam rubber, which is completely washable. But by far the greatest number of toys have cotton-batting stuffing. If the cotton batting has been packed too loosely, it shifts and leaves the toy bunchy in spots when it is washed. A well-packed toy with firm seams can stand washing with little chance of damage.

The outside covering material of a toy really determines the way you'll wash it. If it is of terry cloth, gingham, flannel, or plush, you may put the toy in the washer. Colors may run a little; use only warm water

and mild suds. Since trimmings that are merely glued on will undoubtedly come off in the washer, remove them first and glue them back on after the toy has dried.

If you have doubts about washing stuffed toys, or if the manufacturer's instructions tell you definitely not to wash them, try cleaning with suds. Make copious suds with warm water in a basin, then quickly swish the toy around in them. Or rub the toy lightly with the suds, using a soft brush or a sponge. Work quickly, rinse with clear water, shake well, and pat dry with a bath towel.

When making homemade stuffed toys, choose your covering fabric, trimming, and stuffing for washability. Shredded foam rubber makes spongy toys that may be washed in an automatic washer and dried in an automatic dryer.

### Ideas About Washing Pillows

Washing pillows with an automatic spinner washer is easy because they can be washed without removing the feathers. Fill the washer with lukewarm water and soap and run it for about 5 minutes. Rinse, then spin as long as water flows out the drain. Place wash in dryer or hang outdoors to dry.

If you tackle the job without a washer, choose a bright, sunny, breezy day to do the work. First transfer the feathers to a roomy muslin bag. To do this, leave an opening in the bag the size of the opening in the ticking, and sew the two openings together. You can shake the feathers into the bag without scattering them. Then unsew the bag and ticking and sew up the bag's opening.

Place the bag in rich, warm suds; work it up and down. If necessary, repeat in clean suds. Rinse thoroughly. Squeeze out as much water as you can. Hang outdoors between two lines. While the feathers are drying, bounce the bag frequently and work feathers with your fingers to speed the drying. Be sure the feathers are *completely* dry before you put them back in the clean ticking. This is important, because damp feathers will acquire a musty odor and may develop mildew.

### Washing Curtains and Draperies

**Organdy Curtains.** With care, they can be laundered in a washer. Soak them in cool water, to remove dust; then place in mesh bag; wash for 2 minutes in hot, sudsy water. Rinse and spin dry. For the perky, billowy kind of starch finish on organdy, a heavy starch is required. Use 2 tablespoonfuls of starch to each quart of boiling water, following directions on the package.

**Glass-Fiber Curtains** should be laundered rather than dry-cleaned. The glass fiber is not absorbent, so soil is easily removed by washing. Squeeze the curtains through suds, rinse thoroughly, shake to remove wrinkles, and hang on the rods. The curtains will dry in a few minutes. Ironing is not required, as they do not wrinkle during laundering.

**Nylon and Dacron curtains** are treated in much the same way, but usually require some pressing.

**Washing Draperies.** Draperies never should be washed unless the label tells you that the fabric is washable. If there is no label attached to the fabric, it is safer to have the draperies dry-cleaned. Also, if the draperies are lined, the lining as well as the drapery fabric itself must be washable. When the draperies are washable, a washing machine is the best means of doing them. Use moderately hot water and a good suds, and wash the draperies for 2 to 3 minutes in the machine. If they are very soiled, better washing results can be obtained if a second clean suds is used. After washing, rinse the draperies in the machine.

Draperies should be hung indoors to dry, so that colors will not be affected by the sun. Be sure the weight is distributed evenly so the draperies will not get out of shape while drying.

**Lace Curtains** need particular care. To keep them the right length and with corners square, we put them on curtain stretchers. This means that they must be measured *before* laundering. After they have been washed and rinsed, starch with a medium starch solution. Remove the water, and shake well. Set up your curtain stretcher to match the original measurements of the curtains. Then stretch this way: Fasten the four corners of the curtain to the stretcher. Then pin the centers of the four sides. To equalize the pull on the curtain, pin one side, then the side opposite. Continue to fasten the centers of unpinned sections until the entire curtain is attached.

### New Rayon and Cotton Lace Tablecloths

**To Wash.** These particular lace tablecloths are unconditionally washable. Put them in your washing machine for 5 minutes or suds them in a tub. Rinse well; squeeze out as much water as you can, and hang double over a line.

**Spots Sponge Off.** One of the reasons a lace tablecloth doesn't need to go into the wash very often is that a damp sponge can take up food spills. The best time to remove stains is when they are fresh, so don't let them stand long.

**Tips for Table Mats.** Lace or crocheted table mats should be washed just like a tablecloth, but to make them lie flat on the table they need a bit of starching. Usually the heavier the mats the thicker the starch solution should be. So if a light starch mixture of 1 tablespoonful to a quart of water doesn't seem to be enough, step it up to a medium starch mixture by using 2 tablespoonfuls. While the mats are damp, stretch them flat on a clean porcelain-enamel tabletop. They won't need ironing.

### How to Take Care of Sheets

As you remove sheets from a bed, take the trouble to loosen the tucked-in edges. Don't pull them free; this may weaken the fabric and shorten the life of the sheets. Be particularly careful to remove the corners of fitted sheets.

When sorting clothes to go to the laundry or for washing at home, never use a sheet as a wrapping for other soiled clothes. This puts a strain on the sheets and may soil them heavily. When you send sheets to the laundry, put them in the bag without folding them. It saves time for you and the laundry.

**Laundering Tips.** Use plenty of hot water and a good soap. Follow with thorough rinsing, to avoid a gray look.

Occasional use of a chlorine household bleach, used as recommended by the manufacturer and completely rinsed out, will help keep white sheets white and colored sheets clear and bright in color.

In hanging sheets, fold them double, hem to hem; then turn about 4″ over the line.

If you have a rotary-type ironer, it is easy to get sheets smooth. When ironing a sheet by hand, save time by folding the sheet from hem to hem; then fold it again, making four thicknesses. Iron first on the plain side and then on the hem side.

**Pastel Sheets Are Not Delicate.** The colors are soft and luxurious, but pastel sheets are made to take washing in their stride. You can send your sheets to a good commercial laundry or put them in your washing machine without a qualm; they'll come out fresh and bright. Don't *think* of washing them by hand.

### Keeping Your Blankets Warm and Beautiful

Your blankets will look better and last longer if you take care of them. Modern laundry facilities have simplified the job of washing blankets. If you have put off cleaning yours, don't delay any longer.

**Keep Blankets Clean.** See that your blankets stay fresh and spotless. Today's sheets provide enough turn-back length to cover blanket bindings fully. Since the blanket is protected by the sheet underneath it and the bedspread on top of it, it can often go several years without a laundering. Blankets on seldom-used beds should be removed and aired several times a year; and if a blanket that is constantly used begins to develop a musty odor, an airing will make it sweet again.

**Blankets Will Need Washing,** and if you have an automatic washer, the task is simple. Some blanket labels still advise you to wash blankets by hand, but we think this back-breaking chore is less effective and certainly lots more work than the machine method. If you have no washer, it's best to send blankets to a good commercial laundry. If you attempt to wash blankets at a local laundry center, you may damage them unless special facilities are available.

**Washing Blankets in Your Washer.** Your washer doesn't have to be a late model so long as it has been kept in good working order and does an effective water-removal job. With either a wringer- or spinner-type washer, no special instructions are necessary if you follow the rules for washing wool. Keep washing time short—2 or 3 minutes—because shrinkage is caused more by agitation (washing action) than by water temperature or kind of washing product used. Water as hot as the hands can stand will do a better cleansing job than lukewarm water. Much of a blanket's beauty lies in its delicate color. We found the "fine fabric" nonsoap detergents best for keeping colors fresh and clear after repeated washings. They rinse out easily and leave wool soft and fluffy. However, they are not intended to remove heavy soil, and for this reason we often use regular all-purpose washday detergents. Use enough so that suds will last during washing.

**Washing Blankets Automatically.** Set the control that sends warm water into the machine. Let the machine fill; then add the detergent best suited to your washer. (As in all washing, be sure to dissolve the detergent.) If your washer has a tumbling cylinder and is likely to oversuds, a nonsudsing detergent is best. It does a thorough cleansing job, and you can use enough to get blankets clean without fear of overflowing suds. When the wash water is ready, put in one blanket and let it *soak,* without running the machine, for 10 minutes. At the end of this time, turn the dial to "Dry," "Spin," or whatever signifies "Extract." Let the machine continue to run until it fills for the rinse, but don't let it go on rinsing. Immediately turn the dial once more to "Extract." Let it spin for the entire length of time. Then the washing is done without effort.

**Drying Blankets the Automatic Way.** Before turning on the dryer, place about 6 average-sized bath towels in the tumbling cylinder. These warm towels cushion the blanket and speed drying by absorbing moisture. Then turn on the dryer and let it heat for at least 5 minutes. At the end of this time, stop the tumbler and put the blanket among the towels. If you have a reminder clock, use it, because a blanket's drying time must be relatively short. We found that 8 minutes would remove almost, but not all, the moisture—which is just as it should be. If wool blankets are allowed to dry completely, the shrinkage may be high. Therefore, we remove an almost-dry blanket from the dryer and hang it over the line, indoors, if possible, to finish drying.

**If You Don't Have a Dryer.** In order to take advantage of this method, you must have a good washer, but a tumbler dryer is not absolutely essential. Line drying can be substituted. It will not leave a blanket quite so soft and fluffy as when dryer-dried; but in all other respects the end result will be the same. If you have sufficient clothesline space, hang the washed blanket over two lines for better air circulation and faster drying; if this can't be done, divide the weight equally over a single line so you won't need clothespins, which tend to leave imprints on soft wool. Once or twice during the drying, gently straighten and pull the blanket into shape, being careful not to distort it. Remember you are handling sensitive wool.

**The Finishing Touches.** When the blanket is completely dry, run your hand over it to see if it feels soft and fluffy enough to suit you. Sometimes when we line-dry very luxurious and lovely blankets, we take the time to brush them well, while they are still hanging on the line, with a fairly stiff-bristled brush and a light, brisk stroke. This raises the nap and helps restore the original fluffiness.

Last comes the binding. Straightening and shaping the binding while the blanket is drying may be all you want to bother with. For perfect finishing, the binding can be pressed. Most blanket bindings are made of acetate satin and, like all acetate, cannot stand too hot an iron. The "Rayon" setting on your iron should be used. The binding will look almost new again if you dampen it slightly before pressing. The simplest way is to lightly sponge the binding with a clean cellulose sponge or a piece of damp cheesecloth. Press both sides of the binding. Some blankets have nylon bindings. They keep their shape and need only a light pressing.

### Washing Electric Blankets

Automatic electric blankets should always be washed, never dry-cleaned, because dry-cleaning fluids may injure the wiring system. We recommend two machine-washing methods that are gentle enough to use on any electric blanket. One is for agitator-type washers, the other for tumbler types. Wash one blanket at a time, and follow the procedure given for your washer.

**Agitator-Type Automatic Washer.** Fill the washer with warm water—about 100° F. Add 1 cup of mild synthetic detergent, and agitate until dissolved. Stop washer. Immerse blanket in washer, and close cover. Do not agitate. Let blanket soak 10 minutes and spin out water. Fill for rinse; spin. Remove blanket, shape over two clotheslines a few inches apart, and let dry. Press bindings with steam or dry iron set at low heat.

**Tumbler-Type Automatic Washer.** Place blanket in washer. Fill washer with warm water, adding ½ cup of low-sudsing detergent. Then stop washer. Soak blanket for 5 minutes; then tumble it 1 minute. Advance dial so water drains out. Then advance dial a second time, and let washer fill for deep rinse; run for 1 minute. Finally, turn dial to give final drain, for 2 minutes, or until drain hose stops ejecting. Remove blanket; dry and press as directed for agitator-type washer.

### Washing a Bedspread

Be sure the spread is washable. (It's best to dry-clean most acetate or silk faille, satin, or taffeta spreads.) If the spread's label gave the proper washing method, by all means follow the directions. Otherwise, use this procedure for such washable spreads as chenille, candlewick, corduroy, crocheted, and seersucker. Shake the spread to remove lint and loose dirt. In a nonautomatic washer, fill the tub as you would for a full load (use warm water for colored spreads, hot for white ones). Add mild soap or deter-

gent to make plenty of rich suds. Arrange large spread (or two small ones) loosely inside the tub. Wash for 5 to 8 minutes, and rinse in warm water. Put spread through spinner, or through wringer at "low" pressure setting, to avoid wrinkles. Shake the bedspread thoroughly, and hang it over a line. Square the corners, and pull the four side hems straight. If you have two parallel lines, stretch the spread across both, spacing evenly. Choose a breezy day, to help fluff chenille or candlewick, and a shady spot, to preserve bright colors. An automatic tumbler dryer is the perfect "fluffer" for soft-napped bedspreads.

If you have an automatic washer, follow the manufacturer's directions. Again, one large spread usually makes a full load. Use warm water for colored spreads, hot for white ones; set washing time for 5 to 8 minutes, depending on degree of soil. Remove the spread from the washer after final spin, and dry in dryer or as above.

Chenille, candlewick, and corduroy need no ironing; brush up the nap, if you like, with a fairly stiff brush, and smooth into shape. Spreads that require ironing should be taken from the line or dryer while they're still slightly damp. Crocheted spreads should be dried on a curtain stretcher, or stretched carefully during drying, to prevent shrinkage.

### Hanging Up Clothes

The job of hanging clothes really begins in the laundry. When the clothes are arranged in advance, they can be taken out of the basket easily and similar pieces can be hung together conveniently.

**Hanging Clothes Is an Art.** There is an art to hanging clothes so they will not become marked from pins or stretched out of shape. First, you need a plentiful supply of clean, smooth clothespins. A clothespin bag that slides along the line will save a lot of steps. Proper use of clothespins will do away with distortions such as shoulders pulled out of place and uneven edges on sheets, pillowcases, and bath towels. Here are a few suggestions.

1. In hanging sheets, first fold them double, hem to hem, and then turn about 4″ over the line and use 4 clothespins, 1 at each end and 2 in the middle. After the sheet is hung, straighten it out evenly by running your fingers down the selvage at the sides. This saves time when dampening and pressing, and the sheet dries evenly.

2. Hang men's shirts by the tail, first folding the two shirt fronts together so that the shirt is double. Now fold 3″ or 4″ over the line and pin at the ends.

3. Hang handkerchiefs over the line—*never* by one corner.

4. Try to find a place indoors for a few parallel lines, so that clothes need not be hung outdoors in freezing weather or on windy days. Freezing or flapping in the wind can cause damage to clothes.

5. Never hang colored clothes in the sun. Shady spots cannot be relied on for any length of time, so it is better to hang colored clothes indoors.

6. Whenever possible, hang clothes so the prevailing breeze will billow out sleeves and pajama legs.

**How to Dry Cotton Dresses.** If you want your cotton dresses to keep their shape and be easy to iron, put them on clothes hangers so that they will dry smooth and straight. Button the buttons, zip the zippers, straighten the seams, pockets, and collar. Hang summer dresses, particularly dark colors, in the shade, so they will go through the season with the lovely bright colors they started out with.

**A Worksaver for Washable Trousers.** You can reduce ironing of washable slacks and trousers to a minimum by using trouser creasers. These are metal, framelike devices, over which the trousers are fitted to dry. They are available in several sizes and make the trousers dry smoothly and with a knifelike crease. Use the creasers to keep the press in woolen trousers, too. Merely fit the creasers into the trouser legs and dampen creases, smooth out wrinkles, and let dry.

**Bath Towels—Are Yours Soft and Fluffy?** If you use a washing machine at home, it is easy to launder a load of bath towels; but can you get them soft and fluffy and luxurious, the way you like them? The only way to accomplish this is to shake the towels vigorously before hanging them on the line. It is easier if two people shake, so perhaps your young child would like to help you.

**Lovely Lingerie.** Knitted garments need special attention when hung to dry. Don't hang them over the line, as they may stretch at the fold and dry out of shape. To avoid this, place slips and nightgowns on clothes hangers that have a smooth, nonrusting finish. Panties won't bulge at the sides if hung with clip-on clothespins.

**Drying Clothes Indoors.** It's no fun to hang clothes outdoors when your hands are freezing and the clothes stick to the line—and they won't dry well, anyway! On cold, stormy days find some place—a corner of your basement or even a play or recreation room—where you can hang clothes conveniently. If clothes are properly washed and thoroughly rinsed, they will be as white as when hung outdoors. However, the wind's billowing the clothes does help to take out wrinkles, so shake your wash well when you resort to indoor drying, particularly pieces that are not to be ironed such as seersucker, towels, etc.

*A convenient spot for drying nylon is over bathtub.*

**Taking the Clothes from the Line.** When you take down the clothes, fold them lightly and stack similar pieces together in the basket. Dampening is important, but don't overdo it. Dampen just enough to eliminate wrinkles.

### Drip Drying

When you buy a blouse, dress, or skirt (or even a man's shirt) woven from one of the new man-made fibers, washing directions may say no ironing is needed; you can hang the garment up and let it drip dry.

Drip-drying clothes is something of a nuisance, because, except for the bathroom, the average home does not have a convenient spot to hang dripping-wet clothes.

But the procedure is convenient for a slip or blouse that is light in weight and dries quickly.

One possible arrangement is to use small plastic hooks that can be mounted with an adhesive on any type of wall. Use two to string a light clothesline from one end to the other, or across the corner, of the tub. There is also a drying rack available that hooks over a towel bar on the wall above the tub and another that fits crosswise between the wall and shower-curtain rod.

## The Weekly Ironing

**Selecting an Electric Iron** is difficult, because there are many different types, each with special designs and features. A heat control regulates temperatures for ironing rayons and nylons, which require low heat, and high temperatures for sturdy cottons and linens. Preferences in weight are personal, but the trend is toward lightweight irons. Good ironing results are obtained with irons as light as 2½ pounds. You can judge what will be comfortable for you by lifting several different irons. Get the feel of the weight and balance by pretending to iron a few strokes. This will give you an idea of how the handle fits your grip, too.

Carefully consider this question. A steam iron offers you the same conveniences as a good dry iron and also provides the luxury of steam. If you like to sew, you shouldn't be without a steam iron. You'll save a lot of time in pressing and ironing.

*Cord Control.* This is not essential, but why do without an accessory that may save irritation and outbursts of temper?

*The Ironing Board.* If the price of the ironing board you want seems high, look at its sturdy construction and think of the years it will last. Be sure it can be opened and closed easily.

Select a good pad and several covers when you buy your ironing board. Coverings that fit the board properly make ironing easier. Buy several covers, so you can launder your ironing-board cover as regularly as you do other household pieces.

*Comfortable Chair.* You may not have to buy a special chair for your sit-down ironing, but if you haven't a sturdy, comfortable kitchen chair, look at chairs that are sold to be used with ironers. They are attractive and designed to be comfortable and prevent fatigue. A chair with casters is particularly convenient.

*Clothesbasket and Rack.* Part of any good ironing ensemble is a clothesbasket on wheels and some sort of rack for holding pieces as you iron them.

**Look Forward to an Ironer.** You'll be surprised at the number of table mats, napkins, curtains, and sport things that have to be ironed, even with only two in the household. The only answer to this problem is an electric ironer.

When you've made up your mind to buy an ironer, first plan where to put it. Ironing is a tidy job; it can be done anywhere in the house where there is light and a convenient outlet.

Store-away and fold-up ironers require very little space. The store-away kind is used on a table—a sturdy card table will do. A fold-up ironer has its own base. Among the deluxe ironers needing a place of their own is one that can be used right in the living room, because its cabinet blends with living-room furnishings. Look for an ironer that fits your type of living.

Both a hand-ironing setup and an electric ironer are needed if all the laundry is done at home. Most women find it easier to press and do fancy ironing with a hand iron. They use the ironer for sheets, men's shirts, curtains, and handkerchiefs.

**Get an Early Start.** Don't wait until the end of the day to iron. You can iron more skillfully when you're not too tired from other housework. Dampening clothes the night before helps you get an early start. It's a good method, except in hot, humid weather. Don't be too ambitious; dampen only what you can handle in one day. When you dampen flatwork— sheets, pillowcases, and towels—spare the water. Sprinkle lightly and evenly, and straighten selvages and dog-eared corners. This saves time later and makes ironing easier.

**Be Orderly.** As you dampen, fold pieces lightly, rolling them makes extra wrinkles. Place folded pieces in the clothesbasket systematically. Separate shirts, pajamas, shorts, towels, handkerchiefs, and napkins.

**Don't Dampen These.** Knit underwear, facecloths, sweat shirts, diapers and crib pads, bathmats, and small rugs do not need dampening. Take them out of the basket before you start dampening, and fold them in neat piles, ready to put away. If you think a once-over-lightly with the iron would improve their appearance, use a moderately hot iron. This is advisable especially for sports shirts and such.

**Have You Tried "Dry Ironing"?** Make use of the moisture already in the clothes by taking them out of the dryer or off the line before they are bone-dry. Fold lightly and cover with a heavy towel or plastic sheeting until time for them to be ironed. Ironing like this applies to sheets, dish towels, shorts, pajamas, aprons—all flat or semiflat pieces.

**Never Iron Bath Towels.** Wash bath towels thoroughly, keep them white with a bleach, and liven them up with vigorous shaking. As you take them down from the line, fold them straight and put them away at once. Not only is ironing bath towels a waste of time, but it actually destroys their soft, fluffy appearance.

### Easier with an Ironing Machine

**Not Less Time, But More Ease.** There seems to be a feeling on the part of some people that an ironing machine should curtail, to a very large degree, the time expended. This is not exactly true, for there is just as much handling of the individual pieces with the machine as there is with the hand method. The important thing is the ease with which ironing is done, and the professional look which can be attained.

The standard ironing machine has a moving roller. The ironing shoe may be either above or below the roller. Choosing between the two is something you must do for yourself. We suggest that you watch demonstrations of both types to help you make your decision. If possible, try the machine yourself to find out which one suits you best.

Portable ironers have moving rollers, but are usually smaller than standard machines. They are light enough to be carried, but often they do not have their own base and must be used on a table. Portable ironers do not have all the automatic features of the larger, more expensive models. Consider these factors carefully before you purchase your machine so you will not be disappointed after it has been delivered.

Generally speaking, portable ironers fit in best in homes without a laundry room or a place where the ironer may be kept permanently and ready for use. If you do have a laundry room or a permanent place to keep an ironer, a standard machine is probably your best choice.

In buying an ironer, think of these things:

1. If an ironer is to be a real saving of energy and time, you must be able to use it with comfort. Before you buy, try different ironers. See that the controls are well within your reach.

2. Ironers with both ends open give more freedom in ironing clothing than those supported at one end.

3. An ironer should have extension shelves at the sides and front. A shelf at the front provides a space for folding towels, napkins, etc., and shelves at the sides provide space for piling clothes as they are ironed.

4. An ironer should be heat-controlled so all types of fabric can be ironed on it.

5. All controls should be quick-acting and responsive to the touch.

6. When choosing an ironer, get a comfortable chair to be used with it.

**How to Acquire Skill.** Women who own an ironer for the first time quite naturally wonder how much of the week's ironing they will be able to do satisfactorily by machine. Right from the start, with little or no practice, flatwork such as towels, sheets, pillowcases, napkins, and table mats can be ironed perfectly. Pajamas, shorts, and simple playclothes can be done almost as easily. But when it comes to dresses, fancy blouses, and men's shirts, you'll need time and patience to turn out a skilled job. Demonstrators of good ironers can turn out work rivaling the best hand ironing, and with practice so can you.

Don't be afraid to ask your dealer for help. Your ironer should have an illustrated instruction booklet showing step-by-step procedures. Keep this booklet, and use it faithfully. Be sure to follow the manufacturer's instructions for care of your ironer, too.

**Preparing Your Ironing.** Proper preparation of clothes for ironing by machine begins at the clothesline. Shake them well before hanging and put them on the line so there'll be no dog-ears to cope with. Hang shirts by the tails, shorts and trousers from the waist, and sheets, pillowcases, and towels with several inches of the hem side over the line so they won't sag and dry out of shape. Dampen just enough to get out the wrinkles. If pieces are too damp, you'll have to put them through the ironer several times. The old rule of dampening the night before holds good for an ironer as well as for hand ironing. Moisture then has a chance to spread throughout the fabric.

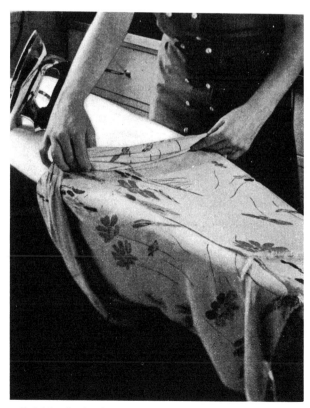

*Fold back the bottom of your nightgowns and your slips when you are ironing the top.*

**The Order of Ironing.** Lay the pieces in the basket so napkins are together, shorts and pajamas sorted, etc. Lightly fold shirts and garments so they will fall in the proper position for ironing as you open them. Place table mats and napkins so they won't need turning over before ironing.

Iron rayons and other light fabrics first; then heat your ironer to a higher temperature suitable for cottons and linens.

**Keep Your Ironer Fit.** Owning an ironer is something to be proud of, and you'll want to care for it as an important appliance. Keep it as spick-and-span and shining as it was when it was delivered to you. Don't use an ironing-machine cover month after month until it becomes scorched and tattered. Extra covers are inexpensive and easy to put on. Keep one or two handy, so you can launder them regularly. A newer type of cover contains a high percentage of asbestos, which makes it less susceptible to scorching than ordinary cotton covers. When you change a cover, take off the padding and fluff it up. This makes for better ironing.

When you finish ironing, let the ironer cool completely, with the shoe away from the roll, before you close it to put it away.

### Your Hand Iron Is Your Valet

Not everyone can afford a laundry completely equipped with modern appliances, but a heat-controlled iron, a well-padded ironing board, and a lint-free pressing cloth are minimum essentials. It's helpful to have a sponge or a small sprayer to apply dampness. If you can, add a sleeve board and a steam iron.

**Temperature Is Important.** The first setting of the dial of most irons is "Rayon." This keeps your iron at a very low temperature. With this heat you can safely press the wrong side of any fabric, even though you do not use a pressing cloth over it. With wool,

rayon, silk, and many combinations of fibers, you undoubtedly can change the setting to the one higher, "Silk," or even the next, "Wool"; but the "Rayon" setting is a safe place to start. When you have found which setting gives the best results with a dress that is a mixture of fibers, you are on the safe side, for the thermostat controls the iron's heat.

**Can All Rayons Be Ironed at the Same Setting?** No. Some can be ironed at temperatures somewhat higher than those for other rayons.

**How to Set the Dial if You Don't Know the Fabric.** If you are ironing a fabric that is unfamiliar, you will have to resort to a little experimenting before you get the right setting of the dial. This happens most frequently with rayons, because the different types make identification difficult. Start with the lowest setting. If this seems too cool, try a little more heat—but test it first on a corner of the garment. If the iron sticks or roughs up the fabric the least bit, you must go back to the cooler setting. Never use a high setting on an unfamiliar fabric. It is better to find your way slowly than to ruin your clothes.

**When Your Iron Is Set for a Particular Fabric, Will It Hold the Right Temperature as Long as You Iron?** For the most part you can depend on the heat control to give you the right ironing temperature. But ironing is not always a cut-and-dried proposition. If you are an exceptionally fast ironer, you may wish to shift the setting a point or two higher. On the other hand, if you iron more slowly than average, or if your ironing is slowed up by a fussy garment, you probably will have to reduce the heat slightly. Adjust the temperature setting to suit you and your individual ironing needs.

**Can All Cottons Be Ironed at the Same Temperature?** There are distinctions among cottons as well as rayons. Cottons range in weight all the way from light organdies to heavy duck. Also, some cottons are starched and others are not. For sheer and starched cottons your iron usually can be set at the low end of the cotton setting, but for heavy and unstarched cottons push it up to the high end.

**Ironing Nylon.** Little if any ironing is required. A quick touching up usually will suffice. As nylon dries quickly, this can be done almost immediately after laundering. With most irons the rayon setting provides a safe ironing temperature, but you may want to experiment on a hidden section of a new garment to find the best setting for it.

**How to Iron.** Too much dampness in a fabric is an incredible time-waster. The best way for a beginner to start is to err on the dry side; then, if the quality of the ironing doesn't suit you, you can step up the

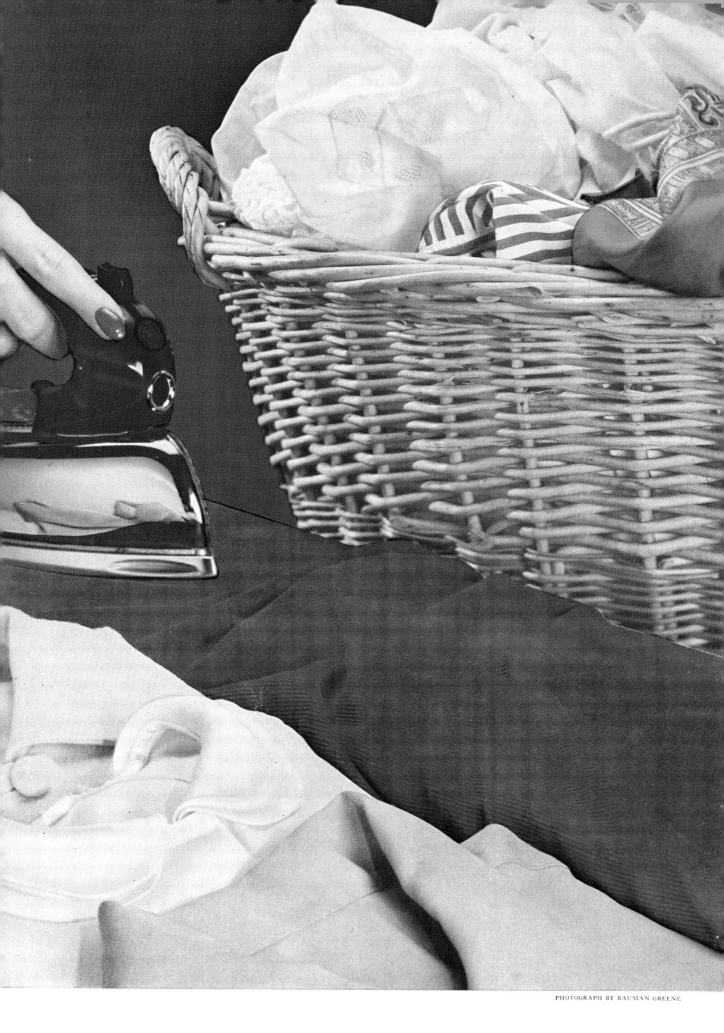

moisture, not by resprinkling the entire piece, but by touching up dry spots with a sprayer or dampened sponge.

One of the most obvious differences between an experienced and a novice ironer is the definite pattern established in handling each piece. The expert always tackles a shirt, shorts, or whatever she's ironing in the same order, and irons each section dry before going on to the next. This saves retracing steps.

**A Good Iron Is Essential.** No matter how efficiently a good ironer works, she can save more time with some hand irons than with others. Here are some of the features that are important when you are considering the maximum ease and efficiency with which ironing can be done.

*Balance.* Poor balance can tire your wrist and other arm muscles and generally slow up ironing.

*Weight.* The greatest ease in ironing comes when the weight of the iron does not exceed 3 or 4 pounds.

*Heat.* It's the heat that smooths the wrinkles, so the iron must provide enough heat for fabrics of all kinds. Modern irons have a rated capacity of 1,000 to 1,100 watts.

*Design.* A well-designed iron has a handle that's comfortable, a fabric dial that's easy to read and adjust, a soleplate large enough to cover a good-sized area with one sweep. Quite naturally, an oversized soleplate covers more ground and speeds ironing.

### Put Your Steam Iron to Work

Perhaps the easiest way to divide steam- and dry-ironing jobs is first to rule out articles that require dampening and dry ironing. These include men's business and dress shirts; heavy linen napkins and tablecloths; handkerchiefs; women's, children's, and other clothes that are starched. Well suited for steam ironing, on the other hand, are virtually all the synthetic fabrics—rayons, nylons, and blended fabrics—used in sport shirts, play clothes, women's clothes, even tablecloths and napkins. Special weaves, like corduroy and wrinkle-resistant finishes on cottons, can be steam-ironed; also knit goods, underwear, dish towels, pajamas, shorts, and lingerie.

If pressing is a major problem, a steam iron is a worksaver. While a steam iron doesn't always eliminate the use of a pressing cloth for fabrics with a tendency to shine, you can double a piece of cheesecloth and steam-press over it, on the right side.

Those unfamiliar with the combination steam-dry iron may be interested to know about the basic differences in design. These account for the varying lengths of time required for irons to start steaming

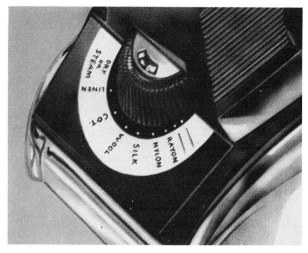

*Set the dial for easier ironing.*

and for them to steam without refilling. The important thing to the user, however, is the iron's over-all size and shape; it should feel comfortable in your hand whether you are using it for short-time pressing or for the whole week's ironing, and it should be fairly light. Steam-dry irons are generally heavier than ordinary dry irons, but they should not be so heavy that using them makes ironing even more of a chore. The idea is to *save* work.

Until fairly recently, many manufacturers insisted that only distilled water be used in their steam irons. Now many of them claim that tap water can be used. Actually, any steam iron will operate on tap water; but in a hard-water area, mineral deposits may clog the steam orifices. When this happens, the iron may need servicing. How quickly this occurs depends on how hard the water is and how much the iron is used. A good rule is to use distilled water in any steam iron. Lacking this, use rain water. But if you do not have distilled water, don't put off steam ironing. Use tap water in an emergency, for it takes a while to build up enough mineral deposits within the iron to cause trouble.

There are a few other things to remember in the good care of your steam iron: (1) Always empty the water after use, preferably while the iron is hot, so that the iron's heat will evaporate the few drops that may be left. (2) If you spill water on the outside while filling the iron, wipe it off with a soft cloth. (3) Follow the manufacturer's directions for use, care, and cleaning.

### Ironing Minute-Savers Without an Ironer

If you have dampened carefully and sorted napkins, dish towels, sheets, and shirts in separate piles, ironing goes faster—you won't have to wait for the iron to heat or cool, as you would in changing from one fabric to another; and sorting into piles for putting away will be taken care of.

Many housekeepers like to start their ironing with acetates, which take a low heat-control setting, and then increase the temperature for cottons and linens. Here's an important point to remember when you iron rayons: most of them can be ironed best when they're almost dry and some when they're completely dry. If you have a steam iron, experiment with it. You'll find many rayons and rayon combinations that can be ironed with a steam iron after they are completely dry. The steam seems to give the needed bit of moisture.

There will be less retouching of wrinkles or ironed sections on dresses, blouses, and similar garments if you iron first the parts that hang over the edge of the ironing board—cuffs, collars, sleeves—and then the body of the article.

**In Ironing Men's Shirts,** be careful with double thicknesses—cuffs, buttonhole bands, and collars. These must be thoroughly dried by ironing on both sides. This is one place where firm pressure on the iron gives a better finish.

You needn't fuss with flat pieces—just run the iron over them until they are smooth and dry. Fold to fit shelves.

**Monograms and Embroidery.** To make monogram and embroidery patterns stand out, place the piece face down on extra-thick material—Turkish toweling is excellent—and iron dry on wrong side. This raises the pattern.

**Handkerchiefs.** Don't fuss with everyday handkerchiefs, but take pains with your choice ones to get edges and corners straight and square. Fold women's handkerchiefs in a square. Fold men's handkerchiefs in thirds lengthwise and in thirds crosswise. To save time, put 3 on the board at once.

**Clothing.** You must do your best ironing with clothing. It takes practice to become skillful. However, if you follow these sugestions, you can develop a technique that makes the difference between mediocre and perfect ironing:

Always iron absolutely dry as you go. This keeps the fabric from wrinkling and requiring repeated ironing. For example, if you don't iron cuffs until all the dampness is gone, they will redampen the adjoining sleeves and you'll have to reiron. This is true of all double thicknesses and heavy seams, such as armhole seams in men's shirts. Ironing until dry may seem slow, but it saves time in the end.

When you iron acetate, the fabric must not only look dry but be dry to the touch. Some blouses, for example, look dry before they are.

Learn to iron with unhurried, well-directed, rhythmic motions, never quick, jerky strokes. Give the heat time to do the work. Don't tire yourself by pressing down on the iron.

First iron sections that can hang off the board—cuffs, collars, sleeves, and belts. Then do the body of the garment.

If shoulder pads aren't removable, iron them as dry as you can before you iron sleeves.

With dresses that button down the front, be careful not to iron too heavily on buttonhole side; if you do, it may sag. To avoid this, press lightly over buttonholes and around buttons.

Be careful of buttons. Some of them may melt or become distorted from the iron's heat. Iron around buttons as best you can, or turn the button side down on a very thick bath towel, and iron over it.

**Plackets.** To iron a placket smooth, first close slide fastener. Iron next to fastener with nose of iron, to smooth out wrinkles in tape, but do not iron directly over it.

**Slips and Nightgowns.** Set heat control according to the fabric. If, for rayon, the ironing goes too slowly at the "rayon" setting, push heat control up a bit. Some rayons can be ironed satisfactorily at "silk" setting. Iron slips and nightgowns on wrong side, with weave of material. Seams should be ironed flat. When the fabric is quite dry, turn to right side, and press double thicknesses. Knit-rayon and nylon slips and nightgowns don't need ironing, but sometimes look better if pressed a bit after they are dry.

**Brassières.** The fullness presents the only ironing problem. To avoid wrinkles, iron toward center of cup, turning brassière on board until entire area is smooth and dry. Then iron flat sections and straps.

**Shorts.** Athletic and knit shorts don't require ironing; but a quick pressing of bands and crotch straightens and stretches them—improvements they frequently need. Press shorts when they are dry.

Shorts of woven fabric need a little more attention, even though they aren't completely ironed. Iron them when they are slightly damp. First, touch up waistband on both sides, then fold the legs of the shorts together, and iron the outside of the legs.

### How to Iron a Shirt

First be sure that the shirts are properly starched and well dampened before ironing.

Second, iron collar on wrong side partly dry, then thoroughly on the right side. Pull material taut, and iron from points in to avoid tiny wrinkles. Move iron slowly, and iron the neckband completely dry, before folding and shaping collar.

Next fold the yoke flat, and iron entire yoke. Be particularly careful to iron it dry, since it is a double thickness. Iron the armhole seams.

The next step is the ironing of cuffs and sleeves. Iron each cuff exactly like the collar. Be sure to nose iron well up into gathers of sleeve, so that the double portion of the cuff and the bottom of the sleeve will be dry. Iron along underarm seam.

Now iron the body of the shirt, first the back and then the two fronts. Hold front pleat taut as you iron it, so that it will be free from wrinkles. Iron on both sides. Starching will keep the pleat smooth and will prevent wrinkling and creasing.

The last but not the least important step is folding the shirt. Lay shirt flat on ironing surface and button top, middle, and last button. Fold under each side of shirt, lengthwise, about one-fourth of width. Lay sleeves lengthwise. Turn over and fold.

### How to Sprinkle Men's Shirts

If you iron 8 or 10 shirts every week, this rapid sprinkling will make the job much easier. Take the dry shirt by the seams at armpits and tail, and let shirt drop into four folds. Fold both sleeves over shirt front. Run fingertips along buttonhole bands. Pile one shirt on top of the other, smoothing as you go.

To sprinkle, lift sleeves, and lightly dampen shirt front and collar. Drop sleeves, one at a time, and sprinkle. Be sure to include cuffs. Fold over from the collar in thirds, sprinkling as you go. You'll become so adept that you'll soon do one shirt after another without putting sprinkler down. Try our method.

### Ironing a Skirt

**To Iron Pleats.** Iron pleats flat on the wrong side first. When you are ready to press the pleats, turn dress to the right side. Using the stitching as a guide, arrange several pleats in a group, spacing them evenly. (Use a ruler or measuring tape if it seems easier.) Pin, and press flat directly on the fabric. Use a pressing cloth if the material shows shine.

**To Iron a Gored Skirt.** If the skirt is cut on the bias, iron with the weave of the cloth—otherwise the fabric may wrinkle and bulge at the seams. At hem, avoid wrinkles by ironing with straight of goods. Smooth gently as you iron.

### How to Make a Blouse Easier to Iron

A blouse doesn't have to be expensive or even frilled with lace or trimmed with a fancy collar to cause trouble in ironing. Sometimes simple tailored blouses are the worst offenders. Unusual weaves are frequently the root of ironing difficulties. Although some weaves iron like a whiz, others take far more time than you want to spend and still don't have a finished look. Here's what to do about them.

**Let It Dry a While.** Hang a troublesome blouse on a hanger and let it dry until the double thicknesses no longer feel wet; then iron. Even if you strike a dry spot or two, it's easier to redampen these spots than to try to iron dry the entire blouse.

**Step Up the Ironing Temperature.** You need not always iron acetate blouses at the dial setting for "Rayon." The "Silk" setting on heat-controlled irons can be used occasionally. It frequently speeds up the job and the extra heat makes garments look better, too. Increase heat gradually to avoid damage.

**Starch for Crisp Vitality.** One of the saddest results of a fair-to-middling ironing job on a blouse is the loss of the fabric's original vitality, the new look that made it pretty. A little starch brings life back to an acetate blouse, and of course, you need starch on cottons, organdies, and batistes unless they have been specially treated. In most cases a light starching will do. A packaged ironing aid will help your iron skim over the blouse.

**Padding Prevents Shine.** Ironing on the wrong side is the first rule in avoiding shine, but when you come to a double thickness, as on a pocket or collar, iron first on the wrong side, then on the right side *over a pad*. A piece of terry toweling or a folded dish towel will do.

**Finishing Touches.** Instead of repeated pressing to touch up your blouse, let it dry thoroughly, then go over it again. Blouses with tiny tucks look wavy when they are not ironed entirely dry.

When you put your blouses away, line them up straight on hangers and give them plenty of room in the closet to hang freely.

## How to Do a Good Job of Pressing

Good home pressing is an art well worth cultivating. Anyone accustomed to using an iron should learn to press dresses, skirts, slacks, men's trousers, etc. Lined jackets and coats, should be pressed by an expert, because, in the hands of an amateur, there's too great a risk of shine and seam marks.

### To Press You Should Have:

A heat-controlled iron (preferably steam)
Pressing cloth, shoulder mitt, and sponge
Ironing board
Sleeve board
Cord control

**To Press Wool.** Always use a pressing cloth. Use the "Wool" setting on your iron. With a treated pressing cloth, a higher setting can be used satisfactorily. Press on the right side over the slightly dampened pressing cloth, and lift the cloth before it is dry.

**To Press Rayon and Silk.** Use the "Rayon" or "Silk" setting on your iron. Press directly on the wrong side of the fabric. Always test the tip of the iron on a free edge of the fabric to make sure it is not too hot. Where touching up on the right side is necessary, use a dampened pressing cloth.

**To Press Velvet.** Use a soft-bristled brush to remove lint and dust from the fabric, or wrap transparent tape, sticky side out, around your hand, and brush with that.

To remove creases and restore the pile, hang the garment over a tub of steaming water or place it on an ironing board and hold a steam iron close to, but not touching, the pile. Dry the garment thoroughly before hanging it in the closet.

Velvet accessories may be freshened by any of the above methods. Hang velvet garments loosely in the closet to avoid crushing the pile.

**Pressing Technique.** 1. Before you press, brush clothes well. Get a well-designed, stiff clothesbrush with good-quality bristles, and go over your clothes thoroughly—even under collars, trouser cuffs, pockets, etc. You'll not only chase dust but give yourself extra insurance against moth damage.

2. A treated pressing cloth is inexpensive and much more satisfactory than an untreated one. Dampen it lightly with a sponge, sprayer, or cloth wrung out of water. Be sure to press on the side of the cloth designated by the manufacturer.

3. Use a true pressing motion—lifting the iron up and down rather than sliding it back and forth as in regular ironing.

4. To press pockets, lapels, and other double thicknesses on the right side, use a pressing cloth and a light pressure of the iron to avoid shine.

5. When pressing wool, don't let the pressing cloth become completely dry. Lift the cloth while it is steaming slightly, and tap the fabric vigorously with a clothesbrush to enliven the material and bring up the nap.

6. Upper parts of sleeves and shoulders are not troublesome to press, if you have a shoulder mitt to slip into them and fill them out. Then you can press on the right side with a pressing cloth and not worry about ironing creases in the fullness.

7. In pressing trouser legs, let the original creases guide you. Straighten each leg carefully, and with the pressing cloth in place, move the iron with a circular motion over inside of the leg; turn, and then press outside.

Whenever you finish pressing a garment, place it on a hanger, centering shoulders so it hangs straight. Button as many buttons as necessary to keep it from sagging, and close the side fastener.

### Getting Rid of Shine:

Some sort of abrasion is the only thing that can be applied at home to reduce shine. If it is attempted, it must be used only with wool, and even then it should be done with caution for fear of damaging the fabric. To remove shine from a blue suit, for example, moisten a sponge or cloth slightly and sponge the shine areas thoroughly. While the fabric is still damp, go over it gently with *fine* steel wool. Stroke the fabric with the steel wool, covering about a 6" or 8" area with each stroke. If the nap is not too worn down, you will improve the appearance of the material and the fabric will take on a dull look while you are using the steel wool. Let dry, and press.

### How to Press a Man's Suit

Start by brushing the suit well—insides of pockets and cuffs, too. Buy a special pressing cloth and a sponge. Dampen cloth evenly, and press around the entire top of the trousers.

Good tailoring calls for uncreased sleeves. Lay sleeve on board with edge overhanging to avoid crease, and press both sides. It's easier to avoid creases with a sleeve board.

Fill out upper parts of sleeves and shoulders with a rolled bath towel before pressing. When these are finished, press back of coat and the two fronts.

Use great care with pockets and all double thicknesses, for fear of markings and shine. Use light pressure, lift cloth before dry, and beat vigorously with brush. Hang the suit carefully.

It stands to reason that the more pressing you can do at home, the lower your professional pressing bills will be. This is why a steam iron makes sense. It banishes wrinkles quickly and easily, but keep these facts in mind:

1. Pressing differs from ironing. You lift the iron up and down. This motion discourages the fabric's stretching.

2. With a steam iron, wool skirts and many rayon dresses can be completely pressed on the wrong side without a pressing cloth. But when you press on the right side, for pockets, lapels, sleves and cuffs, use a pressing cloth and light pressure to prevent shine marks.

3. Cheesecloth is the handiest kind

## Steam-Iron Pressing Hints

*Fill out those hard-to-press shoulders on suits with a plump pressing mitt, and iron right over your palm.*

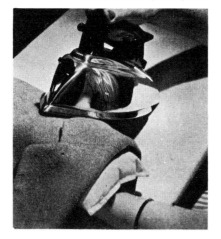

of pressing cloth to use with a steam iron. A double thickness protects the fabric and doesn't interfere with the steam needed to eliminate wrinkles.

4. If there's a nap, press with it, not against it. On smooth fabrics, press with the grain, either lengthwise or crosswise.

5. Your steam iron and a sheet of tissue or waxed paper make veils look as fresh as those on new spring hats.

6. A cloud of steam and a brisk brushing will rejuvenate the most bedraggled hat. It's the best way to banish rain spots.

7. Let pressed clothes hang freely before you put them away, as steam pressing leaves a bit of invisible dampness.

## How to Press Your Suit

A few minutes' attention each time you wear it will make the suit look perfect.

Watch out for these pitfalls in pressing:

1. An overheated iron. Wool scorches quickly, and crisp acetate or silk suits stiffen or melt from too much heat.

2. Shine or "slick" marks from pressing on the right side, particularly double thicknesses. Press on the wrong side, if possible, or use a lightly dampened pressing cloth.

3. Damage to buttons and other accessories on the suit. The heat of the iron damages plastic buttons. If you are working fast, you may loosen buttons by hitting them with the iron.

**To Press the Skirt:** Merely turn the skirt inside out and slip it over the ironing board with the open seams facing you. Starting at the hem edge, press each gore toward the waistband (including the band). Nose iron under seam edge to avoid pressing over the double seams (thereby avoiding shine). When the skirt is pressed, remove it from the board, close the zipper, and immediately hang it from the loops on the inside of the waistband.

If the skirt is pleated, first secure each pleat at the hemline with a straight pin, then press.

**A Touch-up to the Jacket:** A lined suit jacket needs little more than a quick touch-up. Don't forget a cloth and a minimum of dampness. Go over the shoulder area, the sleeves, and the two fronts. Don't use "sweeping" strokes when you press. Instead, lift the iron up and down with a light stroke.

## Pressing Ties

To press a tie without causing a flattened-out look, cut a cardboard insert to fit each half of the tie. Slip the inserts inside the tie; using cheesecloth as a pressing cloth (to prevent shine), press with a steam iron.

### You and Your Dry-Cleaner

**What Dry-Cleaning Is.** Essentially, dry-cleaning is a method of washing and rinsing garments in dry-cleaning fluid, which is continuously being clarified. This washing removes general soil and some stains.

A thorough inspection is made to identify stains that dry-cleaning fluid did not remove. They are given separate treatment—"spotting," the dry-cleaner calls it—which involves special techniques, skill, and an expert knowledge of the chemistry of stains and of the construction, dyes, and finishes of fabrics.

**Help Your Cleaner Do a Better Job.** Send clothes to be cleaned before they become badly soiled, and as soon as possible after they're stained. Stains are very difficult to remove after they have aged. If possible, identify stains—especially special inks, glues, gums, and lacquers—by pinning a note on the garment. Many stains cannot be removed in the general dry-cleaning process, but require special detergents and techniques. A good cleaner knows the chemistry of stains.

Between dry-cleanings, don't press garments stained with fruit juice. Even though the stains are small and barely noticeable, the heat of the iron may turn them into permanent brown spots.

Don't blame the dry-cleaner if acetate clothes take

on a reddish cast. This is fume fading, caused by products of combustion in the air.

**Pick Your Own Pockets.** Remember to search pockets before sending clothes to the cleaner's. Especially remember the watch pocket below the waistband of men's trousers and the small change pocket in the right-hand pocket of men's coats. These are favorite repositories for bills, coins, and valuables. If matches left in pockets are not discovered, they may ignite during the deodorizing process, which follows dry-cleaning, and start a serious fire.

### Dry-Cleaning at Home

Dry-cleaning at home, because of the many dangers, should not be attempted on a large scale, but occasionally it may become necessary on a small scale.

Dry-cleaning is similar to washing fine things by hand in a washbasin. You squeeze the article to remove soil, rub neckline and cuffs with extra effort, rinse, press out the moisture, and allow to dry. The amount of work involved is no more or less than in soap-and-water cleaning. Wear household gloves; without them, cleaning fluid seems to dry the skin. Have a window open and a fan on while you are working. Cleaning fluid often dissolves plastics, so remove all plastic buttons, buckles, trimming, etc., before cleaning.

Unlike water, cleaning fluid doesn't remove creases or pleats, so pressing dry-cleaned clothing is much simpler than ironing laundered clothing.

Flammable dry-cleaning fluids are serious fire hazards. Even the small pilot light on a range some distance from where the cleaning is done is enough to cause an explosion. Rubbing the fabric while it is wet with cleaning fluid also may produce a spark. The fumes of nonflammable fluids are toxic and have been known to cause very serious illness when used in a quantity sufficient for dry-cleaning.

Because most people who attempt to dry-clean their clothes at home do not have a sufficient amount of fluid for both cleaning and rinsing, they seldom do as good a job as even an average professional cleaner.

**Home Stain Removal.** Although we do not recommend general home dry-cleaning, we do suggest that you remove fresh stains at home whenever possible. For detailed instructions on removing specific stains, consult the next chapter.

**Wet "Dry"-Cleaning.** Clothes badly soiled by perspiration or food stains require wet-cleaning with water and a detergent. This is literally a gentle hand method of laundering. Don't be alarmed if your cleaner suggests it.

The reason most dry-cleanable garments are sold as such is that their styling may make ironing after washing difficult, or the fabric will shrink excessively or stretch out of shape in washing. Thus, when the cleaner finds it necessary to wet-clean such garments, he measures them first. Then, in finishing, he is careful to restore them to the original measurements. This is accomplished with special pressing and steaming equipment available only to a professional cleaner. If a garment is badly stretched or shrunken after wet-cleaning, retreatment by a good dry-cleaner may restore its original size and shape.

If you notice yellowing at the neck or upper back of your clothing, call it to the cleaner's attention. He will use a special type of semiwet soap or solvent, or even water, to treat these discolorations.

**Cleaning Before Storing.** Always have clothes cleaned before storing them. Long storage without cleaning ages many stains, making them very difficult to remove.

Cleaning before storage is also a good protection against damage from insects. The clothes moth on wools and the silverfish on cottons and rayons are attracted first to areas with food stains.

**What the Cleaner Can't Do.** Cleaners can't restore faded colors or color that has been removed or changed by a stain. They can measure shrinkable garments before cleaning and usually can restore them to original dimensions in pressing and reshaping. Cleaners cannot dry-clean belts held together with adhesives that dissolve in cleaning fluid, so they are frequently returned uncleaned.

# How to Remove Stains and Spots by Simple Home Methods

Stains sometimes are too complicated for home treatment. They may present problems in chemistry calling for technical knowledge. It is reasonably safe to take out the kinds of stain for which methods are given here. Follow these precautions:

1. Treat the stain promptly. Fresh stains react better than old ones.

2. Do not use stain remover on colored or dry-cleanable clothes without experimenting with a sample from some inconspicuous section.

3. Do not treat a stain on a garment with over-all soil.

4. Do not tamper with light-colored fabrics.

5. Do not attempt to remove stains from hard, smooth fabrics like gabardine and covert.

6. Be wary of taffeta, moiré, and other crisp fabrics frequently treated with finishes that water-spot quickly.

7. If in doubt about what caused the stain, try only cool water and cleaning fluid or powder. (If you sponge the fabric with water first, let it dry before trying any kind of cleaning fluid.) If you are making no progress, stop experimenting and send the garment to the dry-cleaner.

8. Sometimes stains are invisible until they are pressed, after which they may be impossible to remove. If you think something has been spilled but cannot find the stain, hold a single thickness of the garment to the light or sponge the area lightly with water. Frequently the stain will then show up as a darker area than the fabric.

All chemicals, bleaches, cleaning fluids, etc., mentioned here are easily available at grocery and drugstores. "Hypo" comes from a photographers' supply store.

Before using a bleaching solution on a colored garment, test it on a hidden section to be sure it will not affect the color.

When directions call for sponging a spot, fold clean cheesecloth into a pad under it. Moisten another piece of cheesecloth with remover, and, starting at the edge of the spot, sponge toward center (except on satin). With all stains except grease, work on right side. Use stain remover sparingly. "Feather out" the liquid around the stain to avoid a definite edge when the material dries. Pat the spot with dry cheesecloth between applications. As you work, the pad under the spot will absorb the stain, so move it frequently.

### Airplane Glue

**Washable Fabrics (Any Color):** On all washable fabrics except acetate, sponge the spot with acetone. Give it a chance to dissolve the glue, then wash in warm suds and rinse. Caution: Never use acetone without testing it. Airplane glue dissolves acetate. If the fabric has been affected, sponge with amyl acetate, wash in warm suds, rinse.

**Dry-Cleanable Fabrics:** Same, but do not wash.

### Alcoholic Beverages and Soft Drinks

**Washable Fabrics (White):** Soak in cool water, wash in warm suds, rinse. For old stains that have turned brown, bleach: On cotton, linen, and rayon, use 1 tablespoonful of household bleach to a quart of water, soak 15 minutes, rinse 3 times. For silk and wool, use 2 tablespoonfuls of hydrogen peroxide to a gallon of water, soak ½ hour or longer if necessary. Rinse twice.

**Washable Fabrics (Colored):** Soak stains in cool water, wash in warm suds, rinse. If stain remains, mix 2 tablespoonfuls of hydrogen peroxide to a gallon of water. Test solution, then soak stains ½ hour or longer, if necessary. Rinse twice.

**Dry-Cleanable Fabrics:** Sponge with cool water. Alcoholic beverages may form a hard-to-remove dye ring.

**Black Marks on Dish Towels**

The most common stains on dish towels are black streaks from cooking utensils. They require hard rubbing with soap directly on the stain. Remove as much as you can before the dish towels are washed and bleached.

**Blood**

**Washable Fabrics (White):** Soak in cool water until stains turn light brown, then wash in warm suds. If the stains are old, add 2 tablespoonfuls of household ammonia to each gallon of soapy water, soak 15 minutes, wash in warm suds, and rinse.

**Washable Fabrics (Colored):** See "White Washable Fabrics." If household ammonia is used, test first.

**Dry-Cleanable Fabrics:** Sponge with cool water.

**Butter**

**Washable Fabrics (Any Color):** Butter stains usually can be removed in washing. If not, see "Grease and Oil."

**Dry-Cleanable Fabrics:** Use cleaning fluid or powder.

**Candle Wax**

**Washable Fabrics (White):** Scrape off as much as possible, then sponge or soak in cleaning fluid. If stain remains, bleach: For cotton, linen, and rayon, use 1 tablespoonful of household bleach to a quart of water and soak 15 minutes. Wash in warm suds, rinse 3 times. For silk and wool, mix 1 cupful of denatured alcohol and 2 cupfuls of water. Soak 15 minutes, wash and rinse.

**Washable Fabrics (Colored):** See "White Silk and Wool," but test solution.

**Dry-Cleanable Fabrics:** See "Washable Colored Fabrics." Sponge with cool water.

*Note:* The method of removing candle wax by placing blotters over and under stain and pressing with an iron should be used only for wax from white candles. Heat may turn dyes into difficult stains.

**Candy (Except Chocolate)**

**Washable Fabrics (Any Color):** Most candy stains come out in the ordinary washing process.

**Dry-Cleanable Fabrics:** Sponge with warm water.

**Carbon Paper**

**Washable Fabrics (Any Color):** Sponge with cleaning fluid. Wash in warm suds, and rinse.

**Dry-Cleanable Fabrics:** Try sponging with cleaning fluid or using cleaning powder. If this does not work, send the garment to a reliable dry-cleaner.

**Chewing Gum**

**Washable Fabrics (Any Color):** Soak in cleaning fluid until gum loosens and can be scraped off. Wash in warm suds, and rinse.

**Dry-Cleanable Fabrics:** Sponge with cleaning fluid.

**Chocolate and Cocoa**

**Washable Fabrics (White):** Scrape off chocolate candy with a dull blade, then wash in warm suds, and rinse.

Stains from chocolate syrup or sauce or cocoa, should be sponged with cleaning fluid or soaked in the fluid before washing. If stains remain, bleach: For cotton, linen, and rayon, use 1 tablespoonful of household bleach to each quart of water, and soak 15 minutes. Rinse 3 times. For silk and wool, use 2 tablespoonfuls of hydrogen peroxide to each gallon of water, and soak ½ hour or longer, if necessary. Rinse twice.

**Washable Fabrics (Colored):** For

chocolate-candy stains, see "White Washable Fabrics."

Stains from chocolate syrup or sauce or cocoa, should be sponged with cleaning fluids. If stains remain, mix 1 teaspoonful of sodium perborate and 1 pint of hydrogen peroxide. Test the solution, then sponge. Wash in warm suds, and rinse.

**Dry-Cleanable Fabrics:** Sponge with cool water. Dry. Sponge with cleaning fluid, or use cleaning powder.

**Cod-Liver Oil**

**Washable Fabrics (White):** Soak stains in cleaning fluid, and rub between the fingers. Wash in hot suds, and rinse. If stains are old or have turned light brown from ironing, bleach: For cotton, linen, and rayon, use 1 tablespoonful of household bleach to each quart of water, and soak 15 minutes. Rinse 3 times. For silk and wool, use 2 tablespoonfuls of hydrogen peroxide to each gallon of water. Soak ½ hour or longer, if necessary. Rinse twice.

**Washable Fabrics (Colored):** Soak in cleaning fluid, wash in warm suds, and rinse. If stains remain, mix 2 tablespoonfuls of hydrogen peroxide to each gallon of water. Test the solution, then soak stains ½ hour or longer, if necessary. Rinse twice.

**Dry-Cleanable Fabrics:** Sponge with cleaning fluid.

**Coffee and Tea**

**Washable Fabrics (White):** Soak fresh stains in cool water, then wash in warm suds, and rinse. If heavy cream was used in the beverage, sponge with cleaning fluid, or let soak in fluid first. If stains remain, bleach: For white cotton, linen, and rayon, use 1 tablespoonful of household bleach to each quart of water, and soak 15 minutes. Rinse 3 times. For white silk and wool, use 2 tablespoonfuls of hydrogen peroxide to each gallon of water, and soak ½ hour or longer, if necessary. Rinse twice.

**Washable Fabrics (Colored):** See "White Silk and Wool," but test the bleach.

**Dry-Cleanable Fabrics:** Sponge with cool water. Dry; then sponge with cleaning fluid, or use cleaning powder. Old or ironed-in stains are impossible, even for a dry-cleaner, to remove.

### Dye and Running Colors

**Washable Fabrics (White):** It is not always possible to remove a dye or streaks that have bled into a garment. Sometimes a bleach or a special color remover works satisfactorily. To bleach cotton, linen, and rayon, use 1 tablespoonful of household bleach to each quart of water. Soak 15 minutes. Rinse well; repeat if necessary. To bleach white silk and wool, use 2 tablespoonfuls of hydrogen peroxide to each gallon of water and soak ½ hour or longer, if necessary. Rinse twice. Special color removers can be used on any washable fabric if directions on the package are followed.

**Washable Fabrics (Colored):** To remove streaks of dye, take out all color with special color remover. (This applies only to light-colored garments; dark-colored dyes rarely can be removed entirely.) Follow directions on the package, then redye.

**Dry-Cleanable Fabrics:** Dye stains cannot be removed by home methods. Consult a reliable dry-cleaner.

### Egg

**Washable Fabrics (Any Color):** Scrape away as much as possible with a dull knife, then sponge with cold water. (Never use hot water; heat sets egg stains.) If stain remains, sprinkle with pepsin powder. Work in well; let stand ½ hour. Rinse thoroughly.

**Dry-Cleanable Fabrics:** Sponge with cold water. Dry; sponge with cleaning fluid.

### Fruit and Berry Stains

**Washable Fabrics (Any Color):** For fruit and berry stains, see "Alcoholic Beverages and Soft Drinks." Fresh peaches and deep-colored berries may need a second treatment.

**Dry-Cleanable Fabrics:** Sponge with cool water; work soapless shampoo into stain. Let stand several

hours, then test white vinegar on a hidden section of the garment. If no color change occurs, apply a few drops, and let remain a minute or two. Sponge with cool water.

### Glue (Not Airplane)

**Washable Fabrics (Any Color):** Soak in warm suds until dissolved. Wash and rinse.

**Dry-Cleanable Fabrics:** Sponge with warm water.

### Grass

**Washable Fabrics (White):** Wash in hot suds, rubbing well. Rinse. If stains remain, bleach: For cotton, linen, and rayon, use 1 tablespoonful of household bleach to each quart of water, and soak 15 minutes. Rinse 3 times. For silk and wool, use 2 tablespoonfuls of hydrogen peroxide to each gallon of water, and soak ½ hour or longer, if necessary. Rinse twice.

Grass stains can be removed by using a special color remover that is available in most drugstores. Follow the manufacturer's directions given on the outside of the package.

**Washable Fabrics (Colored):** Wash stains in warm suds, rubbing well. If stains remain, mix 1 teaspoonful of sodium perborate to 1 pint of hydrogen peroxide. Test the solution. Then soak stain ½ hour or longer, if necessary. Rinse twice. For stubborn stains, sprinkle sodium perborate on damp material. Let stand ½ hour. Rinse twice.

**Dry-Cleanable Fabrics:** Sponge with cleaning fluid, or use cleaning powder. Mix 1 cupful of denatured alcohol and 2 cupfuls of water. Test. Sponge stains with solution. Sponge with cool water and allow to dry. If stains remain, repeat process.

### Gravy

**Washable Fabrics (Any Color):** Soak in cool water, wash in warm suds, and rinse. Dry, then sponge with cleaning fluid or let soak in fluid.

**Dry-Cleanable Fabrics:** Sponge with cool water. Dry. Sponge with cleaning fluid, or use cleaning powder. Repeat if necessary.

### Grease and Oil

**Washable Fabrics (White):** Soak washable cotton, linen, and rayon in very hot suds, then rinse. Sponge old stains with cleaning fluid or let soak in fluid before washing, then wash in hot suds and rinse. Sponge silk and wool with cleaning fluid or let soak in fluid, then wash in warm suds. Rinse. Do not boil silk or wool.

**Washable Fabrics (Colored):** Sponge with cleaning fluid, or soak in fluid. Wash in warm, not hot, suds and rinse.

**Dry-Cleanable Fabrics:** Sponge with cleaning fluid or use cleaning powder, working from wrong side of material.

*Note:* Do not attempt to remove grease or oil stains by pressing with an iron on a blotter. The heat may set the stains permanently.

### Ice Cream

**Washable Fabrics (White): Vanilla Ice Cream:** Soak in cool water, wash in warm suds, and rinse.

**Fruit Ice Cream:** Soak fresh stains in cool water; wash in warm suds, and rinse. If stains remain, bleach: For cotton, linen and rayon, use 1 tablespoonful of household bleach to each quart of water, and soak 15 minutes. Rinse 3 times. For silk, and wool, use 2 tablespoonfuls of hydrogen peroxide to each gallon of water, and soak ½ hour or longer, if necessary. Rinse twice.

**Chocolate Ice Cream:** Sponge with cleaning fluid or soak in fluid, then wash in warm suds, and rinse. If stains remain, use household bleach for white cotton, linen, and rayon; hydrogen peroxide for silk and wool. Follow directions for removing fruit ice cream stains.

**Washable Fabrics (Colored):** Vanilla ice cream: See "White Washable Fabrics." Chocolate and fruit ice cream: See "Washable White Silk and Wool," but test bleach.

**Dry-Cleanable Fabrics:** Sponge with cool water. Dry. Sponge with cleaning fluid.

### Ink

Inks differ in composition; try several methods of stain removal. So-called washable inks usually are removed if washed either before or just after the ink has dried. Inks in the "permanent" class are made to last and rarely can be removed, although the following methods should at least lighten stains. If they do not respond, take the article to a reliable dry-cleaner.

**Washable Fabrics (White):** Place absorbent pad beneath stain and moisten stain with cool water; blot immediately. Repeat until almost all ink is removed, then wash in hot suds to which a few drops of household ammonia have been added. Rinse. If stains persist, bleach: For cotton, linen and rayon, use 1 tablespoonful of household bleach to each quart of water, and soak 15 minutes. Rinse 3 times. For silk and wool, use oxalic acid. (Ask druggist for a 5 per cent solution. Oxalic acid is poisonous. Handle it carefully.) Soak stains 15 minutes, rinse 3 times. To last rinse add a few drops of household ammonia.

**Washable Fabrics (Colored):** Rinse in cool water, then wash in warm suds to which a few drops of household ammonia have been added. Rinse. If stains remain, bleach as for washable white silk and wool.

**Dry-Cleanable Fabrics:** Sponge with cool water. If stains remain, make a solution of 1 cupful of denatured alcohol and 2 cupfuls of water. Test, then sponge with solution. Sponge with cool water.

*Note:* The old-time theory that milk removes ink stains is not only false but harmful, because milk complicates removal of the stain. Milk adds a protein stain, which makes removal of the original ink spot all the more difficult.

### Ink—Ball Point

**Washable Fabrics (White):** Place an absorbent pad beneath the stain and lightly moisten the stain with denatured alcohol and blot immediately with a second cloth. Repeat until there is no more ink coming out. Wash in warm suds and rinse.

**Washable Fabrics (Colored):** See "Washable Fabrics (White)," but test the alcohol.

**Dry-Cleanable Fabrics:** Test the denatured alcohol to be sure there is no effect on color. Moisten stain as suggested in "Washable Fabrics (White)," and sponge with warm suds followed by clear water.

### Lemon Juice

**Washable Fabrics (White):** Fresh stains usually are removed in washing. If stains are old or have turned light brown from ironing, bleach: For white cotton, linen, and rayon, use 1 tablespoonful of household bleach to each quart of water, and soak 15 minutes. Rinse 3 times. For white silk and wool, use 2 tablespoonfuls of hydrogen peroxide to each gallon of water, and soak ½ hour or longer, if necessary. Then rinse well twice.

**Washable Fabrics (Colored):** Wash in warm suds. If lemon juice has changed the fabric's color, rinse stains freely in cool water. Then hold stained fabric over fumes from a bottle of household ammonia. If the color has not been destroyed, the fumes should restore it. Ammonia affects some dyes, so have white vinegar ready to sponge on quickly if color changes too much. Then rinse well twice.

**Dry-Cleanable Fabrics:** Sponge with cool water. If lemon juice has changed the fabric's color, use ammonia fumes and white vinegar, as above. Sponge with cool water.

### Lipstick

**Washable Fabrics (Any Color):** Although lipstick stains sometimes are removed in washing, it is better to soak them first in cleaning fluid, then wash in warm suds, and rinse.

**Dry-Cleanable Fabrics:** Sponge with cleaning fluid, or use cleaning powder.

### Mascara

**Washable Fabrics (Any Color):** Stains usually come out in washing.

**Dry-Cleanable Fabrics:** Sponge with cleaning fluid, or use cleaning powder. Mix 1 cupful of denatured alcohol and 2 cupfuls of water. Test, sponge with solution, then with cool water.

### Meat Juice

**Washable Fabrics (Any Color):** Sponge with cool water. Let dry. Then sponge with cleaning fluid. Wash in warm suds, and rinse.

**Dry-Cleanable Fabrics:** Sponge with cool water. Let dry. Then sponge with cleaning fluid, or use cleaning powder.

### Medicines

Your chances of success are greatest if the stained articles are washable. Dry-cleanable fabrics, particularly if stained with dark medicines like argyrol or silver nitrate, should be sent to a reputable dry-cleaner. Medicines with a sugar-syrup base frequently can be removed by washing in warm suds, and a thick, gummy medicine sometimes responds to this treatment:

**Washable Fabrics:** Soften stain by rubbing with Vaseline. Let stand 15 minutes; then soak in cleaning fluid. Wash in warm suds, and rinse.

**Dry-Cleanable Fabrics:** With a dull blade, scrape off as much of medicine as possible. Sponge with cleaning fluid. Repeat several times if necessary. If the medicine has no such identifying characteristics, try one or more of the methods given below. (Note in directions when solution should be tested on a hidden section of a colored garment, to be sure it will not affect the color.)

### Argyrol

**Washable Fabrics (White):** Soak in cool water; then wash in warm suds. Rinse. If stains remain, bleach: For cotton, linen, and rayon, use 1 tablespoonful of household bleach to each quart of water, and soak 15 minutes. Rinse 3 times. (Among white cottons, muslin and terry towels hold argyrol stains tenaciously, and bleaching merely lightens rather than removes them.) If this fails, sprinkle on powdered pepsin while stains are damp. Work it well into cloth. Let stand ½ hour or longer, then rinse. Put a few drops of tincture of iodine on stains. Let stand 10 or 15 minutes, then soak or sponge with a solution made with a few crystals of photographer's "Hypo" dissolved in ½ cup water. Rinse twice.

For white silk and wool, use 2 tablespoonfuls of hydrogen peroxide to each gallon of water, and soak ½ hour or longer, if necessary. Rinse twice.

**Washable Fabrics (Colored):** See "Washable White Silk and Wool," but test bleach. If stains remain, use powdered pepsin, sodium thiosulfate, and tincture of iodine, as above.

**Dry-Cleanable Fabrics:** Should be sent to a reputable dry-cleaner as promptly as possible.

## Arnica

**Washable Fabrics (White):** Mix 1 cupful of denatured alcohol and 2 cupfuls of water. Sponge or soak stains in solution. (Do not soak in cool water, for this sometimes spreads stains.) Then sponge or soak in solution made of a few crystals of sodium thiosulfate dissolved in ½ cupful of water. Rinse twice. If stains remain, use color remover, according to directions on package.

**Washable Fabrics (Colored):** See "White Washable Fabrics"; but do not use color remover, unless you wish to take out the color and redye.

**Dry-Cleanable Fabrics:** Mix 1 cupful of denatured alcohol and 2 cupfuls of water. Test the solution. Sponge stains. Sponge with cool water.

## Cough Medicine

**Washable Fabrics (Any Color):** Wash in warm suds. If stains remain, try the treatment suggested for removing silver nitrate.

**Dry-Cleanable Fabrics:** Sponge with cool water. If stains remain, send garment to a reliable dry-cleaner.

## Iodine

**Washable Fabrics (White):** Fresh iodine stains usually are removed if soaked in cool water, then washed in warm suds, and rinsed. If stains are old, use 1 cupful of household ammonia and 2 cupfuls of water, and soak 15 minutes. Then wash in warm suds, and rinse twice.

**Washable Fabrics (Colored):** See "White Washable Fabrics." However, if household ammonia is used, test the solution. Then soak 15 minutes. Wash in warm suds, and rinse. (If ammonia has changed a fabric's color, it sometimes can be restored by immediate application of white vinegar.)

**Dry-Cleanable Fabrics:** Mix a few crystals of sodium thiosulfate and ½ cupful of water. Test the solution. Sponge with solution, then with cool water.

## Mercurochrome

**Washable Fabrics (White):** Rinse out as much as possible in cool water. Mix 1 cupful of denatured alcohol and 2 cupfuls of water. Sponge or soak stains in solution, then wash in warm suds, rinse, and bleach. For cotton, linen, and rayon, use 1 tablespoonful of household bleach to a quart of water. Soak 15 minutes, rinse well. For silk and wool, use 2 tablespoonfuls of hydrogen peroxide to a gallon of water, soak ½ hour or longer, if necessary, and rinse twice.

**Washable Fabrics (Colored):** Rinse out as much as possible in cool water, then mix 1 cupful of denatured alcohol and 2 cupfuls of water. Test, then sponge or soak stains in solution. Wash in warm suds and rinse with water containing a few drops of household ammonia. If stain remains, use hydrogen peroxide as for white silk and wool, then soak in white vinegar until stain disappears.

**Dry-Cleanable Fabrics:** Mix 1 cupful of denatured alcohol and 2 cupfuls of water. Test, then sponge stains in solution. Sponge with cool water containing a few drops of household ammonia. If stains remain, sponge with white vinegar and cool water.

## Paregoric

**Washable Fabrics (Any Color):** Mix 1 cupful of denatured alcohol and 2 cupfuls of water. Test the solution for a colored garment. Then sponge or soak stain, and wash in warm suds. Rinse.

**Dry-Cleanable Fabrics:** See "Washable Fabrics," but sponge with cool water instead of washing.

## Silver Nitrate

**Washable Fabrics (Any Color):** Sponge with cool water to get rid of as much of stain as possible. Then wash in warm suds. If stains remain, mix 1 part tincture of iodine to 3 parts of water. Test solution for a colored garment, then sponge. If stains remain, make a solution of a few crystals of sodium thiosulfate dissolved in ½ cupful of water, and sponge. If stains are not removed, repeat applications of iodine and sodium-thiosulfate solutions. Finally, wash in warm suds.

*Note:* Silver-nitrate stains cannot always be removed from washable fabrics; but the treatment suggested is worth trying, because it won't make the stains worse and in most cases it will considerably lighten them.

**Dry-Cleanable Fabrics:** Stains rarely can be removed satisfactorily.

## Mildew

Mildew attacks the fibers of fabric and weakens them. It is impossible to remove unless stains are discovered in the early stages.

**Washable Fabrics (White):** Wash in warm suds, then rinse. If stains remain, bleach: For cotton, linen, and rayon, use 1 tablespoonful of household bleach to each quart of water, and soak 15 minutes. Rinse three times. For silk and wool, use 2 tablespoonfuls of hydrogen peroxide to each gallon of water, and soak ½ hour or longer, if necessary. Rinse twice.

**Washable Fabrics (Colored):** See "Washable White Silk and Wool," but test bleach solution before using.

**Dry-Cleanable Fabrics:** Mildew stains are likely to be found only in very hot, humid climates. In these exceptional cases, take the stained garment to a reputable dry-cleaner.

## Milk and Cream

**Washable Fabrics (Any Color):** Cream stains usually are removed in washing. If grease remains, soak in cleaning fluid. Wash in warm suds, and rinse.

**Dry-Cleanable Fabrics:** Sponge with cleaning fluid, or use cleaning powder.

## Mud

**Washable Fabrics (Any Color):** Let dry, then brush off. Wash in warm suds, and rinse.

**Dry-Cleanable Fabrics:** Sponge with cool water. If greaselike stains remain, sponge with cleaning fluid or use cleaning powder.

## Mustard

**Washable Fabrics (White):** Work glycerin into stains, then wash in warm suds. Rinse. If stains remain, bleach: For cotton, linen, and rayon, use 1 tablespoonful of household bleach to a quart of water, and soak 15 minutes. Rinse 3 times. For silk and wool, use 2 tablespoonfuls of hydrogen peroxide to a gallon of water, and soak ½ hour or longer, if necessary. Rinse twice.

**Washable Fabrics (Colored):** See "Washable White Silk and Wool," but test bleach solution before you use it.

**Dry-Cleanable Fabrics:** Mix 1 cupful of denatured alcohol and 2 cupfuls of water. Sponge stains with solution, then with cool water.

## Nail Polish

Follow directions for removing airplane glue.

## Paint and Varnish

Oil-base paints and varnish are more difficult to treat than quick-drying oil-emulsion paints.

**Washable Fabrics (Any Color):** With a dull blade, scrape off as much paint or varnish as possible. Rub Vaseline into stain. Then soak in turpentine (U.S.P. quality, or at least highly refined) until stain has softened. Rub occasionally. Wash in warm suds. Rinse.

**Dry-Cleanable Fabrics:** Sponge with U.S.P.-quality turpentine. If stains remain, take garment to a reliable dry-cleaner.

## Finger Paints

**Washable Fabrics (All Colors):** Soak stain in clear, cold water, then wash in warm suds. Rub lightly if paint has dried. Rinse.

**Dry-Cleanable Fabrics:** Place bath

towel under stained area. Sponge lightly with damp cloth on right side of fabric. Dried finger paints can be removed by softening with cleaning fluid, then sponging with water.

## Pencil Marks (Indelible)

**Washable Fabrics (Any Color):** Sponge with cleaning fluid, or let soak in fluid. Then wash in warm suds using stiff-bristled brush if the stain seems to be stubborn. Bleaching is usually of no value.

*Note:* Do not use water first, as this spreads dye and makes stain harder to remove.

**Dry-Cleanable Fabrics:** Stains rarely can be removed, but treatment suggested for candle wax, using cleaning fluid and denatured alcohol, is worth trying. If stains remain, send garment to a reliable dry-cleaner.

## Pencil Marks (Lead)

**Washable Fabrics (Any Color):** Marks usually are removed in washing. If not, rub suds in, wash in warm suds, and rinse.

**Dry-Cleanable Fabrics:** Mix 1 cupful of denatured alcohol and 2 cupfuls of water. Test, then sponge stains, first with solution, then with cool water.

## Perspiration Stains and Odor

**Washable Fabrics (White):** Yellowish stains cannot always be removed, but occasionally washing in warm suds and bleaching will take them out. For cotton, linen, and rayon, use 1 tablespoonful of household bleach to each quart of water, and soak 15 min-

utes. Rinse 3 times. For silk and wool, use 2 tablespoonfuls of hydrogen peroxide to each gallon of water, and soak ½ hour or longer, if necessary. Rinse twice.

When a white washable garment (such as a blouse) has picked up a fugitive dye from a suit or coat lining, follow the treatment given for dyes and running colors, using a special color remover.

**Washable Fabrics (Colored):** Perspiration frequently changes a fabric's color. Sometimes the color can be restored by holding the stain over the fumes of a bottle of household ammonia or by sponging it with white vinegar. (Sometimes both methods are needed.) Then wash in warm suds, and rinse. If stain remains, make a solution of 2 tablespoonfuls of hydrogen peroxide to each gallon of water. Test the solution. Then soak the stain ½ hour or longer, if necessary. Rinse twice.

To get rid of perspiration odor that washing in warm suds has failed to remove, soak in a solution made with 3 tablespoonfuls of salt to each quart of warm water 1 hour or longer, if necessary.

**Dry-Cleanable Fabrics:** A perspiration-stained garment should be sent to a reliable dry-cleaner for thorough cleaning. Do not wash dry-cleanable fabrics or attempt to use hydrogen peroxide on them to restore color.

When a dress or suit has an underarm odor that dry-cleaning has failed to remove—and you are willing to chance a method that may make it wearable—try washing underarm sections with warm suds. Gather section in left hand, and tuck rest of garment under your arm. If suit jacket is lined, loosen lining so jacket can be treated separately. Work soiled section in suds until it is thoroughly clean. Squeeze, and rinse. Then pat as dry as possible with bath towel. When both underarm sections have been treated, straighten garment, and place it on hanger to dry. Then press, or send to dry-cleaner if necessary.

## Rubber Cement

**Washable Fabrics (Any Color):**

Apply Vaseline to stain to loosen it. Let stand 15 minutes. Then sponge or soak in cleaning fluid. Wash in warm suds; rinse.

**Dry-Cleanable Fabrics:** As above, but do not wash.

## Rust

**Washable Fabrics (Any Color):** Wash in warm suds. Rinse. If stains remain, use oxalic acid. (Ask druggist for a 5 per cent solution. Oxalic acid is poisonous. Handle it carefully.) Soak 15 minutes. Rinse 3 times. Add a few drops of household ammonia to the final rinse.

**Dry-Cleanable Fabrics:** Rust stains are rarely found; they cannot be removed by home methods. Consult a reliable dry-cleaner.

## Salad Dressings

**Washable Fabrics (Any Color):** Stains from French dressing, mayonnaise, and similar salad dressings usually are removed in washing. If grease stains remain, soak in cleaning fluid. Wash in warm suds, and rinse.

**Dry-Cleanable Fabrics:** Sponge with cool water. Let dry. Then either sponge with cleaning fluid, or use cleaning powder.

## Scorch

Heavy scorch means the fibers of the fabric have been injured and the scorch cannot be taken out. Slight scorch on cotton, linen, and rayon frequently can be removed; silk and wool seldom can be restored.

**Washable Fabrics (White):** Wash in warm suds. Rinse. If stains remain, bleach: For white cotton, linen, and rayon, use 1 tablespoonful of household bleach to each quart of water, and soak 15 minutes. Rinse 3 times. For white silk and wool, use 2 tablespoonfuls of hydrogen peroxide to each gallon of water, and soak ½ hour or longer, if necessary. Rinse twice.

**Washable Fabrics (Colored):** Wash in warm suds. Rinse. If stains remain, mix 2 tablespoonfuls of hydrogen peroxide to each gallon of water. Test the solution. Then soak stains ½ hour or longer, if necessary. Rinse twice.

**Dry-Cleanable Fabrics:** No satisfactory home method has been devised. Send to a reliable dry-cleaner.

## Shoe Polish

**Washable Fabrics (White):** Stains from paste shoe polish and white shoe dressing usually can be removed by washing in warm suds. If grease stains remain (as from a paste polish), soak in cleaning fluid; wash again in warm suds, and rinse.

For stains from colored, liquid shoe dressing, see "Paste Shoe Polish."

To get rid of dye stains, bleach: For white cotton, linen, and rayon, use 1 tablespoonful of household bleach to each quart of water, and soak 15 minutes. Rinse 3 times. For white silk and wool, use 2 tablespoonfuls of hydrogen peroxide to each gallon of water, and soak ½ hour or longer, if necessary. Rinse twice.

*Note:* Liquid shoe dressings do not always respond to treatment, and brown shades for leather and suede are less likely to come out than black.

**Washable Fabrics (Colored):** Wash stains from paste and liquid shoe polish in warm suds, and rinse. If grease stains remain, soak in cleaning fluid. If dye stains remain, mix 2 tablespoonfuls of hydrogen peroxide to each gallon of water. Test solution, then soak stains ½ hour or longer, if necessary. Rinse twice.

**Dry-Cleanable Fabrics:** To remove stains from liquid or paste shoe polish, sponge with cool water. Let dry. If grease stains remain, sponge with cleaning fluid, or use cleaning powder. Dye stains cannot be removed by home methods.

## Tar

**Washable Fabrics (Any Color):** Tar stains are not always removed from even washable fabrics. Soften stain by rubbing with Vaseline. Let stand 15 minutes; then soak in cleaning fluid. Wash in warm suds, and rinse.

**Dry-Cleanable Fabrics:** With a dull blade, scrape off as much tar as possible. Sponge with cleaning fluid. Repeat several times, if necessary.

## Urine Stains

**Washable Fabrics (Any Color):** Mix 2 tablespoonfuls of household ammonia to 1 cupful of water, and soak stains in solution. If this does not restore color, sponge with white vinegar. Wash in warm suds. Rinse. If stains remain, the dye probably has been destroyed.

**Dry-Cleanable Fabrics:** Send to a reliable dry-cleaner for thorough cleaning.

## Vaseline

**Washable Fabrics (Any Color):** Sponge with cleaning fluid, or let soak in fluid. Wash in warm suds, and rinse.

**Dry-Cleanable Fabrics:** Sponge with cleaning fluid, or use cleaning powder.

---

### STAIN-REMOVAL SUPPLIES

Keep all stain removers together on a handy shelf, but out of the reach of children. Label all the jars and bottles; be sure to mark "Poison" plainly on the poisonous ones. To have a complete shelf, you will need to keep at least three kinds of cleaning agents—bleaches, absorbent powders, grease solvents.

Absorbent powders — for grease spots. Chalk, corn meal, talcum powder, or cornstarch

Bleaches
   Hydrogen Peroxide — a mild bleach for any material
   Oxalic Acid—for rust stains
   Chlorine Bleach—white cottons and linens

Sodium thiosulfate, or photographer's "hypo"—removes iodine stains and yellowing caused by chlorine.

Solvents
   Turpentine—for paint stains
   Denatured Alcohol—be sure to mix alcohol with 2 parts water when using on acetate rayon or colored material.
   Acetone or Amyl Acetate—for fingernail polish stains
   Dry-Cleaning Fluid

Washing agents
   Soap or Detergent

Equipment
   Cheesecloth, white blotting paper, medicine dropper, bowls, cotton swabs, measuring spoons and cup

# STAINS ON HOUSEHOLD ITEMS

## Bathtubs and Basins

When bathtubs are old and fixtures have been misused, rust stains and discolorations often are troublesome. There is a special cleanser for this purpose. Sprinkle cleanser on a damp cloth; rub discolored surface until stains are removed. Rinse, and wipe dry. Treatment must be repeated periodically, because rust will form again.

## Floors

**Grease on Cement Floors:** Make a solution of a water-softening compound (¼ cupful to each gallon of hot water). With stiff brush, scour stains. Use an abrasive household cleanser at the same time. Rinse well. If stains remain, sprinkle water-softening compound; moisten, let stand a few hours; remove and rinse.

**Ink and Other Stains on Marble Floors:** Marble never should be treated with acids or strong solutions, because they remove the polish. Ink: Saturate a thick pad with undiluted household bleach; leave it on the stain several hours. Other stains: Use a paste of household cleanser mixed with hot water. Apply a thick coating; let remain several days, then lift off. Special cleansers and stain remover for marble can be purchased.

**Stains on Unfinished Wood Floors:** Treat with a household cleanser and steel wool. To bleach, use a household bleach in a solution of one cupful to each gallon of warm water. Apply, and let stand 15 minutes. Rinse, and dry. Repeat if necessary.

## Mattresses

**Blood:** Mix cornstarch to a paste with cold water. Apply thickly to stain, and brush away when dry. Repeat until stain disappears.

**Perspiration:** Sponge very lightly with warm water to which a few drops of vinegar have been added. Sprinkle powdered pepsin over stain, and work well into ticking. Let stand several hours, keeping pepsin slightly moist. Dry; brush off powder.

**Medicine:** Removal of medicine stains is not often successful. However, it is worth while to try removing color and grease. For color stains, sponge with a solution of 1 cupful of denatured alcohol and 2 cupfuls of water. Sponge with warm water. Let dry. For greasy stains, sprinkle on cleaning powder; let stand until it absorbs grease; then brush off.

**Urine:** Sponge very lightly with warm, salt water made with ½ cupful of salt and 1 quart of water.

## Rugs and Carpets

**Beverages** (alcohol, tea, coffee, and soft drinks): Sponge stained rug area with lukewarm water; repeat several times. Then sponge with suds made with 1 teaspoonful of detergent to 1 cup of lukewarm water. Rinse by rubbing with a cloth wrung from clear water.

**Chewing Gum:** Apply dry-cleaning fluid around outside edges of gum or cover with rug-cleaning powder. Wait several minutes; then lift up gum with dull edge of knife.

**Animal Stains:** Sponge stained areas with several applications of clear lukewarm water. Then with medicine dropper, apply solution of white vinegar and water, in proportion of 1 teaspoonful of white vinegar to 3 teaspoonfuls of lukewarm water. Allow this solution to remain on stain for 15 minutes; then sponge with suds made from 1 teaspoonful of detergent to 1 cup of water.

**Candy, Chocolate or Sugar Stains:** Scrape off crusty surface with dull knife or spatula. Sponge with clear, lukewarm water, working from outer edge of stain toward center. Sponge with suds made as above.

**Mud Stains:** Let nap dry completely; then take up with vacuum cleaner.

**Nail Polish:** With eye dropper, apply amyl acetate (available at drugstore) directly on stain. Wait a few minutes; then sponge stain with clean cloth, working from outer edge toward center. (Stains of this kind and attempts to remove them with thinner or nail-polish remover may damage rugs made of synthetic fibers or blends. Cleaning by professional rug cleaner is safest.)

**Paint, Varnish, and Shellac:** For paint or varnish, apply turpentine with eye dropper and sponge from outer edge toward center. Follow with application of dry-cleaning fluid, sponging in same manner. For shellac, apply denatured alcohol with eye dropper. If stains remain, call professional rug cleaner.

**Rust:** Too risky for an amateur. Call professional rug cleaner.

**Ink:** Only washable-ink stains can be treated with any success; permanent inks rarely respond. First, with a blotter, take up as much ink as possible. Then sponge with clear water. Sponge toward center, to avoid spreading ink. If stains remain, apply a saturated solution of oxalic acid (poisonous). Sponge with cloth wrung out of clear water. Repeat.

## Upholstery

Upholstery is difficult to treat for stains, because it isn't possible to put an absorbent pad under the material. Test remover on an inconspicuous section of the upholstery. Then treat as for rugs and carpets.

## Wallpaper

**Grease on Wallpaper:** Mild grease stains can be removed by fuller's earth or a rug-cleaning powder moistened with dry-cleaning fluid. Spread paste on spotted surface; let it remain until dry. Then remove with soft, clean cloth. Repeat if necessary. Sometimes a ring is visible after powder has been removed. If so, apply a mixture of powder and water. Let dry and wipe off.

**Food Stains on Wallpaper:** Brush off any clinging food, and if the wallpaper is washable, sponge with cloth wrung out of warm suds. If stains remain, use treatment above.

## Walls and Woodwork

**Crayon Marks on Painted Surfaces:** Wash with special liquid paint cleaner. If marks are still visible, sponge with cleaning fluid. If a ring remains, apply a mixture of fuller's earth and water. Let dry, and wipe.

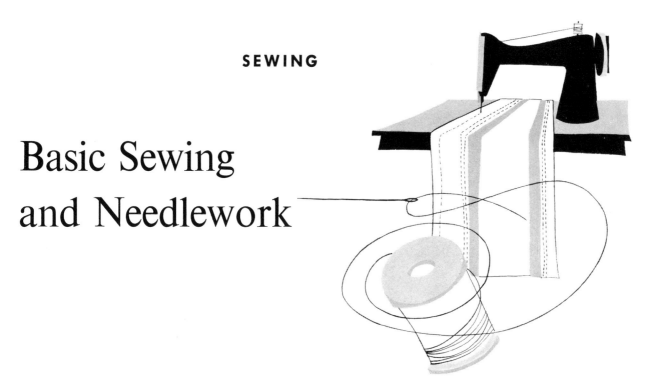

# Basic Sewing and Needlework

## SEWING AND NEEDLEWORK

Sewing can be a source of considerable pleasure. Like most things, if you are good at it, you will enjoy it; or maybe the truth is that if you enjoy it, you will be good at it.

Some women like to sew because they can afford to have more things that way. They can make clothes for less money than they can buy them, and they can be almost sure they will not see the same dress on anyone else. This also holds true in sewing for your home. Draperies and slipcovers you make yourself will suit your taste in your home and not be duplicated all over the country.

In addition to having more things by making them yourself, the money saved can be applied to something that might otherwise be beyond your means. Many a home dressmaker has been able to buy furniture or a major appliance with what she was able to save over a period of time. There is also a certain sense of satisfaction in being able to create something. Sewing need never deteriorate into drudgery since a product results from your efforts.

These things are true of all needlework. A hand-knit dress costs a lot of money if you have to buy it. But if you make it yourself, it costs only whatever you pay for the material plus an infinitesimal amount for the equipment: the needles. And in knitting and crocheting there is the further satisfaction of not wasting time: when you get good at it, you can carry on a conversation or listen to a lecture while you are working on it.

Embroidery is a means of making something quite ordinary into something entirely your own, whether it is a towel you are monogramming or a dress you are making over from a drab thing to a glamorous garment.

Some women are unable to get started in sewing or other needlework because they are afraid it is too complicated. Actually, it is quite easy and based on a few simple stitches no matter how intricate the completed product looks. Don't underestimate your own ability. Start on the simpler things. You will probably become interested and soon want to do something you will be proud of.

### Equipment for Hand Sewing

#### Thread

**Cotton.** Use mercerized cotton thread for sewing cottons, linens, and dull-surfaced synthetic fabrics. Unmercerized cotton thread comes in black and white and is suitable for general use. Cotton thread size is indicated by number—the larger the number, the finer the thread. Sizes range from 8 to 100. Colored mercerized thread is usually made in size 50— sometimes designated as size A or OO-X. Black or white mercerized threads are made in sizes 8 to 60.

Unmercerized black comes as fine as 70; unmercerized white, as fine as 100.

**Silk.** In addition to sewing silk fabrics, silk thread is suited to wool and synthetic fabrics with a high sheen. For ordinary sewing, it comes in one size, A.

**Nylon.** Nylon thread possesses great strength and elasticity, and is excellent for sewing the new synthetic fabrics, plastic film, heavy thicknesses of fabric, and any item that requires extra strength. It is also used for darning, mending, and machine embroidery.

**Special-Purpose Threads.** Size D silk, sometimes called buttonhole twist, is used for embroidery, eyelets, button loops, and other decorative purposes, as well as for finishing buttonholes. Special-purpose cotton threads include heavy-duty thread for draperies, buttons, upholstery, heavy fabrics; buttonhole twist, carpet thread; quilting thread; darning cotton, plain and mercerized; and basting thread with a glazed finish.

**Color.** Thread should be slightly darker than the fabric. It appears lighter when stitched on fabric than on the spool. Buy enough colored thread when you start to make a garment. Although color numbers are stamped on the end of the spool, shades are changed as often as twice a year so you may not be able to match a color by its number. Be sure to buy boilfast cotton thread as it is resistant to fading from sunlight and laundering.

### Needles

For general sewing, needles called "sharps" are most suitable. These have small, round eyes and are sold in sizes 1 to 12 (12 is the finest). Sizes 11 and 12 are used for special work, such as beading. "Betweens," which are similar to sharps but shorter in length, are used for the fine, close stitching of tailoring. Embroidery or crewel needles have long eyes, to take a number of strands of thread. Darning needles, which resemble embroidery needles, have larger eyes.

## NEEDLE AND THREAD GUIDE

Use this guide to select the right thread and needles for sewing various types of fabric:

**Filmy Materials,** such as net, organdy, ninon: 100 cotton thread, size 10 needle.

**Sheer Materials,** such as lawn, batiste, chiffon, rayon crepe: 80 to 100 cotton thread or A silk; size 9 needle.

**Lightweight Materials,** such as gingham, sheer wool crepe, taffeta: 60 to 80 cotton or A silk; size 8 needle.

**Medium-Light Materials,** such as poplin, percale, chintz, faille, wool flannel, wool crepe: 50 to 70 cotton or A silk; size 7 or 8 needle.

**Medium-Heavy Materials,** such as gabardine, velveteen, 30 to 50 cotton or A silk; size 6 needle.

**Heavy Materials,** such as sailcloth and denim: 16 to 24 cotton, heavy-duty cotton, or D silk; size 4 or 5 needle.

**Very Heavy Materials,** such as canvas: 8 to 12 cotton or heavy-duty cotton; size 3 needle.

### Thimble

A thimble is a "must," and is usually worn on the middle finger of the right hand. Be sure the small round grooves or millings are deep enough to hold a needle and that they extend down the sides.

### Pins

Straight pins are sold in three gauges—fine, medium and heavy. For general sewing, use medium gauge, usually called "dressmaker" pins. The fine gauge pins, often called "silk" or "satin" pins, are for sheer fabrics. Use heavy gauge pins on such materials as heavy coatings or upholstery fabrics.

### Scissors and Shears

Scissors have handles of equal size. Shears, used for heavier work, have one handle larger than the other. There are many types of scissors and shears and they come in different lengths. Try several lengths to find which is most comfortable.

**Sewing Scissors** have one sharp-pointed and one rounded blade. The pointed blade is good for ripping;

the rounded one keeps the scissors from marring the table when cutting fabric.

**Embroidery Scissors** are good for ripping, cutting notches in corners, snipping threads, and other fine work.

**Pocket Scissors** have rounded, blunt ends on both blades to keep them from poking through fine fabrics.

**Buttonhole Scissors** cut the buttonhole slit without requiring a fold in the fabric. By turning a screw, they can be adjusted to cut any size buttonhole from ¼" to 1¼".

**Dressmaker's Shears** have bent handles to permit the blade to be placed flat on the table, making it easier to cut straight lines. They are especially good for following a pattern that is pinned onto a fabric.

**Pinking Shears** cut a zigzag edge that resists raveling and gives a finished edge to the fabric. Some cut fabrics of all weight; others are for either light or heavy fabrics.

**Household Shears** are for heavy-duty work. They are good for cutting heavy paper, cardboard, and heavy fabrics.

# BASIC STITCHES FOR SEWING

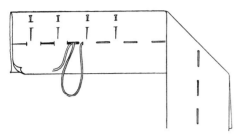

**Running Stitch:** Made by passing the needle in and out of the material in a horizontal line; usually several of these stitches are taken on the needle before the thread is pulled through.

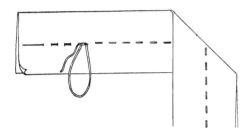

**Basting:** *Even basting*—half-inch running stitches used to hold two pieces of cloth together. *Uneven basting*—a long followed by a short stitch with both on the needle at one time.

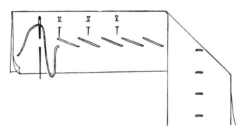

**Diagonal Basting:** A slant stitch on top and a straight up-and-down stitch underneath. Used for holding two or more thicknesses of material.

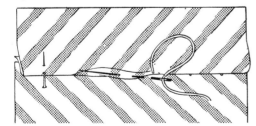

**Slip Basting:** For matching stripes or plaids, or fitting on the right side. Take right side of one piece, fold under indicated allowance and still keeping stripes exactly in line, slip needle along on fold of upper layer, draw it through and take a short stitch in under layer.

**Back Stitch:** Take a small running stitch. Pass needle back over running stitch to wrong side and over twice as much space as original stitch. Bring needle to right side and down to wrong side at end of running stitch.

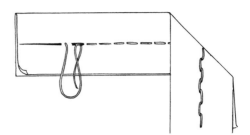

**Overcast Stitch:** Trim edges and make diagonal stitches over raw edges. Always keep stitches twice as far apart as they are deep and never draw stitches tightly or edge will look uneven.

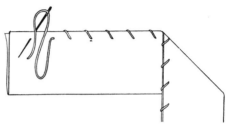

**Catch Stitch:** Fold raw edge over. Working from left to right, take a tiny stitch in the hem or seam and then in the material with the needle pointing to the left. Keep an even slant between stitches.

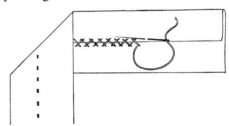

**Overhand:** Fold edges of material and baste together. With needle at right angles to fabric edge, slant stitches on wrong side and take straight stitches on right side.

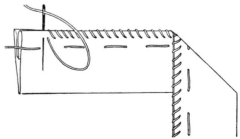

# HEMMING OR FELLING

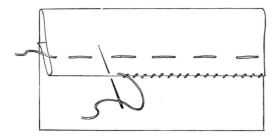

**Hemming or Felling:** Fold edges and baste. Conceal thread under fold. Using a small slanting stitch, take up a thread or two in the cloth and in the fold.

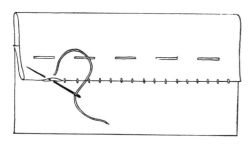

**Vertical Hemming:** The stitch is taken perpendicular to the edge of the hem.

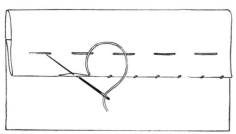

**Blind Hemming:** Take up a thread on under side, then a few threads on the fold. The stitches should not show on right side of work.

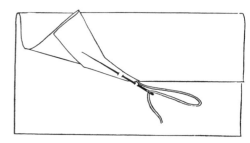

**Slip Stitch:** With running stitch, take a portion of thread in cloth and a few threads in fold to make sewing invisible on both sides.

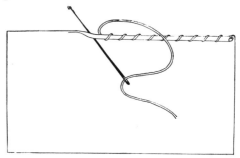

**Whipping:** On wrong side, turn edge and roll an inch or two at a time. Use plain hemming or overcast stitch, passing needle under roll.

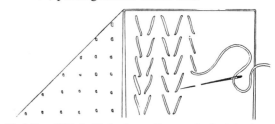

**Padding Stitch:** Take long diagonal stitch inside and short stitch outside. Stitch loosely. Used to hold a second piece of material in place.

# SEAMS

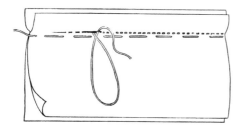

**Plain Seam:** With edges even, place right sides of two pieces of material together and baste. Sew with running stitch or machine. Press seam open or turn to one side of stitching.

**Pinked Seam:** Make plain seam. Pink edges.

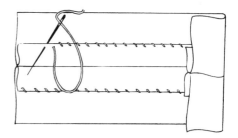

**Overcast Seam:** Stitch and press seam open, then overcast edge of each side. Always work from right to left and do not draw stitches tightly. This is a very durable seam for medium-weight fabrics.

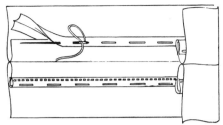

**Bound Seam:** Make plain seam. Bind each edge with bias binding. For unlined garments.

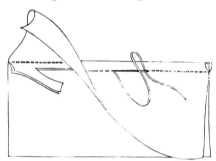

**French Seam:** A seam within a seam. Make a plain seam half the depth of seam allowance on outside of garment. Trim close to stitching. Turn and make a second seam deep enough to take up remainder of seam allowance and to cover raw edges on inside.

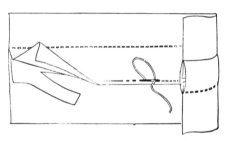

**French or Flat Fell Seam:** Make plain seam. Trim one side to within ⅛″ of stitching. Fold other edge over to line of stitching. Use running stitch or machine close to turned edge. Sometimes called false French seam.

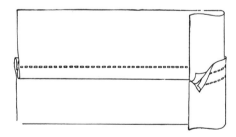

**Welt Seam:** Make plain seam. Trim one side narrower than other. Fold wider side over narrower one. Stitch on outside about ¼″ from seam line. Or leave broad side unfolded and overcast.

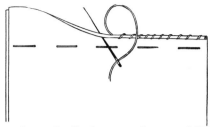

**Rolled Seam:** Roll edges together carefully to avoid puckering. Hem while rolling, putting the needle under the rolled edges.

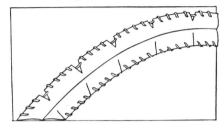

**Curved Seam:** Clip edges. Overcast or pink them. Press open or together. If one edge is slightly longer than the other, ease in longer edge.

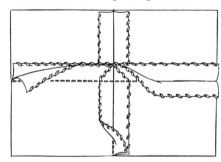

**Crossed Seams:** Stitch and press first seam. Stitch crossing seam. Trim first seam at corners to reduce thickness and press.

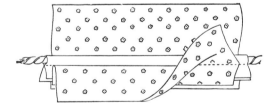

**Piped and Corded Seams:** Baste bias strip or cording on seam line. Stitch to second piece of material as for regular seam. To reinforce, and to make a tailored finish, stitch on right side.

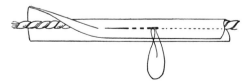

**Cording:** Cover cable with bias strip.

# HEMS

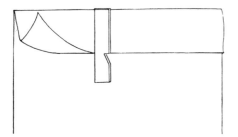

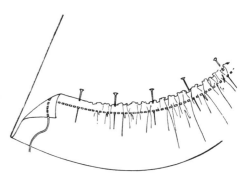

**Turning a Hem:** This is the finish of a piece and should be uniform in depth. Mark it evenly with a ruler or a gauge with a notch. Straight edge of notch indicates depth of hem. Trim hem evenly and proceed with a suitable finish.

**Circular Hem:** Mark hem in usual manner. Gather edge by using running stitch or long stitch on machine. Draw up gathers to fit and fasten thread.

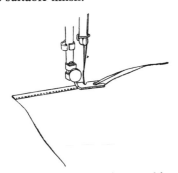

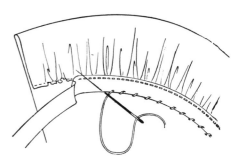

**Hemming Attachment** on the machine turns the fabric and stitches it in one operation.

**Finishing Circular Hem:** Stitch bias binding over gathers and sew hem in place.

## GATHERING AND SHIRRING

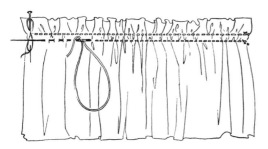

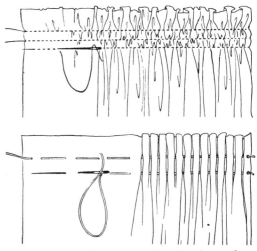

**Gathering:** Knot thread. Draw thread up from wrong side and reinforce with back stitches. Take short, even running stitches. If a great amount of material is to be gathered into small space, take a long stitch on right side and a short stitch on wrong side. Draw fullness up to desired size and wind excess thread over pin. Secure with small overhand stitches or cut material of required size, turn under raw edge and hem against gathers on wrong side.

**Machine Gathering:** With regular presser foot, loosen tension and lengthen stitch. Fasten threads at one end and draw up under thread. With gathering foot, use a long stitch and a tight tension. To increase fullness, lengthen stitch.

**Shirring:** Parallel rows of gathering where the stitches in each row must be directly in line with stitches in the row above. Reinforce with a stay piece as explained in gathering. The gathering foot attachment on the straight sewing machine shirrs as it sews; while the new zigzag and automatic machines gather and shirr by a simple application of the zigzag stitch over cord or perle cotton.

# PLEATS

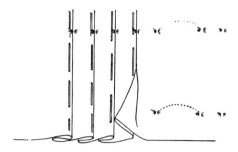

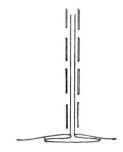

**Side Pleats:** Match marked lines, baste, and stitch close to edge on right side. Stitch from the bottom up to assure pleat hanging straight. Tie thread ends securely on wrong side.

**Inverted Pleats:** The same in appearance as the wrong side of a box pleat.

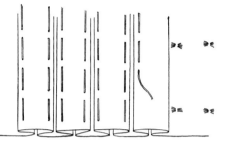

**Box Pleats:** Formed by two side pleats turned in opposite directions.

**Pinch Pleats:** Make a large pleat. Divide evenly into three small pleats and press firmly. Stitch across lower edge of heading and along side to top edge.

# DARNING

Darn on right side. Never make a knot. Work far enough from hole so mend will not pull out. Stitch loosely. Small loop at each turning prevents puckers.

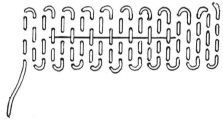

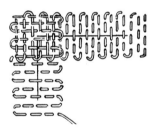

**Three-Cornered Tear:** Stitch at right angles to opening. Darn lengthwise tear completely, then crosswise tear so stitches overlap at corners.

**Straight Tear:** Leave end 6″ or more. Sew back and forth. Catch thread through stitches of last row and clip. Run thread left hanging at beginning through first row and clip.

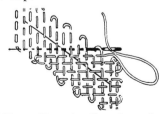

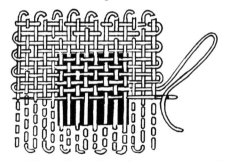

**Diagonal Tear:** Darn in direction of tear. Then at right angles to first group of stitches.

**Darning a Hole:** Cut hole so it is square or oblong. Weave stitches very closely over hole.

**Machine Darning** is much faster than darning by hand.

# SEWING MACHINES

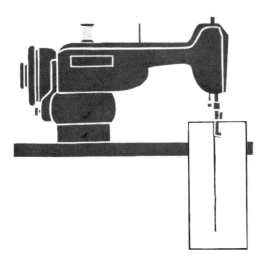

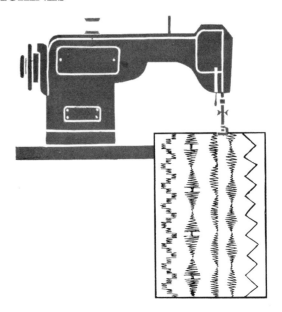

**Straight Sewing Machines** have a needle that goes straight up and down. As the fabric passes beneath it, a straight line of locked stitches is formed. The bobbin carries the lower thread. A machine with a round bobbin gives smooth action, without tangling or vibration. On up-to-date machines the speed control, tension, stitch length, and threading are easy to manage. With a bit of skill, straight sewing machines can produce smart, decorative stitches by using novelty threads and machine embroidery by manipulation of the fabric under the needle. Most models provide a built-in light, forward and reverse stitching, and automatic bobbin winding.

If the machine has a long bobbin which travels in a back-and-forth path, there is more vibration than with the round-bobbin type. It is, however, a less expensive machine and usually has fewer de luxe features.

**Zigzag Sewing Machines** (also called swing-needle) sew a normal, straight, lock stitch. By throwing a lever or turning a dial, they stitch in a zigzag line with the needle traveling from side to side as well as up and down. With a change in the width of the zigzag and/or length of the stitch, a variety of decorative stitches can be created. It takes practice to learn to move the lever or dial with precise rhythm. Once the skill is acquired, an almost unlimited variety of stitches can be designed.

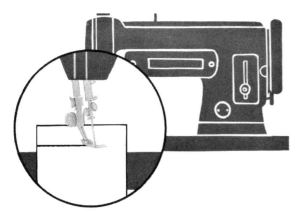

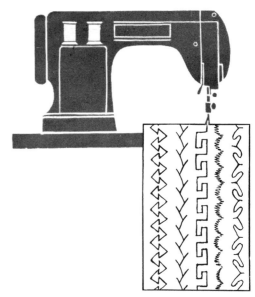

**A Slant-Needle Machine** does straight sewing. The needle and pressure foot are slanted slightly to give better visibility. This machine has many features especially designed for comfortable sewing.

**Automatic Zigzag Sewing Machines** have cams or wheels to change the width and/or length of the stitch so that the machine automatically forms the decorative stitches. These machines turn out far more intricate designs than can be produced by the non-automatic zigzag machines.

Zigzag and automatic machines can do several operations such as buttonholing without attachments. They hem with a blind stitch, sew on buttons, overcast seams, attach lace, appliqué designs, sew stretchable seams on jersey and do mending, darning, and patching easily.

### Needles and Thread

For good sewing results, use needles and thread of the correct size for the fabric. A heavy needle makes unsightly holes; a fine one may break or bend. Keep a selection of sizes, and match them to thread and fabric, using your machine instruction booklet as a guide. When replacing a needle, be sure clamp is tightened properly.

### Oiling

A sewing machine needs frequent oiling. Follow the instructions in your booklet and be sure to use the special sewing-machine oil recommended by the manufacturer. Before oiling, dust the machine carefully with a light brush to remove lint and threads from feed dog, bobbin case, and shuttle. After oiling your machine, stitch a scrap of material to make sure no excess oil is left to soil your work.

### Attachments

Almost all straight sewing machines come with a set of attachments, including hemmer, binder, ruffler, and presser feet of various types. They have been designed to help the home sewer put a professional finish to her work. Practice using them on scraps of fabric.

## SEWING FOR THE HOME

### Glass Curtains

*Measuring and Cutting*

Carefully measure from the top of the rod (see illustration). Windows may vary slightly, particularly in old houses, so measure each one. The curtains may hang to the sill, the bottom of the apron, or the floor —or any in-between length. After you decide the finished length, *add* the depth of the bottom hem, top hem (casing wide enough to hold rod), and heading. Allowing three inches each for top and bottom hem is adequate, although some prefer a wider bottom hem.

If you do not know whether or not the material has been treated to control shrinkage, allow 1″ per yard and make double hems. Treated materials do not need a shrinkage allowance. For the average window, 2 widths of 36″-wide material are sufficient; but if the window is oversized, measure the width and make the curtains 2 to 3 times as wide. The sheerer the fabric, the fuller the curtain should be. The lengths may be sewn together or hung in separate strips.

To cut the curtain lengths, spread the fabric on a large, smooth surface, measure carefully—with a yardstick or steel tape *not a tape measure*—and use sharp scissors. Draw a thread or follow the pattern line as a guide for cutting a straight line. Trim off all selvages.

**Tailored Curtains.** Hems may be of the same width on both sides of the strip or narrower on the outside edge; an inch is a good width for the inside hem. For a narrow hem, use the narrow-hemming attachment of your sewing machine; make a medium or long stitch, depending on the fabric. Practice on a piece of curtain material. For a wide hem, turn in ½″ on raw edge, and crease; then turn full width of hem, and

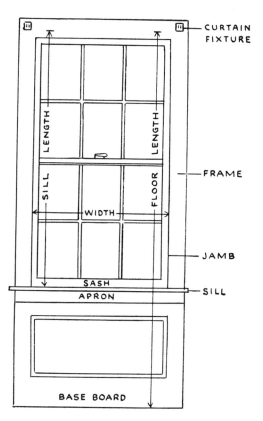

pin at right angles, measuring to keep hem even. Baste, or press without basting, and hem with machine. Make side hems first, then bottom hem. Baste in top hem (casing through which rod will run), and hang the curtains to make sure they are the proper length. Adjust if necessary. Sew casing and bottom hems from edge to edge, finishing ends securely by stitching back.

**Ruffled Curtains.** The width of the ruffles is a minimum of 4″. Cut 4½″ strips, keeping every strip the same width and straight on the thread. You will need 2½ times or more the distance along all edges to be ruffled. The sheerer the fabric, the fuller the ruffle should be. The edges of the ruffle may be hemmed with the narrowest hemmer or picoted for a quick, attractive finish. Use the hemstitching attachment. First figure how many yards of ruffling you need. Carefully mark required number of strips down length of fabric. For hemmed ruffles, cut on lines; sew strips together; hem. To picot two edges at once, hemstitch along lines; cut strips apart on line of hem-stitching. Sew strips together, and they are ready for the next step.

The ruffling attachment saves time and work, because it will ruffle the strip and sew it to the curtain in one operation. If you do not have a ruffling attachment, turn the raw edge under as you gather the ruffles in preparation for mounting them on the curtain. They can be mounted on top of or under the curtain edge. If on top, turn the raw edge of the curtain toward the right side and the raw edge of the ruffle under. Then place the ruffle on the curtain, pin, and stitch. Reverse procedure to place ruffle under curtain edge. Use 2 rows of stitching to finish.

## LINED DRAPERIES

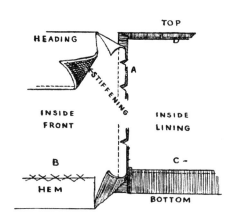

1. Measure and cut as for glass curtains, adding allowance for at least 3″ top and bottom hems. If fabric is not preshrunk, make a double bottom hem which can be let down in case of shrinkage.

2. Turn up, press, and stitch bottom hems in drapery fabric.

3. For top stiffening, cut crinoline or lightweight buckram in crosswise strips of the same width planned for top hem (usually 3″). Pin stiffening along top edge of drapery. Turn top edge of fabric over stiffening. Fold down heading, pin, and baste. Trim extra fabric at corner. Stiffening is not always necessary; use of it depends on the "body" of the fabric.

4. Cut lining-fabric lengths 4″ to 5″ narrower and 1″ to 2″ shorter than the drapery fabric so that drapery-fabric hem shows on underside. Turn top of lining under ⅜″, and stitch (*Figure 1D*). Hem bottom so that finished length just covers top of drapery hem ( *Figure 1C* ).

5. Lay drapery and lining fabrics flat, right sides together, and stitch one side. Clip seam (*1A*) so drapery will hang straight.

6. Then turn and stitch ⅜″ hem on all the raw edges of the lining fabric.

7. Turn and baste narrow hem on other side of drapery fabric (*Figure 2F*). Miter corners.

8. Turn lining fabric smoothly across back of drapery fabric. Miter corners at top and bottom of hem, and whip down (*Figure 2G*).

9. Slip-stitch lining to drapery fabric at top. Do not stitch lower hems together.

10. Insert weights in bottom hems.

11. Pleat the top of the drapery either by hand or use one of the automatic pleating devices available at the drapery findings counter. Pleats are made in uneven groups depending upon the amount of extra fullness allowed. The width of the drapery minus the covered space gives the amount to be taken up in pleats. A simplified method for making professional-looking pleats is made possible through the use of a stiffened tape.

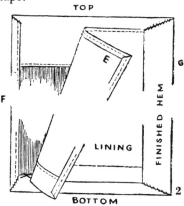

**Unlined Draperies**

Unlined draperies are made like glass curtains, with stiffening (if desired) at head, and pleats like lined draperies. Washable fabrics are particularly suitable for this type of drapery.

# SLIPCOVERS

**Materials.** Choose a firmly woven fabric. The amount will depend on the pattern chosen as well as the size and type of furniture to be covered. The fabric salesman can figure out the yardage from this information: the type of chair (Lawson, wing, club, etc.) and the type of cushion (plain, T-shaped). Give him the measurements for the height, the width of the back, the width and depth of the seat and the height of the arms.

When buying fabric, decide which seam finish is to be used. Welting of the same fabric is always good, or buy ready-made welting to match one of the colors in the pattern. If you make your own welting, buy cable cord to cover with the fabric. A general rule is to make a welt or whatever kind of seam finish is chosen, wherever there is an exposed seam in the chair. Buy a zipper for each cushion, and one for the back of each cover.

the tuck-in. Pin the sides along the seamline and cut the lower edge. Chalk the sewing line on all pinned edges, allowing 1″ seams. Continue pinning, chalking, and cutting on seat, front, and outside arms. Pin, chalk, and cut inside arms, making sure the pattern is the same on both arms. Notch seams at all points.

**Sewing.** Remove cover and turn, so that the seams can be sewn on the wrong side. Pin and sew from notch to notch, sewing the two inside and back seams first. These are plain seams. The rest must be finished seams. Leave opening at back seam for zipper.

Face the zipper opening, inserting the welting on the front edge at the same time. Baste the zipper as close to the metal as possible, with the welting covering the center of the zipper. Be sure the open end of the zipper is at the bottom.

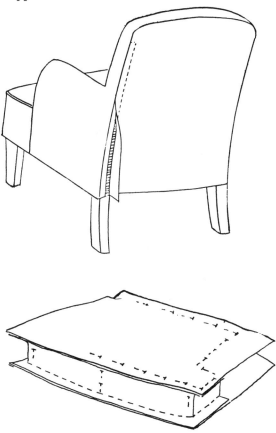

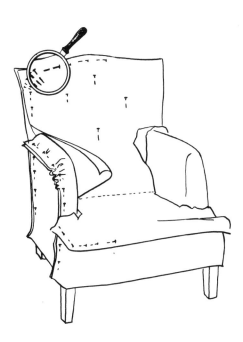

**Fitting and Pinning.** Work with the right side out, using the lengthwise of the fabric at all times. Always place pins lengthwise to form seam lines. Occasionally place pins through center of each piece to hold it in place.

Place the fabric on the back of the chair to center the design, using a tape measure to check it. Pin the fabric along the back of the chair. Smooth the fabric down, tucking in the sides where the arms meet the back and at the seat, allowing at least 4″ to 5″ for

**Cushions.** To make a boxed cushion, place fabric on cushion top with pattern in such position that the pattern is continued from the back of the chair in proper sequence. Cut second piece to match. Cut boxing piece the depth of cushion and long enough to extend all around the cushion. Pin, chalk, and cut edges, leaving lower back seam open for zipper. Use same seam finish as on body of chair.

# DRESSMAKING

## Equipment

To make a dress, there are certain things you should have.

Pinking shears
Cutting shears
Small scissors
Needles
Machine needles
Pins
Dress material
Thread to match material
Zippers
Buttons
Snap and gripper fasteners
Pattern
Yardstick
Tape measure
6″ measure
Tailor's chalk
Skirt marker
Sleeve board
Ironing board
Iron
Thimble
Sewing machine in perfect condition

## Selecting Pattern and Material

The beginner should choose a pattern of few pieces and a solid-color material. A medium-weight cotton is easy to handle. After gaining a little experience in dressmaking, you will be able to use patterns of many pieces. Matching plaids and stripes will not be a problem after the essential steps of dressmaking are mastered.

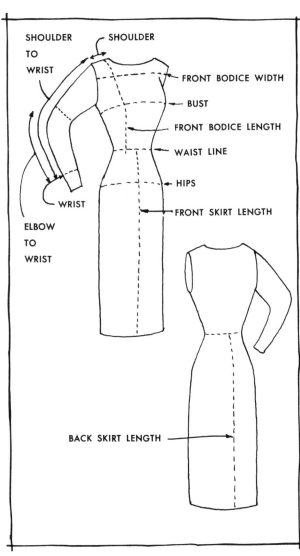

## Altering a Pattern

To make a dress that fits well, use a pattern that fits well. Since all figures are not alike, alter the pattern before cutting into the fabric. Pattern alterations are actually very simple. A slash here and a fold there can make patterns fit most figures.

**Proper Measurements.** Patterns are bought by bust measurement, but your other measurements may vary from those listed on the pattern.

Compare your figure measurements with the pattern. There are two good ways to do this. Either measure a dress that fits properly or have your body measurements taken over one of your dresses.

Be accurate to the fraction of an inch, to assure perfect fit of the garment. Take these measurements:

1. Bust (fullest part)
2. Natural waistline
3. Hips (7″ below waist and fullest part)
4. Sleeve length (shoulder to elbow; elbow to wrist, with elbow bent)
5. Wrist
6. Sleeve width (above elbow at fullest part)
7. Shoulder (neck to armhole seam)
8. Front bodice length (shoulder seam at neck over the bust to waistline)
9. Back bodice length (base of neck to waist)
10. Front and back skirt lengths (center of waist to hemline)
11. Front and back bodice widths, armhole to armhole, 4″ below shoulder seam

Now measure the pattern. Don't include seam allowances. Lay the pattern pieces flat on the table. Pin all darts, pleats, and gathers; pin parts of pattern pieces together if there are several parts to them (such as a yoke on a waist piece). When measuring, measure from seamline to seamline. The waistline, wrist, and front and back waist-length measurements of the pattern and your body should be the same. The hipline on a fitted-skirt pattern should measure at least 1″ more than your body. The bustline of the pattern should measure about 3½″ to 4″ more than your body.

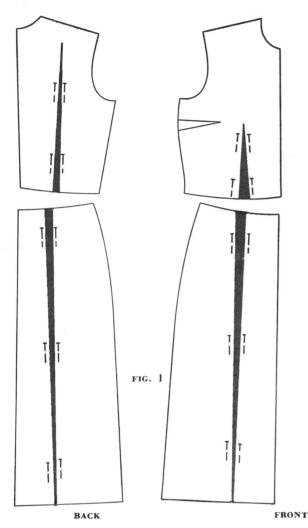

FIG. 1

BACK                    FRONT

shoulders slash the pattern in the same way, but spread the edges of the slash instead of sliding one over the other.

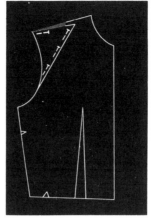 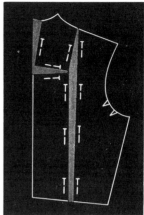

Fig. 2.    Fig. 3.

**Round, Full Back** *(Fig. 3):* Slash the back waist piece lengthwise, from the center of the shoulder straight down to the waistline. Lay over a sheet of paper. Spread the edges of the slash apart the necessary amount. At the fullest part of the back, slash across from the center back to the vertical slash; spread slash far enough to give ease at the fullest part. Now extend center backline to make a straight edge, as shown in gray in the illustration. Pin pattern pieces to the sheet of paper beneath. (Later, when starting to sew fabric, make a small dart at the shoulder; also ease in extra fullness or make a dart at the waistline.)

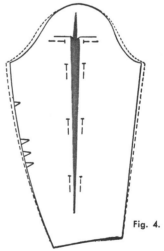

Fig. 4.

**Thick Waistline** *(Fig. 1):* Slash both the front and the back skirt pieces, as illustrated, to about ⅛″ from the bottom edge. Slash the back waist piece from the bottom edge to just below the shoulder and the front waist piece to point of bustline. Spread the edges of the slash apart the necessary amount, tapering them from the waistline to the bottom edge on the skirt pieces and from the waistline up on the waist pieces. Place a sheet of paper beneath each slash and pin the edges of the slash to it. Leave the sheet of paper pinned to the original pattern (do this for all the alterations).

**Narrow Shoulders or Broad Shoulders** *(Fig. 2):* For narrow shoulders slash the front waist piece and the back waist piece from the center of the shoulder to about ⅛″ from the armhole notch shown on your pattern. Slide one edge of the slash over the other for the necessary amount and pin. Place a sheet of paper underneath and pin pattern to it. Since the original shoulderline is no longer straight, form a new shoulderline, as shown in gray in the illustration. For broad

**Heavy Arm Muscles** *(Fig. 4):* Slash sleeve piece, beginning about 1″ from the top and cutting toward, but not all the way to, the wrist. Spread open at the top to the required width. Form darts at the sides of the slash at the fullest part of the arm, thus flattening the pattern piece. Place a sheet of paper underneath the slash and pin the sides of the slash to it.

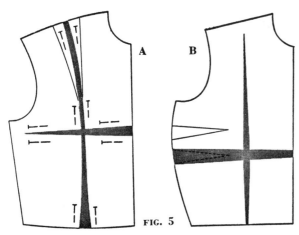

FIG. 5

**Large Bust** *(Fig. 5): For pattern with shoulder dart (Fig. 5, A).* Slash the front waist piece straight across the front below the end of the dart, from the center frontline almost to the underarm; slash vertically from the top through the center of the shoulder dart down to the bottom edge. Lay over a sheet of paper. Spread pattern pieces the necessary amount and pin to the paper.

*For pattern with underarm dart (Fig. 5, B).* Slash front waist piece straight across the front just below the underarm dart. Slash from the bottom edge to just below the shoulder. Lay over a sheet of paper. Spread the edges of the slashes the necessary amount and pin to the paper. Mark a new underarm dart, as illustrated, where the pattern is slashed.

### Cutting Out a Dress

**Guide Sheet.** Study the illustrated guide sheet included in every good pattern. There are several diagrams, showing how the pattern should be placed on fabrics of different widths. Also, diagrams are given for different sizes and variations of the pattern.

Choose the layout for your size, the width of the fabric, and the version of the pattern you plan to make. To avoid mix-up, mark this layout by circling it with a colored pencil.

Study the meaning of the various symbols.

**Grain Line.** The importance of the grain, or straight of fabric cannot be overemphasized. A fabric is woven with warp (*lengthwise*) and filling (*crosswise*) threads. These threads must be kept in position and not distorted; otherwise the finished garment does not hang properly. First, be sure one end of the fabric is straight. Pull a thread at the end of the fabric, and cut across the pulled-thread line. If the crosswise threads are not straight, pull fabric diagonally in opposite direction until the threads are squared with the selvage. Carefully press the fabric if it is creased or even slightly wrinkled.

**Placing Pattern on Fabric.** Put back into the enve-

lope any piece of the pattern, such as an extra collar, which you are not using. Press pattern pieces with warm iron. To cut a double thickness of fabric, bring together the two selvage edges and the straightened end. Pin them into place. Snip selvage edges so they do not pucker.

If you plan to cut two pieces, such as sleeves, which have to be left and right, on a single thickness of fabric, be sure to reverse the pattern when you cut the second piece.

On material with a printed design (running in one direction) or a definite surface or nap—satins, woolens, velvets—all pattern pieces must be placed in the same direction. Plaids and stripes must be matched at the seams. Whenever there is a pattern or design that requires matching, a small loss of material must be expected.

When placing the pattern on the fabric, follow the layout selected on the guide sheet.

Place pattern pieces so markings indicating straight of fabric (grain line) are parallel with the selvage. To be sure these lines are parallel, measure carefully with ruler from ends of grain-line markings on pattern to selvage.

Pin grain line first; then pin around outside of pattern, using plenty of sharp-pointed pins. Pin all the pieces on the fabric before you start to cut.

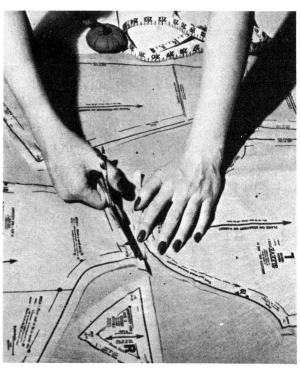

**Cutting.** With sharp shears, cut exactly on pattern's cutting line with long, even strokes. Use a sliding motion, so the fabric is not raised from the table.

**Pattern Markings.** All pattern markings have a meaning. Snip the notches with the point out, to form a tab, so the seam is not weakened. On a fabric that frays easily, mark notches with tailor's chalk.

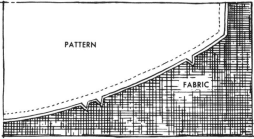

Indicate all pattern markings—darts, pleats, tucks, etc.—with tailor tacks (see directions on pattern guide), pins, chalk, or a tailor tacker. Before you remove the pattern, run basting thread down center front and center back. These basting lines will serve as guides when you are fitting your dress.

### Putting a Dress Together

After the garment has been cut, handle it as little as possible, to avoid mussing and creasing. While fabric is flat on the table, remove pattern pieces. Then pin together the skirt seams, matching notches carefully, and hand baste, allowing for the exact seam width. Take out pins as you baste.

There are three kinds of basting: pin, hand, and machine. On seams without strain, such as skirt seams, long, running hand stitches are adequate. On seams where there is strain—shoulder seams, for example—a shorter stitch, with an occasional back stitch, is preferable. As your skill increases, you'll find you can sew some darts and seams after pin-basting only; but don't try this until you are sure of your size and pattern and have become skillful in handling fabrics.

**Stay Stitching.** A "stay stitch" is a long machine stitch run along the cut edges, to prevent the fabric's stretching before the final stitching. "Stay-stitch" any off-grain edges, such as neck, sleeves, waistline of skirt, and waist to hip on fitted skirt. On materials that stretch, run a "stay line" around placket openings, too. Run a second row of machine basting on the sleeve ¼″ from the edge between the notches. This will be used later to gather in the fullness at the top of the sleeve.

**Basting.** Before basting darts, use a ruler and chalk to mark along line of notches, so stitches will be in a straight line. Then baste from the widest place toward the point. Be sure to end all points of darts at the same place. Baste pleats or gathers, etc.

Baste side seams of the bodice and sleeve seams,

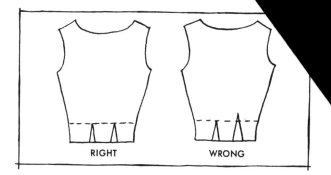

turning darts down, and then the shoulder seams, matching notches. Turn darts on shoulders toward neckline. Pin sleeves in armhole. Hold right sides of material of blouse and sleeves together, with opening toward you. Pin together, first the underarm seam, then center of sleeve at the shoulder seam, matching sleeve and blouse notches. Ease the fullness between the notches by pulling the machine basting thread; distribute fullness evenly. Pin in place. Then finish pinning the armholes, and baste.

The next step is joining the blouse and skirt. Pin at side seams, center front, and center back. Adjust fullness of blouse; then baste, turning darts toward center of blouse.

**Try on for Fit.** Try on garment right side out, wearing a belt of type to be worn with dress. Be sure to wear a foundation garment. If your measurements were accurate and the necessary adjustments carefully made, your garment should fit. A dress fits properly when the lengthwise threads are perfectly straight down the center front and center back and crosswise threads are straight across figure and parallel to the floor at bustline and hips. (Lines will vary on a bias-cut dress.)

There shouldn't be strain at any point. The skirt should hang straight from the hips, with no pull or cup under. Be particular about the sleeves. The underarm seams should fall in a straight vertical line; the darts or gathers in long sleeves should come at the elbow. There should be room to move the arm freely, but no wrinkles. Make adjustments by pin fitting. Always keep the center front and center back lines vertical. If you take in a seam at any point, be sure the take-in is not tapered abruptly. After pinning, baste, and try on the garment again. Repeat until you are satisfied with the fit.

**Stitching.** When you are satisfied with the fit, begin stitching. Stitching and pressing go hand in hand. Never cross an unpressed seam with another seam.

Stitch the darts from the side to the point, and press. Stitch pleats from bottom up, to avoid puckering.

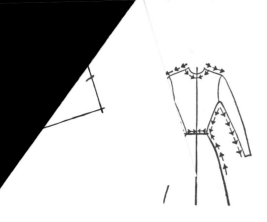

Follow the diagram for the direction in which to stitch seams. Make the proper seam allowance. Stitch seam from the armhole to the wrist, with the side darts or gathers toward you so you can see to guide fullness. The darts always should be turned toward the lower edge of the sleeve.

To stitch sleeve in armhole, place the sleeve toward you, so you can guide the fullness with your fingers as you stitch. Be careful you don't make little pleats. Begin stitching just before armhole seam, and overlap stitching when you complete sewing in sleeve.

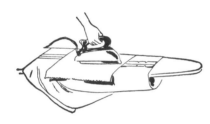

**Seams.** Open seams, and press flat. A few fabrics show press marks on the right side. However, if you place a strip of thin paper between seam and fabric before pressing, marks will not show.

A needle, or velvet, board is desirable for pressing pile fabrics. Place the fabric, pile side down, on the board. Then press lightly with iron, or cover with press cloth and dampen lightly before pressing.

**Shrinking Sleeve Tops.** Some dressmakers prefer shrinking in the fullness at the top of a sleeve when it is basted; others prefer to do it after stitching. For the inexperienced dressmaker, it is probably better to do the shrinking before the final stitching. A tailor's pressing mitt or sleeve cushion is a great help in pressing a sleeve so it hangs correctly. Or press it over the end of a sleeve board. Turn the sleeve inside out, and

press around seam. Then place about 1″ of the sleeve on the sleeve board or sleeve cushion. Use the tip of the iron, and press lightly toward the seam to shrink in the tiny gathers. To press the shoulder and armhole seams, place the shoulder seam over the end of the board, pressing armhole seam toward sleeve.

**Turning the Hem.** Before turning the hem, let the dress hang for a day or two, especially if it has a bias or circular skirt.

Wear heels of the height you expect to wear with the finished dress. Put on the foundation garment that you plan to wear under the dress. If the dress has a belt, wear it.

Actual measuring has been simplified by commercial skirt markers. There are types with which you can mark your own hem; others require the aid of another person.

To mark your own hem without a skirt marker, stand beside a table; using the table edge as a guide, put chalk marks or pins in an even row *below* the hips. Or, rest one end of a yardstick on the floor and measure a line below the hips. Then take off the dress, and measure from this line to hemline.

Turn up hem along marked line; pin. Match seams. Baste close to fold at bottom of skirt, and press on wrong side. Then use ruler or hem gauge to trim to even depth.

Depth of hem depends on amount of fullness in the skirt and the weight of the fabric. Follow hem allowance of your pattern. Usually a hem is 2″ deep when finished, except on very wide skirts where narrower hems are necessary.

After trimming hem to an even depth, press with steam iron or through damp cloth to shrink out extra fullness so hem will lie flat. Tiny, even darts or gathers also may be used to adjust extra fullness.

Finish hem with hand stitching or blind-stitch attachment of sewing machine.

### Zippers

Choose the length indicated on your pattern, in a color and weight for your fabric. Select the type best suited for the closure on your garment. Among the types available, with either plastic or metal teeth, are the following:

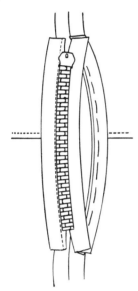

**Dress-Placket Zippers** have a bridge top-stop, which holds the two top sides of the tape together to prevent strain on the underarm seams.

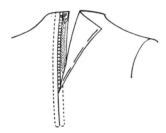

**Neck Open-Type Zippers** are open at the top and made in suitable lengths for sleeve, neck, and shoulder openings, pockets, and children's clothing. This type can be used as a decorative trim at necklines or on pockets. It may also be used for a dress placket if the tapes are stitched across the top to hold them together. (Otherwise, zipper may pull open.)

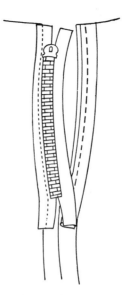

**Skirt-Placket Zippers** have an automatic locking slider to keep the placket from pulling open, and sturdy teeth to give extra strength. This type is also used on shorts and slacks.

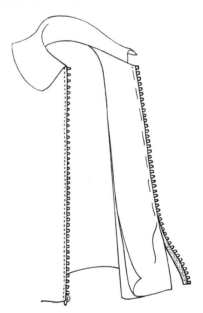

**Separating Zippers** are designed for jackets, coats, blouses, and ski suits where complete coat-type separation is desired. They are made in both light and heavy weights. The heavy type is made with a nontarnishing metal finish and extra-wide tapes for extra rows of reinforcing stitching.

**Trouser-Fly Zippers** have a special lock that withstands the weight of heavy steam presses.

### Inserting a Zipper

Always fit the garment before inserting the zippers. Carefully follow the detailed instructions that accom-

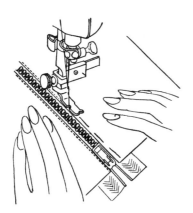

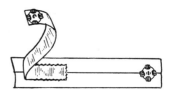

**Snap Fasteners**

Carefully mark position of socket on underlap and of ball on the upper part so that the pressure will come from the ball part of the fastener. Sew with over-and-over stitches. Secure with buttonhole stitches.

pany each package. Seams should be ¾" or more, and the placket should be slightly longer at the top than the zipper. The fabric should be eased to the zipper tape. Keep the zipper closed and the tab turned up while you sew. When machine-stitching, use a zipper or cording foot.

Sheer, lightweight fabrics should be eased when stitched to a zipper. Reinforce thin fabrics with seam tape instead of self material for facing. Seam tape will give more body to the fabric and will let the zipper lie flat.

Fabrics which have a tendency to give should never be stretched into the zipper. Use a muslin facing to overcome stretching.

For best results on velvet, hand-stitch the zipper to the garment.

Washable fabrics on which zippers are used should have a shrinkage of less than 1 per cent. If the fabric shrinks more than the tape, the resulting bulge of the zipper will mar the garment.

**Buttons**

Use a double thread suitable for weight of button and type of fabric. If fabric is thin, use tape or other reinforcement under it.

A stem is needed under the button to allow room for the buttonhole. To make a stem, take three small stitches on the right side of the fabric. Bring thread up through one hole of the button. Place pin over button. Take several stitches over pin and through button and fabric until button is secure. Pull out pin. Lift button. Wind thread tightly around threads between button and fabric. Fasten thread securely. When sewing a shank button, place pin or wooden pick (for longer stem) directly on fabric, just under button shank.

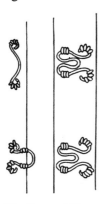

**Hooks and Eyes**

Place hook so end comes about ⅛" from edge, and eye so that it extends just over the edge. Sew both with an over-and-over stitch around the curved edges. Secure with several buttonhole stitches. Where the edges lap, the straight eye or blanket-stitched bar is set back from the edge, usually on the seam.

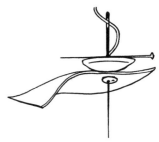

When putting a large button on a coat or tailored garment, sew a small button on the wrong side of the fabric. This gives added support and conceals the stitches.

Buttons are sized by "line," with 40 lines to the inch. Standard-size buttons run from 15 line (⅜") to 120 lines (3").

Buy one or two extra buttons to replace lost or broken ones when you buy a style that may be difficult to replace.

## Buttonholes

Mark position and length of buttonhole on fabric with tracing wheel and tracing paper, or with pins. Make sure markings are along a thread unless buttons are to be placed on the bias. The buttonhole is usually placed a distance equal to half the width of the button from edge of garment. Check position by lapping the buttonhole side over button side. Lap right over left side on women's and girls' garments; left over right on men's and boys'. Place pins along this line. Use a measuring gauge or ruler to make sure buttonhole markings are accurate.

Buttonholes may be horizontal or vertical. A vertical buttonhole is more satisfactory at a point of strain.

Buttonhole size is usually 1/8" larger than the button. A thick button requires a larger buttonhole.

**Worked Buttonholes.** Mark position by a line. Stitch close around this line, by hand or machine. Cut on line, and overcast cut edges.

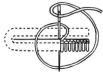 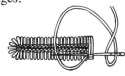

Buttonhole-stitch around edges. Ends may be finished with a fan at one end or bars at both ends. Bars are better for vertical buttonholes, as they are stronger. Make a bar by placing two long stitches across inside end of buttonhole; buttonhole stitch *across,* not around, end of buttonhole.

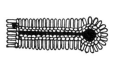 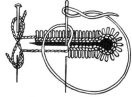

**Tailored Buttonholes** are made by punching the end toward the garment edge with a stiletto. The punched end and the edges are finished with a buttonhole stitch. The other end is finished with a bar. For a corded edge, work buttonhole over a strand of heavy thread or twist held taut over a pin. Work a bar at square end.

**Machine-Made Buttonholes.** A special automatic buttonhole-making attachment is available for most sewing machines. Automatic zigzag machines make buttonholes without attachment.

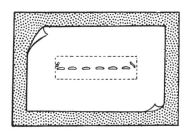

**Bound Buttonhole.** Cut a piece of material (true bias or straight, preferably bias) 2" wide and 1" longer than finished buttonhole. Place piece over line for buttonhole, right sides together. Stitch 1/8" around marking, making square corners. Count stitches at ends so they are of same width.

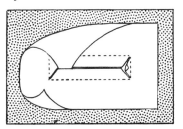

Cut through both layers of fabric to 1/2" from end. Cut into corners diagonally and pull strip through slash to wrong side.

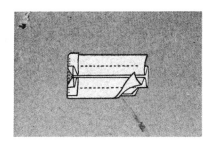

Turn seam away from slash and make inverted pleat at ends to form piping with edges at center. Overcast edges of piping together at center of pleat. Baste, then stitch triangular pieces at ends of piping. Stitch along length of buttonhole.

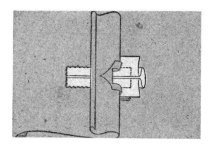

If facing is used, cut slit in facing in back of each buttonhole. Cut diagonally at ends of slash, turn under raw edges of facing, and hem or slip-stitch to buttonhole.

# KNITTING

## Equipment

There are many types of thread and yarn on the market for knitting and crocheting. Listed below are the main types which are sold under various trade names.

**Thread** is made of twisted strands of cotton, silk, linen, or synthetic fibers. It has a smooth finish and is uniform in size.

**Yarn** is twisted more loosely than thread and is made of wool, cotton, synthetic fibers, animal hair, alone or in combination.

**Germantown** is a 4-ply long staple wool. It is smooth, lightweight, and warm. *Ply* refers to the number of strands twisted to make the yarn.

**Knitting Worsted** is usually a 4-ply yarn loosely twisted for rough usage. It is a utility yarn.

**Sports Yarn** is a tightly twisted 4-ply yarn, not as coarse and heavy as knitting worsted.

**Fingering Yarn** is a 2- or 3-ply yarn, not as tightly spun as sports yarn.

**Floss** is a 2-ply yarn hairy in texture with fine but strong fibers.

**Saxony** is 2-, 3- or 4-ply, uniform in texture, made from the finest wool.

**Angora** is 2- or 3-ply, soft and fluffy, made of the hair of the Angora rabbit, usually in combination with other fibers.

**Bouclé** is a novelty yarn on which loops are formed by uneven twisting of the thread.

**Rug Yarn** is usually 4-ply and is available in cotton, wool, synthetic fibers, alone or in combination.

**Needles for Knitting** come in sets of 2 or 4, or as 1 circular needle. In the 2-needle set, only one end of each needle is pointed, and the work is flat. In the 4-needle set, each end of the needle is pointed, and the work is tubular. Both ends of the circular needle are pointed, and the work is tubular.

The gauge pictured below gives the actual size of knitting needles on the American standard. In the Canadian and English standard, the higher the number, the smaller the needle. Notice that this number-

ing method is also used for double-pointed steel needles.

## Abbreviations and Glossary

k—knit
p—purl
st(s)—stitch(es)
yo—yarn over
sl—slip
beg—begin(ing)
psso—pass slipped stitch over knit stitch
rpt—repeat
bet—between
lp—loop
mc—main color
cc—contrasting color
dec—decrease(s, ing)
inc—increase(s, ing)
in(s)—inch(es)
tog—together
dp—double pointed

*, the star symbol, indicates that the directions immediately following are to be repeated. "Work" means to continue in pattern stitch, always keeping the continuity of the original design. When using "yo" be sure you are making an additional stitch.

In all instructions always measure straight up and down unless otherwise stated.

Pattern stitch: Always make a swatch of your pattern stitch, before commencing garment; and as you knit your swatch study the trend of the stitch. This is necessary in shaping your garment.

Garter stitch: Knit every row. It will take 2 rows to make 1 ridge.

Stockinet stitch: K 1 row, p 1 row.

## Stitch Gauge

*Stitch Gauge,* which appears at the beginning of all instructions for knitting, is most important to size and fit. Gauge is the number of stitches per inch *you* knit with a certain size needle and a specific yarn.

| "HERO STANDARD" NEEDLE GAGE NUMBER—AMERICAN STANDARD | | | | | | | | | | | | | | |
|---|---|---|---|---|---|---|---|---|---|---|---|---|---|---|
| 0 | 1 | 2 | 3 | 4 | 5 | 6 | 7 | 8 | 9 | 10 | 10½ | 11 | 13 | 15 |

DIAMETER IN MILLIMETERS

| 2 | 2½ | 2¾ | 3 | 3½ | 3¾ | 4¼ | 4¾ | 5 | 5¼ | 5¾ | 7 | 8 | 9 | 10 |
|---|---|---|---|---|---|---|---|---|---|---|---|---|---|---|

| 13 | 12 | 11 | 10 | 9 | 8 | | | | | | | | | |
|---|---|---|---|---|---|---|---|---|---|---|---|---|---|---|

CORRESPONDING DOUBLE POINTED STEEL SIZES

**HERO MFG. CO., INC.**
*Manufacturers of*
"Hero Standard" Needles
MIDDLEBORO, MASS.

| 4 | 3 | 2 | 1 | 0 | 00 | F | G | H | I | J |
|---|---|---|---|---|---|---|---|---|---|---|

CORRESPONDING CROCHET HOOK SIZES

Before starting your knit article, make a sample swatch of the pattern stitch with the needles and yarn specified. Count number of stitches and rows *you* get to the inch. If you get MORE stitches to the inch than the stitch gauge calls for, you are working tightly, so change to a LARGER needle; if you get FEWER stitches to the inch, you are working loosely, so change to a SMALLER needle.

The important thing to remember is that the size of the needle and the yarn used do not matter so long as your stitch gauge is correct. Check your gauge as you progress—remember that you are only human, and your moods will show in your knitting and crocheting.

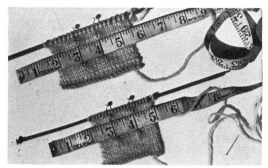

*Same number of stitches, same size needles, and same yarn, but different knitters. This shows the importance of working a stitch gauge before you knit an article.*

**To Cast On:** Make a slip knot, leaving a long end (allow 1″ for each st) and slip needle into loop. (1) *With the loose end make a loop over left thumb and with the strand attached to the ball, make a loop over the left forefinger. (2) Insert needle into thumb-loop and draw through yarn attached to ball.

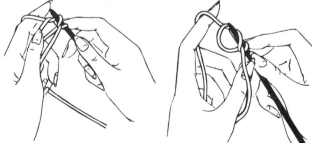

(3) Drop yarn from thumb and tighten stitch slightly. (4) Repeat from * for desired number of stitches.

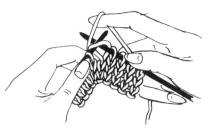

**To Knit:** Hold needle with cast-on stitches in left hand between thumb and index finger. Place yarn in back of work. Insert right-hand needle through first stitch on left-hand needle, taking it from front and below. Pass yarn around the point of right hand needle, going first behind and then in front. Draw yarn through, formng a stitch on right-hand needle. Slip stitch off left-hand needle and pull new stitch tight enough to be easy to knit in next row.

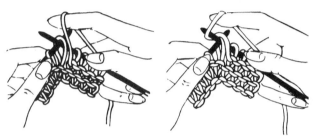

**To Purl:** Hold needles in same way as for knitting but with the yarn in front of work. Insert point of right-hand needle through front of first stitch on left-hand needle from right to left. Pass yarn around back of right-hand needle taking yarn over and below needle. Draw this loop through the stitch. Slip the stitch off the left-hand needle and keep yarn to the front of the work. Pull the stitch to required tension.

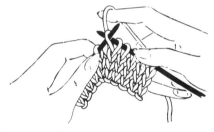

**To Increase:** Knit twice in same stitch. Knit the st as a plain st, and before taking it off the needle, knit again into back of same stitch.

**To Decrease:** Knit or purl two together.

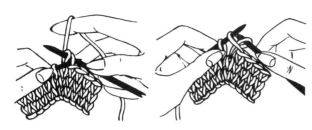

**To Bind Off:** Knit 2 stitches. *Pass first stitch on right-hand needle over second stitch, leaving 1 stitch on right-hand needle. Knit another stitch, again having 2 stitches on right-hand needle. Repeat from * until desired number of stitches are bound off.

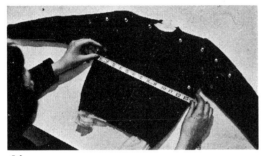

## Blocking

There are two methods that may be used. In the first, join the seams with a slip stitch, using a crochet hook, or join with a back stitch, using a blunt-end needle. Always take care in setting in the sleeves; overlook the pointed corners of the cap, to give a smooth, rounded arch to the shoulder line—these corners on the inside never will be noticed. Immerse in cold water enough Turkish towels to cover both sides of the garment. Wring dry, and lay half of them on a large, flat surface. Lay the garment on the moist towels. Crush tissue paper into long strips and place inside the edges of the sleeves, along the shoulder seams and down the side seams. Press in rustproof thumbtacks an inch apart at the shoulder seams, just inside the exaggerated ridge made by the crushed tissue paper. Stretching the armhole to the proper size and bearing in mind the size of the bust or chest, press in tacks 1″ apart, again inside the ridge of the side seams. Keep the bust measurement for at least 4″ below the armpit. Now start graduating to the waist measurement. Always keep the ribbing as small as possible, to retain its natural elasticity. For sleeves and skirt, follow the same principle. Finally cover the garment with moist towels and let it dry thoroughly before removing towels; then steam seams lightly. The crushed tissue paper helps to prevent that ugly "pressed-in-seam" look.

In the second method, with the strictly dressmaker finish, each piece is blocked separately. Cut heavy paper to the exact sizes the pieces are to measure, allowing for small seams. It is advisable, especially when combing a fabric and a knit piece, to use a regular dress pattern, cutting exact duplicates of the tissue-paper sections in heavy paper for knit parts. Baste knit parts to paper pieces. Place a damp pressing cloth over pieces and steam, but do not press. Never allow the weight of the iron to rest on the garment. Let the pieces dry thoroughly before removing them from the heavy paper. Remove basting threads and join seams, handling knit pieces as you would any piece of fabric. Set in sleeves, easing fullness of cap around top of armhole and being careful not to bind the armhole with tight stitches. Make darts, tucks, shirrings, etc., as in tailoring. It is essential for perfect fit to baste all pieces together. Try on, and make necessary adjustments, before actually sewing the garment. After sewing, steam all seams slightly.

## Blocking Measurements

| *Children* Sizes: | 2 | 4 | 6 | 8 | 10 |
|---|---|---|---|---|---|
| Chest (in inches) | 22 | 24 | 26 | 28 | 30 |
| Shoulder to lower edge (varies) | 12 | 13½ | 15 | 16½ | 18 |
| Side seam (varies) | 8 | 9 | 10 | 11 | 12 |
| Across back at underarm | 11 | 12 | 13½ | 13½ | 14½ |
| Across each front at underarm for cardigan | 6½ | 7¼ | 7¼ | 8½ | 8¾ |
| Length of long sleeve (approx.) | 10 | 11 | 13 | 14 | 15 |
| Width of sleeve at upper arm | 8½ | 9 | 10 | 11 | 11½ |

| *Women* Sizes: | 12 | 14 | 16 | 18 | 20 |
|---|---|---|---|---|---|
| Bust (in inches) | 32 | 34 | 36 | 38 | 40 |
| Side seam (varies) | 14½ | 14½ | 15 | 15 | 15½ |
| Shoulder to lower edge (varies) | 21¾ | 22 | 22¾ | 23 | 23¾ |
| Length of sleeve seam | 17 | 17½ | 18 | 18 | 18½ |
| Across sleeve at upper arm | 11½ | 12 | 13¼ | 14 | 14½ |
| Short sleeve seam | 4½ | 4½ | 4½ | 4½ | 4½ |
| Across each front at underarm for cardigan | 10 | 11 | 12 | 13 | 14 |

*Men*

| | Chest | Waist |
|---|---|---|
| Size 36 ............ | 36 | 32 |
| 38 ............ | 38 | 34 |
| 40 ............ | 40 | 36 |
| 42 ............ | 42 | 38 |

# CROCHETING

Crocheting is an interlocking of loops, formed by a single needle or hook. To many, the manipulation of one needle makes it easier to crochet than to knit. Crocheting is more frequently used for articles for the home than for wearing apparel.

## Abbreviations and Glossary

ch—chain
sc—single crochet
hdc or sdc—half double crochet
dc—double crochet
tr (tc)—treble crochet
dtc—double or long treble crochet
rnd(s)—round(s)
sl st—slip stitch
sk—skip
sp—space(s)
bl—block
p—picot
yo—yarn over

*, the star symbol indicates that the directions immediately following are to be repeated.

"Work" means to continue in pattern st, always keeping the continuity of the original design. When using "yo" always be certain that you are making an additional loop.

In all instructions always measure straight up and down unless otherwise stated.

Pattern st: Always make a swatch of your pattern st, before commencing garment; and as you make your swatch study the trend of the pattern. This knowledge is necessary in the shaping of the article.

**Crochet Hook Sizes:** See chart on page 282.

**Stitch Gauge:** See page 282.

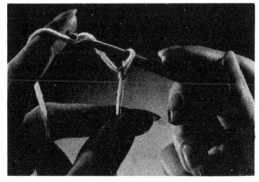

**Chain Stitch.** Make a slip knot and place loop on hook which is held in right hand. * Wrap yarn around hook and draw yarn through loop on hook, permitting 1st lp to drop off. Rpt from * for desired number of chain stitches.

**Single Crochet.** Make chain desired length. Insert hook into 2nd chain stitch from hook, *yo, and draw yarn through stitch (2 loops on hook), yo, and draw yarn through both loops on hook. Rpt from * in each stitch. Row 2: Turn, ch 1. * Insert hook in top of next st, going through both strands of stitch (unless otherwise stated), yo, and draw yarn through both loops on hook. Rpt from * across row. Rpt Row 2.

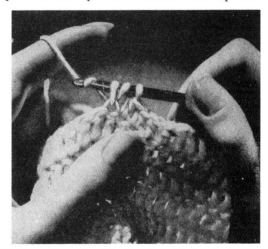

**Half or Short Double Crochet.** Make chain desired length. * Yo, insert hook in 3rd ch from hook and draw up loop (3 loops on hook), yo, and draw yarn through 3 loops. Rpt from * in each chain. Row 2: Turn, ch 2, * yo, insert hook in top of next st, going through both strands, yo, and draw yarn through stitch (3 loops on hook), yo, and draw through 3 loops. Rpt from * across row. Rpt Row 2.

**Double Crochet.** Make chain desired length. * Yo and insert hook in the 4th ch from hook and draw up a loop (3 lps on hook), yo, and draw through 2 lps (2 lps on hook), yo, and draw through last

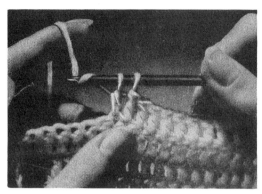

2 lps. Rpt from * in each chain. Row 2: Turn, ch 3, * yo, insert hook through top of next st, going through both strands of the stitch yo and draw through st (3 lps on hook), yo and draw through 2 lps (2 lps on hook), yo and draw through last 2 lps. Rpt from * across row. Rpt Row 2.

**Treble Crochet.** Make chain desired length. * Yo twice, insert hook in fifth ch from hook, and draw up a loop (4 lps on hook); yo and draw through 2 lps (3 lps on hook); yo and draw through 2 lps (2 lps on hook); yo and draw through last 2 lps. Rpt from * in each chain. Row 2: Turn, ch 4, * yo twice, insert hook through top of next st going through both strands of the stitch, and draw up lp (4 lps on hook); yo and draw through 2 lps (3 lps on hook); yo and draw through 2 lps (2 lps on hook); yo and draw through last 2 lps. Rpt from * across row. Rpt Row 2.

**To Make a Ring.** Join last ch to first ch.

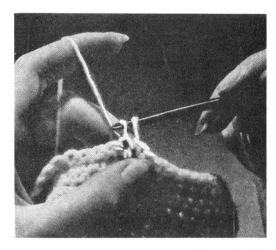

**Slip Stitch.** Make a chain desired length. Insert hook into second ch on hook, yo and draw through ch and loop at same time. Repeat in each chain. Row 2: Turn, ch 1, * insert through top of next st, yo, and draw through top of st and loop at same time. Repeat from * across row. Repeat Row 2. This stitch is used to form a tight edge, such as the band on a beret.

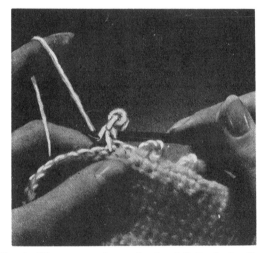

**Picot.** There are 2 methods. Method 1: Sc in foundation, ch 3 or 4, depending on length of picot desired, and slip stitch in top of sc. Method 2: Work a sc, ch 3 or 4 for picot and sc again in same space. Work as many sc's between picots as desired. This is often used as a trim in a contrasting color.

**To Increase.** Make 2 sts in 1 st.

**To Decrease.** Draw yarn through each of 2 sts. Complete st in usual manner.

**Blocking.** See page 284.

As a general rule, metal crochet hooks are used with tightly twisted threads such as cotton or silk. Bone hooks are usually used on wool and synthetic yarns. Large wooden hooks are used to obtain a lacy effect with loosely twisted yarns.

# EMBROIDERY STITCHES

**Threaded Running Stitch:** Weave a thread in and out simple running stitch. Contrasting color may be used for weaving.

**Outline or Stem Stitch:** Work from left to right and keep thread below needle.

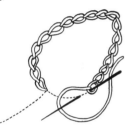

**Chain Stitch:** Bring needle up to right side. Hold left thumb over loop of thread and insert needle near where it first came out. Do not pull thread tightly. Bring needle out short distance forward and over loop of thread.

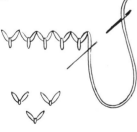

**Y Stitch:** Pass needle up through cloth a little left of center. Place needle a little to right of center and take a slant stitch, bringing needle up through center below first stitch. Take straight stitch on center line to complete Y. The Y stitch becomes a *Fly Stitch* when stem of Y is shorter than horizontal stitch.

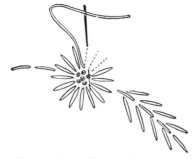

**Stroke Stitch:** Large single stitches used to form flowers, leaves or tiny squares.

**Fern Stitch:** Work long single stitch to center of line; bring needle up at beginning of center line. Return to beginning of first stitch and up above and to left of center line. Insert at beginning of first stitch.

**Feather Stitch:** Take one short slanting stitch on right side of line, pointing needle to left, and the next stitch on the opposite side of line, pointing needle to right. Can be made in a variety of ways by keeping stitches straight on one side of center and by groupings of 2 and 3 stitches to either side of center line.

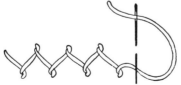

**Creton Stitch:** With thread always under needle, stitches are made at right angles to the work above and below a center line.

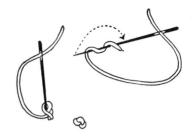

**French Knots:** Bring needle to right side. Wrap thread around needle 2, 3, or 4 times, holding it near cloth. Insert needle near place it came out. Draw thread close to form knot.

**Lazy Daisy Stitch:** Bring needle to right side at center of flower. Hold left thumb over a long loop of thread —the length of the petal—and insert needle as close as possible to place where thread came out. Take long stitch on wrong side to end of petal, keeping loop under needle. Fasten end of loop with short stitch. Bring needle back to center for next petal.

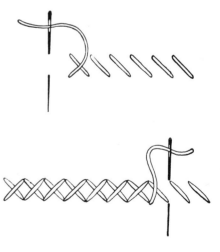

**Cross Stitch:** To form the first slanting stitch, work from right to left; then work from left to right to form cross.

# NEEDLEPOINT

Needlepoint is worked on single- or double-thread canvas. Both types are made in fine, medium, and coarse sizes. The tapestry or worsted needle used is usually long, strong, and blunt, with an oval eye wide enough to thread easily. The size depends on the size of canvas and thread.

Needlepoint canvas is sold with a stamped design, underlaid (*tramé*), or the design can be worked from a chart. In *tramé* pieces, a thread is laid between the narrowly spaced threads of the double-thread canvas, and the stitches are made over the underlaid threads.

Needlepoint tapestries are usually made in petit point or gros point stitches or both. In pieces combining both, all petit point sections are worked first.

When beginning work, leave an end 1″ long on wrong side and "catch in" by stitches as you work. At the end of the yarn, run needle through several stitches on wrong side. The yarn should never be longer than 30″ or it will tend to work thin and tangle. If the yarn curls while working, allow thread and needle to hang a moment so yarn can untwist.

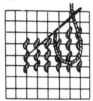

**Petit Point or Tent.** This stitch produces a small slanting stitch on the front and a longer slanting one at the back. At the end of a row, turn the work upside down and make a small upright stitch to bring the needle into position for the next row, as every line is worked from right to left.

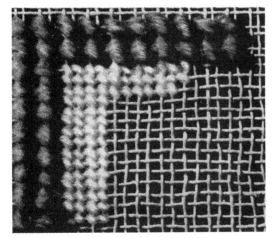

Petit point is usually worked on single-thread canvas. If part of the design planned for double-thread canvas is to be worked in petit point, the stitch

itself is always worked over just a single thread of the canvas. To aid in keeping an even stitch, wet the desired section and separate the horizontal and vertical double threads of the canvas, forcing the threads into even rows.

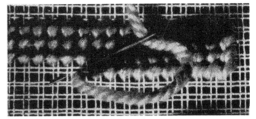

**Gros Point.** A larger edition of petit point. It is worked in the same manner as petit point but over two threads in height and width, usually on double-thread canvas.

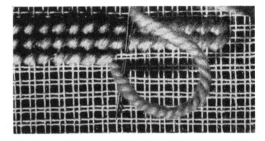

**Half-Cross.** Draw needle through square of canvas at lower left-hand corner. Insert needle into next square above and draw it through square directly below. This forms the first slanting stitch. Continue in this manner, always moving over one square to the right and keeping needle in vertical position which forms a straight stitch on wrong side. When row is finished, turn work upside down. Thread and work is then in position to work toward right. Practically all stamped, or *tramé* (underlaid), pieces are worked in half-cross stitch as it takes about one-quarter less thread than the gros point stitch.

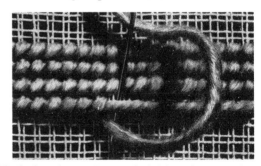

If design is to be underlaid, bring needle and thread up through canvas from right-hand side. Carry thread across top between narrow row to left side. Work in half-stitch.

**Blocking.** Sponge on wrong side until wool and canvas are very wet; or roll in very damp Turkish towel and leave it until entire piece is quite damp. Stretch into shape and tack face down on a board with rustproof thumbtacks, tacks to be no more than ¾" apart. Allow to dry thoroughly before taking up —for 1 to 3 days, depending on weather conditions. It is not necessary to press, but if desired, after piece is thoroughly dry, cover it wrong side up with a damp smooth towel and steam with hot iron. Do not allow iron to touch needlepoint.

**Mounting Finished Work.** Great care is needed in mounting the finished piece, particularly if for furniture. In that case, it should be blocked and mounted by an experienced craftsman when possible. Pillows are usually hemmed and joined to a back of heavy fabric. Picture panels, wall hangings, and bellpulls should be faced with tape and backed with heavy sateen; small rings are sewed at intervals across the top, and the hanging is suspended from a rod. Wall pictures are framed like paintings. Hem or face rugs with tape or line with felt or sailcloth.

## HOOKED RUGS

The foundation for hooking is of burlap, monk's cloth, gunny sacks, or canvas. If gunny sacks are used, they should be washed, boiled, and dipped in hot starch to which a pinch of powdered arabic has been added. To give a glossy surface on which to design, iron while damp.

**Hooking with a Crochet Hook.** Work from the right side of the rug. Hold the yarn or strip of cloth between the thumb and forefinger of the left hand, underneath the foundation, and the hook lightly in right hand. Insert hook through foundation, and then catch end of yarn and pull through foundation. Skip a few threads of material and insert hook through again; pull up gently and leave a loop.

**Hooking with an Automatic Needle.** Work from the wrong side of the rug and use the hook to push rather than pull loops through foundation. Be sure yarn or strip runs freely through needle and does not catch. Always insert needle vertically, bringing end of yarn on the right side of foundation. Withdraw needle just clear of material. Slide and insert again.

**To Clip.** Run a double-pointed steel needle through the loops and pull the loops up firmly from the foundation before cutting. Remove steel needle. For cutting, use long, narrow, sharp scissors. Slide one point of scissors in through the loops and cut about 1" of loops at a time. When working next row of loops, push clipped loops back so no strand will be caught in the descending hook.

**Blocking.** With a sponge or piece of Turkish toweling wrung out of hot water, go over the entire top or looped side of the rug to dampen it. Place the rug face down on a smooth surface covered with clean paper. Put rug in shape but do not stretch tightly. Walk on it as much as possible. This sets and flattens the stitches and keeps them in place.

If the edges of the rug are unfinished, leave enough unhooked foundation all around to have about 3" to turn under and hem. Or turn a narrow edge and bind with strong fabric or carpet binding. If liquid rug sizing is available, spread an even coat over entire back; allow sizing to dry thoroughly, then line.

**To Line Rug.** Cut lining 1½" more than the width and length of the rug all around. Place the lining flat on the table. Place the rug on the lining, having the 1½" project on all sides. Baste the rug onto the lining about 2" in from the edge all around. Turn the rug over so the lining is on top. Using a strong thread, make large stitches and catch-stitch lining onto back of rug. Remove basting.

Although there are yarns especially treated for rug making, many hooked rugs are made of old materials. Woolen yarns and fabrics are best, but cotton, linen, silk, and synthetic fabrics as well as stockings may be used.

## IN-A-WALL SEWING ROOM

1 and 2: Fabric storage boxes
3: Work-in-progress shelf
4: Pattern box
5: Steam iron
6: Sit-down ironing board
7: Sleeve board
8: Notions

9: Dress form
10: Scissors-and-spool board
11: Pull-out table on casters
12: Swivel lamp
13: Two drawers for sewing machine attachments
14: Storage cabinet
15: Folding doors with two full-length mirrors

# Simple Repairs
# Made Easy

### A Tool Kit of Your Own

Every home needs a tool kit in case of minor emergencies, and to save unnecessary repairman's expense.

A good way to store tools is on a wall panel provided with hooks. The wall panel is good because the tools are within easy reach, and they are not easily lost; when one is missing, the obvious blank space is a telling reminder to find the tool and put it back. The simple board with L-hooks shown here is excellent for a few basic tools.

Perhaps a better wall panel is a pegboard. These perforated hardboard panels can be bought at hardware stores and lumberyards, along with an assortment of holders and hooks to fit any tool. As you buy more tools you can rearrange the tool plan on the board. Then as a final touch, you can buy cut-out tool silhouettes, with adhesive backing, and place them on the board, to indicate the exact position of each tool.

The pegboard should be framed before it is hung. Half-inch molding should be fastened to the back of the edges of the panel with small finish-

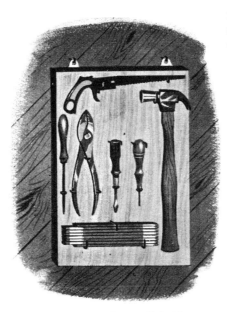

*A wall panel that will hold your most-often used household tools.*

ing nails. This molding makes a space between the board and the wall to allow for the part of the hooks which project through.

If the board is to go on a plaster wall, fasten it with Molly bolts. Hold the board in the desired position and mark with a pencil through the holes

in the 4 corners. With a drill bit the same diameter as the Molly bolts, drill 4 holes through the plaster. Insert the Molly bolts all the way in, and set them by turning the screws down tightly with a screwdriver. Remove the screws, reposition the board, and put the screws back in. Turn them down tightly again.

These are the tools you will need most often:

Medium-size claw hammer
Large and small screwdrivers
Pliers
Adjustable wrench
Half-round, double-cut file
Wood rasp
Six-foot rule (folding or steel tape)
Cross-cut saw
Hack saw
Try square
Twist drill and set of drills
Knife
Putty knife
Small pinch bar
Oil can (pump-type is best)

One last word: *Buy good tools.* A tool is only as good as its working edge or surface, and there is nothing that can take the place of good material and proper temper.

### Replacing Cord Plugs

To replace a plug in a connecting cord, trim the frayed portion of the cord, then strip off about 2" of the outer covering, being careful not to cut the insulation on wires. Slip the plug onto the cord, and separate the wire conductors. Remove about ½" of the insulation from ends of wires, and scrape them with a knife until bright. Twist each wire end.

If the plug will accommodate it, tie an Underwriters' knot, as illustrated, so about 1½" of each conductor projects from the knot. Pull down knot so it is in base of the plug. This prevents strain on the terminal connections in case the plug is pulled from the outlet by the cord. It is wise, however, to remove a plug by grasping its base.

Loop a wire around each of the prongs, and twist it around a terminal screw, tucking wire completely under screw head in a clockwise direction, with no more than one turn of wire. Tighten screws, and trim with scissors any strands that may be exposed. Then replace the fiber panel to cover the exposed wires.

### Light-Duty Lamp Cord

Light-duty "rip cord" wire, with rubber or plastic insulation, is now used on lamps, clocks, and radios. Make quick and simple repairs on this type of wire with the self-wiring plug. It opens to receive the rip cord and then snaps shut to puncture the insulation automatically and make contact with the conductors.

To protect inquisitive children who are still at the creeping age, use "babyproof" outlets, which foil the youngsters' dangerous experiments with metal toys and things they may find on the floor.

### Changing Fuses

Replacing a fuse takes only a few moments and does not present any great hazard. Grasp the fuse by its top and unscrew it like a light bulb. Put in a new fuse in the same way. As an extra precaution, keep one hand behind your back to prevent touching a surface that is grounded, and stand on a rubber mat (or wear overshoes) if the fuse box is above a concrete floor. Then you will be as well protected as electricians who use this method to work on high-voltage circuits. Of course, the main switch on the meter box can be pulled down to disconnect the entire electric supply, but this will put out all the lights and stop all the electric clocks.

Most homes have large main fuses supplied by the power company to protect its meters; if the entire house is without electricity, one of these may have blown. The power company will quickly respond to a call to replace these fuses.

Ordinary, plug-type screw-base fuses for household use are sold in 15, 20, 25, and 30 ampere sizes to fit various kinds of wiring circuits. It is important to use the correct size for a circuit—never a larger size. An oversize fuse may cause the wires to overheat and start a fire inside the walls. Fifteen-ampere fuses are the largest that should be used in ordinary branch circuits.

When you buy fuses, make sure they are listed or approved by the Underwriters' Laboratories. This information will be stamped on the outside of the fuse, or it may be seen through the transparent window in its top. This window also helps you recognize a blown fuse by seeing if the flat wire is broken.

A fuse blows when a defective appliance or lighting fixture causes a short circuit, or when a circuit is overloaded by connecting too many appliances. Always look for and eliminate the cause of a blown fuse before replacing it.

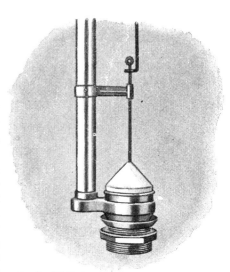

### Leaky Toilet

Constant leakage of water into a toilet bowl usually can be stopped by replacing the rubber ball valve in the bottom of the water tank. Shut off water supply, and flush tank to empty it. Remove tank cover. Holding rubber ball firmly, unscrew rod to which it is attached. If rod cannot be unscrewed, cut it with pliers and get a new one. Replace rod, and screw it into the new ball. (Size of new ball and over-all length of rod, if a new one is used, must be the same as those replaced. Both may be bought in hardware stores.) Turn on water, and fill and empty tank several times, to make sure the new ball valve is working properly.

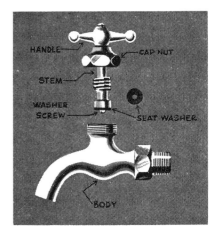

### Leaky Faucets

Badly worn washers are usually the cause of leaky faucets and, at times, of noisy ones. Most faucets are of the compression type, consisting basically of body, valve stem, bonnet, and handle. The washer is fastened by a brass screw to the lower end of the threaded valve stem. This is forced against the valve seat in the body by turning the handle to shut off the water. The washer should be replaced if the faucet leaks or drips continuously. Only moderate force should be used to close a faucet when washer and seat are in good condition. More force signals for repair.

To replace a worn washer, first shut off the water from the leaking fixture or faucet. Second, remove the hood, or bonnet, which may be over the cap nut. Third, loosen the cap nut; then turn the valve stem completely out of the body of the valve. Use care to avoid damaging the finish of the valve or fixture on which you are working. If you do not have a special wrench for this purpose, place a piece of cloth or heavy paper between the jaws of your wrench.

Washers may be obtained in assorted sizes from hardware stores or plumbing-supply stores. Select a washer that is the same size as the worn one, so it will fit the seat in the body of the valve. Remove the worn washer, and clean the section in which it fits. Replace the washer; secure it to the valve stem with a new screw. Be extremely careful when you remove the old screw, to prevent splitting the head. If it splits, you may have to cut a new slot to remove the screw, or tap it out with a prick punch. Great care should be used, too, to avoid breaking off the screw in the bottom of the valve stem.

If the new washer does not stop the leak, perhaps the valve seat itself has been damaged. If so, the seat may be reamed smooth with a valve reamer designed particularly for this purpose. The tool comes with a set of reamer discs that usually fit any valve in the home. It is inserted in the top of the valve body in such a way that the bonnet of the valve automatically keeps the reamer disc in perfect alignment with the valve seat. Turning the handle while tightening the bonnet soon gives a perfect seat.

## Clogged Radiator Valve

When a radiator valve becomes loose or clogged with dirt, it often causes leaks or noises. Try tightening the valve. If, after working the adjusting mechanism, you find the valve still doesn't do its job, it is clogged and a cleaning is needed. Turn off radiator and let it cool. Then unscrew valve at stem and remove. If clogging is minor, hitting valve several times against palm of hand may loosen dirt. If this does not remedy the trouble, immerse valve in white vinegar, kerosene, or hot soap and water, and let stand until liquid has time to fill interior. Allow cleaner to seep out; then swish valve back and forth in pan of clean water to remove all traces of cleaner; dry. If valve still proves unsatisfactory, replace it with new.

## Hanging a Mirror on a Door

If the door or cabinet is very smooth, roughen the surface with a fine grade of sandpaper to provide a good bonding area. Then spread a rubber-base adhesive (such as Miracle cement) on the back of the mirror, applying it about ½" in from the 4 edges. Press the mirror firmly in place on the door, then allow 24 hours for the adhesive to set.

## Fixing Clogged Drains

**Required:** a wrench large enough to fit around the cleanout plug at the bottom of the trap, a pail to catch the water from the trap, a rubber force cup (sometimes called a plumber's friend), some stiff wire about 3' long with a hook at the end, a can of drainpipe cleaner, flexible wire 10' to 20' long (sometimes called a snake).

Pipes become clogged for a number of reasons. Sometimes a gradual coating of grease, which picks up lint and hair, does it. Sometimes a foreign object lodges in the pipe. When this occurs, a rubber force cup is useful. Fill the drainpipe with cold water, place the cup over the fixture outlet, and work the wooden handle on the cup up and down. This will often force small objects past the trap and into the large waste pipe. If the rubber force cup won't work, try drainpipe cleaner. (When using cleaner, be sure you don't spill it on your skin. If you do spill some, flood the area at once with vinegar and water, and rinse it thoroughly. Do the same with floor coverings and clothing.) If neither the force cup nor cleaner works, you'll have to use a wire or the snake to do an inside job.

Place the pail under the trap plug and remove the plug. After the water empties into the pail, scrape the inside walls of the trap with the stiff wire. Do a thorough job. Then replace the cleanout plug. If this doesn't work, the obstruction in the pipes is beyond the trap. Remove the trap cleanout plug once more, and work the flexible snake back through the drainpipe. As you push it in, both rotate it and work it back and forth (this motion is very important). The end of the snake should reach the obstruction and dislodge it. Work the snake out, replace the cleanout plug, and turn on the water.

This major pipe-cleaning job should not be required often. To avoid it, keep a strainer over the sink drainpipe, use a regular, prepared-for-the-purpose cleaner every week, and be scrupulous about keeping refuse and liquid fats out of the drain.

## Frozen Pipes

If the pipe is accessible, wrap rags around it; then saturate rags with boiling water. Start at the point nearest the faucet or fixture serviced by the pipe. Leave the near-by faucet open to encourage flow.

To thaw out sewer or waste pipe, wrap cloth so that boiling-hot water slowly seeps down to joint below. Start at bottom of pipe and work up, so melted ice can run out of system.

Slower method is to use lamp or heater, but be careful not to ground it. Handle the appliance with care; stand it on a rubber mat. Put V-shaped piece of reflective metal or foil above the pipe to speed job.

### Replacing Sash Cord

First remove the sash itself—from inside the house. Begin by removing, from the side with the broken cord, the vertical molding that holds the sash in place. If nailed, not screwed, start prying at the bottom with a stiff putty knife; finish with an old screwdriver or flat chisel. Take care not to break the molding and not to mar the paint too much. If there's a weatherstrip on the sill, it may be necessary to remove this, too. To remove an upper sash, first remove the lower sash and the wooden strip dividing the sash grooves. Usually this strip is not fastened and can be removed with the fingers or by gripping with rag-padded pliers. If paint-stuck, run a thin knife blade along its sides.

Remove the cover of the sash-weight box. This cover forms the lower part of the sash groove. Usually it is held by a screw at top or bottom. To locate, look for horizontal cracks in the sash groove. With the cover

off, the sashweight can be removed from the box and the broken cord untied.

Pass the end of the new cord over the pulley. Push the cord down until it can be grasped through the opened sash-weight box. If the cord is too kinky to do this, tie it to a piece of twine, the other end of which is weighted. Lower the weighted end of the twine over the pulley, and pull the cord through. If replacing all cords on a window, the use of bronze sash chain instead of cord will make a job that may last as long as the house. Tie cord to sashweight, and replace weight in box.

Cut free end of cord longer than need, to allow for knotting; pass end through hole in side of sash. Knot end, and press knot into the hole. Tap knot so it will lie flat and flush with the side of the sash. Now run the window up and down to see if the cord is too long. You can tell this by the weight's hitting the bottom of the pocket before a lower sash is fully opened or an upper sash is fully closed. If too long, shorten at sash-weight end. Replace cover and molding, and lubricate pulley with a few drops of oil.

### Repairing a Sagging Door

If a door sags or hangs unevenly, striking the upper part of the jamb or dragging along the lower outside corner of the threshold, the fault may be traced to loose hinges. Often the weight of the door will gradually cause the upper hinge to work away from the doorjamb.

To check, open the door and try pushing and pulling it to and from the hinges. If some movement occurs, the hinges need readjustment. Sometimes merely tightening the screws remedies the trouble. Try this easy method first.

In other cases, the screw holes have become enlarged and will not hold the screws firmly in place. When this occurs, as it often does in old doors, remove screws and hinges, then fill holes with plastic wood or small hardwood plugs wiped with glue. When plastic wood has hardened, replace hinges and screws.

### Fixing a Window Lock

Locks on meeting rails of double-hung windows often won't close because of expansion or contraction of the wood, or uneven house settling.

Study both meeting rails and remove the part of lock attached to lower rail. Measure difference in height between upper and lower rails, and cut a small block of wood exactly this thickness, and large enough to accommodate removed part of lock. Now drill holes in the block exactly same size and in same position as those in the lock.

Place the block in position on meeting rail, superimpose lock, and screw both to lower rail. Use screws that will go through extra thickness. Paint block to match sash.

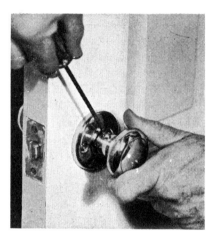

### Fixing a Loose Doorknob

The remedy for a loose doorknob is simple. In most cases, the fault lies with the screw that holds the knob to its shaft. It may be loose, missing, or worn.

First, tighten the present screw. If this does not work, then the screw must be replaced.

Buy the type of screw that has a blunt end. Be sure it is the proper size for your doorknob. If the knob still wobbles, the shaft is probably worn beyond repair and should be replaced.

### Caring for Screens

First remove all loose dust from the screens; then rinse them off with a hose and brush, using soap or detergent, if necessary. Make sure the screens are dried thoroughly before painting. Repair small holes with screen-wire patches of the same material. These may be obtained at the hardware store or made from small squares of screening (remove edge wires, turn up at the edges, and crimp neatly on the opposite side).

If there are large holes or rips, rescreening is necessary. On raised-molding screens, pry off the molding with a chisel and pull off the wire, lifting out all the tacks. Fasten new screen wire across the top with ⅜″ (3 oz.) tacks of material similar to that of the screen. Space the tacks 1″ or 1½″ apart. To tighten the wire on a full-length screen, bow the frame by raising it on ⅞″ strips at the ends and clamping it down at the middle. Then tack the lower end of the screen and let the frame spring straight. A coat of paint near the edges before the molding is replaced decreases the possibility of later rusting at this vital point. Trim surplus with a knife or chisel.

If the screen is of the flush-molding type, remove the fragile molding by careful prying with a putty knife or wood chisel against the edge of the screen. Lift only where the brads are placed, and work them out together, little by little. Remove the paper spline, and save it for replacement; then lift out the screen. The new screen wire should be cut accurately to just fit the square rabbet of the molding. Notch each corner back to the inner side of the recessed edge; if the screen has a crosspiece, notch for that, too. Then roll it down into the recess with a "screen wheel" (available at hardware stores) or a "vulcanizing stitcher" (from an automobile supply house). First roll the top, then the bottom, then the sides.

Apply screen paint every year to preserve black steel screen wire; use a good outside paint on the frames. Galvanized screening is painted only in alternate years. Spar varnish, thinned slightly with turpentine, prevents copper and brass ("bronze") screens from staining woodwork. Plastic screens do not require painting. To apply screen paint, use a piece of carpet tacked to a wooden block, to avoid clogging the screen

holes with paint. To make the painting easier and less messy, place the screens on two sawhorses. Drive two nails, with their heads protruding about an inch, into each sawhorse. Let frame rest on the nails. Then you'll have no trouble painting edges.

## How to Remove a Door

Door repairs often require that the door itself be removed. First open the door and support the outer corner with a small wood block, layers of heavy cardboard, a chisel, or any other flat, firm object.

Take bottom hinge apart first. Insert a screwdriver between pinhead and top of hinge and try to ease the pin out gradually with an upward motion. If it proves stubborn, tap end of screwdriver with hammer.

When replacing door, reverse process, securing top hinge first. Pins should now slip easily back into place.

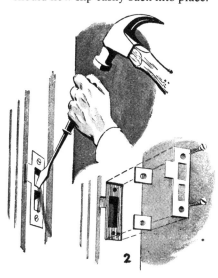

**2**

## If a Door Won't Latch

First, find out if the strike plate is too high or too low by squinting at it as you slowly close the door. If it is only slightly out of position, you may be able to jog it into place by tapping it with a screwdriver or cold chisel (*Fig. 1*). If this doesn't work, remove the plate and cut out a new rabbet with a wood chisel. If the door has warped slightly, so the latch has difficulty engaging the strike plate, enlarge the latch hole with a small file (*Fig. 2*). If the doorframe has spread, so the latch does not quite meet the plate, shim the plate with thin pieces

of wood or cardboard inserted under the strike plate.

## Fixing a Broken Window

It's easier to replace broken window glass if you remove sash from frame and lay it on a solid, flat surface. To remove sash from double-hung windows, first take out side strips (thin moldings that hold sash in position), and unfasten pulley cords or spring balance.

Knock out remaining pieces of glass with hammer. (Always use gloves when working with glass.) Remove putty and glazier's points with narrow chisel or screwdriver.

Scrape wood where glass will rest. Coat scraped wood with linseed oil or thinned paint. This seals wood so it won't absorb oil from new putty, making putty dry and crumbly.

Before setting glass in place, spread thin bed of putty over oiled wood. Frame is now ready for glass.

Measure 4 sides of frame that is to receive glass; note any irregularities. Have glass cut 1/16″ or ⅛″ shorter than opening, to allow for putty bed, expansion, contraction. Press glass into place.

Glazier's points—flat, triangular metal pieces—offer additional help in keeping glass in place. Use 3 or 4 to a side; push them firmly into sash with a screwdriver held flat against glass.

With palms of hands, roll putty into thin, pencil-like rolls. Place rolls end to end, around glass where it abuts sash. Make sure it is fresh and use only the best quality. With putty knife, press putty gently but firmly along sash. Putty should form small, triangular ramp between glass and wood frame. Many people find that using a special putty knife with an arrowhead-shaped blade expedites and simplifies the job. You can buy one at a paint or hardware store.

Remove putty stains on glass with cloth dipped in turpentine. Let putty dry for a day or so before painting to match the sash.

**Materials Needed:** glass, putty, putty knife, linseed oil, hammer, small screwdriver, glazier's points, turpentine, small brush, and gloves.

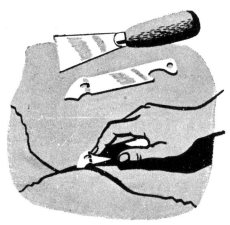

## Fixing Plaster

Plaster cracks are of two kinds: hairline cracks that sometimes develop as a result of uneven drying of plaster, and the wider, more serious cracks that result from house settling or from the use of undersized or green floor joists. Fixing hairline cracks is simple. Buy a pound package of patching plaster at any paint or hardware store. Mix a little with water, according to directions, to a workable, softer-than-putty consistency. Put a bit of the mixture on your thumb, and run it lightly over the crack; those who don't like the feel of plaster on the skin may use a flexible putty knife. But in any case, first wet thoroughly the plaster around the crack. Otherwise, the patching plaster probably will fall out as soon as it dries.

Some cracks are too fine for the thumb method. For these, use white lead thinned with turpentine to a gluey consistency. Apply with a piece of old cloth. Another quick method is to use a plaster pencil: simply rub the pencil over the cracks.

Settling cracks may vary from $\frac{1}{16}''$ to $\frac{1}{4}''$, or more. Usually it is advisable to cut the crack into an enlarged "V" shape, with a deeper opening at the back than in the wall surface. Use a knife or, even better, a beer-can opener. When the patching plaster is forced into this wedge-shaped crack, it hardens into a keystone shape that prevents it from falling out.

After you cut the wedge shape, soak the old plaster thoroughly with a sponge or heavy cloth. It will absorb a surprisingly large amount of water. You can't overdo it. Then apply the patching plaster, forcing it well into the crack so that it spreads in back wider than the surface gap. A wide-blade putty knife (3") is handy here. It makes a much smoother job, particularly if the plaster is uneven. When the patching plaster is dry, smooth it down with the sandpaper.

### Patching a Hole in the Wall

Clean out any loose plaster and then undercut entire perimeter of the hole with a chisel. New plaster will be forced into this undercutting and be locked permanently into place when it hardens.

Second step is to cut piece of wire netting approximately the size of the hole. Press it into the hole. Loose wire ends will hold the piece of netting in place temporarily.

Third step is to wet edges of the old plaster thoroughly. The purpose of this wetting is to prevent old, dry plaster from drying out the fresh plaster before it hardens.

Fourth step is to prepare a mixture of patching plaster and water. (Buy patching plaster at the local paint or hardware store.) Make the mixture nicely spreadable, neither too wet nor too dry. Apply it with a putty knife or a smooth blade.

Fifth step is to smooth out the plaster with a finishing trowel. A few confident strokes and the patch will have a nearly perfect surface. Let the plaster dry.

Sixth step is to sandpaper the dry patch. Wrap the fine sandpaper around a small wood block. Dust the patch, and give it a coat of size. You are now ready to paint or retouch.

### Buying and Using Paintbrushes

**Buy Good Quality Brushes**—either pure bristle or synthetics such as nylon—because they'll last longer, enable you to do better work. There are about 15 types used by professionals, but the home-owner can do nicely with the following selection (though he may well have several of each type) : a 4"-wide flat paintbrush,

usable also for enamel; a stucco-wall, or an oval paint and varnish brush for all large areas—4" wide for a man, 3" for a woman; a 2"- or 3"-wide varnish brush, also usable for enamel; a flat sash and trim tool, 3" wide, and another of 1" width for finer work.

**How to Tell a Good Brush:** This is a task for an expert, but here are some pointers. "Flags," or split ends, are essential for holding the paint and spreading it evenly. Bend the bristles as a test of springiness or elasticity. Buy a brush that tapers down toward the "flag" end; this means long and short bristles have been properly blended. See that bristles are thoroughly set in the ferrule. It is best to

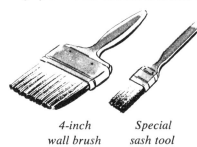

*4-inch
wall brush*        *Special
sash tool*

buy only from a reliable dealer, and by brand name if you know one. If you must have an inexpensive brush, ask the dealer.

**How to Use a Brush:** Even the best new brushes have a few loose bristles. Dislodge them by revolving the handle rapidly between your palms, or by tapping bristles sharply on your hand. Soak a new brush in linseed oil for a couple of days, then squeeze out the oil and comb bristles straight. Dip a brush into the paint to a depth of about 2"; never overload it; tap out excess against inside of can. Always apply paint with bristles flat against surface, and don't poke ends into corners. Hold a brush firmly but lightly; feel comfortable in its use. Don't let a brush stand on its bristle ends.

**How to Clean a Brush:** If a brush is to be in use for several days, suspend it overnight in linseed oil, using special hooks to keep bristle ends from touching bottom. Don't let a brush stand in water. Always clean brushes which are not to be used (get a set of rules from your dealer). Basic procedure is to soak the brush in one of the many special brush cleaners; see that the solvent is worked well up into the bristles; comb out paint from time to time until bristles appear clean. A final rinse in turpentine is effective, or soap and water may be used. When brush is dry, comb bristles straight and wrap in paper to keep out air and to preserve shape. These suggestions are for brushes used in oil-base paints. Natural-bristle brushes used for shellac should be cleaned with alcohol. Lacquer thinner is used for brushes that have been used in lacquer. Brushes used for calcimine or

*Hang brush in oil overnight*      *Store the clean brush in paper*

casein paints should be washed thoroughly in water at the end of every working day. This is important. If they are to be put away, let them hang until completely dry. Comb out bristles and wrap immediately in heavy paper. Then lay them flat.

**Painting with a Roller**

**Step 1.** After all the cracks have been filled, the old paint surfaces must be washed thoroughly. Window sills and sashes, even in the cleanest rooms, usually have a dirty film. Greasy walls, especially in the kitchen, need a washing if the paint is to stick. Use a good detergent, or use what the painters use: trisodium phosphate dissolved in water. Use a sponge.

**Step 2.** Remove the switch plates and electric canopies (the bell-shaped metal devices on ceiling fixtures).

**Step 3.** Get all the gear together: bucket, sponges, detergent, newspaper, stepladder, shellac, sash brush, 4″ wall brush, paint roller and tray, paddles, and 1 gallon of paint for each 350 square feet of wall area.

**Step 4.** Be sure to read the label on the can. Paints vary. Rubber-base water paints **can** be thinned with water. Flat oil paints **must** be thinned with turpentine. Drying times, too, vary—from 20 minutes to 24 hours. Some paints require a sealing prime coat. Some cover in one coat; some in two. Some can go over anything— from calcimine to wallpaper. In other words, before you start, make certain you know everything the manufacturer feels you should know about the paint. Read even the label's very small print.

**Step 5.** Stir the paint. If you're smart, you'll have the paint dealer mix your paint on his electric agitator. The machine will do a pretty fair job if the paint is fresh, but you'll still have to give paint a final stirring before use. (The dealer will supply free stirring paddles.) If the paint is old and has settled to form a tough paste on the bottom of the can, you may have to stir it thoroughly (use every bit of elbow grease you can muster) and then strain it through an old nylon stocking. After the paint is mixed, pour some into the tray.

**Step 6.** Carefully read the directions that come with your paint roller. They vary for different models. And be sure to note how to clean the roller after using it. (This must be done the moment you have finished.) If you use water paint, hold the roller under the water tap for a minute before dipping it into the tray. If you use oil paint, let the roller plunge directly into the paint. Roll it in the tray a few times, so you get the feel of the tool and saturate it evenly. (If you prefer, you may use the type of roller that holds about a pint of paint in its hollow cylinder. This type does not require dipping.)

**Step 7.** There's one more step before starting. Try out the roller on a piece of cardboard to see whether it paints evenly, and to check on the color. If you're satisfied on both counts, you can go to work. Start with the ceiling, never the walls. Using your 4″ brush, paint around the edges of the ceiling (rollers cannot paint close to corners). If you are painting the walls and ceiling the

same color, paint the edges of both at the same time. If the walls are to be a different color, keep the ceiling paint off the walls. Before painting the ceiling, cover your head with a scarf or an old hat.

**Step 8.** Now you're ready to use the roller. Set the paint tray on the ladder shelf. Dip the roller into the tray and squeegee it on the ramp. Make several crisscross strokes in the middle of the area you are to paint. This gets surplus paint off the roller and distributes it so that you can smooth it out evenly. Work fast, but not too fast (if the roller spins too rapidly, the paint will spatter). Go over the area with long, parallel strokes. If you notice a thin spot, give it a second treatment before moving on.

**Step 9.** Windows and doors must be painted with a brush, although the panels can be done with the roller if you prefer. A brush must be used on the sash. A sash guard is extremely helpful.

**Step 10.** Follow the same procedure with the walls as you did with the ceiling. Brush-paint all inside corners, baseboards, and small surfaces. If two people paint, one can do the brush painting, the other the roller painting.

**Step 11.** The wonderful thing about roller painting is that you don't have to be a professional to achieve good-looking results. The secret is to work fast and continuously. Keep the paint flowing, so that edges won't have a chance to dry and leave ugly overlap marks. After you have spread your paint with crisscross or zigzag strokes, always finish off with long, easy, vertical ones. This will smooth out inequalities in the paint coat and give an even finish. As soon as you complete the work, clean both brush and roller.

**How to Clean a Roller**

Paint rollers are both easy to use and easy to clean. But the cleaning must be done immediately after painting. To delay cleaning even for half an hour may mean that the roller cover never can be cleaned.

The first step in cleaning is to remove the roller from the handle by unscrewing the nut that secures it to the shaft. If the roller has been used with water-thinned paint, wash it in soap and lukewarm water; squeeze out the excess water; then immerse the entire roller in a bucket or can containing paint thinner, turpentine, or mineral spirits. (Do not use alcohol or lacquer thinner; they may do damage.) Agitate the roller in the container, lift it out, squeeze out excess liquid, and wipe it with a clean cloth. To clean a roller that has been used with oil paint, just wash it in a container of paint thinner, turpentine, or mineral spirits. Should any paint get on the handle or metal portions of the roller, remove the paint by rubbing it with a cloth moistened in the proper cleaner.

After cleaning the roller, reassemble it and replace end nut. Lubricate the shaft occasionally with light oil.

### Painting a Window Sash

Periodically, window sashes begin to peel, crack, and look dirty. When they reach that state, clean and repaint them, using this quick, easy-to-follow method.

1. Materials: sash brush, detergent, sash paint, painter's shield, 3/0 sandpaper, paint scraper, putty knife, putty, stiff scrubbing brush, rags, 4″-long wood block.

2. Scrape away all loose, scaly, or peeling paint with paint scraper (special tool available at hardware stores).

3. Eliminate slight irregularities of wood surfaces by rubbing wood with sandpaper. For easy handling, wrap sandpaper around wood block.

4. Scrub sill and sash thoroughly with detergent to remove stubborn dirt, grease, and grime that frequently accumulate there.

5. Fill all cracks in wood with good grade of putty. Apply carefully and evenly with putty knife for best results.

6. Check sash for loose or cracked putty that was used to seal windowpane to sash; remove loose putty and fill neatly with fresh putty, using putty knife.

7. Open window about 3″ top and

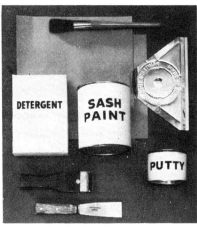

bottom; paint as much of sash as you can without moving window. Use sash brush with painter's shield, as shown, wiping painter's shield with rag each time it is moved. Raise bottom, and lower top, of sash to paint portions missed, taking care not to touch newly painted surfaces. Do not completely close top or bottom of sash while painting.

8. One hour after painting, move top and bottom of sash up and down several times to make sure paint does not bind windows. Repeat raising and lowering procedure 2 hours after painting.

### Estimating Quantities

Don't guess about quantities of painting materials you'll need. Measure carefully each and every surface to be painted. Multiply height by length or width to get number of square feet. To measure a triangular surface, measure width by half of height. (Amateurs can consider window openings as solid area.) Take measurements to your dealer. He has a table of average covering capacities for all types of paint, for various surfaces, for new and old work, one- and two-coat jobs, etc. He'll figure out the quantities you'll need. Remember, it's better to have a little left over than to run short.

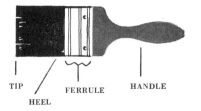

TIP      FERRULE      HANDLE
HEEL

### Finishing Furniture

**Varnish—on Old Furniture:** Apply plenty of varnish remover—flow it on freely. After 15 minutes, give it a second coating. Scraping with putty knife may be begun in another 20 minutes, but a very hard surface may require a third application of remover. When flat surfaces have been stripped, work into corners with a rag soaked in alcohol. Varnish or shellac will come off more readily, as a rule, than paint. Wash with soap and water, rinse and let the piece dry overnight. If the wood is open-grain, a filler should be applied; brush it on with the grain, and wipe it off across the grain. Then apply varnish as directed on can label. Varnishes of the polishing, rubbing, or cabinet type dry to a high gloss and should not dull or obscure the grain of the wood. Velvety finishes may be obtained by rubbing each coat when dry with a paste of pumice or rottenstone in either oil or water. Varnishes which dry to a dull finish may also be obtained.

**Stains:** Oil stains composed of a color pigment in linseed oil or turpentine are easiest to apply and are highly suitable for furniture finishing. They are transparent, clear, and bright. The wood should first be sanded with the grain. If paste filler is used, it goes on after the first coat of stain. Spread the stain evenly. Wiping soon after application of the stain makes a lighter color and shows more of the grain.

**Enameling:** On new wood, or old wood from which the finish has been removed, first apply an enamel undercoater tinted to match the finish color. Sand smooth when dry, and dust off. Then flow the enamel on, give it plenty of time to dry thoroughly hard in a dust-free place, then dry, sand and dust again before applying the final coat.

**Bleaching:** Several acids, such as oxalic, are used by professionals, but it is suggested that a commercial bleach be obtained from your dealer and applied in strict accordance with the directions given by the manufacturer. Then finish with a lacquer or a varnish of the palest type.

**Linseed Oil:** This is an old standby for reviving and beautifying old furniture surfaces. Boiled oil is the thing to buy. It is applied with a cloth and rubbed vigorously with the open hand. The excess oil should be wiped off at the end of 1 hour, and several days' drying time allowed between applications. Such a finish may then be waxed to produce a soft, velvety sheen.

## When You Open the Can

In cans of paint and enamel, you'll probably find a semisolid at the bottom of the can, with liquid on top. These must be thoroughly mixed. There's a standard procedure: First, pour off most of the liquid into a second container that is clean. Then stir contents of original can with paddle or stick until the liquid has been absorbed by the solid. Now gradually restore surplus liquid to original can, stirring constantly. Finally, pour paint back and forth between cans. This is called "boxing." If you wish, strain the contents through screen wire or cheesecloth for greater smoothness. Many modern house paints must be used as they come in the can, or thinned in strict accordance with label directions. This is highly important to remember. Why? They are chemical formulations, and the maker has put them into scientifically correct proportions of oil, pigment, and thinners, to give maximum durability and effect. To overthin with turpentine, and particularly with linseed oil, will destroy the balanced ratio of the product.

# A SHORT GLOSSARY OF PAINT TERMS

**Alkyd:** A synthetic resin, made with phthalic anhydride, glycerol, and fatty acids.

**Alligatoring:** Refers to cracks resembling the hide of an alligator. Common cause is application of thick films which prevent undersurface from drying.

**Antique:** A finish usually applied to furniture to give the appearance of age.

**Back Primed:** When paint is applied to the back of woodwork and exterior siding to keep out moisture, it is said to be "back primed."

**Bleaching:** Restoring discolored or stained wood to its normal color or making it lighter by using oxalic acid or other bleaching agents.

**Bleeding:** Movement of a dye or stain from stained wood or an undercoat into subsequent coats. Usually occurs as the result of solubility in the vehicle portion of the top coat. Can often be prevented or reduced by the application of an intermediate coat of shellac, aluminum paint, or emulsion paint.

**Blistering:** Usually caused by moisture in a wall, or moisture entering painted wood through some indirect source, such as poor joints or careless carpentry work.

**Blushing:** Cloudiness in the surface of a film, usually caused by drying under improper conditions.

**Calcimine:** A paint composed of calcium carbonate or clay and glue.

**Calking Compound:** A semidrying or slow-drying plastic material used to fill crevices around windows, chimneys, etc.

**Casein:** The protein of milk and the principal constituent of cheese. Used extensively in the manufacture of water paints.

**Cement-Base Paint:** Composed of Portland cement, pigment, and other ingredients. Sold as dry powder; mixed with water.

**Chalking:** The decomposition of a paint film into a loose powder on the surface.

**Checking:** Formation of short narrow cracks in the surface of paint.

**Drying Oils:** Oils which are converted to solids when exposed to the oxygen in the air. Linseed oil, tung oil, and perilla oil are the three principal vegetable oils of the drying class.

**Efflorescence:** A deposit of water-soluble salts on the surface of masonry or plaster, caused by the dissolving of salts present in the masonry, migration of the solution to the surface, and deposition of the salts when the water evaporates.

**Emulsion:** A preparation in which minute particles of one liquid, such as oil, are suspended in another, such as water.

**Filler:** Used to fill wood pores before applying a paint or varnish.

**Flaking:** Detachment of small pieces of paint film.

**Flatting Oil:** A varnishlike composition used to reduce paste paint to a flat paint.

**Glazing:** A process of applying transparent coatings over a painted surface to produce blended effects.

**Hiding Power:** The capacity of a paint to obliterate colors beneath it.

**Latex Paints:** These are synthetic emulsion base paints, easy to apply, quick drying and soluble in water.

**Leveling:** The formation of a smooth film on either a horizontal or vertical surface, independent of the method of application.

**Livering:** An increase in the consistency of a paint, which results in a liverlike mass.

**Peeling:** Detachment of a paint film in relatively large pieces. Paint put on a damp or greasy surface may "peel." Sometimes due to moisture.

**Primer:** The first coat in any painting operation.

**Resin:** A solid or semisolid organic material, chiefly of natural vegetable origin, or derived synthetically. Color is usually yellow, amber, or brown.

**Sand Down:** Remove the gloss of an old finish and smooth it prior to refinishing.

**Sealer:** A coat of paint intended to close or seal the pores in a surface.

**Size:** A sealer.

**Spar Varnish:** Durable varnish designed for exterior surfaces. Resistant to rain, sunlight, and heat.

**Tack:** The stickiness of a surface between the time of a coating's "setting up" and of its being "print-free."

**Texture Paint:** One which may be manipulated by brush, trowel, or other tool. In a multicoat system, any intermediate coat.

With building costs high and going higher, it's important to inspect your house carefully and periodically. Best results are obtained by a methodical check from basement to roof. You can make small repairs yourself—work that, if done promptly, will forestall a more costly job later.

The following check list will help you detect decay, deterioration, and damage so you can take corrective steps at an early stage.

**1. Foundation.** Examine walls for masonry cracks and crumbling mortar. Look for open joints between wood sills and foundation walls and around basement-window frames. Check, too, condition of frames for corrosion and rot. Fill and repair any openings where water may enter.

**2. Exterior Walls.** On wood finishes, check for loose, warped, and split shingles or siding; on brick or stone walls, for cracks and soft mortar; on stucco surfaces, for blisters and loose pieces. Repair and repaint.

**3. Trim and Cornices.** Look for open joints and warped, loose, and rotted trim; these are good starting places for bad leaks. Calk open joints and cracks; repaint.

**4. Roof.** Examine roof for any broken, missing, warped, or loose shingles. Inspect ridges for warping, corrosion, and pulled nails. Look for pinhole leaks by studying underside of roof from attic on sunny day.

**5. Gutters.** See that there are no holes, loose hanger straps, pulled nails, open sections, or missing strainers. Check the pitch of gutters for proper water flow and disposal through downspouts. See that water is carried well away from house to dry well or sewer.

**6. Flashing.** Inspect flashing around chimneys; plumbing stacks; doors; windows; roof ridges, hips, and valleys, for looseness, corrosion, or lack of paint.

**7. Chimneys.** Check to see that chimney caps are not loose or cracked and that exposed masonry is secure and well painted. Look for leaks where chimneys pass through the attic of the house.

**8. Steps and Porches.** Watch for structural defects, deteriorated materials, or insecure fastenings. Masonry is subject to cracks, spalling, and wear, while woodwork may warp, crack, rot, and wear. Poke wood near ground with icepick to detect decay.

**9. Windows.** Survey for cracked panes, loose putty, open joints, dry rot, or corrosion. Check shutters, storm sash, screens, and awnings, including fittings and hardware, for defects. Reputty, fill, and paint.

**10. Doors.** Inspect for defects in wood paneling, glass, weatherstripping, and hardware. Examine sills and thresholds for wear and soundness of nailing. Refit or rehang where loose or ill-fitting.

**11. Basement Walls and Floor.** Scan entire area for excessive dampness, discoloration, cracks, and looseness of any kind. Inspect joints where walls and floor meet, to detect leakage. Check wood framing for warping, rot, or termites. If moisture is noticeable, inspect exterior to find source. Is it due to improper drainage, or leaky gutters spilling water close to foundation wall? Drain water *away* from house.

**12. Plumbing.** Go over system for signs of rust and leakage. Inspect drains and traps for possible clogging, faucets for leaks. Check whether flush valves and other mechanisms are functioning properly. Check water pressure.

**13. Hot-Water Heater.** Examine the water for rust and dirt, the tank for corrosion, and the condition of insulation. Also, see that the hot-water relief valve is in working order.

**14. Wiring.** Inspect cords and plugs on all electrical appliances, and all exposed wires, to see that the insulation is in good condition. Arrange to eliminate dangerously long lamp cords. If lights dim when appliances are turned on, circuits may be overloaded. Have an electrician check wire sizes and circuits to determine whether system can safely handle your new electric appliances.

**15. Floors.** Look and listen for loose boards, cracks, squeaks, worn finish, or open baseboard molding. In addition, check subflooring, bridging, and condition of floor coverings. Jump up and down in middle of rooms to check rigidity of floors.

**16. Walls and Ceilings.** Search for cracks, water stains, ceiling sags, or wall bulges. Tap plaster lightly to locate loose spots.

**17. Tilework.** Find any loose, discolored, or cracked tiles. If there are any openings between the tiles and bathroom fixtures, fill to keep out moisture.

**18. Stairs.** Check for squeaks, wear, loose and defective boards, or weak hand rails. Note condition of covering and pads.

**19. Attic.** Examine roof rafters and beams for warping, rotting, or serious cracks. Look carefully for inside water stains due to roof leaks. Check condition of insulation: is it tightly fitted, evenly placed?

**20. Decay and Termites.** Check all wood members in contact with masonry or earth for signs of decay or termite infestation. Poke sills and timbers at grade level with icepick to detect softness and decay.

**21. Moisture.** Where paint blisters, peeling, and other signs of moisture or condensation in walls and ceiling occur, check and correct source. Unexcavated areas under house are a common source; they should be covered. Damp basements, poor ventilation, unvented burners, clothes washers and dryers, are other sources of moisture that can be controlled.

## 13 Ways to Save Fuel

**1. Clean the Heating Plant.** Soot on the walls and in the flues of your heating plant acts as an insulator, keeps part of the heat from doing its job of generating steam, hot water, or warm air. Get rid of it by cleaning the heating plant at least once a season. Best have a professional cleaner with modern mechanical equipment do this job, if you don't want dirt scattered throughout the house. Have him clean your smoke pipe and chimney at the same time.

**2. Check the Insulation.** The insulation on the outside of your heating plant makes fuel go further by keeping heat from escaping. See that it is in good condition. For the same reason, don't neglect to insulate the pipes of your hot-water or steam system, and your hot-water storage tank. Cracks in smoke pipes and chimneys may let deadly gases seep into the house. Have these cracks sealed.

**3. Be an Expert Fireman.** If your hand-fired furnace seems wasteful of fuel, maybe you are using the wrong kind or size of coal. Or perhaps you are shoveling on the fuel without regard to the finer points of firing, such as adjusting checks and dampers correctly and keeping the grates and ash-pit clean. Ask your heating plant's manufacturer for an instruction booklet, or consult your fuel dealer.

**4. Check Oil Burner or Gas Furnace.** Make sure your oil burner or gas-fired boiler is operating with top efficiency and fuel economy; have it tested for needed adjustments or repairs by a capable serviceman who has the scientific instruments required to make a flue-gas analysis, learn flue-gas temperatures, and otherwise find out whether fuel is being wasted.

**5. Insulate Your House.** Uninsulated houses waste as much as 30 per cent of their heat through side walls and attic. Because heat loss is greatest through the roof, you'll probably notice a marked improvement in fuel consumption if you insulate the attic. Side walls are more difficult than attics to insulate, and usually the benefit is not so great. Best get reliable advice on the problems presented by your particular house before having side-wall insulation installed.

**6. Install Storm Sash and Doors.** Properly fitted storm sash and storm doors cut heat losses by reducing air leakage and providing an insulating air space. Using weather stripping and caulking cracks and gaps around door and window frames are effective means of reducing air leakage.

**7. Use Window Blinds and Draperies.** We usually think of these as useful for decoration and for privacy. Seldom do we think of them as helpful in saving fuel. Yet they can help. Simply see that they are drawn at night. They will reduce heat loss through the window glass.

**8. Reduce House Temperatures.** The simplest, most direct way to save fuel is to keep the house temperature from climbing. Keep it at an economical 65° F. in the daytime, and lower it to 55° or even 50° F. when the family goes to bed. If your heating plant is not automatically controlled, get the habit of watching the thermometer and checking the fire before the temperature gets out of bounds. Reduce the temperature also when the house is being ventilated or when no one is at home.

**9. Tame That Hard-to-Heat Room.** If you have a hard-to-heat room, don't try to make it comfortable at the expense of overheating adjoining rooms. Instead, find out why it is hard to heat. Make sure that its source of heat is adequate, that its radiators are not air-bound or poorly vented. An unsuspected reason may be the location of the thermostat controlling the house temperature. Have this checked by your heating plant's serviceman.

**10. Shut off Unused Rooms.** One room fewer to heat means less fuel consumption. Shut off the heat in unused and even little-used guest-room, storeroom, sewing room, etc., and keep their doors closed. If there are water connections, have them turned off and drained to prevent freezing.

**11. Use the Fireplace.** An open fireplace is a good auxiliary source of heat, especially in mild weather. But don't use yours for prolonged periods unless you are sure the chimney is clean and in good repair. Otherwise, you risk a chimney fire. Keep the damper closed when the fireplace is not in use.

**12. Don't Waste Hot Water.** Hot water wasted is fuel wasted. So when you are doing the dishes, bathing, or just washing your hands, don't be too lavish with the hot water. Use only enough to do the job.

**13. Use Room Heaters.** On many days, especially in the fall and spring, only a gas, oil, or electric room heater is needed to take off the chill. If you use one, make sure it is in good, safe operating condition. If any kind of electric heater is needed in the bathroom, be certain that it is built in. Do not use a portable electric heater. Water pipes and damp surroundings make the shock hazard great. Don't use oil or gas heaters in closed rooms. Adequate ventilation is necessary to insure proper combustion and to remove the products of combustion. Keep the heaters away from curtains and draperies, and guard against their being tipped over.

### Know Your Safety Controls

A burst water pipe, a gas leak, an electrical short circuit—these household disasters are rare, but you must know exactly what to do if they happen. You must know the location of the cut-off valves and main switch, and how to operate them.

*Gas* enters the house through the basement wall nearest the main. The meter and shut-off valve are probably located there. Try it to see that you know its functions.

*Electricity* is usually controlled by a master switch on the basement wall, near the meter. Its action should be clearly marked: "On" and "Off."

*Water,* like gas, comes in from a street main. The shut-off valve is next to the meter. Its action may be stiff. Try it to see if it works, even if you must use a wrench.

*Oil burners* have their own special emergency switch. It should *not* be in the same room with the furnace, but it should be readily accessible. The switch looks like a regular light switch, except that the plate is red.

Put conspicuous tags on all switches, and be sure everyone in the house knows exactly how they work and where they are.

| WHAT CAUSES ACCIDENTS? | | WHAT YOU CAN DO TO PREVENT THEM |
|---|---|---|

**FALLS**

**Slippery Floors**
Apply floor wax in thin, even coat, let dry, and polish to hard finish, if it is the kind that needs rubbing. Promptly wipe up spilled liquids, grease, or food.

**Small Rugs**
Don't use at head or foot of stairs or in doorways; prevent skidding at other places with rug-anchoring materials or by tacking down. Discard rugs that wrinkle or curl at corners.

**Dangerous Stairs**
Provide guard rails for all stairs, especially cellar, porch, and back-entry steps. Keep stairs in good repair, carpeting securely fastened, stairs free of obstructions.

**Slipping in Bathtub**
Equip bathtub with a "nonskid" mat, a receptacle for the soap (to keep it from underfoot), and a securely fastened rail to grasp when getting in and out.

**Climbing on Chairs**
Don't be too lazy to get the stepstool or stepladder when storing things on high shelves, hanging curtains, etc. Your stepstool should have a wide base for stability; your stepladder, some means of locking securely in place. (*See information on ladders on page* 00.)

**Poor Lighting**
Don't skimp on lights in hallways, on stairs, in closets, and dark corners. Have a flashlight or light switch at bedside. Make it easy to switch on lights before entering any room and before ascending or descending stairs. Light your porch steps, garden path, and other outdoor danger spots, too.

**ELECTRIC SHOCKS**

**Dampness**
Don't use radios, curling irons, other portable electric appliances in the bathroom, and especially not when you're in the tub. Use a cord, not a metal chain, on light socket. In laundry make sure all wiring and fixtures are suitable.

**Unsafe Appliances**
Keep all electrical equipment in good repair. Inspect connecting cords frequently for worn insulation, damaged plugs, exposed wires; replace when beyond repair.

**EXPLOSIONS**

**Dry-Cleaning**
Don't use gasoline, benzine, or other inflammable fluids for cleaning fabrics. Use only noninflammable fluids.

Don't start fires with kerosene or gasoline. Don't fill oil ranges or lamps without extinguishing the flame.

**POISONING**

**Bathroom Cabinet**
Mark poisons and dangerous medicines plainly, and keep out of your bathroom cabinet and preferably under lock and key in some fairly inaccessible place. Then they won't be taken by mistake. This goes, too, for candy-coated laxatives and pills tempting to children.

**SUFFOCATION AND ASPHYXIATION**

**Carbon Monoxide**
Never run your car's engine in the garage, unless doors and windows are open and air circulates freely, and even then for only a short time.

If you use gas for fuel in your kitchen range, take care that liquids do not boil over and put out the flame, particularly when the kitchen is left unguarded.

If you burn coal for fuel in kitchen range or furnace, adjust dampers so coal gas will be carried off by the chimney and not collect in the house—especially at night when the fire is banked and the family is asleep.

Ventilation is important in rooms heated by oil, gas, or kerosene heaters. Oxygen used by a heater must be replaced and the products of combustion gotten rid of. Don't sleep in a room with a portable heater in use.

# Safety Hints, Fire Prevention, and First Aid

### A Safe Kitchen

Records show that more serious accidents occur in the kitchen than in any other part of the house. Observe these simple precautions:

To reach high shelves, use a good stepstool, not a chair or other makeshift.

Apply wax to linoleum and wood floors in a thin, even coat. Too much wax makes floors slippery. If the wax isn't the no-rubbing kind, rub it long and well, to make a hard, dry finish. Promptly wipe up spilled food, to help prevent falls.

Don't keep lye, insecticides, and other harmful substances in the kitchen. Then they can't be mixed accidentally with food.

To avoid accidentally brushing against them, keep pot handles turned inward so they don't project over the edge of the range. This reduces the risk of scalds from upset pots.

When you are working about the range, wear a simple, trim-fitting, short-sleeved dress. Frilly, filmy garments, especially those with long, flowing sleeves, ignite easily. Also hazardous are dressing gowns and negligees made of flannel, chenille, brushed rayon, and other high-napped fabrics.

Some plastic and plastic-coated fabrics are highly flammable and should not be used for aprons or curtains. Avoid especially plastics of the pyroxylin type. These ignite with explosive suddenness and burn so rapidly it is almost impossible to extinguish the flame.

Have good, shadow-free lighting over all work surfaces. Good lighting helps you work with the deft sureness that lessens the chance of accident. When you are cooking, keep children, especially toddlers and crawlers, out of the kitchen. Many children have been burned or scalded while meals were being prepared.

Cuts and scratches, the most common of household accidents, can almost be eliminated if you follow reasonable safety rules like the ones suggested below.

### Can Openers

Always use a can opener that operates with a revolving motion and presses down the freshly cut edge of the can. Some wall-mounted can openers have a magnet that lifts the top from the can after it has been cut. This is desirable, because it eliminates the need for handling sharp

edges. Avoid the pry-type can opener, for it turns up sharp, jagged edges that may cut you when you are removing the top.

### Knives

Use the correct size and type of knife for each cutting job—a small knife for paring fruits and vegetables, a large one for slicing bread and carving meat. Pay attention to your work.

It's *safer* to have knives sharp. A sharp knife does not require as much pressure as a dull one, and so is less likely to slip and injure the user.

Always direct cutting strokes away from your body. This will help avoid injury if the knife slips.

Wash and dry each sharp knife separately, always keeping the edge turned away from your hand.

Keep sharp knives in a special rack that shields the cutting edges.

It is dangerous to run while carrying a scissors, knife, or other sharp-edged or pointed object. Move carefully when carrying these tools.

Many cuts result from carelessness in handing sharp objects to someone else. Always offer them to another person handle first, with the sharp edges held away from the body.

## A Safe Bathroom

Falls in bathtubs rate high in the total of bathroom accidents. A sturdy handhold fastened conveniently—and securely—at the side of the tub or shower is an aid to balance when climbing in and out, and a godsend should feet start to slip. Standing on a bath towel when taking a shower will take the skid out of almost any tub. Bath crystals and water-softening compounds may make bathtubs more slippery than usual, so take extra care when you use them. There are bathroom rugs with nonskid backs, which take a gluelike hold on tile floors. They're washable, too.

Electric shocks are especially dangerous in bathrooms because of water pipes and damp surfaces, which are excellent conductors of electricity. You can avoid shock hazard by remembering not to switch lights on or off when standing in the tub, or when your hands are damp or touching faucets or other water connections.

Use electric shavers and curling irons only in the bedroom. If your bathroom light operates by a metal chain, be sure the chain has an insulating link or a cord fastened to its end.

Check water temperature before stepping into a bath or shower. It may save you from being badly scalded. Your hand is a pretty good indicator for your own bath, but when bathing babies or small children, use a bath thermometer—don't guess. Water at 100° F. is warm enough for a baby. Never leave small children unguarded in the bathtub.

Keep water temperatures down if you have an **automatic hot-water heater.** You should adjust its control with consideration for the requirements of your home appliances. If you don't own a dishwasher, adjust the heat control so that the water at the tap registers about 125° F. This is hot enough for most purposes, but it is not scalding. If you do have a dishwashing unit the control should be set to give a tap temperature of about 140° F. Water of this temperature may be scalding. Each member of your family should be warned to exercise care in its use at kitchen sink, in the bathtub, lavatory, etc. Keeping water temperatures as low as is practically possible for efficient service is a good safety measure and will prove an economy measure for the fuel bills too.

## Safety with Electrical Appliances

Don't depend on amateur wiring. Makeshift wiring is a fire and accident hazard. House wiring should be done only by a licensed electrician who not only knows the requirements for safety, but will install wiring that is adequate from the standpoint of service and utility. House wiring, whether new construction, or additions or alterations, requires special knowledge and skill.

Long connecting cords trailing across rooms, under rugs or along baseboards are a fire hazard and a tripping hazard, and, for children especially, may even be a shock hazard. Do not allow connecting cords to touch hot radiators or pipes.

Use connecting cords of correct types. There are cords for lamps, for heating appliances such as smoothing irons, for washing machines, etc.— each made to do a specific job. When replacing a connecting cord, get the same kind of cord that was originally on the appliance. See that it carries the approval of the Underwriters' Laboratories.

Keep cords in good repair. Discard badly worn cords. If the outer surface of the cord is frayed, several layers of electrician's tape around the cord usually will make a safe repair. If the cord is badly damaged, do not attempt to repair it.

Fuses are safety valves. When a fuse blows it is a sign of trouble—a short circuit or an overload. Do not replace blown fuses until you have located and corrected the trouble. Do not use substitutes for fuses. Do not use fuses which are not approved by the Underwriters' Laboratories. Use only approved fuses of the correct rating for each circuit. The rating in amperes is marked on the fuse. It is dangerous to attempt to overcome fuse-blowing trouble by using a fuse of higher rating. If you have decided that the fuse blew because you had too many appliances on the circuit, the remedy is obvious: Spread the load of the appliances by plugging them into different circuits.

Disconnect promptly all appliances when you are through using them, especially heating devices such as irons, curling irons, etc. This will help keep the Fire Department away.

Washing machines and ironers can be made safer for use in damp surroundings by electrically grounding their frames. Your electrician can do this properly. Know how to operate your washing machine safely. Know what all the controls are used for, especially if you have a wringer. Release pressure on wringers by operating the pressure release, when you are not using the washing machine. When you are wringing clothes, give the job your full attention. Do not wear loose, flowing clothes that may be caught in the wringer rolls. Keep children out of the room when using your washing machine.

Kitchen appliances should be used away from sinks so that it is not possible to touch an appliance and a water faucet at the same time.

Do not attempt to adjust, oil or clean any electrical appliance while it is connected to the electricity supply. Even though the appliance has a switch to control its operation, pull the plug.

Bed warmers. Don't use electric warming pads, smoothing irons, or makeshift heaters as "bed warmers" where they will be operated while you are asleep. They can prove a fire hazard or even a shock hazard.

Have appliances repaired promptly. As soon as any appliance shows signs of trouble, send it to a competent repairman. Do not attempt to do the work yourself. A professional repair job is usually not only safer but will help to make the appliance last longer. Even though they appear to be working satisfactorily, it is a good idea to have your appliances inspected at regular intervals by a competent repairman. They will last longer. When cleaning electrical appliances, do not put the electrical parts in water. Follow the manufacturer's instructions. Radio or television servicing should be done only by competent repairmen. Do not tamper with the instrument yourself and never touch the electrical parts while it is connected to the electricity supply.

Buy only approved electrical appliances and equipment. Look for the label of the Underwriters' Laboratories on appliances, connecting cords, wiring supplies, etc. This is your assurance that products comply with recognized safety standards in design and construction.

## Safety with Gas Appliances

Gas leaks are dangerous. Any odor or other evidence of the escape of unburned gas calls for prompt action. Extinguish all flames. Do not use a lighted match, candle, or other flame to find the leak. If the location of the leak, such as an open cock or unlighted pilot on the range, is not immediately discovered, open doors and windows, and call your gas company, licensed plumber or other qualified serviceman to locate and correct the trouble. *If there appears to be a large leak, get out of the house without delay.*

When lighting gas burners have the match lighted and hold it near the burner before turning on the burner cock. If the flame flashes back and burns inside the burner, turn off the gas, wait a moment, and then relight. If the flashback continues, the burner needs to be readjusted and cleaned before further use. The air shutter near the cock of each burner should be kept clean and set to give a regular blue flame. Too little air may cause a yellow flame which blackens pans and wastes fuel. If the gas flow to the burner is properly adjusted, keeping the air shutter clean will give the proper flame.

Automatic lighting of range burners—top stove, oven and broiler—is provided in many modern gas ranges. If it fails to operate, call your gas company, licensed plumber, or other qualified serviceman.

All types of pilot lights on kitchen gas stoves sometimes go out and allow gas to escape because they need cleaning. This can be done with a fine wire about hairpin size. If the pilot needs readjustment to light all near-by burners, turn the regulating screw to the left to increase the size of the flame, and to the right to decrease it. If the pilot light on your automatic hot-water heater goes out, follow the manufacturer's directions for relighting it, or call your gas company, licensed plumber, or other qualified serviceman.

Loose burner cocks should be repaired or replaced immediately to prevent leaks, and eliminate the danger of being turned on unintentionally.

Keep range burners clean. A clean and properly adjusted burner will give a regular, blue flame. If your range burner flame tips become irregular or show yellow tips, clean out the small holes on the face of the burner with a fine wire. Range units should be periodically cleaned with a brush, wiped with a damp cloth, and well dried. Unless manufacturer's literature indicates otherwise, don't immerse the burners in water since you may start them rusting inside. When cooking, turn down the heat before you have boil-overs. It will help keep burners clean, and avoid the danger of the flame being extinguished and unburned gas escaping. For the same reason, do not leave pots to boil in an unguarded kitchen.

Gas refrigerators shut off automatically if the flames goes out. In lighting the burner follow the instructions on the refrigerator. Adequate ventilation is necessary for the proper operation of a gas refrigerator. The openings at the bottom of the refrigerator, the space behind, and the ventilating screen should be kept clean and unobstructed. The room where the refrigerator is located should have outside ventilation.

The safest way to connect gas appliances is with iron pipe or semi-rigid gas tubing. If flexible tubing must be used, make sure it is a type tested and approved by the American Gas Association Laboratories, with special ends designed for use as gas connections. When using flexible tubing, turn the gas on and off by using the cock at the end of the house piping where the flexible tubing is attached. Then gas can't escape when the appliance is shut off, should the tube spring a leak. *Do not use flexible tubing which is cracked or damaged.*

Venting is important. Any gas appliance burning comparatively large volumes of gas should be connected to an adequate flue or chimney. Be sure that the pipe connecting the appliances to the chimney is kept open at all times. Do not stuff your range's flue with steel wool or similar materials in order to decrease smoke or grease deposits on near-by walls. It interferes with safe operation.

Ventilation is necessary in rooms heated by gas heaters. Oxygen used by a heater must be replaced and products of combustion gotten rid of. In no case should gas heaters without flues be operated in rooms while you are sleeping.

Buy approved gas appliances. Look for the seal of approval of the American Gas Association Laboratories before buying. This seal is your assurance that the gas appliance which displays it complies with the National Safety Requirements of the American Standards Association.

Do not buy so-called "gas-saving" devices. If they had any merits or if they were necessary for effective operation, manufacturers would incorporate them in their appliances. Their use may impair the safe and economical operation of your range or other gas-burning appliances.

## Safety with Oil-Burning Appliances

Scrupulously clean oil ranges, heaters, and lamps for best operation and greater safety. Keep wicks trimmed and wick controls operating smoothly. Have damaged parts replaced.

Do not fill oil-burning appliances or lamps when they are lit. Be sure to use the proper fuel. Adjust the flame height to avoid smoking.

Ventilation is necessary in rooms where oil-burning appliances are used. Do not go to sleep in a room with a portable oil heater burning.

Use care in placing heaters so they cannot come in contact with curtains, bedding, furniture, etc., or be upset by people in passing.

### Safety with Coal- and Wood-Burning Appliances

Flues and chimneys must be kept clear, clean and in good condition. The operation of drafts and dampers must be understood for safety as well as for maintaining a proper fire. Particularly at night, when the fire is banked, dampers must be adjusted to make sure that coal gas will not escape into the house. Never open the firebox feed door on your furnace, or the lids on your range, as a means of checking the fire. It disturbs combustion and may let coal gas escape into the house.

### Keeping Children Safe

More babies and small children fall victim to accidents than to any of childhood's most dreaded diseases. Practice simple precautions like these:

Until babies are 3 or 4 months old, they smother easily. So don't dress the baby in clothes that might tighten around his neck. In cold weather put more clothes on him, so he'll be warm even though he kicks off the blankets. Don't give your baby a pillow. Don't put him to bed with older children or adults.

When you carry your baby on the stairs, keep one hand free and on the guard rail, so you won't trip or lose your balance. Keep a gate at the head of the stairs until the baby can be taught to use stairs safely. A separate low guard rail on stairs, for older children's use, is a good idea, too.

Have only the necessary few safety pins on hand when you undress or change the baby. Keep the pins closed, and reduce the risk of harm if a pin is mislaid and the baby finds it.

Keep small hands from prying about an electric baseboard outlet by blocking it with a heavy chair or other piece of furniture. A special type of outlet to protect children is available. Keep electric fans and other alluring appliances out of reach.

Danger from burns will be lessened if you have a protection built around the hot radiator and a screen in front of the fireplace, if the child is not allowed near the kitchen stove, and if utensils on the stove are placed so that no one can knock them off by the handles. Use safety matches and keep them in a high place away from investigating fingers. You have only yourself to blame if your child falls out of bed, off a dressing table, from a baby carriage, high chair, or any high object. Do not leave him unprotected. If you can not keep your hand on him every minute, use a safety strap or put him safely in his crib or play pen and see that the sides are securely fastened. When out-of-doors, stay by the baby carriage. If you have a well-screened porch, then the baby can safely sleep or play there. If you have grounds around the house, fence in the part of the yard where you leave him, so stray dogs will be prevented from knocking over the carriage. Also arrange to keep an eye on the baby from a window while you work.

A home and yard can become a safety zone for small children. Start with well-fitting screens which cannot be dislodged, latches or hooks high above small fingers, and a gate at the top or the bottom of the stairs, depending on where the baby's room is. Bars on nursery windows are a safeguard.

Closet doors which lock when closed, or which cannot be opened from the inside, have kept many a child a prisoner. Bathroom doors which may be locked from the inside are a special hazard, as a child can turn a lock before he has learned how to unlock it. The catch can be removed and a hook and staple or bolt placed high for adult use.

When you buy furniture for the child's room, ask for paint which is leadproof, and thus avoid the possibility of the child's chipping off pieces of paint, swallowing them, and developing lead poisoning. Keep dyes of all sorts, dry-cleaners, water-bug or rat poisons, carbolic acid and other disinfectants—in fact, everything that should not go into a child's mouth—safely out of reach.

Avoid accidents by removing the opportunity for them to arise. No child can put peas or beans in his ears or nose unless he has them to play with. You can prevent your youngster from swallowing objects by keeping away from him all small, detachable, and dangerous things, such as nutshells, corn kernels, half-smoked cigarettes, buttons, pins, coins, beads, crayons, lipsticks, screws, nails, etc. Take the squeakers out of squeaking toys before they fall out.

### The Baby Sitter

While she is taking care of your child, a baby sitter is in a very responsible position. It's only fair—and safe—to give her the instructions and information she may need.

Instruct your sitter to:

1. Keep aware and awake, and look in on the sleeping child frequently during the evening to see that he is adequately covered and in a comfortable position.

2. Take careful note of the surroundings, and eliminate any hazards that might cause an accident.

3. Lock all outside doors after you leave, and admit no strangers.

4. Keep the child away from electric appliances, open fires, stoves, medicines, and stairways.

5. Keep matches, sharp objects, and toys you have not specifically said the child could play with out of reach.

6. Feed the child only when and what you have specified.

7. Give the child no medicine unless you've instructed her to. A Band-aid for a slight scratch or cut is all the medical aid a baby sitter should undertake to supply. If something more is needed, she should use the telephone to call on outside help.

You should leave your sitter:

1. The telephone number where you can be reached.

2. The telephone number of the family doctor.

3. The telephone numbers of the police station and the fire department.

### Ladder Safety

Have a sturdy step stool or step-ladder that is designed for home use. Make sure this ladder is well constructed of good materials, so that it will not topple when open. Open it fully. Snap down the metal braces on the sides. Be sure they're tight, and the ladder sets level, before you start climbing. To take the wobble out of an old ladder, tighten the tie-rod nuts with a small wrench, or drive screws into the edges of all steps.

Stand firmly on the steps; mount no higher than the second step from the top. Wear low-heeled shoes, a not-too-long skirt. Above all, never, never lean away. That stretch may start you tumbling down.

Never place a ladder in front of a door unless the door's locked shut or is wide-open. A person entering may throw you into a tailspin. Don't use the ladder as a trapeze: don't stand on the paint shelf or pivot on one leg. A new and higher ladder costs considerably less than a doctor's bill.

### Firearms

If you have any kind of gun around the house, observe the following safety rules scrupulously.

1. Never point a gun at anything you don't mean to shoot. Even though you're convinced that the gun is unloaded, pointing it at random is a foolishly hazardous procedure. And a shocking number of accidents are still attributed to the fact that someone didn't know a gun was loaded.

2. Before examining or cleaning a gun, always open the breech and check to make sure the magazine is empty.

3. When checking the barrel of a gun, always look through the breech end, never through the muzzle end.

4. Never bring a loaded gun into the house.

5. Store a gun and its ammunition

in separate places. If there are any children (your own, the neighbors', or visitors') around the house, be sure that both firearms and ammunition are locked up.

6. When learning to shoot, or when teaching someone else, choose a well-protected range. Never attempt backyard target practice.

7. Never carry a loaded gun while traveling in a boat or automobile.

8. When hunting with a loaded gun, keep the safety on. Always "break" or open the breech of a loaded gun before climbing over a fence or other obstacle, and put the gun over the fence ahead of you.

9. Never lean a loaded gun against a wall, fence, or tree.

10. Never allow a person unfamiliar with firearms to handle a gun.

11. Be sure that young people, especially, are carefully instructed in the handling of firearms, and that they never use them except under adult supervision.

12. Remember that these rules apply to *all* firearms. The .22 rifle, for example, is just as dangerous and deadly a weapon as any other.

### Is Fabric a Fire Hazard?

Newspaper stories telling of tragedies caused by clothes' catching on fire have created a whole host of fears. If you, too, have worried about the danger of this kind of accident to yourself or your children, we have reassuring news for you. Such catastrophes are actually very rare, and can easily be made even rarer if you observe a few precautions.

#### Facts about Flammability

First, you should understand a few facts about fabrics. All ordinary fabrics will burn—that is to say, all of them can be destroyed by fire. This certainly constitutes a hazard to your clothes and rugs and draperies, but actually it is a relatively slight threat to your person. It is the speed with which a fabric burns that determines whether careless handling of a cigarette will just burn a hole in your dress or cause serious injury. Most

fabrics burn rather slowly, and there's plenty of time to put out the fire before it reaches your skin or hair, or causes a flash burn. However, there are some fabrics and some finishes that ignite so easily and burn so rapidly that special precautions should definitely be taken when you wear them near a flame.

One of the factors determining the degree of flammability is the fiber of which the fabric is made. Other things being equal, cotton and rayon burn faster than wool, silk, acetate, or nylon.

#### Texture Is Important

Other factors—for example, the way the fabric is woven—also affect flammability. If the fabric surface is shaggy—if it has a pile, a nap, or tufts—it burns much more quickly than if it is smooth. Remember this when you are wearing combinations. Blends are fabrics made from yarns in which two or more fibers are blended together. Blended yarns produce fabrics with a surface nap, such as gabardines and suitings in general.

Combination fabrics are those made of a combination of yarns, each one of which is spun entirely of one fiber. The French crepe widely used for lingerie, for example, contains warp yarns of acetate fiber in filament form and filling yarns of filament rayon. Combination fabrics are smooth-surfaced.

Today's fabric designers have new materials and new techniques at hand. They can "engineer" fabrics to predetermined specifications, producing softness; bulk; washability; absorbency; beauty; strength; warmth with a minimum of weight; ability to resist shrinking, stretching, wrinkling, or abrasion; and ability to take permanent pleating.

Many man-made fibers are thermoplastic and will melt if a high enough temperature is used. When fabrics made from these fibers are pleated or creased at temperatures slightly under the softening point, they form permanent creases. When these fibers are blended with nonthermoplastic fibers, the resulting fabrics can still be very durably pleated.

# FIRE AND FIRE PREVENTION

Fires are accidents which, unlike falls, burns, poisonings and other "personal" accidents, can happen when you are not there. Often they are due to equipment which is faulty through natural wear and tear, or because it is improperly used or installed. This is all the more reason why you cannot be indifferent to the possible existence of fire hazards in your home, but should make sure by regular periodic inspection that they are eliminated before they can do harm. Of course, personal carelessness or ignorance of danger causes many fires, too.

**Chimneys, Flue Passages and Heating Plants** should be inspected and cleaned at regular, yearly intervals. See that they are in sound operating condition. Metal smoke pipes passing through wooden partitions, floors, or walls, should be insulated with an air space and metal shields. If smoke pipes are close to wooden surfaces, the surfaces should be covered with asbestos or some other fire-resistant material.

**Use Metal Cans** and other containers for ashes and rubbish. Do not use wooden barrels or boxes. Ashes, particularly wood ashes, are deceptive, and may be hot enough to start a fire even though they appear to be dead.

**Empty Your Ash Trays** into metal containers, too, but first make sure that there are no cigarette stubs still smoldering. Provide convenient ash trays about your house.

**Screen Your Open Fireplace.** It will keep popping embers and sparks off your rugs and furniture.

**Do Not Use Your Open Fireplace for Long Periods** unless you are sure that your chimney is clean, in good repair, and properly constructed for continuous operation. Many homes have been destroyed because these precautions were not taken. Do not burn resinous wood, such as pitch pine, in an open fireplace. It will form a greasy, sooty deposit in your chimney which may give a foothold to a serious chimney fire.

**Burning Rubbish or Dead Leaves Outdoors** should not be attempted on windy days, near buildings, or near dry grass or underbrush. In any case, do not leave such fires to burn unguarded. Stand by with a filled water pail, or attached garden hose, ready to control the blaze should it start to get out of hand. After the fire has burned down, make sure the fire's ashes are dead before you leave them, by dousing with water.

**Candles, Matches, and Other Naked Lights** should not be used when exploring cellars, attics, closets, and other dark places. If electricity is not available, use a flashlight.

**Grease Fires in Kitchen Range Ovens or Broilers** usually can be smothered by turning off the burners, throwing a handful or more of salt or soda on the flame, and shutting the oven door. Do not use water. If this does not put out the fire, use a chemical fire extinguisher, or call the Fire Department.

**Oily, Greasy, Paint-Smeared Rags** should not be kept about the house. Discard them immediately after use, preferably in your covered, metal garbage or waste can. Such rags can ignite spontaneously and, under favorable conditions, may burst into flame if kept even a few hours.

**Keep Cellars, Attics, and Closets** free of rubbish, old newspapers and magazines, discarded furniture and the like. They increase the chances of starting a fire, and are fine food for flames.

**Don't Hang Long Window Curtains** near your kitchen range because the wind might blow them against the burners.

**Christmas Trees.** Electric tree lights have almost done away with the extreme fire hazard older generations used to run when they used candles on their trees. Almost—but not entirely. When tree lights are not in good condition, they can be a fire —and a shock—hazard, too. Before you dress your Christmas tree, examine the lighting sets for bare wires, and cracked or damaged plugs and lamp sockets, or other damage. Do not use damaged sets until they have been repaired to safe condition. Indoor lighting sets should not be used outdoors, where the shock hazard is especially great because of moisture in the air and ground. Use sets designed especially for outdoor use. Refuse to buy any tree-lighting set— whether for indoor or outdoor use— if it is not listed as approved by the Underwriters' Laboratories.

## Automatic-Sprinkler Systems

Fires in basements and attics often go undetected before they reach major proportions. Automatic-sprinkler systems in these places can nip fires at their start. The sprinklers are connected to the water system of the house and automatically release a blanketing shower when rising temperature in their area signals danger. Installation costs are moderate. Four automatic-sprinkler heads usually are enough to protect a 30' x 30' basement.

## Fire Alarms Save Lives

Perhaps the greatest threat to your family is a fire that starts when you are asleep and is not detected until escape is cut off. An automatic, electric fire alarm is excellent protection. Such an alarm is activated by thermostats located in the basement, kitchen, garage, and other danger spots. The alarm bell, placed in a central location, such as an upper hallway, rings loudly when the temperature in the area of any of the thermostats rises to about 140° F. A transformer, plugged into any convenience outlet, provides the necessary current. These alarms are easily installed—any handyman can do the job by following directions—and their cost is surprisingly low. Battery-operated alarms are available, too. Batteries, however, must be replaced regularly.

# HOW TO FIGHT A FIRE

Prompt action often can prevent a small fire from becoming a major catastrophe. Collect your wits, size up the situation, and decide whether or not you can cope with it. If there is any doubt, don't take chances. Promptly get yourself and everybody else out of the house, and call the fire department. In every case it is best to have someone call the firemen, even though you feel sure you can extinguish the blaze. Firemen urge this; so you won't have reason to feel embarrassed, if, on arrival, they find their job completed.

Operators are accustomed to having the word "Fire!" shouted over the wire. They are trained to handle hysterical people and are adept at extracting an address before the caller hangs up. They have to cope daily with terrified women who cry that the fire is "in the attic" or "down in the cellar" but never give the address. If they are unable to learn the actual address before the caller hangs up, the service assistant gets in touch with the telephone plant and traffic system and the call is traced. But tracing a call loses valuable time in an emergency.

Don't attempt to fight a fire that has spread beyond a very small area. It is nearly always futile and hazardous to continue fighting a fire that is too far gone to be extinguished in about 30 seconds.

**Fire Drill for Your Family** is a wise precaution. If all members know what to do in case of fire—particularly at night—there will be less chance of their becoming panic-stricken and being trapped, or injured. Study the layout of your house and devise ways and means of escape, especially from upper stories.

**In Case You Smell Smoke** and the door of the room is closed, do not open the door if it feels warm to the touch. This means that the air is probably superheated on the other side of the door, and breathing superheated air is usually fatal, even though no flames are present.

## Use a Fire Extinguisher

The best weapon for fighting most small fires is a fire extinguisher of a type approved by the Underwriters' Laboratories. One outstanding exception is a person's clothing catching fire. Smothering the flames with a rug or wool blanket is best in such an emergency. Water is effective on ordinary fires, but it is seldom so quickly available, especially in the necessary quantity, as an extinguisher kept in a handy place. Water may spread the flames from burning grease, oil, and other flammable liquids; it presents a dangerous shock hazard in electrical-equipment fires unless the current is turned off or the equipment disconnected.

**All-Purpose Fire Extinguishers.** Keep fire extinguishers in strategic places—the kitchen, basement, upstairs hall, attic, and garage. Choose an Underwriters-approved type suitable for use on small fires of ordinary combustibles (paper, wood, cloth, etc.); grease, oil, and flammable liquids; and electrical-equipment fires. According to the National Fire Protection Association, the following extinguishers are suitable:

**The Vaporizing-Liquid Type.** This is the familiar cylindrical type containing carbon tetrachloride. It is operated by pumping a handle back and forth. Heat turns the liquid into a smothering blanket of heavy vapor. The most popular size holds a quart of liquid and throws a stream a distance of about 20 feet. It is emptied in about 45 seconds.

**The Carbon-Dioxide Type.** Extinguishers of this type contain carbon-dioxide gas under pressure. Opening a valve releases the flame-smothering gas through a funnel-like nozzle, which is directed at the fire. It has a maximum range of about 8 feet but is most effective when held close to the fire. Recharging must be done by the manufacturer. This type is especially good for extinguishing fat fires in broiler ovens. The carbon-dioxide gas is odorless, tasteless, and won't harm food in any way. It disappears and leaves no damages behind.

**The Dry-Chemical or Compound Type.** This type contains a nonflammable gas that forces specially treated bicarbonate of soda through a short hose. Operating a small wheel or lever releases the gas and, in turn, the dry compound. On striking the flame, the finely powdered bicarbonate of soda decomposes instantly to form smothering carbon-dioxide gas in large volume. The discharge travels about 10 feet, and it lasts up to 30 seconds.

## Fire-Fighting Technique

If possible, stand between the fire and a door. Then, if the flames get out of hand, you can beat a hasty and safe retreat. In the case of ordinary combustibles and electrical equipment, aim the stream from the extinguisher directly at the burning object, not at the smoke or flames. Aim just above the surface of burning grease, oil, and flammable liquids to avoid splashing and spreading the flames. Move the nozzle of the extinguisher slowly, from side to side.

If the fire is on the floor, start at the end nearest you and sweep it out as you go. Start at the bottom to put out a fire that is beginning to climb curtains or woodwork.

To prevent reignition of an electrical-equipment fire, make sure the equipment remains unconnected until it is repaired.

Ventilate the room thoroughly as soon as the fire is safely out, especially if your extinguisher is of the carbon-tetrachloride type. High concentrations of carbon-tetrachloride fumes are irritating to the nose, throat, and lungs, and may be strangulating or toxic.

Small house fires are of three types: rubbish fires (Class A); liquid fires—fats, oil, grease, and paint (Class B); and fires in electric equipment (Class C). A pail of water is an excellent fire extinguisher for a small rubbish fire; but never, never use it on a grease (Class B) or electric-equipment (Class C) fire. Instead you should have, and know how to use, at least one good fire extinguisher—one bearing an Underwriters' Laboratories Seal.

Liquid extinguishers containing foam, or soda acid are effective against Class A and B fires. Carbon-dioxide extinguishers are excellent combatants of Class B and C fires. If your home is to have only one type of extinguisher, the carbon-dioxide type is recommended. It is fairly expensive, but it is well worth the money.

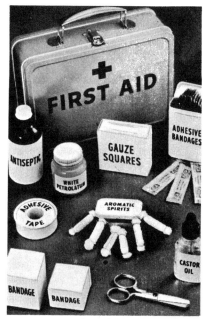

## First Aid

Every home should have a first-aid kit for meeting those little emergencies that crop up in spite of precautions. Listed below are the basic supplies and equipment needed to treat minor injuries. They can be bought almost anywhere at small cost.

1. A box or container to hold the supplies and keep them handy in one place. If you prefer to buy a ready-made first-aid kit, you can find both large and small sets all assembled and ready for use.

2. One-inch compresses on adhesive tape, in individual packages.

3. Sterile gauze squares, about 3" x 3", in individual packages.

4. Burn ointment (small jar of white petrolatum).

5. Small bottle of mild antiseptic, such as tincture of thimerosal.

6. Roll of ½" adhesive tape.

7. Aromatic spirits of ammonia, in ampoules.

8. Small bottle of castor oil or mineral oil with dropper, for use in eyes.

9. Scissors.

10. One-inch and 2" roller bandages.

It is particularly important to know how to stop bleeding; how to give artificial respiration in cases of drowning, suffocation, or electrical shock; what to do to ease the pain of burns and scalds; how to recognize when persons are suffering from shock to their nervous systems, and what to do for them. But an inexperienced person should practice first aid only on the most minor injuries, such as small cuts or mild burns. If you aren't absolutely sure of the approved treatment, or if the injury is more extensive than that commonly encountered, see a doctor immediately.

The American Red Cross has an excellent book on first aid. Every home should have a copy of it. What is more important, local Red Cross chapters give first-aid courses. Take one of these courses if you possibly can. Red Cross representatives also give talks to groups not only on first aid but on other specific subjects such as artificial respiration for drowning and suffocation.

There are many other organizations and sources from which helpful material on first aid may be obtained: insurance companies such as the Metropolitan Life Insurance Company. Another source may be your state departments of Health and Labor. The Federal government also publishes such booklets; they can be obtained from the Superintendent of Documents, U.S. Government Printing Office, Washington 25, D.C. Local branches of the National Safety Council may be able to furnish you with helpful booklets.

The information obtained from any one of the above sources should help you determine the course of action when emergencies arise.

## Your Medicine Cabinet

Your medicine cabinet, which should be a source of aid and comfort, can turn into a real hazard if it isn't given proper attention. Avoid making common mistakes.

1. Don't keep anything except necessary staple articles (tooth paste, mouthwash, lotions, etc.) in a medicine cabinet that is accessible to children. Store all other items (medications, prescription medicines, antiseptics, etc.) elsewhere—in a closet or a special box that can be locked or placed out of children's reach.

2. Don't keep anything poisonous *anywhere* unless it is clearly labeled as such. Even with this precaution, it's wise to have a separate storage place for such items.

3. Don't keep half-used prescription medicines for a long time unless you consult your doctor about (*a*) the lasting properties of the prescription; and (*b*) the advisability of using it again, and the purpose for which it can be used.

4. Be especially careful about pleasant-tasting cough syrups, laxatives, tooth pastes, etc., which are attractive to children. The very young may eat these if they can reach them.

5. Don't forget to examine and arrange your medicine cabinet frequently. Discard half-evaporated bottles of antiseptics, etc., which may have become unfit for use. Have a regular schedule for doing this. A good idea is to keep a card posted inside the cabinet door listing the dates for checking.

6. Don't allow any box or bottle without a label, or one whose label has become illegible, to stay in the cabinet. If you are not absolutely sure of the contents, so that you can put on a new label, discard them.

7. Always read a label twice before using a medicine or antiseptic.

8. Don't leave discarded razor blades on the shelves of your medicine cabinet. Have a disposal system for them that will eliminate any chance of accident.

9. Always screw bottle caps on tightly. This not only assures a longer life for some medicines, cosmetics, etc., but makes the bottles more difficult for small children to open.

10. To keep labels from getting moist and dog-eared and slipping off, dry the bottle thoroughly; print a label, giving the name of the medicine, what it is for, and the dose; stick it on, and varnish or shellac over it.

## Poisons

Most poison labels give instructions for administering antidotes. Remember to look for these instructions in case of accidental poisoning. Follow them promptly.

# More Leisure Through Better Management

## A WORK PLAN THAT WORKS

If you feel hurried while you're trying to get through the day's work; if some days seem more crowded with work than others, try following a plan. It will help you spread the work more evenly through the week; it is a reminder of work to be done and so will help to keep special tasks from piling up.

The routine of preparing meals, washing dishes, making beds, and tidying the house is easy enough to follow. Usually it is the special work, done only now and then or once or twice a week, that piles up—the week's washing and ironing, vacuuming rugs and carpets, keeping Venetian blinds clean, putting up clean curtains, cleaning soiled areas on upholstery, polishing furniture and silver, etc.

### Take Time to Plan Ahead

On Friday or Saturday morning, or at any convenient time, jot down a schedule of special tasks for the coming week, beginning with Monday. Planning your meals ahead for half the week is a help in many ways. You may find it satisfactory to divide the washing and ironing, to avoid overcrowded days. Going over one or two Venetian blinds and using the vacuum cleaner on one rug each day won't take too much time, and this usually finishes that work by Friday. When you wash the dishes, polish any silver that shows tarnish.

Have each day carry its quota of special tasks. If a change in plans is necessary one day, shift any work left undone to the next day. Keep your plan flexible, and fit it to the needs of your household.

### Let the Family Help

If you have a full-time helper, plan her work, too. If you have part-time help or no help, enlist your family's co-operation. Children can be interested in helping as soon as they can run about—picking up their toys, hanging up their clothes if hooks are low enough for them to reach.

Ask each member of the family to pick up his clothes, clean basin and tub after using them, air and make bed before leaving for school or work.

Have the family take turns setting and clearing the table, washing dishes, tidying the living room, using the vacuum cleaner, dusting, and polishing.

To avoid that morning rush, remind the family (and yourself) to plan the night before the clothes to be worn next day. Are stockings, gloves, shoes clean? Are buttons missing? Are there rips to be mended?

### Managing the Meals

Check staple groceries by going over your shelves; list supplies that are running low.

Plan your menus at least 2 or 3 days in advance;

order perishable foods for these meals, if there is room in your refrigerator or freezer.

When you plan menus, choose dishes that can be prepared quickly and cooked just before dinner, or can be made the night before, cooled, and put into the refrigerator, ready to serve or to finish and cook the next day. For example, make a cold dessert or casserole. Or, while getting dinner, cook next day's stew, fricassee, or pot roast. Then cool, and put in refrigerator. Add vegetables, finish the next day.

Post a sheet of paper, ruled for a week's menus, in the kitchen. Then jot down ideas for luncheons or dinners as you think of them or as the family asks for old or new favorites. Before you realize it, most of your next week's meals will be planned.

In the morning, look in your refrigerator to check up on leftovers and necessary marketing for dinner.

Be ready to make changes in your market list (therefore in your menus) when you place your orders, in case some of the foods you planned to use are not available.

An oven roast or pot roast is a good choice for the week end, because you can use leftover roast for one or more dinners the first part of the following week.

## Making and Serving Meals

Use doilies or table mats that are easy to wash and iron or can be simply wiped off. Or use paper mats and napkins.

Serve salad-bowl salads. Arranging individual salads takes time.

Frequently choose course-in-one main dishes, such as casseroles, hearty salad bowls, soups that combine meat, fish, or cheese with vegetables, and stews or pot roasts with vegetables.

Save on dishwashing by serving hot food, when possible, in dish in which it was cooked—skillet, Dutch oven, or casserole. Or serve meat and vegetables on one hot platter or chop plate.

Now and then, arrange main course in kitchen on hot individual plates. Serve the more watery vegetables, such as tomatoes, in side dishes, and place a spoon at each plate, for liquid part.

Use a tray when you set and clear the table. It's a great stepsaver.

If dining table is narrow or small, serve main course and dessert from an extra table.

Fill pots and pans with cool water as soon as they're emptied, and leave them on the range to soak, for easier washing.

After breakfast or supper, wash dishes, rinse with hot water, and leave in dryer or on drainboard, covered with a towel.

## A Dozen Ways to Kitchen Efficiency

Do you ever look around your kitchen and wonder how you possibly got it so cluttered while you were cooking such a simple meal? If you do, maybe these time- and labor-saving suggestions will help you get time out in the daily kitchen work.

1. You can save time, energy, and nerve strain by using utensils and equipment for their intended purpose.
   a. Pot holders, not dish towels, should be used for handling hot things. Using pot holders saves wear and tear on your dish towels, and helps prevent accidents. If you want to avoid a steam burn, *never* use a damp cloth to handle a hot utensil.
   b. Institute recipes give instructions for the size utensil best suited to the recipe. If, for example, your fruit-pie recipe calls for a 9″ pie plate, you are risking a poorer product and a soiled oven by trying to use an 8″ one. Make an inventory of your utensils. If you don't have all the sizes you need, it would be wise to get them.

2. Treat yourself to a really adequate supply of covered refrigerator dishes. They save much valuable space, for they take less than the miscellaneously sized bowls you might otherwise use.

3. If you pack many lunchboxes, you will save precious minutes when you need them most, by assembling your lunchbox equipment—paper napkins, waxed paper, cardboard containers, extra vacuum corks, etc.—in one place, either on a pantry shelf or in an accessible kitchen drawer.

4. In sifting flour, save bowls by using waxed paper instead. Have two squares of waxed paper, one on which to sift the flour before measuring, the other on which to sift the mixed dry ingredients.

5. Pare vegetables and fruit onto a piece of paper toweling or newspaper. Then you can fold over the corners and discard the whole business without having to do any extra cleaning.

6. Save the paper bags from your groceries, to use in your garbage can when you run out of regular garbage bags. Then the garbage can will be much easier to keep clean. Of course, treated garbage-can liners, being moisture-resistant, are best of all.

7. Plan your trips to the refrigerator so you can take out several needed things at one time. This may save you many steps during the course of preparing one meal.

8. Save yourself trips to the dining room at breakfast time by stacking the bowls for ready-to-serve cereal, carrying them to the table with the cereal box, and filling them there.

9. Rinse your egg beater under running cold water right after you have used it. This takes only a second and may save minutes of hard work later on.

10. Especially if you are a beginner at making pastry, you will find that a canvas pastry cloth for your pastry board and a stockinet for your rolling pin make handling and rolling out the pastry much easier.

11. If your oven is still warm after the dishes are washed, you can put your cast-iron utensils, which need very thorough drying, the egg beater, and any other hard-to-dry utensils there until dry.

12. After you've used your meat grinder, run a piece of bread through it to clean off the knives before you wash it. It will be much easier to clean.

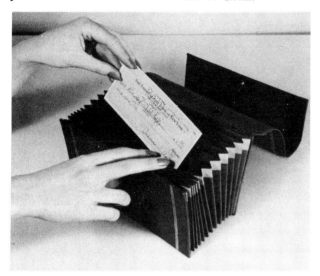

## FILE IT TO FIND IT

Did you ever spend an exasperating half-hour rummaging in vain for a receipted bill, the new address of a friend, a recipe you had clipped, or a direction booklet? A simple filing system would have saved you all that time and worry.

### A Card File

Some records are kept best on 3″ x 5″ cards. For these you'll need a card-filing box and colored cards with index tabs, to help classify and segregate properly the information filed—addresses, phone numbers, dental records, etc. Get the cards and box at a stationery store.

### Recipes and Menus

Clipped recipes will be easy to find if you paste them on cards and keep them in your card file. Use colored index cards to separate and classify the different kinds—casserole dishes, desserts, sauces, etc.

Use the same system to file menus that have made a hit with your family or that you've enjoyed as a guest —dinners, buffet suppers, etc. Keep a file record, too, of menus you have served guests, so you won't repeat when the same people are guests again.

### Your Household Inventory

An inventory of your furniture and furnishings may prove useful in several ways. If you take out fire and burglary insurance, for example, it will help you estimate the amount of insurance. If there should be a fire or burglary, an inventory would help determine the damage or loss when you settle your claim with the insurance company. It would prove useful, too, if you rented your house furnished.

To inventory household goods, make a careful list of the contents of your home—furniture, rugs, draperies, pictures, ornaments, books, silverware, china, table and bed linen, clothing, etc. After each item, record the date purchased, where purchased, and the price, which may be estimated if necessary.

Classify the contents of each room, or list them alphabetically. Some insurance companies provide printed inventory forms that make the job easy. It is a good idea to keep a copy of your household inventory in your safe-deposit box.

### Booklets, Catalogues and Patterns

Filing folders about 9″ x 12″ are convenient for ready reference to instruction booklets for appliances, patterns, catalogues, bulletins, etc. These folders are sold in most stationery stores. Get folders with index tabs, and mark on the tabs the titles of the booklets or a description of the material—for example, "Refrigerator Instruction Booklet," "Upholstery-Shampooing Directions," "Hooked-Rug Designs." Arrange the folders in alphabetical order, and keep them in a desk drawer or in a box.

### Receipted Bills and Canceled Checks

A receipted bill or a canceled check saves trouble if you are billed a second time. If you pay with cash, be sure bills are receipted. Keep the receipted bills, arranged alphabetically according to the names on the billheads, in a 9″ x 12″ folder.

Canceled checks and receipted bills for gas, electricity, telephone, and similar services may be discarded after the next bill is received and shows your account to be correct; though you may wish to keep them until you have estimated your income tax. It is wise to keep indefinitely records of payments of such things as taxes, insurance premiums, mortgage interest, and medical bills.

## Storing Things

When you store clothing and other things for a season or longer, label everything clearly. Garment bags, in use, should have labels, unless the bags are transparent. So should everything stored on shelves in packages and boxes. Labels should be attached where they can be read at a glance, so the contents of shelves or closets needn't be disturbed. Large boxes or trunks containing many different things should have large labels listing the contents. This saves endless hunting. Use labels the same way when you are packing to move to a new home. Then boxes can be unpacked as needed.

## A Sentiment File

This is for family dates of all kinds—the birthdays, anniversaries, and special occasions that take pre-celebration planning. Just a few business-like cards kept in a box on your desk will jog your memory for these important dates. When writing to friends or relatives whom you don't see often, the file helps, too. You can't always remember how old children are, for example, so whenever you get a birth announcement, make a note of the name and date of birth.

## An Appliance File

In order to talk to service people intelligently, make a file arrangement on appliances. Use a card for each appliance and write the serial and model numbers, the period of warranty, and the dealer or serviceman's name and phone number. Information like this right at your fingertips will help you get prompt and courteous service.

## Important Papers

Into the safe-deposit box go all Very Important Papers—birth certificates, deeds to property, copies of wills, insurance policies, etc. But keep a listing at home of everything in the box, including policy numbers and renewal dates of insurance.

Keys on rings carried by individuals may be used so often that they are identified at a glance. But household keys, which should be available to every member of the family, need tags for identification and a central storage place in the house.

A bulletin board in the kitchen is handy for making up shopping lists. Just jot down needed items as they occur to you.

A notebook in your desk will help. In it write the serial numbers of stock certificates and bonds, of insurance policies and other important papers, social-security numbers, bankbook and passport numbers, and so on. Then, if in a moment of normal human carelessness something of importance is lost anyway, you will be able to report the loss promptly and accurately and replace the missing document with a minimum of time and trouble.

Less important but vital papers may be kept in a wall safe and placed in a closet wall, where it will be hidden from prying eyes, or in some wall where its door can be covered by a picture. These little safes are fire-resistant except in the most extreme blaze. They are fitted with typical dial locks.

## Essential Phone Numbers

Beside every telephone there should be a plainly written, easy-to-read list of emergency numbers to prevent your having to fumble through the directory or address book or ask for information. Keep your emergency list, either printed or typed on a plain white card near the telephone. Affix it to a memorandum pad with transparent tape, or thumbtack it where you can see it. The list should be revised when necessary. In addition to fire, police, and ambulance service, the list should contain such of the following numbers as your household may need:

DOCTORS
General practitioner
Pediatrician
Obstetrician
Specialists
Dentist
Veterinarian

DRUGSTORES
List two, in case one is busy

HOSPITALS
Your nearest physician's hospital

NURSES
Registered nurse
Practical nurse

PERSONAL
Your husband's business number
Your husband's secretary's home number
Your next of kin (out-of-town numbers, too)
Your nearest neighbor
Your minister

MONEY
Your bank
Your loan society
Savings bank

TRAVEL
Railway station
Bus terminal
Airport

HOUSEHOLD
Electric company
Gas company
Water company
Plumber
Furnace service

DOMESTIC
Day help
Agency
Baby sitter

MISCELLANEOUS
Garage
School
Newspaper
Locksmith

TELEPHONE SERVICE
Long distance
Information
Repair department
Business office

LEGAL
Your lawyer

This sort of list is invaluable to you under stress. And in emergencies when it is necessary for friends, neighbors, or even strangers to make telephone calls for your benefit, such a list will save an incalculable amount of time, trouble, and confusion.

*Tape a square of cardboard to your shopping bag for a neat pocket for your list. If you prefer a "see through" pocket, use cellophane.*

## When You Move to a New Home

### Duties before Moving

1. Change-of-Address Cards. Your postman or post office will supply postage-free change-of-address cards at no charge. Send your new address to the post office. Notify local stores, public utilities, insurance companies, automobile-license bureau, doctor, dentist, bank, friends, income-tax bureau, the magazines to which you subscribe, etc., as well as the paper boy, milkman, and other tradespeople who come to your house.

2. Gas, Power, and Telephone Service. Arrange for the companies to transfer their services, so that you will not be without them at either your old or new locations. If you are moving to a new town, arrange for the transfer of your bank account. Pay charge accounts and end-of-the-month bills for gas, electricity, and telephone services. Tell the new post office the date of your arrival, to expedite delivery of mail.

### Packing Procedures

When you do the packing yourself, the mover is not responsible for breakage, so use care! Find out whether your mover will supply barrels, cartons, and packing materials for your use in packing. If he won't, you should begin buying or collecting them. Newspapers are seldom a problem, but barrels are usually hard to obtain unless there is a cooperage near your home. Grocery and other stores may be able to supply empty shipping cartons. Heavy wrapping paper, tissue paper, stout twine, and sometimes excelsior are available at most hardware, stationery, and department stores.

Select a moving company as carefully as you would a bank. There are several ways to investigate service and reliability. Find out whether the mover is a member of a trade association or an agent for a large line of interstate vans, and check through those channels. Make sure the mover has a well-established business with a reputation for good service. Insist on satisfactory references. Compare costs.

1. Pack china in barrels, with 2 or 3 inches of excelsior or shredded newspaper on the bottom of each, as a cushion. Wrap each piece in soft paper; then protect it on all sides with packing material. Put the heaviest pieces at the bottom of the barrel, plates next, and the lightest, most fragile pieces on top. Place a thick, cushioning layer of packing material on top of these.

2. Roll table lamps, vases, etc., in packing material, then in soft paper, and pack them in separate barrels.

3. Wrap lampshades in tissue paper and place them in separate cartons.

4. Wrap kitchen utensils in newspapers; pack them in sturdy cartons, with excelsior or shredded or crumpled newspaper between the layers.

5. Put silverware in its original containers, or wrap it in cloth or tissue paper, and pack it in boxes.

6. Provide some sort of adequate covering for mattresses and box springs.

7. Pack books in small cartons.

8. To protect large pictures and mirrors, wrap them in paper, fasten them with heavy cord, and affix a warning label saying "Glass—Handle with Care."

9. Wrap small pictures in newspapers, and pack them in cartons. Carefully crate any valuable paintings—or have them crated by a professional who makes a specialty of such work.

10. Use suitcases, cartons, garment bags, etc., for clothing, handbags, and shoes. Pack separately clothes and other necessities for the family to use until you're settled in the new home.

11. Put identifying tags on every suitcase, box, and crate; then you can unpack the most-needed articles first.

12. Send out rugs, carpets, draperies, etc., for cleaning so they will be ready for your new home.

For safety's sake, keep all stairways and halls clear. Arrange to send young children out of the house, or at least have some responsible person guard them to prevent accidents.

It is customary to tip the packing and moving men and others who help, such as the apartment-house freight-elevator man. The size of the tip depends on the amount of work done.

# THE FAMILY BUDGET

Good money management is essential to good home management. Not only does it make for happier family living, but it helps to stretch dollars through planning for present obligations and provision for future emergencies. No two families can plan alike. Only you can say what your budget must cover. But you must follow certain basic steps if you are to make the most of your money.

1. Decide whether you wish to operate on a weekly, semi-monthly, or monthly budget. Divide your total net annual income accordingly.

2. Subtract all regular living expenses (food, clothing, operating expenses, car, allowances, recreation, telephone costs, etc.)

3. Subtract all fixed obligations (rent or mortgage payments, insurance, taxes, installment payments, school or college costs, etc.).

4. Set aside something for an emergency fund.

5. Put the rest in family savings.

If your income does not stretch to cover all these categories, you are living beyond your means and some adjustment is necessary. Here is a typical budget to guide you:

| | |
|---|---|
| Food .................................... | 25% |
| Home operating expenses ............... | 12% |
| Clothing .......................... | 15% |
| Transportation ...................... | 6% |
| Shelter ........................ | 25% |
| Savings ........................ | 5% |
| Other ........................... | 12% |

Remember, this budget is only typical. The best plan for you is one which you and your family have set up together and with which you are satisfied. Adjust these percentages to fit your specific needs and wishes, but *bear in mind that an increase in one category must be compensated by a decrease in another.*

# *Acknowledgments*

The editors wish to thank the following sources for permission to reprint copyrighted material: for "Mr. and Mrs. Wilson" and "Boat Races at Deauville," p. 38, F. A. R. Galleries, N. Y.; for "Still Life," p. 38, N. Y. Graphic Society; for Swedish print, p. 38, Reed and Stevenson, N. Y.; for illustration p. 55, Westinghouse Electric Corporation; for photos p. 56, material and illustrations p. 57, and photos p. 58; National Canners Assoc. for illustration p. 140; National Livestock and Meat Board for illustrations pp. 147–150; Lighting Laboratories of General Electric Company, Lamp Division; for material pp. 171–172, Libbey Glass, division of Owens-Illinois Glass Company; for material pp. 173–175, The Wine Institute; for photo p. 175, Harry R. Failing, Gump's, S. F. (courtesy Wine Institute); for material pp. 176–178, International Silver Company and Sterling Silversmiths Guild of America; for illustration top p. 184 and illustrations p. 185, International Silver Company; for illustrations p. 228, Westinghouse Electric Corporation; Pittsburgh Plate Glass Co. for the Color Wheel.

# Index

## HOW TO MEASURE

Correct measuring of ingredients is a must. All measurements are level!

### Choosing Measuring Cups

*For Dry Ingredients:* Buy 2 1-cup measuring cups, each with the 1-cup line at the rim. Or for one of these cups, buy a nest of 4 graduated measuring cups, consisting of a ¼-cup, ⅓-cup, ½-cup, and 1-cup measure. Such a nest of cups makes accurate measuring easy.

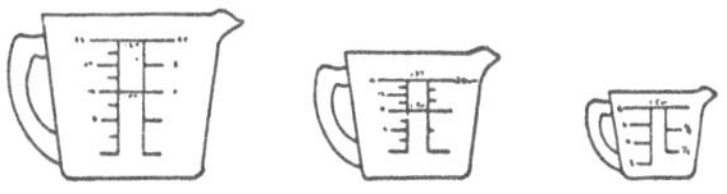

*For Liquid Ingredients:* Buy a 1-cup measuring cup that has the rim *above* the 1-cup line to avoid spilling. The 2-cup and 1-quart measuring cups are also very convenient.

### Choosing Measuring Spoons

Buy one or more sets, attached to a ring, containing the following spoons: ¼ teasp., ½ teasp., 1 teasp., and 1 tablesp. In a good set, 16 tablesp., or 48 teasp., should equal 1 cup.

### Measuring Dry Ingredients

Use a measuring cup with the 1-cup line even with top. Or use a nest of graduated

measuring cups. Use a set of measuring spoons.

*Baking Powder, Salt, etc.:* Dip measuring spoon of correct size into dry ingredient until full; lift out and level off with edge, not flat surface, of knife or spatula.

If it's necessary to measure half spoonfuls, first measure a level spoonful; then divide contents lengthwise with knife, and push off half.

*Brown Sugar:* Roll out lumps with rolling pin. Sift. Spoon into measuring cup, packing firmly enough to hold shape.

*Granulated and Confectioners' Sugar:* If lumpy, sift. Spoon lightly into cup, leveling off with edge, not flat of spatula or knife.

*Flour:* 1. Sift onto waxed paper or into bowl. Do not sift directly into measuring cup.

2. Spoon sifted flour lightly into cup until

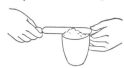

cup is full. Do not pack or shake.

3. Level off with edge, not flat surface, of spatula or knife, without packing it down.

### Measuring Liquids

*Milk, etc.:* Set measuring cup (one with rim above 1-cup line) on level surface, keeping measuring line at eye level. Fill cup as desired.

*Vanilla, etc.:* Pour extract into measuring spoon. If thick, like molasses, level off with edge, not flat surface, of spatula or knife.

### Measuring Shortenings

*Shortening:* Scoop from can or package and pack firmly into graduated measuring cup. Level off with edge, not flat surface, of knife or spatula; remove from cup.

*Butter or Margarine:* Measure as for shortening. If you're using a 1-lb. print of butter or margarine, each ¼-lb. stick equals ½ cup, or 8 tablesp. Half of a ¼-lb. stick equals ¼ cup, or 4 tablesp. For 2 tablesp., cut off one fourth of ¼-lb. stick.

*Melted Fat:* Measure before or after melting—the amount will be the same. However, it's simpler to measure it after melting.

Salad oil, often used instead of melted fat, is measured in a measuring cup or spoon.

## EQUIVALENT MEASURES

| | |
|---|---|
| Speck | Less than ⅛ teasp. |
| ⅓ of ¼ teasp. | Pinch * |
| ⅓ of ½ teasp. | Pinch * |
| ½ of ¼ teasp. | ⅛ teasp. |
| 3 teasp. | 1 tablesp. |
| ⅓ of 1 tablesp. | 1 teasp. |
| ⅓ of 2 tablesp. | 2 teasp. |
| ⅓ of 5 tablesp. | 1 tablesp. + 2 teasp. |
| ⅓ of 7 tablesp. | 2 tablesp. + 1 teasp. |
| ½ of 1 tablesp. | 1½ teasp. |
| ½ of 3 tablesp. | 1 tablesp. + 1½ teasp. |
| ½ of 5 tablesp. | 2 tablesp. + 1½ teasp. |
| ½ of 7 tablesp. | 3 tablesp. + 1½ teasp. |
| 2 tablesp. | ⅛ cup |
| 4 tablesp. | ¼ cup |
| 5 tablesp. + 1 teasp. | ⅓ cup |
| 8 tablesp. | ½ cup |
| 10 tablesp. + 2 teasp. | ⅔ cup |
| 12 tablesp. | ¾ cup |
| 16 tablesp. | 1 cup |
| ⅓ of ¼ cup | 1 tablesp. + 1 teasp. |
| ⅓ of ⅓ cup | 1 tablesp. + 2⅓ teasp. |
| ⅓ of ½ cup | 2 tablesp. + 2 teasp. |
| ⅓ of ⅔ cup | 3 tablesp. + 1⅔ teasp. |
| ⅓ of ¾ cup | ¼ cup |
| ½ of ¼ cup | 2 tablesp. |
| ½ of ⅓ cup | 2 tablesp. + 2 teasp. |
| ½ of ½ cup | ¼ cup |
| ½ of ⅔ cup | ⅓ cup |
| ½ of ¾ cup | 6 tablesp. |
| 2 cups | 1 pt. |
| 2 pt. | 1 qt. |
| 1 qt. | 4 cups |

*\*Pinch is as much as can be taken between tip of finger and thumb.*